D1559684

# FROM FEDERATION TO COMMUNION

# FROM FEDERATION
# TO COMMUNION

## The History of the
## Lutheran World Federation

Edited by
*Jens Holger Schjørring*
*Prasanna Kumari*
*Norman A. Hjelm*

*Viggo Mortensen, Coordinator*

FORTRESS PRESS                    MINNEAPOLIS

FROM FEDERATION TO COMMUNION
The History of the Lutheran World Federation

First published by Fortress Press in 1997 in cooperation with the Lutheran World Federation, Department for Theology and Studies.

*Library of Congress Cataloging-in-Publication Data*

From federation to Communion : the history of the Lutheran World
    Federation / [edited by] Jens Holger Schjørring, Prasanna Kumari,
    Norman Hjelm ; Viggo Mortensen, coordinator.
        p.    cm.
    Includes bibliographical references and index.
    ISBN 0-8006-3110-2 (alk. paper)
    1. Lutheran World Federation—History.    I. Schjørring, Jens
Holger.    II. Kumari, Prasanna, 1950–    .    III. Hjelm, Norman A.,
1931–    .    IV. Mortensen, Viggo.
BX8004.L9.F76    1997
284.1'06'01—dc21                                                      97-16506
                                                                                 CIP

The paper used in this publication meets the minimum requirements of the American National Standard for Information Sciences—Permanence of Paper for Printed Library materials, ANSI Z329.48–1984.

Manufactured in the U.S.A.                                          AF 1-3110
01    00    99    98    97        1    2    3    4    5    6    7    8    9

# Contents

# List of Illustrations

head are the cochairs, Bishop Hermann Dietzfelbinger of Munich, Lutheran, and Cardinal Hermann Volk of Mainz, Roman Catholic. Cardinal Johannes Willebrands is seated next to Cardinal Volk.

28. Fourth Meeting of the Lutheran-Orthodox Joint Commission, Crete, 1987.

*Chapter 8, pages 319–22*

29. Participants from the Huria Kristen Batak Protestan at the Minneapolis Assembly, 1957.

30. Dr. Kunchala Rajaratnam of India here giving a lively account of his four decade involvement with the LWF. He is flanked by Professor Jens Holger Schjørring, left, and Dr. Viggo Mortensen, right.

31. Women at the Hanover Assembly, Sister Eva Lyngby, Denmark, first woman elected to the LWF Executive Committee, is on the right.

32. André Appel, LWF General Secretary, with some of the more than forty participants at the International Lutheran Women's Consultation held in Båstad, Sweden, 1969.

33. A demonstration during the Budapest Assembly, 1984, concerning the role of women in the LWF.

34. Participants in the first International Consultation of Lutheran Women Theologians, Karjaa, Finland, August 1991.

35. Herman Rao, a student from India, distributes rice to the Rev. Roland Payne of Liberia, during a youth demonstration on world hunger at the Evian Assembly, 1970.

36. Youth Workshop on HIV/AIDS, sponsored by the LWF and the WCC, Windhoek, Namibia, May 1993.

37. Ms Clarice Cid Heisler de Oliveira of the Evangelical Church of the Lutheran Confession in Brazil, lector at a Eucharist at the Curitiba Assembly, 1990.

*Chapter 9, pages 345–46*

38. The LWF coordinated international and ecumenical funding for legal aid during a trial in Swakopmund, Namibia, when six Namibians were charged under the Terrorism Act of the apartheid regime.

39. Delegates to the Pre-Assembly Youth Conference, held prior to the Curitiba Assembly, participating in a demonstration of the "Mothers and Grandmothers of May Square" for 30,000 children who disappeared during the post–1976 military dictatorship of Argentina.

40. and 41.
LWF General Secretary Ishmael Noko met in March 1966 in Gaza City with Yassir Arafat of the Palestinian Liberation Organization (plate 40) and in Jerusalem with Israeli Prime Minister Shimon Peres.

ASSEMBLIES OF THE LWF

42. Dr. J. P. van Heest, President of the Evangelical Lutheran Church in the Kingdom of the Netherlands, signing the first Constitution of the LWF at the 1947 Lund Assembly. Other persons at the signing included, seated from the left: Dr. Abdel Ross Wentz, U.S.A. and Bishop Hanns Lilje, Germany; archbishop Erling Eidem of Sweden, last President of the Lutheran World Convention and presiding

# Foreword

IN 1997 the Lutheran World Federation (LWF) celebrates its golden anniversary. To mark this occasion the Council of the LWF commissioned the writing of the history of the organization. Three authors, with the help of many other dedicated individuals, young and old, have completed the project.

The authors of the history that you are now reading do not claim completeness. However, they have succeeded in placing in your hands a reader-friendly survey of a colorful and eventful search for inter-Lutheran unity. They have focused on specific themes and developments that emerged during a period of approximately fifty years. These years have been marked by just about everything that is human: high and low points, detours, delays, timidity, boldness and courage, theological tensions, quarrels, apprehension, voluntary withdrawal and suspension of membership, inner growth in self-understanding, complete and incomplete work, happy celebrations, moments of forgiveness and reconciliation.

The launching of the LWF in 1947 with its vision for a global Lutheran movement was indeed a bold step, given the political context of those times. It was a complex exercise that brought people and communities together who, although sharing essentially the same confession and theological heritage, had obvious cultural and political differences. The delegates assembled in Lund in July 1947 came from nations that had been at war. It was not easy for those delegates, affected as they were by such a devastating war, to leave behind their national experiences. The formation of a global movement like the Lutheran World Federation in the face of all these odds was in itself more than a human act.

The content of the LWF Assemblies demonstrates that the vision of *world Lutheranism* was not limited to things Lutheran. The LWF understands itself as a movement within the one ecumenical movement for the sake of the one church catholic. The Lutheran churches themselves and through the instrument of the LWF have engaged in bilateral dialogue with other Christian World Communions with an expressed goal for visible unity.

Reading this book makes clear that what began as a Euro-American movement has gradually become much more than a response by those from "cold climates." The churches in other parts of the globe have laid spiritual, theological, and structural claim to this movement. This claim is expressed in many areas of the life and work of the LWF, such as the call to recognize that all theological reflections are contextually bound. Women and youth have made an impact on the structures of the LWF member churches and those of the governing bodies. The various constitutional amendments and structural changes at the level of the LWF as an organization reflect the constant need to renew the movement. One such claim was the presentation of a document from the Ethiopian Evangelical Church Mekane Yesus to the LWF entitled, "On the Interrelation between Proclamation of the Gospel and Human Development." This document represents a claim and a keen desire to make a contribution to the life and work of the LWF from a church in the South. The discussion and action regarding the *status confessionis* was yet another point in the life and work of the Federation that reflects common ownership among the churches of the LWF.

The chapter "Affirming the Communion: Ecclesiological Reflection in the LWF" confirms how the Lutheran churches over the years have grown together. They have cooperated in programs of proclamation and service and at the same time have acknowledged that the gift of communion with God in Christ calls for a life of interdependence among themselves. Pulpit and altar fellowship implies that the "federal" concept no longer adequately describes this global movement. Since 1947 Lutheran member churches have asked themselves again and again the question of the nature of the LWF. Is the LWF more than a confessional movement? How does it serve the church catholic? What about the churchly character of this organization? In more recent years the LWF has understood itself as a communion of churches enjoying pulpit and altar fellowship. Does this self-understanding in any way raise the question of an appropriate renaming of the LWF? Is the name "Lutheran Communion" not better than "Lutheran World Federation"? The concept of *communio* is not only biblically and theologically rooted; it also challenges Christians to live a life that is both rooted in and transcends current societal fragmentation marked by racism, nationalism, ethnicity, and gender oppression.

It is my conviction that this book will be a valuable discussion-starter in theological seminaries, faculties, pastoral conferences, and congregational meetings. Those who seek to engage in interconfessional dialogue have in this book an excellent resource.

*Ishmael Noko*
Geneva, July 1996                                          General Secretary

# Preface

THE PREPARATION OF THIS VOLUME, conceived as appropriate to the fiftieth anniversary in 1997 of the founding of the Lutheran World Federation (LWF), has developed in complicated ways. Clearly, this anniversary—which occurs as the third millennium comes to the horizon—presents an occasion for serious historical and theological reflection on the heritage of the past fifty years and such reflection should assist the federation in facing the prospects and challenges of the future. Yet how is a book such as this to be shaped if historical and theological integrity is to be its hallmark?

Oral, documentary, and archival research has been essential to the preparation of *From Federation to Communion,* and the support of a large group of knowledgeable and committed colleagues who are wide in experience and fully inclusive in representation has been gratifying. Prior to such research and cooperation, however, it proved necessary to develop a fundamental approach, constructive yet critical, to the writing of this history. What has here been produced makes no claim to uniform excellence; it should be seen solely as a faltering yet crucially important first step in the uncovering of the memories that must accompany an informed and dedicated journey to the future.

A history of an organization such as the LWF requires a decision between an outline built around purely institutional and programmatic developments and an outline that traces basic themes that are to be found spread throughout the Federation as an entire entity. We have chosen neither a purely chronological nor departmental approach; the volume does not proceed year by year, nor does it present the discrete story of individual LWF departments. Rather, we have attempted to trace the "trajectories" of fundamental concerns or themes of the federation's life—diaconic service, mission, theology, ecclesiology, ecumenism, inclusiveness, and witness in public life. While these concerns predominate in certain departments or offices, their trajectories most frequently cover a wider spectrum of LWF life. Obviously, an important consequence of this decision is that the present volume is selective in what it describes; it is not a comprehensive directory of all LWF activities or events over the past decades. To develop in the Federation a viable "institutional memory" requires coherent, selective, and relevant principles of critical discernment, and the present description of trajectories is our attempt to aid in that development.

Another crucial decision has guided our work: To what extent should this be a *critical* study of the history of the LWF? The authorization of this project by the LWF council has never been interpreted as a mandate only to tell a story of Lutheran successes. In describing the trajectories of LWF concerns, it has seemed to us inevitable that questions be asked and judgments made, otherwise the volume would lack basic integrity. The pithy words of Polybius about the writing of history apply, we trust, to what is offered here:

> That historians should give their own country a break, I grant you; but not so as to state things contrary to fact. For there are plenty of mistakes made by writers out of ignorance, and which anyone finds it difficult to avoid. But if we knowingly write what is false, whether for the sake of our country or our friends or just to be pleasant, what difference is there between us and hack writers? Readers should be very attentive to and critical of historians, and they in turn should be constantly on their guard. (*History*, bk. 16)

The closeness of this history in time and the proximity and dedication of those who have collaborated in its preparation to the institution itself make an authentically critical approach difficult. There are temptations both to silence when judgments should be made and to carping when prejudice or personal bias determines the questions. We have attempted to withstand these temptations, although we must acknowledge that in some of the chapters that follow we have achieved only limited success.

It is important also to point out that this volume is a history of a very short time in the course of the Lutheran story, and it is limited even in that time to only one aspect of the story. This is not a history of the Lutheran churches, either individually or regionally. Further, it must be pointed out that there are tensions, perhaps inevitable, within the LWF itself that are admittedly reflected in this book—between the secretariat in Geneva and life in the member churches, between the dominant churches and agencies of the North and the newer, smaller, and less wealthy churches of the South. The story of the LWF is not simply the story of the secretariat, that is, of Geneva, nor is it the story of the hegemony of European and North American churches. How well these pages reflect these truths is perhaps not ours to judge.

The nine basic chapters of this volume describe from a variety of angles how the Lutheran World Federation has moved, over five decades, to

become an authentic expression of *communio*. This is not simply, in our
view, a matter of constitutional development, theological wordsmanship,
or administrative arrangement. Relations of *diakonia* and mission, relations between North and South, new patterns of shared and inclusive
responsibility—these are, in the LWF, growing if yet imperfect realities,
expressions of new ecclesial and ecumenical understandings of communion. These understandings have been born in debate, struggle, and controversy, but the Federation's history shows that they are coming to living
reality. The title of this volume, *From Federation to Communion*, is not
meant to be a provocation or an instance of special pleading—it was
selected prior to the proposals contained in the foreword to the book by the
present general secretary of the LWF. It is intended simply to describe a
clear development in the Federation's general self-understanding.

*Chapter 1—The Lutheran Church in the World Today: The Founding of
the LWF.* A large amount of published material on the formation of the
LWF in 1947 and its prehistory, especially the story of the Lutheran World
Convention, is available. This chapter centers only on certain aspects of
that story, concentrating on the impetus provided by the prehistory, the
Lutheran commitment to reconciliation and relief work after World War
II, and the dialectic between Lutheran identity and ecumenical unity,
together with a review of the convictions and contributions of those who
participated in the formation of the LWF. The chapter title was the theme
of the 1947 Lund Assembly.

*Chapter 2—From Federation to Communion: Five Decades of LWF His-
tory.* This chapter is an overview of five decades of LWF history, necessary
to establish a basic framework for the ensuing thematic considerations. It
provides a survey of the basic concerns of the Federation through a selective review of programmatic, constitutional, and structural developments,
a review of LWF assemblies in terms of themes and outcomes, and a critical indication of dominant leitmotifs that have been sounded in these
decades.

*Chapter 3—Let Us Help One Another: Service in the LWF.* World service and development have, since 1947, been central to the life of the LWF.
This chapter surveys decisive turning points, achievements, and challenges, concentrating on questions of the theology of "proclamation and
development," the practice of interchurch and humanitarian aid, ecumenical patterns of *diakonia*, concerns for both the alleviation of suffering and the identification of the "root causes" of such suffering, and the
fostering by the LWF of community development in the Third World.

*Chapter 4—Faithful to the Fundamental Task: Mission in the LWF.*
Alterations in basic understandings and commitments to global mission
have marked the LWF in various contexts and periods of its history: "home

missions" and "foreign missions"; the trusteeship of "orphaned missions" after two world wars; mission fields as "younger churches"; mission as church cooperation; the relation of mission to politics, church aid, and development; ecumenical impulses and commitment to mission. Progressions in LWF structures and programs are, in this chapter, surveyed in terms of the development of such understandings of and commitments to mission.

*Chapter 5—Continuity and Change: Theological Reflection in the LWF.* The trajectory of theological reflection and understanding is, in this chapter, traced in a wide variety of manifestations. Focal issues in Lutheran theology—justification, tradition and the role of the confessions, ecclesiology, worship and sacraments—are surveyed in the context of global Lutheranism as are specific theological concerns that are directly related to themes covered in other chapters of this volume. Present concerns for new and varying contexts—for example, North–South dialogue—in which theological reflection is pursued are noted, and the structural ways in which at different points in its history the federation has dealt with theological issues are reviewed and assessed.

*Chapter 6—Affirming the Communion: Ecclesiological Reflection in the LWF.* Lutheran ecclesiological identity has preoccupied the LWF as a matter facing each member church as well as the global Federation itself. The self-understanding of the LWF and hence of member churches has gone through mutations and turned corners—from "free association" to "communion." This chapter surveys the debates concerning the ecclesiological character of Lutheran churches and those concerning the global communion of Lutheran churches and raises the question, Is there a world Lutheran Church?

*Chapter 7—To Serve Christian Unity: Ecumenical Commitment in the LWF.* The twentieth century has seen the rise of the modern ecumenical movement, and the LWF has come into being within the horizon of that movement. Relations between the Federation and the World Council of Churches, the course of bilateral ecumenical dialogues, and the growth of Christian World Communions have both brought significant ecumenical achievements and raised sharp challenges for Lutheran churches. This chapter evaluates those achievements and challenges in its review of themes such as "confessional identity" and "reconciled diversity," which have given specific force to the ecumenical consciousness of global Lutheranism.

*Chapter 8—Dimensions of Communion: Inclusive Participation in the LWF.* "Inclusive participation" is in many ways a theme that is integral to virtually each chapter of this volume, for the movement toward inclusiveness is not merely statistical but substantive in relation to all of the book's themes. From being a Eurocentric, male-dominated entity at the time of its founding, the LWF has become a communion marked by genuinely inclusive participation. The story of this development—its accomplishments and its unmet challenges—is told in this chapter in respect to the involvement of churches from Asia, Africa, and Latin America and the participation of women, youth, and the disabled.

*Chapter 9—Responsibility for the World: The Public Role of the LWF.* The LWF was established in a time of political and social upheaval, and its response to the impact of pervasive injustice, change, and unrest throughout its history must be measured. The revolts of the 1960s, apartheid in southern Africa, relations to "liberation movements," involvement in peace negotiations, tensions between East and West, and commitment to the struggles of the less privileged—these issues have preoccupied the Federation at many points, programatically, structurally, and ideologically, and the volume's final chapter recounts this story.

The nine chapters of *From Federation to Communion* are followed by what is called a "Handbook of the Lutheran World Federation." This briefer section of the book is designed to provide capsule summaries of each of the eight LWF assemblies—venues, surrounding circumstances, programs, and main actions—together with biographical sketches of Federation presidents and general secretaries. These biographical sketches have of necessity been limited to those who have carried the official responsibilities associated with presidents and general secretaries. Clearly, many other persons—men and increasingly women and youth—have played and are playing key roles in the life of the LWF, but for obvious reasons the Handbook limits its biographical material to these official personages. Also, the decision has been made that greater attention should be paid to evaluating the contributions of persons and the significance of events in the earlier period of LWF history than in more recent times.

It is to be noted that at the end of each of the book's nine chapters and at the end of each section of the Handbook there is a brief bibliographical note that refers to sources, published works, and archival material used in the related portion of the book. It is clear that these are partial and highly selective notes; they are in no way exhaustive lists either of available material or of material actually used in the preparation of the relevant sections. While this book has been prepared with every effort at maintaining the highest standards of accuracy and integrity, it does not aim at being an academic treatise. Were it to be such a treatise, its use would doubtlessly be limited to scholars. It is hoped that this volume will be of help and appeal to a broader spectrum of readers.

The preparation and publication of a historical review of the first fifty years of LWF history were first proposed after the Eighth Assembly of the

Federation in 1990, and subsequently approved by the Federation Council. Responsibility for the management of the project has been lodged in the LWF Department for Theology and Studies, of which the Rev. Dr. Viggo Mortensen is director. An initial consultation concerning the project was held, with the generous support of the German National Committee of the LWF, June 14–17, 1993, at Kloster Wennigsen near Hanover, Germany. At this meeting some thirty persons, who themselves embodied a "living memory" of the LWF, reflected on the character and substance of the history. Papers presented at this consultation and the vigorous discussions they stimulated went far to clarify the purpose, approach, and shape of the final volume. In addition, smaller consultations and interviews have been conducted.

The actual preparation of drafts and manuscripts was under the leadership of the editorial group that has signed this preface. A large number of other persons were consulted, and many contributed—from their experience, knowledge, and expertise—to the research for and writing of this book. It can be asserted that the present volume is truly the result of a broad and open process of joint work by colleagues. In some instances the contributions of this wide circle of coworkers involved the actual preparation of full or partial chapters; in other instances they involved research and the development of outlines or ideas of substance; in yet other cases they involved critical readings leading to helpful revisions. The names of those colleagues who prepared texts are indicated in notes attached to relevant chapters and Handbook sections; a full listing of the persons and agencies who have contributed so generously and helpfully to the final publication is to be found in the acknowledgments. Together these persons constitute a wide spectrum of the global and inclusive Lutheran family. To each of these persons—and to many others who in correspondence and conversation showed support and offered ideas for this venture—a considerable debt of gratitude is owed.

It is, further, important to note the enormous amount of substantive work given to the project by one of the members of the editorial group, Jens Holger Schjørring, Professor of Dogmatics and the History of Theology at the University of Aarhus, Denmark. Over the course of a lengthy sabbatical, provided by the University of Aarhus and supported by the Danish Council for Interchurch Relations, he was able both to give leadership to the editorial group and to undertake essential research and the preparation of draft manuscripts. His coworkers on the editorial group wish to express their thanks to Professor Schjørring for his dedicated leadership and scholarship and to his university and church for making his work possible. It is also to be noted that in addition to his reviews and contributions to the substance of each chapter and section of the book, the

Rev. Norman Hjelm of the Evangelical Lutheran Church in America provided full editorial oversight of the entire manuscript.

While the editorial group was given full independence in the pursuit of its work, the LWF Department for Theology and Studies provided both substantive and technical support. Dr. Mortensen assumed the role of "project manager" and is to be generously thanked for his enthusiastic support and unfailing and disciplined leadership in bringing the endeavor to fruition. His colleagues in the Department for Theology and Studies, Ms. Inge Klaas and Ms. Iris Benesch, brought skill, commitment, and good humor to their essential tasks of support. Additionally, Ms. Dorothea Millwood of the Federation's Office for Communication Services devoted countless hours to the translation of large portions of the book so that publication could occur in both English and German editions. Professor Heinrich Holze of the Faculty of Theology at the University of Rostock, Germany, formerly on the staff of the Department for Theology and Studies, competently reviewed all translations into German. Finally, Ms. Birgitta Kok of the LWF Archives provided considerable assistance to those who did research for this book, and also, together with Ms Katarina Unell of the Office for Communication Services, helped locate, identify, and select the photographs that accompany the text of the book. To each of these persons, members of the Geneva Secretariat of the LWF, the editorial group wishes to express its deepest gratitude. They have contributed immeasureably to the task at hand.

While *From Federation to Communion* is not to be regarded as an "official" publication of the Lutheran World Federation, the governing body of the Federation and the Geneva staff have, as indicated, exhibited uncommon commitment to the project. We are especially grateful to the LWF president and the general secretary, Dr. Gottfried Brakemeier and Dr. Ishmael Noko, for their encouragement and contributions; their helpful and stimulating statements—Foreword and Afterword—enhance the volume greatly.

While so many have with positive results graciously and enthusiastically participated in the preparation of *From Federation to Communion*, it obviously remains that responsibility for errors—of fact or judgment—rests with the editorial group.

A recent study by the American Faith and Order group has proposed a number of principles for the writing of ecumenical history (*Telling the Churches' Stories: Ecumenical Perspectives on Writing Christian History*, ed. Timothy Wengert and Charles Brockwell [Grand Rapids: Wm. B. Eerdmans, 1995], pp. 3–20). It seems appropriate to refer to three of the fourteen principles for the writing of Christian history identified in this study:

An ecumenical history of Christianity assists groups of Christians to define their own voices within the conversations among communities of faith and to issue their special challenge to these communities. (Principle 9)

An ecumenical history of Christianity approaches its task in the spirit of repentance and forgiveness, avoiding defensiveness with regard either to social location or to particular theological, methodological, or ecclesial traditions. (Principle 12)

An ecumenical history of Christianity acknowledges that no historical account can claim complete objectivity, but seeks fair-minded empathy with the particular stories that comprise the ecumenical history of the Christian people. (Principle 14)

*From Federation to Communion* has been written, it can well be claimed, as a history of one Christian World Communion with such principles as these in mind. The story is far wider—globally and locally—than that recounted here. The stance of those who have contributed to the volume is always particular and shaped by locations which are never universal and only partially objective. Yet if the volume succeeds in stimulating others to recount their histories, if it succeeds in aiding the creation of usable historical memory, it will have made a contribution. Our goal is that *From Federation to Communion* initiate a process of research, study, and reflection through consultations, seminars, and publication leading to the creation—globally, regionally, and locally—of a theologically informed awareness of history within the Lutheran churches of the world today. Such awareness is essential to the life and mission both of the Lutheran communion and the whole *oikumene.*

Aarhus, Madras, Philadelphia                          *Jens Holger Schjørring*
The Feast of All Saints                                        *Prasanna Kumari*
November 1, 1996                                              *Norman A. Hjelm*

# Acknowledgments

Many persons—from different generations and from all corners of the globe—have contributed to *From Federation to Communion*. A large number of persons were consulted as the volume assumed structure and outline; some have assisted in the preparation or actual writing of chapters or sections of the book; many have reviewed and carefully evaluated parts of the work while it was in process; and others contributed insights based on research, personal memory, and experience. The editorial group, which must alone bear responsibility for the volume's shortcomings, wishes to express deep gratitude to the following persons who have so graciously supported and contributed to this record of the history of a deeply loved LWF.

Emmanuel Abraham
André Appel
Mercia Bachmann
Iris Benesch
Eugene Brand
Risto Cantell
Yadessa Daba
Helmut Edelmann
Dennis Frado
James Greig
Bernhardur Gudmundsson
Udo Hahn
Béla Harmati
Gunnar Heiene
Stewart Herman
Michel Hoeffel
Howard Hong
Anneli Janhonen
Musimbi Kanyoro

Arthur M. Allchin
Ivar Asheim
E. Theodore Bachmann (†)
Gottfried Brakemeier
Reinhard Brandt
James Crumley
Martin Dreher
Julius Filo
Hendrik Frederik
Eric Gritsch
Karoly Hafenscher
Holger Bernt Hansen
Wolf-Dieter Hauschild
Christa Held
Hans-Volker Herntrich
Heinrich Holze
Andrew Hsiao
Mikko Juva
Peter Kjeseth

Inge Klaas
Birgitta Kok
Günter Krusche
Per Larsson
Risto Lehtonen
Eckehart Lorenz
Dorothy Marple
Robert Marshall
Carl H. Mau, Jr. (†)
Dorothea Millwood
Amani Mwenegoha
Brian Neldner
Todd Nichol
Ishmael Noko
Mika Palo
David Preuss
Eugene Ries
William Rusch
James Scherer
Henrik Smedjebacka
Gunnar Staalsett
Anita Stauffer
Stephen Sykes
Lars Thunberg
Vilmos Vajta
Eva von Hertzberg

Gottfried Klapper
Georg Kretschmar
Erasto Kweka
William Lazareth
Anza Lema
Käte Mahn
Friedrich Manske
Daniel Martensen
Harding Meyer
Viggo Mortensen
Gyula Nagy
Clifford Nelson
Karsten Nissen
Hans Otte
George Posfay
Kunchala Rajaratnam
Michael Root
Björn Ryman
Emmanuel Gebre Silassie
Bodil Sølling
Margret Stasius
Lloyd Svendsbye
László Terray
Katarina Unell
Per Voksø
Vitor Westhelle

Additionally, generous financial contributions from several organizations and individuals aided greatly in bringing *From Federation to Communion* to completion. Deep gratitude is expressed for such contributions to the LWF National Committees in Denmark, Germany, Norway, Sweden, and the United States; to Danchurchaid, Finnchurchaid, and Norchurchaid; to the late E. Theodore Bachmann, to the late Carl H. Mau, Jr., and to Bishop Herbert Chilstrom.

# Bibliographical Note

At the end of each chapter and handbook section, a bibliographical note is appended that indicates the principal sources—published and unpublished—that illuminated the research for the material in question.

Since 1929 a number of introductions to the Lutheran churches of the world have appeared. Most helpful in the preparation of the present volume has been the comprehensive volume by E. Theodore and Mercia Brenne Bachmann, *Lutheran Churches in the World: A Handbook* (Minneapolis: Augsburg, 1989). This volume was preceded by four others: Alfred Th. Jørgensen, Paul Fleisch, and Abdel Ross Wentz, eds. *The Lutheran Churches of the World* (Minneapolis: Augsburg, 1929); Abdel Ross Wentz, ed., *The Lutheran Churches of the World* (Geneva: Lutheran World Federation, 1952); Carl E. Lund-Quist, ed., *Lutheran Churches of the World* (Minneapolis, Augsburg, 1957); and Mercia Brenne Bachmann, *Lutheran Mission Directory* (2d ed.; Geneva: Lutheran World Federation, 1982).

*Official Proceedings of LWF Assemblies*

*Proceedings of the First Assembly of the Lutheran World Federation.* (Lund, 1947). Edited by Sylvester C. Michelfelder. Philadelphia: United Lutheran Publication House, 1948.

*Proceedings of the Second Assembly of the Lutheran World Federation* (Hanover, 1952). Edited by Carl E. Lund-Quist. Geneva: Lutheran World Federation, 1952.

*Proceedings of the Third Assembly of the Lutheran World Federation* (Minneapolis, 1957). Edited by Carl E. Lund-Quist. Minneapolis: Augsburg, 1958.

*Proceedings of the Fourth Assembly of the Lutheran World Federation* (Helsinki, 1963). Edited by Kurt Schmidt-Clausen. Berlin/Hamburg: Lutherisches Verlagshaus, 1965.

*Sent into the World: The Proceedings of the Fifth Assembly of the Lutheran World Federation* (Evian, 1970). Edited by LaVern K. Grosc. Minneapolis: Augsburg, 1971.

*In Christ—A New Community: The Proceedings of the Sixth Assembly of the Lutheran World Federation* (Dar es Salaam, 1977). Edited by Arne Sovik. Geneva: Lutheran World Federation, 1977.

*Budapest 1984—"In Christ—Hope for the World:" Proceedings of the Seventh Assembly.* General editor Carl H. Mau, Jr. *LWF Report No. 19/20, February 1985.* Geneva: Lutheran World Federation, 1985.

*I Have Heard the Cry of My People: Proceedings of the Eighth Assembly, Lutheran World Federation* (Curitiba, 1990). Edited by Norman A. Hjelm. *LWF Report No. 28/29, December 1990.* Geneva: Lutheran World Federation, 1990.

In the present volume, these official records are abbreviated as *Proceedings,* followed by the location of the assembly under consideration. Moreover, the *Official Minutes* of each of these assemblies, available through the LWF in Geneva, have also been consulted in the research for the present volume.

# The History of the
# Lutheran World Federation

CHAPTER

# 1

# The Lutheran Church in the World Today: The Founding of the LWF

## Historical Setting

WORLDWIDE COOPERATION among Lutheran churches is intimately connected with the aftermath of two world wars. In postwar contexts we find the settings for the signal events of both 1923 and 1947.

The constituting assembly of the Lutheran World Convention took place in 1923, just five years after the end of World War I. The location was Eisenach, a key place in the course of German history, where Martin Luther had stayed in 1521 and 1522 at the celebrated Wartburg Castle. Participants at the assembly thus had their attention directed to events in German history central to the entire Lutheran heritage.

Simultaneously, the concern of delegates was marked by a shared feeling of obligation toward brothers and sisters whose lives had been devastated by the recent war. This widespread devastation, moreover, was exacerbated by political developments which in 1923 were seen as a serious threat to the formation of all kinds of community. From the German point of view the Treaty of Versailles was not only unjust, but "a treaty of dishonor" or even a "murderous treaty." Germans doubted that good relations could be established with former enemies who were not content only to impose severe peace conditions on the central powers, Germany and Austria-Hungary, but also felt it necessary to impute sole guilt to those central powers as a kind of moral justification for the then current political conditions. These doubts were increased just a few months prior to the Eisenach assembly when the French marched into the Ruhr in order to force the Germans to complete the payment of their debts even though

*Jens Holger Schjørring, Aarhus, Denmark, is the author of chapter 1.*

the German economy was in disastrous condition and the German people were suffering from massive hunger.

These dark shadows continued to dominate the second assembly of the Lutheran World Convention in Copenhagen in 1929. The Germans that year "commemorated" the tenth year of the disgrace of Versailles, and many who participated in the assembly insisted on a common resolution of protest against that treaty. Again, at the third assembly in Paris in 1935, discord threatened even more, for that was the time when the Church Struggle in Germany required the attention of the entire ecumenical community of churches. The fourth assembly, moreover, planned for Philadelphia in 1940, was canceled because these many disturbances and tensions had ushered in World War II.

To be sure, the unsettling atmosphere which for Lutherans marked the aftermath of World War I was to some degree overcome by the feeling that common enemies nevertheless had to be faced. Lutherans from all over the world wanted to manifest a united reaction to the aggressively anti-Christian actions of Soviet Communism. Further, there was a felt need for solidarity among Protestants in the face of what was then perceived as a strong movement of "re-Catholicizing" taking place in many European countries.

In 1945 these early, difficult relationships between Lutherans were reborn. The myth of the phoenix comes to mind, for it proved possible to reestablish and further develop the connections established after World War I only to be cut off by the second war. This event silenced the skeptical voices of friend and foe alike. Could not the image of the phoenix be used to characterize this remarkable reawakening? The bird of beauty, seemingly destroyed as it burns, is miraculously reborn, rises from the ashes, and soars toward the sky with the same glory as before. At least something of this image comes to mind in relation to the founding of the Lutheran World Federation in 1947. Those who had labored so diligently and under such difficult circumstances after World War I had seen their hopes shattered at the outbreak of World War II and for a long time saw no chance of renewal. But a rebirth, phoenix-like, took place.

The situation in 1945, when the bombs had rained their destruction, was desperate, like that of the phoenix burnt to ashes. There were endless masses of people who lacked even the most basic essentials for daily life; bitterness and hatred dominated; the structures for international cooperation created after World War I to prevent future catastrophe had proved completely illusory. How could even Lutherans, bound by a common faith, set out again to create community? Such questions need to be asked, if the atmosphere at the time of the founding of the Lutheran World Federation is to be understood. These questions lead to one of the basic considerations which this chapter will pursue: How are we to measure the continuity and discontinuity between the two attempts, in 1923 and 1947, to create Lutheran fellowship and cooperation?

Even if it is true that the general political environment provides the immediate historical setting for early twentieth-century endeavors toward international community among Lutheran churches, it would be gravely misleading to describe those endeavors solely as a reaction against certain patterns in international politics. The origins of Lutheran cooperation should not be seen merely as self-defense against external threats. These origins must also be seen in terms of the desire to share mutual reflection on a common heritage of faith in spite of the barriers of nationality, language, and culture; to share worship as integral to confessional community; to share a common strategy of mission at a time when war had exacted a great toll on the churches in "the mission fields"; to share in theological learning and research; and, not least, to organize a network for actions of solidarity that would offer aid to sisters and brothers who as refugees often were suffering the deprivations of war—hunger, homelessness, disability. Such factors as these, arising from the inner life of churches, when put in the context of national and international social and political realities, go far to provide an appropriate description of the setting for the founding of the Lutheran World Federation.

Clearly, then, the second twentieth-century attempt to forge international Lutheran fellowship and cooperation was connected with the aftermath of World War II. In this there are parallels to the setting, more than two decades earlier, when the Lutheran World Convention was established. Yet in 1947 there were also important factors of discontinuity with the prehistory of the LWF.

## Three Dominant Blocks:
## German, American, and Nordic Lutherans

IT IS POSSIBLE to compare 1923 and 1947 as complicated struggles to come together in spite of suspicion and sacrosanct nationalism—in other words, as efforts to realize nonpolitical visions in an international situation that provided no confidence at all for the viability of such visions. Consequently, one feature of the origins of Lutheran cooperation in this century was the competition between pioneering leaders and between blocks of participants, a rivalry that stemmed from divergent interests and expectations.

Yet it would be a distortion if the events of both 1923 and 1947 were to be regarded only as results of hard negotiation, as stories of compromise where the participants were forced to sacrifice points of principle. Rather, the achievements of these two innovating events came about because of the contributions of both individuals and national churches. Only if these realities of serious cooperation and shared visions are seen in connection will it be appropriate to investigate the role of individuals and national churches. Such investigation, to be sure, will then also reveal costly struggles for power on the part of leading personalities, individual churches, and blocks of churches.

The Lutheran World Federation was founded in 1947 upon four pillars. These pillars shaped the common vision and, at the same time, led to divergent views. We shall develop our exposition in terms of these four pillars:

- rescue for the needy
- common initiatives in mission
- joint efforts in theology
- a common response to the ecumenical challenge

Sharing these four concerns, the churches that formed the Federation took their stand at Lund in 1947 under the straightforward theme, "The Lutheran Church in the World Today." Sometimes they diverged from one another because of differing experiences and goals, but always they shared a sense of common obligation for the establishment of a new organ of international Lutheran fellowship and cooperation.

Before examining in some detail the characteristics of the three dominant blocks of churches involved in the founding of the LWF, attention must be paid to a fourth group. We refer to the "minority churches," even though this group had so many single participants that it hardly comprised a block. These minority churches were in a situation that had been unique and troubled for generations. They were impoverished—particularly the Lutheran churches in Russia and Eastern Europe—to the extent that the more prosperous churches had for long been conscious of an obligation to provide material aid. Moreover, they were invariably situated in confessional tension with majority churches, usually Roman Catholic or Orthodox, which often had extremely close ties to governmental authorities. If, in what follows, we concentrate on the three main blocks of national churches, it is not without an awareness of the importance of these minority churches. What is said here by way of generalized characterization is to be supplemented by further information provided throughout the present volume.

*The Lutheran Churches of Germany*

Germany was, of course, "the motherland of the Reformation." However, its leading role in the establishment of international Lutheran cooperation was not only due to its history but also to far more recent contributions. A case in point: the German universities as places of theological reflection and research exerted an influence far beyond national borders. For centuries, theologians from all parts of the world had studied at German universities in the regular course of their academic work. The specific character of Lutheran theology in respect to scholarship and research can largely be ascribed to the German university tradition. Moreover, other aspects of German culture—for example, poetry and hymnody, in which a person like Paul Gerhard excelled, and music, marked especially by the accomplishment of Johann Sebastian Bach—have been of great importance to the entire Lutheran family. To these influences from Germany should also be added elements of practical church life: liturgy, parish education, and the development of Christian institutions of mercy and social ministry.

German Lutheranism contributed strongly to the confessional consciousness of Lutheranism throughout the world. There was primarily the Reformation heritage itself, but also the legacy of Lutheran opposition to the "confessional union" instituted by the Prussian king in 1817 and inspired by the national revival that arose during the Napoleonic invasion. "Confessional Lutheranism" was developed further in response to liberal Protestantism, which in Germany played a major role in church life throughout the nineteenth and early twentieth centuries.

As far as the political context is concerned, the Lutheran churches of Germany went through a transition during the time of their involvement in the movement toward international Lutheran cooperation. For one thing, these churches had lived in a close alliance with the state (*"Thron und Altar"* and *"landesherrliches Kirchenregiment"*) right up to the formation of the Weimar Republic in 1919. In addition, the Lutheran churches shared the overall German inability to accept the results of World War I and the conditions of the Treaty of Versailles. The consequent tendency toward national frustration and international isolation was supplemented by the tension between movements of confessional orthodoxy and those calling for Protestant interconfessionalism.

The Lutheran churches of Germany contributed many leading figures to the movement for international Lutheran fellowship. Bishop Ludwig Ihmels (1858–1933) from the Church of Saxony was a pioneer at the 1923 assembly in Eisenach and continued to hold positions of leadership until his death. His colleague from the Church of Hanover, Bishop August

Marahrens (1875–1950) carried for long a similar responsibility. As will be discussed below, however, he was so deeply marked by the nationalist propaganda of the Nazis that, even though he was prominent in the Confessing Church, he became, so to speak, a stumbling block in the period of preparation for the rebirth of international Lutheran cooperation after the Second World War and in 1945 was forced to retire as president of the Lutheran World Convention. Marahrens's position of international leadership was subsequently assumed by his successor as Bishop of Hanover and second president of the Lutheran World Federation, Hanns Lilje (1899–1977; cf. pp. 430–37 below).

### The Lutheran Churches of North America

The Lutheran churches in Germany were split into regional churches (*Landeskirchen*), reflecting centuries of territorial autonomy. The North American churches, somewhat in contrast, were organized in terms of their dependency—in terms of immigration, language, and tradition—on the churches of their respective "old countries." To be sure, the important and influential National Lutheran Council had been in existence since 1918, but it remains a fact that regional, linguistic, and cultural divisions persisted as barriers to Lutheran unity in America for a long time thereafter. Nevertheless, the American churches were deeply imbued with the feelings of common obligation which marked the life of the Lutheran World Convention and, later, the Lutheran World Federation.

American Lutheranism in the period under consideration was marked by strongly conservative movements which resulted in serious internal tension regarding the definition of confessional integrity. There were many who adhered to a rigorously orthodox if not outright fundamentalist view of the Bible and to a vigorous opposition to liberal interpretations of the creeds. This tendency manifested itself in extreme hesitancy regarding ecumenical fellowship. Traces of this conservatism—still very much alive in the separatistic Lutheran Church–Missouri Synod—continue to play a role in Lutheran church life in America today.

This deep conservatism, however, did not altogether block actions toward solidarity between American Lutherans and their fellows in other countries. On the contrary, the Americans played a leading role from the very beginning in providing aid to needy brothers and sisters. Not only were the Americans willing to provide considerable sums of money for the operational budgets of relief and aid programs, but they also proved to be efficient in terms of organization. The mark of American Lutheran leaders was particularly felt in these regards. The pioneering leader of the Lutheran World Convention was the American John Morehead (1867–

1936) who, during his service in the first decade of international Lutheran cooperation, was widely known as "Mr. Lutheran." No less prominent a role was taken by Sylvester C. Michelfelder (1889–1951; cf. pp. 481–87 below) who, from Geneva, became after 1945 the main organizational figure behind world Lutheranism, serving as the first Executive Secretary of the Lutheran World Federation. Michelfelder was succeeded by another American, Carl Lund-Quist (1908–1965; cf. pp. 488–93 below).

## The Nordic Lutheran Churches

There is ample reason for describing the churches of the Nordic countries as a homogeneous group, even allowing for minor differences between them. When viewed in an international perspective, these Nordic Lutheran churches stand out as majority churches, enjoying an unbroken Lutheran tradition since the Reformation and remaining intimately connected to their nation states. In this international context, these churches most often acted as a united body, especially in regard to the Lutheran World Federation. In respect to inner-Nordic relations, however, there were a number of points of conflict, for example, the tension between Iceland and Denmark, its former colonial ruler; the Norwegian offense at the political domination on the part of its neighbors, Sweden and Denmark; or Norway's resentment at the alleged failure of Sweden to show solidarity during the Second World War. In respect to Finland, its first point of political orientation was clearly its relation to the mighty neighboring power in the east, the Soviet Union.

Within the international community of Lutheran churches, the Nordics were destined to play a mediating role. They had been politically neutral during the First World War, and that was a significance fact at Eisenach in 1923. They were small countries without exclusive links with Germany. In point of fact, it was essential to the self-understanding of the Nordic Lutheran churches to have open relations—in respect to church life and theology—with both the European continent and the English-speaking world.

This international outlook was impressively demonstrated by the church leader and Archbishop of Uppsala, Sweden, Nathan Söderblom (1866–1931). He was an ecumenical leader of considerable importance, having been leader of the Universal Christian Conference on Life and Work held at Stockholm in 1925, an important milestone in the course of the modern ecumenical movement. As we shall see, however, many conservative Lutherans looked askance at him, considering him a "liberal" theologian. His fellow Swede, Anders Nygren (1890–1978; cf. pp. 421–29 below), who was elected the first President of the LWF at the Lund Assembly in 1947, was another Nordic church leader of genuinely international consequence.

The Church of Norway offered a leader of the same stature in Eivind Berggrav (1884–1959) who was in fact extremely close to both Söderblom and Nygren. Berggrav was not only a prominent theologian and the Bishop of Oslo but also the leader of his church in its opposition to the Quisling regime during the years of Germany's occupation of Norway, 1940–1945. Even before World War II, moreover, Berggrav had led his church in the establishment of many ecumenical contacts with churches in both Germany and the English-speaking world.

The Danish church did not produce individual figures who occupied similar positions of international importance. However, Alfred Theodor Jørgensen (1874–1953) was a prominent member of the executive committee of the Lutheran World Convention from its inception and continued to play a leading role in matters of organization, structure, and identity up to the founding of the LWF. At the Lund Assembly, Jørgensen was the only surviving "founding father," and he was elected to the first LWF Executive Committee on which he served until his death.

## The First Pillar: Rescue for the Needy

THE STORY of Lutheran cooperation in the twentieth century is rooted in the setting created by two world wars. Given this context, relief work was a necessity—perhaps *the* necessity of the moment.

### After World War I

The Lutheran minority churches of Eastern Europe were in particularly dire straits at the end of the First World War. Material needs were pressing and urgent; food and clothing were desperately needed. Simultaneously, these churches were in a difficult struggle for their very survival. In some places they faced massive pressure from majority churches of a differing confessional background; in other places the pressures were more political and ideological.

It is against this background that the contribution of John A. Morehead, first president of the Lutheran World Convention, is to be understood. His meetings with suffering fellow Lutherans from Eastern Europe convinced him of the need to organize relief work, and it was not least this pioneering labor which contributed so decisively to the formation of the Lutheran World Federation.

Extracts from Morehead's reports concerning relief work in Russia after

World War I present a vivid picture both of the atmosphere at that historic moment and of the enormous difficulties that had to be overcome. These difficulties were not simply created by the famine and privations following the widespread drought of the 1920s. Just as often the churches faced political harassment and even systematic persecution that damaged their public structures, schools, diaconal institutions, and administrative organs. It was particularly difficult to maintain structures for the education of clergy. In this situation it was an elementary requirement that relief should be effective and should arrive at the areas—often remote and barely accessible—where the need was greatest. At the same time, circumstances, political and churchly, required that relief be given with discretion and tact. Both material and other forms of relief were required, as was demonstrated in the maintenance of aid to the school for clergy founded in St. Petersburg / Leningrad in 1924.

In this context, Morehead raised questions and proposed strategies for discussion within the executive committee of the Lutheran World Convention. In a letter to Alfred Theodor Jørgensen, of August 10, 1924, he wrote:

> Unfortunately, a true picture of the hard circumstances in which our Lutheran brethren in Russia are placed is not given without statements as to the oppressive attitude of the present government, notwithstanding its declaration of freedom of conscience, etc. For example, during the concluding service of the General Synod, [Theophil] Meyer [Bishop of Moscow] was cited to appear before the Intelligence Department of the Soviet Government the following day. He was subjected to an inquisition for two hours and finally dismissed with a warning.

> There is threat of another famine in Russia. Our Lutheran people are terribly impoverished there. They were unable to hold this meeting without financial help from the [U.S.] National Lutheran Council to pay travelling expenses and to provide meals at the restaurant in Moscow. They will not be able to make this new organization of the Synod effective without help from their Lutheran brethren in other lands. Cannot our executive committee of the Eisenach Convention do something to line up the Lutherans to give united help to our brethren in Russia? (papers of the Danish National Committee of the Lutheran World Convention, Copenhagen, Rigsarkivet)

A year later, on April 17, 1925, Morehead wrote again to Jørgensen to seek support for larger contributions to Lutherans in Russia:

> Unfortunately, the anti-Christian and anti-church policies of the Soviet Government are such that we dare not give any public sign that we are in relation with the Lutheran church of Russia, that we are sending them assistance, and especially that we are supporting the church there, lest it may increase the difficulties of our brethren in Russia and even lead to the imprisonment of the

pastors. The Soviet Government definitely declined to give a visa to the pass-port of the Commissioner of the National Lutheran Council, whom we sent to Russia, but who waited in vain at Riga for a month for permission to go to Moscow.

But we have a private channel through which we can safely send money for private delivery to the Oberkirchenrat of our Lutheran church in Russia, of which Bishops [Theophil] Meyer and [Arthur] Malmgren are of course leading members. They urgently need money to support this churchly organization, to maintain the ninety active Lutheran pastors and other needy families of the church, and to assist the famine stricken in Siberia. (ibid.)

Morehead in the meantime faced difficulties in the donor churches in the United States. People there were not willing to allow Morehead to use money collected in the American Lutheran churches for the purposes he had in mind. Leading figures within the churches wanted to tie an eccle-siastical-confessional condition to relief so as to make certain that it really was fellow believers within the confessional family who were receiving support. This was described in clear terms by Morehead in a letter to Jør-gensen, July 7, 1925:

One fact that we cannot change, even if we would, is this, that the Lutheran church bodies of America will not support any theological seminary of a union character anywhere. The only way to secure the hearty and generous support of the Lutherans of America for this vital enterprise of a Lutheran training school for pastors in Leningrad is to develop it as a real Lutheran insti-tution under the entire control of the Lutheran Church of Russia and in entire conformity with the historic position of the Lutheran Church. (ibid.)

On this point there was a clear difference of view between the Ameri-can Lutherans and the majority of the Europeans. In Europe a great part of relief aid was distributed through inter-European and interdenominational services such as those based in Switzerland and organized by Adolf Keller (1872–1963), founder of the European Central Bureau for Relief to the Protestant Churches. As far as Denmark was concerned, for instance, relief work after World War I was organized on a national basis, represen-tatives of the national church being part of the same committee as repre-sentatives of other philanthropic organizations. Thus, this disagreement between the Americans and the Europeans became a particularly sensitive point of conflict in the Lutheran World Convention, and these divergences persisted for a considerable length of time.

A challenge of quite a different kind arose from the Convention's atti-tude toward other confessions and toward interconfessional work. Here too was a pronounced difference between those who wanted to follow a strictly defined Lutheran line and those who pleaded for a line which was more open to dialogue. As far as the Convention's attitude toward Roman Catholicism was concerned, however, there was far greater unanimity. Indeed, it can be said that the solidarity of the Convention was strengthened by a common conviction that the aggressive "re-Catholicizing" of the 1920s needed to be countered. Again, we get a vivid impression of the situation from a letter of Morehead to Jørgensen, June 12, 1924:

> It seems perfectly clear that at its next meeting our committee may find a proper field of service in the common study of the problem of Rome. The situation in this connection has grown very much more serious since our meeting in Copenhagen. It may be that the committee may find it possible to express itself in the form of recommendations or otherwise on this subject. It will mean much if all the forces of the Lutheran Church can be brought to understand the seriousness of Rome's offensive. Perhaps the committee may do something also to stress the Evangelical way of meeting this adversary. To my mind, this is not merely a well planned counter-Reformation on the part of the Vatican. In my view, according to her age-long policy, Rome is planning a worldwide special drive to win all parts of Christendom to reunion within the visible organization of the Roman hierarchy so far as may be possible by the use of every measure at her command. Witness the formation of a Catholic union and the establishment of a theological school in Vienna for the purpose of winning the Eastern Orthodox Church to the one true mother church of Rome! Witness the proclamation of a holy year by the Pope in which is stressed the unity of all Christians within the bosom of Rome! The organization of the laymen of the Roman Catholic Church in the Knights of Columbus in America is very significant. The two newly appointed cardinals in America make no secret of the fact that the aim of Rome here is to win a dominant place by political and spiritual methods in American life. In the second sermon Luther preached after his return from Worms, he makes it clear that the Word of truth, not force, is the power that will weaken the papacy. The increase of the number of devoted confessors of the positive Evangelical faith through the preaching of the Gospel by word and by printed page should, to my mind, be the central thought of the counter-offensive. (ibid.)

### After World War II

A few months after the May 1945 end of the war in Europe, a comprehensive Lutheran relief operation was set in motion to aid those on whom the war had inflicted the greatest suffering. The secretariat was in Geneva, but it was the Americans who played the major role in initiating the work. They contributed large amounts of money to the operation and also sent highly qualified collaborators to head up the operation—persons such as Sylvester Michelfelder (cf. pp. 481–87 below), Stewart Herman (b. 1909), and Howard Hong (b. 1911) who first went to Europe in 1945 under the auspices of the YMCA and returned in 1947 to work with Michelfelder.

The needs were extensive and not restricted to certain sections of Europe. Many Lutheran churches were in dire need of help, and there were many who were prepared to help. Needs included medical assistance, the resettlement of displaced persons, food for the starving, and accommodations for those who had lost their homes. To illustrate the extent of the need: about ten million Lutherans of a total of about seventy million Lutheran Christians in Europe were refugees, having had to leave the place they called home. This need could not be met by governments alone but required the support of private organizations, including the churches. It was again the case that the countries of East Europe were particularly hard hit. After the ravages of the Nazi occupation, the Communist takeover gave rise to new floods of refugees and to persecution and oppression for those who remained behind. Despair was great among the refugees, as it was among those who remained in their homelands, and the despair was both physical and spiritual.

Other countries were in need as well. Countries that have since come to be reckoned among the world's wealthiest, such as Norway and Finland, had been badly affected by the war and were in great need of assistance from abroad. A country like Denmark, which had not suffered as much as many other countries also occupied by Germany, was nevertheless faced with an immense challenge by its decision to take in large numbers of refugees, particularly from the East. Between the autumn of 1945 and the summer of 1947, 250,000 refugees were received by Denmark, a country of merely 4,000,000. The presence of so many refugees created new confrontations. The bitterness of the Danes that resulted from the German occupation was now often turned against the refugees, who were frequently Germans or ethnic Germans, as though they were personally responsible for the Nazi misdeeds. In this situation of tension, a group of Danish clergymen who were committed to support for the refugees made a public statement: "We fought against Nazism because it would not recognize a fellow human being in a Jew. In the same way we shall fight against a new Nazism which will not recognize a fellow human being in a German." There was clearly a need for a specifically churchly contribution to the solution of such tensions. But the general order of priority in relief work, in Denmark and in other lands, was to be found in the familiar slogan, "First bread, then the catechism."

In precisely this historical situation the Nordic churches felt most strongly that they had an obligation they could not reject. Obviously they had to support all efforts to provide relief to those in the greatest need, but they also felt it imperative to take initiatives to rebuild confidence in former adversaries so that peaceful relations might be recreated between neighbors. The Danish theologian Kristen Ejner Skydsgaard (1902–1990), later known as one of the outstanding Lutheran observers at Vatican II, had such an undertaking in mind when he pointed to the necessity of collaboration between the Nordic Lutheran churches. Skydsgaard affirmed that only together could those churches resist the temptation to create "an iron ring of isolation and hatred around Germany." Such an undertaking required more than financial support and personal goodwill if relief work was to be truly constructive and if a new period of genuine fellowship was to be created. It was necessary that Germany's former adversaries should be aware of the deep feelings of many Germans who were possessed by intense frustration at being what they considered the victims of unjustified retribution on the part of the victors. Many in Germany saw themselves as having no prospect of a better future.

There can be no question that the famous "Stuttgart Declaration" of October 1945 stands as one of the most significant ecumenical events in the history of the twentieth century. In this declaration leaders of the German Confessing Church acknowledged before representatives of many ecumenical organizations that they bore guilt for the war and its devastations. This acknowledgment of an insufficient confession of faith was accompanied by an expression of repentance and a confession of sin. Now they asked to be allowed to take part in the building of a new Christian community.

However important and essential that declaration of guilt was, it must also be recognized that both in 1945 and afterwards considerable numbers of church people in Germany could not fully accept unilateral and collective guilt. They could confess their own sin and guilt, but they regarded the expression of unilateral and collective guilt as a misplaced generalization that made way for additional ignominious suffering on top of all that had already been experienced. To this was added a great deal of bitterness at what was perceived to be the harsh attitude of the occupying powers after the German surrender. Thus the international community of Lutheran churches saw a particular need to express a common will to mutual reconciliation that could bury such suspicion and bitterness once and for all.

In this situation Sylvester Michelfelder had a deep appreciation of the importance of such a pastoral approach. It is crucial to point this out, for it has frequently been maintained that the American Lutheran participants in post–World War II relief work lacked sympathy with European traditions and ways of thought. The exact reverse is evident, for instance, in a report which Michelfelder prepared after journeying through Germany in November and December 1945 in the company of American colleagues. The group met with Martin Niemöller (1892–1984), the internationally known leader of the Confessing Church who had himself spent eight years in a Nazi concentration camp. Niemöller had tried to explain the feelings of the German people in relation to current conditions and, not least, in relation to the Stuttgart Declaration of guilt. He spoke to his American guests in the following way:

> The echo from ministers and congregations has been rather poor, since a good deal of contradiction has become evident. Even more refusals have come from such parts of the population which do not belong to the church in the proper sense. By far the greatest obstacle seems to be that every work of guilt is met with the statement: "Certainly Hitler and his gang have been criminals, but the new situation is worse and everybody knows well enough." People are suffering from hunger and it is a well-known fact that people are starving in the eastern provinces; people are suffering from cold; above all, people are without hope that things might be altered for the better in the near future or even years; the economic situation is pressing on minds and souls; the more so as family life is broken down; some have been arrested without cause, others have been arrested without knowing the cause of their arrest or imprisonment; they have been unable to communicate with their families—just the same, people say, as under the Nazi rule.

> If the church is to fulfill its mission of leading our nation to repentance and a new beginning according to Christian rules and principles, there must be a new course of dealing with a nation on the part of the powers of occupation. Otherwise the soul will harden irrevocably, let the church do and say what she may. In the beginning of the occupation quite another attitude was prevailing. Then there was a feeling of release of hope, even of guilt, and thankfulness. People knew at that time that the Allies had fought and suffered for our redemption and we are indebted to them forever! This feeling will be found nowhere now, and souls have been hardened nearly unto despair: "All men are liars." (LWF Danish National Committee, Rigsarkivet, Copenhagen—Box: "Lund 1947")

Even as donor churches from outside the European continent were meeting the most elementary needs for daily survival, it became possible to devote attention also to the reconstruction of church buildings. In the light of the persisting tension between the Germans and their conquerors, as we have described it, the fact that church leaders from neutral, prosperous Sweden should have asked Swedish congregations to give toward the rebuilding of churches in bombed-out Germany speaks with a particular eloquence. Behind this initiative there lies at one and the same time a sensitivity to the Germans' jarred nerves, a respect for the signs of a church renewal in Germany, and a recognition that the churches of Sweden only needed to give from their abundance in order to come to the support of their fellow believers who were in great distress.

Despite its poor external setting, the life of worship in Germany is now expressing a remarkable renewal. No one goes to church out of routine, people go because they have a real need for prayer and praise with other Christians and for shared participation in the Word and in Communion. It is reported in many places that the size of congregations despite the circumstances frequently has grown rather than diminished.

What most strikes a foreigner is the almost total lack of decoration in all these emergency churches and temporary places of worship. The first thing is that the places should be suitable for meetings, an aesthetic consideration comes afterwards. One dean in Kiel relates how during a whole winter they succeeded in nailing together pieces of wood so as to make a door and entrance to the town's biggest underground church. Before this the wind and the snow had blown right in.

You do not need to have seen these emergency churches in order to understand that the very simplest decorations are acceptable. A freezing cold cellar acquires the feeling of a church if one puts an altar cloth on the table, or perhaps a crucifix on the wall.

The German church has expressed the wish that we from the Swedish side should help them to give a worthier liturgical character to their very temporary places of worship. We therefore issue an invitation to the Swedish congregations and to individuals to meet this request. (the Papers of Anders Nygren, Lund, the University Library)

## The Second Pillar: Common Initiatives in Mission

THE HARDSHIP imposed by the Treaty of Versailles made it difficult for the Germans to adjust to the realities of world politics after 1919. It was an essential element in the restrictions imposed by the treaty that the Germans allow their colonies to be transferred to an international mandate administered by the League of Nations. As a consequence of this, German missionaries were forced to give up their work in what had been their mission fields. It was thus a matter of urgency for these "orphaned missions" to find new mission agencies willing and capable of replacing the Germans. This process was one among several which caused the Germans to feel humiliated and deprived of their national dignity. Bitterness was often directed toward those who replaced them, mainly the Americans but also to a considerable extent the Swedes. Understandably, this tension in regard to missions was one of the barriers to progress in the development of global cooperation among Lutherans after World War I.

In this situation Lutherans from many countries felt a common responsibility to make a serious attempt at cooperation in missions in spite of palpable suspicions and divergences. The first World Conference on Missions, Edinburgh 1910, had agreed on a resolution that urged the churches to cooperate in the interest of efficiency and credibility. and it was something of the spirit of that resolution which was needed among Lutherans after World War I.

A solution was found in the 1920s with regard to the immediate needs of the orphaned missions. Nevertheless, the Lutherans did not succeed in taking further steps to genuine understanding and cooperation after the Eisenach assembly of the Lutheran World Convention. This failure can be illustrated by two instances. First, efforts to establish a theological seminary in India failed. Had there been success, these efforts would perhaps have proved that it was possible to advance beyond the very general resolutions of the Eisenach assembly. Second, there were tensions within the committee in charge of planning the second assembly of the Convention for Copenhagen, 1929, precisely over the question of invitations to missionary churches to participate as full delegates in the assembly. These tensions were signs of an initial inability to deal in an adequate manner with the question of cooperation in mission.

Such tensions had not been forgotten when the Lutheran churches convened at Lund in 1947. This made it necessary that a thorough discussion of the mission responsibilities of the churches be on the assembly's agenda. The seriousness of these discussions is evident in the report of the second issue group and in several of the plenary resolutions. The atmosphere had changed radically from that of the 1920s. There was now a deliberate will to reintegrate the German missionary societies, and strong formulations in several resolutions indicate that all Lutheran churches were being urged to cooperate in missionary efforts, not only among themselves but also with the International Missionary Council. A serious attitude toward the latter agency was seen as an integral part of a common Lutheran ecumenical obligation.

This plea, of course, was based on the missionary character of the Christian gospel. The second section of the official report from Lund is entitled, "Performing Her Mission in a Devastated World: Evangelism and Stewardship." There it is stated that "the obligation to carry the Gospel to every human being is a sacred responsibility entrusted to all Christians." Moreover, the section makes specific recommendations "to foster a unified approach in spite of differences among the home fields and sending agencies." The determination evidenced at Lund to avoid rivalry among mission agencies and to seek cooperation on the home fields is to be followed by the formation of unified churches so that "the national churches formed under various mission societies may develop into self-subsisting churches." Clearly the missionary imperatives expressed in the Lund report still took place within the horizon of colonialism, as is apparent from the fact that in 1947 it was not yet common to talk even of "younger churches." Nevertheless, it is to be observed that there was a strong recommendation to move toward "indigenous, self-supporting church[es]." It was also recommended to move toward the restoration of orphaned missions to their original agencies "as soon as the latter are again able to assume their support and control." It was made clear that in respect to mission, there should be a motivation "to transcend national barriers" and to insist upon an essential combination of evangelism with "faith and action." Thus reconstruction and rehabilitation were seen to be at the core of the missionary obligation of the Lutheran churches. We shall see in due course how this new vision of cooperation in mission worked out in the years that followed.

## The Third Pillar:
## Joint Efforts in Theology

AT THE CONCLUSION of World War II the primary theological concern of the Lutheran churches was the critical rethinking of Lutheran identity. The war had great consequences for Lutheran self-understanding in relation to ecclesial identity, to ethical judgments concerning society and nation, as well as in relation to the human isolation brought about by the sufferings of armed conflict. The wounds were deep, and healing was an immense task for the churches. It was crucial to remake personal friendships and it was necessary to reestablish organizational structures and links between structures.

When healing occurred, it was possible to deal with the past. But in many instances a critical confrontation with the immediate past itself brought new problems. In many countries bitter conflicts developed regarding the role of both governments and citizens in the war, and even extensive judicial actions were taken. Understandably, these events cast a kind of shadow over the churches, particularly in cases where church leaders were charged with having compromised their Christian responsibilities by undue compliance or even alliance with the Nazi authorities.

The Lutheran churches of Germany were obviously shaken by this painful examination of what had happened under Hitler. The pain was intense both for those who were accused and for those who were given the authority of judgment. In a number of spectacular instances, such investigations acquired ecumenical significance when criticism was directed toward Lutheran leaders and theologians who had held positions of trust and responsibility. The repercussions caused by all of this became particularly important for the founding assembly of the Lutheran World Federation at Lund in 1947. We shall examine certain individual cases.

## August Marahrens

Already during the first months after the end of the war, a number of the international Lutheran leaders who were involved in relief work in Germany made it clear that under no circumstances would it be possible for Bishop August Marahrens, until that time the President of the Lutheran World Convention and Landesbischof in Hanover, to continue in his position of responsibility and trust. Sylvester Michelfelder was altogether convinced of this and, independently, the views of the Swedish Archbishop Erling Eidem (1880–1972) took the same direction. Eidem was particularly important in this connection, because he had played a significant ecumenical role in respect to the German church struggle and because he bore the prestige of being successor as Archbishop of Uppsala to the ecumenical leader, Nathan Söderblom. Moreover, since Eidem was Vice President of the Lutheran World Convention he was to become, upon Marahrens' resignation, its President.

When the Lutheran World Convention's Executive Committee met in Copenhagen in December 1945 it was soon clear that in respect to Bishop Marahrens the North American and the Nordic members were in complete agreement. Marahrens had, in point of fact, resigned his post after strong external pressure, but he did not accept the substance of the criticism directed toward him, viz., that his activities during World War II in respect to the Nazi government had actually compromised his ability to provide international leadership within the Lutheran churches. The executive committee noted with regret that in announcing his resignation, Marahrens had not given a satisfactory reason for his decision. Nevertheless, the resignation took place, and Archbishop Eidem was named president *pro tem.*

The resignation was an extremely sensitive issue at the Copenhagen meeting and became more painful afterwards in spite of the fact that those pressing for it tried to act as gently and tactfully as possible. Marahrens himself reacted bitterly and with repeated attempts at self-justification. Moreover, he received some support in his position from many who were close to him in his own church, a fact that needs to be seen in connection with the deeply emotional atmosphere that characterized much of the German church at the end of 1945. We need, however, to look more closely at the incident: What were its historical causes? Why is it that the case of August Marahrens illuminated so clearly deeper theological questions relating to issues of Lutheran identity and political ethics?

Marahrens had been among the first members of the German confessional movement that grew up in protest against Nazi-inspired elements that had infiltrated German theology and church politics in 1933–34. In opposition to the threat that came from the "German Christian" ideology, Marahrens hesitated not a moment in calling for church resistance based on principles of the Lutheran Reformation. He maintained this confessionally based resistance within his own *Landeskirche* and also as a leader in the national "confessing movement." Yet Marahrens took this line of resistance in respect to the church's *confessional* identity while at the same time taking a positive attitude toward the government's *political* authority. In fact, he did not hesitate in making enthusiastic public pronouncements in support of the politics pursed by the Nazi authorities after 1933.

An instance of this occurred when Marahrens was in Copenhagen in 1936 to take part in the celebration of the 400th Anniversary of the Reformation in Denmark. As President of the Lutheran World Convention, he was a prominent guest at the celebration. In a newspaper interview he was asked by Danish journalists about the situation of the Confessing Church in Germany and was also requested to comment on the general political situation in his country. In the course of his response he said:

> Secularization (the making worldly of the life of a nation) we can see in its full development in Soviet Russia; that is why the whole German people and the Lutheran church in particular supports Hitler in his courageous struggle against Bolshevism. The people of the Confessing Church are careful to fulfill their duties as citizens and are deeply grateful to Hitler for making Germany a bulwark against Communism. We will help Hitler and the German people on the basis of the gospel, but naturally we can only go as far as our Christian conscience will allow. (from the Danish newspaper, *Kristeligt Dagblad*, now in the papers of the Danish National Committee of the Lutheran World Convention, Copenhagen, Rigsarkivet)

Marahrens maintained this basic attitude even though racism and persecution became more and more evident—not least to critical observers abroad—as the motivating force behind the Nazi party ideology. Additionally, during the war itself he stressed his own national patriotism and in the early years of the conflict, was enthusiastic in his praise of the armed forces' success. After the failed coup of July 20, 1944, Bishop Marahrens expressed relief that the Führer had escaped attack from unpatriotic forces.

If the showdown with Marahrens in 1945 was so uncomfortable, both within Germany and in the wider international connection, it was due primarily to the realities of his public conduct during the war. But these specific instances must be seen against the much wider background of a distinct tradition within Lutheranism. This strain of Lutheranism was marked by an unquestioning, patriarchal understanding of authority and by a manifestly inadequate sense of the connection, which at times must become critical, between confessional fidelity and appropriate obedience to political authority. In the Germany of World War II political authority was marked by such totalitarian ideology, fanatical racism, and militarism as to cause it to forfeit any right to be considered a "true Christian authority."

Hanns Lilje, who succeeded Marahrens as Landesbischof in Hanover and also quickly emerged as a leading spokesman for a new generation of German Lutherans, had a quite different approach to political authority. He tried to a certain extent to protect Marahrens, in the hope of preventing an overly hasty legal action; but his actions nevertheless made it clear to non-German church leaders that he was one of those who possessed the ability to lead the Lutheran church in Germany into a new period. That confidence finds remarkable expression in a letter from Michelfelder to Lilje dated October 3, 1946:

> I'm very anxious to hear what is happening to the Lutheran churches' program in Germany. I sincerely hope that nothing will happen to upset the program of the EKiD [the Evangelische Kirche in Deutschland, the Evangelical Church in Germany]. I also hope that Pastor Niemöller will not press it too much that the EkiD should become a church in the full sense, but remain a Bund or Federation. This is no time to be rocking the boat, and I want to urge upon you again, this is no time for you to quit the boat either. Stay with it and help to bring this good ship through in these perilous seas. We now know what Byrnes [James Byrnes, the American Secretary of State] has told the German people; we also have heard the announcement of what the [War Trials] Tribunal at Nürenberg has done. We all realize more every day how much we need to back you up and you can count on me and the Lutheran World Federation for all the help that we can give you. I have now accepted the executive secretaryship of the Lutheran World Federation and will give it everything I have, but I can't do much alone. I will need such faithful spirits as you to back me up. Germany will be an important part of this Lutheran World Federation and we need every man. Now I don't know who is going to appoint your delegates or who will select the one who shall take Bishop Marahrens' place on the executive committee. The executive committee was unanimous in accepting his resignation not only as president of the Lutheran World Convention but also as a member of the executive committee. We all realize that this is a delicate subject and I know how you feel about it, but we have to consider the cause

rather than an individual. (Lund Assembly, correspondence manuscripts, Box 1, LWF Archives, Geneva)

### Carl Stange

As painful as the events surrounding August Marahrens was another confrontation which also possessed a clear international dimension: the conflict over Carl Stange's leadership of the Luther Academy in Sondershausen/Thuringia. Stange (1870–1959) was professor of systematic theology at the University of Göttingen and a Luther scholar of considerable importance.

The Danish theologian A. T. Jørgensen had argued convincingly, in the assemblies of the Lutheran World Convention, 1923 and 1929, that international cooperation between Lutheran churches would not be complete unless an international, traveling "Luther Faculty" were created. In the form originally envisioned by Jørgensen the idea was never realized; but in a modified form the proposal was taken up by Carl Stange. Stange had for many years been a leading figure in connection with efforts to provide confessional Lutheranism in Germany with a highly qualified and professional theological expression. From 1932 onwards he made use of his experience in this field to establish a Luther Academy in Sondershausen with himself as director. The most important part of the work of the Academy was an annual summer conference of internationally recognized Luther scholars. Stange attempted to get official recognition for his efforts, in part by persuading Archbishop Eidem of Sweden to become chairman of the Academy's council in 1934, and in part by maintaining regular contact with the leaders of the Lutheran World Convention.

Each year the Academy's international conference included a series of lectures by invited speakers. Undeniably this event served as a meeting place for theologians and clergy from many countries even after the increasingly divisive church struggle in Germany created a growing lack of unity among conference participants. For his part, Stange based his policy as leader on the view that the meetings should be held without political or ideological interference, and he pursued this aim by forbidding non-German participants to offer critical comments about the political situation in Germany. At the same time he, more or less reluctantly, gave in to pressures from the German authorities with the result that the meetings were not altogether politically neutral. In fact, there was an increasing perception, particularly on the part of Nordic participants, of Nazi-inspired infiltration into the work of the Luther Academy, a perception which Stange himself attempted to explain away.

The holding of these conferences naturally became more complicated after the outbreak of war in 1939, but nevertheless they continued. After 1945 it was quite clear to the non-German members of the Academy's council—in particular to Archbishop Eidem and his Danish colleague, New Testament scholar Frederik Torm—that the conference program could not be continued or resumed without a thorough revision of the whole institution and its program, including the withdrawal of Carl Stange as director.

This confrontation was painful—and typical of the period. It revealed that expressions of international church cooperation can become extremely difficult if participants are subject to constant pressure from their home countries, particularly when those countries are under dictatorial rule. In such circumstances even theologians are often pressured to act as apologists—consciously or unconsciously—for their own governments. This pressure militates against the expression of criticism from outside under the pretense that such criticism represents a failure of solidarity and insight. The result is that there is a rejection of criticism from without even as there is capitulation to massive pressure from within.

When the new Lutheran World Federation's Commission on Theology began its work, it quickly became clear that the Luther Academy in Sondershausen could not be given the status of a center for theological study as originally envisioned by Carl Stange and others. More directly, it became clear that Stange's work could not be given any kind of official status within the Federation.

### Karl Barth—A Critical Voice from Outside

The cases of August Marahrens and Carl Stange indicate that at the end of World War II the international Lutheran community was required to engage in a kind of internal self-criticism. At the same time, there was considerable critical scrutiny from external sources. Most notably, there was weighty and sharp criticism directed both toward Martin Luther himself and toward his successors by the renowned Reformed theologian Karl Barth (1886–1968). Since in the present ecumenical climate this conflict between Barth and the German Lutherans maintains a great deal of currency, it is worth reflection here.

Immediately at the end of the war, Barth published a series of small books that dealt with the situation that resulted from the collapse of Nazism. All of these works gave attention to the Sisyphean tasks of national and ecclesiastical reconstruction. Barth had considerable empathy and personal solidarity with the Germans, even though some of his writings had particularly harsh titles, e.g., *Wie können die Deutschen gesund werden?* 1945 (*How Can the Germans be Cured?* English edition,

1947). For a time he gave up his academic work in his Swiss homeland in order to contribute to the task of rebuilding theological studies in the German universities. Through all of this, however, Barth did not yield in his insistence on the necessity of a thoroughgoing, critical self-examination as the inescapable precondition if the Germans were to free themselves from their imprisonment to the evil powers that had ruled the nation and made the Germans victims of their own war machine.

In Barth's critical diagnosis he pointed to the fateful line concerning social problems that stretched from Luther himself to contemporary Lutherans. Barth thought that this line could be amply documented from the time of the German church struggle. In his view the Lutherans had constantly held back from the struggle and were unwilling to come to grips with the root of the Nazi evil. Further, in the postwar situation Barth detected a continuation of the Lutherans' weak attitude to social challenges, notably in the maintenance of a special Lutheran position over against the radical wing of the confessing movement. He saw the Lutherans as determined to pursue a course of reconstruction and restoration opposed to those who, under the leadership of Martin Niemöller, wanted a radical cleansing and a new beginning in an all-Protestant ("Evangelical") church, the Evangelical Church in Germany (EKiD). This attitude so angered and pained Barth that in 1945 he could not free himself from the conviction that it represented Lutheranism pure and simple. When during those years Barth encountered Lutheran theologians from other countries, he would not budge an inch from this uncompromising judgment.

During a 1947 ecumenical conference at Bossey in Switzerland, however, Barth came into cordial contact with the Swedish Lutheran theologian, Anders Nygren, who later that year was to become the first President of the Lutheran World Federation. He later wrote that Nygren showed him "quite a different Luther" from the one he knew in Germany (cf. Eberhard Busch, *Karl Barth* [Eng. tr., Philadelphia: Fortress Press, 1976, p. 342]). Yet when he was later invited to contribute to a *Festschrift* for Nygren's 60th birthday he refused, thus showing his characteristic capacity for indignation and his tendency to see a specific instance always in the light of universal conflicts and principles. From his contact with Nygren it is clear that his understanding of Lutheran identity was shaped in a quite one-sided way by the German experience of his time. Yet the questions he raised were and remain important. In a letter of December 17, 1949, to Sylvester Michelfelder, Barth gave the following explanation of his refusal to participate in the Nygren *Festschrift*:

> You will understand that when I hear the word "Lutheranism" I think of the Lutheranism that I know personally—and know only too well—that is, German Lutheranism. And now I am afraid, that if I were to handle the theme

[Dialogue with Luther and Lutheranism] I could hardly avoid that the tone would be sharp and bitter. I have so much against the German Lutherans (from Meiser to Schlink, from Althaus to Asmussen, from Gogarten to my old friend Georg Merz—with the exception of a few individuals like Iwand, Ernst Wolf, and Heinrich Vogel); their stubborn confessional romanticism, their obstinate connection with political reaction, their unenlightened ritual Romanising, their poor showing in the time of the Church Struggle, and now last of all their sabotage of the unity of the EKiD through their separation into the VELKD [Vereinigte Evangelisch-Lutherische Kirche Deutschlands, the United Evangelical Lutheran Church of Germany, founded 1948]. (papers of Anders Nygren, Lund; copy in LWF Archives, Geneva)

When one considers such a passionate and deeply penetrating complaint, one can only, in hindsight, regret that its serious ecumenical content was never placed in a more constructive context. Naturally enough, the justification for some of Barth's complaint would have to be considered; but account would also have to be taken of his misrepresentations. Barth was unable to give an adequate characterization of those elements in the Lutheran view of the church that were irreconcilable with his own; he was simply not able to carry on a balanced discussion concerning either episcopal church order or a sacramental way of worship. It must be concluded that the ecumenical opportunity presented by Karl Barth's challenge to Lutheran identity never really reached fruition.

### Dietrich Bonhoeffer

The contribution of Dietrich Bonhoeffer (1906–1945) to a post–World War II reformulation of Lutheranism's theological identity is of an altogether different character. In the years immediately following the war, Bonhoeffer was not at all widely recognized; indeed, he was not known at all outside a very narrow circle. But in light of more recent research and on the basis of thorough documentation we now know that Bonhoeffer was himself preparing a penetrating critical revision of the Lutheran theological heritage. Bonhoeffer's theological roots were solidly within Luther's understanding of Christianity, and his effort was to work for a renewal of contemporary Lutheranism by going back to its origins.

In the course of his ecumenical activity during the war, Bonhoeffer made contacts that gave him a well-rounded picture of international Lutheranism. Twice he came into contact with Anders Nygren: first in 1936 during a journey to Sweden, which he made with a group of his students from the theological seminary of the Confessing Church at Finkenwalde, and again on his journey to Sweden in 1942, when he wished to gain the ear of non-German friends, particularly the Anglican Bishop George Bell, regarding his plans for conspiracy against Hitler.

During his visit to Sweden in 1942 Bonhoeffer sent a letter to Nygren in which he reminded the Swedish theologian of their previous contact and mutual understanding in 1936. In grateful acknowledgment of the hospitality which he and his group of students had received on that occasion, and in reference to fundamental agreements he had reached with Nygren on that occasion. Bonhoeffer wrote on April 11, 1942:

> I must use this brief moment to tell you, that we—despite all the terrible things which have happened in between—stand unaltered in the same cause and the same struggle—this you must believe, even though you hear very little from us—and that we are more conscious of our fellowship with Christians of all lands than ever before. Only in this way shall we be able to overcome these terrible times. (papers of Anders Nygrens, University Library, Lund)

As we now know, shortly after this Bonhoeffer was imprisoned, and just before the end of the war he was executed. It is noteworthy that Nygren in an undated memorandum from after the war put down the following recollection of Bonhoeffer and his visit to Lund in 1936:

> Bonhoeffer and his young friends all belonged to the resistance movement. Most of the time was spent discussing the position of the church. But what impressed me was that Bonhoeffer was not only absolutely clear in his negation of the Nazi system—at that time many were indeed clear—but that he also had a clearly positive answer to the questions of the time. Here, I thought, is one of the men who can take responsibility when this awful system will break down. (ibid.)

Referring to Bonhoeffer's letter of 1942, quoted above, Nygren ended his notes with the following words, "He held his position until the bitter end."

### "Forward to Luther"—A Reevaluation.

At the founding assembly in Lund, 1947, the atmosphere was full of joy and relief because efforts toward Lutheran unity were again being pursued after the interruption of the war. Once again it had become possible to undertake joint efforts in emergency aid and in missions, to bring confessional community to a stage of practical realization, and to establish a common program of theological study designed to reconsider Luther's theology and the Lutheran heritage. As indicated already, each of these challenges involved considerable difficulty, not least the last mentioned one.

Under these circumstances one might have expected an overly defensive posture to have marked the course of the Lund assembly. Here the achievement of Anders Nygren stands out. Having been elected the first president of the new Lutheran World Federation and not being personally subject to the accusations directed toward his German Lutheran colleagues, he boldly proclaimed the heritage of Luther as being the source of a vital message for the present era. (cf. pp. 426ff. below).

Nygren had absolutely no thought of apologizing for his position. He was utterly convinced that the message of Luther and the Lutheran reformers contained a power of renewal applicable precisely to those areas most needed in the wake of World War II. He heard Luther as one who speaks to society as a whole and not only to the church and its theology. Thus Nygren's powerful slogan, "Forward to Luther," appeared as the very essence of a new appraisal of Lutheran solidarity. This conviction especially marked the first two assemblies of the LWF, Lund in 1947 and Hanover in 1952.

Nygren, however, was not alone in his theological vision of Lutheran renewal. Three other persons from the same period bear witness to the same commitments.

### Eivind Berggrav

Eivind Berggrav, primate of the Church of Norway, had been an undaunted leader of the Norwegian resistance movement during the years of Nazi occupation. Against this background he spoke with particular authority to the assembly at Lund.

His particular concern was to affirm that inspiration from Luther had given him certainty during the struggles of the war. To be sure, Berggrav had already made this point at previous international events held prior to the Lund Assembly, but it made a long-enduring impact when at Lund he expanded on the deep resources given him by Luther. The image he used was Luther's description of the Christian response when faced with "a drunken coachman." In critical circumstances a reconsideration of Luther had convinced him of the obligation to take a stand against injustice, a radically different stance than that of unconditional obedience and national patriotism often adopted by Lutherans, not least many in Germany during the Hitler years. According to Berggrav one ought thus not only to speak of a *right* to resistance but of an *obligation* to resistance as long as injustice was so apparent that the authorities had forfeited their mandate to maintain justice. In international and ecumenical perspective Berggrav's point acquired particular importance, because he insisted that in such an emergency situation—when faced with "a drunken coachman"—the whole Christian community was challenged; it was not only the local or the national church that was involved.

For his part, Berggrav understood the elementary standards of law in terms of a natural law which for him provided the foundation for all authority in society, government, school, family, and congregation. He had no doubt that there was an urgent need for ecumenical response if any single member of the body of Christ was struck by injustice:

> The blow strikes the whole church as well as each separate unit of the same. If anyone is persecuted and tortured because of his convictions and without any legal grounds, the Church, as the guardian of the human conscience, must stand solidly on the side of the sufferers. . . . A truly evangelical church must, therefore, take a stand against any attempt to interfere with or subjugate the individual conscience by the exercise of authority or violence. And if individual units or persons be displaced against their will and be made to suffer because of a firmly based conviction common to many believers, the Church must not and can not act as if it did not concern her. The Body of Christ would in such a case suffer and sins would be committed against the communion of the several members. (*Proceedings,* Lund, p. 115)

These prophetic words, obviously, spoke straight to the conscience of those gathered in assembly. Simultaneously, they pointed to the future. There is, in fact, a striking similarity between the words of Bishop Berggrav and the insights expressed some thirty years later when the Lutheran World Federation declared a *status confessionis* in respect to the rupture of church fellowship in Southern Africa in light of official governmental policies of apartheid.

In the postwar context Berggrav expressed his understanding of Luther in yet another setting, historically no less significant. In the same year as the Lund assembly, 1947, a volume was published in England entitled *Luther Speaks: Essays for the Fourth Century of Martin Luther's Death* (London, 1947). It had been prepared by a group of pastors and theologians from Northern and Western Europe, most of whom had taken refuge in England during World War II. Among the authors were several exiled German pastors who had been involved in the initial phases of the church struggle but had subsequently left Germany either voluntarily or as refugees. Other authors came from the Nordic countries, and Eivind Berggrav added particular weight to the publication by writing a preface. Dated June 1, 1946, that preface contains the following passage:

> I do not say that Luther was our only source of strength in our battle against Nazism and all which that implies. The most important source was the New Testament. But Luther's words were current, they showed us very clearly and powerfully what we should do. Above all, he was the very best remedy to expel all "Lutheran" servility to the state and secular authorities, and to char-

acterize Hitlerism undauntingly. (*Luther Speaks*, pp. 10ff.; cf. an important lecture given in Norway by Berggrav in 1941 and subsequently illegally distributed, "When the Driver Is out of His Mind: Luther on the Duty of Disobedience," in E. Berggrav, *Man and State* [Eng. tr., Philadelphia: Muhlenberg Press, 1951] pp. 300ff.)

## Lajos Ordass

The Hungarian Bishop Lajos Ordass (1901–1978) was another prominent Lutheran church leader who spoke with a similar authority as a witness to confessional integrity. Ordass was a churchman who did not bow to those who tried to maneuver him out of leadership but consistently resisted political persecution of his church.

Shortly after the war Bishop Ordass received an invitation to visit the Church of Sweden. He was inclined to accept the invitation, even though he soon came to realize that the Hungarian government's Department for Home Affairs was rapidly becoming a center of oppression and ill will. He became strikingly aware of this reality when he learned that these authorities had in a sophisticated way infiltrated themselves into the spiritual sphere of the life of the Lutheran Church in Hungary. In 1946 the Department for Home Affairs, having launched a campaign of oppression, attempted to prevent Ordass from traveling abroad. In the end, however, he did travel as a direct result of generous intervention from friends in other governmental offices.

Having realized that all of these obstacles were to be permanent features of the Hungarian public administration, Ordass did not dare immediately to return to Budapest. He thus continued his travels in the knowledge that by so doing he could not be prevented from participating in the 1947 Lund Assembly. At that assembly he was elected one of the vice presidents of the new Lutheran World Federation; and he maintained the distinction of leadership in the Federation for more than two decades, even when he was under detention or in prison in his own country. In point of fact it might accurately be stated that Ordass was kept in a position of LWF leadership precisely because his colleagues in international Lutheran leadership wanted to assure him and his church of their sympathy and support.

At the Lund Assembly Ordass preached one of the major sermons, "We Must Work While It Is Day." This sermon struck the international congregation deeply; it was clear that Ordass would not tolerate any tendency toward escapism or defeatism: "Many even in the church who have gone through hard struggles to the very limit of their courage and strength and to the very brink of despair, ask today 'Is there any day?'" With pastoral intensity he refused to accept even the slightest defeatism, pointing instead to the confidence that is inherent in the biblical exhortation to awake from sleep because the night is over and the day is at hand. Ordass went on: "Let us therefore cast off the works of darkness and let us put on the armor of light." He concluded the sermon with the admonition of his text, "Let us work while it is day." (*Proceedings*, Lund, pp.141ff.)

It is true that Bishop Ordass's sermon did not have the direct political implications found in the address of Bishop Berggrav. Yet no one present in Lund was left in doubt as to the deepest intention in Ordass's heart. The sincerity of his concern was cast in bold relief when, upon his return to Budapest, he was arrested and subsequently dismissed from episcopal office. Even when he was allowed to reassume those duties, new trials and dismissals awaited him.

### Hanns Lilje

Hanns Lilje stands as a third example of a Lutheran bishop who actively resisted tyranny. In 1936 he had been elected Executive Secretary of the Lutheran World Convention in light of his theological competence, which had in part been shaped by international experience. He had attended a mission conference in India in the 1920s and had also been a visiting scholar in the United States for a considerable period of time. When this experience is added to Lilje's linguistic training he can be seen as embodying a new kind of international orientation, strikingly different from that of the previous generation of German Lutheran church leaders. Since as a president of the Lutheran World Federation his life and accomplishments will be described more completely in another section of this book (cf. pp. 430–37 below), we shall here dwell only on his activities at the Lund assembly. Those activities are to be seen in direct connection with the fact that he had been imprisoned during the war on account of his cooperation with those Germans who actively conspired against Hitler.

As was the case with Berggrav and Ordass, Lilje showed no sign of self-righteousness at his own role during the war, nor did he seek to justify the activities of his church. On the contrary, he maintained that, seen from a Christian point of view, judgment can not be directed toward any single church. A genuine Lutheran understanding of the nature of the church requires a sober self-criticism and sense of guilt in every human being. In consequence Lilje stated:

> We have learned the wholesome truth that the judgment of God is coming upon the nations of the world—not only upon one or two nations, but upon all nations where the name of Christ has been proclaimed and where a Christian church existed. This church, we confess, was powerless to prevent mankind's plunge into darkness and chaos. But we ourselves, we personally, share responsibility for this catastrophe; we were disobedient, we were self-

ish, we were cowardly, we were sinful. A church is truly Lutheran only if it fearlessly proclaims this judgment of God over all the nations and if it, above all, humbly and penitently submits to its judgment itself. (*Proceedings*, Lund, p. 143)

Against the background of this theme of judgment, Lilje went on to proclaim God's promise, the gospel of the resurrection. The proclamation of the Easter gospel enabled him to conclude optimistically, in a tone of spiritual renewal: "Away with defeatism, with hopelessness and despair." In place of such feelings of frustration he pointed to the words of joy, "Serve the Lord with gladness!"

## The Fourth Pillar: A Common Response to the Ecumenical Challenge

THE PREPARATIONS for the Lund assembly were themselves an integral part of the struggle to build up realities of cooperation and unity among Lutherans. During the same period another ecumenical endeavor was taking shape, an endeavor that has probably had farther-reaching consequences when seen within the perspective of the modern history of Christianity as a whole. It was the foundation of the World Council of Churches, which finally took place in Amsterdam in 1948 after a delay of more than ten years, caused by World War II.

The development of the two organizations had been parallel from the beginning. The Lutheran World Convention since its inception in 1923 had seen its role as precursor to a *confessional* supplement to the pan-Protestant association which in the 1920s had already been in preparation for more than a decade. A strong case can be made that many participants in the events of 1923 were ambiguous about even an informal "coexistence." Many were more inclined to insist upon a specific and even prior unity among all Lutheran churches, thus forming a kind of confessional alternative to the multi-confessional association foreseen by others.

Early drafts of a constitution for the World Council of Churches (WCC) had been in circulation since the late 1930s; implementation had been postponed by the outbreak of World War II. By the time the WCC was established in 1948 in Amsterdam the Lutheran churches had already been faced—when they met at Lund in 1947—with the basic question, should the Lutherans aim at a policy of both/and or either/or?

The proposal for "both/and"—both the LWF and the WCC—had been the strategy of the ecumenical leader Nathan Söderblom from the very start of his work for the unity of the church. In this he was supported by fellow Lutherans who in actuality were of far more conservative confessional convictions than he, e.g., the German Wilhelm von Pechmann and the Dane Alfred Th. Jørgensen, both of whom were charter members of the Lutheran World Convention Executive Committee.

Or was the proper course of action more of an either/or—either the LWF or the WCC—an alternative that assumed that only a clear cut distinction would permit wholehearted dedication to the heritage of the Lutheran confession? This latter view was championed by a number of the leading first-generation American participants in international Lutheran cooperation. The confessional conservatism of such Americans even went so far as a rejection of solidarity with Archbishop Söderblom on the basis of a claim that his liberal position was an obstacle to the formation of genuine Lutheran identity. In similar spirit, these Americans felt unable to participate in the celebration of the Eucharist at the second meeting of the Lutheran World Convention in Copenhagen in 1929.

Clearly the problem had a complex historical background. When, however, the dominant position of leading Lutherans was taken into account, it became evident that the majority stood for confessional openness and ecumenical engagement. This was especially the case with respect to theologians and leaders from the host church at Lund, the Church of Sweden, most notably Archbishop Eidem and Professor Nygren. Their position took on great significance in the international perspective, because the Church of Sweden had a centuries-long reputation as a strong bastion of the Lutheran tradition. At the same time, however, the Church of Sweden had played a prominent role in the movement toward transconfessional unity among the churches. In this context one needs only to recall Swedish involvement in the Universal Christian Conference on Life and Work held at Stockholm in 1925 or the important ecumenical achievements of the bilateral dialogue between the Church of Sweden and the Church of England between the two world wars. Indeed, the development of Anglo-Scandinavian Conferences for Theologians during this period had been supported wholeheartedly by Eidem as well as by Nygren.

In similar fashion, the leading bishop in Norway, Eivind Berggrav, wished to combine loyalty to his own confessional inheritance with ecumenical openness. During the years 1938–39 when, against the background of an imminent danger of war, he had led efforts toward an international peace initiative, Berggrav had been in steady dialogue with Willem A. Visser 't Hooft (1900–1985), the chief architect of the World Council of Churches. Even allowing for sharp disagreements with Visser 't Hooft, Berggrav felt so deeply indebted to the cause of ecumenical unity that at times he was somewhat hesitant about efforts toward specifically inter-Lutheran cooperation. His reservations on that score, however, quickly faded away and, as has already been seen, his participation at the

Lund Assembly gave yet another testimony to the breadth of his ecclesial convictions.

The same strategy of both/and was articulated after World War II by two of the Danish leaders, Hans Fuglsang-Damgaard, Bishop of Copenhagen (1890–1979), and Alfred Th. Jørgensen, the only remaining member of the original Executive Committee of the Lutheran World Convention as constituted in 1923. Outside the Nordic countries there were also spokespersons for the both/and position—Lajos Ordass, for example, and Hanns Lilje, who in 1947 had just succeeded August Marahrens as Bishop of Hanover.

With regard to the American representatives there was actually a marked shift of opinion. In the earlier time of the Lutheran World Convention the American church leaders had definitely been in favor of a purely confessional movement, but after 1945 their successors supported a comprehensive, inclusive ecumenical strategy.

Cooperation between the WCC and the LWF also seemed appropriate in light of other, even more obvious, factors. In Geneva the secretariats of both international organizations were housed in the same building. These shared facilities, at 17 route de Malagnou, corresponded with a deliberately cooperative emphasis in policies advocated especially by the Americans. Sylvester Michelfelder, for example, had a job description which gave him responsibilities in both organizations. Michelfelder, however, did not feel the slightest disjunction from the fact that his responsibilities were within two structures. Whether he was traveling in his capacity as Executive Secretary of the LWF or reporting to his home church, the United Lutheran Church in America whose support—not least economic—was urgently needed, he strongly advocated the double strategy. The same line was adopted by other prominent American church leaders, persons like Franklin Clark Fry (1900–1968) (cf. pp. 438–44 below) and Stewart Herman, whose leadership within both the Lutheran and the ecumenical communities was undoubted.

However obvious the dominance of the inclusive—both/and—attitude may appear, a basic difficulty of principle remained. A persistent doubt as to the viability and tenability of uniting both sets of interests was increased by impressions from two regional churches which were to play crucial roles in the formation of opinions in 1947. The first such region was India. After years of difficult negotiation, an agreement was reached that very year, 1947, involving the formation of The Church of South India, a union on a broadly pan-Protestant basis. The Lutheran churches in the region, nonetheless, decided to maintain a confessional distance and did not commit themselves to the new body, a decision which was not well received in many quarters both within and beyond India.

No less controversial was the course of church politics in Germany after 1945. Historical differences, largely regional, were combined with disagreements regarding actual points of decision in such a way that the German debate became extremely sharp. There was, as one instance of debate, the well known divergence between the "Prussian Union" which included Reformed, Lutheran, and United Churches, on the one side, and the traditionally Lutheran *Landeskirchen,* on the other. This divergence had only been exacerbated during the church struggle in the Nazi period when the "destroyed" Union churches were forcibly required to submit to the authority of the Berlin government while the "intact" churches, largely Lutheran, retained a certain independence. The church struggle, partly in consequence of this intensified divergence, was carried on in a much more uncompromising way in the destroyed churches while the Lutheran intact churches lived in relative calm. As a result of this, leaders in the destroyed churches accused—sometimes bitterly—their colleagues in the intact churches of not being fully committed to the struggle. The confrontation heightened, and a serious blow was dealt to solidarity within the Confessing Church when the Lutherans formed a separate council of churches in 1936, a body which subsequently agreed to negotiations with bodies controlled by the state.

This conflict was picked up again and intensified after the war when the Lutherans founded their own association of regional churches, the United Evangelical Lutheran Church of Germany (VELKD), alongside the joint association of Protestant churches (to which members of the VELKD also belonged), the Evangelical Church in Germany (EKiD). This dispute went far beyond the borders of Germany, not least because internationally prominent theologians and church leaders such as Karl Barth and Martin Niemöller were vocal in their sharp criticisms of the Lutherans.

The situation within Germany was extremely critical. However, in a wider international framework the German theologian Hans Ehrenberg (1883–1958), who left Germany for England in the late 1930s since he was a Christian of Jewish origin, succeeded in defining a more constructive point of departure for the debate. From England he had carefully observed the church struggle within Germany and in 1947 he published a series of open letters to his German Lutheran friends, typified by the young Heidelberg theologian Edmund Schlink (1903–1984), who had taken a firm position within the Confessing Church. Ehrenberg entitled his letters, published only in German, "Lutheranism: Ecumenical and German."

Ehrenberg's main concern was to combine two issues. First, he was determined to remain loyal to the heritage of the Confessing Church, most notably its Barmen Declaration of 1934; second, he was eager to widen the horizons of discussion ecumenically, largely on the basis of his experiences in England. In exile, Ehrenberg had learned to live within what he termed a "department store of Christianity," even as he had been deeply impressed by the traditions of the dominant Church of England. In this regard he had become convinced that a common heritage bonded Lutherans and Anglicans, founded on a common understanding of worship and liturgy. Neither church, he felt, was a sacramental church in the Roman Catholic sense, nor were they "churches of the sermon" in a Puritan sense. The crucial mark of Anglicanism as a *via media* seemed to Ehrenberg to be very close to his own understanding of Lutheran ecclesiology, the core of Lutheran identity, as a *via centralis.*

On the basis of this understanding of both Lutheranism and ecumenism, Ehrenberg felt compelled to face the broader international ecumenical challenge. This meant that he was obliged to raise a number of critical questions with his German Lutheran friends, based largely on his anxieties about the particular approach taken in the formation of the VELKD. He passionately maintained in this whole discussion that the German Lutherans would be wise to exercise a greater degree of self-criticism.

For Ehrenberg the whole question of confessional identity was focused on a proper understanding of the nature of the church, an issue that was simultaneously the only clue to constructive ecumenical dialogue. It was a comprehensive ecclesiology which alone could prevent a narrow understanding of identity determined only by individual elements in the creeds, whether particular articles from the historic, ecumenical creeds or from, say, the Barmen Declaration. As an alternative to this narrowness, Ehrenberg advocated a comprehensive ecclesiology, including an understanding of the church's worship: "The corporate concept of the nature of the church is the common denominator, which is suited to define a future Lutheran understanding of her position, ecumenical and German at the same time." (*Luthertum, ökumenisch und deutsch,* p. 64, Gütersloh, 1947)

Consonant with this ecclesiological approach, Ehrenberg found stimulation from twentieth century Swedish Luther research. He mentioned particularly the work of Gustaf Aulén (1879–1977) and Anders Nygren. Ehrenberg had direct lines to the Nordic theological tradition, as evidenced in his cooperation with the publication of *Luther Speaks* (cf. pp. 29–30 above). Ehrenberg found particular affinity between his own ecclesiological views and the Swedish identification of the core of Luther's theology as the connection between christology and redemption, on the one side, and ecclesiology, on the other. On the basis of this insight, Ehrenberg could propose an ecclesiological starting point for both a new global union of Lutheran churches and a deep ecumenical commitment to "one, holy, catholic, and apostolic" church as confessed in the creeds.

At this point there is, to be sure, a striking similarity between the views of Hans Ehrenberg and Anders Nygren, the first president of the Lutheran World Federation, concerning Lutheran identity and the ecumenical challenge. Nygren for his part was not willing to reduce his vision simply to criteria which might be required for a redefinition of the confessional heritage. Using his watchword, "Forward to Luther," he looked to a recapturing of Lutheran identity even as he took seriously the imperative, stemming from Luther's well-known phrase, that the one church comprise "the whole of Christianity on earth."

## Conclusion: Two Movements toward Lutheran Unity

IT WOULD BE IMPOSSIBLE to describe the foundation of the Lutheran World Federation without also considering the foundation of its predecessor organization, the Lutheran World Convention. It is now appropriate to place the question, In what way did the Lutheran World Federation, founded in 1947, differ from the Lutheran World Convention which convened for the first time in 1923?

1. At Lund in 1947 those who gathered had acquired experience, both positive and negative, that enabled them to erect pillars for the new organization on firm ground. They knew much of what was necessary and much that had to be avoided, and were thus in a position of considerable confidence. The convention of 1923, in contrast, had an experimental character with no certainty that the cooperation which was intended would prove either tenable or lasting.

2. The work of the Lutheran World Convention, from 1923 onward, was carried on by individuals. Regardless of their personal dedication and regardless of their general efficiency, however, a steering committee given purely to individuals carried with it great risks—of a lack of decisiveness, of resentments based on personal controversies, of a lack of higher authority. Additionally, the individual character of the Convention meant also that its leaders were not necessarily representative of their various constituencies. In contrast, it was of decisive importance that the cooperation established in 1947 was explicitly that of a federation not of individuals but of churches.

3. The Lutheran World Convention was a community of individual church leaders solely from Germany, North America, and the Nordic countries. Even though these same groups were the vast and powerful majority among those who gathered at Lund in 1947, there was representation—limited, to be sure—from mission churches and even from independent churches in what has come to be called the Third World. The very

fact of this limited participation came to be a matter of crucial importance. Some felt that this greater variety of participants carried with it the
risk of threatening the consistency that had been built up during the Convention's life. It became quickly apparent, however, that the Lutheran
World Federation required this globally more adequate and inclusive representation both for the effectiveness of its work and for the reality of its
claim to international Lutheran unity.

4. The situation in Germany after World War II was decisively different
from that after World War I. The latter situation was determined largely by
national anger at the terms of the Treaty of Versailles and its controlling
international organizations. To be sure, the October 18–19, 1945, Stuttgart
Declaration of Guilt ("Die Stuttgarter Erklärung: Ein Schuldbekenntnis")
presented by leaders of German Protestant churches to an international
ecumenical group, was questioned by large elements within the German
churches. Much of the church atmosphere in Germany at this time threatened to tear to pieces the unity that had been so dearly purchased during
the church struggle. Nevertheless, a comprehensive analysis leads to the
conclusion that at the end of World War II the German churches, so crucial to the new Lutheran World Federation, possessed a genuine will to
self-examination, a sincere desire to turn away from the dark shadows of
the past. In 1947 at Lund the leaders of the German Lutheran churches
were determined to be open to new possibilities for international cooperation, including the possibilities presented by the ecumenical movement.

5. It was ecclesially, confessionally, and theologically crucial that at the
time of the founding of the Lutheran World Federation there were strong
signs, internationally discernible, of an eagerness to revise accepted understandings of Luther and of the Reformation heritage. This was not least
true in respect to matters of social ethics, often regarded as the Achilles'
heel of Lutheranism. In this situation the German Lutheran churches had
much to give and much to receive; an international approach was required.
Thus it was that the LWF early in its life saw itself as an international
forum for common theological studies that were to lead to new points of
orientation for churches of the Lutheran confession.

6. Between 1923 and 1947 there was virtually a seismic shift in the
international ecumenical atmosphere. The formal establishment, in 1948,
of the World Council of Churches provided new opportunities for cooperation and communion. Similarly, it was possible even in 1947 to see new
possibilities of relationship with the Roman Catholic Church differing
totally from the spirit of indignant confrontation that marked the period
between the two world wars. Even in 1947, then, the new realities of ecumenical respect and dialogue which were to appear in subsequent decades
could be foreseen.

7. Perhaps the most far-reaching difference between the situations of 1923 and 1947 was the new willingness to reformulate ecclesiological questions. The establishment of the Lutheran World Federation brought with it a willingness to look again at the very nature of the church through the eyes of a renewed Reformation heritage. This had consequences both for Lutheran and ecumenical unity. It cannot be doubted that at Lund some of the most penetrating contributions in this regard came from theologians of the host church, the Church of Sweden. The first President of the LWF, then professor and after 1948 Bishop of Lund, Anders Nygren deserves particular mention in this connection. But this concern for the nature of the church was widely shared. A few theologians of importance to the subsequent life of the Federation should be mentioned: Regin Prenter of Aarhus, Denmark (1907–1990), who was to become the first chairperson of the LWF Commission on Theology; the new generation of German theologians including Peter Brunner (1900–1981) and Edmund Schlink. Vilmos Vajta (b. 1918) should also be mentioned. He had come from Hungary to Lund to study with Anders Nygren; subsequently he became the director of the Department of Theology of the LWF and the first Director of the Institute of Ecumenical Research at Strasbourg.

It was thus a common willingness to face the question of the nature of the church that paved the way, even in 1947, for a cooperation among the Lutheran churches of the world that transcended mere pragmatism. The Lutheran heritage supplied the basis for a renewed understanding of the worship of the church, of the shared existence of local, regional, and national expressions of church life, and of commitment to the ecumenical enterprise within the global community of Christian churches. Here, at the foundation of the Lutheran World Federation, was the dynamic that gave power to a federation which was to see itself as a communion of churches suited to go beyond initial obstacles.

## Bibliographical Notes

I. Archives, unpublished documents

LWF archives Geneva.
Anders Nygren Papers, University Library, Lund.
Danish National Committee of the Lutheran World Convention, Rigsarkivet, Copenhagen.
A. Th. Jørgensen Papers, Rigsarkivet, Copenhagen.
Per Pehrsson Papers, Landsarkivet, Göteborg.
Lars Boe Papers, St. Olaf College, Northfield, Minnesota.
August Marahrens Papers, Hanover.
Hanns Lilje Papers, Lutheran Church Archives, Hanover.

II. Printed documents

*Proceedings*, Lund.
*Junge Kirche*, 1933ff.
*Kristen Gemenskap*, 1928ff.
*The Lutheran World Review* (1948–1950).

III. Monographs and Selected Writings

Berggrav, Eivind. *Man and State.* Trans. by George Aus. Philadelphia: Muhlenberg Press, 1951.

Busch, Eberhard. *Karl Barth: His Life from Letters and Autobiographical Texts.* Trans. John Bowden. Philadelphia: Fortress Press, 1976.

Ehrenberg Hans. *Luthertum, ökumenisch und deutsch.* Gütersloh: Bertelsmanns, 1947.

Grundmann, Siegfried. *Der Lutherische Weltbund.* Köln/Graz: Böhlau, 1957.

Heiene, Gunnar. *Eivind Berggrav. En biografi.* Oslo, 1992.

Jørgensen, Alfred Th. *Filantrop og Skribent.* Copenhagen: Gad, 1949.

Lilje, Hanns. *Memorabilia: Schwerpunkte eines Lebens.* Stein/Nürnberg: Laetare Verlag, 1973.

*Luther Speaks: Essays for the Fourth Centenary of Martin Luther's Death* by "a group of Lutheran ministers from North and Central Europe at present in Great Britain with a foreword by the Bishop of Oslo." London: Lutterworth, 1947.

Nelson, E. Clifford. *The Rise of World Lutheranism: An American Perspective.* Philadelphia: Fortress Press, 1982.

Schmidt-Clausen, Kurt. *Vom Lutherischen Weltkonvent zum Lutherischen Weltbund.* Vol. 2 in *Die Lutherische Kirche in Geschichte und Gestalt.* Gütersloh: Gütersloher Verlagshaus Gerd Mohn, 1976.

Solberg, Richard W. *As Between Brothers: The Story of Lutheran Response to World Needs.* Minneapolis: Augsburg, 1957.

Terray, Lázsló G. *He Could Not Do Otherwise: Bishop Lajos Ordass, 1901–1978.* Trans. Eric W. Gritsch. Grand Rapids: Eerdmans, 1997.

Wadensjö, Bengt. *Toward a World Lutheran Communion: Developments in Lutheran Cooperation up to 1929.* Uppsala: Verbum, 1970.

1. Lutheran World Convention, founding meeting at Eisenach, Germany, 1923.

2. Executive Committee of the Lutheran World Convention and Visitors, Uppsala, Sweden, 1946.

# 2

# From Federation to Communion: Five Decades of LWF History

## Survey and Analysis

As WE HAVE SEEN, the Lutheran World Federation was founded both out of necessity and in the light of a vision. It was founded, moreover, in a very particular historical context that conditioned the very shape of Lutheran cooperation. It would obviously be a serious error to idealize the founding of the Federation apart from the complexities and difficulties which marked subsequent developments. Original inspirations are neither helpfully nor realistically viewed in abstraction or in isolation.

Accordingly, we shall now review the interaction between the ideals of the founders and the struggles that followed. This survey will be accompanied by an analysis that is intended to provide points of judgment—regarding obstacles to progress, genuine accomplishments, and instances of failure—for subsequent investigations of what has actually been achieved in the LWF since its establishment in 1947. This chapter will thus have several foci.

First, it will provide basic information that will shape an approach to each of the themes of subsequent chapters. This survey intends to do more than offer a historical key to subsequent expositions of individual issues. It intends also to provide criteria for linking the original vision that we have described in terms of "four pillars"—rescue for the needy, common initiatives in mission, joint efforts in theology, and common response to the ecumenical challenge—and its realization or transformation in concrete historical circumstances. Only if this linkage is traced will it be possible to take seriously the essential interrelationship between the four

*Jens Holger Schjørring, Aarhus, Denmark, is the author of chapter 2.*

pillars, the degree to which the emphases of these pillars have shaped the overall work of the Federation, and even the way in which inadequate interaction between the pillars has at times weakened the LWF as a communion of churches.

This linkage will, second, provide criteria for what we trust will be an unprejudiced view of the accomplishments—and failures—that have marked the first five decades of LWF history.

Third, we shall in this chapter attempt to define a method for locating key turning points in the Federation's history. Such turning points reveal not only memorable peak events but also moments of trial, of critical encounter between conflicting interests, and even of the compromise of original visions.

We will not be able to claim that the present endeavor is in any sense a "critical" account of the history of the LWF unless we are able to do justice to each of these foci. Before embarking on this chronological journey through the five decades of LWF history, however, we must also pay attention to the overarching patterns of cooperation within the Federation. We point to seven *leitmotifs* characteristic of the global fellowship of Lutheran churches, factors that cut across the themes or trajectories that have determined the structure of our total study. These factors point to issues and events that appear repeatedly in subsequent sections of this book. They have an essential mark in common: Each one transcends the boundaries of the themes of this study; they are to be understood as decisive for understanding the interplay between the original vision of 1947 and subsequent developments.

## 1. Relationships among Member Churches

It was a major accomplishment of the Lund Assembly that a framework for cooperation was created which allowed for proportionate involvement from each of the three original blocs of participants—German, North American, and Nordic. This balance did not prevent or paralyze the main issues of the agenda from being faced straightforwardly. No less important was the fact that this balance of power did not, as things turned out, prove detrimental to the role of the minority churches even though it was difficult for these churches initially to have much influence.

It will be basic to our analysis of the five decades of LWF history to observe how the interactions between these blocs of member churches played out. Obviously, World War II provided the immediate background for the initial phase of member church relationships. Growing tensions between East and West (Europe and North America) soon, however, became a key factor in these relationships, the division of Germany by the

Berlin Wall being of crucial importance. In this developing context it became important for the Federation to insure the full involvement and fair representation of Lutheran minority churches from Central and Eastern Europe. This task became increasingly delicate as contrasting views of appropriate relationships between church and state became apparent and as these minority churches in certain instances actually tended to become in their own right what can only be described as subregions of the Federation even when no formal structure was created.

The image of an orchestra is perhaps helpful. As the ensemble of Federation member churches played, there was a constant risk of permanent disharmony simply on the basis of the dominant role played by Americans in the Geneva secretariat, particularly in early LWF years. Modulation was necessary, and it was provided largely by the Nordic churches, most specifically in relation to Eastern Europe by the Finns and Swedes. Further, as though questions regarding Eastern Europe were not complex enough, the main blocs of member churches were at the start in considerable danger of drowning out the harmonies provided by other minority churches, from Southern and Western Europe as well as, increasingly, from other continents.

To be sure, there was participation from the beginning from churches outside Europe and North America. At the outset this participation was clearly minimal; such churches were represented in LWF circles largely by leaders from missionary organizations and not by indigenous persons. This pattern, however, changed visibly during the second decade. Global decolonization from about 1960 on led to a rapid growth in the number of LWF member churches. Yet such patterns of change did not occur without clashes of interest. Churches from the South presented a challenge to those from the North, not least in respect to a more just sharing of influence in LWF decision-making bodies. Not until the Fifth Assembly of the LWF, at Evian, could a marked shift toward fuller recognition of the right of churches from the South to proportionate voice and vote be noted.

*2. Different Types of Church Polity:*
*Organization and Tradition*

Lutherans churches differ from most other world communions in placing greater emphasis on doctrinal tradition than on matters of structure and forms of ordained ministry. Within the Lutheran communion, churches with an episcopal tradition are in full communion with churches of congregational polity. There is a clear pluralism in the structure of Lutheran churches. In this situation of pluralism, Lutheran churches, in their patterns of international cooperation, have wanted to learn from and support one another by both organized and informal programs of exchange. The conditions for such exchange have obviously changed enormously over the past fifty years, as have available financial resources for travel and effective communication. To achieve an instructive unity in the midst of this pluralism has remained a clear task of the LWF.

### 3. Structure: Constitutions, Secretariat, and National Committees

The Federation has had three different constitutions during the first five decades of its life (cf. Appendix). The present study of those decades requires clarity in viewing and analyzing those constitutions, shifts in structure, and reformulations of basic mandates.

At the outset, the pattern of a relatively small but representative executive committee with clearly mandated commissions was adopted in order to give a strong role to member churches and to provide expertise within the departments of the secretariat. This was initially viewed in a consistently decentralized way. There have, quite obviously, been dramatic shifts in this view. Different patterns of representation have been called for—regional, ethnic, gender, clergy/laity—which in the eyes of some have been at the expense both of the member churches as such and of overall competence and in the eyes of others have provided for new and important equities in inclusive participation and decision making.

The five decades have also seen significant shifts at other points of LWF organization. At the time of its founding, the necessity of establishing an efficient secretariat was generally acknowledged. At the same time, many were anxious that a powerful bureaucracy, subject to pressures of power, finance, and personal ambition not be created. The resulting structural proposal—for an efficient secretariat in Geneva and uniformly organized "national committees" (with functional subcommittees) in each country where there was more than one LWF member church—was itself a pattern foreign, for example, to the Nordic churches and assumedly to the churches of Germany. It was clearly a structure which had its origins in the United States.

What was desired and carefully crafted was a constructive relationship between the secretariat and member churches marked by an unhindered exchange of ideas in both directions. In the Federation's original constitution this desire was expressed by underlining the "autonomy" of member churches and the Federation itself as a "free association of Lutheran churches," language that remained unchanged until 1990. The initial desire has, with varying forms of structural implementation and theological awareness, remained constant through five decades. Yet there have also been widely varied expectations both of member churches and their national committees, and of the secretariat itself.

### 4. The "Four Pillars"

In chapter 1, which dealt with the establishment of the Federation, four pillars were seen to provide the basic support, if not the foundation, for the construction of the LWF. Those pillars were scarcely able in 1947 to be transformed immediately into workable mandates and strategies for programmatic commissions and departments. As that transformation developed, the programmatic units of the Federation—commissions, departments, desks—were never expected alone to assume total responsibility for particular pillars. Each of those pillars concerned the entire Federation and each of its units. Each theme is to be understood here as a set of issues inherent to the Federation's struggle to reach specific goals; they are not to be thought of as visible signals regarding administrative strategies at any given time. The four pillars, then, will aid in identifying turning points in LWF history, in examining the several patterns of interaction which together have formed the life of the LWF, and in discerning the origins of the goals and strategies of LWF concerns, programs, and activities.

### 5. Mission, Development, Service

Shared efforts to establish rescue and relief operations for the needy at the conclusion of World War II and the development of cooperative actions in world mission were two of the pillars upon which the Lutheran World Federation was established. Initial relief work was viewed in terms of an immediate situation of great urgency, and it was felt then that in time such work would be rendered superfluous. This was obviously not to be the case. Service came to be a permanent part of the Federation's life, and its mandates had to be redefined to reflect long-term perspectives. "Development" and "the creation of sustainable structures" became major rubrics within the LWF. Subsequently, sharp questions were put concerning the relationship between service, broadly understood in terms of development and mission, and the proclamation of the Christian gospel. To trace these questions—which far exceed individual programmatic units—will be a major concern of the following chapters.

### 6. The Lutheran Heritage and Present Realities: Confessional Integrity and Ecumenical Commitment

The founders of the Lutheran World Federation were committed to seeing that the tradition associated with Martin Luther was carried forward to new generations. This represented a challenge far beyond the orbit of academic scholarship. The watchword of Anders Nygren, first president of the Federation, "Forward to Luther!" was a statement of his conviction that this heritage was applicable to the present life of every church-goer. Accordingly, the Federation from the beginning saw it as one of its tasks to stimulate both theological research and church renewal in order to bring the two together at every level including that of parish life. Here again, the fact of Lutheran pluralism must be acknowledged: The LWF throughout the five decades of its history has been concerned to relate the Lutheran tradition to the variety of styles of worship, piety, and social witness found in Lutheran churches of the world. Not least in respect to clarifying the Lutheran tradition regarding the witness of the churches in the social and political spheres has the Lutheran World Federation been faced with an enormous task with both ecumenical and geopolitical implications.

In addition, the reality and vitality of the modern ecumenical movement has consistently occupied the Federation. This concern has included a critical questioning of the relationship of the specifically Lutheran tradition to the quest for a wider visible church unity. This *leitmotif* is itself to be the subject of chapter 7. It occurs and reoccurs, however, throughout our exposition.

### 7. Key Issues in Varied Contexts

The LWF, in its relatively short history, has been required to deal with certain central issues that have reoccurred in a variety of settings. These issues have, to be sure, been approached as theological concerns, but their force has been concrete and practical as well. Here we summarize the way in which three such issues have appeared in varied forms.

*Justification and justice.*   The Federation has never finished its theological task of clarifying the essential articles of the Lutheran confession in a way that is acceptable to all Lutheran churches around the world. Indeed, this task is probably by nature one that will never be brought to completion.

As an example, the question of the relationship between justification by faith, the most basic article of the Lutheran confessions, and justice in the world is a perennial one, which the LWF has faced in a variety of connections and in a variety of ways. There is probably no single interpretation of this relationship that can claim to be the correct one satisfactory to all. Consequently, one can observe in the fifty years of LWF history changing models for the interpretation of the relation of justification to justice. At times questions of social ethics seem to determine the model; at other times particular concerns for human rights are determinative.

*Status confessionis.*   Disputes about this thorny issue, rediscovered for the present generation as part and parcel of the North-South tension within global Lutheranism, have had ramifications far beyond the various ways in which Lutherans have appropriated either the "two kingdoms" theory or traditional points of ecclesiology. The issue has taken on immense importance not only for definitions of fellowship between Lutheran churches but perhaps equally as crucially for the working out of modes of ecclesial life in contemporary societies.

*Secularization.*   As early as the Lund Assembly, attention was paid to dangers stemming from "the secular powers in our time," by which were then meant chiefly the totalitarian ideologies of Nazism and Communism. Initially, theologians and leaders from the churches of North America and Northwestern Europe regarded the churches of the Lutheran confession as a sacred space behind secure walls that offered protection against the dangers of such secular ideologies. Ironically perhaps, it came to be one of the messages of persons from the minority churches of Central and Eastern Europe that the liberal traditions of both the European folk churches and American denominations were themselves strikingly susceptible to the virus of secularism. In later decades the issue has been passionately taken up within younger Lutheran churches, chiefly in the South, where the value of preserving the Reformation heritage has been seen in the light of failings, if not apostasy, within the older churches.

These three issues—others could have been chosen—illustrate the steady oscillation between uniformity and pluriformity which has marked the communion of Lutheran churches within the LWF. A *leitmotif* to be discovered throughout the present survey is thus the reoccurrence of tensions between the continuity of the Lutheran tradition and forces creating discontinuity.

This, therefore, is the frame for our investigation. The original vision of those who founded the Federation will interact with such *leitmotifs* to form an approach to the basic themes or trajectories covered in subsequent chapters. To return to the image of an orchestral performance, we might say that the voice of the LWF was tuned to the four pillars, but that history will show that no constant beat is guaranteed. There will be moments of discord, of shrill collision, as well as of unforgettable melody and rich harmony. The common score is to be the broad Lutheran heritage as lived in churches throughout the world, but that score will be marked both by disruptions of history and pluriformity and by new variations leading to deeper communion in faith, life, and witness.

## The First Decade

THE TASK FACING the Geneva secretariat of the Lutheran World Federation immediately after the Federation's first assembly at Lund in 1947 was to draw out the organizational consequences of the assembly's decisions. Satisfaction at the results of the assembly was, however, tempered both by the anxieties of the postwar situation itself and by the challenges facing Lutheran churches in light of that situation.

Sylvester Michelfelder, the first LWF Executive Secretary (a title later changed to General Secretary), had no doubt that among his primary obligations was to convince every church delegation to return to its own constituency with a mandate for the establishment of LWF national committees. Only then, he thought, would it be possible to involve the people in the congregations in the Federation and thus to prevent the newly formed body from quickly degenerating into an exclusive, elitist organization. He invested all of his experience gained in his home church in the United States in this task of building up networks of laity dedicated to global Lutheranism. His assignment was thus to create tenable working structures in the Geneva secretariat and at the same time to stimulate the formation of national committees in the member churches.

In a Handbook for National Committees and Study Committees, issued in 1948 as a follow-up of the Lund Assembly, Michelfelder outlined his goal of a reciprocal relationship between the secretariat and the national committees. Only through such cooperation would it be possible for the Federation faithfully to respond to the challenges of the time. Accordingly, he suggested the formation of subcommittees within national committees that would mirror the structure in Geneva. He proposed fifteen areas of activity that would occupy national committees, international commissions, and the Geneva headquarters:

| | |
|---|---|
| Theology | Education |
| Evangelism | Stewardship |
| World Missions | Inner Missions |
| Men of the Church | Women of the Church |
| Youth | Students |
| Ecumenical Relations | International Affairs |
| Interchurch Aid | Publicity |
| Publication | |

Exhausting weeks of ceaseless effort marked Michelfelder's attempts to put this plan into effect. His initial confidence turned into a matter-of-fact soberness when he evaluated his efforts two or three years after the Lund Assembly. Writing to Hanns Lilje, who had become Bishop of Hanover and whom he considered the person best qualified to become the second president of the Federation, and in anticipation of the Second Assembly already scheduled for 1952, Michelfelder described his disappointment. The members of the LWF Executive Committee, he felt, had demonstrated passivity and a lack of vision at their 1950 meeting at Tutzing, Bavaria, and he viewed this as a serious setback. On September 5, 1950 he wrote to Lilje:

> I left Tutzing quite confused, as you perhaps observed. There was much time spent on jots and tittles. There was much attention given to crossing the t's but it was very difficult to get either the Executive Committee or "Committee I" to rise to the importance of the great things for which the Lutheran World Federation stands. I fear that the Executive Committee did not read the voluminous document sent out from my office before and if they did, they forgot a good part of the things which were laid out. At least, they were seldom referred to. This may be due entirely to a faulty or a too wordy preparation on my part. Perhaps I expected too much. When I read the voluminous Minutes, I find that most of the important things were left to the Geneva office to implement. This can mean several things. It can mean an unwillingness to face up to it or it can mean a willingness to leave it to the Geneva office. In either case the responsibility upon the Executive Secretary and upon the Geneva office is overwhelming. I am somewhat disturbed by the shock that the members of my staff, who were present at Tutzing, received from the way the meeting itself impressed them. There is not much that I can do about this except to tell them that they probably expected too much. (Lilje Papers, Hanover, L III 418)

*Early Regionalization.*   The conclusion of the first decade was marked by a paradox that actually revealed an essential characteristic of the period: the number of LWF member churches increased significantly even as a marked regional consciousness developed. The influence of the three dominant blocs of members—from Germany, the Nordic countries, and the United States—gradually diminished, and that led to a demand for the establishment of new forums for the articulation of the concerns of new member churches.

Latin America constituted a specific challenge. An LWF Committee on Latin America was authorized at the Hanover Assembly of 1952. Stewart W. Herman, of the United Lutheran Church in America, who had served in Germany and Geneva for a number of years, was appointed the committee's first director and in that capacity presented his first report to the Third LWF Assembly held in Minneapolis in 1957. In that report Herman gave clear evidence of the need to clarify the specific challenges arising from developments among the Lutheran churches in Latin America. Satisfaction was to be taken in the fact that Latin America was represented at Minneapolis by ten delegates and twenty visitors from eleven countries, which accounted for "three times as many countries and three times as many representatives as at Hanover." Moreover, Herman pointed out that these numbers represented an extension of perspective regarding the LWF as a whole: Latin America offered an extension of *length* by adding two Americas (Central and South) to the North, one of *breadth*, because the Lutherans in Latin America represent a variety of traditions and ethnic backgrounds, and also an extension of *depth*, because two theological seminaries were to be found there, in Argentina and in Mexico. Stewart Herman concluded that this "extension" should be acknowledged by the entire Lutheran World Federation as a mark of progress:

> For all Lutherans this is not merely a remote challenge with intriguing possibilities. It is an immediate responsibility. Divided though we are by national origins, by language and even by doctrinal differences, our 750,000 brethren in Latin America—mostly of European origin—represent the largest confessional group among five million Protestants. The future of this region directly involves us all. But it would be ridiculous to pretend that this responsibility can be referred to the Latin American Committee and be forgotten, just as it would be ridiculous for our Committee to take credit for the totality of the Lutheran work as we see it today. (*Proceedings*, Minneapolis, p. 133)

Herman was careful to mention without evasion the political realities to be found in Latin America as well as the spiritual challenge which that context gave to Lutheran churches:

> Latin America is an undeveloped world bursting with new growth. Rich natural resources are being converted into abundant wealth entailing all sorts of economic dislocations. Almost every South American republic can be labeled as an area of rapid social change. The population is increasing three times faster than the rate of growth of the rest of the world. Both the Roman Catholic Church and the Protestant churches are becoming acutely aware of the tremendous religious challenge. (ibid.)

Herman did not leave any doubt, however, about the impending task. He took a certain pride in mentioning "that today there is no South American republic without at least one pastor to care for the Lutheran diaspora." At the same time, however, difficulties within the diaspora situation prohibited a premature celebration of hopes for a flourishing church life among Lutherans. He pointed to four immediate steps which, though modest in scope, had to be taken: "to send out pastors," a task more difficult than many might imagine; "to help the people organize a congregation and obtain a parish center"; "to link the widely scattered parishes more closely together"; and, finally, to "foster the growth of self-supporting synods" (ibid., p. 134).

Stewart Herman, at Minneapolis, was deliberate in his determination to present the Latin American challenge to the LWF in such a way that it would be perceived as a significant step for the general self-understanding of the LWF as an agency of global cooperation. There was no longer to be room for the monopoly on power exercised by those blocs of churches present at the founding of the Federation:

> There is no doubt that people must be spoken to in a language they can under-stand. But anyone who contends that the basic language of the Lutheran Church must be German or Swedish or English or some other tongue of the sixteenth-century Reformation simply does not understand the Reformation. The language of the Lutheran Church is the language of the people—any people. (ibid., p. 135)

During this first decade of the LWF the Lutheran churches of Africa were facing a challenge of similar proportions to that in Latin America. The LWF Commission on World Missions convened an "All Africa Lutheran Conference" in Marangu, Tanganyika, November 12-22, 1955 (cf. *Marangu: A Record of the All-Africa Lutheran Conference,* LWF Department of World Mission, Geneva, 1956). Approximately one hundred fifty delegates attended, many of whom were missionaries or representatives of missionary agencies. A number of LWF leaders participated, among them Hanns Lilje, who was then LWF President, Franklin Clark Fry of the United States, then a President of the World Council of Churches as well as a Vice President of the LWF, Fridtjov Birkeli (1906–1983) of Norway, Director of the Department of World Missions, and Fredrik A. Schiotz (1901–1989) of the United States, chairperson of the LWF Commission on World Mission.

It was characteristic of the time that the joy among African Lutherans was tempered by anxiety and hesitation. On one hand, they were encouraged by the mere fact that they were able to travel and attend the conference at Marangu; on the other hand, they hesitated to present open, critical statements because of possible reactions from either the colonial powers or the missionaries and their agencies. In light of these facts, the delegates from Ethiopia, which was then one of the few independent African states, insisted on a closed session reserved to indigenous African delegates to the conference. That closed session brought about a change in the overall atmosphere of the conference: a mood of confidence emerged and common agreement was reached among the African participants. In their report to the plenary they made mention of five urgent requests that were later summarized in the following way by Dr. Emmanuel Abraham

(b. 1913), leader of the Ethiopian Evangelical Church Mekane Yesus in a communication to the Emperor of Ethiopia, Haile Selassie:

1. The African delegates feel that it is very desirable that an institution for advanced theological education be established as soon as possible in Southern Rhodesia, Liberia, or Ethiopia.

2. Until such an institution is established, it would help greatly the young Churches if scholarships were granted to enable deserving Africans to study in European and American universities.

3. It is desirable that local institutions in the various countries in Africa be developed more fully so that the standard of training for teachers, pastors and evangelists may be more in line with the rising educational standards in Africa.

4. It is strongly felt that it would strengthen the young Churches in Africa if more responsible positions [i.e., in organizations such as the LWF] were filled by Africans to enable them to realize more fully their responsibility for the work.

5. It would greatly help the propagation of the Christian faith in Africa if Missionaries in their relations with Africans showed a better example of fighting all kinds of discrimination. (quoted in Emmanuel Abraham, *Reminiscences of My Life* [Oslo: Lunde Forlag, 1995] p. 316; also discussed orally by J. H. Schjørring with Dr. Emmanuel Abraham and Dr. Emmanuel Gebre Selassie, September 1993, Addis Ababa)

As will become apparent, the "root causes" of later church struggles in South Africa were already evident in the mid-1950s. The historical significance of the Marangu conference of 1955 is given full evidence in the report, already cited, which Emmanuel Abraham subsequently presented to the Ethiopian Emperor. In that report Dr. Abraham referred directly to racial discrimination in South Africa as an obstacle to the Lutheran presence throughout the continent.

Generally speaking, the activities of the Missionaries are gratifying and fruitful, but it was clear from what was said and left unsaid that the Africans living in South Africa are experiencing great difficulties due to racial discrimination. The South African blacks were averse from speaking about the oppression they were enduring because of differences of race, the reason being fear of being subjected to worse treatment on returning home. In spite of the fact that it was apparent that the spirit of equality and unity prevailed in the Conference where the people believed they were genuine Christians who followed Luther's faith and example, it was painful to observe at times that differences engendered by race and color were looming large. The reason being that, although it was a novelty for most of the Africans at the Conference to talk to the whites freely even in spiritual matters, some of the blacks had to speak candidly about the obstacles placed in the way of the extension of the Kingdom of Christ and the whites, not accustomed to hear such remarks from the blacks, showed feelings of displeasure. Even then, appreciating the truth of what was said, the whites got over it quickly. The Africans were often reluctant to repeat in the Conference what they told us plainly outside. We understood this was because they did not trust one another or were unwilling to offend the whites who paid for them to go to the Conference. (ibid., p. 315)

Concerning the same Marangu conference, a statement by the local Lutheran bishop, Stefano Moshi (1906–1976) of the Northern Diocese in Tanganyika, was also noteworthy. He commented on another basic African concern, in fact precisely a concern that was to inform the development of guidelines for church cooperation in the "Two-Thirds World." Bishop Moshi pleaded that the LWF take steps toward the creation of structures that would enable African Lutherans to move toward church autonomy, including self-determination for the indigenous people in matters of administration, economy, and spirituality:

A third higher step for training native leadership is the church office. In the mid-age of a church the head of the church is a missionary president. There should be native workers such as vice president, and church secretary and treasurer. They will share church and mission problems and help good understanding between the church and the mission. The native leaders will get a clear picture of the whole church. They will learn its weak and strong aspects and reasons why and find out the remedy. They will know how the church is making progress administratively, spiritually and economically. The church office thus will be a school for native leadership. The native workers in this office should not be like figures only, but they should have the mission and the church affairs and policies made clear to them. It may happen that in some church such native leaders may be in the dark as to what is going on in the mission and the church policy, and very little training of the leadership would be gained. On the other hand the native leaders should be patient and wise enough to discuss any policy which they think is not fair in a friendly and brotherly way. (cf. Marangu, pp. 56f.)

At the end of the first decade of the Federation, Lutheran churches joined together in what became perhaps the largest project in Federation history, the formation of Radio Voice of the Gospel, the preparation for which began in 1957, with its transmitter in Addis Ababa, Ethiopia. This radio station was dedicated to development and education as well as to ecumenical witness; it achieved international renown—its signal reached at times to the Far East—and provided an additional point of identity for the Lutheran presence in Africa. Its operational life was limited to fourteen years; in March 1977 it was nationalized by the Ethiopian Provisional Military Administrative Council. (cf. below pp. 161–63; and Manfred

Lundgren, *Proclaiming Christ to His World: The Experience of Radio Voice of the Gospel, 1957–1977* [Geneva, 1983])

As in Latin America and Africa, there was also during this period considerable ferment within the Lutheran churches of Asia. While more decisive regional consultations were held in Asia during the second decade of LWF history, the churches there were facing issues of considerable importance. Two can be mentioned here. First, the Church of South India had been formed in 1947 without, as it developed, Lutheran participation; the ramifications of this Lutheran noninvolvement continued to be of importance both ecumenically and in respect to the identity and witness of the several Lutheran churches in that area. Second, in Sumatra, Indonesia, considerable attention was paid to the reception into LWF membership in 1952 of the Huria Kristen Batak Protestan (HKBP). Ecclesially and ecumenically, the significance of this reception lay in the fact that the HKBP had no statement of formal subscription to the Augsburg Confession or other traditional Lutheran documents. The HKBP's own confession, adopted in November 1951, was judged by the LWF to be in harmony with Lutheran standards and, accordingly, this church became a member church of the LWF. The theological and ecclesial significance of this reception must be counted as of signal importance.

In April of 1956 a conference that bore a certain similarity to the Marangu All-Africa Lutheran Conference was held by representatives of European minority churches in Semmering, Austria, under LWF auspices. It is yet another instance of the tendency in the mid-1950s toward a new self-consciousness and sense of cooperation among smaller and less affluent Lutheran churches in various parts of the world. While the intent of the Semmering event was basically to provide a forum for pastors of minority churches to deal with issues of parish ministry and not to move toward some form of regional organization, the conference must be seen as part of a growing self-awareness of Lutheran churches sharing similar contexts for life and ministry. The most urgent needs that arose after World War II in Europe had been met. Yet, many of the minority churches present at Semmering were living under intense pressure, most notably those living in one-party states ruled by the Communists, but also those from other "diaspora churches," which often faced extreme intolerance and hostility from majority churches of other confessions, usually Roman Catholic or Orthodox bodies. Such situations presented challenges that far exceeded needs for material assistance and financial support. In these circumstances it was crucial that the small Lutheran churches avoid the kind of unhealthy preoccupation with internal matters that centered exclusively about self-preservation, and it was equally crucial that they not view their own church bodies as being without blemish. Superintendent

Professor Fritz Zerbst from the Evangelical Church of the Augsburg Confession in Austria made a substantial contribution to the development of self-awareness in these diaspora churches:

> Melanchthon had a very pessimistic view of the small number of conscious Christians in the world. Of course, it was not his intention to divide the church into the rare true Christians and the fake Christians. But singling out the few is immediately dangerous—when we say that the few, the minority, that is the true church. When we say this, the minority church is forced into a self-understanding according to which it includes the true Christians merely due to its minority status. Quite a few visitors come to the diaspora in the expectation of finding the true church. They are, in advance, ready to adjust their later reports to this line. The minority church neither is an ideal construct, nor is it a *civitas platonica.* (*Amt und Gemeinde,* edited by the bishop of the Evangelical Church of the Augsburg Confession in Austria. Special issue on the minority church conference of the LWF, Semmering, 23–27 April 1956, vol. 7, no. 6, 1956, p. 12; trans. supplied)

## The Second Decade

### *The Balance between Member Churches.*

The growing participation of churches from outside the three original groupings—German, Nordic, and American—was a dominant theme in the second decade of the LWF story. This evolution was given an added dimension by striking changes in the overall composition of church delegations to LWF assemblies. In 1957 those delegations were still largely dominated by senior church leaders and prestigious university professors, nearly all of whom were male. In 1970, at Evian, the composition of the groups had changed radically: laity, women, and youth were now far more visible. This development gives evidence to the fact that the second decade witnessed a continuation of the growing involvement of churches and persons from the Southern Hemisphere in the life of the Federation (cf. chapter 8 below).

Of particular importance during this period were the changing relations between the churches of Western and Eastern Europe. The Berlin Wall was erected in 1961, signaling, among many other things, a new situation for the churches of the German Democratic Republic, a situation that led directly to the creation of a separate LWF national committee for the churches of East Germany. Also, this was the period when Lutheran churches in the three Baltic countries became members of the Federation, Estonia and Latvia in 1963 and Lithuania in 1967. At the same time, further, the establishment of the Christian Peace Conference in the early 1960s, an ecumenical organization whose policies strongly reflected the positions of the Soviet Union, created a serious dilemma for Lutheran churches in Eastern Europe. In general, the LWF and its member churches remained as independent as possible from the influence of the Christian Peace Conference. These developments created a new and difficult context for the work of the Federation in Eastern Europe, not least in respect to its programs of interchurch aid. Political oppression, imprisonment, severe censorship, and violations of human rights were matters of course for the churches. Many left the East; those who stayed and remained faithful to the church and its message found themselves at great risk (cf. chapter 3 below).

One of the great moments of the LWF's Third Assembly, at Minneapolis in 1957, was the sermon preached by Bishop Lajos Ordass of the Lutheran Church in Hungary. The enthusiastic welcome given to Bishop Ordass, who served two separate terms as a vice-president of the LWF (1947–52, 1957–63), must be understood in its context. Less than a year before, in 1956, the rebellion of the Hungarian people had been brutally put down by the Russian army. Bishop Ordass was seen as an outstanding leader of the resistance, a brave witness to Christ who stood in opposition to the powers of darkness identified with the Marxist government of Hungary which was actually a tool of Soviet expansionism.

Ordass's sermon centered about the freedom and unity that are given only through Christ. He made no direct reference to political issues or to his own personal situation, but the congregation of several thousand persons applied his message to circumstances in the Lutheran Church in Hungary whose bishop, Ordass, witnessed courageously to the gospel without giving heed to political or personal consequences (cf. above pp. 30–31 and pp. 370, 466 below).

### Theology: Consensus and Fragmentation

The Third Assembly of the Lutheran World Federation was a milestone in respect to the role of theology in the life of the LWF. Both the Commission and the Department of Theology emphasized in their reports that much had been accomplished since the Second Assembly in 1952. A broad spectrum of topics had been broached in that period, from the establishment of an international forum for Luther research to a serious consideration of liturgical matters of immediate relevance to member churches and their parishes. In reporting on this latter issue, it was pointed out that there was common agreement regarding principles of worship quite apart from any consensus regarding standard forms of worship. In commenting on a proposal that the Commissions on Theology and Liturgy be merged, the report made the following substantive points:

> Such a merger [of the two commissions] will not mean a submerging of liturgical study in other aspects of theology. For it may be claimed that the theology which the majority of the members of our congregations learn most clearly and impressively is the theology that comes through the forms of worship—through Baptism and confirmation, through prayers and praise, through confession and communion, through the observance of holy days and weekly services, through word and hymn, through act and attitude and the spirit that prevails in the house of the Lord. This is the daily bread of the congregations of Christ and the health of the Church is best manifested in what pastor and people do as they participate in the "communion of saints." There may be more conspicuous duties that challenge the attention of the Lutheran World Federation but none more basic or pervasive than those related to the building up of the people of God in congregational worship. (*Proceedings*, Minneapolis, p. 144)

In this survey it is crucial for us to observe the fact of *consensus* concerning matters of theology demonstrated at the Third Assembly. This was evident not only in respect to specific recommendations but also and perhaps more importantly in respect to the felt desire that a common Lutheran identity be expressed in both theological exposition and liturgical practice. The celebrated "Theses" of the Minneapolis Assembly concerning its theme, "Christ Frees and Unites," prepared under the leadership of Franklin Clark Fry, who was elected LWF president at that assembly, stand as a focus for this theological consensus. Never since has any LWF assembly succeeded in expounding its theme both with such theological clarity and with such direct relation to strategy and practice (cf. pp. 220, 373 below).

The Fourth Assembly of the LWF, Helsinki 1963, presents a striking and almost violent contrast to the consensus reached at Minneapolis. As is well known, at that assembly the LWF was unable to adopt a common statement concerning the most central Lutheran theological concern, justification by grace through faith. This contrast between consensus and fragmentation has given rise—not surprisingly—to misperceptions, rumors, and legends, and it is essential that a proper analysis of the facts be presented. To be sure, no single factor explains the "Helsinki failure," but the following points must be taken seriously:

1. By 1963 the mechanisms and procedures deemed proper to an LWF assembly had become far too complicated for leaders and staff. One celebrated example should be cited. At a certain moment in the debate surrounding the proposed statement on justification (Assembly Document No. 75) there was complete confusion in the plenary concerning the exact

nature of the vote. Franklin Clark Fry, LWF president and well known as a church parliamentarian, was probably too quick in his own presentation of the four variations of the topic which were up for vote. This caused difficulties for those doing simultaneous translation and great unclarity among those who were to vote.

2. At Helsinki there was far too little time reserved for plenary discussion and debate. Even prior to the assembly there had been sharp criticism of the heavy schedule and the amount of time allotted for both group and plenary work had been judged unacceptable.

3. The authority of Federation leadership was no longer such that any proposal at all would be automatically accepted. The most prominent leaders in the debate—Franklin Clark Fry; Hanns Lilje, former LWF president; Vilmos Vajta; Director of the Department of Theology—found themselves subject to sharp questioning and disagreement in a way which had not happened previously in the Federation.

4. At the time of the Helsinki Assembly the overall theological and ecumenical situation was in the process of considerable change. The theological dominance of the three "blocs" was being reduced; representatives from minority and younger churches were claiming a greater role in the debates. Ecumenically, this was the time both of the Second Vatican Council and of the first stirrings of "liberation" and "political" theologies. These factors combined to create new theological expectations—e.g., regarding the relationship of justification to justice—which were perhaps unprecedented in twentieth-century Lutheran theological reflection (cf. pp. 377ff. below).

The problems, issues, and expectations that arose at the Fourth LWF Assembly were only to become more pronounced in future years. What was being seen in the early 1960s was the demise of a certain style of doing theology and the birth of new methods and the raising of new questions. It was not at all clear that the Lutheran World Federation at this point in its history was prepared to deal with what were finally to be seen as its own theological questions.

## The Third Decade

### *Transition in Assemblies*

The first four assemblies of the Lutheran World Federation, from 1947 to 1963, produced feelings of satisfaction. Not only was there joy at the very ability to convene in a setting of community, there was also a commonly felt need to join in unified response to external challenges, whether from prevailing political circumstances and ideologies or from other world communions. These first four assemblies had notably all taken place in countries from the main groupings of member churches which had dominated the Federation since its founding.

During the LWF's third decade, however, important reflections concerning the character of an assembly took place. An assembly, virtually an institution in itself, was seen to be unnecessarily complicated; negative judgments overshadowed positive estimations. This was voiced with strikingly clear foresight in a report drafted by the General Secretary, André Appel of France (b. 1921) and presented to the LWF Executive Committee at its 1969 meeting in Copenhagen. The first point on the agenda for that meeting dealt with major structural questions. Appel's report included the following observation:

> To look at an assembly as we did in the past, as a kind of Lutheran Jamboree, Ashram or Kirchentag, and at the same time as a certain type of a "synod," adding the duties and joys of a study consultation, is just obsolete and impossible. Besides, we are more than before trying to take into account the specific context and especially the life of our host church. Have we set our goals too high? (Report of December 5, 1969, signed also by Darrol Bryant, Marc Chambron, Ulrich Duchrow, Olof Joëlson, and Günther Schulze; 1969 Meeting of the LWF Executive Committee, Exhibit C)

It is perhaps no exaggeration to state that the fundamental point of these observations has never received the attention it deserves. Even so, several other features of the assemblies after 1963 are striking as indications of changes in the ethos of the Federation.

The political context of assemblies has played an increasingly important role. This was especially true in respect to the dramatic circumstances in which the Fifth Assembly, 1970, took place. It was scheduled for Porto Alegre, Brazil, after Weimar in the German Democratic Republic proved impossible as a venue, but was moved, not without controversy, to Evian-les-Bains, France (pp. 382ff. below). Political contexts, however, proved to be just as important at each of the following assemblies. Moreover, from the 1977 assembly at Dar es Salaam, Tanzania on, LWF assemblies have taken place without exception outside the orbit of the three blocs of churches. Furthermore, ever since 1963 LWF assemblies have found themselves newly and deeply concerned with sensitive social-ethical issues. This fact, on the one hand, represented the courage and willingness to address new challenges and, on the other hand, it has resulted in a widespread impression that controversial socio-ethical questions have most often been approached in the Federation without sufficient grounding in the common theological heritage of the Lutheran tradition.

Thus if theology played a role in the interpretation of a shared heritage and in the formation of communal obligations among the member churches of the LWF in the first two decades of Federation history, the subsequent decades have been marked by a deep concern for—if not a preoccupation with—sensitive and controversial issues in social, political, and economic arenas. Among such issues we could name the "root cause" study of social and economic injustice, women's concerns, and the "China studies," all of which came to the fore in the LWF in the early 1970s.

### Structural Renewal

The 1960s were for the Lutheran World Federation a long journey of discussions in anticipation of structural changes. At the meeting of the executive committee in Copenhagen in December 1969, a proposal for restructuring was adopted and subsequently approved at the Evian Assembly the following year.

Prior to the adoption of this plan a preliminary report had been circulated which pointed to the fact that a need for restructuring—structural renewal—had been felt within the Federation as early as 1962 when "the need for clarification of responsibilities and jurisdiction" was expressed. The process which followed proved more comprehensive than anticipated because it involved structural factors of an extremely diverse nature: (1) the relationship between member churches and the Geneva secretariat; (2) the relationship between programmatic commissions and the LWF Executive Committee; (3) the interplay between commissions and departments; (4) the balance between the Northern and Southern Hemispheres; (5) financial resources; and (6) a redefinition of the mandate for each of the commissions and departments.

The necessity of structural change was occasioned by the obvious need for a simplification of the LWF administration. At the same time, however, it was stimulated by a renewed and dynamic vision made apparent in the following list of advantages and disadvantages to a new structure which would place a greater emphasis on LWF regional structures. The lengthy list of advantages may be summarized in six points: (1) the desirability of decentralization; (2) the recognition that the changing ecclesial life in Africa and Asia was increasing the numbers of autonomous churches; (3) the desirability of liberating commissions from functional and technical administrative responsibilities in order that they might concentrate on matters of comprehensive strategy; (4) the need for a clearer expression of regional identity within the Federation, including the need better to understand the problems of particular regions and to stimulate indigenous leadership; (5) the need for better contact between member churches and the Federation as a whole and the concurrent need to present the LWF in its entirety rather than as individual departments; and (6) the need more adequately to deal with current social and political developments (cf. *Report of the Special Committee on Structure and Function,* March 14, 1962).

Disadvantages of the proposals, on the other hand, were seen to include the danger of overemphases on partial aspects of LWF work, the difficulties in coordinating special requests from regions, and the danger of fostering pressure groups that were described as "vested interests and competition" (ibid.).

Additionally, the 1962 report balanced the advantages of a functional structure that would utilize regional consultants with corresponding disadvantages. This proposal was seen as one that would best equip the Federation to express global concerns, "a better possibility of weighing global needs, clarification of purpose and function of the commissions and comparatively small changes in the organizational structure." Its disadvantages were seen, in a strikingly self-critical way, as centering about the danger of "unhealthy concentration in Geneva," the difficulties in maintaining equal contact with all groups of member churches, and the danger of overlooking the special wishes and needs of given regions (ibid.).

The work of this Special Committee on Structure and Function continued into 1969 when the following recommendations were presented:

1. "That the structure of the Lutheran World Federation be based upon global concept and function." In explication of this it was stated that members of LWF commissions should have double responsibilities, to "represent the wholeness of the LWF" and to "provide special knowledge."

2. "That the Executive Committee and the Commissions on Theology, World Mission, and World Service be the basic operational units." It was foreseen that such a simplification would encourage overall exchange of information and promote greater cooperation, thus paving the way for a more efficient and transparent LWF administration. The proposal indicated that "the Commissions should operate through functional Departments with the following general areas of responsibility:

Theology: Worship and Spiritual Life; Theology of Stewardship and Evangelism; Faith and Order; Research; Preparation of Studies for LWF Assemblies

World Mission: Missionary Outreach [with several specifications]; Inter-Church Aid; Congregational Life

World Service: Migration and Resettlement; Disaster and Emergency Relief; Community Development Projects; Medical and Charitable Institutions; Self-help and Rehabilitation; Volunteer Services.

It is crucial to underline that in this listing the name of the Department of World Mission was changed to the Department of Church Cooperation, reflecting, above all, the resistance among representatives of the non-Western churches to an alleged prolongation of the historical alliance between the missionary movement and Western imperialism or colonialism. Also vigorously in favor of the name change were representatives of member churches of Eastern Europe whose churches were to be closely related to the new department since Inter-Church Aid was transferred to that unit from World Service. To persons from Eastern Europe, heavily influenced by their socialist environment, the word "mission" had a subversive Western connotation which would complicate cooperation between Eastern European churches and the LWF. This issue gave rise to a lengthy and spirited discussion at the Evian Assembly, which revealed sharply divergent points of view.

3. A specification of the responsibilities and procedures of Geneva staff, most notably a strengthening of the role of the general secretary. Also made explicit was the concern for closer cooperation between commissions and the corresponding departments of the secretariat, and an authorization of commissions to give guidance to the departments in questions of principle and policy.

4. It was further proposed to enlarge the Geneva staff by appointing regional consultants, thereby "emphasizing the legitimate concerns of the main geographical regions."

5. It was proposed to review the number and function of study commissions with the purpose of reducing their number and insuring their attachment to a particular programmatic department. At the same time it was recommended that a member of the Geneva staff should serve as liaison with each study commission. This proposal eliminated the Committee on Latin America as a special unit within the Federation, an action seen as a move toward the combining of programmatic structure with regional initiatives and concerns. Finally, it was recommended that all budgets be consolidated and that an "Office for Public Information and Promotion be established." This report had been drafted in a committee composed of Rudolf Weeber (1906–1988), LWF Treasurer, of Germany, as chairperson; Etienne Jung, Vice President of the Church of the Augsburg Confession in France; and William D. Schaeffer of the United States.

### 1972–73: The Turning Point

The restructuring process just described was from an internal point of view the necessary precondition for broad scale renewal within the LWF. The role played by the 1970 Assembly at Evian in this renewal is described elsewhere in this volume (cf. pp. 382–96 below); we shall here survey other aspects of this extensive transformation, which took place some twenty-five years after the Federation was founded. In order adequately to do this, we must be reminded of the global context within which the LWF found itself at the time.

The world's political situation at that time was one of continued confrontation: wars in the Middle East, the Soviet invasion of Czechoslovakia, the war in Vietnam. New tensions arose in the early 70s even before the repercussions of the earlier military conflicts were settled: apartheid in South Africa was extended by that country's occupation of Namibia; the oil crisis of 1973 added to the unsettled situation in the Middle East; inner instability marked the "First World" as countries in the "Two-Thirds World" struggled for influence in spite of the unrest caused by long processes of decolonization and by grossly weak economies; the contrast between North and South, often described in economic and political terms, reached even deeper levels of value and lifestyle. Ideologically, the times were further marked by the rise, not least among youth throughout the world of a "New Left," which was an often inchoate protest against the many corruptions of the entrenched power that accompanied the political, military, economic, and racial policies of most Northern nations. In many respects the early 1970s found the world at sharp crossroads.

To what extent did the major decisions of the LWF reflect global political tendencies? What were both the continuities and discontinuities between the founding intentions of 1947 and the life of the Federation twenty-five years later?

Ecumenically, too, this was a time of considerable ferment. The Assembly of the World Council of Churches held at Uppsala, Sweden, in 1968 was striking evidence of the intrinsic relationship between ecclesial questions and those of the social order, particularly questions of inclusiveness, not least the matter of equal rights for women and youth, and racism. These were issues also on the agenda of the LWF. Further, the process of renewal in the Roman Catholic Church in the wake of Vatican II paved the way for a thorough reconsideration of bilateral relations between Roman Catholics and Lutherans (cf. chapter 7 below). Even more broadly, this must be seen as a time when the connection between social ethics and human rights, and the systematic understanding of the classic Christian faith was being reinterpreted. Movements such as liberation theology, black theology, political and "hope" theology, and various forms of Christian-Marxist dialogue were attaining considerable currency, with appropriate variations, throughout the world.

In this global and ecclesial context the Lutheran World Federation entered a period of profound transformation. It is important to give brief consideration to several developments that contributed to this transformation.

*Proclamation and Development.*   On March 9, 1971, Dr. Emmanuel Abraham, President of the Ethiopian Evangelical Church Mekane Yesus (EECMY), sent on behalf of the General Assembly of that church a message of concern to the LWF General Secretary, André Appel. The concern was that the LWF urge its member churches and their service organizations to amend their aid criteria to include direct support for the work of evangelization, leadership training, and church building. The response from Geneva suggested that the EECMY prepare a detailed study of its economic situation. The church's executive committee, however, decided to prepare a theological analysis of its concern. A document, signed by eight officers of the EECMY, entitled "On the Interrelation between Proclamation of the Gospel and Human Development" was, accordingly, forwarded to the Federation in May 1972.

The document underlined the inability of the church "to cope with the fast growing congregational work and the opportunities for evangelistic outreach in this country [Ethiopia]." In this emergency situation, the call of the church for assistance from outside was seriously complicated if not compromised "by the prevailing imbalance in the assistance given to the Church by its Overseas partners." On the one hand, the EECMY had gratefully received aid for development projects that met the criteria set by the donor agencies: "The Church could not responsibly let the opportunities to get funds for development projects go by without making the fullest possible use of them. Over a number of years, the Church has therefore considered it her responsibility and privilege to work out project requests which would meet the criteria decided by the Donor Agencies." On the other hand, the document pointed out that "the Church, in faithfulness to her Lord, realized her obligation to proclaim the Gospel to the ever-growing crowds expecting more than bread." In this situation of growth the church had turned to overseas mission organizations for help, since it could not possibly deal with the need on the basis of its own resources. The Mekane Yesus Church, however, had not been heard in respect to these requests.

Emmanuel Abraham and his colleagues in the EECMY made no secret of the anger and bitterness which was felt in their church in light of this imbalance of support, and they urged that the entire matter be taken up within the context of the role of the church on the entire continent of Africa: "From the African point of view it is hard to understand this division [between proclamation and development] and the dichotomy created in the West and reflected in the criteria for assistance laid down by the Donor Agencies." The statement from Ethiopia was not limited to an expression of challenges and needs. It went far beyond the customary deferential tone of Southern recipients of aid by presenting a critical account of the thought patterns which directed the strategy of the agencies from the North. Referring to frequently used distinctions between rich and poor, developed and underdeveloped countries, it stated:

> We are using only generally adopted socio-economic measurements to determine which society is rich or poor, developed or underdeveloped. The standard of human life and that of society is normally evaluated in terms of economic growth and material wealth or in technology and production. Based on this materialistic Western concept of development and in an effort to find a remedy at least two things seem to have been largely overlooked, namely a) that there are values in life beyond those of modern technology and economic betterment without which man's development will never be meaningful and lasting [and] b) that man is not only the suffering creature who needs help, but that he is also the most important development agent. (*Lutheran World*, Vol. XX, 1973, pp. 187–92)

At several points in the following chapters, this statement on "Proclamation and Development" and its impact will be examined. It is important here, however, to indicate why the statement has assumed such importance in Federation history: First, it reflects in a pivotal way the continuing growth of self-consciousness on the part of LWF churches in the Southern Hemisphere; this self-consciousness is shown in the clear desire of those churches to be heard, to exert influence, and to be taken with new seriousness. Second, it stands as a clear indication of the differing contexts—South and North—in which the churches of the Federation live and work. The "old" churches, frequently frozen in traditionalism and decline, are seen in contrast to the younger or "new" churches whose life is increasingly marked by dynamic growth. Finally, "Proclamation and Development" dramatized for the global Lutheran communion the necessity of caution in applying one and the same theological concept—in this case, the classical Lutheran view concerning the two kingdoms—to situations that are diverse in time, place, and milieu.

*Status confessionis.*    Although the question of racial injustice had been recognized by the Federation as a burning issue as early as the first All-Africa Lutheran Conference in 1955, the fact that it remained an unsettled—more correctly, a worsening—issue made it a point of major concern in the 1970s. Racial oppression had become extreme in both South Africa and occupied South West Africa (Namibia), and Lutheran churches in those countries were divided in their response. Consequently, international Lutheran attention was increasingly focused on the matter, and this reached a climax in debates on *status confessionis*, debates that culminated in the 1980s when, at the Budapest Assembly, the membership of certain churches in the LWF was suspended (cf. pp. 71–73, 230ff., 399ff., 408–9 below).

*The Leuenberg Agreement.* The Leuenberg Agreement, submitted to Lutheran and Reformed churches on the continent of Europe in 1971 and adopted in 1973, represented a general departure from fixed positions of unconditional confessionalism that had long marked the relationships between those churches. This agreement recommended full "pulpit and altar fellowship" between those churches in light of the conviction that points of historical division—in particular, matters concerning eucharistic presence and predestination—were no longer seen as church-dividing. The Lutheran World Federation, through its General Secretary, André Appel, together with the World Alliance of Reformed Churches and the Faith and Order secretariat of the World Council of Churches, in a common communication of March 30, 1973, endorsed this transformative ecumenical development, which was designed to foster fellowship between "the Lutheran and Reformed churches in Europe along with the Union churches that grew out of them, and the related pre-Reformation churches, the Waldensian Church and the Church of the Czech Brethren." Implications of the Leuenberg Agreement beyond the European continent have yet to be fully realized.

*The Role of LWF Studies.* Signs of transformation—or at least of reorientation—were nowhere more spectacular than in the LWF Department of Studies. In chapter 5, specific features of the pioneering study project, "The Identity of the Church and Its Service to the Whole Human Being," will be assessed. This project was widely discussed, not only because it voiced basic concerns of the churches, but also because from its start it was marked by a note of provocation. Debate soon reached outside the Department of Studies and its commission, and the broad leadership of the Federation was brought into a heated situation. This controversy became more intense as other initiatives of the Department of Studies—the "China Study," programs fostered by the Women's Desk, and work on "root causes" of social and economic injustice—themselves became the object of discussion, debate, and in some cases severe criticism (cf. chapter 5).

The issue within the Federation was sharp. Overheated debate created the impression that the Department of Studies had become a locus for onesided outbursts of ideological propaganda in glaring contrast to the consensus building pursued in LWF theological work in the first decade of its history. Simultaneously it must not be forgotten that for many within the Federation—not least some voices from the South (not those who were deeply suspicious of being "coopted" for the radical causes being taken up by some in the North) and polarized youth in general—it was precisely "Studies" which virtually alone was showing the courage necessary seriously to take up burning issues that were first identified at the Evian Assembly of 1970. These controversial debates, in regard both to substance and method, were at the heart of LWF life during this crucial watershed period.

*The 1973 Meeting of the LWF Executive Committee.*   The foregoing developments within the LWF justify describing the third decade of the Federation's life as an authentically epochal turning point. Such momentum was, moreover, historical in that the Federation in 1972 celebrated its twenty-fifth anniversary. That celebration combined remembrance of the founding of the LWF with questions concerning its response to new challenges.

In direct prolongation of the 1972 observance, the Federation in 1973 witnessed yet another anniversary, that of the first conference of the Lutheran World Convention held at Eisenach, Germany, in 1923. In fact, the 1973 meeting of the LWF Executive Committee was held in Eisenach, a historical event also because it was the first LWF meeting to be held in East Germany, the German Democratic Republic. At this meeting, however, participants had no opportunity merely "to recollect in tranquillity" accomplishments of the past. Urgent questions of immediate importance demanded their full attention, even though the climate for open discussion was not always easy in light of the constant presence of government observers.

Chief among those questions, perhaps, was the matter of LWF relations to churches in Central and Eastern Europe, churches in countries under Marxist domination. The decision, not incidentally, to hold the 1973 Executive Committee meeting in the German Democratic Republic itself represented a deliberate determination to reconsider relations with churches behind the iron curtain.

The LWF was not alone in facing these questions. The overall political climate of the early 1970s was marked by a general reorientation of East-West relations. The European Security Conference was giving birth to hopes for a formal affirmation, by both sides, of a common will to refrain from military aggression, to allow for weapons control, and to assure a common respect for human rights. The so-called "New East Policy" (*Ostpolitik*) of the West German government under Willy Brandt, was itself seen as a stimulus for pragmatic cooperation involving also the churches.

In the context of this milder climate in international politics it was felt by many LWF leaders that the time had come for a reconsideration of relationships with churches in countries under Marxist rule. To be sure, there had already been subtle shifts in this direction, not least due to the work of Paul Hansen (1920–1992) first as a staff person of Lutheran World Service and subsequently the Department of Church Cooperation (cf. chapter 3 below). The fruits of that quiet work, many thought, should now become more public. Would not pragmatic cooperation with authorities in the socialist countries make life easier for the churches—congregations, pastors, and leaders—in those countries? Would it not be wise to develop a cautious but open policy of negotiation without abandoning loyalty to the true identity of the universal church?

Such a thorough reorientation in relations with the churches in socialist countries was not met in the LWF with total approval. Yet the advocates of such a policy won the day, not least among the majority of representatives from the churches of the Southern Hemisphere, the new generation of leaders from Central and Eastern Europe, and among many from the West who saw such a strategy as a welcome continuation of breakthroughs begun at the Evian Assembly in 1970. André Appel, General Secretary of the LWF, expressed himself as being obligated to support this general reorientation in policy, although he did not disguise his hesitations:

> In capitalistic, liberal societies, it is—in principle—possible to proceed to critical evaluations of the prevailing system. But in societies where the state controls all phases of life—even the church—public criticisms are considered a danger to the security of the country. This creates a real problem for international organizations which are used to treating all issues in the open. ("Reflections on Eisenach," *Lutheran World*, Vol. XX, no. 4, 1973, p. 343)

Obviously, a host of questions had to be faced in this debate. Was it possible to pursue a policy of pragmatic cooperation without betraying the interests of those who had resisted Communist oppression in the past, among whom were persons such as Bishop Lajos Ordass, of Hungary who in 1973 was still under house arrest? Was it a workable policy to confirm the advocacy of "inviolable" human rights, individual and corporate, when Marxist governments exerted pressures designed to prevent open criticism of their policies?

Further, to gain a clear picture of this crucial meeting of 1973, it is important to pay strict attention to the North-South—as well as the East-West—relationship. Mention has already been made of the importance of the "Proclamation and Development" debate that originated in Africa, and it is also important to note that this was a period in which intensification of work on world mission—associated with such leaders as Josiah Kibira (1925–1988) of Tanzania, James Scherer (b. 1926) of the

United States, Soritua Nababan (b. 1933) of Indonesia, and Horst Becker (b. 1926) of West Germany—marked the efforts of the Department of Church Cooperation. It is worthwhile, further, also to consider a statement presented to the executive committee by Manas Buthelezi (b. 1935) of South Africa who, while he was at Eisenach as a representative of the Commission on Studies, can be regarded as a spokesperson for the churches of Africa.

Dr. Buthelezi made specific reference to the theological tradition that since 1947 had been dominant in the LWF; he expressed serious doubt as to whether or not this tradition, if left unchallenged, would allow the LWF to take its new global responsibilities seriously. He went straight to the point:

> I think it is important for people who cry for this [i.e., the traditional] theological profile to realize that it is just not as simple as all that, that you can pick up a few theologians, German theologians, American theologians, Scandinavian theologians, who are of course more sophisticated in theologizing compared to people from Asia and Africa; then you say that you have really done your work seriously. What if I also say that my problems of faith are just as important? Maybe there is no history of expertise in our theologizing, but I feel we are also members of the LWF. How will the LWF answer to our concerns? (Minutes, LWF Executive Committee, 1973, Exhibit G 2, App, pp. 2f.)

It must, not incidentally, be pointed out that the full-scale request of the churches from the South—as represented in Buthelezi's intervention—gave rise to an emotional opposition. This was partly due to the fact that the demand that their voices be given full recognition was largely framed within the context of the work of the Department of Studies. While the work of that department and the controversy surrounding that work was not limited to North-South projects, the connection did give rise to concerned opposition.

In this broader connection, an ad hoc committee was formed by the executive committee at Eisenach to deal with the whole spectrum of questions raised by the work of the Department of Studies. This group gave a clear affirmation to the numerous remarkably courageous innovations of the department. Yet, it also pointed directly to the fact that "Studies" had given rise to an opposition which was both unnecessary and intolerable. The ad hoc committee added that this opposition was not only within the Geneva secretariat but came from outside as well:

> It is not clear that the Department has always been sensitive to the traditional theological methods which are practiced in most of our member churches. We fear that the striving for new forms of study and expression (although they are not to be condemned in themselves) may cause an unacceptable amount of confusion and tension in our Federation.

It appears that the Department staff, although more careful than in prior years, has not yet understood adequately the need to work cooperatively as a team with other staff of the LWF and with leaders of our member churches. We feel it necessary to stress that study methods which involve contact with individual congregations and units of member churches, present a danger unless the member churches involved are shown every consideration before such contacts are made. (Minutes, LWF Executive Committee, 1973, Exhibit E 8, p. 2)

This question of "traditional theological methods" has become perennial and highly contested in the life of the Federation.

## The Fourth Decade

### Status Confessionis

A continuous development marked the life of the Lutheran World Federation from its Fifth Assembly at Evian in 1970 through the Sixth Assembly at Dar es Salaam in 1977. Discussion concerning *status confessionis* in response to the fact of racial injustice within both societies and churches of South Africa and Namibia dominated the fourth decade.

As background to this discussion it must be seen that there was a causal relationship between earlier concerns about South Africa and actions begun in the 1970s prior to the Sixth Assembly. Violations of basic human rights exemplified by the policy of racial segregation pursued by the government of South Africa, presented precisely the challenge which prompted the LWF at its Fifth Assembly to speak on the issue in concert with other ecumenical bodies, including the World Council of Churches. It is, accordingly, appropriate to view the struggle against racism as central to the growing concern within the Federation for social ethics, a concern notable to the Federation's development after 1970.

It would, however, be misleading to view this growing concern for social ethics as though the Federation were developing political strategies alone without reference to the classical Christian creed or, in more specifically Lutheran terms, without drawing the proper consequences of the distinction between Law and Gospel. Such a view had in fact been developed in criticism of the whole ecumenical movement ever since the Uppsala Assembly of the World Council of Churches in 1968, which was often characterized as an assembly marked by an ethical surplus and an ecclesiological/theological deficit.

In respect to the LWF in the 1970s, such characterizations must not be too easily dismissed. Nevertheless, even though balance in judgments is required, it was exactly the connection between ecclesiological reorienta-

tion and the application of fundamental ethical standards that lay behind
the crucial resolution which was adopted in Dar es Salaam in 1977:

> Being together here as LWF member churches under the theme "In Christ—A
> New Community" we know that we are in solidarity with all those who stand
> for humanness. The LWF should propose to its member churches that they
> compare the legal codifications on human rights in the national laws in their
> own areas with the Human Rights Conventions, and report thereon. We espe-
> cially encourage our member churches to walk in obedience in the way that
> God's care for human beings prescribes. (*Proceedings*, Dar es Salaam, p. 178
> [statement 42])

Continuing along the same path, the Sixth Assembly stated regarding
South Africa:

> Under normal circumstances Christians may have different opinions in polit-
> ical questions. However, political and social systems may become so per-
> verted and oppressive that it is consistent with the confession to reject them
> and to work for changes. We especially appeal to our white member churches
> in southern Africa to recognize that the situation in southern Africa consti-
> tutes a *status confessionis*. This means that, on the basis of faith and in order
> to manifest the unity of the church, churches would publicly and unequivo-
> cally reject the existing apartheid system. (ibid., p. 180 [statement 56])

and on confessional integrity:

> Confessional subscription is more than a formal acknowledgment of doctrine.
> Churches which have signed the confessions of the church thereby commit
> themselves to show through their daily witness and service that the gospel
> has empowered them to live as the people of God. They also commit them-
> selves to accept in their worship and at the table of the Lord the brothers and
> sisters who belong to other churches that accept the same confessions. Con-
> fessional subscription should lead to concrete manifestations in unity in wor-
> ship and in working together at the common tasks of the church. (ibid., pp.
> 179ff.)

The intense discussions concerning *status confessionis* at Dar es Salaam
led to the fateful decision taken at the Seventh Assembly at Budapest,
1984 in its "Statement on Southern Africa: Confessional Integrity":

> The Seventh Assembly of the Lutheran World Federation, having studied and
> heard extensive reports regarding the situation in Southern Africa:
>
> 1. REAFFIRMS the resolution of the Sixth Assembly (Dar es Salaam 1977) on
>    Southern Africa: Confessional Integrity.
> 2. STRONGLY AND URGENTLY APPEALS to its white member churches in
>    Southern Africa, namely the Evangelical Lutheran Church in Southern
>    Africa (Cape Church) and the German Evangelical Lutheran Church in
>    South West Africa (Namibia) to publicly and unequivocally reject the sys-

tem of apartheid (separate development) and to end the division of the church on racial grounds.

3. Regretfully concluding that no satisfactory fulfillment of this goal has as yet been achieved, FINDS that those churches have in fact withdrawn from the confessional community that forms the basis of membership in the Lutheran World Federation. Therefore, the Assembly is constrained to SUSPEND THE MEMBERSHIP of the above churches, intending that such action serve as a help for those churches to come to clear witness against the policy of apartheid (separate development) and to move to visible unity of the Lutheran churches in Southern Africa. (*Proceedings*, Budapest, pp. 179–80)

It was in 1991 that the council of the LWF, after a lengthy process of pastoral guidance, visitation, and judgment, which accompanied marked shifts in the lives of both churches, lifted the suspension of these two churches.

### Questions of Balance: North-South, East-West

The debate on *status confessionis* created a symbol of unity for LWF churches in the South as they dealt with their enduring struggle against racial oppression. That struggle became for those churches a touchstone for the credibility of international Lutheran solidarity across the boundaries dictated by race and ethnicity. The member churches from the North, however, did not achieve uniformity on this issue. While there was no effort in the North to disregard the issue, there was no full agreement on, for instance, the implementation of sanctions against South Africa. A dominant conclusion about this decade must be that while the churches of the South had a commonly shared determination to remain in solidarity, there was in several areas an increasing fragmentation among those from the North.

Simultaneously, there were several indications of common cause between leaders from the churches of the South and those from the churches of Central and Eastern Europe. The mere fact that it was possible to elect Bishop Josiah Kibira of Tanzania and Bishop Zoltán Káldy (1919–1987) of Hungary, each of whom can count as a spokesperson for the direction just indicated, as successive presidents of the Lutheran World Federation is witness to this common cause.

Yet, when final reckonings are taken, the two assemblies of this period, Dar es Salaam in 1977 and Budapest in 1984, left the impression of controversy largely based on so-called nontheological factors. It was a sign of the times that the consciousness of a common Lutheran heritage no longer possessed sufficient dynamic to define common priorities against a shared background and a common obligation to the present, on the one hand, and diverse concerns and interests on the other.

## Communication

The importance of growing divergence and fragmentation between member churches of the LWF was highlighted in 1977 when it was decided to give up the publication of the LWF quarterly journals, *The Lutheran World/Lutherische Rundschau*. Up to 1977 these periodicals had served as a forum for discussion among all English- and German-speaking member churches on all issues related to the work of the Federation. It is surely true that there were several reasons given for the decision to abandon publication of *The Lutheran World*, among them being the clear need to strengthen a broader program of communication within the Federation. Nevertheless, it is not to be questioned that *The Lutheran World* had served as a communal forum for reflection, largely theological, a function that in a certain way has not been subsequently maintained.

Even before the nationalization of Radio Voice of the Gospel by the Ethiopian government in 1977 the LWF had reviewed its entire program of communication, a review which resulted in the establishment in 1975 of a Committee and Office of Communication within the general secretariat. In 1980 a full Department and Commission on Communication was established. Significantly, the communication work of the Federation antedated even the 1947 Assembly at Lund: at the behest of Sylvester Michelfelder an information service, *News Bulletin—Lutheran World Convention*, was inaugurated in March 1946.

The work of the department created in 1980 was various: information and documentation, with a global news and information bureau continuing to publish *Lutheran World Information* and *Lutherische Welt-Information* in English and German editions; communication consultancy in support of a wide variety of communication projects in LWF member churches, largely in the Two-Thirds World; LWF interpretation, publications, and promotion; reflection and research on global communication issues; and relations with ecumenical and secular media. Noteworthy among the many activities of the Department of Communication has been the support of regional communication entities and services within the Lutheran community of churches. The *Informationsdienst lutherischer Minderheitskirchen in Europa* (IDL, Information Service of European Lutheran Minority Churches), which operated first in Budapest and then in Vienna from 1982 to 1994, was an extremely important news service that served churches in Central and Eastern Europe at a time when there was very little communication allowed among those churches.

Additionally, the department has given continued support to Lutheran communication entities in Latin America, Asia, and Africa.

That all of this communication work has had an ecumenical dimension is attested by the LWF's participation, with other ecumenical groups (most notably the World Council of Churches), in the 1994 establishment of *Ecumenical News International* (ENI) a global ecumenical news service the creation of which has allowed *Lutheran World Information* and *Lutherische Welt-Information* to concentrate more creatively on news and information applicable directly to the Lutheran community of churches.

In the 1990 restructuring of the Federation, comprehensive communication work was continued, although communication consultancy—the support of communication projects in member churches and the pursuit of research in the field—was transferred (over some objection) to the new Department for Mission and Development. Other aspects of the work have been maintained in an Office for Communication Services within the LWF General Secretariat.

## Ecumenical Progress

While theological reflection as a specific task of the Federation was during this decade taken up by the challenges that we have briefly sketched above, it remained a vital factor within the compass of the LWF's involvement in ecumenical concerns.

Two important—for some, even spectacular—occasions of historical remembrance offered the opportunities for intensified ecumenical endeavor: the 450th Anniversary in 1980 of the *Confessio Augustana* and in 1983 the 500th Anniversary of the birth of Martin Luther. Each event brought about initiatives, even on a global scale, which were designed to closen relations between the Lutheran and Roman Catholic communions. In 1977 at Dar es Salaam the Assembly of the LWF welcomed "endeavors which aim at a Catholic recognition of the *Confessio Augustana*" and expressed "the willingness of the Lutheran World Federation to engage in dialogue with the Roman Catholic Church on this subject" (*Proceedings, Dar es Salaam,* p. 175). In 1984 it was pointed out that "(I) [the Sixth Assembly] noted that voices were speaking about the possible recognition by the Roman Catholic Church. While such formal recognition did not take place, it was a year in which Roman Catholics and Lutherans, on many different levels, considered that important Christian confession together" (Report of the General Secretary, Carl H. Mau, LWF-Report 17/18, 1984, p. 67).

A number of consultations and conferences in 1983 were devoted to the celebration of Martin Luther as a stimulus for renewal in theology and church life today. These events usually took place in situations where there was generally little connection between academic theological research and the actual concerns of church leaders and laity. The initiatives relating to the anniversary of the birth of the Reformer thus provided at least a modest occasion for reinvigorating the church's concerns with central theological and ecclesial issues.

Finally, the dialogue between Lutherans and the Jewish people was yet another field in which considerable progress was made. It was of great significance that at the Budapest Assembly a major address was given by Gerhart M. Riegner, retired General Secretary of the World Jewish Congress and Co-Chairperson of the International Jewish Committee on Interreligious Consultations. This event represented the first time that a representative of Judaism formally addressed a gathering of Lutheran Christians (cf. p. 408 below; also cf. LWF Report, 1984, pp. 255ff.).

## The Fifth Decade

IF THE QUESTION of *status confessionis* provided the hallmark of the fourth decade of the history of the Lutheran World Federation, the question of the self-understanding of the Federation as *communio* marked the fifth decade. This issue, further, provided impetus for the preparation and implementation of major structural changes authorized at the Eighth Assembly in Curitiba, Brazil, 1990. Principal aspects of this discussion are covered in chapter 6, where the question of the identity of the Federation is dealt with, and in the review of the Curitiba Assembly itself. Here we shall provide a brief historical assessment of this debate concerning the nature of the LWF and of the implications of the restructuring of 1990.

The decisions of 1990 by the LWF Assembly and subsequently by the LWF Council need to be understood as part of an historical development, even if some critics are inclined to see it as a complete innovation and departure from the original understanding of the nature of the Federation. In contrast to this latter view, there is clearly a basic, inner logic to developments from the watershed assembly at Evian in 1970 through and after the Curitiba event. This continuity can be demonstrated by five factors which when taken together and in context provide impetus for the journey which the global fellowship of Lutheran churches expressed in the LWF has taken in what some have called the movement "from Federation to Communion."

1. The Federation had, since Evian, been acting in *koinonia* or *communio*. Decisions such as the suspension of the membership of the two all-white churches of southern Africa "bear unambiguous witness to a sol-

idarity between churches which allows even such serious discipline to be exercised in the interest of building the communion." Further, "(t)hese expressions of the developing sense of communion (*koinonia*) to be found within the LWF could be amplified by reference to other existing practices, such as the making of common statements on matters of church and public importance on behalf of all member churches, the representation of Lutheranism in international ecumenical dialogue through the Federation, etc. Together, such elements in the history and action of the LWF bear witness to a communion (*koinonia*) which needs now to continue its growth toward self-consciousness as that might be expressed in the LWF" (Report of the Executive Committee on LWF Restructuring, August 1989, I [4]).

2. The legitimate desire of the churches from the Southern Hemisphere for a greater role in the decision making processes of the Federation led clearly in the direction of a new understanding of fundamental relationships between all member churches. Arguments against this desire, whether based on tradition alone or on control by financial strength, have yielded to arguments reflecting present realities and a basic ecclesiological conviction regarding equal and just representation. This question of representation in all aspects of Federation life and work has resulted in a new concern for regional balance as well as a deep concern for the just representation of women, youth, and disabled persons (cf. chapter 8).

3. At least since Evian, the Federation has been occupied by a quest to discover a balance between its doctrinal identity and its commitment to justice, peace, and human rights. At Budapest and Curitiba this quest for a proper interaction was a governing factor in new formulations of LWF self-understanding, the adoption of a new constitution, and the development of strategies for program committees and departments. *Communio*, among other things, has provided a key to developing a balance between questions of faith and ecclesiology and commitments to witness and mission. It has, further, provided an understanding—although not the only possible understanding—for new developments in respect to structure and administration.

4. The growing ecumenical concerns of the LWF, largely in its bilateral work but also in its role within the global conciliar movement, are well and logically served by the notion of *communio*. In point of fact "the ecclesiology of communion" is a dominant theme in all ecumenical encounter at the end of the twentieth century, and the LWF has taken a leading role at many levels of that encounter. In addition to allowing the Federation increasingly to speak on behalf of its member churches in ecumenical matters, the new constitution possesses a doctrinal basis that properly balances confessional identity with ecumenical commitment and fellowship,

viewing each as essential to a proper understanding of the global communion of Lutheran churches expressed in the Federation.

5. The role of the Geneva secretariat is clearly illuminated by *communio*. On the one hand, it is provided with a clearer understanding of the
proper mutuality in both decision making and operation between all
member churches and the secretariat itself; on the other hand, traditional
program units—service, mission, theology, ecumenism, international
affairs and human rights, communication—are given space to adjust to
changing contexts and new initiatives.

At the 1987 meeting of the LWF Executive Committee in Viborg, Denmark, when a Committee on Restructuring was formed with Bishop James
Crumley (b. 1925) of the United States, as its chairman, it was made clear
that relevant decisions of recent Federation assemblies would guide its
work. Thus it was that decisions concerning *status confessionis*, pulpit
and altar fellowship between member churches, and the self-understanding of the Federation provided, directly and by implication, impetus for
restructuring:

> Restructuring, then, was to be undertaken in the context of the life and work
> of the entire Federation. Ways were to be found to assist the member churches
> in expressing their relationship as communion in mission and service. It is not
> enough to construct a new Geneva structure; if the need is to be met, a thor-
> ough reexamination of the LWF would be required. The Geneva secretariat
> must, of course, be a major component of the restructuring process since it is
> the instrument established by the churches for coordination and mutual assis-
> tance. Additional reasons for addressing the issue of Geneva restructuring
> have been seen to be: the need for greater departmental integration, the desire
> to make the Secretariat a more effective instrument and, financial constraints
> which require the trimming of the LWF budget. (*From Budapest to Curitiba*,
> LWF Report 27, 1989, p. 41)

The full text of the LWF Constitution adopted in 1990 at Curitiba
appears as an appendix in the present volume; a review of the negotiations
leading to its adoption is to be found in the survey of the Curitiba Assembly (cf. pp. 416–18 below). It is appropriate here, however, briefly to indicate some of the more far-reaching implications of this action that
developed under the strong and at times contested leadership of the Federation's General Secretary at the time, Gunnar Staalsett (b. 1935) of the
Church of Norway (cf. pp. 509–14 below).

It is perhaps in the structure and workings of the LWF Council that the
implications of *communio* are most dramatically visible. Membership in
the council, which is now the chief governing body of the Federation
between assemblies, is divided evenly between representatives of member
churches in the Southern Hemisphere and representatives from the

Northern Hemisphere. This equality is based on a judgment, ecclesiological in nature, concerning the fundamental identity of churches, not on criteria such as historical, numerical, or financial strength. The LWF Constitution of 1990 has a new view of authority within the global communion:

> Authority within the total LWF communion must be shared insofar as possible. Authority presupposes that responsibility is to be found in specific places and in designated persons or units, and those to whom such responsibility is given are held accountable for carrying out their duties. In the communion power—related to responsibility and authority—is properly limited so as not to become destructive to the communion. Both authority and power are used to serve, not to control. (Report of the Executive Committee on LWF Restructuring, August 1989, III, [6])

Another major change resulting from the restructuring had to do with the creation of program committees as a replacement for commissions. In the previous LWF structure the commissions did their work quite apart from the former executive committee and thus fundamental LWF program planning was separated from basic policy making within the Federation. Program committees now consist in persons who have been elected by an assembly to the LWF Council, augmented by persons specially chosen for technical expertise. The attempt has been to create a unified approach to matters of policy and of program.

The general secretariat in Geneva, the administration of the Federation and its activities, has in the new structure been reduced in size in order to accommodate financial realities. Most notable—and perhaps controversial—has been the creation of the Department for Mission and Development, which combines the activities of the former Department of Church Cooperation with elements from the former Departments of World Service (the Community Development Service), Study (the women's, youth, and education desks), and Communication (consultative services in communication).

Historical accuracy and honesty require that it be acknowledged that the debate that led to the restructuring of the Federation in 1990, as authorized by the Curitiba Assembly, was a painful and at times bitter one. The final decision was taken by the narrowest of votes, and it has taken time to restore relationships and to reconcile serious internal differences. Never in its history had the Lutheran World Federation faced an issue more divided, a striking irony in view of the fact that the issue had to do with the deepest of unities, *communio*. This irony is thrown into deeper relief when it is recalled that the first LWF Constitution was approved in 1947 unanimously, and the structural changes of 1969–70 met with broad general approval.

The 1990 restructuring involved additional ambiguities. There is a stated policy to achieve democratic balance—in respect to region, gender, ethnicity, and race—in all LWF decision-making bodies. This concern for inclusiveness—gender, laity, youth, the disabled—has become a clear and praiseworthy goal of the Federation (cf. chapter 8). Notwithstanding this, however, it is frequently asked whether the restructured LWF provides sufficiently for competence, professional skill, and experience as criteria for involvement in decision-making bodies as well as staff. Finally it remains to be seen whether the concept of *communio* is allowed to become a powerful ecclesiological reality, or whether it is reduced to being a mere rationale for administrative arrangements.

## The Four Pillars

WE CONCLUDE this survey of five decades of LWF history by returning to "the four pillars" that have been identified as key to the establishment and subsequent development of the Federation: rescue for the needy, common initiatives in mission, joint efforts in theology, and a common response to ecumenical challenge. Our survey has shown that each of these pillars has been, over the five decades, subject to change at both the periphery and the center. When in the chapters that follow we pursue fundamental trajectories stemming from these pillars—service, mission, theology, ecclesiology, ecumenics, inclusiveness, and international affairs and human rights—we will observe this change as a dynamic evolution that reflects various degrees of both continuity and discontinuity. Has the original vision of faith, manifested in the four foundational pillars, faded away in this history? Have unifying concerns dominated the life of the Federation, or have fragmenting realities prevailed? What have been the effects of specialization, on the one hand, and global concern, on the other?

Perhaps most crucially—some would say, fatefully—it has been the role of theological reflection that has apparently been transformed the most in the course of these fifty years. The pillars of service, mission, and ecumenism have, to be sure, also undergone continuous adjustment to new contexts. Yet, these three themes have maintained a clearly discernible identity. It is theology that has been tossed about most violently in the storms of fifty years. The reasons for this striking change—in fact a reduction—in the Federation's expectations from theological research and reflection are doubtlessly many and complicated and actually are part of a global movement away from that view of the role of "traditional theology" that dominated the church—Western and Northern—for generation after generation. In light of this reality the Lutheran World Federation, perhaps

now lacking the systematic incentives that Lutheran theology has classi-
cally provided both for self-understanding and for a clear vision of mission,
as it views its future in light of both its history and its new contexts and
as it continues its movement "from Federation to Communion," needs
more than ever to focus theologically on its faith, identity, and mission.

## Bibliographical Notes

I. Archives, Unpublished Documents

LWF Archives, Geneva.
Hanns Lilje Papers, Lutheran Church Archives, Hanover.

II. Written Statements and Oral Interviews

Emmanuel Abraham, Addis Ababa.
André Appel, Strasbourg.
E. Theodore Bachmann†, Princeton, New Jersey.
James R. Crumley, Philadelphia, Pennsylvania.
Steward Herman, Shelter Island Heights, New York.
Miko Juva, Helsinki.
Robert Marshall, Chicago, Illinois.
Carl H. Mau, Jr.†, Geneva and Philadelphia, Pennsylvania.
Gyula Nagy, Budapest.
Emmanuel Gebre Selassie, Addis Ababa.

III. Printed Documents

*Luthern World/Lutherische Rundschau*, passim.
LWF Reports, passim.
*Proceedings* (all LWF Assemblies)
Abraham, Emmanuel. *Reminiscences of My Life.* Oslo: Lunde Forlag,
    1995.
*Amt und Gemeinde,* ed. Bischof der Ev. Kirche A.B. in Österreich. Sonder-
    nummer über die Minderheitskirchenkonferenz des LWB, Semmering,
    23. bis 27, 7/6 (1956) 12ff.
Lundgren, Manfred. *Proclaiming Christ to His World: The Experience of
    Radio Voice of the Gospel, 1957–1977.* Geneva: The Lutheran World
    Federation, 1983.
*Marangu: A Record of the All-Africa Lutheran Conference.* Geneva:
    Lutheran World Federation, Department of World Mission, 1956.

3. First All-Africa Lutheran Conference, November 1955, Marangu, Tanganyika.

4. Consecration of Rajah B. Manikam as Bishop of the Tamil Lutheran Church in India, January 1956. This event was followed by a meeting of the Asia Lutheran Conference in Madras, India.

5. Third Latin American Lutheran Conference, April 1959, Buenos Aires, Argentina. Stewart Herman is speaking.

6. Participants in the LWF Church Leaders Consultation, with LWF Council and staff, June 1994, in Geneva.

7.  Joint campus of the Lutheran World Federation and the World Council of Churches, 1947–1964, 17 route de Malagnou, Geneva.

8.  The Ecumenical Centre, route de Ferney, Geneva, which houses the LWF, the WCC, and other ecumenical organizations, was opened in 1964.

# 3

# Let Us Help One Another:
# Service in the LWF

"LET US HELP ONE ANOTHER." With these words John Morehead of the United States opened a major address at the First Assembly of the Lutheran World Convention held in Eisenach, Germany, in 1923. There is no doubt that at the earliest stages of twentieth century Lutheran cooperation there was a determination that such an enterprise should have at its heart aid to those who had been ravaged by World War I.

The scene repeated itself at the conclusion of World War II. Once again Lutherans from North America took the initiative by asking Sylvester Michelfelder to go to Europe to assess the extent of the need and to organize ways of rescuing the many whom the war had left in dire straits (cf., chapter 1, above; pp. 481ff. below). No survey of the history of the Lutheran World Federation can fail to take note of the essential role of service, *diakonia,* at the beginning and throughout the course of that history.

This pioneering work in the wake of World War II served as the initiation of the full scale, highly organized programs of diaconic service which have remained at the heart of LWF life and work. Without the concreteness of dedicated operational service and mutual aid, early efforts at international cooperation among Lutherans would perhaps have drowned in an ocean of idealism without the moorings of binding commitment. The impetus came from North America but was quickly joined by the churches of Europe. "Faith in action" provided the first steps toward global Lutheran fellowship. Through five decades the Federation has developed a remarkable record of efficient, operational projects of aid, relief, and service that has cast light on the dark circumstances of misery and victimization that have largely marked twentieth-century life.

*Jens Holger Schjørring, Aarhus, Denmark, is the author of chapter 3.*

The narrative that follows can be but a selective survey. This selectivity, as we shall see, will also involve judgments and even controversial questions that, no matter how tentative or one-sided, are not to be avoided. We see the story of service unfolding in three phases.

1. The initial period of the story was determined by the effects in Europe of World War II at least through 1960. Service was focused on activities of relief, reconstruction, assistance to displaced persons, and resettlement programs. Interchurch aid, moreover, involved spiritual care as well, notably programs of stewardship and evangelism. Outside Europe, in this period, a number of LWF projects were undertaken in the Middle East, in Hong Kong, and in Latin America. Additionally, during this time, the LWF secretariat and its Commission on World Service refined basic mandates and strategies.

2. The story in its second period was played out during the 1960s. Service activities as carried out by the Federation were no longer centered in Europe but shifted to the Southern Hemisphere. Simultaneously, as pointed out in chapter 2, a self-consciousness was developing among Lutherans on each continent which led to a certain degree of regional awareness. These developments coincided with global decolonization, the emergence of new nations marked by deep instability, and the difficulties inevitably attendant on processes of social and political change and transition. During this period, moreover, new and independent Lutheran churches were being established throughout the world amid unprecedented challenges.

Within the LWF, the 1960s saw the establishment of a new interdepartmental entity, an office for Community Development Service (CDS), an important attempt to meet the needs of a new situation. A Secretariat for Social Affairs was also established during this decade, which brought about direct cooperation between those responsible for world service and the Department of Theology; its mandate was to define basic roles and responsibilities for the church and theology in the global society of the time. Finally, it was during this period that the Lutheran churches of West Germany, the Federal Republic of Germany, took a leading position among "donor" churches and agencies supporting the work of service.

3. The third period of the present story covers the time from 1970 to the present. A new structure, developed in 1969 and approved at the Evian Assembly in 1970, was assumed by the Lutheran World Federation, and this involved a reformulation of basic mandates for Lutheran World Service. In 1990 the most recent restructuring of the Federation again gave rise to new definitions of the task and witness of world service.

During this time, moreover, concrete events, sometimes of a spectacular nature, marked the story of service within the LWF. A very basic discussion concerning "proclamation and human development" followed the issuance in 1972 of a penetrating letter on that matter from the Ethiopian Evangelical Church Mekane Yesus (cf. pp. 65–66 above). In those years also there was considerable debate regarding "root causes," human rights, and the adoption of appropriate political measures for the struggle against injustice in society. The experience of the Community Development Service led to a growing consciousness of structural renewal in societies and to integrated development projects. More recently, the rending of the iron curtain in Europe, the fall of the apartheid regime in South Africa, and a vigorous peace process in the Middle East, among many shifts in the global geopolitical scene, have provided a virtually new framework for the social service of the churches. Internally, finally, the Federation witnessed considerable tension and disagreement between the departments responsible for service, on the one hand, and studies, on the other, and to a lesser extent also between the Departments of World Service and Church Cooperation.

## Ambiguities and Complexities

IN OUR PRESENTATION of this story, which frequently has epic proportions, it is important not to slip into a kind of romanticism. To recount elements of this story requires that attention be paid to particular contexts and historical circumstances, and this will inevitably involve evaluation and at times critical judgments. Such evaluation will lead to a consideration of the long-term as well as the immediate effects of the work of aid and assistance, and that will in turn lead to vexing questions of both principle and method that seem inevitably to accompany the serving witness of world Lutheranism. It is important that such issues as the following not be avoided in our consideration.

1. There is irony, in the first place, in characterizing the work of service as an impressive achievement. Prosperous donors are often condescending in the face of suffering; sacrifice becomes mere benevolence which allows life to continue uninterruptedly after a brief pause for charitable activity. Giving at times leads to no lasting change, much less to authentic recognition of the lack of dignity which characterizes the life of recipients. Persons and agencies in the Northern Hemisphere have often been inured to the deep shock of the misery of the Two-Thirds World, not least when the media tell the story of such misery as though it were a prime-time thriller. These ambiguities force the question as to whether or not service, in spite

of noble intentions, really avoids participation in the perpetuation of global degradation.

2. The relationship of service to political reality—ambiguity and compromise—is an enduring dilemma. Can they be separated? Does one inevitably involve the other? At times in the course of its diaconic witness, the LWF has been characterized as a "multipurpose organization" which requires that its serving arm, Lutheran World Service (LWS), have only humanitarian/diaconic aims, while other entities within the Federation properly take up advocacy on issues of human rights and social justice. Unless LWS as an operational service unit maintains a kind of "transparency" and is seen as free of political or ideological goals, its work will be compromised. This view was sharply advanced by Bruno Muetzelfeldt (b. 1918), Director of Lutheran World Service from 1961 to 1980, who insisted that the task of service be pursued single-mindedly lest it be identified with social and political concerns in a way which would lead to its failure. The relationship, then, between diaconic and sociopolitical matters—both appropriate concerns of an organization such as the LWF—needs persistently to be faced.

3. A third question has to do with whether the LWF has pursued its service with an aim to developing self-support on the part of recipients, or has, knowingly or unknowingly, imposed on recipients patterns of life that are foreign to the integrity of their identity. Has service, not least in the area of long-term development as carried out by the CDS, encouraged self-determination, or has it actually kept recipients in a vicious circle of dependency?

4. Whether the rendering of service should be undertaken confessionally or ecumenically is a fourth issue. At the start, the LWF saw its work of service as an expression of confessional solidarity—service toward fellow Lutherans in need. In short course, however, the strategy was redefined in light of the clear fact that emergency situations know no barriers of confession, religion, race, or nationality. The impulse toward aid was, moreover, further stimulated by comparable efforts as undertaken by such Christian organizations as the World Council of Churches (WCC) and the Roman Catholic Church through Caritas Internationalis, and by organizations not religiously identified such as the Red Cross, the United Nations, Oxfam, et al. In the course of LWF history this question of principle was complicated by strategic issues, for example, the divergence in the 1960s between WCC relief and assistance programs, which adopted a nonoperational strategy, and the clearly operational strategy of Lutheran World Service. It is an issue that in one form or another has persisted through fifty years of LWF history and remains open to new initiatives and approaches.

5. Service, for the LWF, has long been marked by a tension between the

concerns of Federation member churches as the recipients of aid and the interests of the Geneva secretariat itself. This is an inevitable tension: any recipient will be prone toward an "inferiority syndrome" and donors toward one of superiority. On which side is Geneva? The pluriformity and complexity of cultural, administrative, and bureaucratic traditions which mark Northern societies frequently clash with the traditions of those in the South who live under near-perpetual conditions of emergency and who possess no viable structures for withstanding need. It has proved difficult to develop attitudes and procedures that level out such disparities, and the role of the Geneva secretariat—the mediator of programmed relief and aid—has not always been well defined or well understood.

6. An issue which has run through five decades of LWF service and has frequently been the subject of vigorous debate, concerns matters of staff recruitment. Initially, when the LWF was creating a service entity virtually from nothing, professional standards for staff were often minimized. Soon, however, and in large part due to the operational character of Lutheran World Service work, a concern for skill and technical expertise developed. Alongside this development there has been an ongoing discussion centering around such issues as "the Christian character of World Service," the importance of professional competence for staff, and the balance between expatriate and local staff.

7. Finally, the Federation has had a steady theological discussion concerning the nature of diaconic service within the church. At times, perhaps, this issue has been taken lightly, but it has always been close to the surface in discussions within the Commission for World Service and in contacts between donor and recipient churches and the Geneva secretariat. The very existence of the LWF testifies to the conviction that the confession of the Reformation has enduring validity, and the Federation has tried consistently to resist splits between the theological/theoretical and the practical/operational. The celebrated—and historically pivotal—discussion of "proclamation and development" in the early 1970s provided a watershed for serious theological reflection on the nature of service within the Federation. Nevertheless, many of these serious theological questions have not been clearly answered and at times seem not to have been taken seriously. This matter persists as an important, albeit difficult and not conclusively decided, element in the history of the diaconic work of the LWF.

None of the above seven issues is new, and none has found easy answers. Nevertheless, in any survey of the Lutheran World Federation's willingness to accept the mandate of service to the people of the world, each must continually be faced.

## Early Initiatives: the First Phase

AT THE CONCLUSION of World War II church leaders in Germany were confronted with an immense task: the desperate need, until then unprecedented in modern history. of millions of persons for emergency assistance
from the ravages of the war. As church leaders they were conscious of an
obligation to address congregations and congregants in a way which
acknowledged the reality of the Nazi horror and which led to a deep awareness of corporate guilt. Yet that would not be enough. It was also required
that the people be mobilized toward the establishment of a new future for
church and society. The task required wisdom, courage, and vision to a
degree that was beyond the capacity of some in high ecclesiastical positions. Solidarity in the form of both material aid and critical advice was
needed from the outside. How could starving and freezing people be re-
educated?

Bishop Theophil Wurm (1868–1953) of Stuttgart/Württemberg, a leading figure in the German Evangelical Church, was key at this point. Even
though more radical elements within the Confessing Church had accused
him of failing to lead his church into open and wholehearted opposition to
the heresy of Nazi totalitarianism in the church, it is undoubted that at
many points he had given strong leadership to the voices of resistance in
Germany's dark times. He had, for example, been outspoken in his public
opposition to the taking of "life not worth living" (unwertes Leben) and,
moreover, he had during the war dedicated himself to a serious effort
toward the reunification of the divided German Evangelical Church. It
was altogether appropriate that Wurm had been elected the first leader of
the reunited Evangelical Church in Germany in August 1945.

In this position Wurm assumed a particularly strong role in the eyes of
international aid agencies, and he took it upon himself to undertake the
essential task of creating understanding for the German situation among
more prosperous Christians in other parts of the world. In a letter of June
12, 1947, to J. A. Aasgaard (1876–1966), president of what was then the
Norwegian Lutheran Church of America, Wurm gave a moving description of the needs of the people of his church:

> When I write to a Christian brother of Norwegian descent, I feel deeply the
> guilt which the German army has incurred by conquering and occupying your
> native country. We bow to the judgment which has come over our people
> because of so many excesses and acts of violence. We also hope for forgiveness
> from you and for sympathy with our distress. Famine and epidemics reign
> here just as they are described in Matthew 24. Apart from the four million
> Germans who were killed in action there are still three million missing or
> prisoners somewhere abroad without the hope of return. In every house and

in every family there is manifold grief. Sixteen million, i.e., 25% of all Germans, have been expelled from the German eastern areas and have lost all their property and the land on which their ancestors lived for more than a thousand years. The large cities have been destroyed by bombs and there is no prospect of reconstruction as yet. Daily hundreds die of malnutrition and starvation, and many thousands have perished from cold last winter. Houses, clothes and shoes, and particularly medicines are lacking. In spite of the relief action of the U.S.A. we are at present living on 750 calories daily, while a person must have 2,500 to live. In the French Zone the daily ration is only 3 gr. fat and 125 gr. bread; in the American Zone 7 gr. fat and 200 gr. bread. Potato provisions are exhausted everywhere and it is still three months until the new harvest. (papers of Johan A. Aasgaard, Luther Theological Seminary, St. Paul, Minnesota)

Relief work was carried out by the German Evangelical Church through *Evangelisches Hilfswerk*, a special agency created for that purpose, and it became an important and cooperative partner for international aid agencies. Through reliable personnel, the *Evangelisches Hilfswerk* developed extremely close contact with the general population, and its strategy was to provide material and spiritual support simultaneously. Much of its work was performed by deacons and deaconesses of the church. The work of these persons was highlighted in a request submitted by Sylvester Michelfelder, representing the Geneva secretariat, to the National Lutheran Council in the United States for an acknowledgment of the German situation and an allocation of funds in response to the need. He described the work of the German deaconesses:

The 80,000 deaconesses in Germany have been working valiantly and against tremendous odds, in relief and reconstruction work among their fellow people. Seeing them move about tirelessly, makes one ask repeatedly how they can carry on under these very great handicaps. It is obvious that the clothing which is assigned to them is limited in quantity and that what they have cannot last indefinitely. I have heard of deaconesses who possess only one outfit, and it can be taken for granted that this adds even greater difficulties to the performance of their services. Anything which we can do from America to strengthen and support them will serve as a great moral encouragement and speed them on in their silent service to those who are suffering within their country.

Michelfelder listed three items in the request for aid: wool for coats, cotton for clothing, and leather for shoes ($2.00 a pair!). An elaborating comment by Dr. Michelfelder mirrored a tension that has endured in LWF service: he mentioned that the items of clothing might best be manufactured in Germany rather than being purchased in the United States. By such means the value of the donated funds would be increased by a factor

of eight or ten. Michelfelder, however, left this matter undecided, requesting advice from the National Lutheran Council "whether this is advisable
and possible" (request of May 20, 1948; Lilje papers, Lutheran Church
Archives, Hanover, 418/L III).

Students, too, were victims of the dire situation in Germany. Accordingly, a program was established to provide food. Commenting on one very
substantial donation of food for theological students, delivered and distributed in the late winter of 1948, Michelfelder wrote:

> It has been my privilege in the course of this last month to be present at sev-
> eral openings of such student feeding programs. I have been invited to attend
> others, but my required presence here in Geneva made the attendance impos-
> sible. During my presence at Tübingen, Darmstadt and Mainz, I brought
> greetings from the giving churches in America and assured the students that
> the food is an expression of our fraternal relationship with those who, like us,
> serve as the Christian vanguard. The gratitude of those who are to be benefit-
> ted by these gifts from America was most cordial and very sincere. Repeatedly
> I was asked to express to the people in America how much this gift of food
> meant to the student body. Directors, professors, graduate students and under-
> graduates all joined in assuring me of their appreciation. It just seemed unfor-
> tunate to me that there could not be more of our giving Americans present to
> witness the wholehearted gratitude that was evidenced by these people. Hear-
> ing these expressions of thankfulness forms one of the high spots of my life
> and makes me feel that the contributed gifts of America have really attained
> their purpose. (ibid.)

Michelfelder went on to discuss the objection that had been made at the
decision to limit this shipment of food to students of theology: "However,
as I have explained previously, it was these students especially who
refused to have the donations limited to themselves and rather insisted
that the scope of those to be benefited be widened. . . . In some cases only
those are recipients who are undernourished and who are able to produce
a doctor's attest to that fact. In other cases again the whole student body
of the Christian *Studentengemeinde* is included."

Finally, Michelfelder expressed his hope, first mentioned by persons in
the *Evangelisches Hilfswerk*, that "improved conditions in Germany during the coming winter will make unnecessary this student feeding program." Nevertheless, he considered the program as one of prime
importance, recommending it strongly. *Hilfswerk*, for its part, pointed out
that this food for students should be seen in a wider context: "It is hoped
that with these two hundred tons of food 9,200 students can receive sup-
plementary food in the amount of 900 calories daily for ninety days"
(ibid.).

Conditions were by no means better in Austria. A request for financial support for pastors' salaries gives ample evidence of the emergency there:

> There are 202 Lutheran pastors in the Lutheran Church in Austria, and 65 Lutheran refugee pastors for whom the church is responsible towards Austrian government and authorities. The salary of a pastor is only one-third of the salary of a school teacher paid by the government. The Lutheran Church does not get anything from the state for pastors' salaries. Even to keep the pastors' salaries at this low level will mean a deficit of $25,000. The church authorities are looking to the Lutherans in America for help, because it seems to be impossible to obtain it from other sources. Owing to the devaluation of the currency in November 1947, the Austrian church lost about 1,000,000 [Austrian] shillings and this is why the situation is now so precarious. (ibid.)

A tour through war-torn Germany in the late 1940s would provide many more examples of service from the Lutheran community of churches. There was an obvious need to expand this service to include churches in Eastern and Central Europe as well. It has already been observed that it was precisely for the sake of these "minority churches" that the first relief operations were established in the aftermath of World War I. Similar problems persisted after the second war. These churches lived as minorities among Roman Catholic or Orthodox communities, and those communities were often neither tolerant nor ecumenical in relation to the smaller groups. Further, these small churches in Eastern and Central Europe were, in the late 1940s, forced to come to terms with the extremely difficult political circumstances characteristic of the period. The new totalitarianism of Marxist regimes dominated by the Soviets, the historic minority status of Lutheran churches in the area, and the deprivations caused by the war formed a new and extremely difficult context. We shall return to the situation of these churches.

But we now must also note the sad fate of thousands of persons expelled from the countries of Eastern and Central Europe, not least from the Baltic states. The internal hardships caused by the war persisted into the postwar period. Many dissidents who opposed the new Marxist regimes were deported to prison camps in Siberia, others decided to seek a better future in Western Europe, and those who remained in their native lands were by no means blessed with a comfortable daily existence.

This exceedingly difficult reality was reflected with sad clarity in another request for financial support from Lutherans in America aimed at the establishment of an LWF Immigration Service. The proposal centered about an actual list of non-German Lutherans who found themselves in Germany at the end of the war and "who cannot return to their homelands and who should leave a Germany already broken and severely overpopulated." The list included a large group of Baltic expellees, with Latvian and Baltic ethnic Germans numbering 100,000 and 75,000 respectively. Their situation is described in some detail:

> Until last summer many of these groups kept themselves together here in Germany, hoping that they could return home. By last November or December a change took place, and now, realizing that return is impossible, they see in emigration the only possibility of a new life. They are not welcome in a country desperate with its own problems of suffering, hunger and destruction. If there is a new invasion by a foreign power [i.e., the Soviet Union], these people, many of them the double victims of communism and fascism, will be among the first to be liquidated.

However, those mentioned here were only a small part of a total of more than ten million refugees coming from East Germany and countries to the East, most of whom also were Lutherans. Referring to this, the request just quoted continues:

> Most of these have been or must be assimilated by a fractured Germany; a few have returned under special conditions to their old land. At present there are thousands living under unspeakable conditions in camps and out. Whenever it becomes possible for more than those who are exceptions to emigrate, there will be great numbers from these refugees.

Much emphasis was laid upon the necessity of expanding the proposed immigration service to a global scale. From the perspective of the Lutheran World Federation it was particularly important that pastoral care be provided for expelled and displaced persons wherever they now found themselves: "At present there are urgent needs of this kind in England, France, Canada and Australia. Unless the churches are counselled and act upon this counsel, and unless the various phases of the movement are coordinated the pastor is left to his own devices and the vagaries of official selection boards."

Even more initiatives came to be associated with the huge task of immigration service and resettlement that faced Lutheran churches in the immediate postwar situation. "The other needed phase of assistance complementary to the development of possibilities is the field work of selection and processing the emigrants. The Jews and Catholics have been working at this since before the end of the war. The Protestants, except for the work of Church World Service in the American Zones of Germany and Austria, and that of the Christian Council earlier, have done little. Inasmuch as 85% of the Protestant refugees under the International Refugee Organization are Lutherans, their need is clearly an inescapable charge upon Lutherans of the world." (The above citations are from the request of May 21, 1948 submitted by S. Michelfelder, Geneva secretariat, to the

National Lutheran Council, U.S.A.; copy in the Lilje papers, Hanover, 418/L III.)

We proceed now to a more systematic survey of the areas to which a commitment to service in the form of aid and relief in the post–World War II situation led the LWF. It will be seen that this commitment to service involved many agencies which were to some degree associated with the work of the LWF Department of World Service which at the end of the 1940s was itself in the process of formation.

## Service to Refugees

We have provided several illustrations regarding the enormous number of persons expelled from their homes in direct or indirect consequence of World War II. While often described merely as "refugees," these millions of people included not only political refugees and expellees but also displaced persons, escapees, persons who for whatever reason had been evacuated from their homes, and persons who were intent on returning to their original territories.

A number of national committees of Lutheran churches took up the challenge of service to refugees. The task, however, was so immense that it required an international and coordinated effort. Accordingly, the Lutheran World Federation established its "Service to Refugees" as a voluntary agency associated with the United Nations' International Refugee Organization (IRO), the successor to the United Nations Relief and Rehabilitation Administration (UNRRA). The challenge was enormous: there were an estimated 24,000,000 refugees and displaced persons, of whom 13,500,000 were non-Germans and 10,500,000 Germans. More than 600,000 were living in camps in Germany, and approximately 190,000 of those persons were Lutheran. The LWF Department of Service to Refugees worked in close cooperation with a corresponding office in the World Council of Churches' Department of Inter-Church Aid and Service to Refugees.

Staff leadership of the LWF program was, in the aftermath of the war, key to its success. It is of more than passing significance that a large number of persons in this period who gave themselves to refugee work ultimately became important figures in the international ecumenical community. Two Americans whose work was integral to the program in its earliest stages were Stewart Herman and Howard Hong. Herman, who in 1948 became head of the Resettlement Division within the LWF Refugee Service, actually arrived in Germany as early as 1945. He subsequently left his mark at several points in the life and work of both the Federation and the World Council of Churches as well as in American

Lutheranism. Hong, who subsequently pursued a distinguished academic career and is, with his wife, well known as the premier English translator of the works of Søren Kierkegaard, was primarily responsible for 190,000 refugees who found themselves in various sorts of camps in Europe.

The original strategy for this work was that the International Refugee Organization would be responsible for material aid to persons in need, while confessional organizations such as the LWF would undertake a spiritual ministry to the same persons. Sylvester Michelfelder at one point enumerated six fields of activity, a listing that clearly and strategically clarified this distinction between material aid and spiritual ministry: (1) provision for religious services; (2) spiritual care and welfare aimed at those who had already been resettled; (3) maintenance of a bureau to give advice and counsel to the refugees; (4) the initiation of programs of resettlement; (5) submission of formal proposals in line with the reparations agreement to appropriate authorities; and, (6) welfare activities which affected the life and work of Lutheran congregations (Lilje Papers, Hanover, L3/ III 420).

In certain areas of Europe this spiritual ministry was seen as an integral part of the Refugee Service, in other areas two distinct offices/programs were involved. In both cases the LWF was primarily concerned that this ministry not be left aside. Michelfelder made this extremely clear:

> But everyone in this organization is acutely aware of the emphasis which should be placed upon a spiritual ministry program, which after all assumes a more important role—since we are all members of the great Body of Christ—than the material aspect. In the individual reports on each country, details and statistics will be furnished with respect to material aid, but as can be readily understood, it is impossible to evaluate by means of statistics the importance of spiritual guidance or the effects this spiritual ministry can and does have in the lives of the people contacted. There is a new awareness throughout Europe of the value of the work of the Lutheran Church, and a reawakened recognition of the need among the distressed and distracted people of the unfortunate lands in which our work is concentrated. (Report to the 1949 meeting of the LWF Executive Committee, Lilje Papers, Hanover, L3/ III 420)

### Stewardship and Evangelism

Pastoral and spiritual care was considered essential to work among refugees and displaced persons, as can be seen from the LWF provision of chaplaincies to refugees en route—often by boat—to new homes. Similarly, the parallel concern of bringing the dynamic force of hope and love into "normal" Lutheran congregations was seen as integral to the postwar reconstruction work of the LWF. In many places in Germany, the church

struggle against the forces of totalitarianism in politics, public administration, and church and cultural life, had developed a spirit of responsibility and activism on the part of clergy and laity alike. This was seen as an
integral part of the legacy of Lutheran identity, faithful to the original
meaning of "the priesthood of all believers," and thus also an essential element in the future life of church and society both.

Work in this area was launched under the title "Evangelism and Stewardship" and carried on within LWF "service branches." Here again, American Lutherans were instrumental in terms of both funding and personnel.
Carl Mau (1922–1995), for example, began his LWF career in 1952 on
assignment to this program; that career culminated in his service to the
Federation as its general secretary (cf. pp. 504–8 below).

### Prisoners of War

Another important responsibility undertaken by the Federation in the
immediate postwar period was the provision of pastoral services among
prisoners of war, Germans and others. Anders Nygren, first President of
the LWF, as early as 1946 had taken an active role in this ministry when
he gave lectures to Germans who were prisoners of war in England (cf.
p. 427 below).

### Interchurch Aid

Throughout the postwar period many European churches were in need of
emergency assistance to the extent that their very survival depended on it.
The burden for such assistance fell on Lutheran churches that were able
and willing to render aid. The aid given took many forms: spiritual/pas-
toral, educational/training, and material. Since many churches were without basic resources, they needed help in the rebuilding of church
buildings, the provision of medical care, food, and clothing, and the fur-
nishing of Bibles, hymnals, and other supplies for parish use.

The problems were not confined to the minority Lutheran churches in
Central and Eastern Europe even though their situation was challenging
beyond measure. Churches throughout the continent were in need. However, it must also be acknowledged that some minority churches persisted
in need since interchurch aid activity was conspicuously not fully
extended to churches in the countries directly occupied by the USSR,
churches that experienced great hardship and even outright persecution
under the new rulers. The Stalin era was obviously not a time when this
work could be carried out among these beleaguered churches.

This latter fact reflected the reality of the "Cold War." Although the

Lutheran World Federation refrained from becoming an instrument of the West, the situation was extremely difficult and had consequences for service priorities. While the role of political authorities was primary in the creation of this difficult situation, it is also in this context that the role of "exile churches" is to be seen. These churches on occasion became vigorously anti-Communist and that in turn perhaps contributed to a certain slowing down of the establishment within the LWF framework of more normal relations with churches behind the iron curtain.

In Western Europe in the years immediately following the war, the churches of Norway and Finland were in need of considerable aid, but after a short span of years they were to be numbered among those churches giving assistance (with regard to Norway, cf. the LWF Archives, WS/ I 1b; concerning Finland, cf. Lilje Papers, Hanover, 418/ L III). The Lutheran Church in Italy also depended on outside sources for its support, and that dependence persisted for a far longer period. Without such support, it would not have been possible to appoint a pastor who could serve the congregations of the Italian Church in appropriate languages: "If the Ev.-Lutheran Church in Italy does not start to sink its root into Italian soil, it will be doomed to perish (with the only exception of the churches in Milan and Rome)," the Church Consistory stated in a report of October 1955 (sent to Reuben Baetz, of the LWF Department of World Service, Geneva, LWF Archives, WS/Ia, 1954–56).

It is important to note that the concept of interchurch aid underwent a significant development during its first decade, not least in respect to the gulf that was perceived to exist between prosperous churches and those under the pressure of poverty and need. From being a project based upon emergency assistance, it developed into a program that aimed at full-scale and mutual exchange. This development is seen in the slogan that was used as an initial framework for the new pattern of relationships, "Preaching—Teaching—Reaching." This was clearly an attempt to go beyond attitudes that created a spirit of condescension on the part of giving churches, and of passivity on the part of the receiving churches. The Director of World Service commented on this strategy in his report to the assembly of the LWF in Minneapolis, 1957:

> After nearly being forced upon each other as "givers" and "receivers" during periods of acute need, the churches within the LWF discovered that they also needed each other during, relatively speaking, quieter periods. Contact and fellowship between churches had almost become a necessity of life. Emergency aid offices both within the LWF and in many member churches developed into departments for mutual assistance. One can no longer think of being without these departments. They belong to the structure of the churches. (Department of World Service, Report 1952–1957, p. 14)

## Programs of Exchange and Service

Cooperation within the Lutheran World Federation at its most basic level involved the promotion of international understanding between sister churches. Not least was such understanding necessary in order to overcome both past isolations and new misunderstandings. Thus it was that a program of service projects involving *exchange* was developed within the Department of World Service. Such projects were to be seen as essential, fully mutual, and continuous in implementation. They were to involve persons from every level of church life—laity (deacons, church workers, youth), students of theology, pastors, teachers, leaders. While the majority of such service projects were initially located in the Euro-American sphere, significant initiatives also took place between churches and among persons outside Europe. We shall survey such initiatives.

*The Middle East: Jerusalem and Israel.* World Service adopted as one of its first—and enduringly important—areas of work the Middle East. The aid program based at the Augusta Victoria Hospital (AVH) in Jerusalem deserves particular attention. Its story involves a wide range of sensitive negotiation and cooperation with other international agencies and with local and national authorities.

The conditions of the Armistice that concluded World War I required the transfer of all German missionary programs to the administrative control of other non-German agencies. Following World War II, the Commission on Younger Churches and Orphaned Missions of the National Lutheran Council (U.S.A.), known as CYCOM (pp. 146–54 below) took responsibility for work in the Middle East, and the Australian churchman Edwin Moll (1892–1961) was designated to explore ways of establishing aid programs in that troubled part of the world.

Moll directed his immediate attention to enabling local Lutheran pastors to function within the previously formed parish structures. This involved arrangements for salaries as well as for securing proper theological training, often in the United States, for younger pastors. Furthermore, he quickly became concerned with securing resources for the development of already existing diaconal institutions, chief among which was AVH.

The "Augusta Victoria" had been built in the late nineteenth century at the initiative of Kaiser Wilhelm II of Germany, and was named after his consort. During the period of the British Mandate in Palestine, it had been used as a military hospital, and from May 1948 through May 1950 it had been operated, on lease from the LWF, by the International Red Cross, which used it to accommodate Arabs who were living in conditions of desperation in refugee camps. After only two years, however, the Red Cross determined that AVH should be handed over to others, since a basic working principle of the Red Cross called for providing assistance only under short-term emergency conditions. After long negotiations with the United Nations Relief and Works Agency an agreement was reached according to which the hospital was to be operated by the Lutheran World Federation and subsidized by the UN itself. Additional negotiations were necessary between the LWF and the German institutions that historically had possessed legal rights to the hospital, notably the Kaiserswerth Deaconess Society. Even though these German institutions were preoccupied with work in the difficult context of their homeland, they were able to arrange a limited contribution toward badly needed physical repair of the hospital, which had been severly damaged during the Arab-Israeli War of 1948. The LWF had to pursue additional fundraising efforts within the international community before the maintenance of the Augusta Victoria could be legally and financially guaranteed.

Even when these steps had been successfully taken, new challenges continued to appear at the AVH. The hospital was situated at a crucial location in Jerusalem, the Mount of Olives. This was obviously a noteworthy historical location, but it was also militarily strategic: the buildings were located in the demilitarized, neutral zone of Jerusalem and were thus under the military protection of the United Nations. It took another round of complicated negotiations, this time with UN authorities, before a long-term agreement could be signed which would permit the hospital to function with reasonable security. The AVH had a capacity of 350 beds; its chapel, the Church of the Ascension, was one of the most remarkable Protestant church buildings in the entire Middle East.

In its Middle East work the LWF operated field offices in Amman and Damascus, but considerable attention was of necessity given to work in Jerusalem. The LWF's Jerusalem field office, the "Middle East Office," was itself headquartered in the Old City of Jerusalem, then in the possession of the Arabs. The director, Edwin Moll, had chosen this location deliberately because he had the firm conviction "that the safety of personnel and its [the LWF's] freedom of action could best be achieved in Arab-held territory" (Report to the LWF Executive Committee, August 1950).

Threats and challenges, however, continued to surround the work of the LWF among the people, largely Palestinians, of Jerusalem. The Israeli authorities consistently ignored the request of the LWF's Jerusalem field office to be allowed to traverse the city's "no man's land." Further, the Israelis were highly restrictive in their administration of property formerly owned by German missionary institutions but now located in the State of Israel. They were prepared for only one concession: the return, in this case to the LWF, of such buildings as were to be used exclusively for worship. Actually, these buildings were of rather negligible value and of limited practical use in comparison to the total quantity of German property in Jerusalem. The fact that the German mission societies were cut off from their own property made negotiations between the LWF and the Israeli government even more tortuous. For the LWF the negotiations were carried on by Edwin Moll, Fredrik A. Schiotz, then secretary of CYCOM and later President of the Federation (cf. pp. 445–49 below), and LWF attorneys from Geneva.

While the Augusta Victoria Hospital was doubtlessly the most noteworthy LWF project in the Middle East, it was by no means the only one. The LWF was also responsible for a number of schools that were largely devoted to vocational training, homes for orphaned children and a large number of other diaconal activities. Most of these projects were carried out in the Kingdom of Jordan, although important work was also carried on in Syria under the leadership of the Danish field worker, Christian Christiansen (cf. p. 122 below).

There is great reason to express respect for the LWF's remarkable Middle East work, not least because of the extremely difficult conditions under which it was carried on. Yet, political and religious adversities notwithstanding, there remains reason to ask whether the work was conceived in the most balanced and comprehensive way possible. Edwin Moll performed his nearly impossible task with talent and diplomatic expertise, often in the face of obstacles put up by the Israeli authorities, obstacles which over time nearly assumed the character of permanent harassment. But—and it must be acknowledged that we now speak on the basis of hindsight—did the general framework of LWF activities—which should have included, for example, serious reflection on the Holocaust, its meaning and effects—adequately account for the reasons behind the seemingly perpetual misunderstandings and suspicion with the Israelis? That this was a time of extraordinarily deep polarity between Israelis and Palestinians is obvious and, since that polarity has by no means been eradicated, it remains a factor in all attempts to deal helpfully with tensions in the area. (Subsequent LWF consultations on "The Holy Land" in 1975 in Geneva and in 1980 in Cyprus continued to be marked by such polarity.)

It surely remains regrettable, however, that for a lengthy period of time there was on the part of the LWF no substantial effort toward deepened dialogue between the people of Jewish faith and the Lutherans themselves, a community whose ambiguous heritage in respect to the Jewish people was indeed a heavy burden. Religious dialogue and efforts at a political understanding of the State of Israel came—and they *have* come—far too late. Internationally, not until 1963 did the LWF enter into meaningful dialogue with the Jewish people, although several Lutheran churches preceded the LWF itself into such dialogue on national bases.

(For a detailed treatment of the LWF strategy in the Middle East, see the unpublished manuscript by Hanna Issa, *Love in Action: the Story of the Lutheran World Federation in the Middle East*, 1970, Geneva, the LWF Archives.)

*The Far East: Hong Kong.*   In the Far East conditions after the war had obviously been shaped by the militant foreign policy and aggression of Japan and by the long and violent civil war in China that had resulted in Communist ascendency and the formation of the People's Republic of China. For the Lutheran World Federation the main involvement was in Hong Kong, and it was an involvement of great significance, even if its challenges were completely different from those in other parts of the world.

Shortly after the turbulent civil war in China, the Communists adopted an uncompromising policy of expelling all missions and missionary agencies. In the face of this policy, the World Council of Churches and the LWF undertook jointly to arrange for the escape and safe return of Westerners to their home countries. As this venture reached completion, a new challenge arose in light of the surfeit of Chinese refugees to Hong Kong. This situation required not only new programs but great resources. As in the Middle East, such resources were forthcoming from the global Lutheran community: material aid, funds and supplies for medical care, provisions for programs of vocational training. The Hong Kong refugee project was conducted under the direction of Ludwig Stumpf (1913–1987) who had himself come from Shanghai where he had been an active member of the German church.

Two main concerns were crucial to LWF strategy in Hong Kong from the beginning. In the first place, a philosophy of "self-help" undergirded each element in the project as well as the development of overall strategy. In the second place, all LWF projects were designed to aid all people regardless of religious background, a conscious policy which was to be observed in LWF service projects everywhere (cf. Reports to the Commission on World Service, Ljubljana, 1955 and to the LWF Assembly in Minneapolis, 1957).

*Latin America.*   There seemed to develop in LWF circles a curious canonical order of the world's continents and their place in global Lutheranism. Stewart Herman, who had been key in LWF service work in Europe directly after World War II, at the 1957 LWF Assembly in Minneapolis described this "order" with both humor and sarcasm: "First there is Europe, the cradle of the Reformation and the source of all theology, followed by North America, constantly clamoring for attention, then Asia and Africa, on which the missionary concentration of the older churches has so long been centered. Latin America is tacked on, if at all, as an afterthought" (*Proceedings*, Minneapolis, p. 131).

Yet, in spite of the relatively small number of Lutherans in Latin America, it really has not been a neglected continent within the Lutheran communion. Even in the interval between the two World Wars, the Lutheran World Convention had taken upon itself to insure the rescue of a particular group of Asian refugees, the Harbin people, and to secure their resettlement in Latin America.

Generally, the Lutheran communities in Latin America were small minority churches nearly overwhelmed by the dominant Roman Catholic Church. They had been established, in the nineteenth and early twentieth centuries, by various European immigrant groups (in Argentina, Brazil, Chile, Columbia, Peru, Venezuela, and parts of Central America and the Caribbean) and thus from the beginning had been churches in a diaspora situation, surrounded by Roman Catholics who were far from ecumenical or tolerant in their relations with other Christian groups. Yet, in spite of their small numbers, these communities were not disregarded by fellow Lutherans. On the contrary, it could be maintained that they received almost special treatment, as witnessed by the establishment of an LWF Committee on Latin America in 1952. It was Stewart Herman who first headed this committee.

An extract from Herman's first report of 1952 gives an impression of the extraordinary difficulties faced during this period when Lutherans were attempting to find a viable place for themselves in Latin America. He wrote of the situation in Venezuela:

On October 26 the first Lutheran church in Venezuela was founded consisting of three distinct linguistic groups but united by a unique constitution into a single congregation. Five languages were used at the main service on that notable Sunday afternoon in Caracas: German, Swedish, Latvian, Hungarian, and English. 425 people were counted in the crowded chapel or standing outside the open windows under the eaves. Scores more of the charter members were obviously detained by a severe downpour which all regarded as a symbol of God's blessing on the newly planted church. The congregation is founded, not on language or nationality, but upon a common confession of faith. It consists of people who wish to worship in their various mother-tongues but all agree that their children must also be able to confess that faith in the language of their new homeland. What stories those quiet people in the pews could tell! Years of exile, loss of home, adventures by land and sea, new beginnings in a foreign land under a tropic sun! Painters and craftsmen from Latvia, musicians and engineers from East Germany, business and military men from Hungary. Mothers and children who have been uprooted and deprived of the most elementary security. I saw one Lithuanian family building its own new home—cement block by cement block—on the edge of a hill in West Caracas. Refugees learn to live by their hands and their wits, or they perish. But these Lutherans are determined to survive. They call themselves the Evangelical Lutheran Church of the Resurrection! (Letter of November 1952, "Latin American Lutheran, 1952–1963")

## Concepts and Strategies

The LWF from the start acknowledged the operational character of its Department of World Service. It is on the basis of such an understanding that we have presented the foregoing narrative descriptions of its work. From that narrative, however, it should be clear that issues of a more theoretical nature have been basic to World Service since its inception. We turn now to a description of the original charter and mandate of World Service and to an examination of the relation between those principles and working procedures in field operations.

At its First Assembly, in Lund in 1947, the LWF approved a set of governing rules that first formulated a straightforward working concept of service: "to support Lutheran groups in need of spiritual and material aid." The governing body which was to have responsibility for the implementation of this was a Department for Service to Refugees to be located in the Geneva secretariat. Even during this initial phase it was clear to the LWF member churches that mutual assistance would have to go beyond emergency measures. In order to provide effective support, the churches saw that a broader scale of mutual responsibility, spiritual as well as material, would be required. Throughout the 1950s this concern was a preoccupation of World Service. Even earlier, however, Sylvester Michelfelder had proposed an LWF structure which clearly defined each element within that structure. The Federation's Executive Committee began its consideration of this proposal at its meeting in Oxford, England in 1949, but it was not until 1953, after the Hanover Assembly, that final agreements were reached. Four sections dealt with the role of World Service within the LWF; it is appropriate that those sections be quoted.

> to provide the member churches with a common international agency, available to them as they seek to meet in Christian love and compassion, human need as it may develop in the world.
> to secure the support of member churches and National Committees for World Service projects through financial grants, material goods and/or personnel.
> to represent the Lutheran World Federation before governmental and voluntary relief and welfare agencies.

to offer National Committees, member churches and their agencies a consultative service as they seek to carry forward their Christian ministry of mercy (cf. Department of World Service Report, 1952–57, p. 6).

These articles clearly articulate certain basic presuppositions upon which World Service was established: (1) Already existing national initiatives (primarily from the United States) needed to be coordinated. (2) Member churches were, however, not to be prevented from carrying out projects on their own initiative even as, on a coordinated basis, they supported LWF work. Indeed, the Commission on World Service at its first meeting stated that the department "should give due regard to the policies and wishes of the cooperating churches, working through or with the national committees." (3) The churches would be required to take into account and when advisable be related to the work of governments and private relief/service agencies. (4) "Consultative service" would involve the provision of theological, geopolitical, and other strategic reflections on diaconic witness by the churches not least in actual congregational life. Not until the mid-1960s was a functioning consultative service added to the structure of World Service, although in 1955 approval was given to the department "to work out a program for the exchange of personnel and information in the area of stewardship and congregational life" (Minutes, Commission on World Service, 1955, LWF-Archives, WS/A I 1955).

These articles, which together formed a mandate for the Department of World Service, were supplemented with rules for administrative procedure. For example, in respect to financial cooperation between the secretariat and member churches it was stated that

> The activities of the LWF-WS shall be kept strictly within a budget of assured financial support. Administration costs shall be kept at a minimum, the larger part of the funds being used for field service and projects. Contributions from cooperating churches may be in the form of a) funds, b) contributed supplies, c) salaried or voluntary workers.

Such regulations reflected the fear, shared by many and strongly expressed at the 1947 assembly, that the LWF might develop into an international "super-organization," trapped in a bureaucracy with uncontrolled budgetary needs, much as had already happened to many other instruments of global cooperation. Although it seems to have been clear to the LWF from the start that international relief work could not be run entirely or even primarily on a voluntary basis, as might have been possible in local or even some national situations, the desire to create in World Service an enterprise operated on the basis of professional skill was not always easy to fulfill. In this connection the regulation that "staff workers shall be chosen, in so far as possible, from the various member churches in order that the personnel shall be representative of the different insights and traditions of the member churches" seems to be an effort at Solomonic compromise.

Two additional emphases of the original mandate and procedure of the Department of World Service should be mentioned. The first underlines both the global character of the LWF's diaconic work and the necessity to attain flexibility in carrying out that work: "The program of LWF–WS shall be global in its perspective and shall be kept as flexible as possible in order to meet with speed and efficiency the needs of emergency and changing conditions." To be sure, in the first decade of its existence the "global" character of World Service work was more of an intention than a fact, even though there were a number of local field projects carried on outside Europe. The second deals with the criterion for selecting service projects: "Aid given by LWF–WS normally shall be determined in the light of its relations to the strengthening of self-help and to the development of ultimate self-support. LWF–WS shall not, except in extreme emergencies, allow funds for needs in situations which seem to imply permanent subsidy." Again, this remarkable statement of intent proved more difficult to implement than was perhaps originally anticipated (Minutes, Commission on World Service, Copenhagen, July 1953; LWF Archives).

The first Directors of the Department of World Service were Henry Whiting (U.S.), 1952–55, Reuben Baetz (Canada), 1955–56, and Bengt Hoffman (Sweden), 1956–61. Members of the first Commission on World Service were Paul Empie (U.S., chairperson), Henrik Hauge (Norway, secretary), Volkmar Herntrich (Germany), Harry Johansson (Sweden), and Henry Schuh (U.S.). This reflects the fact that in its early years the Lutheran World Federation found its leadership rather evenly divided between persons from the United States, Germany, and the Nordic countries; the minority churches of Europe were seldom among the leadership, and the young churches of the South were virtually absent from such positions. Even so, the concern that churches outside the Euro-American community be increasingly received as fully a part of the global fellowship of Lutheran churches, the *communio*, was recognized as an important goal from the very founding of the Federation.

## Open Questions

In the introduction to this chapter, reference was made to "vexing questions" which seem to accompany the entire narrative of service within the LWF. These critical issues have been acknowledged and faced throughout the five decades of Federation history, although the way in which they have been dealt with appears as an uneven story. In the first phase of the present account, questions such as the following appear as important.

1. The staff of World Service in its first historical phase was largely from Lutheran churches of the North, most notably from the National Lutheran Council in the United States. What were the consequences, acknowledged or unacknowledged, of this fact?

2. Were service operations limited to Lutherans alone, or were they directed to anyone in need, regardless of faith, race, or nationality? It was, quite obviously, initially intended, in the immediate aftermath of World War II, to extend aid to needy brothers and sisters who occupied the same household of faith. When, however, the LWF began its witness of service outside Europe, especially in the Middle East and in Hong Kong, these limits were lifted. This has remained a fundamental issue of both policy and program for the Department of World Service.

3. Was the diaconic work of the LWF based upon a confessional or an ecumenical strategy? From the time of the very first service projects there was, within the Federation, serious theological reflection concerning this question. It is instructive that the first American members of the LWF staff held joint appointments with the World Council of Churches. When this fact was seriously reviewed and evaluated, Paul Empie (1909–1979), in his double capacity as chair of the Commission on World Service and as Director of Lutheran World Action, the relief program of the American Lutheran churches, wrote to Dr. John Mackie, Director of the World Council's Department of Interchurch Aid and Service to Refugees:

> As you know, one of the objectives of the LWF is to promote Lutheran participation in the ecumenical movement. With us this is a matter of deep conviction and concern, and not merely a matter of pious words behind which it would be easy to ignore the spirit, while making a gesture toward the letter. We believe in the ecumenical movement and we are anxious that the Lutheran contribution to it should be a substantial one and a constructive one. (Letter of June 11, 1953; LWF Archives, WS I, 1b, Commission on World Service, 1953–54)

4. There is clear evidence that from the start, LWF assistance to churches was aimed at developing patterns of self-support in the receiving churches. Was this goal met? It was consciously the intention in projects of interchurch aid and, even more notably, in the work in Hong Kong. This question appears throughout five decades of service.

5. Could material and spiritual aid be held together? The necessity of extending material assistance was patently clear in the post–World War II situation, but even then there was a stated goal of extending this to areas of spiritual or pastoral care. Early on the issue was formulated as one of "both / and." From this awareness it was inevitable that there should be

continued reflection on the penetration of ideology into church programs. Franklin Clark Fry for one, third president of the Federation (cf. pp. 438–44 below), in pleading for comprehensive aid to the German churches let it be known that he opposed "the use of starvation as an instrument of foreign policy." And, to be sure, reflection on the life of the church in the world received considerable attention at the Lund, Hanover, and subsequent assemblies, and in the 1950s such events of major consequence as the 1956 revolt in Hungary even deepened that reflection. Yet it is worth asking whether World Service saw these issues at this early time. Concerns for "root causes" and "structural development" did not appear until later in World Service and then as part and parcel of the way the LWF dealt with matters of social ethics. Initially, service was often seen as a provisional task for the Federation, as is clear from Stewart Herman's comment that he began his work with no clear idea about the duration of his term: "We were convinced that it would be a matter of assisting in bringing Germany back to normal conditions, and then, after a span of a few years, it would be all over" (oral comments, 1994). In due course, as global service became a permanent part of the life of the LWF, basic work on theological, political, and socioethical questions became a necessity for the Department of World Service itself.

## The Move Outside Europe: The Second Phase

A BROAD TRANSFORMATION in the ministry of service of the Lutheran World Federation began around 1960. No single decision—not even at a particular meeting or consultation—determined the transformation. There were, instead, a variety of factors which during this period brought about the change.

1. There was no longer a need for a refugee program in Europe, although the events of 1956 in Hungary had been a major concern of Lutheran World Service.

2. Outside Europe, in the Southern hemisphere, new states were formed in the 1950s and 1960s as a result of liberation struggles of various kinds. These states were in desperate need both of recovering from the effects of their colonial past and of achieving for themselves a new awareness of independence. In most cases conditions were desperate, and there was enormous need for emergency aid and long-term support from the established churches. These new circumstances required of the Federation a redefinition of both the mandate and strategy of service.

3. The Federal Republic of Germany, West Germany, was at this time rapidly becoming a major donor to relief work after having so recently been a major recipient.

4. The organizational structure of the LWF secretariat was reshaped. Two such changes involving service operations were noteworthy: the establishment of the Community Development Service (CDS) in 1962, and the creation of a Secretariat for Social Affairs in 1965.

5. In the mid-1950s the Federation had sponsored important regional conferences that had led to the formation of continental entities as a recognition of the need for a differentiated approach to service in different parts of the world. These initiatives can perhaps be seen as the first stirring of a desire for "regionalization," although that desire became more articulate at later stages in LWF history. They did, however, clearly contribute to the formation of such regional ecumenical groupings as the All Africa Conference of Churches and the East Asia Christian Conference. For the Federation directly these regional initiatives resulted in shifts in representation on decision-making bodies such as the Commission on World Service and the Governing Board of the CDS. These shifts were long in being carried out and were frequently extremely difficult.

6. In the 1950s new issues and themes which impinged on the LWF's understanding of service began to emerge and in the 1960s they came into full daylight. Relationships between "donors" and "recipients"; the interaction between a traditional view of service based on compassion and charity and a new concern for structural development; internal connections between traditional understandings of the church's mission and newer patterns of interchurch aid and operational service—directly to confront such matters created for the Federation the occasion both for new approaches to service and for serious and at times even divisive conflict.

The transitional character of this period in LWF history was made apparent during the 1962 annual meeting of the Commission on World Service. Paul Empie, the chairperson, expressed a certain anxiety that the programs presented for examination by the commission were still too much geared toward the post–World War II situation: "Those features of the program which were traditional but no longer of urgent importance should, as far as possible, be eliminated in order that resources be released for new and constructive projects." From another position, however, Henrik Hauge of Norway, commission secretary, maintained that there was a different danger which deserved no less attention, namely, that the implementation of new programs might be determined by the acceptance of new priorities which were ephemeral in character: "In evaluating the program it would also have to be borne in mind that its validity is not automatically impaired by the item being traditional, nor should Christian agencies be unduly influenced by the popular and dramatic appeal of new types of programs in areas which now are front-page news" ( Minutes, Commission on World Service, 1962, LWF Archives). These issues, which brought about transformation in the service program of the Lutheran World Federation, were—like so many other serious matters in the Federation's history—to be long-standing and difficult to solve, even as they provided a context for new and creative initiatives in LWF work.

### Africa: Tanzania

Tanzania in the early 1960s was quite obviously one of the countries which could most benefit from Lutheran World Service. Since its time as a German colony (Tanganyika), Tanzania had been a field of intense Lutheran missionary activity. Moreover, the first president of this nation, which attained independence in 1964, Julius Nyerere, created an atmosphere marked by vision and accountability largely by his ability to be a reconciling figure between factions—tribes and religions—within the overall Tanzanian community.

In the years immediately after Tanzanian independence, the number of refugees in the country had been enormous. From Mozambique, Rwanda, Burundi, and the Congo (now Zaire) thousands upon thousands of refugees had streamed into Tanzania; in 1963, 30,000 refugees were given aid by LWF agencies. The most important reason, accordingly, for opening a Lutheran World Service field office in Tanzania was to initiate a program of aid and resettlement for these refugees, and that program took shape in the formation of the Tanganyika Christian Refugee Service (TCRS).

Some background to this initiative is of considerable interest. Bishop Bengt Sundkler (1909–1995) of Sweden, serving then as Bishop of Bukoba in the Evangelical Church of Northwestern Tanganyika, turned to Geneva in a desire to respond to the need posed by the refugees. He referred to local initiatives, but pointed out that the need far exceeded what the local church could do. Bruno Muetzelfeldt of Lutheran World Service replied to Sundkler:

> The LWF, in keeping with its tradition of assistance throughout the world to refugee groups is also prepared seriously to consider the possibility of raising funds and resources, and if necessary, personnel, to help the refugees in Tanganyika. However, in accordance with our policy, we act only in cooperation with the local Lutheran Church in the area concerned. It is for this reason that we are turning to you for your advice and comments, before taking further action. If it is your feeling that in the needs described to us by the United Nations High Commissioner for Refugees and other recent visitors to Tanganyika, LWF could be of assistance, we would immediately be prepared to make a survey of the refugee situation in Tanganyika, with a particular emphasis on the needs of the refugees in North-West Tanganyika, which we were informed is the most critical area of need. In other words, the basic assistance to refugees, according to our present information, would be required in

the Bukoba area of Tanganyika. (Letter of May 22, 1962 from Muetzelfeldt to Sundkler; LWF Archives, Tanganyika Christian Refugee Service)

It did not take long before appropriate actions were taken. With the purpose of coordinating the specific measures that had already been taken, the Tanganyika Christian Refugee Service (TCRS) was launched in 1963. As the program turned out to be of considerable significance for future programs in Africa, it is worthwhile to quote from the proposal for a definition of its nature, a proposal that had been drafted by the Department of World Service in Geneva in consultation with the World Council of Churches.

> The following two methods of providing help to refugees shall be used:
> 1. Utilization of existing organizations and facilities by financing or subsidizing specific services which such bodies are able and willing to render. In view of the extensive facilities available through the churches in Tanganyika, it is anticipated that a substantial part of the program will be carried out by direct utilization of the facilities available through these churches and their services, it being understood that financial assistance provided through the program will not substitute resources currently available to these churches but rather provide the necessary means to enlarge the services of the churches in order to meet specific refugee needs. At the same time secular organizations may also be used as an instrument to carry forward specific services to refugees, it being understood that only such secular channels are used as are consistent with the Christian character of the program's purpose.
> 2. The development of direct operations to provide such assistance for refugees as cannot be readily given through existing church or community facilities. (From Programme Proposals for Ecumenical Assistance to Refugees in Tanganyika, prepared by Brian W. Neldner and Joseph Thomsen, then director of Luthern World Service in Jerusalem; document provided by Neldner)

The policy of the LWF was that these refugee settlements should be self-supporting within four years of their establishment, and that after eight years they should be fully integrated into the local society. By and large, this schedule was kept in Tanzania, even though the flow of refugees into the country has continued and even increased up to the present time.

The TCRS was significant also for its ecumenical character. The LWS field office operated on behalf of both the Federation and the World Council of Churches, and its policy was shaped in cooperation with the Tanzanian government, the United Nations, and the Christian Council of Tanzania. Relations as they developed over many years between the TCRS and the LWF member church, the Evangelical Lutheran Church in Tanzania, demonstrated both the commitments and the tensions of "confessional/ecumenical" work.

Another reason for placing a focus on service in Tanzania was the nation's overwhelming need in the area of health care. At the time of its independence there were only 650 physicians to serve the 9,000,000 citizens of Tanzania; a minimum of 4,500 was needed. Since it was becoming true that churches and mission agencies were contributing nearly 50% of the total support for medical service in Tanzania, supplemented by governmental grants-in-aid, it seemed obvious that the churches should be fully involved in the structural reform of the nation's health care system. Thus it was that a German physician, Dr. Otto Walter, who was serving at a hospital in Bumbuli, Tanzania, designed a plan for the establishment of a new hospital near Moshi, near Mount Kilimanjaro. Dr. Walter proposed that a medical center be built, equipped with the best available technical equipment and having about 400 beds. Walter maintained that if necessary funding could be secured, this hospital could potentially be a national center for the education of medical assistants, nurses, and midwives. Dr. Walter in his proposal laid out an essential aspect of development strategy: the wisdom of implementing the project in two phases. The first phase would be devoted to the recruitment of suitable personnel; the second, the implementation through building and actual operation of the center.

The Kilimanjaro Christian Medical Center, which resulted from Otto Walter's proposal, came to be the largest single project to be supported by the Community Development Service of the Lutheran World Federation (LWF Archives: WS/IA 4 a; memorandum of O. Walter, March 2, 1961; cf. also Christa Held, CDS Overview, 1962–1990).

*Asia*

In the early 1960s Lutheran World Service initiated projects in India, Pakistan, and, later, Bangladesh. The Bengal Refugee Service was set up by an ecumenical group of church agencies with the purpose of providing help for refugees from East Pakistan. These agencies undertook this work on the basis of initiatives and proposals called for during the World Refugee Year, 1960. The National Christian Council of India had entered into cooperation with Inter-Church Aid and the Service for Refugees of the World Council of Churches, and Lutheran World Service agreed to supplement and provide 20% of the total costs of this venture provided that the partners agreed "to select one of two identifiable projects, against which the LWF–WS contribution could be applied" (LWF Archives, WS/ I a, 1961/62, report from a "journey of negotiation" by Bruno Muetzelfeldt, November 7–15, 1961). Within a short time a considerable number of additional projects followed in the same region, ranging from resettlement and agricultural development projects to emergency aid for work among the thousands of suffering people in Calcutta.

## Continuing Commitments

Although, as has been indicated, circumstances in the 1960s caused a shift in much of World Service attention to Third World concerns, at the beginning of this decade, a Secretariat for Minority Churches in Europe was established within the department. The Danish churchman Paul Hansen was responsible for this work both when it was in World Service and subsequently when it was transferred to what became the Department of Church Cooperation. This is an important story, which spans several decades and several locations within the LWF structure. Its focus was largely on Lutheran churches in Eastern Europe under Socialist governments, and obviously there were political and social ramifications to its work. It is a matter treated in more detail in other sections of this book (cf. p. 69 above and pp. 170–71 below.

The story of the Augusta Victoria Hospital in Jerusalem was another ongoing element in the work of the LWF Department of World Service. Increasingly this hospital took on significance as the only major hospital primarily serving the Palestinian population. As such it also became a base for small, mobile clinics which served people in Gaza and on the West Bank. For a long period of time this enterprise has persisted as an unsung— for obvious reasons—point of reconciliation in the midst of the extreme tension between Israelis and Palestinians.

To be sure, the need for emergency services in Jerusalem decreased in the early 1960s as open hostilities themselves decreased. To a certain extent, the work of the Augusta Victoria shifted toward welfare and educational initiatives on behalf of the Arab population. The spacious hospital buildings could house modest centers for vocational training in line with recommendations stemming from the World Refugee Year. At the same time, negotiations with the original German owners of the hospital moved toward the attainment of such legal agreements as would make possible the provision of necessary subsidies for the foreseeable future (LWF Archives, WS/I A, 1961-62, report of Bruno Muetzelfeldt on projects in Jordan, November 1961; cf. also, Muetzelfeldt's Director's Report to the Commission on World Service, 1959, 1966-67).

During the War of 1967 the Augusta Victoria Hospital was severely damaged in the fighting and, as might be expected, a new influx of refugees meant that emergency assistance from the hospital was again needed. This happened just at the time when plans were being formulated to recast many of the programs at the hospital from relief to self-help. Simultaneously, programs for the areas of Jerusalem that were occupied or annexed by the Israeli government were adapted to new administrative conditions. The restoration of the hospital was an immediate necessity and was successfully carried out (cf. Hanna Issa, *op. cit.* [p. 102 above]).

In Hong Kong the flow of refugees continued unabated after the 1950s; in fact it increased. Ultimately, LWF refugee services were handed over to the Hong Kong Christian Council on December 31, 1975.

World Service aid projects in Hong Kong became more pronouncedly programs of self-help and thus established a pattern for use in many places. The idea was to give assistance to persons only on the basis of case-by-case investigation, a procedure that led to heightened accountability, to the elimination of indiscriminate largesse in accordance with "sound principles of social work," and to giving recipients incentive toward personal rehabilitation. Muetzelfeldt commented on this: The strategy of self support "moves us away from an ongoing commitment toward an indefinite and large number of people by artificially raising their standard of living beyond the point of absolute necessity." The disadvantage of the strategy was, inevitably, an increase in administrative costs (LWF Archives, WS/I 1a, Director's report, December 1961).

An enduring challenge to the work of Lutheran World Service in Hong Kong proved to be the difficulty of forming local committees, of persons from the local churches, strong enough to take on new responsibilities. Bruno Muetzelfeldt lucidly described this challenge:

> It is a great pity, however, that the Lutheran church in Hong Kong will not be sufficiently strong within the foreseeable future to be charged with taking over our Hong Kong operations, or even substantial parts of it. From this it follows that for considerable time to come the Lutheran witness in this community must be conducted through the instrumentality of the Department of World Service, in the hope that the Lutheran church in Hong Kong can be increasingly involved in this program. (LWF Archives, WS/I 1a, December 1961; cf. Director's report to the Commission on World Service, 1966/67)

### The Community Development Service

Three factors were instrumental in the decision of the executive committee of the Lutheran World Federation, at its meeting in Warsaw in 1961, to approve the establishment of the "LWF Community Development Liaison and Validation Service," later named more simply the Community Development Service (CDS).

First, the experience of Lutheran World Service projects in younger Lutheran churches had created an impulse toward concrete community development. Such events as the "Freedom from Hunger" campaign of the United Nations had stimulated a general move from emergency measures to the creation of sustainable structures with respect not only to food supply but also to medical care, educational initiatives, and agricultural production.

Second, there was a general and firm desire within the LWF to establish and implement creative programs outside Europe, thus taking into account both the actual demographic proportions of the global family of Lutheran churches and clear disparities between overall living standards in the Northern and Southern hemispheres.

Third, there was a recognition within the LWF of the need to bridge gaps between the Departments of World Service and World Mission. More appropriately, perhaps, it could be said that there was a need to create a constructive working relationship between the two departments. As has already been noted, the LWF has often found itself in a position of converting points of potential duplication, competition, and irritation into fields of common and complementary work.

In its effort to develop criteria for the definition and implementation of working projects, CDS reflected, on the one hand, on the need to deal with problems which were observed in existing service operations and, on the other hand, on deliberate strategies to develop something new that would creatively break out of previous strategies. The essential criteria developed were to provide for and/or expand activities in the fields of social and economic welfare; to serve entire communities; to enlist the support of local Christian communities, thereby developing a sense of social responsibility in those communities; to be church-owned or church-related; and to be of high priority. Projects submitted to CDS in order to receive funds which would be available from other sources would not be considered. Moreover, terms of reference were added to provide CDS with consistency in its strategic planning and its administrative procedures (cf. Christa Held, *op. cit.*).

A governing committee was established for CDS, consisting of two members each from the Commissions on World Service and World Mission. The first chairman of this group was Fredrik Schiotz. At the LWF Assembly in Evian, France, 1970, Eugene Ries (b. 1926) of the United States was appointed Associate Director of the LWF Department of World Service and the Director of CDS, CDS being seen as an entity within World Service. Ries served in that twin capacity until 1980, when he succeeded Bruno Muetzelfeldt as the Director of World Service. Christa Held (b. 1931) of the Federal Republic of Germany then was appointed Director of CDS, a post she held until her retirement in 1993.

From the outset it was made clear that no CDS projects would absorb resources otherwise available for regular LWF program budgets. Staff were not to "limit the freedom of action of either churches or donors to make direct contacts and agreements," and it was pointed out that "responsibility for the effective implementation of projects should rest with the recipient" and not with CDS.

Although CDS was from its beginning seen as an initiative reflecting the interests of churches in the Southern Hemisphere, the first members of the Governing Committee were exclusively from Northern "donor churches." The chairperson was from the United States; there were two Scandinavians and two from the Federal Republic of Germany. It was not until 1971 that the composition of the committee began to reflect the actual character of CDS programs, when Joel Ngeiyamu (1920–1994) of Tanzania was elected to the chair and two members came from Indonesia, one from Brazil, one from the United States, and one from West Germany.

As referred to above, one of the factors behind the creation of CDS was the desire to bring the Departments of World Service and World Mission into a closer working relationship. Accordingly, the administrative structure of CDS—based on a working decision in the Geneva secretariat and operative 1964–70—was the result of a compromise between these two departments. This intention, of a formal compromise which was really based on a fear of conflict, proved in the eyes of many to be hopelessly inefficient. An example: the area secretaries of the Department of World Mission were made responsible for CDS activities in Asia and Africa, while staff from the Department of World Service carried responsibilities for Latin America and for overall fund raising.

A fundamental criticism of CDS in its early years was taken up by its Governing Committee itself—remarkably enough, as early as 1963. On the basis of experiences gained from a journey to field projects, it was reported with an extraordinary awareness of the need for honest self-evaluation that

> the biggest problem is finding imaginative projects. When thinking of community development projects, the churches often think in terms of the work they have been doing so far, which leads to the extension of hospitals, schools, establishment of charitable homes. There is also a tendency to think of providing money for the church, employment of church people, serving their own members first instead of helping the whole community. Often the question arises of who should run a project. Some churches feel unable to take over the extra burden, but maybe are hesitant to turn over the administration into the hands of an outside expert. (Christa Held, op. cit.)

### The Secretariat for Social Affairs

The establishment of a secretariat for social affairs within the Department for World Service in 1964 took place at a time when there was both a discussion of LWF structure and serious consideration of theology and social ethics. There is an obvious relation between the establishment of the Community Development Service as a program entity and a secretariat for social affairs as an office for study. The latter initiative is also to be seen in light of the debates concerning justification and justice at the 1963 Helsinki Assembly, a debate that had surely not come to a conclusion (cf. pp. 377–79 below). The substance of this unfinished contention was identified as the first point on the agenda of the new secretariat, with a rec ommendation that there be collaboration between this new office and the LWF Department of Theology.

Even twenty years earlier, Lutheran theologians from the Nordic countries had set forth a distinctive interpretation of Lutheranism in which the gospel was understood to include an emphasis on the sociopolitical responsibility of Christians. As has been seen in chapter 1 above, this interpretation represented a rejection of both the patriarchal conservatism that often emerged from a theology centered about "the orders of creation" and all pietistic separations of the "two kingdoms." In the intervening time this discussion had remained a central issue among Lutherans, not least in Europe, and especially in Germany where the 1960s were marked by serious debates over political ethics. Simultaneously, members of indigenous Lutheran churches in the Southern hemisphere, whose lives were largely determined by historic colonial subjection and by economic deprivation, wanted open discussions of social questions in light of their own political realities.

The German theologian Christian Walther (b. 1927) was appointed to head up the new secretariat for social affairs. In 1966 a volume, *Faith and Society: Toward a Contemporary Social Ethic*, was published as a supplement to the LWF journal, *Lutheran World*; this book should be seen as a characteristic result of the new study initiative. It contained two contributions from the United States, by Joseph Sittler and Carl Reuss; two from Germany, by Wolfgang Trillhaas and Trutz Rendtorff; and one from the Nordic countries, by Tor Aukrust. Walther himself was the editor of the volume.

## A Strategy for Service: The 1960s

In the 1960s two individuals left indelible marks on the policy and implementation of service in the life of the Lutheran World Federation. The first was Paul Empie of the United States, who had been involved since the founding of the Federation and who served as chairperson of the LWF Commission on World Service throughout the 60s. The second dominant figure was Bruno Muetzelfeldt of Australia, who became Director of the Department of World Service in 1961, retaining the post until 1980. Muetzelfeldt was a theological conservative who was always suspicious of new fashions within the discipline. He was, however, a remarkable administrator who was able efficiently to lead World Service through a period of continuous growth.

It is not an exaggeration to state that in the 1960s World Service head-quarters—the Geneva secretariat—attained a new strength. The fact remained, however, that the gap between service efforts and world reali-ties, especially in Third World countries, only widened. Despite the exten-sive relief and development activity of the LWF and of many other organizations, governmental and nongovernmental alike, the situation throughout the developing countries continued to deteriorate. In his report of 1967–68, Muetzelfeldt commented on political instability in the world, a reality that he regarded as a threat to anyone of goodwill because, as he said, "It adds an ominous dimension to the signs of frustration expe-rienced by so many in their endeavor to build, rather than to destroy." Referring to the relief work that would be required following the Vietnam War, he went on, "The mind just staggers in the face of the stupendous sums spent on destruction" (Report to the Commission on World Service, 1967–68).

New instances of political unrest, stemming from new economic and social difficulties, added further to the already apparent calamities. Accordingly, Muetzelfeldt seriously asked whether Christian relief opera-tions were not facing the danger of weariness. He considered it too vague to ask only about "compassion fatigue"; he suggested rather that the expression "compassion despair" be used. Muetzelfeldt attempted to pen-etrate to the psychological root causes of that deadlock which he saw as threatening to bring about stagnation in any policy of relief:

> The processes of sound economic development are too slow for those who want to see quick results. The population explosion tends to undo more than the patient efforts towards economic growth accomplish. Thus the sheer size of the task staggers the imagination, and the multiplicity of the almost immeasurable proportions of the problem throw the mind into confusion, and the incomprehensibility of it all has a deadening effect on the conscience. (Report to the Commission on World Service, 1967–68)

In light of this dreadful dilemma, Muetzelfeldt focussed upon the rela-tionship between public, governmental resources for relief and the efforts carried out by church and other private agencies, a key issue for all dis-cussions of relief and development strategy. He considered it essential that Christians exert self-criticism in regard to their failure to influence the policy of their own governments:

> One wonders whether the Christian church, so active and also effective in organizing social welfare programs at home and abroad is exerting the requi-site moral influence on the governments for the purpose of fostering

large-scale support for the underprivileged masses of the world. One wonders whether the individual Christians, many of whom are not only generous but sacrificial in their giving toward church-sponsored programs, adequately utilize their political influence to stimulate greater concern for government action in social and economic assistance.

It was Muetzelfeldt's own conviction that state taxes would never be able to replace compassion, even though he admitted that exactly the interaction of the two required the full attention of all aid agencies: "Here a whole area of Christian service needs more extensive exploration; not to substitute for the sacrificial gifts, not to replace Christian motivated programs, but to add a further dimension to the totality of Christian social responsibility" (ibid.).

Muetzelfeldt's concern to mobilize all possible resources in order to insure the expedient administration of service projects did not, however, flag in the face of largely negative experience. Neither did his concern for the "operational" character of the Department of World Service cause him to refrain from theological examination of the nature of the work. In his report of 1966–67 he commented on the establishment of the Secretariat for Social Affairs, referring at the same time to the 450th anniversary of the Reformation, and specifically to a sermon of Martin Luther on Luke 6:36ff. Muetzelfeldt wanted to pay due attention to the basic Lutheran distinction between faith and works as a presupposition for sound commitment to political responsibility on the part of Christians. Having touched upon this burning theological issue, he presented a very critical view of the "theology of revolution" which at that very moment was for many—including persons in the LWF—an object of interest and approval. Muetzelfeldt for his part warned against paying undue attention to that wave of fashion. Yet he accompanied that warning with a refusal to exempt the churches from self-critical examinations of defects in their own history of service:

> Alongside of the genuine appreciation of the evident readiness of the church to cast aside an unhealthy conservatism which has inhibited its social consciousness for far too long, there is now a growing concern that the pendulum may be swinging too far in the opposite direction through an over-anxiousness to atone for the past neglects and the desire to be 'with it.'" (Report to the Commission on World Service, 1966–67)

## Expansion, Debate, and Reorientation: The Third Phase

FAR-REACHING SHIFTS can be seen at significant points in the work of service as carried out in the LWF from the time of the Federation's Assembly at

Evian in 1970 to the present. Five concrete matters should be singled out as indicative of this process of transition.

1. The emphasis in service programs, by definition as well as implementation, clearly moved from Europe to the "Two-Thirds World," even as the gap between North and South in terms of socioeconomic realities widened drastically. The agenda of World Service was determined by this clear fact and by the tensions attendant to it. New definitions of aims and strategies were necessary.

2. In the 1970s new points of crisis appeared or, in some cases, remained explosive: the tensions between East and West which were not confined to Europe alone; open questions concerning sociopolitical ideologies as raised in the church's struggle against all forms of injustice; new questions regarding human rights. Most dramatically, perhaps, the crucial matter of the church's role in combating the policy of apartheid in South Africa embodied most of these critical issues.

3. The structure of the Federation's Geneva secretariat was changed twice during this period of time: first as a result of executive committee decisions taken in 1969, and second as a result of the restructuring approved by the LWF's Eighth Assembly in Curitiba, in 1990. These changes were significant and not without controversy.

4. This process of restructuring, designed in each instance to facilitate greater internal cooperation in the Geneva secretariat, in actual fact frequently resulted in misunderstanding, frustration, and rivalry. This proved particularly the case with respect to interdepartmental matters but also regarding the manifold relations between Geneva, member churches, and, for World Service, field staff.

5. A number of debates—some of which were of decisive and far-reaching importance for this book—occurred during this period, notably, the discussion on "proclamation and development," on the root causes of social and economic injustice, and on the relation between confessional and ecumenical strategies of service.

However important such matters proved to be, marked even by conflict and considerable disagreement, the period also exhibited signs of steady progress and dynamism as new challenges arose in field projects whether they dealt with emergency situations or issues of long-range development.

### Europe

Although, as noted, there was a perceptible shift in service concerns from Europe to the "Two-Thirds World," a certain nuance must be made. The minority churches of Europe, most notably in Eastern Europe, were still in great need of support from the outside, as the Federation in 1969 shifted responsibility for service to such churches from the Department of World Service to the Federation's mission department which had been renamed the Department of Church Cooperation. The complexity of the European situation was further typified by the fact that Lutheran churches in what was then East Germany, the German Democratic Republic, were beginning their own work of supplying aid to suffering countries outside Europe.

The main burden of service to European churches was in the direction of those communities living under Marxist rule. For example, the Lutheran Church in Hungary, a country of relative prosperity, reported in 1967 that "the support from abroad was having a most stimulating effect on church life and the congregations' willingness to sacrifice." There was no intention to withhold such support, although increasingly attention was being given to measures designed to increase self-support within minority churches. Such was also the goal in respect to minority churches in Western Europe where economic and social circumstances made self-support a far more attainable goal.

The case of the small Lutheran church body in the United Kingdom may serve as an example of how interchurch aid in Western, noncommunist Europe was now to be approached. At its 1970 meeting, when the Commission on World Service made a final assessment of its work in Great Britain, it stated:

> We do not deem it wise and appropriate that the LWF support of Lutheran activities in Great Britain be envisaged as further large-scale objectives. Rather, in our judgment, such support should be continued on the basis of limited but specific goals.

This intention—which implied that minority churches should not be supported "for whatever reasons" by the LWF—was specified further:

> The LWF should recognize and accept the responsibility to assist groups of continental Lutheran traditions which manifest earnest convictions that they should continue to worship and to bear witness to the Gospel in such traditions. Such assistance, however, should be rendered only to the extent to which these groups put forth genuine efforts to support themselves to the maximum of their abilities. As any of these groups decline in number, further support should be contingent upon its willingness to work more closely or to merge with another Lutheran group in Great Britain in such a way that Word and Sacrament may be available to those remaining at all age levels.

The challenge was seen not solely in financial terms; it was also ecumenical:

> Although it is always the clear obligation of every Christian to witness to Christ to those around him who are not in the Christian household, the LWF

cannot be a party to efforts financed from abroad, especially designed to evangelize amongst the British population. It sees its role as assisting Lutherans in Great Britain to bear testimony to the Lutheran tradition at its best, and in so doing to stimulate and enrich the work of other Christian communions there in the ecumenical context and spirit of our day, in the process of which Lutherans will also be enriched. (Director's Report to Commission on World Service, 1970)

The fundamental task of the LWF in Great Britain, after 1969 through the Department of Church Cooperation, was to enable the Lutheran community to move toward financial self-support in an overall ecumenical atmosphere. The important service of the Federation in supporting two Lutheran lectureships—at Mansfield College, Oxford from 1957 to 1995 and at Selly Oaks Colleges in Birmingham from 1970 to 1994—is to be seen both as providing a foundation for a strong Lutheran clergy and as an ecumenical contribution in the United Kingdom from world Lutheranism.

## The Middle East

During the 1960s a double strategy had been defined relative to LWF service and activity in the Middle East: on the one hand, to strengthen tendencies toward self-support and, on the other hand, to pursue negotiations with original (German) owners of property now entrusted to the Federation and with appropriate international agencies, especially the United Nations, to insure continued financial support from other external sources. As is perfectly clear, general political developments in the region—provocation and retaliation—have not allowed the LWF to withdraw from its own basic commitments. Whether the current peace process will substantially change this situation remains to be seen.

The projects operated until 1977 by the LWF in Syria have been recognized as remarkably successful, especially given the political context in which they have been carried out. It has been stated that the LWF has been "the only international Christian organization which has an operational program in Syria that has continued without interruption since 1952." In the same connection the good relationship with "the concerned government agencies as well as UNRWA officials" was noted (Proceedings, LWF Commission on World Service, 1969).

Substantial support for the Augusta Victoria Hospital in Jerusalem has continued to be required, not least in light of both the serious disrepair of the physical facilities and the unabated flow of patients requiring treatment. After 1970 there were serious negotiations with different partners aimed at establishing cooperative ventures at the hospital. Importantly, the Israeli government also participated in these discussions, giving approval to the payment of compensation for damages caused during the Six Day War of 1967. Similar talks were held with representatives of the OPEC nations, which was deemed appropriate because in 1987 the hospital was requested to reserve 20% of its services for serious cases from the Gaza Strip which was "chronically underserved" (Report of the Director of World Service, 1987). The major contributions to the Augusta Victoria, however, were supplied by German agencies in response to the work of Dr. Otto Walter of the Federal Republic of Germany who had been commissioned to coordinate the renovation of the hospital.

## The Far East

Hong Kong, the earliest working field for the LWF in Asia, also witnessed the first steps taken in Asia toward self-support: Financial and administrative responsibility for service projects there were transferred to the Hong Kong Christian Council in December 1975 and the distribution of emergency food was, when required, to be in the form of "food for work" (Proceedings, Commission on World Service, 1972, 1973). It was in this period, too, that the LWF first investigated the possibility of carrying out service projects in the People's Republic of China. Beginning in the early 1980s, emergency projects, in light of droughts and floods, became possible, and short-term assistance was given.

The largest single program of LWF service in Asia has been in Bangladesh. The Cooch Behar Refugee Service was established there in order to help refugees from what was then East Pakistan. In addition to service for refugees, this program also enabled the establishment of small-scale industries, provided agricultural assistance, and organized rehabilitation programs for women. All of this was done with the explicit intention of moving toward self-support via such programs as "food for work" (Report of the Director of World Service, 1972–73).

India has also been the location of considerable World Service work. Projects there have included a number of integrated rural development initiatives, several of which have been aimed at reducing the number of refugees flowing toward the desperately overcrowded city of Calcutta. The need for major work in the cities of India has obviously only increased over time. A special unit for providing emergency and rehabilitation services has been overtaxed in its work amidst the many natural disasters which seem perennially to devastate the land (Report of the Director of World Service, 1987).

Lutheran World Service, in the period under examination, also established important programs in other Asian countries—among them, Nepal (a fresh water project), Indonesia, the Philippines, and Papua New Guinea, where emergency project assistance was given. In Cambodia, World Service was one of the major agencies comprising the first Non-Governmental Organization consortium after the fall of Pol Pot. From this developed a closely coordinated program with the WCC. It is to be recalled that Cambodia was completely isolated diplomatically by the West for more than a decade after the fall of Pol Pot and, apart from India and the countries of the Eastern bloc, it was only the NGOs and the Red Cross that provided aid.

### Africa

Africa in recent years has become a major focal point for international relief programs, including those of the Lutheran World Federation. Not incidentally, certain Lutheran churches on this continent—for example, in Madagascar, Ethiopia, Tanzania, and Nigeria—have been among the fastest-growing churches in the world. It is, however, the dire situation of the entire continent that has required massive international response. The African story of ethnic and religious tensions, of inappropriate national boundaries determined by colonial powers, of dictatorships, civil wars, and political confusion has been tragically exacerbated by realities of drought, famine, and refugee flight. These facts have prevented progress on struggles to create sustainable social and economic structures, to improve agricultural and industrial production, and to raise levels of general education and health care. The LWF has responded to the emergency both upon request from well established and newly formed churches, and in situations where no local Lutheran church is present as a viable partner. Space limitations require that the following account be limited to certain specific descriptions of this work.

Zimbabwe, which became an independent state in 1980, presents a case in point. Independence meant the displacement of the previous white minority government by a black majority government. The new government faced an immediate and enormous challenge in the repatriation of thousands of Zimbabwean refugees who sought a return to their homeland. The government entrusted major responsibility for this task to the LWF which responded by the establishment of a World Service operational program. The number of refugees resettled was in the vicinity of 41,000, according to a report which was presented in 1981, and the work was carried on in spite of multiple tensions between the Federation and the Christian Council of Zimbabwe, between the World Service field operation and the Geneva secretariat, and between the emergency relief arm of World Service and the LWF Community Development Service.

In Namibia, especially during the many years of that nation's struggle for liberation from the dominance of the white powers of South Africa, there was long-term need. Countless Namibians were living in exile, others were in prison, and still others were struggling for their existence in deprived economic and social conditions. Although many relief and development projects, carried out with the Lutheran churches, were directly sponsored by Lutheran agencies such as Finchurchaid and Danchurchaid, the LWF was initially involved through its Community Development Service and subsequently through other arms of World Service. The Federation thus included among its efforts the direct sponsorship of the administration of the Namibian Council of Churches, the reconstruction for the Ovambokavango Lutheran Church (later the Evangelical Lutheran Church in Namibia) of printing and communication facilities which had twice been destroyed in bomb attacks, as well as projects in health care, education, and the development of a more adequate water supply. For Namibians in exile, the LWF sponsored, with Anglican and Roman Catholic partners, significant ecumenical chaplaincies in Zimbabwe and Tanzania.

New chapters in the Namibian involvement of Lutheran World Service came after the independence of the country was achieved in 1989. A major responsibility presented itself and was taken for aiding in the repatriation of exiled Namibians and for this a field office was opened for the duration of the program. An important component of this work was the resettlement of several thousand Namibian Bushmen who had been conscripted to the South African army. Additionally, the post-1989 period witnessed the implementation of new concepts for operational service work under the direct auspices of the Evangelical Lutheran Church in Namibia itself.

Other diaconic efforts have been carried out by the LWF throughout Southern Africa both during the period leading up to the overthrow of apartheid in South Africa and since that momentous change. Many of these programs centered about the return of refugees to their native countries, including educational and vocational adjustments upon their return. Important in this work has been ecumenical work in the so-called "Frontline States," where new contacts have been forged between Christian churches, liberation movements, and official governments.

The role of World Service in the midst of the political struggles that have for several generations marked the African continent is well illustrated by the daring LWF relief operation directed to the liberated zone in Mozambique, a zone held after 1970 by FRELIMO, the vigorous liberation movement. This work with FRELIMO was perhaps the most important program of assistance in Mozambique, and led directly to the positive reception of international Christian relief and development work when the country attained its liberation. The story of this effort is in many respects like that of an international mystery: The program was conducted under great secrecy from Tanzania and involved the clandestine transport through war zones of hundreds of tons of material needed in schools and hospitals.

It has been to Ethiopia that Lutheran World Service has devoted major attention, most publicly in response to the several famines which began in 1984–85. Even earlier, the LWF had responded to the famine of 1973–76, and in 1980 an ecumenical program, the Interchurch Response for the Horn of Africa (ICRHA) had been established by three major American agencies, Church World Service, Catholic Relief Services, and Lutheran World Relief. ICRHA has been described as "one of the most successful recent instances of ecumenical cooperation," and its work led, in part, to an international initiative taken in 1984 by Eugene Ries, then Director of the LWF's Lutheran World Service. In February of that year at a meeting called in Geneva, the Churches Drought Action in Africa (CDAA) was formed by the Lutheran World Federation, the World Council of Churches, the Roman Catholic agency Caritas Internationalis, and the Catholic Relief Services. At the Geneva press conference announcing the formation of CDAA, Dr. Emmanuel Abraham, President of the Ethiopian Evangelical Church Mekane Yesus, stated, "Many African countries have been suffering for fifteen years from drought. The call for common action in this emergency situation from the Catholic and Protestant agencies is becoming ever stronger. Almost every third African is or soon will be suffering from hunger."

The first steps taken by CDAA have been described in the following way:

> To establish a common context for the anticipated appeal, members agreed to conduct an inventory of their current aid programs in Africa, to project new ventures for the next one to two years. . . . The new commitments were to be over and above the aggregate $270 million total already designated by the agencies for their current programs throughout Africa. . . . [In June 1984 it was] reported that the cooperating agencies had already given assurances for $100 million, the full amount of the appeal: $54 million in cash and 112,413 tons of food valued at $500 per ton, or $56 million. In addition, the Lutheran World Federation and Caritas Internationalis had each committed $100,000 for a comprehensive study on the root causes of hunger in Africa, to be led by Dr. Sibusisu Bengu, a South African on the staff of the Lutheran World Federation. (Richard W. Solberg, *Miracle in Ethiopia: A Partnership Response to Famine* [New York: Friendship Press, 1991, p. 50])

Only such international, ecumenical cooperation could implement the emergency projects needed to provide even a modicum of relief in Africa. Whole regions not defined by national boundaries needed a sustainable strategy for the future, ranging from a countermove against deforestation, construction of water supplies, and cultivation of seedling crops to education and especially agricultural research. In Ethiopia these needs had to be set against a background of internal political stagnation after nearly a decade of oppressive Marxist dictatorship, civil war in the northeastern provinces and especially in Eritrea, and the hordes of refugees streaming into the country from famine- and war-torn Somalia and Sudan.

The saga of famine and relief aid in Ethiopia needs, further, to be seen also in the context of relations between the Ethiopian Evangelical Church Mekane Yesus, the Lutheran church affiliated with the LWF, and the dominant Ethiopian Orthodox Church. Those relations had never been easy and persist even to the present in being marked by charges of proselytism and other tensions that have even resulted in violence toward the Lutherans. Nevertheless, the years of the most severe crises for the Ethiopian people saw the Orthodox and the Lutherans, together with the small indigenous Roman Catholic Church, brought together in a Joint Relief Partnership (JRP) in 1986 when the name Churches Drought Action in Africa ceased being used in favor of the names of individual participating agencies. International relief agencies, in point of fact, made their participation in JRP conditional on full ecumenical cooperation between the Ethiopian churches. The achievement of the JRP, in terms of both its serving work to the Ethiopian people and its ecumenical advance, has been described by Richard Solberg:

> The crowning achievement of the JRP has been the realization of what many have called the "Ecumenical Miracle." The integration of the Roman Catholic and Lutheran relief networks through Caritas Internationalis and CRS [Catholic Relief Services] and the Lutheran World Federation has in itself been a witness to the way in which human need can draw individuals and churches together in common missions of mercy. But the JRP also became the instrument to break down walls that for fifteen hundred years had separated the Ethiopian Orthodox Church [EOC] from most other members of the Christian community. . . . The full participation of the EOC in the JRP—expressing a common commitment to Christ's mission to feed the hungry—has continued beyond the crisis that brought the churches together. As he returned from the ecumenical journey in March 1986, Archbishop Garima of the Ethiopian Orthodox Church expressed thanks to God on behalf of all the partners "that during the sufferings of millions of people we were able, irrespective of denominations, to think and act as Christians in the service of the needy people of Ethiopia." (ibid., p. 179; cf. also Report of the Director of the Department of World Service, 1985-86, 1987; and the Report of the Director of the Department for World Service, 1993)

World Service work in Africa has also been marked by significant programs in, among other places, Zambia, Botswana, and not least in Uganda, a nation severly hit by the AIDS pandemic. World Service's bold but dangerous program to air-lift material aid to the people of the Southern Sudan has been given well-deserved attention. In addition to the danger inherent in the air-lift, the overall political situation in that country wracked by long-term civil war has added political dimensions which some have even called ambiguous to the LWF's work. In Mauretania a most significant initiative has been taken by World Service in the development of a program of reforestation in a Moslem country where there is no appreciable Lutheran presence. This project has been described as having "taken on an importance of national proportions" (Reports of the Director of the Department of World Service, 1981, 1987). The more recent, and yet only partially resolved, civil war in Liberia provided yet another opportunity for significant relief and refugee work on the part of the Federation. In the midst of this struggle the need for new patterns of closer cooperation between ecumenical relief organizations has yet again become apparent. Reflection on this need, both in Liberia and throughout sub-Saharan Africa, resulted in 1995 in the formation of ACT, Action by Churches Together, a merger of emergency operations as carried out in Africa by the Lutheran World Federation and the World Council of Churches. The long-range ecumenical significance of this new cooperative venture will perhaps provide new patterns for the global diaconic witness of the churches.

### Central and Latin America

As already indicated, the LWF formed a Committee on Latin America in 1952 (cf. p. 50 above), to which Stewart Herman gave creative leadership. After initial activities in Latin America, however, relatively little direct attention was given by the LWF to work on this continent until 1983. At that time there was what might be termed a "rediscovery of South America," with the recognition that it shared the structural problems common to the entire Two-Thirds World. Its Lutheran churches were numerically small and had little economic capacity, even though in 1970 the Evangelical Church of the Lutheran Confession in Brazil had been heavily involved in the drama surrounding the Fifth Assembly of the LWF (cf. pp. 382–96 below). Accordingly, in 1983 a subcommittee on Latin America was formed to report to the LWF Commission on World Service in concert with the annual statement of the Director of World Service. This committee recommended the establishment of "an interdepartmental task force on Latin America to coordinate the Lutheran response to the many severe problems and challenges of this troubled area." Moreover, it suggested that a high-level delegation travel to Central and South Amer-

ica "to establish contacts with Lutheran churches and with the authorities, and in order to assess the needs of the area, particularly of the
churches there" (Report of the Commission on World Service, 1983).

In 1988 the Governing Committee of the Community Development
Service met in Argentina. This gave the visitors the opportunity to obtain
direct impressions of the Latin American situation. During that meeting
representatives of many Latin American Lutheran churches reported on
realities in their churches and lands, a presentation "which was enriching
and moving, as many live and work in politically unstable countries,
where changes are hoped for or in process. The churches often have to be
the voice of the voiceless and take a stand in question of exploitation or
disregard of human rights" (Held, CDS Overview, pp. 35ff.).

We shall cite only two examples of LWF service in Latin America. Peru
has been the recipient of a number of integrated rural development projects. The programs, however, have experienced several reversals, partly
because of continuous guerrilla activity and partly because of natural disasters. Yet, the activities have never been given up; their range can be measured by the fact that in 1987 the national development agency of the
Evangelical Lutheran Church in Peru had 28 fulltime and 165 temporary
staff (Report of the Director of World Service, 1987).

Haiti, too, has been the recipient of World Service efforts in Central
America. This involvement—programs for refugees, support of human
rights efforts, agricultural projects—has become particularly urgent during
recent years of governmental change from military oppression to a fledgling democracy (Report on the Caribbean, Haitian-Dominican Republic
Program, submitted to the Department of World Service, 1993).

### Debates during Transition

As previously noted, in the 1970s, midway in the course of the five decades
of LWF history, the Federation's life was marked by serious ambiguities.
On the one hand, there was a clear determination that in an intentionally
comprehensive way the Federation should "break new ground"; on the
other hand, this could not be done without contentious debate, even harsh
controversy (cf. p. 120 above; cf. also p. 109 above). It is appropriate in the
present context that the role of "service" in this significant period of transition be investigated.

*Evangelism and Structural Development.*   The statement of the
Ethiopian Evangelical Church Mekane Yesus "On the Interrelation
between Proclamation of the Gospel and Human Development," communicated to the Lutheran World Federation in May 1972, went directly,
albeit by an intricate pattern of exchange, to crucial elements in the basic

self-understanding of the Federation that had been developed over nearly twenty-five years. There can be no question that the key implication of the controversy regarding the relationship between donor agencies and the LWF secretariat was fully recognized by the Commission and Department of World Service, but it remains doubtful whether the matter of that relationship was brought to a balanced, long-term resolution.

The results of the LWF Consultation on Proclamation and Human Development held in Nairobi in October of 1974, a consultation in direct response to the Ethiopian initiative, were carefully examined by the Commission on World Service. A formal statement, approved by the commission, began with a self-affirmation. The first paragraph of the statement claimed that the entire issue had already been thoroughly considered by the commission even as it acknowledged with gratitude that an opportunity to consider further the issues and challenges had been presented in Nairobi. In particular, the commission welcomed the necessity of redefining "proclamation" as it involved "both verbal witness and diaconic work such as assistance in development." Moreover, the commission in its statement advocated *a flexible approach to the connection between spiritual need and material assistance* in light of the multiplicity of conditions within which the churches of the global Lutheran community lived. The commission further recognized the urgency of keeping self-reliance and not apparent or hidden dependency as an ultimate goal and criterion for the LWF's work of service: "Care must be taken therefore that support from outside does not create dependency, but fosters local initiative and increases the capacity of the project-carrying church in personnel, structure and resources." Additionally, the commission expressed its determination to replace any dominance of the wealthy churches by giving increased responsibility in decision making to the churches in the Southern Hemisphere: "In view of the present food and economic crisis in the Southern Hemisphere, the churches as an expression of Christian concern and love should play an increasing role in situations of desperate need." Finally, and no less important, the commission's resolution underscored that service projects ought to originate with the churches of the recipient country except in cases where an emergency situation made it impossible for local churches to act (Summary Background and Recommendations for Action, Commission on World Service minutes, 1975).

A critical evaluation of this issue, from the ease of hindsight, would reveal that these recommendations were built on a cautious consensus that did not necessarily come sharply to grips with the problems expressed in the original statement of the Ethiopian church. The complexity created by a great diversity of concerns actually preserved important elements of the gulf between donor and recipient churches. In retrospect, this excessive caution by Lutheran World Service concerning unresolved issues, a caution primarily intended to protect relief operations from governmental interference, may unnecessarily have prolonged tension in the relationship, for example, between World Service and the Mekane Yesus Church.

*Donor Agencies and Recipients.* It has not been possible in the LWF to pass beyond the use of overworked phrases such as "donor agencies" and "recipient churches." Over many years, this has given a certain stagnation to crucial and enduring debates. As World Service became involved in greater and greater transition after the Nairobi Consultation of 1974, the relationship between these donor agencies which represented "giving churches" in wealthy countries, and recipient churches of impoverished and suffering lands, continued to provide a focal point for debate. The problem was taken up and given provocative expression in a volume, *The Politics of Altruism: A Study of the Political Behaviour of Voluntary Development Agencies,* published by the LWF in 1977. Its author was a Danish political scientist, Jørgen Lissner (b. 1945), at that time a member of the Geneva staff of the LWF Department of Studies.

Lissner pointed to the dilemma that existed between the interests of the voluntary agencies, i.e., income maximization, and the value system which was intended to define their program priorities. He maintained that donor agencies were similar in their behavior to political entities designed to effect an increase in economic influx, even if those same agencies also claimed that their work was carried out solely in the interest of recipients.

It was not Lissner's intent to disregard the positive aspects of Christian service. He gave particular attention to the then thirty-year work of Lutheran World Service, work carried out in a spirit of personal dedication to Christian witness. He saw a quality of spiritual motivation and efficiency which gave the staff of World Service a credibility vastly different from "ivory-tower academics" or "journalists in transit." Yet he maintained that it was still necessary to view the positive distinctions of service staff in the light of the fact that their agencies enjoyed a "quasi monopoly in the Third World."

*The Politics of Altruism* also presents a clear exposition of the dualism between the mechanisms that produce wealth in the rich countries and those that cause poverty in the developing countries. Additionally, Lissner carefully examined the connection between "root causes" of political, social, and economic deprivation that are indigenous to developing countries and those that are imposed from without. From this analysis the volume presented strongly critical judgments toward high-income nations regarding the ever widening gap between themselves and countries marked by increasing poverty. In this perspective is to be seen the sharp contrast between the need of developing countries for structural aid and the tendency in donor agencies to perpetuate a concentration on emergency services. Lissner, finally, also made a strong case for a creative co-existence between projects which emphasized "service and relief" and measures aimed at achieving "justice and liberation."

Jørgen Lissner's work elicited wide-ranging response, including sharply critical judgments. Since the publication of *The Politics of Altruism* several of his concerns and attendant responses have become a part of ongoing discussions within the Federation. Specifically, the establishment of an office for "Research and Social Action" within the Department of World Service, which is to receive more detailed attention below, was part of an overall effort to develop a "wholistic" concept of service designed to deal precisely with Lissner's concerns. The whole matter of a dichotomy between projects based on relief and those based on structural development has been given serious attention, perhaps most recently in the important exposition of a strategy for service presented by Brian W. Neldner (b. 1933), Director of the Department for World Service from 1990 to 1995, in a paper presented in South Africa in September 1994 on "The Humanitarian Imperative" (LWF Archives).

It is proper, nevertheless, to ask whether or not the Federation as a whole has given sufficient attention to the concerns expressed from the "receiving" churches (and nations) of the Southern Hemisphere. The Indian churchman and economist Kunchala Rajaratnam (b. 1920) who has served as a layperson both on the LWF staff and on many of its governing agencies, for example, has given unrelenting attention to these concerns. The research center established, under Dr. Rajaratnam's direction at the Gurukul Theological Seminary in Madras, India, for the study of economics and development (Center for Research on New International Economic Order, CRNIEO) has been one of several centers for pursuing both reflection and action regarding relationships between donor agencies and recipient churches.

*"Root Causes."* "Service" programs were often, during the first decades of the life of the Federation, seen as being based on an individualistic anthropology and as being concerned largely for what was often described as "mere ambulance service." Judgments of this sort are simplistic and miss the mark, although they must be seen as part of a far-reaching debate within the LWF. The early 1970s witnessed rounds of discussion aimed at bringing about a basic reorientation concerning methods for establishing priorities for service projects and programs. New positions in this regard were marked by a vigorous inclusion of human rights concerns and an inclusion also of reflection regarding the "root causes" of injustice of all forms.

The executive committee of the LWF in 1974 began giving an impetus to this reorientation. An interdepartmental study that received considerable attention had been produced concerning these questions and the Commission on World Service at its 1976 meeting pursued the matter thoroughly. The commission agreed to encourage increased LWF commitment to a process of "conscientization" as an essential precondition for fully and responsibly involved participation at all levels connected with the work of service. This commitment, further, was to extend toward making further progress in the struggle toward self-reliance in churches of the developing world.

These discussions, approached with great seriousness, led to a thoroughgoing reexamination of the mandate of the Commission and Department of World Service.

> Its [World Service's] primary role was seen in relation to these root-causes of social and economic needs relating to underdevelopment of human and material resources in the developing countries. . . . Its activities will therefore be concentrated on responding to needs and requests which directly relate to the elimination of causes for social and economic privation and underdevelopment. The development of the material and human resources in the developing countries also has a constructive bearing on the struggle for justice and human dignity, as it increases the potential of the oppressed and underprivileged to shape their own destiny. (Cabinet paper on "Root Causes of Social and Economic Injustice," Agenda, Commission on World Service, 1977, Exhibit to D.1.C., p. 145)

This interdepartmental statement is excellent in its balanced definition of common concerns and relationships between departments of the LWF secretariat and between the secretariat and member churches. The debate really had to do largely with the place of diaconic work in the context of the church's social and political responsibilities, between the witness of "feet washing" and that of "public, prophetic protest." It might be asked, however, whether once again consensus was achieved in the LWF at the expense of a full ventilation of the controversy. The terminology of the discussion, for instance, lent itself at many points to ideological rhetoric, including that colored by Marxist views. The lines were not clearly drawn: some of one ideological stripe from the Southern Hemisphere found allies in the North, and those of differing views were also spread in the same way. Many concerned about dealing with the root causes of social and economic injustice combined those concerns with a more general political protest against the dominant liberal market economy. The fact is that such tensions—present in the LWF—were not always openly articulated.

The same is true about another controversial feature of the same debate: how human nature is to be understood in relation to social and political

structures. The emphasis on root causes came close at times to being captured by what can only be described as Marxist anthropology, in which
unjust structures are seen as the main cause of human estrangement and
poverty, and improved economic conditions as themselves providing the
only way of insuring human dignity. In contrast, many maintained that an
authentically Christian view of human nature starts from human sin as
causative of injustice, and that ultimately only the grace of redemption in
Christ leads to renewal and lasting liberty. Bruno Muetzelfeldt in 1979
gave the following description of the World Service commitment to hold
justice and liberation together:

> In all of this, however, there needs to be the realization, that, seen from a
> theological perspective, the so-called "root causes" are really only symptoms
> of the underlying cause of human rebellion against God's will and purpose.
> This root cause will disappear neither in response to development aid nor
> through the introduction of any new economic order. It yields only to the
> gospel of Christ's redeeming grace. (Report of the Director of World Service,
> 1979)

In 1987 a different nuance was given to the same issue by Muetzelfeldt's
successor as Director of World Service, Eugene Ries: "Hunger and poverty
are, ultimately, rooted in economic, social, cultural and political injustices
that hinder a fair distribution of the world's resources and the realization
of human potential, dignity, security and community" (Report of the
Director of World Service, 1987).

Such contrasts of perspective must not be construed rigidly as exclusive
alternatives. The debate on root causes was, for the Lutheran World Federation, an extremely rich one, essential to the work of diakonia. It helped
the Federation, even when at times sharp differences were not fully articulated, to deal substantively and creatively with the question of the relationships between service, sociopolitical realities, and the most
fundamental confession of Christian faith.

*A Confessional and/or Ecumenical Strategy.*   At several points in the
foregoing discussion, another recurrent issue has raised itself: Should the
work of Christian service be carried out on a strictly confessional basis, or
should it be pursued ecumenically?

The question must be seen in context. The LWF from the immediate
post–World War II period provided in its emergency services one viable and
effective model for service. Churches and their agencies and indeed the
World Council of Churches itself provided other models. Contrasts were
those between confessional and ecumenical approaches and also between
operational and nonoperational strategies.

One response to this question has been repeatedly made: that the LWF must give to the question an answer that allows for both/and. Yet there has not been unanimous acceptance of this position. Perhaps most notably, Ulrich Duchrow (b. 1935), Director of the LWF Department of Studies, 1969–77, in his volume *Conflict over the Ecumenical Movement: Confessing Christ Today in the Universal Church* (David Lewis, trans.; Geneva: World Council of Churches, 1981; German original, 1980), passionately attacked several aspects of LWF strategy. In particular, he criticized the Department of World Service which, he alleged, acted only out of a narrow confessionalism in its eagerness to maintain a position of economic privilege. In Duchrow's view the LWF was to be seen in the most parochial of terms, acting as a financial mastodon with little genuine concern for the actual interest of the underprivileged.

The question has subsequently been taken up in a vastly different and more constructive manner by Brian Neldner, Director of the Department of World Service, 1990–1995. He has referred to allegations from the outside that the LWF strategy for service is to be seen only within a confessional framework that is in fact "a constraint, an irritant, or an embarrassment" (Report of the Director of the Department of World Service, 1991). In the same report Neldner pointed out that even if staff were willing to become "an ecumenical foundation," the majority of LWF member churches would most likely have serious objections. Consequently, Neldner could see no other course than to continue acting as a confessional agency with as many joint ecumenical ventures as appropriate.

A number of such ecumenical ventures have attracted considerable attention. The Churches Drought Action in Africa, its successor in Africa, the Joint Relief Partnership, ecumenical efforts against apartheid in South Africa, and venerable ecumenical programs in Hong Kong are cases in point. More recently, Action by Churches Together (ACT), a joint program in Africa between the LWF and the World Council of Churches to which reference has also been made above, provides a remarkable example of potentially effective ecumenical work. ACT was born out of discussions between the LWF and the WCC and their related agencies. An initial proposal which gave guidelines for further negotiations and for widening the conversation with member churches was brought to the LWF Council in 1994. The Council in 1995 approved the establishment of ACT.

Referring to such cases, Brian Neldner has suggested a "third option" that avoids both confessional isolation and ecumenical fusion. He has rightly insisted that such fusion might in actuality be contrary to the convictions of many groups in the constituency—donors, national churches, and individuals alike. But the question remains whether it might be possible to make joint ecumenical operations part of a more flexible overall strategy for World Service. Would it be realistic, Neldner has asked, to create "working partnerships for major emergencies or operations on a case-by-case basis"? (ibid.).

*Structure, Administration, and Strategy.* "Restructuring" in the Lutheran World Federation, as has been demonstrated at several points in this volume, has not always successfully dealt with fundamental problems. The restructuring of 1969, for example, proved unable to remove palpable tensions between departments in the Geneva secretariat. Indeed, some have maintained that the decisions of 1969 exacerbated those tensions. The 1970s saw heated controversies between different offices in the secretariat and between different groups—commissions, to name one—within the Federation's constituency. While these problems were often simply those of adjusting to new administrative arrangements or those that inevitably arise between individuals, the main difficulties were actually inherent in the general challenges of the time as this account of "Debates during Transition" bears witness.

The period saw particular tension—if not animosity—between the LWF Department of World Service and its Department of Studies. Not only were the two directors, Bruno Muetzelfeldt and Ulrich Duchrow, in frequent disagreement, but it is also clear that the conflicts were rooted in rather different theological and ideological positions. This is reflected in the report of the 1977 meeting of the Commission on World Service, a meeting in which the discussion about root causes was a focal issue. Referring to some of the consequences of the 1969 restructuring decision to transfer a study desk from World Service to Studies, the report comes to the following acrid conclusions:

> Commission members also pointed to the special nature of the LWF involvement in these issues. Biblical theology rather than political ideologies should determine the church's involvement. . . . Members of the Commission on World Service expressed some surprise that a report of the Commission on Studies dealt critically with the area of work of the Commission on World Service and regretted that a document such as the one prepared by the Commission on Studies was prepared without prior reference to the Commission on World Service, which was directly involved and had extensively dealt with some of these issues. (Minutes, Commission on World Service, January, 1977)

As a result of this bitter conflict, the Commission on World Service decided to reestablish a study desk of its own, which subsequently became the Office for Research and Social Action (cf. Report of the Director of World Service, 1978–79). It was to this desk that analysis of root causes was assigned and it is a clear sign of the time that the first occupant of the office was Dr. Sibusisu Bengu (b. 1934), a black South African layperson whose academic field was political science. Bengu dedicated himself to the struggle against apartheid and other ideologies causative of social and economic injustice.

In 1980 Bruno Muetzelfeldt retired as Director of World Service and he was succeeded by Eugene Ries, an American who had been Associate Director of the Department and Director of the Community Development Service. As Director of CDS, Ries was succeeded by Christa Held of Germany, who remained in that position until 1993 (the CDS, as a result of the Curitiba restructuring, became part of the Department for Mission and Development in 1990). Ries retired as Director of World Service in 1990, when Brian Neldner, an Australian, became Director. Neldner in turn retired in 1995, and Rudolf Hinz (b. 1941) of Germany became Director of World Service.

The LWF restructuring of 1990, approved at the Curitiba Assembly, led to major strategic decisions for the Department for World Service (in this restructuring the names of LWF departments began to use the preposition "for" rather than "of"; additionally, the restructuring called for governing entities to be referred to as "Program Committees" rather than "Commissions"). According to decisions of the commission, special attention was now to be given to developing a balance between service projects in rural areas and those in "fast growing urban concentrations," to strengthening capabilities for disaster prevention, to lifting up a concern for ecological issues within the context of development education, and to pursuing careful studies of the "New International Economic Order" in order to contribute to a "more equitable division of wealth between nations." Further, it was at this time quite explicitly stated that LWF service projects should be focused on sustainable development as well as relief, in order to aid the preservation of human rights and to attain more equitable participation and inclusiveness (cf. Proceedings of the Program Committee on World Service, June 1990).

## Concluding Observations

A REVIEW of fifty years of service within the life of the Lutheran World Federation, even within the present limitations of space, reveals an impressively successful accomplishment. Through the generosity and sacrifice of churches and of committed donor agencies, which have been blessed with material strength, and through the skill and dedication of field staff and the leadership of an efficient secretariat, an achievement of considerable scope has been made possible.

Our sketch, however, has also indicated that the actions of mercy and service are never exempted from the ambiguities of social, political, and economic contexts. It is a fundamental Christian insight that those who are engaged in diaconic work are among those most subject to the temptations both of pride and of sacrificing only out of abundance. It is appropriate to point out that the service projects of the LWF—coming from the prosperity of the Northern churches to the overwhelming needs of the South—cannot be evaluated without a recognition that even such actions, undertaken in good will, carry within themselves elements of relativity, ambiguity, and contradiction.

Triumphalistic conclusions are, therefore, inappropriate. The history of service within the Lutheran World Federation, we have attempted to show, has from the very beginning been marked by a serious attempt to face the hard questions and ambiguities that mark both today's world and the witness of the churches within it. Virtually no challenge or criticism can be raised regarding Lutheran World Service that has not first been raised, in commission and department, by those responsible for the work itself. It belongs to human and institutional reality that honesty and insight do not of themselves prevent consequences that are far less than perfect.

The Lutheran World Federation has in numerous ways, not least within its work of service, recognized the root causes that lie behind social and economic injustice. It has also frequently been able to discover mechanisms that provide for at least relative progress in alleviating such injustices. Its participation in debate on such matters—with political groups, research institutions, and other nongovernmental agencies—antedated even the celebrated "Brundtland Report" of the United Nations, which gave high priority to such concerns. For example, the report of the Commission and Department of World Service to the Sixth Assembly of the LWF in Dar es Salaam in 1977 stated:

> The fact that in many situations disengagement could be effected demonstrates the importance of involving the local community right from the beginning in the planning and development of any program designed to assist them. Colonialism comes under many forms and one of the more subtle and yet pernicious ones is a paternalistic humanitarianism which helps effectively and yet perpetuates a dependency on the external benefactor. Help should not constitute an imposition of outside concepts, but ought to be consistent with the priorities set by the people themselves, relevant to their needs, in concert with their political aspirations and compatible with their cultural environment. By integrating its services into the overall plans and policies of the countries concerned and by encouraging those whose destiny is at stake to have a share in a common partnership of service, both the technical and practical base is established to allow for an orderly transfer to local management. Thus economic support and technical aid need not do violence to human dignity and impoverish further by generating dependencies. Instead its goal is to

strengthen local initiatives and promote development through indigenous resources. (Report of the Commission on World Service, *Reports 1970–1977* [Geneva: Lutheran World Federation, 1977] p. 200)

This sober statement represents literally decades of thoughtful research and debate, even as it also reflects concrete service activity which, in any realistic assessment, appears as a minuscule contribution to immense global problems. The urgency of the questions that World Service has faced remains: To what extent have the LWF's efforts to promote self-reliance proved successful? Has there always been a genuine will to delegate necessary and deserved responsibility to partners in the South? Has there consistently been a readiness to admit the real proportions of the clash of interests present in the global partnership of Lutheran churches?

The Lutheran World Federation, like other ecclesial and ecumenical bodies, has been privileged to be something other than an "old" colonial power with instrumental agencies. Precisely this difference allows the communion of Lutheran churches to avoid the creation and perpetuation of the domination of headquarters and donor agencies over field projects and recipients. The work of service, most ideally, requires both a shared Christian vision and the skills and efficiencies of a truly global agency. Much of the strength of LWF service initiatives lies in the untiring efforts of personnel, professional staff and volunteers alike. That dedication to a common vision has seldom led to rank amateurism is a clear fact. And yet here, too, questions remain: Has the work of service, based upon the solidarity of the common faith of Lutheran churches, consistently been demonstrated toward all who are in need regardless of their ethnicity, nationality, or religion? Has it proved possible to employ staff solely on the basis of professional skill? To what extent is confessional solidarity the proper factor for determining the accountability of staff and local groups involved in the work of service? The history of Lutheran World Service demonstrates the utter necessity of facing such questions even when the answers are partial, relative, or unclear.

Fifty years of cooperation in service in the Lutheran World Federation have been marked by both solid accomplishment and ongoing debate and controversy. Nevertheless, the dominant note—beyond instances of disagreement and even collision of interests—has been one of corporate action based on consensus. To be sure, the documents of both the Commission and the Department of World Service at times demonstrate a disproportionate desire for consensus and an avoidance of controversial or difficult decisions. Yet it has been the conviction of World Service that only through consensus is it possible to convey to all the desired reality of mutual understanding and common will. The following statement, made by the Governing Committee of the Community Development Service toward the end of its existence, is instructive:

> There was agreement that there must be a will and determination to be open for change; constant reflection should lead to a new vision. It was expressed that church structures may often hinder decision making processes and that all churches should be ready to challenge governments on difficult issues. New patterns of international decision making were discussed, and more participation of the south in decision making on granting of funds was requested. (CDS Overview, p. 37)

This statement reflects not only the accumulated experience of thirty years for the LWF Community Development Service; it also seems to be a clear description of the most appropriate overall strategy for the work of service within what is now understood as the global communion of Lutheran churches, the *communio*. It is the reality of communion that has made admirable accomplishment possible, and it is the communion that compels this ministry to proceed. It is, moreover, this reality that makes a strategy based both on consensus and on a willingness to learn from qualified opposition, criticism, and even controversy, a productive and viable way for the work of service to proceed.

**Bibliographical Notes**

I. Unpublished Documents

LWF Archives, Geneva.
Particularly:
Eggins, Edwin. "The Right Answer: An Account of Twenty-five Years of Lutheran World Service."
Held, Christa. *CDS Overview: 1962–1990.*
Issa, Hanna. "Love in Action—In His Service: The Story of LWF in the Middle East." 1970.
Senft, Kenneth C. *The Lutheran World Federation and the Displaced Person.* (Unpublished) M.Div. Thesis, Lutheran Theological Seminary, Gettysburg, PA 1952.

J. A. Aasgaard Papers, Luther Theological Seminary, St. Paul, Minnesota.
Hanns Lilje Papers, Lutheran Church Archives, Hanover.

II. Written Statements and Oral Interviews

Holger B. Hansen, Copenhagen.
Christa Held, Geneva.
Stewart Herman, Shelter Island Heights, New York.
Howard Hong, Northfield, Minnesota.
Risto Lehtonen, Helsinki.

Anza Lema, Dar es Salaam.
Carl Mau (†), Geneva and Philadelphia, Pennsylvania.
(N.B. Dr. Mau provided a great deal of research from the files and records of Lutheran World Service, Geneva).
Brian Neldner, Geneva.
Eugene Ries, Geneva.
Björn Ryman, Uppsala.
Bodil Sølling, Copenhagen.

III. Field Office Reports, Lutheran World Service

Ethiopia (1971–92), Nepal, India, Mauretania, Uganda, the Caribbean, Haiti.

IV. Printed Documents and Monographs

LWF Reports, passim.
*Proceedings* (all LWF Assemblies).
Bachman, John W. *Together in Hope: 50 Years of Lutheran World Relief.* New York: Lutheran World Relief, 1995.
Bachmann, E. Theodore. *Epic of Faith: The Background of the Second Assembly.* New York: National Lutheran Council, 1952.
Dahlgren, Sam. *Politik och Kyrka: Lutherska kyrkor I Östeuropa.* Stockholm: Verbum, 1989.
Duchrow, Ulrich. *Conflict over the Ecumenical Movement: Confessing Christ Today in the Universal Church.* Trans. David Lewis. Geneva: World Council of Churches, 1981.
Herman, Stewart W. *Report from Christian Europe.* New York: Friendship Press, 1953.
Hessler, Hans-Wolfgang. *Five Aspects of Development Work: An Analysis Based on Three Projects in Asia, Africa and Latin America.* Geneva: LWF Documentation, No. 2, April 1979.
Lissner, Jørgen. *The Politics of Altruism: A Study of the Political Behaviour of Voluntary Development Agencies.* Geneva: Lutheran World Federation, Department of Studies, 1977.
*Proceedings* (All LWF assemblies).
*Proclamation and Human Development:Document from a Lutheran World Federation Consultation, Nairobi, Kenya, October 21–25, 1974.* Geneva: Lutheran World Federation, 1975.
Ryman, Björn. *Förlåt oss våra Skulder: Tredje Världens skuldkris och kyrkorna.* KISA Rapport Nr. 4, Uppsala: Lutherhjälpen, 1989.
———. *Lutherhjälpens historia.* Stockholm: Verbum, 1997.
Solberg, Richard W. *As Between Brothers.* Minneapolis: Augsburg, 1957.
———. *Miracle in Ethiopia: A Partnership Response to Famine.* New York: Friendship Press, 1991.

9. Displaced persons being assisted by LWF staff member Kenneth Senft of the United States at Camp Valka, Nürnberg, 1949.

LWF Photo 1953

10. Augusta Victoria Hospital, Mount of Olives, Jerusalem, 1953. For security reasons, the LWF was requested by the UN to fly its flag above the hospital. As the Federation had no flag, Sylvester Michelfelder promptly designed one.

11. Signing an agreement between the UN High Commissioner for Refugees, the United Republic of Tanzania, and the LWF concerning rural settlement projects in Tanzania, 1967. LWF World Service persons are: first row, third from left, Bruno Muetzelfeldt; second row, third and fourth from left, Brian Neldner and Eugene Ries.

12. The treadle pump, developed by Rangpur Dinajpur Rural Service (LWF/World Service, Bangladesh) is a classic example of appropriate irrigation technology for small farmers.

13. An LWF/World
Service reforestation
project in Nouak-
chott, Mauretania.

14. Women ploughing as part of an LWF/CDS project in Peru. Loans from the
project made possible the purchase of oxen.

# 4

# Faithful to the Fundamental Task: Mission in the LWF

AS FAR AS THE MIDDLE of the nineteenth century, a common concern for mission was one of the driving forces for Lutheran unity. Some early landmarks of international Lutheran cooperation in mission were the emergency appeal for North American diaspora missionary helpers sounded at the Hanover Pentecost Conference of 1842 and Karl Graul's 1845 invitation on behalf of the Leipzig Evangelical Lutheran mission "to the Lutheran church in all lands" to unite in support of Lutheran mission work in India.

In 1868, several German Lutheran territorial churches met in Hanover to form the General Evangelical Lutheran Conference (AELK), a forerunner of the Lutheran World Convention. From 1868 to 1923 it met twenty-three times to facilitate international Lutheran cooperation in missions, as well as to champion the confessional principle as the basis for ecumenical relations. Delegates from sister churches in Scandinavia and North America were invited to attend meetings after 1870.

The First World War, dividing Lutherans of the North Atlantic region into hostile political camps, was particularly troubling for inter-Lutheran communication and solidarity. Yet the strong common commitment to Lutheran mission demonstrated in the nineteenth century once again become a key factor in forging international Lutheran solidarity. The Lutheran World Convention (LWC), meeting at Eisenach in 1923, barely five years after the armistice that ended World War I, identified "works of mercy," "foreign missions," and "care of migrating Lutherans" (*Diaspora-pflege*) as priority concerns of international Lutheranism (*LWC Proceedings*, Eisenach, 1923, Eng. ed., p. 13).

*James A. Scherer, Oak Park, Illinois, is the author of chapter 4.*

The Eisenach LWC meeting was overwhelmingly western in composition, being attended mainly by Germans, Scandinavians, and North Americans. A single Tamil Evangelical Lutheran Church leader from India was present, together with an American missionary serving in India and another from China. The agenda at Eisenach reflected anxious concern for the preservation of threatened Lutheran mission stations in the Southern Hemisphere, especially those established by German Lutheran missions. German mission groups were strongly represented at Eisenach.

Dr. Siegfried Knak of the Berlin Mission declared cooperation in foreign missions to be the clearest expression of the "real ecumenical quality in Lutheranism" (ibid., p. 67). Dr. Abel Ross Wentz (1893–1976) of the United States, summarizing his impressions of Eisenach, spoke of "the essential unity of Lutherans in all lands" as an occasion for praise. He envisioned "a glorious future" made possible by a unitary Lutheran organization stretching across oceans, beyond seas, rivers, and mountains, and leveling barriers of language and nationality (ibid., p. 177). Clearly, this idyllic vision of a newly united world Lutheranism—following the pain and division of World War I and the bitterness of Versailles—could not have arisen without the influence of the missionary factor.

The second meeting of the Lutheran World Convention in Copenhagen (1929) recognized the presence of Lutheran church leaders from India and Japan. It received an extensive report from the Jerusalem meeting of the International Missionary Council (1928). Pastor Appadurai of India spoke of the movement toward Lutheran unity in South India, while Pastor Inadomi of Japan pleaded that "the Lutheran Church in all the world [might] help the Church in Japan to realize her high aim to fulfill her God-given task" (*LWC Proceedings*, Copenhagen, 1929, Eng. ed., pp. 193, 197).

A special convention committee appointed by the Copenhagen meeting received resolutions (1) "call[ing] on all Lutherans everywhere to do their utmost to further the great cause of spreading the Gospel," (2) urging more unity and cooperation among Lutheran mission groups, (3) asking that the theological message of Lutheranism to the world be made more explicit, and (4) requesting increased Lutheran representation in the International Missionary Council (ibid., p. 204). The strengthening of ties between Lutheran "inner mission" workers in all countries was recommended. Similar concerns were voiced when the Lutheran World Federation was formed in 1947.

## Orphaned Missions

THE CONVERGENCE OF LUTHERANS around missionary work as a stimulus to Lutheran solidarity had a strong historical catalyst: orphaned mission aid.

Generous and enthusiastic support for increased Lutheran participation in global mission, as evidenced at Eisenach 1923, Copenhagen 1929, and later at Lund 1947, cannot be understood apart from special undertakings and commitments which, while closely related to the genesis of both the LWC and the LWF, took place outside the structure of those organizations.

Following the First World War, and during and following the Second World War, intense efforts were made by Lutherans and non-Lutherans on both sides of the Atlantic to rescue German and other orphaned missions, or "missions affected by war," as they were sometimes called. While there were marked differences between the situations of the First and Second World Wars, insofar as relations between Lutheran churches were concerned, heroic measures to save German and other missions threatened by war were a common feature of both periods.

At the outbreak of war in 1914, German overseas missions were concentrated overwhelmingly in British overseas colonial territories in Asia and Africa or in former German colonies occupied by Allied forces. German missionaries serving in these colonies were interned or repatriated, and their fledgling mission churches were generally cut off from both missionary leadership and mission board support.

Among the urgent problems facing the Continuation Committee of the 1910 Edinburgh World Missionary Conference were how to preserve these mission efforts from extinction and how to keep orphaned churches operating on an emergency basis. A special legal problem was how to prevent German mission properties from being seized as wartime reparations. When hostilities ended, there was the further need to enable German missionaries to return to their prewar fields as quickly as possible. Solving these problems required tact, diplomacy, and deep sensitivity to feelings on both sides of the wartime divide.

The consequences of orphaned mission assistance, though neither intended nor foreseen, were a powerful stimulus to Lutheran solidarity. Orphaned mission aid contributed to international Lutheran cooperation and to the healing of the breach between Lutherans on opposite sides of the war. In the following decades, emergency wartime instruments of cooperation would be forged into permanent operational arms of international Lutheran cooperation.

The United States–Canadian National Lutheran Council (NLC, 1918), working in conjunction with its missionary counterpart, the Lutheran Foreign Missions Conference of North America (LFMC), raised $700,000 in emergency aid for seven German and two Finnish mission societies after World War I. It dispatched orphaned mission funds to Africa, China, India, and Japan between 1918 and 1930. It also recruited and supported experienced missionaries who were assigned to superintend work in orphaned

German fields. This cooperation was a forerunner of the NLC Commission on Younger Churches and Orphaned Missions (CYCOM, 1948–52), and of the LWF Commission (CWM, 1947) and Department (DWM, 1952) of World Mission.

Under Article 438 of the Versailles Treaty (1919), the Edinburgh Continuation Committee secured recognition of the "supra nationality" of mission properties and arranged for German orphaned missions to be placed under the trusteeship responsibility of another group holding the same faith. It was agreed that Lutherans, working through the NLC and LFMC, would assume sole responsibility for Lutheran orphaned missions, while the newly organized International Missionary Council (IMC, 1921), successor to the Edinburgh Continuation Committee, would take major responsibility for non-Lutheran orphaned fields.

This led to the extensive entry of American, Canadian, Swedish, and Australian Lutheran missionaries into former German Lutheran fields. While this was normally done on a temporary trusteeship basis, in some cases it resulted in agreements for the permanent transfer of former German fields to other Lutheran mission agencies. In South India, the Church of Sweden Mission took over responsibility for Tamil mission work from the Leipzig Mission. American Lutherans in India came to the aid of the Hermannsburg, Breklum, and Gossner mission fields. In Papua New Guinea, missionaries of the Neuendettelsau and Rhenish missions were replaced by representatives of the United Evangelical Lutheran Church of Australia and the American Iowa Synod. In East Africa, American Augustana Synod missionaries assumed trusteeship responsibilities on behalf of the Leipzig, Bethel, and Berlin missions. In 1927 Augustana relinquished these and secured its own field in Central Tanganyika.

Permanent transfers included the United Lutheran Church in America's purchase of the Berlin Mission's China (Shantung) field, the Joint Ohio Synod's acquisition of the Hermannsburg Mission's India (South Andhra) field, and the Iowa Synod's replacement of the Rhenish Mission in its Papua New Guinea (Madang) field. These changes gave a great boost to the principle of internationalizing support for threatened mission fields, with a view to making them less vulnerable to disruptions caused by war.

The Second World War—a kind of déjà vu for orphaned missions—dealt a second heavy blow to Lutheran world missions. Not only were German mission societies affected (the Hitler regime as early as 1935 restricted the transfer of funds gathered for German overseas missions) but this time mission societies of Denmark, Finland, and Norway were also prevented from sending funds abroad. The IMC and the NLC again quickly agreed that Lutherans should be responsible for helping Lutheran missions affected by war, while the IMC would assume responsibility for non-Lutheran missions.

The NLC collected and administered orphaned mission grants from U.S. and Canadian Lutheran churches amounting to $6 million dollars between 1939 and 1952. The Church of Sweden Mission and the Swedish Evangelical Mission provided similar emergency help and undertook added trusteeship responsibilities in Tanganyika. Australian Lutherans provided personnel for the Neuendettelsau mission field in Papua New Guinea. In all, twenty-three mission fields served by two Finnish and fifteen German societies were assisted. These programs and activities form the immediate missionary background of the first LWF Assembly at Lund.

## The Lund Assembly

THE 1947 LUND ASSEMBLY, described by the first LWF Executive Secretary as "the most significant gathering ever attempted by Lutherans of the world" (S. C. Michelfelder, *Proceedings,* Lund, p. 5), served to reinforce and consolidate preassembly mission developments. It also foreshadowed new advances.

Lund built on positive experiences of orphaned mission assistance. It gave expression through the new LWF Constitution to the nature of the LWF as a free association of autonomous Lutheran churches seeking "to bear united witness before the world to the Gospel of Jesus Christ" and "to cultivate unity of faith and confession among the Lutheran churches of the world" (LWF Const., III, 2, a,b). The LWF could act as the agent of member churches in matters assigned to it. This included missionary cooperation between member churches and their related mission agencies.

The keynote address at Lund by Ralph Long (1882–1948), Executive Director of the U.S. National Lutheran Council, singled out orphaned mission assistance as a "ray of light" shining in the darkness of the wartime years, giving hope and courage to prepare for better things during peacetime years. "Out on the far-flung lines of Lutheran missionary enterprises the light shone brighter than elsewhere," said Long. The American churchman doubtless reflected personal pride in the achievements which his own agency, the NLC, had made and would continue to make through its Commission on Younger Churches and Orphaned Missions, the immediate predecessor of CWM and DWM (*Proceedings,* Lund, p. 129).

The report of Section II at Lund, dealing with the mission of the Lutheran Church in a devastated world, presents a comprehensive understanding of Lutheran mission (ibid., pp. 61–84). Lutheran mission, said the report, is determined by two factors: "confessing the truth" and the special needs of the world in our time. The broader context of Lutheran world missions included evangelism ("telling the good news") and stewardship ("doing the work of the Lord"), understood as good fruits by which faith is tested and carried out in the spirit of serving love. All were seen as functional activities indispensable to the life of the church.

The fundamental impulse for world missions, as Lund saw it, was "the saving work, the example, and the commission of Jesus Christ." The church as the body of believers must live and proclaim the gospel abroad, else it will incur the Lord's condemnation and perish; the church in every nation and every local congregation will propagate its faith in every possible direction. The missionary impulse is a "most vital principle" in the life of the church: "the obligation to carry the gospel to every human being is a sacred responsibility entrusted to all Christians."

Unity of faith among Lutherans the world over, while tolerating divergence in practice, was seen as something distinctive of Lutheran mission. Lutherans acknowledged the supreme authority of God's Word, affirmed the central position of Christ and his work, upheld justification of the sinner by grace through faith, and maintained "the absoluteness of Christianity" in relation to non-Christian faiths.

At Lund Ralph Long boldly challenged the assembly to develop a comprehensive plan of missionary cooperation through a common Lutheran agency, and a united global strategy. Resolutions from the Lund Assembly mandated "full cooperation on the home fields," steps toward Lutheran union in mission areas, and the "formation of nation-wide Lutheran churches." Lund called for the immediate implementation of these directives through the creation of a new Commission on World Missions (CWM)—popularly referred to in the 1950s and 1960s as the LWF's "world mission parliament." Five years later, at the LWF Hanover Assembly (1952), this Commission was equipped with an efficient executive arm known as the Department of World Mission (DWM).

The Lund Assembly marked an important step in the crucial transition from a mainly Western-oriented and directed Lutheran sending effort toward one that, especially after Evian (1970), reflected the autonomy and interdependence of Lutheran churches in all six continents. Despite its transitional character, Lund showed that it had deeply absorbed prophetic lessons from the wartime experience, particularly as related to the provision of emergency assistance, negotiating trusteeship arrangements, and internationalizing mission work. At Lund it was recognized that no return to the older pattern of Western missionary paternalism was possible.

The Lund Assembly authorized the LWF Executive Committee "to promote the widest possible cooperation of Lutheran churches throughout the world" on behalf of orphaned mission fields, with a view to preserving them and returning them to their former supporting agencies as soon as possible. It supported proposals of the International Missionary Council that called for consultation between societies exercising temporary trusteeship rights over former German mission fields and representatives of German mission societies in matters affecting the future of those areas. The aim was to forestall permanent claims to possession by temporary trustees, except where mutual agreements existed to transfer a field permanently to the orphaned mission trustee.

In a most significant policy statement, Lund proposed that "in each area a National Lutheran Church may be developed, including all Lutheran churches in the area, so that an indigenous, self-supporting Lutheran church may carry forward in a unified way the work of the Kingdom in that area." Member churches were asked "to encourage the formation, as soon as practicable, of united Lutheran churches in the various mission fields."

The Lund Assembly set forth a vision of ecumenical mission far in advance of where most Lutheran churches and mission agencies were at the time. It also gave authorization to new instruments of international Lutheran cooperation which would decisively change relations between mission agencies and emerging Lutheran churches. Without fully grasping the long-term consequences, Lund encouraged the growth of autonomous Lutheran churches in Asia, Africa, Latin America, and Oceania and their development toward greater selfhood and maturity. This step would in time transform the LWF from a predominantly North Atlantic community into a worldwide *koinonia* of churches.

## CYCOM, CWM and DWM

THE NEW COMMISSION on World Missions (CWM), appointed by the LWF Executive Committee in response to the Lund Assembly resolution, met for the first time at Oxford in 1949. CWM and its successor after 1970, the Commission on Church Cooperation (CCC), would continue to meet every year, normally gathering each time in a different country at the invitation of a mission society or an LWF member church.

CWM's main function lay in providing a forum for mutual consultation and discussion of common policy issues and mission opportunities. Its annual meetings were also the venue for geographically or functionally organized consultations. Only rarely did CWM/DWM become operational, as for example in the case of Radio Voice of the Gospel, and then only for a short duration. Even though CWM possessed only deliberative authority, it faced suspicion in the early years of wanting to act as a "super-missionary society," coercing independent mission agencies into becoming part of united Lutheran structures against their will. CWM in response adopted a policy statement assuring independent societies and boards "that there would be no encroachment" on their rights and functions.

CWM, at its annual meetings, provided a neutral setting for younger churches and mission agency leaders from around the Lutheran world to learn to know each other as persons, to exchange experiences and insights, and even to develop beneficial and lasting friendships. In time a spirit of positive goodwill, trust and cooperation developed. CWM became the annual occasion for meetings of regional and functional coordinating committees. It brought together representatives of missions and churches working in the same area or facing common problems. Average attendance at CWM meetings numbered 150 persons.

In certain countries, for example, Taiwan, Papua New Guinea, and Madagascar, CWM facilitated the uniting of Lutheran mission staffs. It led to the formation of Lutheran coordinating committees for Tanganyika, Ethiopia, and South Africa. It is credited with influencing Lutheran unity developments in India and Japan. CWM assisted in negotiations with the government of Israel over compensation for confiscated lands and with Jordan and Ethiopia for the return of mission property.

CWM meetings featured plenary presentations on important topics, such as the Lutheran concept of church autonomy, partnership between younger churches and mission agencies, Lutherans and the ecumenical movement, the challenge of Islam, the church and the Jewish people, salvation and healing, use of mass media, and many others.

Until the LWF Hanover Assembly (1952), however, CWM had no executive arm and continued to rely heavily on the National Lutheran Council's Commission on Younger Churches and Orphaned Missions (CYCOM) for administrative assistance. By 1952, CYCOM was ready to phase out its emergency orphaned mission assistance program. (Only in Tanzania would the NLC continue to carry administrative responsibilities for former German fields.)

At its 1952 annual meeting in Hamburg, CWM received and endorsed a proposal that the New York office of CYCOM be closed, and that its responsibilities be taken over by a new LWF Department of World Missions to be established in Geneva under the authority of the LWF Executive Committee. The Hanover Assembly, concurring with this recommendation, made the new DWM Geneva staff responsible for orphaned missions and, "in cooperation with an inclusive group of representatives from younger churches, the Lutheran mission boards and societies, to continue and extend the field of cooperation among the younger churches, the mission boards and societies."

A six member Commission on World Missions, known as "CWM Proper," was now created, and it became in effect the board for the Department of World Missions. CWM meetings were, however, open as before to representatives of mission societies and younger churches. The Department of World Missions welcomed its first full-time director in the person of Dr. Fridtjov Birkeli of Norway, who took office in 1954. Until his arrival, former CYCOM Executive Secretary, Dr. Fredrik A. Schiotz, served in an interim capacity as DWM Director.

The transitional character of CWM/DWM as an agency for world missionary cooperation is clearly reflected in these developments. The LWF Executive Committee limited CWM/DWM's sphere of operation to missionary cooperation in Asia, Africa, and Oceania. CWM Proper consisted of six representatives selected from Lutheran churches in Asia and Africa and from mission boards and societies in Europe and North America. CWM's rotating membership included three each from the North and the South. DWM directors until quite recently were former western mission executives, assisted by Asian, African, and Western staff colleagues.

Latin America formed no part of CWM/DWM. For supervision of Lutheran diaspora ministries in Latin America, the Hanover Assembly created a Committee on Latin America, headed by Stewart W. Herman, with its office attached to the NLC in New York. (In 1965 the LWF Office for Latin America was transferred to Geneva.) Eastern Europe, with its minority churches, was also excluded from CWM/DWM and placed under the supervision of a minority churches secretariat within the Department of World Service. This office was responsible for interchurch aid and consultative services to Lutheran diaspora and minority churches in Eastern Europe.

Prior to Evian 1970, CWM/DWM remained a one-directional arrangement for missionary cooperation in two continents. It coordinated mission sending by Western mission agencies and mission receiving by churches in Asia, Africa, and Oceania. It became an effective clearing house (one former CWM leader described it as a "stock market") for donors and receivers to coordinate grant requests, jointly plan programs, and discuss strategies. At no time did it represent the evangelistic outreach and planning of Lutheran "majority" churches in Europe or North America, apart from their overseas mission departments.

Despite the visionary head start given to international Lutheran missionary cooperation by the Lund Assembly, CWM/DWM failed to carry forward the vision of mission in six continents to its next logical stage. CWM/DWM did not become a multi-directional global forum for sharing mission resources and drawing up international mission strategies between Lutheran churches in all six continents. Still beholden to mission agency initiatives and western funding sources, it did not adequately recognize the pressing claims of emerging churches in the Third World, and their desire to participate as decision makers and full partners rather than as mere recipients of western benevolence.

Among CWM/DWM's achievements were the holding of continent-wide All-Africa and All-Asia Lutheran Conferences (for example, Marangu, 1955, cf. pp. 52–54 above; Ranchi 1961), the launching of a highly significant communication venture (RVOG, 1963), the introduction of new programs for theological education and research in Asia and Africa, the joint establishment with the WCC of the Christian Medical Commission (CMC), and the provision of scholarship and other leadership training programs.

## Evian 1970: A Turning Point
## for LWF Mission Involvement

THE FIFTH LWF ASSEMBLY met at Evian, France (1970), in a meeting transferred only weeks before the date of the assembly from its intended site in Porto Alegre, Brazil. Evian's missionary theme, "Sent into the World," had been purposely chosen to dramatize a serious Lutheran commitment to mission in the entire world. The report of Section I, "Sent with the Gospel," was an eloquent presentation of the concept of holistic, church-centered evangelization, based on the call of baptism.

However, the sudden and controversial decision by LWF officers to change the venue of the assembly because of human rights violations in Brazil, and because necessary conditions for holding an assembly in that country could not be assured, had immediate consequences. It pointed to important new dimensions of the meaning of mission in the modern world. After Evian, concern for human justice as an aspect of mission could not be ignored. In the turbulent atmosphere of the Evian Assembly, it proved impossible for the LWF to arrive at a simple consensus on issues of world mission. The Sixth Assembly at Dar es Salaam (1977) would push this tendency still further by making opposition to *apartheid* an expression of faithfulness to the church's mission.

Of greater long-term significance than the Evian Assembly's report of Section I, "Sent with the Gospel," however, was the decision taken by the LWF Executive Committee prior to Evian to restructure all mission-related activities of the LWF and to consolidate them in a new Commission and Department of Church Cooperation (CCC/DCC). This was a decisive turning point in the life of the LWF. It marked the final transition from an era in which CWM/DWM had been mainly responsible for defining LWF mission theology and policy to one in which LWF member churches assumed that responsibility.

The shift involved changes in both the theological understanding of mission and in structural relationships between missions and churches. The LWF restructuring of mission was preceded and undoubtedly influenced by the integration of the International Missionary Council (IMC) into the World Council of Churches, which had taken place at the WCC New Delhi Assembly (1961). Many of the concerns voiced with regard to integrating mission into the life of the churches before the IMC-WCC merger were also heard in connection with discussions on the proposed new LWF structure. Some of them actually erupted in floor debates at Evian.

Restructuring at Evian was carried out with the intention of making mission the responsibility of every LWF member church—east or west, south or north—and an expression of the church's total life. "Mission was grasped as the total task of the church in the world. Evangelism was at its centre and it included as integral elements diaconic service, prophetic witness for justice and the sharing of spiritual and material resources," said a later report from CCC to the Sixth Assembly. .

Accompanying this holistic understanding of mission were structural changes that eliminated parallel and overlapping programs run by different LWF departments and made mission services more accessible to all churches. The main functions of the former CWM/DWM were now brought together with programs of the Committee on Latin America and of the European minority churches secretariat formerly within the Department of World Service. Work of the earlier LWF Commission on Stewardship and Evangelism was also incorporated. The new Commission and Department of Church Cooperation (CCC/DCC) was to become the common carrier for all these mission emphases and activities.

These proposals ran into opposition at Evian. In introducing such far-reaching structural changes, the executive committee had not given an adequate theological rationale for doing so, nor did it offer a clear theological vision of the meaning of mission. Accordingly, many felt that abolition of the older CWM/DWM structure and its replacement by a Commission and Department of Church Cooperation signaled a betrayal of the LWF commitment to mission or, at the very least, a weakening of the central place which mission had occupied in the post-Lund structure.

For some—especially for independent mission societies that faced the loss of their secure place in the new structure—the sweeping structural changes introduced at Evian meant the eclipse of a trusted and familiar pattern of world mission cooperation by an integrated and as yet untried structural experiment. The new Commission on Church Cooperation was designed as a forum and an instrument of cooperation for representatives of Lutheran churches from all six continents, with no representation provided for mission societies. The numerous coordinating committees which formerly met in conjunction with CWM now began to meet on their own. CCC/DCC attempted to accommodate the needs of mission agencies in this period by organizing special consultations and fostering mutual contact through a *Lutheran Mission Directory.*

On the floor of the LWF Assembly at Evian, many controversial issues came into focus during a heated debate on the proposed name of the new commission. Was mission still to be understood primarily as the select task of specially called individuals called "missionaries," the majority of them sent by Western agencies? Or could mission now be embraced as the task of the whole people of God in every place? What was implied by the new integrated concept of mission? Were member churches prepared to give their blessing to a proposal whose consequences they could not yet fully grasp?

"Alarmed and concerned over the omission of the word *mission* from the proposed new structure," said one recommendation from the floor, "we recommend that the name of the proposed 'Commission on Church Cooperation' be changed to 'Commission on Church Cooperation in World Mission.'" A similar recommendation had received strong support at the final CWM meeting in St. Louis (1970) just prior to Evian.

Those supporting the motion, including both mission society representatives and some Third World church leaders, argued that deletion of the word "mission" was a betrayal of the assembly theme, "Sent into the World." Their concern was for the continuing place of mission in the life of the LWF. "Mission implies more than cooperation", reads the Evian account; "it means proclamation, and therefore the word *mission* is necessary."

On advice from the Policy and Reference Committee at Evian, however, the motion to add the words "in World Mission" to the name of the new commission was defeated. Even so, the Fifth Assembly later unanimously adopted a statement introduced by Gunnar Staalsett of Norway. His resolution urged member churches and related mission agencies "faithfully to work for the proclamation of the gospel to all nations." While the Evian Assembly adopted the proposed new structure and the new name for the commission, there was clearly widespread questioning of the wisdom of these decisions and ambiguity about their meaning for the future of missionary cooperation in the LWF.

Those supporting the new structure and new name proposed by the executive committee had weighty arguments on their side. At Evian, "mission" was still a term loaded with negative connotations, and suggestive of Western colonial domination. Newly independent churches in countries which had undergone decolonization were being admitted to the LWF as full members on the basis of their autonomy and equality. They did not wish to be regarded as wards of Western mission societies, as appeared to be the case in the old CWM/DWM structure.

The late Stefano Moshi, then Presiding Bishop of the Evangelical Lutheran Church of Tanzania, in arguing against inclusion of the term "mission," put it this way: "Mission, being Western mission domination, belongs to the past. The churches in Asia and Africa are equal partners to the churches in the West. We, therefore, want the name 'Church Cooperation.'"

Other factors pointed to the need for a more integrated mission structure. Apart from programs on stewardship and evangelism, the LWF had not yet challenged its own Western member churches to do mission among their own population. Now large folk churches in Western Europe were experiencing shrinking membership and participation. Handicapped in their outreach to youth and to a secularized population, they recognized that growing churches in the Third World might have something to teach them about vital faith and evangelization.

In some European countries, particularly West Germany, independent mission societies were being integrated into territorial church structures as mission departments. The aim was to enable these churches to take responsibility for doing mission "at their own doorstep" as well as at the ends of the earth. In North America, where by the end of the 1960s church growth had reached a plateau, Lutheran churches were placing renewed emphasis on discipleship training and evangelism activities. The traditional separation between mission overseas and homeland evangelism was proving anachronistic.

In Eastern Europe, where Lutheran churches had by 1970 largely "normalized" their relationships with socialist regimes—symbolized by the "church amid socialism" in East Germany, and the "church of diakonia" in Hungary—churches began to feel a call to proclaim the gospel in word and deed, not as a counterideology, but as a message of hope. These churches needed to act discreetly, not antagonizing state authorities, nor tending to upset the delicate balance. Anything suggestive of an anticommunist "mission crusade" had to be avoided. Thus the proposal to add "World Mission" to the name of the new commission did not receive support from these churches.

Under the pre-Evian structure, the LWF had related to East European "minority" churches mainly in terms of interchurch aid, special services to clergy and congregations, and support for consultations. The new structure would continue these services but also provide the challenge to focus on mission opportunities within the atheistic Marxist context. The possibility of holding the Seventh Assembly in Budapest, Hungary (1984) was a major fruit of this policy.

The LWF Committee/Commission on Latin America had served immigrant churches of diverse national backgrounds and provided ministry for diaspora congregations scattered throughout the continent. Most of these preserved the languages and cultures of the countries from which they came. Under the new structure, Latin American immigrant Lutherans would be linked more closely to churches growing out of mission efforts. They were encouraged to relate to Spanish and Portuguese vernacular languages and to local cultural contexts, as the large Brazilian member church had already begun doing during World War II. The aim was to foster a sense of mission in the total Latin American Lutheran community. This development was greatly facilitated by the holding of a series of Latin American Lutheran Congresses and conferences of Latin American Lutheran church presidents.

In addition to geographical factors, it was important that the missionary intention be seen as permeating all functional activities of separate LWF units. Diaconic service, community development, witness for justice, interchurch aid, theological education, evangelism, ecumenical relationships, worship, studies, and communication were not to be seen as activities competing for scarce resources but, in principle if not in fact, as all having the church's mission task as their central aim.

According to new CCC mandates, "all inter-church relations were now to be developed with the goal of enabling both giving and receiving churches to fulfill their mission obligation, inside and outside their own national boundaries, not in isolation or through domination, but as true partners in a common global task of mission." The implication was that all member churches, whether rich or poor, were both givers and receivers. The integrated structure would mean something new, not only for relations between the LWF and its member churches, but also for the inner workings of LWF commissions, departments, executive committee, and general secretariat.

Composition of the new twelve-member Commission on Church Cooperation, reflecting its enlarged scope, included two persons each from Eastern and Western Europe, North America, Latin America, Africa (including Madagascar), and Asia (including Oceania). Annual meetings, normally about ten days in length, were held in different member countries and continents on a rotating basis. Most often, three or four day consultations were appended to CCC annual meetings.

CCC meetings included local visitation programs to enable members of local host churches to become acquainted with LWF representatives, and vice versa. In addition to the twelve members of CCC proper, invitations were sent to representatives of national committees, regional and local church representatives and consultants. DCC staff members were also in attendance.

## Further Restructuring before Curitiba

IN 1987 the LWF Executive Committee mandated a further study on restructuring prompted by both theological and practical considerations. Theologically speaking, the aim was to develop a structure which would express a new vision of relationships between LWF member churches going beyond federative association toward communion (*koinonia*) in Christ. At the same time, practical considerations demanded that the LWF move toward adopting a more economical structure that would permit the Federation to carry out all its operations within a balanced budget.

The need to reduce expenses as part of restructuring would lead to greater centralization of policy making and would result in fewer decisions taken at local or regional levels, fewer meetings and consultations, and a 20% reduction in headquarters staff. The proposed structural recommendation, adopted by the LWF Executive Committee in 1989 prior to the LWF Eighth Assembly (Curitiba, 1990), had immediate implications for CCC/DCC, as it had emerged after Evian. In the new structure, commissions such as the Commission on Church Cooperation ceased to exist as separate bodies and were replaced by Program Committees of the new LWF Council.

The mission function within the LWF would now be carried out by a new Department for Mission and Development (DMD), significantly reclaiming the term "mission" jettisoned at Evian. After Curitiba, *diakonia* and development would be recognized as integral expressions of mission and incorporated into the work of DMD. The newly constituted LWF Council, combining functions and responsibilities of the former executive committee and the major commissions, became the sole policy and decision making body of the LWF between assemblies.

The council itself was divided into five program committees, one of which was the Program Committee on Mission and Development. Four experts on mission and development were to be chosen as consultants; they meet annually at council meetings along with council members assigned to the Program Committee on Mission and Development, but had no voting rights in council plenary sessions. In comparison to the representative process that obtained at earlier CCC meetings, it has been argued that the input of LWF member churches into the decision-making process has now been greatly reduced.

The specific assignment of the Department for Mission and Development, under the post-Curitiba structure, was to "encourage and support Lutheran churches, agencies and other groups as they endeavor to create, develop and maintain ministries faithful to the fundamental task of the church to participate in the whole mission of God to the whole world." Mission and ministry were conjoined as aspects of this "fundamental task."

Under the new mandate, traditional mission agencies were again granted a participatory role in the LWF mission program similar to the one which they had enjoyed under CWM/DWM, but from which they tended to be excluded by CCC/DCC. Information sharing and practical cooperation between the LWF and mission organizations were intensified through special consultations between DMD and Lutheran mission agencies.

Some departmental roles and functions were modified under the new DMD mandate. Studies relating to mission and evangelism were now carried out by the department. The former Community Development Service (CDS), providing member churches with opportunities to respond to local development needs through project assistance and expertise, was transferred to DMD.

The new department was mandated to provide member churches with consultative services in the field of communication. It was also made responsible for special LWF programs in such areas as Women in Church and Society, youth, Christian education, theological education, and leadership training. DMD was organized with area desks having programmatic responsibilities related to a broad range of assignments. In effect, DMD became general administrator for the majority of LWF projects affecting member churches.

In this final period leading to the LWF Ninth Assembly scheduled for 1997, the structural arrangement for international missionary cooperation was more streamlined and centralized than at any time in the fifty-year history of the LWF. At the same time, its agenda was becoming more diffuse. Fewer staff executives were involved, and fewer mission-related meetings and consultations were held. And yet the total scope of the department's work was expanded. Critics of the structural change maintained that the LWF was moving beyond the definition of mission adopted by Evian toward one which was in danger of becoming totally amorphous in the post-Curitiba period. DMD was becoming, in effect, an ecclesiastical bureaucracy providing interchurch aid, diverse mission services, and church development assistance. Mission and development were combined in a single department. More varied activities were undertaken under the umbrella of "mission" than previously. Mission, as the "fundamental task of the church," and closely identified with "the whole mission of God to the whole world," was expanded to embrace a comprehensive range of services geared to the upbuilding and strengthening of the worldwide Lutheran family. This reflected DMD's new and broader mandate. But it also raised the question of whether the specificity of mission had been lost in the new structure.

## Important LWF Mission Initiatives and Programs

### Radio Voice of the Gospel

The opening of Radio Voice of the Gospel (RVOG) in the environs of Addis Ababa, Ethiopia, on February 26, 1963, was described at the Helsinki Assembly that same year as "none other than a miracle of God" (*Proceedings,* Helsinki, p. 403). The project had been initiated by the LWF Broadcasting Service as authorized by the Federation's Commission on World Mission in 1957.

In the late fifties the transistor had become available, making the reception of radio messages possible everywhere. Radio fitted into the oral tradition in the developing world, so it could be predicted that radio would become a privileged medium of communication in many developing countries. In 1959, Dr. Sigurd Aske (1914–1991) of Norway was appointed the first director of the radio project and in 1961 general director of the LWF Broadcasting Service.

RVOG was unique in religious broadcasting for a variety of reasons. In a summary way it can be said that its program philosophy was based on three principles: the radio ministry should serve the mission of the church, be contextual and true to life, and be culturally relevant. Since programs had to be produced in the areas where they would be heard, RVOG did not accept program packages produced in Europe or North America. (Manfred Lundgren, *Proclaiming Christ to His World: The Experience of Radio Voice of the Gospel, 1957–1977* [Geneva: Lutheran World Federation, 1983], p. 169).

RVOG's programming was designed to meet the needs of the whole person, as an individual and a member of society. It aimed at being 70% educational and cultural with an emphasis on development education, and 30% evangelistic. This holistic understanding of the churches' ministry was seen as being biblical as well as corresponding to the African understanding of life as an entity. This "30/70" policy was only a guideline, and the reality was often different. It was even the view of some that the programs should be seen as 100% Christian insofar as they catered to the total needs of the whole human being.

RVOG also provided professional support to area studios in the form of technical and production training and various consultative services. Much emphasis was placed on awareness building and media education among church workers in order to strengthen the follow-up work of the churches.

An area was considered for regular broadcasts only if there was a local church ready and able to assume the responsibility for program production and follow-up work. However, there were two exceptions—areas closed to regular church and mission work (China) or where the political situation constituted a special need (South Africa) (Lundgren, p. 163).

At the peak of its operation in 1972, RVOG was broadcasting an average of twenty hours a day on two 100-kw shortwave transmitters located in Addis Ababa and nearly seven hours a day on medium wave. During its relatively short history, RVOG broadcast 117,301 hours of programs in twenty different languages, produced in nineteen area production studios in Africa, the Middle East, and Asia. Broadcasts to Latin America, though technically possible, were never carried out.

A very important part of the operation were the daily newscasts in seven languages broadcast from the newsroom in Addis Ababa and staffed by professional journalists using international wire services. Even though increasingly subject to censorship by the Communist government of Ethiopia, the RVOG news service managed to maintain its integrity and in general had a reputation for reliability and objectivity. However, a distinction had to be made between the concept of integrity and the Western concept of "free flow of information." To a large extent, the newscasts made up the positive image and reputation of the station (Lundgren, pp. 191–96). In turn RVOG contributed significantly to building up the image and credibility of local churches in society, as the radio medium was put at their disposal and thus given a chance to speak with a culturally relevant voice in society. RVOG also enhanced the LWF's external image as many people identified the LWF with it.

RVOG was broadly ecumenical, including among its partners the Near East Christian Council, the World Association for Christian Communication, the Ethiopian Orthodox Church, the Lutheran Church—Missouri Synod , and other agencies. The work of RVOG and other communication efforts led quite directly to the formalization of LWF communication work within the Geneva secretariat and ultimately to the establishment of the LWF's Commission and Department of Communication in 1980.

On March 12, 1977, fourteen years after its inauguration, Radio Voice of the Gospel was nationalized by the Provisional Military Government of Ethiopia. Its Addis Ababa buildings and equipment were confiscated and used for the services of the Radio Voice of Revolutionary Ethiopia. At that time there were 212 staff members at RVOG in Addis Ababa, with a budget for 1976 of $1,228,015. Its capital cost amounted to $2.4 million and the total running cost of its operation since 1963 was $12,436,007.

At the time of its nationalization, RVOG's 12 production studios with over 200 staff lost their outlet and had considerable difficulties in continuing their communication ministries. However, most of them are still operating, broadcasting over shortwave transmitters in Africa (FEBA Seychelles and TWR South Africa and Swaziland) or over local and national outlets. Several have been transformed into communication centers that use a multimedia approach in their work. Through its Department for Mission and Development, the LWF continues to support them financially and with consultative services. The impact of RVOG's efforts in building communication awareness among the churches can be seen in the diversified use of media in their ministry and mission. The long range impact of RVOG can perhaps best be identified in the ongoing requests from the churches to reestablish the LWF Broadcasting Service in Africa.

In 1988 the Ethiopian government agreed to the payment to the LWF of Birr 1,200,000 in compensation for the takeover of RVOG and to returning its collection of taped African music. This money has now been allocated for buildings and equipment for communication ministry of the member churches in Ethiopia and Eritrea.

## Proclamation and Human Development

From early 1971 until October 1974, Lutheran missionary thinking was deeply troubled by a recognized dichotomy between evangelization and human development, and separate funding for each, as aspects of mission work. The issue was raised as early as 1971 and later formulated in a statement by the Ethiopian Evangelical Church Mekane Yesus (EECMY).

Composed by eight members of the EECMY Executive Committee and circulated among LWF member churches under the title "On the Interrelation between Proclamation of the Gospel and Human Development," the statement raised questions about development aid criteria in general. It quickly zeroed in on the wide disparity between generous funding by Western donors for economic and social development, in comparison to the meager assistance offered to EECMY for evangelization.

The Ethiopian member church, then undertaking evangelistic outreach in unevangelized areas and experiencing unprecedented numerical growth, found itself simultaneously challenged by demands of social development activities and by responsibility to provide spiritual nurture for its rapidly growing membership. For the EECMY, the deeper issue was one of a "responsible church ministry" that balanced the "commission to preach the gospel of Jesus Christ to all nations" with the obligation to "heal brokenness and make people whole," that is, to restore God's plan of creation. A related issue was the identity and integrity of an independent African church that felt its hands tied by aid criteria set by overseas donors, which did not match the African church's own objectives and priorities.

Discussion provoked by the EECMY letter led to the holding of an international consultation on Proclamation and Human Development in Nairobi, Kenya (October 21–25, 1974) that dealt with two main topics, "A More Responsible Church Ministry" and "A More Flexible International Aid-Relationship." The consultation report concluded that proclamation takes place through both word and deed, and that there is a basic unity between mission and service. It urged that LWF programs be designed to serve the whole person and that vertical and horizontal dimensions of church outreach programs not be divided. The consultation also warned against relationships that created dependence or fostered paternalism. This discussion was helpful in clarifying relationships between LWF policies and programs of mission, service, and community development (see pp. 65–66 above, *et passim*).

### Joint Christian Ministry in West Africa

In the late seventies, the Commission on Church Cooperation became midwife to the "Joint Christian Ministry in West Africa" (JCMWA), a new ecumenical mission organization designed to serve needs of the Fulani-speaking peoples who inhabit the southern edge of the Sahara and extend from Senegal on the west to the Central African Republic. It was a Lutheran initiative to bring together churches of the region and their overseas partners for a common ministry in which mission and service concerns would be integrated. In addition to LWF member churches, several Anglican dioceses and other Protestant churches and communities in the area became founding members of the new agency.

The background for this ministry lay in the expanded activity of the LWF Radio Voice of the Gospel (see pp. 161–63 above), which had started broadcasts in the Fulani language from its West Africa studio, aimed at the nomadic, nominally Muslim population of this region. Positive responses to Fulani radio broadcasts pointed to the need for a broad-based ministry for which the LWF mission unit would carry initial organizational responsibility.

Interested partners, including both Lutheran and non-Lutheran churches and mission organizations, were invited to the 1978 CCC meeting to discuss the challenge. In the early 1980s a series of planning meetings was held in Senegal, Cameroon, and Nigeria, following which JCMWA became operational. Jos, Nigeria, was chosen as the site for the administrative and coordinating office for the new agency.

The main emphases of the JCMWA were to provide Fulanis, traditional cattle people, with a variety of practical services, such as vaccinations, animal husbandry services for their herds, agricultural and literacy training, and help to bring Christian Fulanis in contact with one another. Christian Fulanis were encouraged to share their new experience of the gospel and Christian community with Muslim relatives and neighbors.

## Consultations and Conferences

IN LATER YEARS the working style of the Department and Commission on Church Cooperation began to move away from annual commission meetings to greater emphasis on a variety of regional, interregional, and subregional consultations, conferences, planning sessions, and workshops. As many as fifty such events were convened at locations on all six continents between LWF assemblies, often in conjunction with the Department of Studies.

These meetings dealt with literally thousands of mission projects and interchurch aid programs important to member churches. Typical subjects were seminars on mission, leadership training with increasing emphasis on women, youth ministries, and theological education. Specialized conferences dealt with ministry to migrants in Europe, evangelism in Lutheran minority churches, theology in the local cultural context, theological education by extension, the Lutheran response to China, urban industrial mission, church construction, church pension programs, family counseling, stewardship and self-reliance, and congregational worship.

In Africa, a series of meetings was devoted to theology in the African context and to the upgrading of theological education. In Asia, APATS (Asia Program for the Advancement of Training and Studies) was organized to meet the needs of Asian Lutheran churches in such areas as theological education, Luther research, and contextual studies. APATS operates in nine Asian subregions. In Latin America the LWF assisted in bringing eight member churches into closer cooperation for mission and theological training. Similar meetings were held in the Caribbean.

In Europe, LWF consultations enabled small minority and large Lutheran majority churches to consult on common concerns of reevangelization, secularization, and renewal for mission. Consultations in Eastern Europe, beginning with an important consultation of European Lutheran

Churches in Tallinn, Estonia (1980), took advantage of the atmosphere of "perestroika" and explored new mission possibilities. Increasingly, the consultation approach became a normal expression of the working life in the LWF, and a useful method of facilitating relationships between member churches in pursuit of common mission objectives.

## Upgrading of Theological Education in Africa

IN THE 1980s, as it became evident that efforts to train pastors and other church workers in Africa suffered from a piecemeal approach, the LWF Departments of Church Cooperation and Studies jointly embarked on a coordinated strategy for the upgrading of theological education in Africa. An Advisory Committee for Theological Education in Africa was convened with the aim of raising standards of theological education across the board, securing necessary facilities within the limits of resources available, and helping to upgrade a few key institutions, known as "magnet seminaries," with the capacity to offer graduate programs and undertake contextual theological research. African Lutheran churches and theological institutions were major participants, but non-Lutheran churches and institutions both in and outside Africa were also represented on the Advisory Committee.

Recommendations of the Advisory Committee, which met in locations across Africa in 1981–85, led to the inclusion of a Lutheran faculty presence at the University of Zimbabwe and at the Protestant Faculty at Yaounde, Cameroon. The committee also supported the launching of a new interracial program in the Department of Theology at Pietermaritzburg, South Africa. Efforts were made to increase the number of trained Africans on seminary teaching staffs, to upgrade theological libraries, and to focus on methods of contextual theological education. Assistance was given toward the expansion of Makumira Seminary in Tanzania and of Meiganga in Cameroon, and the moving of Paulinum in Namibia to a new location in Windhoek. Short courses and intensive seminars dealing with nation building and the challenge of socioeconomic development were planned for African church leaders and pastors.

## A Lutheran Theology of Mission

AN UNDERLYING CONCERN of the LWF since the Lund Assembly (1947) has been clarification of the specifically Lutheran contribution to the ecumenical mission of the church. In 1982 an Interregional Consultation on Mission and Evangelism held in Stavanger, Norway, became the focal point for Lutheran mission theology and strategies (LWF Report 13/14, 1983). The Stavanger meeting was preceded by LWF regional consultations and by major mission conferences organized by the World Council of Churches and the Lausanne Committee on World Evangelization.

The aim of Stavanger was to provide an opportunity for Lutheran churches to consider their common missionary obligation, to evaluate fruits of ecumenical mission meetings, "to articulate a contemporary Lutheran theological position on mission and evangelism," and to explore frontiers and opportunities for joint missionary effort. A message directed to local congregations of LWF member churches stressed the importance of local congregations and individuals for mission and evangelism.

In 1984 The Seventh Assembly of the LWF, meeting in Budapest, called for the preparation of an LWF statement on mission and assigned the task to the Commission on Church Cooperation. The purpose of the statement was to help Lutheran churches become more deeply aware of God's mission to the world and of the churches' participation in that mission, to stimulate renewal of missionary commitment among Lutheran churches and congregations, and to further cooperation in "united witness before the world to the gospel of Jesus Christ."

An international working group convened by CCC met to prepare three drafts of a working paper on mission. The statement was completed and published in November 1988 as "Together in God's Mission: An LWF Contribution to the Understanding of Mission" (*LWF Documentation* 26, 1988). It was then sent to member churches for study and implementation. A four-session study guide, "Together in God's Mission," was later developed by an international team to assist congregations and churches to reflect on the meaning of mission and to provoke cooperative action for united witness.

The LWF statement takes a self-consciously trinitarian approach to the mission of God and of the church, deliberately excluding other biblical and confessional themes. "What," it asks, "does confession of the Triune God mean for mission in today's world?" It limits use of the word "mission" to "God's saving work" and the church's participation in it, and rules out more general uses of the term. This stands in sharp contrast to the broad understanding of mission adopted by the LWF in its post-Curitiba structural realignment.

The LWF mission statement declares that "participation in the mission of God is the central purpose of the church" and that "the mission of the church is derived from God's own mission." The continuity of the church's mission in changing historical contexts and differing cultural situations is based on God's own activity revealed in Jesus Christ and in the sending of the Holy Spirit. The church is a sign of the presence of God's reign within history, participating in God's mission to bring justice and salvation to humanity and to reconcile a broken creation.

Mission, says the LWF statement, belongs to the very being of the church and is thus not an optional activity. The church's apostolic character refers primarily to its missionary nature. The church's role is rooted in the gospel and the sacraments, through which Christ continues to give himself, and its goal is not the church itself but the world. Through the witness of the missionary church, God calls peoples to conversion and baptism, offers them newness of life in communion with Christ, and invites them to participate in God's saving activity in the world.

Participation in God's mission is "the task assigned to every Christian in baptism," belongs to all local congregations, and is the common responsibility of the whole church. The nature of the church's mission is always servanthood as exemplified by Christ. Faithfulness in mission implies pursuit of the unity and united witness of the whole church.

The LWF statement on mission includes further observations on the changing religious, cultural, social, economic, and political contexts of mission, including rapid population growth and technological change. It seeks to define contemporary mission frontiers and challenges, mentioning especially those posed by other religions and ideologies. It calls for ongoing dialogue with Judaism. As particular mission frontiers and challenges, it mentions secularization, urbanization, refugees and migrants, and the poor.

"Together in God's Mission" makes a case for special attention to youth and women. It describes theological and practical criteria for the missionary renewal of the congregation. It presents new models for mission practice and advocates the sharing of resources and the development of joint mission strategies. Guidelines for "Joint Action for Mission," as adopted by the Budapest Assembly, are appended. These call for joint action by local churches and their international partners in responding to new mission challenges and opportunities.

### Mission and Evangelism in Europe and North America

Prior to the adoption at Evian (1970) of a six-continent mission structure, LWF member churches in Western Europe and North America and their related mission agencies were seen primarily as sending bodies and donor agencies. Their role under CWM/DWM was to provide mission resources and strategies for Lutheran mission efforts and emerging churches in Asia, Africa, and Latin America.

The radically new post-Evian structure had the effect of making every Lutheran church both a sender and a receiver, simultaneously a church in mission and a mission field to be evangelized (or reevangelized). Growing awareness of the declining influence of large European folk or territorial churches, the beleaguered situation of Lutheran minority churches, and stagnant growth in North American churches, made a new approach to evangelization timely.

CCC/DCC had no area desks for mission cooperation in Western Europe and North America, but under its mandate to study the needs of churches and to assist them in programs of evangelization it was able to organize significant regional consultations on evangelization. In 1972 a special visitation and consultation program called "Villach 72" was held in Austria, attended by representatives from 38 countries, with the aim of promoting the sharing of experiences in mission outreach.

A more ambitious consultation for churches in North America, the Nordic countries, and Germany was convened at Loccum, Germany, late in 1978 (LWF Report 4, "Mission and Evangelism: Report of a Regional Consultation," Loccum, 1978). Taking seriously the missionary situation faced by large Lutheran churches and the context of secularization, materialism, and the invasion of new religious movements, Loccum advanced the thesis, "Mission begins on our own doorstep."

Loccum participants were challenged with a strategy for reevangelization that included the thorough renovation of territorial church concepts and structures, and the renewal of congregations as "the first and most important field for home mission." Education for mission should aim at making pastors active missionaries and witnesses to the alienated, rather than mere shepherds of the flock. The pastoral task was to recruit coworkers and coordinate evangelistic witness. Lay persons, representatives of the church in the world but also of the world in the congregation, were depicted as the real missionaries of the twentieth century.

CCC, at its final meeting prior to the Curitiba Assembly (Rome, 1989), recommended that the LWF make mission and evangelism in Europe and North America a priority issue for member churches. It endorsed plans for a series of local consultations and recommended creation of an ad hoc Advisory Committee on Mission and Evangelism in Europe and North America. This Advisory Committee, meeting successively in Celle, Weimar, Strasbourg, New York, and Amsterdam, drafted a report on "The Missionary Congregation" (1989) that included eight marks of a missionary congregation, plus further recommendations to the LWF and several models for equipping church members for congregational renewal.

## LWF Role in Rediscovering Missing Soviet Lutherans

The Lutheran presence in Russia, stemming from the immigration to Russia of ethnic Germans during the reign of Peter the Great, but also related to the existence of Finnish-speaking communities and groups sharing ties to the Baltic Lutheran churches, has always been scattered and marginal. Lutherans gained recognition under the Russian imperial law of 1832 and organized into consistorial districts in the Baltic provinces, in St. Petersburg (for Western Russia), and in Moscow (for Central Asia and Siberia).

Lutherans survived the 1917 October Revolution, but the situation for them and other religious communities suddenly became precarious under the dictator Joseph Stalin. Between 1928 and 1938, church organizations were crushed. More than two hundred remaining Lutheran parishes with 920,000 members were forced to close; their properties were confiscated and their seminary in Leningrad shut down. Ninety-eight theologically trained pastors serving open churches were sent into internal exile. The last open church in Moscow was closed in 1938.

Another massive blow was struck in 1941 when, at the time of the Nazi invasion of the USSR, all ethnic Germans living west of the Urals were deported to Central Asia and Siberia to provide slave labor. For more than half a century Lutheranism miraculously survived in eastern towns and rural villages, despite lack of an official ministry or church structure, and without Bibles, hymnals, or prayer books. Pietist tradition and training served local lay leaders—more often than not elderly persons and women—well as they met in house gatherings and informal prayer meetings to maintain their Christian identity.

The dramatic story of the rediscovery of these "lost" Lutherans in the former Soviet Union, and the LWF role in helping to reestablish a Lutheran church presence, begins in 1955 with the gathering of an officially registered congregation in Tselinograd, Kazakhstan. In the 1960s several independent Lutheran congregations in Central Asia asked Latvian Pastor Harald Kalnins (b. 1910) of Riga to visit them regularly as their superintendent and to oversee registration of congregations, appointment of pastors, and arrangements for informal training of congregational leaders. In 1976 the LWF Europe Secretary, Paul Hansen, was able to accompany Kalnins, and by 1978 the LWF was granted permission to send Bibles, hymnals, and worship orders. Subsequently, additional shipments of Bibles, hymnals, catechisms, and other worship materials took place, along with visits from German and Scandinavian churches.

In 1989 Kalnins was consecrated bishop for registered Lutheran congregations which were organized into districts with deans, and regions headed by superintendents. During the nineties synodal organizations were formed in Siberia and Ukraine, congregational properties in large cities were returned to their owners, old churches reopened, and some new churches built. The Evangelical Lutheran Church in Russia and Other States (ELCROS), the German ethnic Lutheran Church, joined the LWF in 1990. The Evangelical Lutheran Church of Ingria in Russia (ELCIR), the smaller Ingrian Lutheran Church supported by Finnish church aid, elected its bishop in 1993 and was also received into the LWF.

## LWF Marxism and China Study Program

CONCERN FOR CHINA in various forms has been a constant within the LWF since the closing of China to the outside world in the early fifties. No other single country has exercised so continuous a fascination for the world Lutheran community. The holding of the Ninth LWF Assembly in Hong Kong in July 1997, within days of the return of the British Crown Colony to the People's Republic of China, is further testimony to this fact.

In 1971, the LWF China study program was begun as a special aspect of the study of the Christian encounter with other religions and ideologies and of the encounter of the church with Marxism in various cultural contexts. The LWF issued a "Marxism and China Study Information Letter," and published several volumes dealing with the situation of churches in Asian, African, Latin American, and Eastern European socialist contexts.

As early as 1968 the LWF Commission on World Mission had raised the question of studying "the New China" in terms of its wider implications for Christian mission. "What," the inquiry asked, "has China to say to the church?" Collaboration was begun with other China study networks, and an ecumenical study liaison group including LWF representatives was established.

Increasingly the discussion moved toward theological and ethical implications of "the New China" for Christian faith and for mission practice. In 1979, with the restoration of diplomatic relations between the United States and China, and the reopening of the Chinese Three Self Patriotic Movement Churches in major Chinese cities, the aims of the LWF China study program were modified to monitor latest developments and conditions in China, to establish friendly relations with the Chinese church, and "to inquire how the experience of the Chinese church can serve the missionary purpose of the church in other parts of the world."

In 1979 the LWF Departments of Church Cooperation and Studies jointly sponsored a China consultation in Geneva and opened a Lutheran Churches China Coordination Office in Hong Kong. Shortly thereafter, visits by the LWF President and General Secretary to offices of the China Christian Council, and participation by Bishop K. H. Ting in meetings of the LWF Executive Committee, led to the establishment of ongoing relationships between the LWF and the Chinese Protestant Church, reorganized in 1980 as the China Christian Council (CCC). In 1993, the LWF Council mandated a new study project on China concerns, to be led by a Chinese theologian assisted by an Advisory Committee, and conducted by the Department for Theology and Studies in close cooperation with the Department for Mission and Development and Chinese Lutheran seminaries.

## Summary and Evaluation

REGARDING Lutheran World Federation experiences and programs in the area of missionary cooperation during the past fifty years we can draw the following conclusions.

*1. Structures for Missionary Cooperation.* Unquestionably LWF structures for missionary cooperation changed during the fifty-year period. Much time—perhaps too much—was spent on structural overhaul. It is too soon to say whether the structural changes have been worth the time and effort. Actual effects of structural changes cannot always be measured in terms of intended results. Sometimes structural changes preceded long-term changes in missionary practice and relationships and functioned as a catalyst for those changes. At other times structural changes merely reflected or validated changes in relationships that had already occurred.

At Lund (1947) the LWF authorized the formation of the Committee of World Mission, the first formal structure for international Lutheran missionary cooperation. At Hanover (1952), CWM, taking note of the termination of CYCOM, the National Lutheran Council's New York based office, created the Geneva-based LWF Department of World Mission (DWM). While CWM was purely consultative, DWM gave the LWF an effective executive arm in Geneva. Mission was still largely understood as one-directional sending activity by western mission agencies into the "non-Christian" world. But changes were occurring in the Lutheran "world missions parliament," as CWM was popularly termed.

CWM's official policy as set forth at Lund was prophetic in reflecting lessons learned from the orphaned missions experience. It foreshadowed the emergence of new structural relationships. CWM encouraged the formation of united Lutheran churches in former mission areas, and called for the internationalization of the Lutheran missionary force. Implementation of these policies would make the sender-receiver relationships anachronistic and undercut the "dominance-dependence" syndrome. It would eventually give rise to a global communion of Lutheran churches mutually engaged in mission cooperation and becoming partners in united witness.

At Evian (1970) CWM/DWM was restructured into the Commission and Department of Church Cooperation (CCC/DCC). This structural re-alignment reflected the emergence of autonomous LWF member churches in former mission areas, the integration of church and mission, and a new understanding of mission as the task of member churches on all six conti-nents. At Curitiba (1990), CCC/DCC was, for practical and theological reasons, replaced by a new and more comprehensive Department for Mis-sion and Development (DMD), reporting directly to the LWF Council.

In retrospect, it may appear that the greatest and most positive result of structural changes, particularly after 1970, was the recognition of the integrity of emerging member churches in Asia, Oceania, Africa, Latin America and the Caribbean. The post-Evian structure recognized the maturing of these churches from dependence to independence, and empowered them for interdependent mission and ecumenical relations. Thereby it furthered their communion (*communio*) and partnership with other LWF member churches. Initially this was accomplished at the cost of disenfranchising independent Lutheran mission agencies, which had been active participants in CWM/DWM, but—especially after 1990—special efforts were made by DMD to bring these mission agencies back into partnership with the LWF.

*2. Definition and Understanding of Mission.*    The working definition and theological understanding of mission also changed over these fifty years. The changes were not always fully understood, recognized, or pub-licly articulated. Controversies could and did erupt over proposed changes in structure and nomenclature which masked deeper differences about the essential meaning of mission. The word "mission" itself was invested with deeply symbolic significance, as its exclusion from the proposed title of CCC/DCC at Evian and its reincorporation into the title of the DMD at Curitiba showed. LWF missionary partnership would be handicapped when proposed structural changes were not accompanied by agreement on the theological and practical understanding of mission. Ironically, the important LWF trinitarian contribution to mission theology, "Together in God's Mission" (1988), has not had much practical effect on the actual work of mission.

Lund (1947) initially reflected a traditional nineteenth-century empha-sis on Western mission sending in fulfillment of the Great Commission, though modified by the experience of orphaned missions. The Lund Assembly challenged the assumption of continued Western control and dominance by proposing that mission trusteeship arrangements for orphaned missions should be short-lived, and recommending that Western leadership give way to the formation of united Lutheran churches in each country and to the internationalization of the Lutheran mission force.

The LWF understanding of mission in the post-Evian period (1970–90) was clearly influenced by the IMC–WCC "integration" discussion and by the emerging ecumenical view of mission as the task of the church in all six continents. It also reflected a Lutheran concept of mission as the task of every Christian through baptism and of every local congregation. Documents prepared for the next restructuring of the LWF at Curitiba (1990) reflect a further shift toward a holistic "missio dei" concept of mission, understood as participation in "the whole mission of God to the whole world" and as the "fundamental task of the church." Some felt that this expansion of function made mission so diffuse and amorphous as to lose all specificity.

The LWF understanding of mission—never precisely defined—has had to bear the burden of a wide range of applications and interpretations. There has been a tendency to move from specific frontier-crossing efforts of evangelization toward the provision of comprehensive interchurch aid and support services for mission. Church-mission integration and ecumenical sharing of resources have produced this effect. When mission is defined as "the fundamental task of the church" and the responsibility of every Christian and every congregation, the specific focus or concentration of mission tends to disappear. .

As a recent adage puts it, "When everything is mission, nothing is mission." Mission is in danger of becoming domesticated as an interchurch activity. When this happens, the eschatological horizon of the proclamation of the message of the kingdom in the whole world tends to be replaced by churchly concerns. In the Lutheran World Federation, the current movement is from *conversio gentium* to *communio ecclesiarum.* Only a proper consideration of the "unfinished task" and an effort to direct mission and evangelization toward specific mission frontiers and unevangelized areas can rescue the church from excessive focus on its own needs and problems. In this sense, *communio* must stand in the service of *conversio.* Those who articulated the meaning and goal of Lutheran missionary cooperation at Lund were quite clear about this.

3. *Actual Performance and Accomplishments.* The LWF has never claimed to be an agent of mission in its own right, but has regarded the churches and their related (or independent) mission agencies as the primary doers of mission. DWM, DCC, and DMD have existed as servants of the member churches, acting in response to instructions from church-appointed commissions such as CWM, CCC, and the LWF Council in determining priorities and procedures. According to their mandates, the

LWF mission units exist to support churches and mission organizations in carrying out their own mission activities; to facilitate contacts, exchanges, and sharing of resources between churches; to provide programs requested by churches when it is not feasible for the churches themselves to conduct such programs, and to develop patterns of ecumenical cooperation in mission.

The LWF has preferred the role of convener of missionary forums, planner of regional or functional consultations, shaper of new strategies, and clearinghouse for ideas and resources. Rarely has it become "operational" in managing or directing mission activities, and then only as temporary administrator. Its mandate has included the initiation of cooperative pilot projects seeking new forms of witness. DWM took temporary responsibility for Radio Voice of the Gospel but later gave it independent life. DCC later acted as midwife to the pilot program known as the Joint Christian Ministry in West Africa.

LWF mission units have not been in the business of claiming credit for their accomplishments. Their real achievements will be found scattered throughout reports from hundreds of policy conferences, theological consultations, regional assemblies, leadership training programs, consultative services, and new mission endeavors. Ultimately, the value of such mission programs will be measured by lives of church workers enriched through contact with fellow workers from other areas or provided with new insights and incentives for mission.

**Bibliographical Notes** _____

I. Unpublished Documents

LWF Archives, Geneva.

II. Written Statement and Oral Interview

Risto Lehtonen, Helsinki.

III. Printed Documents

LWF Documentations, passim.
Particularly:
*Together in God's Mission: An LWF Contribution to the Understanding of Mission.* Geneva: LWF Documentation 26, November 1988.
LWF Reports, passim.
Particularly:
*Mission and Evangelism: Report of a Regional Consultation, Loccum, 1978.* Geneva: LWF Report 4, March 1979.
Scherer, James A. ". . . that the Gospel May be Sincerely Preached

*Throughout the World: A Lutheran Perspective on Mission and Evangelism in the 20th Century."* Geneva: LWF Report 11/12 (November 1982).

*Stavanger 1982. LWF Interregional Consultation on Mission and Evangelism.* Geneva: LWF Report 13/14 (April 1983).

*From Dar es Salaam to Budapest, 1977–1984.* Geneva: LWF Report 17/18 (April 1984).

*From Budapest to Curitiba, 1985–1989.* Geneva: LWF Report 27 (November 1989).

*The Lutheran World Convention, Eisenach, 1923.* Philadelphia: United Lutheran Publication House, 1925.

*Proceedings* (all LWF Assemblies).

*Proclamation and Human Development: Document from a Lutheran World Federation Consultation, Nairobi, Kenya, October 21–25, 1974.* Geneva: Lutheran World Federation, 1975.

*The Second Lutheran World Convention, Copenhagen, 1929.* Philadelphia: United Lutheran Publication House, 1930.

IV. Monographs

Hogg, William Richey. *Ecumenical Foundations: A History of the International Missionary Council and Its Nineteenth Century Background.* New York: Harper Brothers, 1952.

Latourette, Kenneth Scott, and Hogg, William Richey. *World Christian Community in Action: The Story of World War II and Orphaned Missions.* New York and London: International Missionary Council, 1949.

Lundgren, Manfred. *Proclaiming Christ to His World: The Experience of Radio Voice of the Gospel, 1957–1977.* Geneva: Lutheran World Federation, Department of Communication, 1983.

Scherer, James A. *Mission and Unity in Lutheranism: A Study in Confession and Ecumenicity.* Philadelphia: Fortress Press, 1969.

Schiotz, Fredrik A. "Lutheran World Missions." *International Review of Missions* 43/17 (July 1954), pp. 311–22.

Wentz, Frederick K. *Lutherans in Concert: The Story of the National Lutheran Council, 1918–1966.* Minneapolis: Augsburg, 1968.

15. Inauguration of Radio Voice of the Gospel, February 1963, Addis Ababa. From left: Emperor Haile Selassie, Dr. Fredrik Schiotz, chairman of the Board of the LWF Broadcasting Service, and Dr. Emmanuel Abraham, president of the Ethiopian Evangelical Church Mekane Yesus.

16. LWF Consultation on Proclamation and Human Development, Nairobi, Kenya, October 1974. Gudina Tumsa of Ethiopia and Ulrich Duchrow of the LWF Department of Studies are shown.

17. Lutheran service in a house church in Alma-Ata, Siberia, 1976. The Revs. Harald Kalnins and Paul Hansen are shown.

# Continuity and Change:
# Theological Reflection in the LWF

THE CHARGE IS FREQUENTLY MADE that theology is imprisoned within tradition. This accusation alleges that theology fails to demonstrate relevance or topicality, or that it is bound to an outmoded, antiquarian vocabulary. Yet, an opposite charge is also frequently heard: theology is all too often obscured by fashion; it has fallen prey to whatever is the current trend. This criticism avers that theological discourse tends often to be shaped by various forms of spiritual patricide; its content is dictated by a desire to create popular interest at the cost of an adequate valuation of the classics.

Curiously enough, it is possible—beneath obvious simplifications—to unearth an element of truth within each of these polemics. Theology does have a double character. On the one hand, it is of necessity traditional, since its primary task is to pass on a message from the past to new recipients. In the biblical tradition, the classic texts—and those who have transmitted them and those who have embodied them—cover three millennia of historical continuity. On the other hand, the interpretation of those classic texts always takes place within a specific context that possesses its own unique contemporaneity. The interpreter is part of a community that itself is determined and shaped by a concrete framework of culture and society as well as by a particular tradition of learning and ecclesial service. It can consequently be claimed that the development and application of Christian theology is conditioned by a great chain of varied historical contexts that culminate in whatever is the present moment of interpretation and critical evaluation. Method in theology therefore includes the interaction between these two poles—tradition and context—and it is precisely this tension that gives to theology its excitement and challenge.

---

*Jens Holger Schjørring, Aarhus, Denmark, is the author of chapter 5.*

This double character of theology—dialectic and polarity—has been as crucial and intriguing in relation to its role in the history of the Lutheran World Federation as in any other arena. The interplay of continuity and change is of crucial importance if five decades of theological reflection in the Federation are adequately to be analyzed. Neither a simple picture of a continuous unilinear development nor one of alternation and change would be adequate to such analysis.

With such reservations as these in mind, we may identify three periods in the role taken by theology in the LWF. (1) An initial period of foundational efforts in which theology was seen as constituting an essential part of the general consensus reached within the Federation. This was a time of "classical theology" promulgated by prominent scholars, both academicians and church leaders, who represented the three dominant blocks— German, American, Nordic—of participants in the early LWF (see chapter 1 above). This period covers the first generation after the founding of the Federation, through the Helsinki Assembly of 1963. (2) A second period is one of provocative theological renewal. This time was marked by "prophetic denunciation," by increased participation of theologians from younger churches, by a growing number of persons doing theology and studies, by the use of critical social theory as a key hermeneutical instrument in a nearly comprehensive revision of the classical heritage. This period covered approximately a decade, from the late 1960s until after the Sixth Assembly of the LWF, at Dar es Salaam in 1977. (3) In the time from the late 1970s to the present, the major attention has been given to developing a "balanced" theology. In this period attention has been given to crafting a role for a theology that mediates between the original basic concern faithfully to identify and maintain the Lutheran tradition as well as the more recent critical concerns. In light of global fragmentation, however, this mediation has been complex and at best partial.

## The Background

IN HIS OPENING ADDRESS at the First International Congress on Luther Research held at Aarhus, Denmark, August 1956, Hanns Lilje, then Bishop of Hanover and President of the Lutheran World Federation, presented a clear picture of the role of theology within the LWF. He acknowledged directly the frequent accusations that Lutheranism was marked by quietism, an indifference to sociopolitical challenges. With subtle irony he responded to these accusations by referring to his own recent contacts with Lutheran churches throughout the world. The activities that had immediately caught his eye were those connected with relief work and cooperation in mission. Lilje took pride in those efforts, considering them indispensable to the whole range of challenges and responsibilities that marked the life of the Federation. Nevertheless, he underscored his conviction that there could be no legitimate transmission of the heritage of Lutheranism without a careful dedication also to the cause of theology. He was utterly unwilling to regard concern for theological clarity as the province only of a limited group of specialists whose interests were focused chiefly on the Reformation era. On the contrary, he maintained, an enduring commitment to theology was required for a decisive contribution to the ecumenical conversations of the time. Moreover, Lilje insisted that he was determined that theology assume a central role within the LWF so that every element of the Federation's life could be examined and guided according to basic theological principles (LWF Archives, TH / VI 5).

To Lilje's far-sighted remarks of 1956 it could well be added that a carefully defined doctrinal basis had always been a focal concern for those involved in the LWF predecessor body, the Lutheran World Convention. In giving emphasis to theology, Lilje was obviously continuing along a well-marked path.

Seen even more broadly, it must be recognized that a quest for theological clarity has motivated all movements for the reform of the church since Martin Luther began his struggle for renewal. His contribution to church renewal, it is to be remembered, began only after a passionate and lengthy debate concerning the theological interpretation of Holy Scripture. Similarly, the incentive behind *Confessio Augustana* (the Augsburg Confession, 1530) was to move beyond what were then recent and arbitrary additions or alterations to the earliest creeds in order to reestablish authentically biblical preaching and teaching within the church.

The present century again challenges the church continually to pursue a concerted effort both to judge theology by a careful interpretation of the biblical texts and to examine its worship in the context of the whole of church praxis. Furthermore, this judgment and this examination can for Lutherans be pursued only on the basis of the historic confessions of the church. There is, to be sure, considerable justification for the pride felt by many Lutherans at their contributions to academic theology and even at their accomplishments in the education of the laity. At the same time, however, the fact can not be disguised that from time to time the Lutheran quest for theological investigation has degenerated into an obstinate insistence on the private insights and opinions of individuals. Simultaneously there has frequently developed within Lutheranism a kind of corporate intolerance of other traditions and confessions. To find a proper balance has been extremely difficult: on the one hand, to avoid both unjustified arrogance on the part of individual theologians and narrow confessionalism on the part of church groups and, on the other hand, to overcome a lack of loyalty toward biblical authority and a lack of fidelity to the confessions.

Against such a background it is thus our task to examine how the task of theological reflection has been carried out within the history of the Lutheran World Federation. We shall examine some of the topics that have been focal through the five decades of that history: the understanding of justification and justice; the connection between "faith alone" and a concern for social justice; and the relationship between confessional identity and ecumenical fellowship.

## The First Period: Commission and Department

### *The First Study Document, 1952*

The first LWF Commission on Theology presented its initial study document to the Assembly in Hanover 1952, "The Living Word in a Responsible Church" (the wording in German indicates a reciprocity between the divine proclamation and the church's response, "Das lebendige Wort in einer lebendigen Kirche"). This document was a full-scale exposition of the gospel, a dense, learned summary of biblical theology interpreted in the light of the historic confessions and at the same time presented with emphatic reference to present challenges in society and culture.

"The Living Word" is the mystery of divine revelation amidst the ambiguities of the world. In this understanding, the incarnation of God in Christ involves a "joyful deliverance of the world from every form of idolatry." This basic dogmatic definition is immediately applicable to the present times: "Our own age has experienced the tyranny of idols, of false political, biological or pedagogical gods that clothed themselves with divine authority, reduced men [sic] to the level of slaves and exacted from them the tribute of life and possessions."

The document asserts that there is no salvation nor liberation from such idols apart from the gospel and its proclamation of the justification of sinners, a proclamation that at the same time points to the only possible way of restoring the dignity of humankind. This characteristic feature of "the Living Word" rests on the presupposition that "the Church both unites and distinguishes between the gospel and the law." If the two are confused or their proper relationship neglected—as has so often happened—the result is the reduction of the law to a set of moral or political propositions. Similarly, "the gospel, without the law, becomes a purely private and inoffensive matter." In both case the result is a dissolution of the basic orders of human life.

Having described the nature of the divine Word as the gospel of incarnation, cross, and resurrection, the study document goes on to describe "the life, which the living Word gives," pointing first to the sacraments of Baptism and Eucharist. Both sacraments are seen in sharp relation to the main challenges of the present world. Baptism is depicted as a response to the loneliness which is a common fate in modern society: "The natural bonds of human society are disintegrating and gradually give way to all kinds of mass organizations which only accentuate the loneliness of the individual. But baptism removes man from this state of loneliness which basically is the loneliness of sin, and calls him into true fellowship with God and with men" (*Proceedings*, Hanover, p. 127).

No less is this also the case in the document's words concerning the Eucharist: "Men today are oppressed by the cruel necessity of self-preservation. In the inescapable struggle between individuals, classes and nations for self-assertion they find themselves under the awful coercion of battling for survival and security of self. In the sacrament of the body of Christ in the Lord's Supper, however, men are drawn by the gift of Christ's true body and blood into the sphere of Christ's sacrificial love, where the spell of self-centeredness is broken and men made free to praise and love" (ibid., p. 129).

The presentation of this study document was evidently a dominating feature of the entire Hanover Assembly. Theology was seen to be at the center of the Federation, as was also apparent in the presidential address of Anders Nygren, which bore the same title as the study document. Without doubt theology at this point in LWF history possessed a unifying power for all assembly participants, and this added even more weight to the work of the Commission on Theology, work which was just about to be taken up. Against this background it is worthwhile analyzing how the commission defined its mandate, how the first work of the commission was evaluated, and how the relationship between the Commission on Theology and the new Department of Theology was initially defined.

## The Mandates of Commission and Department

It was the intention of the first members of the LWF Commission on Theology to let theology articulate the basic identity of the Federation as a whole. At the same time they were aware of the danger that this might result in a "theocratic rule of theological experts."

This concern became apparent when the commission expressed its determination to arrive at an adequate definition of the core of the gospel

and thus implied that the primordial role of theology was in fact penultimate to the preservation of a genuine biblical theology and the faithful
reinterpretation of the confessions. Members sought for a suitable modesty which would avoid any kind of exaggerated view of the importance of
theology; such modesty was essential in order to secure on theological
issues a conversation of equals between all who were involved in the common task of the LWF.

Thus it was a view of the maximal role of theology that was reflected in
the conviction that theology indeed articulated the identity of the LWF
generally. More particularly it was this view that gave to theological
reflection the responsibility both for a critical evaluation of the Hanover
Assembly and for the substantive preparation for the next assembly. This
dynamic toward an all-embracing role for theology referred to much more
than the specific contributions made by the academic theologians who
comprised both the commission and the staff. Theology was seen as a key
issue in the mutual exchange of experience and insight which would be
crucial if the international character of the Federation were to be made
manifest. This view of theology was expressed by the LWF Executive Secretary, Carl Lund-Quist, in February 1952, when he expressed his appreciation of the plans to establish a Department of Theology. Lund-Quist
supported these plans because he saw clearly the need to establish a
department that would guarantee an exchange of ideas that could reach far
beyond the confines of academic work, ideas that could touch the experience of all within the churches of the Federation. In this connection he
referred to plans "to establish a publication center, a center for the collection of materials on the history of the exiled churches and for the better
exchange of theological students, professors and church workers." It was
the general secretary's desire to make important theological literature
available in as many languages as possible.

"For too long," Lund-Quist added, "we have been encrusted with the
wrong kind of nationalism and sectionalism which have stifled real interchange of ideas and spiritual life. We must find a way to cross the barriers
of language, geography and race." He left no doubt that serious theological
work, expressed even in the life of congregations, was a central task in the
building up of closer contacts between the member churches. Without
such communication the LWF would fail to take up an essential part of its
task as a global communion. Lund-Quist concluded: "We have large gaps
to fill in making possible real stimulation and cooperation between the
churches of the North and Central Europe, between the old world and the
new, between the younger churches and older churches, between minority groups and Folk Churches. The responsibility for lifting the sights to
look on the task of the church as one which goes beyond national bound-

aries or racial bonds, is still a most real task. The new department can not do all of this, but it can lead to a beginning in assisting the churches and their people to see this opportunity" (LWF Archives, TH/ II 1, Commission on Theology).

A differing point of view, that of moderating the role of theology for the sake of preserving the genuine contributions which theology could make, was expressed at the same time by the first chairperson of the Commission on Theology, Regin Prenter (1907–1990), Professor of Systematic Theology at the University of Aarhus, Denmark.

Prenter saw it as his foremost obligation to express unvarnished truth about the procedure and content of the Hanover Assembly. He pointed out that the theme of that assembly had been formulated far too widely. Since the time provided for discussion in Section I (Theology) had been very limited, and since the introductory presentations had been far too comprehensive, the results had generally been superficial. Accordingly, Prenter maintained that for the future the only tenable procedure would be to choose a more precise and modest assembly theme and to include more time for discussion by the participants.

Moreover, and perhaps more surprisingly, Prenter distanced himself from the view that it should be the task of theology to create the foundation for the work of all other LWF sections. No, Prenter argued, such a view might easily create the mistaken impression that there could legitimately exist something like a particular theology for LWF headquarters. The only legitimate foundation, he maintained, was reflection on the biblical sources and the heritage of the Reformation; this reflection could provide a basis common to every section of the Federation. If this basis proved weak or created fatal diversity in years to come, it would be wise to face such a calamity openly rather than to disguise it artificially behind a veil of inappropriate "bureaucratic theology." Prenter regarded the kind of theology that he opposed as an arrogant theocracy of theological experts, and he maintained that such a theology could never be in harmony with the true character of Lutheranism. Instead, he pleaded for a definition of the role of the Department of Theology *alongside* other sections and/or departments. He urged his colleagues to accept the possibility that they— as theologians—might receive important insights from the experience of other sections, whether "Evangelism and Stewardship," mission, or youth. It was, however, far from Prenter's intention to advocate a diminished role for theology; he rather regarded it as an imperative to give a sober and to some extent modest description of the mandate of the Department of Theology in order to develop a method that would in the long run prove tenable and credible.

Prenter's plea for a sober minded self-criticism among theologians was expressed against a background of general support for a prominent role for theology within the LWF as a whole. There was a consensus in respect to both content and method for the carrying out of theological projects. In regard to this consensus Prenter could be confident.

In all essential matters, Regin Prenter was in complete agreement with another key figure of the first generation of LWF leaders, Vilmos Vajta (b. 1918) who was appointed the first Director of the Department of Theology. Vajta had left his homeland, Hungary, during World War II and had come to Sweden in order to pursue studies with Anders Nygren. He had been ordained in Hungary and was received as a pastor in the Church of Sweden at the same time as he completed his doctoral work on Luther's theology of worship. This work of Vajta on liturgy and sacrament subsequently played a major role in international theological discussions (Vilmos Vajta, *Die Theologie des Gottesdienstes bei Luther* [Göttingen: Vandenhoeck & Ruprecht, 1954]; Eng. ed. *Luther on Worship: An Interpretation,* trans. and condensed by U. S. Leupold [Philadelphia: Muhlenberg Press, 1958]).

Prenter and Vajta followed the same line in respect to the relationship between the LWF Commission and Department of Theology. The aim of the department was drawn up in the following way:

1. To promote fellowship and cooperation in study among Lutherans;
2. To engage in such theological studies as are assigned to the department by the [LWF] Executive Committee;
3. To assist the churches in meeting their needs for the strengthening of congregational life.

These goals were to be reached by coordinating an exchange of personnel—professors, students, pastors, and laity; by making available to the LWF Executive Committee studies based on the main actions of assemblies and by proposing themes and lines of study for future assemblies; and by pursuing a number of further initiatives associated with communication, publications, and exchange programs.

All of these recommendations presupposed close cooperation and mutual understanding between the Commission and the Department of Theology. The commission was, in point of fact, defined as a supervisory committee (LWF Archives, TH II 1. Commission on Theology. Establishment. Annual Reports). The first reports of both commission and department were marked by a spirit of harmony. Prenter, in his report, laid particular emphasis on the necessity of continuous communication and cooperation between the two. He and Vajta both pointed to the danger that either commission or department, or both, might concentrate upon internal processes or goals in order simply to get along to the detriment of absolutely essential conversation and integration with external groups and bodies. Toward this end they urged the delegation of responsibilities, the building up of national commissions on theology among LWF member churches, paying further attention to the exchange of journals and other publications, and frequent travels by the director of the department. Only such openness and communication could make for genuine consensus as well as for the necessary exchange of critical views (LWF Archives, TH/ II 2. Commission on Theology, Copenhagen, 1953, first regular meeting of the commission).

## International Congress on Luther Research

An early and significant initiative with respect to theology in the life of the Federation was the international symposium for Luther scholars held in Aarhus, Denmark, in August 1956. This conference had been organized by the staff of the new Department of Theology, headed by its director, Vilmos Vajta; its host was the chairman of the LWF Commission on Theology, Regin Prenter, who was himself a professor in the Faculty of Theology at the University of Aarhus. As has also been noted, the President of the Lutheran World Federation, Hanns Lilje, delivered the opening address to the eighty participants who came from fourteen countries.

Lilje, in his address, emphasized the widespread concern among Lutherans to evaluate Luther's theology as "living Word" and urged that that priority should be developed as an ongoing process. Only in these terms, Lilje asserted, could the work of Luther scholarship be prevented from degenerating into a rigid confessionalism. This was in reality a warning against a fundamentalistic theological arrogance—here Lilje's position was similar to that previously made by Prenter in the theological commission—which would convert serious Luther scholarship into merely a self-conscious exposition of Lutheranism as such. Lilje explicitly took his distance from the arrogant, confessionalistic view of theology often developed by Lutheran church bureaucrats. In contrast he embraced a theology which, rightly understood, would exist in service to both freedom of thought and clarity about the true identity of the church.

In light of the growth, internationally, of interest in Luther research since 1956, it may be surprising for readers today to note that Bishop Lilje deplored what he termed a lack of real understanding of Luther. Most specifically in respect to the English-speaking world, Lilje observed an appalling lack of objective information and understanding of Luther both as a person and a theologian. This deficit in knowledge and understanding caused frequent misunderstanding and on occasion massive distortion of historical realities. In these terms the LWF President expressed his best wishes for the Congress as an integral part of the work of the Federation.

The Aarhus conference was clearly a success, and there was widespread interest in continuing the enterprise. There was both general acknowledgment that the Congress would in fact strengthen the life of LWF member churches and a clear desire to maintain LWF sponsorship of the Congress' work. After considerable discussion it was decided by participants in the Aarhus conference that for the sake of freedom of research an independent continuation committee be established, but that close links with the LWF should be preserved. The LWF would continue its financial sponsorship of the Congress, and the staff of its Department of Theology would serve the continuation committee (LWF Archives, Th / II.1; Commission on Theol; Correspondence 1957). It is significant that the International Congress for Luther Research has continued its work to the present day as an independent enterprise yet with continued ties to the LWF. The Federation continues to give financial support chiefly in enabling scholars from younger, Third World churches to participate.

The Norwegian theologian Ivar Asheim (b. 1927) succeeded Vilmos Vajta as Director of the Department of Theology in Geneva. Asheim did not initiate any immediate or radical changes in the work of the department; he was determined to continue already existing efforts and projects with whatever adjustments were absolutely necessary. He saw his primary obligation to be the continuation of study concerning "justification by grace through faith" in order that that doctrine could be continually clarified and applied. It was important that the dogmatic core of this classical Lutheran doctrine be connected with the issue of justice in modern society with full attention to the developing ecumenical context. Thus it was that basic issues in social ethics came to be seen as integral to the work of the Department of Theology. These issues were approached in terms of the relation of the church to society and culture, and in terms of fundamental considerations of themes such as freedom, liberation, and hope.

This agenda for the Department of Theology, under the leadership of Ivar Asheim, made necessary a critical reinterpretation of the Lutheran doctrine of "the two kingdoms," a doctrine which more than any other had for a generation been under fire not least within the Lutheran churches themselves. Twentieth-century history, particularly on the European continent, has—to many—demonstrated the perennial risk facing the Lutheran tradition of separating the kingdom of the world from the kingdom of Christ. Asheim was determined to face this challenge. He was convinced of two things: that the experience of churches from the southern hemisphere, in their new contexts, could illuminate this reinterpretation; and that insights from nontheological disciplines should be integrated into the study. This was, in point of fact, actually an anticipation of the controversial debate over the proper nature and role of theology which in subsequent years was to mark the Federation.

In this period of LWF life, further, it is to be noted that questions about the relationship of Christianity to other world religions were beginning to appear. Even as the original work of theological reflection in the Federation continued, new issues—including questions of ecumenism, as raised by Vatican II, and ecclesiology, which are discussed in other chapters of this book—were on the horizon at the close of this "Initial Phase."

## The Second Period: Prophetic Denunciation

AS THE BROAD SURVEY of LWF history in chapter 2 indicates, the 1960s were a period of transition that called for new patterns of thought and practice. There were also, in this period, new and explicit challenges to the role to be played by theological reflection within the life of the Federation. The most crucial of these challenges were six, each of which will be subsequently reviewed:

1. The restructuring of the Federation in this period called for new definitions of the role of theology.
2. The involvement of churches from the "Two-Thirds World" made a redefinition of basic strategies urgently necessary.
3. Global—and ecumenical—shifts in theology impinged directly on the work of theology in the LWF.
4. Theological leadership was no longer confined to academics and ecclesiastics from the north.
5. Fundamental paradigms and frameworks for the doing of theology were changing.
6. Political shifts that altered basic sociopolitical theories had direct bearing on the theological enterprise and gave to questions of social ethics a new and basic role in that enterprise.

1. Prior to the 1960s, the period now under review, theology was most frequently regarded as an intellectual, abstract activity confined to the academic ivory tower; it was held to lack contact with or relevance to the life of the churches. The inability of the Commission on Theology at the Helsinki Assembly of the LWF in 1963 to present a generally acceptable report on the doctrine of justification gave rise to an antitheological spirit, albeit most were prone to adopt this spirit without properly investigating the story of Helsinki itself (cf. pp. 375–81 below *et passim*). Myth and legend rather than genuine understanding resulted. Furthermore, the establishment of the Lutheran Foundation for Interconfessional Research,

the Institute for Ecumenical Research at Strasbourg, France, was seen by
some as a new provision for the basic theological work of the Federation.
Indeed, the sharing of roles and tasks between the Department of Theology in Geneva and the Institute at Strasbourg was bound to lead to some
unclarity as to the relation between the two.

The "restructuring" of theological work in the LWF typified by the
establishment of the Strasbourg Institute is further to be marked by the
change in name of the Geneva department to "Department of Studies."
This change was seen by many as part of the move away from classical
theology in response to the concrete needs of the member churches and
their people. Traditional theology, the province of professional academics,
was seen as giving way. "Studies" indicated a widespread desire to redefine
the role of theology, and in a new way more closely to relate the work of
both commission and department to life in the member churches.

2. Churches in the countries of the south, having recently obtained
political independence, sought in the Federation new forms of authentic
and just participation. In 1962 it was pointedly noted, by a commission
reviewing the entire structure and function of the LWF, that "the work of
the Department of Theology has been concentrated chiefly in Europe and
North America." Subsequently, in 1969, a restructuring was proposed that
was based on even further-reaching views: "There is a need for a broader
outlook and function in serving churches in developing countries and in
the outreach in the older churches in Europe and North America." The
master narrative of the Lutheran World Federation in its first generation—
"the Lutheran heritage in Europe and North America"—was now opening
toward the south and the new churches. This, as many eager reformers
desired, called for a complete renewal.

3. The period of the late sixties was broadly marked as a new beginning,
involving in certain respects a confrontation between diverging features of
tradition held to be incompatible with new realities. Such tensions were
not absent from Lutheran theology. The LWF Commission and Department of Theology by this time had already begun certain studies designed
as acts of critical self-examination; the reevaluation of the two-kingdoms
theology and a thoroughgoing examination of the issues of anti-Semitism
and the relation of the church to Israel were instances of such studies. To
do this it was necessary to complement traditional theological work with
well-grounded insights from, for example, the social sciences, with
unknown consequences for the role of theological reflection within the
Federation.

4. The first generation of the LWF's history had given remarkable proof
of the dynamic power embodied in classical Lutheran theology. This
theology had been dogmatic in both method and content as well as con-

sensus-creating in its impact and had thus achieved a balance between tradition and renewal. At the same time, however, it is proper to describe this work as, to use a felicitous phrase of Professor Vîtor Westhelle, "the sages' discourse," insofar as those who had created the balance were university professors and theologically well trained church leaders from Europe and North America. In this situation, then, both world political realities and serious reflection on the nature of church fellowship and the ministry of all faithful persons demanded that theological conversation within the LWF be opened to a far wider community than ever before.

5. The fundamental paradigm for theological reflection that had been so convincingly followed by the Commission and Department of Theology during the first two decades of the history of the Lutheran World Federation was defined by the classical tradition of European universities. In the late 1960s voices were vigorously raised demanding that this tradition be supplemented—some even said, replaced—by a new paradigm that accounted for the encounter between Christianity with other world religions and for the new realities of ecological crisis, peace ethics, human rights claims, and north–south tensions.

6. In direct line with these calls for change, the rise of the social sciences as a serious academic discipline resulted in its inclusion in the overall agenda for a new kind of theological reflection in the LWF.

To take all of these challenges seriously, however, required that the matter not be limited to theologians alone, as though they could somehow connect traditional theological discourse to new concerns and new methodologies. The problem did not appear simply as a call for adding something to what was already present. A fundamental revisioning was necessary. Classical theology had to be placed in a radically widened framework with new attention to mutuality and dynamic interaction, and sensitivity to such hitherto unrecognized global realities as racial oppression, social injustice, and the exploitation of natural resources.

## How the Change Appeared

In order more concretely to illustrate the force of the preceding rather theoretical analysis, it will prove helpful to give a few specific examples of how these changes in the LWF understanding of the role of theology in its life were carried out.

In the work of the Swedish theologian Gustaf Wingren (b. 1910) the oscillation between continuity and change is vivid. Wingren had been appointed Professor of Systematic Theology (Dogmatics) at the University of Lund at exactly the time of the First Assembly of the Lutheran World Federation, 1947. He was then identified as the youngest spokesperson for the "Lundensian Theology" associated with Anders Nygren, Gustaf Aulén, and Ragnar Bring, an identification he later rejected. By nature Wingren was a passionate debater, and his writings were marked by polemical confrontations with such theological luminaries as Karl Barth, Rudolf Bultmann, and even his mentor, Anders Nygren himself. His capacity for systematic analysis was internationally noted through his contributions to the critical reinterpretation of Martin Luther and was abundantly demonstrated at the Hanover Assembly of the LWF in 1952 when he delivered a major platform address on "Lutheran Theology and World Mission." In this perspective it is clear that Wingren was representative of "the sages' discourse" as carried out in the early years of LWF history, even though he was not in an ongoing way involved in the LWF before 1970.

In the crucial period around 1970, however, Gustaf Wingren, who was then a member of the LWF Commission on Theology, played a leading part in the reexamination of the role of theology in the life of the Federation. He did not hesitate to take up the challenges posed by secular ethics, nor did he refrain from new controversies. At the Evian Assembly of the Federation, 1970, he appeared both as a senior representative of classical northern European Lutheranism and as one committed to theological revision and renewal. It was seen, in LWF circles and beyond, as a spectacular sign of ecumenical reorientation that Wingren was one of those who publicly proposed, to no official avail, that the Nobel Peace Prize be awarded to the Brazilian Roman Catholic Archbishop, Dom Helder Camara.

Professor Heinz-Eduard Tödt (1918–92) of Heidelberg, Germany, was another representative of the classical European tradition who subsequently advocated a thorough renewal in Lutheran theology. Tödt was a leading expert on the theology of Dietrich Bonhoeffer and he was thoroughly committed to Bonhoeffer's criticism of conservative Lutheranism's patriarchal tendencies in political ethics. Tödt's keynote address at the Evian Assembly of the LWF, 1970, "Creative Discipleship in the Contemporary World Crisis," was doubtlessly the most penetrating statement for theological innovation at that assembly (see pp. 390–91 below).

These two persons, Gustaf Wingren and Heinz-Eduard Tödt, indicate that to some extent the process of theological renewal in the LWF was initiated by scholars from the churches of northern Europe. Yet at the same time new and crucial contributions to this renewal were being made by persons from the younger churches of the south. A signal instance of this contribution was provided by the declaration "On the Interrelation between Proclamation of the Gospel and Human Development" issued by the Evangelical Ethiopian Church Mekane Yesus in 1972. The significance of this statement, which is thoroughly considered in chapters 2, 3, and 4 above, was enhanced by the fact that one of its chief authors and advocates was Emmanuel Abraham (b. 1913), a prominent Ethiopian diplomat at the time, layperson, and president of the Mekane Yesus Church. Dr. Abraham, who had participated in the first All Africa Lutheran Conference held at Marangu, Tanganyika in 1955, came to be one of the leading personalities within the LWF, giving one of the major addresses at the Budapest Assembly in 1984. The importance of the declaration on "Proclamation and Human Development" and the discussion it provoked can hardly be overestimated; it contributed greatly to the revisioning of the role of theology in the Federation. A few comments on its theological significance are appropriate here.

The order of things in the declaration's title—*proclamation* and then *human development*—is no coincidence. It was the basic intention of the declaration to give witness to the gospel. Without explicit reference to Luther, the Augsburg Confession, or any other classical document in the Lutheran tradition, it presents an emphatic exposition of the nature of the church (the proclamation) as based upon salvation through Christ and marked by the presence of the Holy Spirit. Proclamation, in this interpretation, neither leaves room for separation between faith and action, nor between the Living Word and its contextual interpretation. "A true theological definition of a responsible church must always grow out of an 'action situation,' or, to go even one step further, true biblical and evangelical theology must always allow for a contextual interpretation of the Gospel and the action strategy of the church, and priorities must be decided upon in faithfulness to this interpretation" (*Proclamation and Human Development*, 13).

With similar clarity the declaration gives a foundational definition of the human person ("man") as a presupposition for a clarification of anthropological concerns that are to be interpreted in relation to a properly clarified connection between proclamation and human development. There can be no service for the wholeness of life, no holistic anthropology, unless the biblical witness to creation, sin, and renewal are taken into account. "The brokenness of man and of the world at large has its real root in the sinful nature of man. Sin is not only situational or an act which destroys the relationships between man and man and between man and God, but it is a reality in itself within the individual. The healing of the brokenness in human life can therefore never be accomplished without the Gospel message of forgiveness which has in itself the power to liberate man from the most dehumanizing power in his own life and in his relationships with other men and God" (ibid., 14). Importantly, it was exactly through such "classical" clarification of the relationship between anthropology and ecclesiology that the actual scene in Ethiopia was exposed. As we shall

see, this declaration, "Proclamation and Human Development," had wide
ramifications for other churches within the Lutheran family as well.

*The LWF Ecclesiology Study*
*as the Chief Testimony to Change*

A watershed—perhaps thus far *the* watershed—in the LWF debate on the
role of theology came to expression in the project of the Department of
Studies, "The Identity of the Church and Its Service to the Whole Human
Being." Hardly any other theological project in the history of the Federation was ever undertaken with comparable creativity and enthusiasm.
Hardly any other initiative taken by the staff in Geneva was ever marked
by the same degree of happy interaction between the secretariat, which
assumed careful and dynamic leadership, and representatives of member
churches, who exhibited extraordinarily high degrees of cooperation. And,
to maintain balanced and honest historical judgment, hardly any other
theological work of the Federation aroused more controversy and debate
on practically all levels than this "ecclesiology study."

Responsibility for the project was in the hands of Ulrich Duchrow
(b. 1935) who in 1970 had become Director of the Department of Theology, soon to become the Department of Studies. Duchrow was a Luther
scholar from the University of Heidelberg, Germany; he thus shared the
same research milieu as Heinz-Eduard Tödt. His dissertation was a histor-
ical-theological examination of the notion of the two kingdoms, analyzed
within its contexts before, during, and after the Reformation. It was
Duchrow's clear intention in his study of the two kingdoms to avoid a
false dualism in interpreting Luther, a dualism which he felt had sadly and
mistakenly dominated modern Lutheranism.

Even though Duchrow had a key if not dominant role in the carrying out
of the ecclesiology study—in inception, implementation, and development—he was himself determined not to exercise such central control as
would impose method and content on participants from the LWF member
churches. It was, rather, his desire to encourage *self-studies* within the
member churches, that is, to allow regulating principles of examination to
be developed from appropriate empirical contexts. Such an "inductive
method," however, rested on the presupposition that ruling guidelines for
the study had been carefully prepared in advance and presented to the participants. Without such guidelines participants would not be able to reach
the ultimate goal of the study: to present a multifaceted overview of the
global community of Lutheran substreams in order to reach comparative
assessments that would facilitate broad, critical reorientations. Accordingly, the point of departure of the study, which was formally launched in

March of 1973, was to be "the context of real history," the daily life of congregations with special attention to their embodiments in specific socio-economic and cultural settings. This point of departure in actual fact led to a noticeable and determined tone of tension and struggle in the study's description, a reflection perhaps both of Duchrow's own concern with the heritage of the German church struggle and of actual tensions in many of the younger Lutheran churches.

The study was intended to foster self-clarification on the part of each member church, and to achieve this an adaptation of current, critical theory from the social sciences was required. From its beginning this analytical study was described as being directed toward "life, structure and action" in dynamic interplay, with the clear intention "to see feed-back or lack of feed-back between the dimensions of faith, institution and practice." The study consciously rejected allegedly abstract methods of traditional theology in favor of a combination of "socio-historical and theological methods as tools for repentance and renewal." Specific areas of concern were singled out as having central impact on the description of the identity of the churches: (1) the development and use of resources (economic and other forms of public support); (2) the participation of women, men, and youth; (3) political conflicts and opportunities; (4) pluralistic cultures; and (5) ecumenical relations applicable to all areas of concern. The use of "socio-historical" methods was, it must be pointed out, accompanied in the study by a deep concern to analyze biblical images of the church for the sake of developing a modern ecclesiology.

The study was marked by a passionate, prophetic approach in its appropriation of a somewhat provocative ecumenical perspective. In its introduction, the ecclesiology study acknowledged its debt to other recent LWF projects, notably "the work on root causes of social and economic injustice and the Two Kingdom studies." Yet it is also acknowledged that there was now a clear necessity to let the project proceed with an authentic ecumenical dimension which had hitherto not been characteristic of LWF theological work. Thus, from its start the ecclesiology study was carried on in an atmosphere of trial and judgment.

The tone of controversy that permeated the ecclesiology study is particularly to be found in its identification of specific areas of Lutheran theology and church life that required critical attention:

1. "The overemphasis on individual salvation and the uncritical going along with so-called autonomous laws of the world."
2. "The uncritical isolation and over-institutionalization of word and sacraments with regard to the other marks of the church, leading to a gap between priesthood and laity, between teaching and living, as well as between Sunday and Monday."

3. "The naive takeover of highly institutionalized, hierarchical (and expensive) patterns of administration and organization from social and political institutions instead of being concerned with alternative models of community."

4. Finally, the lack of concern for ecumenical openness, and instead adherence to "unecumenical confessionalism," the consequences of which have been worsened "in a colonial and neo-colonialistic world situation."

The study could well be described as a merciless showdown. These negative judgments concerning areas of Lutheran theology were, to be sure, supplemented by considerations concerning "cells and signs of repentance and renewal." The adoption of methods shaped by critical social theory was to be counterbalanced by an exposition of the healing role of crisis and of "living alternatives—concretely liberating Gospel, meaning base-communities as alternatives to established, hierarchical churches, who are insisting on their power and privileges." A new spiritual community was suggested, based upon sharing and solidarity. This led to open questions: "Is it at all possible to shape the church as a large organization according to the spirit?" and, "Is it at all possible to transfer the model or parts of the model of a community in the spirit of Christ to large, complex and technologically mediated systems?"

It would go beyond the boundaries of the present chapter to review each of the case-studies produced within the framework of the ecclesiology study. Two printed "Final Volumes," of 777 and 271 pages (1977; cf. Bibliographical Notes, p. 212 below), leave the reader with a picture of world Lutheranism distinctive in its identity and pluralism, its present challenges and future prospects, and its multiplicity and yet also its communion.

"Final Volume I" covers the continents. Africa is represented by case studies from Ethiopia, Madagascar, Tanzania, Namibia and Southern Africa, and Liberia; Asia by the Indian Lutheran churches, Hong Kong, and Indonesia; North America by the United States; Latin America by Mexico, Chile, Argentina, and Brazil; the Nordic countries by Finland, Sweden, and Norway; the European continent by the Federal Republic of Germany and the German Democratic Republic. "Final Volume II" comprises a report by a study group—Trond Bakkevig of Norway, William Everett and Karl Hertz of the United States, Judah Kiwovele of Tanzania, and Gerta Scharffenorth of Germany—that had been commissioned to present a summary and critical evaluation of the findings presented in the case studies. This concluding evaluation was undertaken within the framework of LWF decisions taken at the Evian Assembly and subsequent global developments; specific reference was also given to the overall situation in Southern Africa and to the LWF debate that originated in Ethiopia, "Proclamation and Human Development." This second volume also included a sketch of Luther's ecclesiology both in its original historical setting and as it had developed since the Reformation. There is a strong affirmation of the key conclusion: there must be a connection between human needs and the proclamation of the gospel, between "what the church is according to its divine institution and what it is to do in the world" (II, 24). It is also maintained that the study, as a significant contribution to a fuller understanding of the life of the churches and their communion together, had been carried out as an exchange of views: "Critical and constructive contributions from partners belonging to other churches enabled participants to transcend the limited scope of their own thinking and gain new insights" (II, 29).

This final statement of the ecclesiology study covers a whole range of essential issues in ecclesiology, together with concrete recommendations to the governing bodies of the Lutheran World Federation. These considerations—from observations concerning ecclesial ministry and authority to matters of service and participation—would seem to have provided material for years of reflection and activity within the Federation. Yet there is reason to ask whether the Federation has ever done justice to the seriousness of these issues as presented in the study. Even as it is to be acknowledged, however, that many recommendations of the study were never put into effect, it is also true that many of the study's conclusions have become matters of intense negotiation.

The study's conclusions possess an urgently pastoral tone: "We believe that the Lutheran community must address itself to the brokenness that exists in its midst; it must do so out of concern not only for the persons involved, for the churches and their traditions, but also to safeguard the integrity of the Gospel it proclaims and its confession to that Gospel. Faithful action in this situation would also be proclaiming the whole Gospel to the whole human being" (II, 248). Pastoral concerns and challenges of this nature touched directly on subsequent issues within the LWF, most dramatically on the matter of the relationship between the nature of the church and human rights, particularly seen in the *status confessionis* discussion (see chapters 6 and 9 below).

## Studies: Vitality and Tension

The ecclesiology study was surrounded, in the Department of Studies, by other projects of diverse yet related character. One set of initiatives was gathered under the theme, "Peace, Justice, Human Rights"; another under the theme "Marxism, China, Missiology, Other Religions"; a third under "Life and Work of the Churches" (for example, worship, the role of women, education, and communication); and finally a fourth was "Interconfessional Dialogue." All of these concerns had grown out of the Evian Assembly and were seen, particularly by younger churches, as issues of considerable importance.

In the 1970s the work of the Department of Studies possessed considerable vitality and vision accompanied by remarkable dedication. At the same time, however, there was tension and controversy around the work of Studies. Some within the LWF perceived that the department had allowed its work to be marked by one-sided politically and ideologically determined strategies. In retrospect it must be acknowledged that at least an element of this criticism was justified.

An illustration of the problem is to be found in the project, "The Encounter of the Church with Marxism in Various Cultural Contexts with Special Reference to China" (cf. pp. 171–72 above). The studies undertaken in this project could well be described as instances of "prophetic denunciation" which were seen as forcing "the Churches and each Christian to see the integration of three closely interrelated dimensions for the theology, life and witness of the church: the theoretical (ideology criticism), the institutional (ways of decision-making and structures of power) and the practical (individual challenge to join in common struggle with the oppressed)." Yet statements such as these were signs of the time, not to be ascribed to narrow pressure groups, whether members of the LWF staff or others within the Federation. In reality these concerns, as has been seen in our survey of five decades of LWF history (chapter 2), were frequently shared by persons from the Two-Thirds World itself. Those (and their numbers were not large) who raised their voices in criticism of these tendencies within the LWF Department of Studies often failed to discern signs and movements that encircled the globe. Yet how is it to be explained that this period, the 1970s, when theology possessed a high profile in the Lutheran World Federation, is so frequently described as a period of tension and controversy rather than as one of far-reaching renewal?

Clearly there was a tone to the initiatives from the Department of Studies that gave rise to feelings of uneasiness and opposition. These feelings came both from significant voices within the member churches and from other departments within the Geneva secretariat of the LWF. It was patently clear, for instance, that the LWF Department of World Service, led by its director, Bruno Muetzelfeldt, was steadfastly in opposition to the work of the Department of Studies. It was equally obvious that there was little willingness in the Department of Studies to take such voices of dissent into serious account. "Prophetic denunciation," as pursued in Studies, was marked by inclinations to be confrontational and to dismiss disagreement as misguidedly reactionary, the complacent reluctance of old-fashioned intellectuals to see the need for change. In connection with the project on Marxism, for instance, the reasons were sought for the lack of participation from some of the larger LWF member churches. The hesitation of those churches was described within the Department of Studies with condescending irony: some "were uneasy about the seeming radicality of the overall approach"; others were thought to have been wary for "internal political reasons," and a still more deplorable group was said not "to have been quite ready to ask these questions and to be questioned by others."

Most likely, such failures on the part of the Department of Studies to accept criticism and a plurality of viewpoints, to combine "prophetic denunciation" with the task of achieving basic consensus concerning Lutheran identity, may help explain why many of the promising initiatives from this period were subsequently set aside or at least postponed.

### Another "Ecclesiology Study"

A project parallel and simultaneous to the major endeavor of the Department of Studies, "The Identity of the Church and Its Service to the Whole Human Being," was undertaken by the LWF–sponsored Institute for Ecumenical Research at Strasbourg. It also was concerned with ecclesiology and dealt specifically with the matter of confessional identity, albeit with the explicit argument that growing ecumenical fellowship posed basic internal theological questions for Lutheran identity. The Strasbourg project—frequently referred to as the "identity study" in contrast to Geneva's "ecclesiology study"—further, aimed at a translation of "the positive results of ecumenical-theological dialogues into actual church fellowship."

The two studies differed in respect to both method and content as they faced diverse contexts within worldwide Lutheranism. Whereas the Geneva "ecclesiology study" had its methodology based in "self-studies," the Strasbourg "identity study" started from a more classical view of both the nature of Christianity and Lutheran identity; the contrast was that of inductive and deductive approaches. The Strasbourg enterprise, however, was not designed as an escape from "engagement" and "action;" it rather involved *the necessity of examining* the fundamental and yet tension-ridden interrelationships between identity and engagement, existence and action. "The question of what Christian identity, Christianity and Christian faith are, again appears as a necessary base, a center of orientation for an adequate and relevant Christian engagement and adequate and relevant Christian service in the world." The classical character of the Strasbourg project is also apparent from the fact that it included detailed investigation of historical developments during and after the Reformation. The project was less ambitious than the Geneva initiative chiefly because it involved fewer participants.

Even though there were differences between the two projects, they nevertheless must be seen as twin enterprises that led to different results. To be sure, the simultaneous implementation of these parallel efforts is remarkable in itself. Their coexistence, however, does not necessarily imply that one was "mistaken," or that one should have been dismissed as a mere waste of resources. On the contrary, a closer relation between Geneva and Strasbourg in this instance could have provided a constructive point of departure for an overall assessment of many crucial issues facing the Federation. Such a clarification, however, was not obtained, most probably because divergent opinions and methods were perceived as points of tension rather than as opportunities for dialogue. Additionally, governing structures within the LWF were diverting the Federation's attention in other pressing directions. The improved cooperation came in the third period when, after the Curitiba Assembly, a third ecclesiology study was launched, directed from the newly established desk for Theology and the Church. A working group on ecclesiology under the leadership of Heinrich Holze (b. 1955) produced a statement "Toward a Lutheran Understanding of Communion" that was received by the LWF Council in 1996.

## The Third Period:
## Theology in an Era of Fragmentation

TO IDENTIFY PRECISELY the year 1977 as another turning point in the development of the role of theology within the Lutheran World Federation requires nuance. The main issue at the Sixth Assembly of the Federation, Dar es Salaam 1977, was the debate on *status confessionis*, an issue that had been fermenting for some time within the Federation and a topic that remained high on its theological agenda through the Seventh Assembly, Budapest 1984. Yet, in spite of the dominance of this concern, there is reason to see the late 1970s as a time in which global fragmentation was beginning. The phrase "global fragmentation" is itself paradoxical: How is it that the search for a holistic mission and theology which had marked the LWF was in point of fact replaced by seemingly unceasing fragmentation? And similarly, why did the Federation's quest for global community seem precisely at this time to be threatened by regional contextualization? This paradox can be discerned at several levels and, since these points touch on the basic role of theology within the LWF, we shall examine several issues that reveal both the difficulty of achieving balance and the risks and tensions inherent in diversity.

1. *Consensus versus controversy.* The preceding chapters have shown that it really was not possible simply to transfer the accomplishments of the first generation of LWF leaders to the changing contexts of the late 1960s and the 1970s. The inclusion of new member churches and the agenda defined by international social, political, and economic realities led to a style of theological reflection marked by provocative divergence, by what has been called "prophetic denunciation." Was this a clear alternative, or might it have been possible that the struggle for convergence could proceed along with the maintenance of uncompromising ideals? Ever since the period in question, a period of dramatic confrontation, this dilemma has presented a major methodological challenge to the quest for an adequate redefinition of the role of theology in the LWF.

2. *Global Lutheran identity versus regional differentiation.* The determination to discern a global identity for Lutheranism ran counter to attempts at contextualization, attempts to take specific and divergent regional realities into account. How could this challenge be converted into a constructive approach that took seriously "both/and"?

3. *Confessional identity versus ecumenical openness.* From the start, the first years of the LWF, the task of defining loyalty to the Lutheran confessional heritage seemed to some observers to clash with ecumenical, transconfessional openness. How could witness and prophecy, which sprang out of inner convictions based upon an historically defined identity, be combined with a willingness to enter into authentic and creative dialogue with persons from other traditions?

4. *Academic discourse versus the common and popularly expressed concerns of the churches.* The criticisms directed toward traditional theology by the laity, particularly young persons, could not be avoided. Charges were leveled against abstract, elitist, North Atlantic viewpoints. It was in part as a consequence of such charges that the LWF restructuring of 1969 proposed the replacement of "Theology" with "Studies." This replacement was aimed at bringing together divergent concerns both within the member churches and the Geneva staff. Could sterile confrontation be replaced by constructive interaction?

5. *Classical theology versus a theology of modern reference.* "Classical" theology was characterized by an interrelationship between biblical, historical, and systematic (dogmatic) disciplines. It had proved difficult, however, to integrate new areas of both practical and academic concern—law, economics, health, education, and so on—into this kind of theological discourse. Could there take place a genuine integration of and fearless engagement between traditional theological study and the "new knowledge"?

6. *Tradition versus renewal.* Theology in its traditional sense was often defined as the unflagging struggle to preserve a threatened heritage. In the

face of this tradition was formed an alliance between rebellious prophets from the older churches and leaders from the younger churches who together advocated "renewal without looking back." Here again: was rapprochement possible?

7. *Central leadership versus grass roots initiative.* Theological cooperation during the Federation's first generation had been fostered by efficient and creative coordination in the Geneva secretariat. The post-Evian period was marked by calls for decentralization, by contextual initiatives founded on base groups and grass root thinking, and this seems to have required a more flexible interaction between global and regional centers. Drastic reductions in the size of the Geneva staff intensified this requirement. In this situation was it to be possible to render services of coordination for the sake of global community without neglecting the integrity of local groups?

These seven antinomies reveal the tension between continuity and discontinuity which marked theological reflection in the LWF after the Evian and Dar es Salaam Assemblies. Oscillation in the face of paradox was apparent and was to be revealed ever more starkly in new projects which were devoted to issues which seemed to possess continuing relevance.

### Justification and Justice

As noted previously, the debate on justification at the Fourth Assembly of the LWF, Helsinki 1963, was designed to sum up what had been on the theological agenda of the Federation during the first fifteen years of its history. Even at Helsinki, however, there was a palpable shift in the terms of theological understanding as compared, say, with the founding period of the Federation. The Helsinki study document mentions "a quiet shift from a theocentric to an anthropocentric approach," a shift that needed serious theological consideration. Moreover, the document highlighted such other changes as the new atmosphere in relation to the Roman Catholic Church, new trends in biblical and liturgical scholarship, and others. As encouraging as this new situation appeared, however, there was a counterbalance of "an erosion of theological terms," that is, secularization as a threatening deprivation of established values which in fact depleted the heritage that nourished preaching in the church and theological discourse in the academy.

At certain points the study document of the Helsinki Assembly contained noticeable instances where application was called for in respect to present conditions in society (nationalism), in culture (materialism), and in church life. But on the whole, the impression left by the document is one of a classical theological contrast between the self-righteousness of man and the righteousness of God, and this was clearly aimed at a "reha-bilitation of theological terminology." Such a rehabilitation would clearly have required an intramural, academic (North Atlantic) approach, seen in opposition to an engagement by the church in political matters that would have called for new church involvements. It was exactly this latter judg-ment—that the document, albeit with goodwill, neglected the main chal-lenges facing the churches, particularly those from the Two-Thirds World—that led leaders from the south to engage in an attempt to restore imbalance. In retrospect, however, the question arises whether or not it was justified to blame the Commission and Department of Theology merely for a failure to connect the values of traditional Lutheran theology with a critical analysis of modern society. The problem was not so super-ficial; it rather possessed a more foundational character and was an early reflection, in 1963, of a turn of epochs, a paradigm shift in the character of theological reflection.

This problem reappeared in the LWF in the 1980s after the storms of the 1970s. In that decade several new initiatives were taken to deal with the basic question—for example, a discussion of the relationship between the classical Lutheran understanding of justification and "liberation theol-ogy," particularly as found in Latin America. These initiatives coincided with a comprehensive evaluation of Luther's theology in the context of the Two-Thirds World. An important conference on this theme was held in Brazil in 1988, designed "to ask ourselves about the reasons that have led to the transformation of Luther's dynamic theology into a static one, of a dialectic theology into a theology of dualism, of a prophetic theology into one that stabilizes established orders" (*Rethinking Luther's Theology in the Contexts of the Third World*, 132). This shift in methodology stands in remarkable contrast to the "Luther Renaissance" which marked the LWF's First Assembly, Lund 1947. One of the lecturers at the 1988 event, the Latin American theologian Ricardo Pietrantonio, gave vigorous expression to the new direction when he urged that there should not simply be talk of liberation but that dimensions from the realms of economics, society, and politics should be integrated into the agenda of theology itself in order to articulate what he labeled "the spirituality of society." With this Pietrantonio turned his back on all forms of Western economic capitalism which to him lack all awareness of solidarity and moral sensitivity. The discussion in Brazil was based largely on this call for political strategies intended to connect justification with justice, in particular to create a con-nection between technological progress designed to bring about lasting improvements in the conditions of life, especially in the south, and an authentically ethical view of life (ibid., 72).

Efforts similar to those of 1988 are reflected in a more recent study prepared by the LWF Department for Theology and Studies (the name given to the department in the course of the LWF restructuring that followed the Eighth Assembly, Curitiba 1990) for a seminar held in connection with the meeting of the LWF Council in Madras, India, 1992. This study, *Justification and Justice,* was the first to be published under the directorship of Viggo Mortensen (b. 1942). It signalizes his wish to stress "the fundamental relationship between the ongoing struggle for justice and the concept of justification, a cornerstone of the Lutheran Reformation" (p. 7). The contribution to this study of the Brazilian theologian Vitor Westhelle (b. 1952) is notable in its identification of a proposed supplement to the traditional emphasis upon Christology in any genuine interpretation of justification. Westhelle suggested the inclusion of a theology of creation in the doctrine of justification in order to "outline positively our experience in the world." Creation, as underscored by Westhelle, must not be understood in a dualistic sense as merely the scene of the history of salvation; rather, as he suggests, it should be understood as "a worldly history in and through which we confess that God creates the space for human belonging" (*Justification and Justice,* p. 35).

"Justification and justice," as an enduring theme for theological reflection in the life of the Lutheran World Federation, can from this brief discussion be seen as one point where a constructive rethinking of the core of the Lutheran heritage is taking place.

## Theology, Pluralism, and the Encounter of Religions

In the 1960s a discussion started within the LWF regarding the relationship between a theology of mission based upon the traditions of the older, established churches on the one hand, and the multifaceted religious picture now presented to the younger churches on the other hand (see chapter 4 above). The issue involved not merely historical practices of mission agencies and practical realities of life on mission fields, it touched on matters of principle as well. The discussion was finally a kind of "farewell" to older, one-dimensional ways of missionary thought and practice, but in its initial stages it was no more than a modest beginning of a major shift. It can be agreed that in the 1960s the imperative to listen to non-Christian religions and cultures was beginning to be heard, but—judged by the standard of more recent research, experience, and insight—it is doubtful that living interaction was yet being set in motion. Did this early phase indicate more than preliminary uncertain steps toward involvement with the issues of pluralism? The LWF was moving toward genuine encounter and even dialogue with non-Christian faiths through a program with different foci undertaken by Arne Sovik (b. 1918) in the 1970s, on Encounter with

Other Faiths and Ideologies. In cooperation with the Dialogue Center in Aarhus, Denmark, a study on "new religious movements" was undertaken, since these groups were emerging in many western and northern countries challenging the churches to respond.

By the 1980s the picture changed gradually. In 1984 a special desk was established for The Church and People of Other Faiths. Such developments were one reminder, among several, that basic theological reflection on the nature of the Christian mission was needed. "Dialogue" was the widely used watchword, although in reality that word itself entailed more challenges than solutions. The task was to define a position in the middle of the road, taking "consciousness of pluralism" as an incentive for the appropriate process of rethinking mission, as a chance for gaining valuable insight which would do justice to the realities of living world religions as well as to the inner situations of the churches, whether "old" or "young." As the first Study Secretary for the Church and People of Other Faiths within the Department of Studies, Paul Rajashekar (b. 1948), a Lutheran theologian from India, wrote in 1988:

> The nature of interreligious encounter is such that it takes us beyond our traditional domain. It involves crossing our set boundaries or perimeters of self-understanding and obliges us to explore rather unfamiliar territories. The further we penetrate such unfamiliar terrain the more we become self-conscious of our identity. Therefore, to avoid the risk of capitulating or relativizing Christian beliefs and convictions under the pressure of the immediate, pragmatic exigencies of our religious situation, we need to be sure about our identity in relation to others. (LWF Report, No. 23/24, 1988, *Religious Pluralism and Lutheran Theology*, p. 13)

The optimism that marks this plea for a pioneering spirit contains more diagnoses of the agenda than well-thought-out propositions for the theological task itself. Without disguising the character of his open-ended proposals for a new program, the same author, Paul Rajashekar, also provided constructive suggestions for the method that appears to be required. Having given up the inner logic of classical, doctrinal thinking and the temptation merely to repeat inherited interpretations, Rajashekar proposed a method of correlation, using "dynamic interaction" as a core principle. He maintained that there can be benefit from exposure to new and enriching ways of thinking not previously known. At the same time, he reflected on the Lutheran heritage from refreshingly new angles, underlining the character of authentic dialogue by proposing a "hermeneutics of cross-reference," proposed originally by the Fathers of the early church. This posture of cross-reference implies

> that Christians, by being attentive to the truth claims of others and especially to the questionings that give rise to different answers in other faiths, are com-

pelled to incorporate those questions and answers in articulating their distinctive claim. It may indeed be that Christians recognize forms of truth in others as being "Christian" not in the sense that they own it, but as expressions of God's universal love. Even radical differences that emerge in mutual encounters may shed light on our articulation of faith and thus enrich us in ways that we cannot predict. This process is a mutual one, and others experience the same with reference to their own fiduciary framework. (ibid., p. 19)

The program continued under the leadership of Hance Mwakabana (b. 1939) and reached an interim conclusion with a consultation in Bangkok 1996 on "Theological Perspectives on Other Faiths: Towards a Theology of Religions."

## Tradition and Renewal in Liturgical Theology

Reflection on the church's worship has from the beginning been a manifestation of theological work in the Lutheran World Federation. Significant change over the five decades of LWF history is, as in other areas, apparent here. An initial Commission on Liturgy chaired by Christhard Mahrenholz (1900–1984) of Germany, one of five study commissions that comprised the early Federation structure, presented a report for the LWF's Third Assembly, Minneapolis 1957, as well as a document on "Basic Principles for the Organization of the Main Worship Service in the Evangelical Lutheran Church." That document, which reflected the atmosphere of the first LWF decade, was based on an interpretation of Luther's renewal of the worship of the church at the time of the Reformation; it was criticized by some. The report breathed the air of cultural homogeneity, as was typical of that era, but was aimed at unity of faith but not uniformity in worship. After the Minneapolis Assembly in 1957, work in worship was integrated into the Commission on Theology, and for the 1963 Helsinki Assembly this resulted in a document on "Prayer in the Life of the Congregation," considering both corporate and individual prayer.

The Helsinki Assembly once again created separate commissions for Theology and for Worship and Spiritual Life. Staffed by Friedrich-Wilhelm Künneth (b. 1933), this new worship commission had members from Ethiopia and Indonesia as well as Europe and the United States. It is thus not surprising that within the work of this office (in addition to a major study on forgiveness, a study of lectionaries, and sending observers to the Vatican II liturgical council) attention was given to questions of what was then termed "liturgical indigenization."

The Evian Assembly reorganized studies efforts once again, and worship was subsumed under the new Department of Studies. Major attention to worship was not given until after the 1977 Assembly in Dar es Salaam, when Eugene L. Brand (b. 1931) of the United States served as part-time -co-opted staff in worship and from 1982 as secretary of the new worship desk. Major attention was given to the cultural context of worship as well as to several other issues (including the centrality of the Eucharist, children and worship, training in liturgy and music for pastors, and the ecumenical dimensions of worship). Brand pointed to the inherent way in which Christian worship is countercultural as well as contextual (*A Lutheran Agenda for Worship*, 1979, p. 26). However, within a few years this desk was also given responsibility for ecumenism and ecclesiology, and gradually the work in worship was concluded.

Following the Curitiba Assembly the new structure provided a Department for Theology and Studies, one desk of which was for Worship and Congregational Life, staffed by S. Anita Stauffer (b. 1947) of the United States. The work of this desk attempted to maintain a balance between an appreciation of Luther's accomplishment in the renewal of worship, and more recent ecumenical developments in respect to both the theology and practice of liturgy. The major focus of the work was the relationships between Christian worship and the cultures of the world—building not only on the prior work of Künneth and Brand but also on the Department of Studies' "Confessing Christ in Cultural Contexts" study of 1975–1983.

It is, therefore, appropriate in this study of the role of theological reflection in the LWF to inquire about the change in focus since the 1950s. What has been its cause? For one thing, the ecumenical climate founded on common theological reflection and with new impressions gained from the worship practices of other Christian bodies has been an instrumental factor in the change. Of equal importance has been the inclusion in the LWF of member churches from quite diverse cultural contexts. This latter fact by itself justifies the importance now given to the question of the *contextualization* of worship. Finally, new insights from the fields of biblical and historical theology offer fresh views both of the origins of Christian worship in Judaism and the early Church and subsequent developments through twenty centuries of history in the world's many cultures.

In the 1990s Worship and Culture Study, Stauffer has provided a clear exposition of a methodology that combines inductive and deductive approaches. The aim has not only been to develop a process for contextualization but to achieve a balance between that which is "authentic and relevant, Lutheran and catholic, local and global, Christocentric and anthropocentric" (*Worship and Culture in Dialogue*, 1994, p. 11), and thus between the transcultural, contextual, and countercultural aspects of worship. American liturgical scholar Gordon Lathrop (b. 1939) has—in connection with the LWF study—given depth to this methodology. He has proposed that it is necessary to regain a view of "the center," the classical service of Word and Sacrament as redefined by Martin Luther: "The first agenda item for a renewed Lutheran interest in worship accessible to local culture will be renewed scriptural knowledge and strong biblical preaching, new clarity about baptismal teaching and baptismal practice, and the establishment of the Lord's Supper as the principal service in all churches every Sunday" (*Worship and Culture in Dialogue*, 142). This focus on the ecumenically recognized "core" or "center" will prove to be anything but a burdensome yoke; it will provide a liberating power to make worship accessible to local culture. Lathrop suggests a method of "juxtaposition" as appropriate, respecting both the "center" and the richness of local contexts, and balancing the contextual with the counter-cultural. The second volume published out of this study, *Christian Worship: Unity in Cultural Diversity* (1996), makes clear the importance of the ecumenical core as the foundation for contextualization. Throughout LWF history it would seem that theological reflection has enriched both the understanding and practice of worship in Lutheran congregations around the world.

## New Themes for Theological Study

The decisive innovations that marked the LWF's theological work during the 1970s—serious attention to the relation of Christian faith to events in the social, political, and scientific spheres as well as the use of the social sciences in coming to terms with these developments—were never disregarded, even though the more controversial, "prophetic" methodologies which characterized the 1970s were minimized in favor of more irenic consensus seeking methodologies.

The former dean of the theological faculty at the University of Aarhus, Denmark, Viggo Mortensen, came to the Department for Theology and Studies in 1991. He reformulated the social-ethical agenda and concentrated on issues within the areas of "Land," "Life," "Peace," "Justice." Although this represented a follow-up of the JPIC ("Justice, Peace, and the Integrity of Creation") agenda in ecumenical social ethics, it was done in an independent way in dialogue with representatives of various social sciences.

In the area of "Land," attention was paid to questions regarding ethnicity and nationalism (*Region and Religion: Land, Territory and Nation from a Theological Perspective*, 1994). In view of the strong statements in the Curitiba Message the theology of life focused on environmental ethics (*Concern for Creation*, 1995), and studies in bioethics led to the book *Life and Death: Moral Implications of Biotechnology*, 1995. Peace ethics was very high on the agenda of the program secretary 1986–1991, Götz Planer-Friedrich (b. 1939), and studies on how to relate certain churches' strong engagement for peace with the notion of *just war* (CA 16) served as background to the LWF Council's controversial stance on the war in the former Yugoslavia in 1993 (*War, Confession and Conciliarity,* 1993). The area of "Justice" dealt with ethics and the economy, and studies were carried out at the regional level, starting in Europe. The consultation "A Just Europe" in 1991 (published 1992) was one of the first attempts at a theological ethical evaluation of the new political situation in Europe. Africa came next and a consultation on "A Just Africa: Ethics and the Economy" was convened at Moshi, Tanzania in September 1993. The published considerations of this consultation were in many ways an extension of discussions regarding political structures, their root causes, and the many dark shadows which had been cast over the world from the time of colonialism. Issues dealt with included the international debt crisis, the global imbalance in technological progress, inequality of access to natural resources, and, of course, the role of the church in "nation-building."

The Tanzanian event was historic in the sense that it brought together for the first time leading staff from the World Bank and the International Monetary Fund with church leaders and theologians representing the Two-Thirds World. Its atmosphere was not one of confrontation or suspicion, but rather one marked by a determination to enter into close cooperation. At this consultation there was positive dialogue and the potential contribution of the churches was clearly taken seriously by the experts in international finance. Watchwords such as "structural adjustment programs" were joined to suggestions for new educational strategies—"education for life"—which would take seriously the role of women in the development of societies. The responsibilities of the churches, it was concluded, should include major accountability for educational initiatives and health care maintenance as well as the making of substantive contributions to the promotion of sustainable development programs and the redefinition and modification of definitions of interdependent foreign aid between nations.

## Conclusion

THIS SURVEY of the role that theological reflection has played in the history of the Lutheran World Federation has been largely centered around a comparison between initial expectations and the present situation, between the original vision and the present reality. A striking element in our review seems to have been the noting of discontinuities:

1. *Consensus based on academic definitions of confessional identity contrasted with global contextualization and fragmentation;*

2. *The dominance of leadership shaped by the traditions of Europe and*

*North America versus far more inclusive and democratic modes of participation.* Theologians and church leaders in the early periods of the LWF were persons—almost always males—who were steeped in the academic and intellectual traditions of the north. This hegemony has given way to much more globally dispersed groups of participants whose theological questions and expectations have produced radically new interests, applications, and achievements.

3. *The common doctrinal identity of Lutheran theology has been greatly tempered by a new and broadly based ecumenical openness.* Ecumenical involvement has, to be sure, always marked the theology pursued within the LWF, even when confessional witness has been expressed confrontationally. The ecumenical situation is far more varied and even confusing today. On the one hand, remarkable ecumenical convergences have been achieved; on the other hands, local—and even regional—"reception" has not necessarily kept pace with those convergences. The seriousness of this imbalance in ecumenical progress is currently exacerbated by the growth of religious movements, even within the classical Christian families, which can be described as "fundamentalist" or, in certain instances, as one-sidedly concerned for single perspectives or issues.

Other signs of discontinuity in the present situation could, to be sure, be added to these three. Yet it is clear that any summary that concentrates only on discontinuities will be misleading. To be complete, our analysis should include signs of continuity as well, signs which now extend beyond formal, institutional connections. The complex interplay between continuity and discontinuity bears witness to the necessity of giving high priority to historical evaluation of the role of theology in the total life of the Federation. The Program Committee for the Department for Theology and Studies conducted in several sessions in the nineties such a discussion that culminated in the presentation to the council in 1995 of Ten Theses on the Role of Theology in the LWF and a proposal for a consultative process on global issues in theology. Thus it was realized that it is essential carefully to examine links and breaks within the LWF's theological development, to compare the heritage given by the founders to present realities. This kind of scrutiny helps to reflect on past achievements and failures, on present opportunities and challenges, and on future needs and prospects.

Moreover, each of the theological issues mentioned in this volume, in this and other chapters, deserves more detailed and continuous attention. Included in this attention would be the assignment "to evaluate the implicit and explicit theology that is operative in the other [LWF] departments" (V. Westhelle). To fulfill this latter assignment would, as implied, be catalytic for the development of better cooperation between LWF departments and deeper conversations on theological matters than presently exists. This would also reopen a debate which has, as we have seen in this chapter, been present in the LWF since the first discussions concerning the mandate proper to the first Department and Commission of Theology (see above, pp. 183ff.).

Even more intriguing, for our present conclusions, are a number of basic challenges facing the Lutheran World Federation in relation to its theological responsibilities. It is a basic task and permanent obligation of theology that it move beyond single issues and projects to envision them from the perspective of the comprehensive context to which they all belong. For example: The immediate value of an analysis of economic structures must be measured in relation to the basic issue of the unification of diverse aspects of life and thought within Lutheran churches. Similarly, for the LWF it is imperative that the accomplishments of projects relating liturgy and human culture be evaluated in respect to the achievements of several generations of Luther research.

Our point is that it belongs to the basic theological task of the LWF to consider connections, or their absence, between present challenges and projects on the one hand, and a comprehensive view of Lutheran identity on the other. In other words, the strength of the initial phase reviewed in this survey was its unifying vision and the integrity of its academic quality. This provided at the very founding of the LWF a consistency which in hindsight now appears to many as an unattainable ideal, especially in light of the more recent tendency in the LWF to develop disconnected networks of organizational subunits tied together only by bureaucratic measures.

Basic theological considerations are quickly dismissed by some as irrelevant simply because their value is subject to no empirical proof. Yet exactly here lies the danger: it is presently far too convenient to approve only "instrumental" projects that can easily and even statistically be measured as useful or relevant. Critical theology —which ought to be a task of distinction within a federation of Lutheran churches worthy of its name and history—must take up this work precisely in order to transcend purely instrumental, albeit popular, standards of judgment.

Obviously, it is increasingly difficult to further this view of the task of theology within the LWF, a complex organization that must be administered on the basis of political balance, efficiency, and accountability. Yet the alternative is clearly not to view theology as "unappreciated," as the victim of a general decline in proper critical understanding whether the decline is caused by secularism or fragmentation. Such lamentations have no merit unless joined with a corresponding willingness, on the part of those whose vocation is the pursuit of theological understanding, to be self-critical even as constructive suggestions for renewal are made.

In consequence, a balanced view of the role of theology within the
Lutheran World Federation requires a precise diagnosis of present conditions within the Federation itself and of the spiritual, cultural, and sociopolitical climate of the times themselves. Theology, when properly
defined, draws upon a heritage and vision which transcends the genius of
individuals and groups. Genuine theology is called to ecclesial reflection
on the invisible majesty of "the living Word"; it is responsible and responsive, as the Hanover Assembly of the LWF declared in its theme. It is thus
a task—to be conceived and carried out ecumenically—for the whole confessing and worshiping church.

With this understanding in mind, it is appropriate finally to question
whether "theology and studies" as presently conceived in the Lutheran
World Federation is adequately equipped for such a far-reaching endeavor.
Or perhaps the question should be put differently: Can the LWF be both
faithful to its heritage and sensitive to its present challenges without taking the role of critical theology into more serious account?

**Bibliographical Notes** _____

I. Unpublished Documents

> LWF Archives, Geneva.
> Franklin Clark Fry Papers, Evangelical Lutheran Church in America
> Archives, Chicago.
> Hanns Lilje Papers, Lutheran Church Archives, Hanover.
> Anders Nygren Papers, University Library, Lund.
> Regin Prenter Papers, State Archives, Copenhagen.

II. Unprinted Manuscripts and Oral Statements

> Ivar Asheim, Oslo.
> Gyula Nagy, Budapest.
> Vilmos Vajta, Alingsås.
> Vítor Westhelle, Chicago.

III. Publications

> Brand, Eugene L., ed. *A Lutheran Agenda for Worship.* Geneva:
> Lutheran World Federation, 1979.
> Duchrow, Ulrich. *Conflict Over the Ecumenical Movement: Confess-
> ing Christ Today in the Universal Church.* Trans. David Lewis.
> Geneva: World Council of Churches, 1981.
> Hedin, Dag, and Viggo Mortensen, eds. *A Just Europe: The Churches'*

*Response to the Ethical Implications of the New Europe.* Uppsala: *Tro & Tanke* 1992:7.

*The Identity of the Church and Its Service to the Whole Human Being,* 3 vols. Geneva: Lutheran World Federation Department of Studies, 1977.

Kirst, Nelson, ed. *Rethinking Luther's Theology in the Context of the Third World.* Geneva: Lutheran World Federation, 1990.

*Lutheran World/Lutherische Rundschau,* passim.

Mortensen, Viggo, ed. *Concern for Creation: Voices on the Theology of Creation.* Uppsala: *Tro & Tanke* 1995:5.

———, ed. *A Just Africa: Ethics and the Economy.* Geneva: Lutheran World Federation, Department for Theology and Studies, 1994.

———, ed. *Justification and Justice.* Geneva: Lutheran World Federation Department for Theology and Studies, 1992.

———, ed. *Life and Death: Moral Implications of Biotechnology.* Geneva: World Council of Churches, 1995.

———, ed. *Region and Religion: Land, Territory and Nation from a Theological Perspective.* Geneva: Lutheran World Federation Department for Theology and Studies, 1994.

———, ed. *War, Confession and Conciliarity: What does "just war" in the Augsburg Confession mean today?* (with German text, *Krieg, Konfession, Konziliarität*). Hanover: Lutherisches Verlagshaus, 1993.

Planer-Friedrich, Götz, ed. *Frieden und Gerechtigkeit: Auf dem Weg zu einer ökumenischen Friedensethik.* Munich: Chr. Kaiser Verlag, 1989.

Rajashekar, J. Paul, ed. *Religious Pluralism and Lutheran Theology.* Geneva: LWF Report 23/24, 1988.

———, and Kishii, Satoru, eds. *Theology in Dialogue.* Geneva: Lutheran World Federation, Department of Church Cooperation and Department of Studies, 1987.

Stauffer, S. Anita, ed. *Worship and Culture in Dialogue.* Geneva: Lutheran World Federation, Department for Theology and Studies, 1994.

———, ed. *Christian Worship: Unity in Cultural Diversity.* Geneva: Lutheran World Federation, Department for Theology and Studies, 1996

Vajta, Vilmos. *From Generation to Generation. The Lutheran World Federation 1947–1982.* Geneva: LWF Report 16, 1983 .

Westhelle, Vitor. "And the Walls Come Tumbling Down: Globalization and Fragmentation in the LWF." *dialog* 36/1 (Winter 1997): pp. 32–39.

18. A meeting of the first LWF Commission on Theology, Minneapolis, 1957.

19. First meeting of the International Congress on Luther Research, University of Aarhus, Denmark, August 1956.

20. Group that evaluated the LWF Department of Studies project, 1973–1977, on "The Identity of the Church and Its Service to the Whole Human Being." From left: Trond Bakkevig, Norway; Karl Hertz, U.S.A.; William Everett, U.S.A.; Gerta Scharffenorth, Federal Republic of Germany; and Judah Kiwovele, Tanzania.

21. Julius Nyerere, first president of Tanzania, center, gave a major address at a consultation on "A Just Africa" sponsored by the LWF Department for Theology and Studies, September 1993.

CHAPTER

6

# Affirming the Communion: Ecclesiological Reflection in the LWF

WHAT IS THE LWF? The LWF Constitution adopted at Lund in 1947 (Article III.1) gave a deceptively simple answer: "The Lutheran World Federation shall be a free association of Lutheran churches." The meaning of "free association" was partially spelled out in the next sentence: "It shall have no power to legislate for the churches belonging to it or to interfere with their complete autonomy, but shall act as their agent in such matters as they assign to it." The LWF would be a cooperative agency in which the Lutheran churches would come together to accomplish tasks they could carry out better together than apart. It would have no authority over its members.

Yet it would be a free association of Lutheran churches. Article II of the constitution, "Doctrinal Basis," implicitly stated what was meant by "Lutheran." The member churches of the LWF would all see "in the Confessions of the Lutheran Church, especially in the Unaltered Augsburg Confession and Luther's Catechism, a pure exposition of the Word of God." Unlike the World Council of Churches (WCC), the LWF would be united by common commitment to a comprehensive confession.

Just here lay the problem: Could churches that share a common confession be linked only by the bonds of a "free association"? If they are one in confession of the gospel, then are they not one in a far deeper sense than the churches of the WCC, and should that oneness not find expression in an LWF that was something more than just a free association?

---

*Michael Root, Strasbourg, France, is the author of chapter 6.*

The debate over varying answers to that question is the subject of this chapter. The debate involved two closely interrelated but distinct questions. The first is directly about the nature of the LWF as a organization. What is it? In what sense, if any, is it itself a church? If not a church, then what? Important for a Lutheran answer to this question is Article 7 of the Augsburg Confession: "For the true unity of the church it is enough to agree concerning the teaching of the Gospel and the administration of the sacraments." If the churches of the LWF share a common Lutheran confession, then it would appear that they possess the agreement this article describes and are thus one in "the true unity of the church." Does this unity imply then that there is, in some sense, a "world Lutheran church"? If so, what is the relation of such a "church" to the LWF? To some, the line of argument that ran from Augsburg, Article 7, to the idea of a world Lutheran church, with the LWF as its institutional expression or instrument, was irresistible. To others, however, such a line of argument called up the specter of a world "super-church," either on the model of the Vatican or of a world spanning denominational bureaucracy. The question "Is the LWF a church?" oscillated between the poles defined by the seeming logic of a particular understanding of unity and by the fear of any authoritative world structure. This question directly about the LWF can be called the ontological question, since it concerns what sort of thing the LWF is or should be.

A second question was also asked. What sort of fellowship or communion does or should exist among the member churches of the LWF? One could imagine a free association of churches that would imply no fellowship of any sort among its members. An association of churches to run a common pension fund would involve its members in no fellowship at the altar, neither in the pulpit nor in the mission of the church. On the one hand, the first LWF Constitution said nothing about pulpit and altar fellowship among the member churches. As was known to all involved, some Lutheran churches, inside and outside the LWF, were not ready to enter such fellowship because they did not believe Lutherans were really one in Word and Sacrament, despite a common confessional subscription. On the other hand, the Purposes of the LWF, spelled out in Article III.2 of the constitution, seemed to imply that the LWF member churches would together carry out some aspects of the essential mission of the church, for example, to "bear united witness" to the gospel. This purpose not only seemed to presuppose that the member churches were in agreement about what constituted a true witness to the gospel (how else could they bear a united witness?) but also seemed to imply that membership in the LWF would involve a certain kind of fellowship, a fellowship in the activity of witnessing to the gospel. This second question can be called the relational question, since it concerns the relations among the member churches rather than the nature of the LWF itself.

The interrelation of the ontological and relational questions is complex. One could decide that the LWF member churches are in communion and still perhaps defend the organization of the LWF as a free association. If the LWF had significant ecclesial characteristics, however, then it would seem to follow that the member churches were a fellowship like that which exists within a single church.

The debate over the nature of the LWF has been more than an intramural organizational squabble. It was a debate over what binds Christian churches together and what follows from that unity for their common life. Thus, the debate was closely bound up with the ecumenical discussions of this same time (see below, chapter 7). The growth of the LWF was part of a wider pattern in which the various Christian world communions have gained in importance and self-consciousness. All have been faced with the question of the meaning and significance of Lutheran or Anglican or Orthodox unity and all have sought an organizational form that corresponds to their understanding of the communion that binds them together. For the most part, these discussions have been carried on in isolation from one another, but they are species of a common genus.

This chapter describes the history of this debate within the Lutheran World Federation. On the whole, those who contended that the LWF must be more than the free association described at Lund in 1947 have carried the day, although only slowly has the nature of this "more" come into focus. The concepts used to describe and discuss the question have changed; world Lutheranism has itself changed. Part of the difficulty is precisely that the LWF has been and still is in evolution. Nevertheless, the underlying question about the "ecclesial nature" of the LWF forms one of the threads of continuity in the LWF's history. Within this continuity, four distinct phases can be noted. The phases are distinguished by the particular question that focused the discussion. From 1952 until the late 1960s, questions relating to the significance of LWF membership drove the discussion. From 1970 until 1979, the question was most often a subordinate one within the discussion of the relation of the LWF and its member churches to apartheid. From 1979 until 1990, the concept of communion and its applicability to the LWF formed the focus of discussion. We are now in a fourth phase of discussion, in which the implications are being explored of the decision made at the 1990 Curitiba Assembly to redefine the LWF as a communion of churches rather than as a free association of churches.

## 1952–1968: Membership and the Great Debate

THE FIRST PHASE of the debate on the LWF focused on two questions about LWF membership. First, what should be the conditions for membership in the LWF? This directly addressed the question of the sort of doctrinal unity the LWF presupposed and sought. Second, what did membership mean for the member church? Did membership involve the member church in some form of fellowship with the other member churches? If so, what was the nature of that fellowship?

The interest that drove the discussion was the nonmembership of a small number of Lutheran churches, of which the most important was the Lutheran Church–Missouri Synod (LCMS) in the United States. While the nonmember churches were not numerically large, they were the object of considerable attention. The Americans in particular were eager to bring the LCMS into the wider Lutheran fellowship, both nationally and globally. Even some non-Americans, however, felt that the LWF would be incomplete if these churches could not be moved to join.

The objection these churches raised against the LWF was simple: the LWF both formally and factually lacked true consensus in the gospel, and yet it carried out ecclesial activities that presupposed such a consensus.

On the one hand, the argument went, true consensus in the gospel requires more than mere subscription to the letter of the confessions; it is a matter of a shared commitment to follow them. The LWF, however, does not test the true commitment of its member churches, and critics had doubts about the Lutheranism of some, even many, member churches. Beyond questions of membership, the Hanover Assembly had, so it was argued, demonstrated the lack of theological agreement in the LWF. Even the official report of the Hanover Assembly had noted the prominence of disagreement within the Theology Section.

On the other hand, it was argued, the LWF carried out activities of a churchly nature that presupposed the presence of such a doctrinal consensus. A committee of the LCMS contended that when the LWF Constitution speaks of the LWF bearing "united witness to the Gospel" (Article III.2a), then "the Lutheran World Federation is . . . acting as only a church can act. (The witnessing subject is the Lutheran World Federation.)" Even though the opening Eucharist at the Hanover Assembly was sponsored by the local host church and not by the LWF, the very fact of such a service "was and remains an impressive and ineradicable testimony to an assumed oneness, a testimony to which member churches are by the fact of their membership committed." The committee concluded that membership in the LWF in fact involved church fellowship (see LCMS in Bibliographical Note, p. 245 below).

The questions of the nonmember churches were pressed within the LWF by the United Evangelical Lutheran Church in Australia (UELCA), a member church but in merger discussions with a nonmember Lutheran church in Australia. In 1954, the LWF Executive Committee responded to a detailed inquiry from the UELCA with the first official pronouncement on the nature of the LWF after the acceptance of the constitution in 1947. The committee stated that, on the one hand, the LWF had in no way retreated from the earlier confessional statement of the Lutheran World Convention, the Copenhagen Declaration of 1929, which spoke of an "unmistakable adherence to the Holy Scriptures and the Confessions inherited from our Lutheran fathers." The executive committee certainly understood itself as bound to the standard of the Confessions in its activities. On the other hand, the "LWF is most certainly a Federation, not a church." Thus, the LWF has no authority over its member churches and the member churches are not coresponsible for LWF actions with which they disagree. In relation to the difficult question of disciplining a member church, however, the response foreshadowed future developments. If a church were to abandon the common confessional basis, the committee hoped that such a church would itself see this action as breaking fellowship and draw the necessary consequence, that is, leave the LWF. If the church did not draw such consequences, the assembly would have to undertake steps to bring about a separation. What is not said is how an assembly would do this, since the LWF Constitution at that time included no provision for removing a church from its rolls (see "Briefwechsel.")

Although the UELCA pronounced itself pleased with the answer it received from the LWF Executive Committee and reaffirmed its commitment to LWF membership, this answer did not convince the nonmember churches. In 1956, the LCMS voted overwhelmingly to remain outside the LWF.

While the executive committee was discussing the question of LWF membership, an important parallel discussion was occurring within the Theology Commission and the newly created Department of Theology in the form of a study project on "The Unity of the Church." This project produced a volume of essays, *The Unity of the Church: A Symposium*, and influenced the Study Document for the Minneapolis Assembly on the assembly theme, "Christ Frees and Unites." This Study Document in turn formed the basis for the theses adopted by the assembly, the so-called Minneapolis Theses.

Taken together, the published papers, the Study Document, and the Minneapolis Theses constituted a major step forward in ecclesiological reflection within the LWF, even though they did not directly address intra-Lutheran unity or the nature of the LWF. By their rejection of any merely invisible unity and their insistence on the centrality of communion in Word and Sacraments, they laid the foundations for the ecclesiology of communion that would reshape the LWF in the 1980s and 1990s.

Between Hanover and Minneapolis, the discussion of the LWF had taken place within the executive committee, not the Theology Commission, and the membership discussion had not been enriched by the broader explorations the commission was conducting. The decisive change following the Minneapolis Assembly was the interweaving of the membership discussion with the more broadly ecclesiological discussion. The assembly, responding to a recommendation of the commission, asked for a study on the nature of the LWF. This nature was unclear, with the result that "entry into the Lutheran World Federation, or membership and cooperation within it, are made unnecessarily difficult." The Theology Commission was now to take up this question, but at this stage membership and the reluctance of the Missouri Synod and its related churches to join the LWF remained the focus of discussion.

In 1958, the commission invited representatives of the nonmember churches to attend its meeting. The discussion was inconclusive and the commission decided that the nature of the LWF would be better discussed as an issue in itself, without direct reference to (or representation of) the Missouri Synod and its affiliates or to their prospective membership. The Theology Commission now pursued the question as "an ecclesiological problem." This decision to separate the questions was fateful. It gave the commission the space to carry on the most theologically penetrating discussion of the LWF in its entire history. It also separated that discussion from the particular concrete issue that was most pressing for certain parts of the LWF leadership, the membership of the LCMS.

The path for the new, more generally ecclesiological approach to the nature of the LWF was broken by Peter Brunner in a paper written for the 1959 meeting of the Theology Commission and published with responses the following year in *Lutheran World/Lutherische Rundschau*: "The Lutheran World Federation as an Ecclesiological Problem." This then-controversial, today oft-celebrated paper redefined the discussion. The questions were now set, not by the objections of the LCMS and its partner churches, but by the reflections on the unity of the church that had occupied the Theology Commission between Hanover and Minneapolis. This shift in context represents an important aspect of the breakthrough in Brunner's paper and the "Great Debate" it sparked off.

Brunner contends that the LWF embodied a two-sided contradiction. "The one side is that a free association of churches, which expressly refuses to be regarded as a church, is constantly being obliged by its doctrinal basis and its purposes to act and live as a church. The other side . . .

consists in the fact that in the World Federation, despite the actually existing and expressly declared identity of the confessional obligation of the members, what is being realized is only a free association of churches but not *unitas ecclesiae.*"

On the one hand, Brunner argues that the LWF, if it is serious about being Lutheran, cannot avoid certain activities that are ecclesial in character, most notably actions of defining doctrine. Again, membership comes to the fore. "By granting or refusing membership the World Federation decides whether the doctrinal basis of the World Federation is actually operative in the church in question." The contradiction "may be formulated as follows: Although, according to the definition of its nature in Article III.1 of the constitution, the World Federation is not itself a church, because of its binding doctrinal basis it is constantly having to act as a church *in concreto* and by its actions make decisions which lie within the scope of ecclesiastical doctrinal decisions."

On the other hand, Brunner argues that if the common doctrinal foundation of Article II of the constitution is seriously intended, then it is unacceptable that the churches of the LWF are not in fellowship. "If there is a consensus in the understanding of the gospel, then it is our spiritual duty to consummate church fellowship."

What sets Brunner's essay apart is its combination of clear analysis and a passionate insistence that "the Spirit yearns for corporeality," that unity cannot "float about in the realm of an invisible ideal." He never spells out what this corporeal realization of unity would be, but the pressure toward a "more" beyond mere declarations of fellowship is evident in his statement that the LWF "can only develop forward spiritually in the direction of a genuine church which is composed of members and spans the globe but still is not a 'Vatican' church." This rejection of any "Vatican" was meant to calm the ever-reappearing fears of a super-church, but such fears were reawakened by Brunner's willingness to question the usually unquestionable assumption of the autonomy of the member churches. "Today it cannot be the business of the Lutheran churches of the world, and therefore of the World Federation, to perpetuate and make an absolute of that ecclesiastical autonomy of the individual churches which Article III.1 of the constitution was obliged to speak of."

Response to Brunner's paper was mixed. Commission members agreed that the lack of explicit altar and pulpit fellowship among the LWF churches was a scandal that needed rapid remedy. Agreement on this point was central to the judgment of the Theology Commission that something was amiss in the LWF and needed correction.

Beyond this agreement, however, reactions fell into three categories. Some agreed almost completely. A second group rejected, sometimes vehemently, Brunner's analysis of the inherent problems within the phrase "free association of Lutheran churches" and insisted that the LWF must never be more than such a free association. A third group of responses accepted much of Brunner's analysis, but then argued that when altar and pulpit fellowship has been declared, the end point in the development has been reached. As Regin Prenter, chair of the Commission, put it: "It is my own opinion in this question that according to CA [*Confessio Augustana*] VII and XXVIII, pulpit and altar fellowship in themselves constitute full church fellowship, and that, along with this, a central organization is not necessary in order to make church fellowship manifest." Prenter desired a strong answer to the relational question and a weak answer to the ontological question. He was clearly concerned by the pressure toward the "more" in Brunner's essay. For Prenter, this "more" could only be some form of church merger. Especially in Prenter's response, one can see the problem created by the lack of a concept that would describe a form of common life that would be more than free association but less than a single, organizationally integrated church structure.

The "Great Debate" sparked by Brunner's essay raised the level of the discussion of the LWF to a new theological level, but what was now to come of it? Brunner had already suggested in his original paper one possibility: an "authoritative commentary" on the opening articles of the LWF Constitution. The Commission took up this suggestion and together produced a pamphlet entitled "The Nature of the Lutheran World Federation: Commentary on Articles II, III and IV of its Constitution," which was distributed prior to the Helsinki Assembly as Preparatory Document Number 4.

The analysis of Document 4 rests on a threefold distinction: the LWF member churches, the LWF, and that which may come about through the LWF. The LWF member churches are defined by a common confessional commitment spelled out in the constitution's Doctrinal Basis. Sharply distinguished from the churches is the LWF as a free association which in no way binds its members. Since the churches that make up the LWF are churches which share a common confession, however, they are capable of carrying out together churchly tasks, such as those enumerated in Article III of the constitution. These churchly tasks, however, do not make the LWF a church. The document insists that the statement, "The LWF carries out churchly tasks," is in fact only an abbreviation for "The member churches carry out churchly tasks through their instrument, the LWF."

Precisely because such like-minded churches carry out common churchly activities through the LWF, one must add a third element to the distinction: that which might come about through the LWF. "We hope that through the activities of the LWF something new in the realm of the spirit and the church will come into being and develop." What this "something new" might be is not said and is not yet describable, but a section on "Federation and Church Fellowship" makes clear that it must embody the Lutheran churches as a united fellowship of churches, manifesting the essential unity of the church in Word and Sacrament. It must involve more than the mere declaration of altar and pulpit fellowship. "For churches in fellowship with each other, a complete isolation in churchly activity is not possible either. There are certain burning, decisive problems which can be solved rightly only by a joint action of the several Lutheran churches"

This hoped-for fellowship is clearly distinguished from the LWF, both in the present and possibly in the future. Even if and when altar and pulpit fellowship is realized among the member churches, the relation between this fellowship and the Federation will need to be thought through. Perhaps, as Prenter argued, nothing more than a free association still would be needed. The document concedes, however, that even in the present this distinction is inevitably blurred. "The instrument and that which may come into being through it are interdependent, and from this a certain tension arises in the nature of the Lutheran World Federation." Since the LWF is a structure within which churches of a common confession together carry out churchly tasks, it itself participates in that fellowship which comes about through it. Implicitly, the document admits that membership in the LWF involves a certain kind of church fellowship in the form of a common participation in essentially ecclesial actions.

This interdependence is particularly if implicitly evident in what the document says about the difficult issue of membership and doctrinal oversight. When a church is received as an LWF member, it must be ascertained whether its practice in fact corresponds to its doctrinal basis. The member churches in turn have a responsibility to make sure the LWF is true to its doctrinal base and to urge, admonish, and help each other in this respect. "Just as the member churches have a supervisory function with reference to the World Federation and its agencies, the latter in turn have a supervisory function with reference to the member churches. Strictly speaking, this means, of course, that the community of member churches has the obligation of supervising the individual member church." The interweaving of the LWF as instrument and the fellowship of churches that might act through it is here evident. The churches as a community have the responsibility of common doctrinal oversight (a remarkable assertion) and they exercise that through the agencies of the LWF.

What is not yet seen in the document is how fellowship might be established among the LWF member churches. On the one hand, it states, "We are agreed that the LWF should strive to the end that the member churches may come to achieve actual church fellowship among themselves." On the other hand, "How this church fellowship is to be brought about in practice is a matter that cannot yet be described."

Document 4 was a foretaste of later developments. It failed, however, in its immediate purpose of providing an "authoritative commentary" on the constitution. What precisely would an authoritative commentary to the constitution be? What authority would it have in relation to the constitution itself? In response to such questions, General Secretary Schmidt-Clausen sought opinions from experts on church law. While in varying degrees sympathetic with the analysis of the document, they found the idea of an authoritative commentary unacceptable. If the commentary were subordinate to the constitution, then one could always appeal away from the commentary to the actual text of the constitution. If it was understood to define more precisely what the constitution said more vaguely, then the commentary "would basically be nothing but constitutional legislation disguised as a commentary." When the Theology Commission met immediately prior to the Helsinki Assembly, it was forced to the conclusion that the idea of an authoritative commentary was "no longer tenable." Document 4 could only serve as a resource document for whatever actions the assembly might take.

Meanwhile, others had quite different ideas about what the Helsinki Assembly should do with the constitution. The question of LCMS membership had not disappeared when the Theology Commission dropped it in favor of the more general ecclesiological problem. It continued to be pursued by President Fry and Executive Secretary Lund-Quist, both of whom were American and highly interested in LCMS membership. They sought from the LCMS a statement of under what conditions it might enter the LWF.

A response from the LCMS Committee on Doctrinal Unity stated that "before we can recommend to the Lutheran Church–Missouri Synod consideration of membership in the LWF, certain changes in the constitution and provisions to assure its effectual functioning are necessary." Two changes are explicitly noted. First, some provision for suspension of members who do not live up to the membership conditions is needed. Second, those purposes which presuppose "agreement in doctrine and practice" need to be modified, so that LCMS membership would not seem to imply its agreement with the doctrine and practice of some member churches. Explicit mention is made of Article III. 2a, which speaks of bearing a "united witness . . . to the Gospel." "If the constitutional changes indicated in our answers . . . are made, we see a possibility of making our witness heard within the LWF.""

The answers given by the LCMS to the questions placed by the LWF officers seemed to open a real possibility for Missouri Synod membership in the LWF. Thus, as the LWF approached the Helsinki Assembly, two quite different, even mutually opposed, tendencies were at work. On the one hand, the attempt to bring the LCMS and its affiliated churches into the LWF would require a clear statement of the nature of the LWF as a free association that did not assume an agreement in Word and Sacrament of the sort necessary for church fellowship. On the other hand, the process at work within the Theology Commission, embodied in Document 4, would further developments within the LWF that were moving it away from its status as a mere free association, even if these developments did not yet burst the bonds of that definition.

At first glance, the Helsinki Assembly seems to have affirmed the former tendency. The constitutional amendments it adopted were developed during the assembly in extended discussions with the observers present from the Missouri Synod. The amendments proposed to the assembly were those requested by the LCMS in its answers to Fry and Lund-Quist. Suggestions for constitutional changes that would have strengthened unity within the LWF were not taken up. The striking lecture on "The One Church and the Lutheran Churches" by E. Clifford Nelson (b. 1911) during the assembly made no immediate difference.

The suggested amendments to the opening articles of the constitution contained two changes that affected the nature of the LWF. The first was the rewording of Article III on the nature and purposes (now called functions) of the LWF. To the first clause was added the statement that the LWF "shall not exercise churchly functions on its own authority." The statement of purposes or functions was altered to read: "In accord with the preceding paragraphs, The Lutheran World Federation shall: a) further a united witness before the world to the Gospel of Jesus Christ as the power of God for Salvation." The "in accord with the preceding paragraphs" phrase made clear that whatever is said about the purposes is not to contradict the earlier statement that the LWF is a free association (although it also implied that it was to carry out its functions in accord with the doctrinal basis in Article II). The insertion of the language of "furthering" a united witness has a twofold effect. On the one hand, the article no longer implies that a united witness by the LWF or its member churches is a present reality or immediate possibility, but only that it is a something the LWF will seek to further. On the other hand, the rewording removed the LWF as the subject of the act of witnessing. Thus, the statement of functions would imply neither that the LWF was itself carrying out a churchly activity nor that sufficient agreement for a united witness already existed within the LWF.

The second change was the addition of a new sentence to Article 4 on membership: "Membership in the Federation may be terminated by vote of the Assembly or by withdrawal." The possibility was thus created of removing from membership any church which explicitly or implicitly abandoned the Doctrinal Basis.

Read with more care and the advantage of hindsight, the Helsinki amendments are ambiguous. They contained an internal contradiction. The logic of the objections from the LCMS and others implied that the LWF should either move toward being a pure free association, without any claim to doctrinal consensus, or that it should operate in a more ecclesial manner and make adherence to a confessional consensus a condition for entering or remaining within the LWF. Very few persons within the LWF, however, really desired either extreme. The two amendments at Helsinki instead tried to incorporate a bit of both. The amendments to Article III on the purposes of the LWF on the whole diminished any ecclesial status that might be ascribed to the LWF, but they also made clear that the LWF carried out "churchly functions" and that the Doctrinal Basis was a standard for LWF activity and not just a membership condition. More importantly, the amendment to Article IV on membership gave the LWF the authority to judge and, in a limited sense, discipline a member church. This latter amendment certainly heightened the ecclesial status of the LWF.

In the long run, it was the amendment to Article IV that was the most significant of the amendments made at Helsinki. The changes in Article III provided rhetorical ammunition to those who insisted on the non-churchly character of the LWF, but they did not bring any change into the actions of the LWF. The amendment to Article IV, however, laid the basis for one of the decisive events in the evolution of the LWF, the suspension of the white churches in Southern Africa.

The consequence of the discussions and actions that culminated at Helsinki should have been the reception of the Missouri Synod and its affiliated churches into the LWF. The LWF would then have included all but a truly tiny minority of churches which identified themselves as Lutheran. But such a climax was not to be. In 1969, the convention that elected J. A. O. Preus LCMS President and inaugurated a general conservative trend in the Missouri Synod also overwhelmingly rejected LWF membership. In addition, when the Australian Lutheran churches finally merged in the late 1960s, the new church remained outside the LWF.

## 1968–1979: Confessional Integrity and Southern Africa

BY THE LATE 1960s, the persons most deeply involved in the earlier discussions about the LWF had either died, rotated out of office, or left the LWF staff. Their replacements had different interests. While the nature of the

LWF never ceased to be a question, the issue was debated between 1968 and 1979 with less intensity and with a conceptually less clear focus than it was in the periods that preceded or that followed. Decisive in this period was not talk but action. The LWF acted and then it considered the meaning of what it had done.

Issues of Lutheran unity and fellowship had been so important at Helsinki that they could not simply be absent from the Evian Assembly, but they played a strikingly small role. Most importantly, the questions had ceased to be defined by relations to the non-member churches. The questions were being redefined as part of the broader reshaping of theology in the LWF (see chapter 5 above). Characteristic is the insistence on placing issues of Lutheran unity and fellowship more explicitly in the context of the church's mission in the modern world. The Report from Section II of the assembly stated: "In light of the New Testament as well as the Augsburg Confession, the mandate and mission of the church appear as primary, and the problem of the unity of the church must be understood from that viewpoint." As a result, the argument ran, "the situation in which the church bears its witness must be taken seriously as a determining factor in the question of fellowship among churches of the Lutheran confession." The focus of consensus is concrete proclamation in the modern situation. "The concern is that we together interpret the gospel anew from the viewpoint of the present context of our witness and formulate this reinterpretation."

The "present context" at the Evian Assembly was dominated by the last minute change of venue and the related issue of human rights. While the Brazilian situation was most in the foreground, the Southern Africa question was also directly addressed by the assembly. The assembly adopted the principles that "in the Lutheran church members of all races should be willing at all times to receive communion together" and that "the Lutheran churches should oppose the principles and practices of racial discrimination and segregation."

The Evian resolution displayed a certain double sidedness that would be typical of the post-Evian debate and of the more forceful 1977 Dar es Salaam resolution. It addressed both the internal church matter of fellowship between churches and also the social-ethical question of the attitude of the Southern African churches to apartheid. While in practice they were intertwined, the two matters related very differently to the mandate of the LWF. It was one matter for the LWF to address issues directly involved in fellowship between the churches and another to address what should be the attitude and actions of the member churches toward their sociopolitical context. A certain oscillation between these two aspects of the issue will be visible throughout the discussion.

In the debate at Evian, the worry was expressed that the LWF was here acting as a "super-church," but the "strong opinion" was also voiced that the resolution must not be weakened. Certainly, the LWF was here entering into the life and practice of member churches in a new way. In an essay written soon after Evian, General Secretary Appel addressed this question: "No one doubts that authority lies with the member churches. But it remains open to what degree autonomy can be viewed as complete independence, whether it can remain unaffected by life together in a fellowship, and to what degree it is possible simply to reject a serious request from churches with which one is bound in faith." Appel here is close to the picture of the LWF in Helsinki Preparatory Document 4, in which the LWF is a means through which churches in a significant fellowship in the faith can engage in mutual admonition. The fellowship has no binding or juridical authority over its members, but the members are not morally free simply to ignore the earnest admonition of the other member churches. Appel equates, however, a request from fellow member churches with an action by the assembly, thus giving a kind of authoritative synodal status to the assembly which constitutionally it did not possess (see Appel 1970). Here, as in various other cases in coming years, the strong sense that the assembly was in fact acting in concert with the wishes of the member churches was permitted to override a strict construction of the constitution.

In this chapter, the path of discussion and action on apartheid and the Southern African churches in the years after Evian can only be followed in relation to the issue of the nature of the LWF. Two issues, corresponding to the already noted double-sidedness of the Evian resolution, focused the discussion. The first was the question of fellowship between the white and black churches. The churches had accepted official resolutions of fellowship. Nevertheless, reports repeatedly indicated that official statements were not translated into practice. In addition, paralleling arguments earlier put forward by Peter Brunner, the black churches insisted that fellowship was more than a formal matter of pulpit and altar. It involved a commitment to a common life, a common life the white churches were accused of rejecting on racial grounds.

The second issue was more straightforwardly sociopolitical: What should be the role of the churches in the struggle against apartheid? Was a witness against apartheid not merely a possible or optional activity of the churches, but an action required by Christian faith? If the white churches were not willing to take a clear stand against apartheid, were they contradicting their existence as churches of Jesus Christ in a way that called for some sort of admonition or even discipline?

A letter in 1973 from the two black churches in Namibia to the LWF

Executive Committee forced the issue. They asked, what does the LWF "consider doing in order to achieve a concrete realization of the decisions of Evian 1970?" How will the LWF relate to those churches which seek to actualize these resolutions and to those churches which do not? How will it relate to churches "which want to actualize these resolutions but which are obstructed in their efforts by other member churches?" Appel noted the difficulty that now faced the LWF: "The LWF has no juridical power over its member churches. However, the theological issue at stake—the manifestation of Christian fellowship in spite of race, culture, and language barriers—is of the utmost importance" (see Appel 1973).

The wording of the executive committee's response indicates the way the implicit authority of LWF pronouncements was being amplified. "The LWF Executive Committee finds the Evian resolutions to be applicable to all its member churches, and therefore is obliged to strongly and persistently remind each member church of its unavoidable obligation in conscience to implement them" (see LWF 1974). No juridical authority is here ascribed to the Evian resolutions and the "unavoidable obligations in conscience" was presumably found to lie in the resolutions' moral content, not in their formal status as LWF resolutions. Nevertheless, that these resolutions could "bind consciences" was a striking statement.

The letter from General Secretary Appel in answer to the Namibian churches went a step further. It stated that if one church hindered another in implementing the resolutions, the LWF "will feel constrained to take concrete action in accordance with the appropriate article in the constitution regarding withdrawal of membership." For the first time, the membership clause added at the behest of the Missouri Synod came into play.

These 1973 statements were the beginning of the process by which the LWF was moved by the pressure of events and the forceful questions of its black Southern African member churches to act in ways that seemed to belie its official status as a free association. The judgment that somehow international Lutheranism had to do something was stronger than any constitutional scruples. Such scruples in fact are hard to find in records of the events, except occasionally in objections expressed by the white Southern African churches.

Even apart from its African setting, the events and statements of the preceding years made it unthinkable that the Dar es Salaam Assembly could plausibly avoid a substantive engagement with the issues raised by the South African situation. The report of the executive committee to the assembly repeated the forceful conclusions that had been typical since at least the mid-1970s: "Lack of clarity regarding this issue [apartheid] is for many a departure from the community we have in Christ." Admonition and warning were again addressed to the white churches: "We regret that the churches of European origin find it so difficult to express adequately their community with their Lutheran sisters and brothers. We believe that in not expressing that community, they are in danger of becoming so much a part of the system of apartheid themselves that they may forfeit their right to continue to be part of the community which they still have with the 'black' Lutheran churches." That "the question of membership in the Federation has been raised" is explicitly noted.

The assembly's Policy and Reference Committee presented a recommended three-paragraph statement under the heading: "Southern Africa: Confessional Integrity." The issue in the first two paragraphs of the statement was the fellowship that must follow from common confession. "Churches which have signed the confessions of the church thereby commit themselves . . . to accept in their worship and at the table of the Lord the brothers and sisters who belong to other churches that accept the same confessions. Confessional subscription should lead to concrete manifestations in unity in worship and in working together at the common tasks of the church."

More controversially, the third paragraph, as finally adopted, stated that while Christians may "under normal circumstances have different opinions in political questions . . . political and social systems may become so perverted and oppressive that it is consistent with the confession to reject them and to work for changes. We especially appeal to our white member churches in southern Africa to recognize that the situation in southern Africa constitutes a *status confessionis*. This means that, on the basis of faith and in order to manifest the unity of the church, churches would publicly and unequivocally reject the existing apartheid system."

Taken as a whole, the statement on "Southern Africa: Confessional Integrity" made two clear assertions and implied a third. First, more clearly than ever before, the LWF had stated that its common confessional basis implied fellowship at pulpit and altar and also beyond. Second, in Southern Africa, the nonrejection of apartheid implied a denial of the gospel whose confession was essential to Lutheran fellowship. The implication could hardly then be avoided that a Southern African church which did not clearly reject apartheid called into question its fellowship with other churches who shared its formal confession.

Our concern here is with the implication of this statement for the nature of the LWF. Most unambiguously, the LWF was now assuming that it was in fact an association of churches who shared a common confession in word and deed, from which fellowship should follow. The first two paragraphs of the statement on confessional integrity gave a stronger answer than previously to the relational question about the LWF, even if to a degree implicitly. More complex were the implications of the *status confessionis* statement. The earlier contention that the LWF had a doctrinal basis but itself did not "teach doctrine" could no longer plausibly be made. The LWF had decided that in a particular situation, a specific action (rejecting apartheid) was so bound up with the gospel that the nonperformance of that action constituted a denial of the gospel. The LWF had made a highly specific doctrinal decision. In addition, the content of the statement meant that if some action were then taken on the membership of the white Southern African churches, it would unavoidably appear to be an act of doctrinal discipline.

In a sense, the implications for the nature of the LWF to be drawn from the statement depend on the kind and degree of authority ascribed to it. The statement had no juridically binding authority with the member churches. Nevertheless, it would be false to see the statement as yet another high-flown moral admonition from yet another powerless ecumenical assembly. The Dar es Salaam statement's authority did not derive from any juridical status of an LWF Assembly but from its place in a process of consensus formation and reception. While the language of *status confessionis* was new, the content of the assembly statement was a logical extension of earlier statements on racism. These roots in a more comprehensive process made up for the assembly's lack of authoritative, synodal status. The authority of the statement resided in its capacity to focus and advance a consensus in formation.

The Dar es Salaam statement on "Southern Africa: Confessional Integrity" was a decisive turning point in the debate on the nature of the LWF, despite the virtual absence of the nature of the LWF as a distinct theme in the discussions. Dar es Salaam was decisive because it established a fact which almost no one wished to see canceled. Something needed to be done; only by treating the LWF as a forum of authoritative decision making could that something be done. That the LWF proved itself useful as such a forum and instrument inevitably reflected on its nature.

While the theme of the nature of the LWF moved out of the spotlight during this period, it did not remain completely undiscussed. What was said, however, pointed in different directions. President Juva expounded with some vigor an understanding of the LWF as a free association, with "world church" as the opposite, rejected term. The general secretaries during this period, however, Appel and Carl Mau, took a different line. Appel wanted an LWF capable of challenging the churches, and thus something more than their mere instrument. Mau, in his first report as general secretary in 1975, spoke of an "ambivalence or dual polarity" within the LWF between its character as an agency or instrument of the churches and its character as a community of churches.

While the ontological question remained in the background during this period, significant progress was made in answering the relational question. The Evian Assembly had called on the member churches to declare that they were in pulpit and altar fellowship with each other and to report such a declaration to the general secretary. The executive committee could report to the 1977 Assembly that the member churches "have almost without exception stated that they are in 'pulpit and altar fellowship' with each other." As with the South Africa question but through a more formal process of canvassing the member churches, a consensus was being developed that could later form the basis for an official LWF action.

This growth in fellowship was all the more important when seen in the context of the ongoing debate about the nature of the unity of the church being pursued in the wider ecumenical world. The development of and debate over the concept of "reconciled diversity" and its affirmation by the Dar es Salaam Assembly cannot here be traced (see chapter 7 below). Significant for the understanding of the nature of the LWF, however, was the growing recognition that fellowship in Christ cannot stop at pulpit and altar. The statement on "Models of Unity" adopted at Dar es Salaam stated: "Unity and reconciliation do not mean mere coexistence. They mean genuine church fellowship, including as essential elements the recognition of baptism, the mutual recognition of church ministries, and a binding common purpose of witness and service." While a phrase such as "binding common purpose" could still be interpreted as requiring little common action or decision making, the rejection of "mere coexistence" is clear.

The first two phases of the discussion of the nature of the LWF seem on the surface quite different, driven by different issues to different ends. Ironically, if one ignores the content of what was done at Dar es Salaam and attends only to certain formal characteristics of the actions, they represent the triumph of ideas pressed on the LWF by nonmember churches in the 1950s. The issue was precisely "confessional integrity": Did churches which officially subscribe to the confessions actually live by their teachings? During this period the LWF did just what the nonmember churches had wanted; it investigated the confessional integrity of member churches. The great difference, of course, was that the issues involved were racism and opposition to apartheid and not biblical inerrancy and the real presence.

The oddity of this period was that momentous actions were taken without the sort of theological reflection which is allegedly typical of Lutherans. To a degree, this absence was a function of the theological shifts of the late 1960s and 1970s. The question about the nature of the LWF had earlier been framed and discussed in the language of the confessional theology of the 1950s. A new language had not yet been developed to reframe the question. That would only occur in the 1980s.

But this absence of reflection also had institutional causes. Whatever the advantages of the many-sided change that had led from the Theology Department and Commission of the 1950s to the Department of Studies of the 1970s (see chapter 5 above), one result was the absence of a body within the LWF that was interested in and capable of an extended analysis and discussion of the ecclesiological issues implied by such actions as the Dar es Salaam resolution. During this period (and, to a degree, during the next also), the Department of Studies not only had other concerns but also was pursuing the theological enterprise in a way that did not mesh well with the realities and problems, practical and conceptual, that came together around the issue of the nature of the LWF.

In part due to this lack of reflection, the transformation of the LWF during this period into a forum of fellowship and common decision making was ad hoc and informal. It was related to the single issue of relations with the Southern African Lutheran churches. The process of consensus formation that was crucial to its credibility had been pursued somewhat willy-nilly, with little methodological or ecclesiological self-consciousness either at the time or immediately thereafter. As a result, very little reflection was done at the time on the conditions under which the LWF might play such a new role. Such reflection would have to await the next phase of the debate, which would begin in 1979.

## 1979 to 1990: A Communion of Churches

THE NEW PHASE of the discussion of the nature of the LWF had a clear beginning, the 1979 meeting of the executive committee, and a clear end, the redefinition of the LWF as a communion of churches by the 1990 Assembly. The temptation is to see this period as a repeat of the 1952–1963 discussion, only with an opposite outcome. Similarities do exist between the two discussions; the underlying issues were broadly the same. These issues were discussed, however, in a significantly changed context. Four aspects of this change should here be noted.

First, all agreed that the churches of the LWF had grown closer together over the years. While the lack of altar and pulpit fellowship among the member churches was an embarrassment during the 1950s, the existence of such fellowship among virtually all LWF churches was now taken as a foundation upon which one could build, even if no declaration of fellowship had yet made its way into the constitution.

Second, the LWF had come to play a much larger ecumenical role. The Roman Catholic decision to invite ecumenical observers to the Second Vatican Council from the various Christian World Communions, including the LWF, rather than from the individual churches, was of decisive importance. In the following years, the LWF entered bilateral ecumenical dialogues with a variety of other Christian World Communions (see chapter 7 below). There simply was no other body that could carry out this task for the Lutheran churches and the churches were appreciative of what the LWF was doing.

Third, the expanded LWF membership from Asia, Africa, and Latin America subtly redefined the questions. The relational question, earlier almost exclusively centered on pulpit and altar, was broadened. What was the significance of the fellowship among the member churches for issues that arose from massive differences in wealth? What sort of material sharing, what sort of partnership in development should follow from fellowship? As can already be seen in the discussion in South Africa prior to Dar es Salaam, these newer member churches often insisted that fellowship must extend beyond pulpit and altar into a wider unity of life. Smaller churches in a minority situation in their countries (as many of these churches were) had a marked tendency to support a stronger, more ecclesial LWF. They were more concerned with identifying with world Lutheranism than in protecting local or national autonomy.

Finally, significant theological advances provided what was absent in the 1950s and 1960s: more nuanced concepts to express widespread but difficult to state intuitions about the LWF. Most important was the steady movement in ecumenical circles toward an ecclesiology centered on the concept of *communio*.

The new discussion began at the 1979 session of the executive committee in Joinville, Brazil. The instigating theme was the relation of the LWF to the WCC, but the papers presented by Daniel Martensen (b. 1936), responsible for ecumenical relations in the Studies Department, and Harding Meyer (b. 1928) of the Strasbourg Institute, addressed the nature of the LWF. Martensen emphasized the implications of the Dar es Salaam "Confessional Integrity" resolution: "The LWF [in this action] answered the question of its ecclesial nature in a positive way; it placed the weight on its ecclesial character rather than on the autonomy of its members." Meyer's paper, more generally ecclesiological in focus, introduced two concepts important for the further discussion: the LWF is "a real communion of churches which share pulpit and altar fellowship; without wanting to be a 'church' in the full sense, it possesses a high degree of 'ecclesial density.'" Through the concept "communion," one could say that the church expressed itself in a different way at the international level than at the

local or national levels. To say that the LWF had churchly qualities need
not mean that it was on the way to becoming the super-church, the world-
spanning bureaucracy so many feared. Lutheranism at the international
level would take the form of a communion of churches, a living web of
churches, and need not itself be organized the way the national churches
were. Through the concept "ecclesial density" one could say that church
is realized by different organizations to different degrees. The LWF had
certain churchly qualities but lacked others. It is more than a common
pension fund, but not a church in the full sense. It was more like a church
than the WCC (in that it had a common comprehensive confessional
basis), but was not a church in the unqualified sense that a local church is.
(Unfortunately, the slightly comic sound of the phrase "ecclesial density"
prevented its wide adoption. The text by Meyer in the bibliographical note
is a slightly altered version of his Joinville paper.)

The executive committee decided that the Martensen and Meyer papers
should be shared with the member churches. With the papers, several
questions were sent to the churches, most notably, whether they would
"welcome the possibility of the ecclesial nature of the LWF" becoming
"more pronounced." This polling of the churches marks an important difference from the first phase of the discussion about the LWF. While the
papers from the Great Debate were published in *Lutheran World/
Lutherische Rundschau*, the debate itself took place within the relatively
closed and theologically sophisticated circle of the Theology Commission.
Neither the executive committee nor the member churches were polled.
The discussion that began in 1979 was not published (for there was no LWF
journal in which to publish them) and the LWF no longer possessed a committee of theology professors comparable to the earlier Theology Commission to pursue the issue in conceptual depth. Nevertheless, the
discussion of the 1980s was far more oriented to creating an effective consensus both of the churches and the LWF leadership.

This survey of the churches was summarized in a report for the
Budapest Assembly: "Self-Understanding and Ecumenical Role of the
Lutheran World Federation" (see LWF 1984). Typical was the response of
the Ecumenical Study Committee of the United Evangelical Lutheran
Church in Germany: "This fellowship of Lutheran churches portrays a
form of church on the universal level. The instrument of this fellowship,
the LWF, participates in this church character, although it is, in accordance
with its organization, a federation of churches."

The survey demonstrated the change in the understanding of the LWF
since 1960, but what should now be done about this change? The executive committee discussed and rejected the idea of proposing an amendment to the constitution's definition of the LWF. Instead, a more modest,

two-pronged approach was taken. First, the executive committee unanimously recommended an amendment to Article III.1 of the constitution which would state that all LWF churches "understand themselves to be in pulpit and altar fellowship with each other." The Budapest Assembly accepted this amendment by an almost 10 to 1 margin; for most it was an affirmation of the self-evident. The only dissenting voices came from a few churches which still had a mission or partnership relation with the LCMS.

The wording of the amendment is worth noting. The LWF Assembly did not create on its own authority a new relation among its members; the amendment rather describes and confirms an existing consensus of the member churches. In the form of the amendment, a particular kind of role and authority of a certain kind of LWF action becomes visible. The LWF officially recognizes and thus in a sense seals the existence of a consensus on some important topics. This action gives the consensus a *de jure*, and not just *de facto*, binding quality. As discussions and actions following the assembly made clear, as a clause of the constitution, the descriptive sentence became normative. To enter (or remain within) the LWF now implied an official relation of pulpit and altar fellowship with all other member churches. Here, paradigmatically, the assembly acted as the instrument and expression of the mind of the communion.

Second, a consultation in December 1983 on the ecumenical issues before the LWF proposed a draft statement for the assembly's consideration on "The Self-Understanding and Task of the LWF." As a statement requiring a two-thirds majority and not as a simple resolution, the significant but less than constitutional authority of the text would be clear and the problem that scuttled Helsinki Document 4 avoided. Like Document 4, the statement distinguishes the Lutheran communion from the LWF. The Lutheran communion, "rooted in the unity of the apostolic faith . . . finds its visible expression in pulpit and altar fellowship, in common witness and service, in the joint fulfillment of the missionary task, and in openness to ecumenical cooperation, dialog, and community." The LWF is "an expression and instrument of this communion. It assists it [the Lutheran communion] to become more and more a conciliar, mutually committed communion by furthering consultation and exchange among its member churches and other churches of the Lutheran tradition, as well as by furthering mutual participation in each other's joys, sufferings, and struggles" (*Proceedings*, Budapest, p. 176).

This statement sought to summarize the results of the discussions and survey that had taken place since 1979 and was adopted with little dissent. It represents a conceptual turning point in the official self-understanding of the LWF. The language of communion now becomes the central category for understanding the LWF. In addition, communion is understood as inescapably visible, expressed in a far-reaching set of common activities and involving a mutual commitment of the churches.

The statement omits, however, an important aspect of the earlier discussion. All mention of a possible ecclesial character, either of the Lutheran communion or the LWF, disappears. "Communion" no longer explicates the ecclesial character of the worldwide fellowship of Lutheran churches, but rather replaces any mention of such a character. In addition, the interrelations within the Lutheran communion, the activities in which the communion expresses itself, and the LWF as expression and instrument of the communion remains unclear. Does the communion exist prior to or even independently of its expression in such forms as pulpit and altar fellowship, common witness, and joint mission? Is the LWF the expression or the concrete realization of this communion?

The significance of the Budapest Assembly's pulpit and altar amendment and its "Self-Understanding" statement were magnified by the assembly's action in relation to the white Southern African churches. As the Budapest Assembly approached and an adequate response to the Dar es Salaam "Confessional Integrity" resolution remained lacking from the white churches, pressure for decisive action by the Budapest Assembly grew. The precise form of such action was suggested by the Pre-Assembly All Africa Lutheran Consultation in Zimbabwe, December 1983. It recommended that "in the absence of any significant and meaningful progress toward church unity and (the 'white' churches') failure to reject publicly the sin of the apartheid system, . . . the Assembly reaffirm the Dar es Salaam statement on *status confessionis* and call upon the 'white' member churches to take positive steps towards church unity, [and] as an interim measure, the 'white' member churches be suspended from the LWF membership until such time that they reject apartheid publicly and unequivocally and move towards unity with other member churches in the area." Suspension, with possible ongoing consultation with the affected churches, would be a more concrete expression of Christian love and concern than simple expulsion. General Secretary Mau noted that such a procedure expressed the understanding of the Lutheran churches as a mutually committed communion in which the members do not abandon one another. The African suggestion encountered the formal objection, however, that the LWF Constitution provided for the expulsion of a member, but not suspension. Substantively, such suspension, precisely because it would be a more pastoral and less merely institutional action, might appear as a form of church discipline difficult to reconcile with the status of the LWF as a free association.

The assembly accepted the argument that the power to expel a member implied the less extreme power to suspend. The wording of the suspension resolution, accepted by a 4-to-1 majority, is again significant. The statement "FINDS that those churches [which have not rejected apartheid] have in fact withdrawn from the confessional community that forms the basis of membership in the Lutheran World Federation. Therefore, the Assembly is constrained TO SUSPEND THE MEMBERSHIP of the above churches" (*Proceedings*, Budapest, p. 180). As in the constitutional amendment on pulpit and altar fellowship, here again the emphasis is placed on a description or discernment; the white churches have in fact withdrawn from the confessional unity upon which the LWF is based. The suspension can then be seen as confirming a state of affairs that already exists more than as bringing a new state of affairs into being. The fellowship amendment and the suspension action thus display similar patterns of LWF action: the LWF only acts in a binding way on the basis of an extensive consensus, developed over a significant time and the product of extensive discussion. The binding assembly action is primarily a discernment and confirmation of this consensus, giving it official form and drawing consequences for the common life of the churches.

Taken together, the constitutional amendment, the "Self-Understanding" statement, and the Southern Africa suspensions placed the nature of the LWF in a new light. The question of the ecclesial nature of the LWF had been avoided, but a new understanding of the LWF was now firmly established: the LWF represented a communion of churches which understood themselves as mutually committed in a way that permitted the exercise of a kind of church discipline. These actions did not settle all questions, but they determined the nature of the following discussion.

As already noted, while the Budapest actions had answered the relational question about the LWF with some clarity, its answer to the ontological question about the LWF itself was less clear. It was this question that would focus the debate in the next years. If the Lutheran churches truly formed a mutually committed communion, could the organizational expression of that communion be only a "free association"?

That this question occupied such a large place in the discussions between Budapest and Curitiba was due in large part to the priority given it by the new general secretary, Gunnar Staalsett. Staalsett made the theme of the emerging and deepening Lutheran communion the refrain of his period as general secretary. His role, however, was not unambiguous. He gave the office of general secretary a higher profile than his predecessors had and was more willing to press a controversial agenda and to provoke and face down public opposition. Without his perseverance, further development of the Budapest results might not have occurred. Nevertheless, his forceful style contributed to the ever latent fears of an unduly authoritative, centralized "super-church." For some, the undesired Lutheran world-church had taken on a human face, and it was Staalsett. Paradoxically, Staalsett's forcefulness became both a significant force for change and a contributing cause of the resistance to change.

The primary forum for the discussion of the nature of the LWF became the yearly reports of the general secretary to the executive committee. Beginning with Staalsett's first report in 1986, each report contained a further development of the concept of communion in relation to the LWF. This forum permitted a connected series of presentations to be developed over an extended period of time. Because the executive committee was a central decision-making body, it was in certain respects an appropriate forum for the discussion. This forum had its limits, however, and these limits contributed to the difficulty of the debate. While each session included the possibility for a discussion of the general secretary's report the discussion time was limited. The reports received some circulation, but were not published. The discussion thus threatened to become a monologue. Most significantly, the wider church audience could not be included as it was in the early 1960s through the publication of essays in *Lutheran World/Lutherische Rundschau*. No forum for a truly public debate now existed. As a result, the possibilities of consensus formation beyond the reach of the discussions held within the LWF institutions was limited.

In Staalsett's presentations, a subtle but significant change occurred. While the distinction between the Lutheran communion and the LWF was not directly denied, the interpenetration of communion and federation was pushed close to the point of identification. Thus Staalsett could say: "LWF—that isn't the Secretariat in Geneva; that is the communion of churches which belong to it" (see Staalsett, *Auf dem Weg . . .*). No simple separation can be made between the common life in Christ and the Spirit that makes the Lutheran churches a communion, on the one hand, and the common activities which are the LWF, on the other. The Federation is the communion of its member churches; the activities and structures of the Federation are aspects of the common life of the churches in communion.

For such an understanding of the Lutheran communion, the definition of the LWF as a free association contradicted its nature. The constitution would need to be amended to bring it into line with what the LWF had become.

For better or worse, the debate over such a constitutional change became complicated (or given greater specificity and reality) by being linked with arguments over a possible restructuring of the LWF. A restructuring of some sort was perceived by many as necessary on financial grounds. When a restructuring committee was appointed in 1987, however, its mandate was to consider structure against the background of the nature of the LWF. The interrelation of the two considerations was furthered by the presence of James Crumley (b. 1925), Bishop of the Lutheran Church in America, as chair of both the Structure and the Constitution Committees.

The fundamental shape of the proposed changes is already visible in the reports of the two committees in 1988. The constitutional redefinition of the LWF as a communion of churches rather than a free association would form the framework for a rethinking of the organization of the LWF. A more organic, less contractual image of the LWF is projected. The churches are joined together by bonds of common faith and life that create communal obligations. Authority is thus to be "shared," rather than "assigned" or "delegated." The communion as a whole does not thus receive authority by delegation from the member churches but shares in the authority that flows from life in the Spirit.

While the proposed new constitutional language continued to speak of the LWF as "instrument of its member churches," reference to the autonomy of the member churches disappeared. The feared "super-church" was not being proposed, but the process of redefining and restructuring was calling into question an autonomy that exists prior to mutual commitment.

While Crumley was careful to deny any simple deduction of a particular structure from an understanding of the LWF as a communion, the exact relation between the redefinition and the restructuring remained unclear to many. In addition, the content of the restructuring proposal, especially the replacement of the executive committee and the various commissions by a single LWF Council, was seen by some as steps toward the bureaucratic super-church they feared. They felt confirmed in their suspicions that any discussion of the ecclesial or "communion" nature of the LWF was a Trojan horse that contained a shift of power from the churches to some centralized body.

During 1988 and 1989, reports from the Structure Committee were circulated to the member churches with requests for response. While the few responses from the churches in Asia, Africa, and Latin America and from the European minority churches were predominantly positive, the responses from the larger European churches and from elements within the American churches were at points negative, even vehemently so. It was often difficult, however, to separate opposition to the redefinition of the LWF as a communion from opposition to the specific restructuring proposals.

A common object of criticism was the equation: "The LWF is a communion of churches." It was argued that the communion of churches is one thing, while its structural expression and instrument is another. As the Danish Church's Council on Inter-Church Relations said: "Communion cannot be adequately expressed within the limits of any structure at all. Communion is above all the fellowship that already exists between the Lutheran churches. . . . Any attempt at equalizing [*sic;* equating?] the LWF with the Lutheran communion should be rejected by good, sound Lutheran theology." Frequently, the use of the concept "communion" to define the LWF was attacked as a pretext for a concentration of power in the LWF. "Communion is here assumed to motivate and to justify the concentration of power in the organization," the Finnish response argued.

In answering the responses, Staalsett sought to reassure the churches that the redefinition in no way challenged the churches' authority over their own affairs. He continued to insist, however, that a true communion among the churches implied interdependence rather than simple autonomy. Nevertheless, a reference to the "autonomous member churches" was now inserted into the proposed new constitutional wording that the executive committee approved for submission to the Curitiba Assembly.

As the delegates, advisers, journalists, staff, and observers gathered in Curitiba for the assembly in late January, 1990, it was by no means clear that the restructuring proposal and the related redefinition of the LWF as a communion of churches would be approved. Since the proposed changes in the constitution were presented in the form of an entirely new constitution rather than in a series of amendments, the redefinition of the LWF included in the first articles and the restructuring implied in the later articles would be voted on together. While Crumley sought to differentiate and interrelate the redefinition and the restructuring, Staalsett pulled the two closer together: "The proposals of the outgoing Executive Committee . . . endeavor to draw out the implications of the Budapest statements on communion for the *constitution and structure* of the LWF." Linking together of the redefinition and the structure proposal created a problem for those who favored the first but not the second.

The redefinition of the LWF as a communion was not the focus of criticism of the new constitution. Only one speaker spoke against the redefinition and in favor of the retention of the language of free association. Strong support for the redefinition came from speakers from Africa, Asia, and Latin America. They emphasized communion as a sharing in which all participate, materially and spiritually both giving and receiving. Professor Simon Maimela (b. 1944) from South Africa emphasized just what some wanted to reject: communion as a concept which interrelated the spiritual and the organizational. For these persons from the Southern Hemisphere, "communion" allowed a more flexible, organic understanding of the spiritual within the social and institutional.

The rancorous debate over the restructuring and the acceptance of the new constitution by precisely the two-thirds majority it needed should not obscure the importance of the decision made at Curitiba. The LWF had made a momentous decision: what in 1947 had been a free association of churches unable to gather unanimously in the Lord's Supper was now officially "a communion of churches which confess the triune God, agree in the proclamation of the Word of God and are united in pulpit and altar fellowship" (Article III.1 of the new constitution).

## Conclusion: Life in Communion

THE DEBATE OVER THE NATURE of the LWF from its founding through the Curitiba Assembly was driven by the internal contradiction of a free association of Lutheran churches. If the churches were in fact Lutheran, then they were one in Word and Sacrament and could not be only a free association. With the Curitiba redefinition of the LWF, this form of the debate over the LWF came to an end. The question is now: What does it mean to be a communion of Lutheran churches?

The shape of a discussion of the meaning of life in communion has not yet become sharply focused and it may not have the single focus of the earlier debate. Nevertheless, certain questions will be unavoidable. First, there are still unresolved issues of self-definition. Curitiba, following the linguistic lead of Staalsett, moved from the distinction between the Lutheran communion and its expression in the LWF to the equation "the LWF is a communion of churches" with the addition that the organizational structures of the LWF express and serve that communion. The implications of this shift have still not been fully understood and institutionally embodied. If the LWF is the communion of churches and the assembly, council, and secretariat are only expressions and instruments thereof, then structures need to be found by which the identification of LWF and the churches can become both more real and more visible. LWF leadership and decision making will need more directly to mesh with that of the member churches. At present, however, rules of procedure and representation in council and assembly militate against such a meshing. The leaders of the member churches play far less decisive a role today than they did fifty years ago. If the LWF is its member churches, then somehow this development needs to be reversed.

In addition, if the LWF is a communion, then the name "Federation" has become misleading. Eventually, some change of name is required ("Lutheran World Communion"?). A change of name would also emphasize that the offices in Geneva are only a secretariat.

Second, the nature of decision making and authority in the LWF still remains undefined. The Budapest Assembly stated that the "unity we seek," a unity that should already be partially embodied in the Lutheran communion, "is a committed fellowship, able to make common decisions and act in common." This chapter has shown that the LWF has been able to make common decisions, even about doctrinal matters, by a slow process of consensus formation, sealed by an assembly action which recognizes the formed consensus. This form of decision making, however, has evolved somewhat unreflectively and its authority remains untested. Similar procedures are being adopted in relation to the possible declaration of the nonapplicability of the Reformation condemnations of the Roman Catholic Church in relation to justification. Can world Lutheranism together make an authoritative statement about the meaning of some aspect of the confessions in the contemporary ecumenical situation? Or, on another topic, what should be the result if the present consensus in the LWF that the ordination of both men and women is theologically correct becomes, as some believe it should, a consensus that the nonordination of women is theologically unacceptable?

Third, what is the meaning for the Lutheran communion of the great discrepancies of wealth among its members? If communion means sharing, what is the meaning of communion for the aid, relief, and development work that has formed so significant a part of the activities of the LWF? What difference does it make that the churches involved are one in a mutually committed fellowship?

Fourth, what significance does a specific Lutheran identity have for the LWF and its members? This question has at least two sides. On the one hand, how should the member churches interconnect their relations within the Lutheran communion and their local and national ecumenical relations with non-Lutheran churches? How does international Lutheran identity and action relate to local and national ecumenical relations which may seek to overcome such distinct identities? On the other hand, what today makes the Lutheran World Federation Lutheran? The LWF is today far more diverse that it was fifty years ago, yet it claims a deeper unity. The question of the meaning of confessional subscription, the question with which the debate about the LWF started, comes back in a transformed shape. What is the shared sense of being Lutheran which forms the context of our common life as a communion of Lutheran churches.

The answer to none of these questions is obvious, nor is it yet clear even how best to frame the most important questions. Life in communion at the international level in its present form is a new reality, possible only through the means of communication and travel that developed in recent decades. Not just Lutherans, but also Anglicans, Catholics, Orthodox, and

others are engaged in discussions about forms of international communion. Lutherans would do well to attend to parallel discussions in other
traditions, especially those with whom we share both a tradition of legally
autonomous national churches and a strong sense of international identity, e.g., the Anglicans and the Orthodox.

Too great a concern with identity and self-understanding, however, can
lead to paralysis. After all, the first of the "functions" of the LWF listed in
the present constitution is to further "the united witness to the Gospel of
Jesus Christ," not to make statements about itself. At the end of his 1959
essay, Peter Brunner says that the LWF is less an *esse*, a being, than a *fieri*,
a becoming. Thanks to the debate and decisions here chronicled, perhaps
that comment is less true today than it was three and a half decades ago.
But the LWF remains a becoming, and so the history of its identity is not
closed.

### Bibliographical Notes

I. Unpublished Documents

> LWF Archives, Geneva.
> Particularly:
> Agenda and Minutes of LWF Executive Commitee and, since 1990, Coun-
> cil meetings.
> Agenda and Minutes of LWF Theology Commission, Commission on
> Studies, and, since 1990, Program Committee for Theology and Studies.
> Correspondence and documents relative to relations between the Lutheran
> Church–Missouri Synod and the Lutheran World Federation.

II. Printed Documents

> Briefwechsel VELKA-LWB. *Lutherische Rundschau* 3 (Geneva, 1953):
> 410–15.
> "The Great Debate," essay by Peter Brunner with comments. *Lutheran
> World* 7/3 (Geneva, December 1960): 237–91. Further comments in
> *Lutheran World* 8/1 (Geneva, 1961).
> LCMS Committee Report on the Lutheran World Federation. *Lutheran
> Witness* (St. Louis, 1956): 122–23.
> *Lutheran World* 11/2 (Geneva, April 1964): 172–203.
> *Lutheran World* 21/1 (Geneva, 1974): 88–90.
> LWF 1974 Executive Committee, "Eisenach: Statement on Namibia."
> *Lutheran World* 21 (Geneva, 1974): 88–90.
> "The Nature of the Lutheran World Federation: Commentary on Articles
> II, III and IV of its Constitution." *Document 4, Fourth Assembly of the
> Lutheran World Federation, July 30–August 11, 1963, Helsinki, Finland.*
> Geneva: Lutheran World Federation, 1963.

Opinions on "the Status of Document 4 [above]." *Lutheran World* 11 (Geneva, 1964): 172–203.

*Proceedings* (all LWF Assemblies).

*Self-Understanding and Ecumenical Role of the Lutheran World Federation. Report on a Study Process 1979–1982.* Geneva: Lutheran World Federation Department of Studies, 1984.

III. Monographs and Selected Writings

Appel, André. "Ein Termin ist gesetzt. Evian im Licht der ökumenischen Rassismus-Debatte." *Lutherische Monatshefte* 9 (Hanover, 1970): 634–37

———. "Reflections on Eisenach 1973." *Lutheran World* 20 (1973): 340–46

Brand, Eugene L. *Toward a Lutheran Communion: Pulpit and Altar Fellowship.* LWF Report 26. Geneva: Lutheran World Federation, 1988.

Department of Theology, LWF, ed., *The Unity of the Church: A Symposium. Papers Presented to the Commissions on Theology and Liturgy of the Lutheran World Federation.* Rock Island, Ill.: Augustana Press, 1957.

Gassmann, Günther. "Wachsende kirchliche Gemeinschaft: Die künftige Rolle des LWB im konziliaren Prozeß." *Lutherische Monatshefte* 20 (1981): 550–52

Meyer, Harding. "Wandlung eines Weltbundes. Für eine Intensivierung der ökumenischen Verantwortung." *Lutherische Monatshefte* 19 (1980): 329–33.

Nordstokke, Kjell. "The Ecclesiological Self-Understanding of the Lutheran World Federation: From 'Free Association' to 'Communion of Churches.'" *Ecumenical Review* 44 (1992): 479–90.

Schmidt-Clausen, Kurt. "Wesen und Auftrag des Lutherischen Weltbundes. Versuch einer Klärung durch die IV. Vollversammlung." Pp. 239–56 in *Reformation als ökumenisches Ereignis: Reden und Aufsätze zu Themen der ökumenischen Bewegung.* Berlin: Lutherisches Verlagshaus, 1970.

Staalsett, Gunnar. "Auf dem Weg zu Einheit und Frieden. Gespräch mit Generalsekretär Gunnar Stålsett." *Lutherische Monatshefte* 25 (1986):168–71.

Zeddies, Helmut. "Confessing in Ecumenical Solidarity: Ecclesiological Aspects of the Declaration of the Status Confessionis." Pp. 105–17 in *The Debate on Status Confessionis. Studies in Christian Political Theology.* LWF Studies. Edited by Eckehart Lorenz. Geneva: Department of Studies, Lutheran World Federation, 1983.

22. Professor Peter Brunner, Federal Republic of Germany, speaking at the Helsinki Assembly, 1963.

LWF Photo—Peter Williams

23. Church leaders from Southern Africa speaking at the time of the suspension from LWF membership of white churches in the region, Budapest Assembly, 1984. From right: Dean Simon Farisani, Bishop Manas Buthelezi; the Rev. Christoph Brandt; the Rev. Willfried Julius Blank; the Rev. Zephaniah Kameeta; Mr. Daniel Tjongarero (partially hidden); and the Rev. Marc Chambron and Mr. Friedrich König of the LWF staff.

LWF Photo—Peter Williams

24. The debate on LWF structure and constitution at the Curitiba Assembly, 1990. From left: the Rev. Augusto Kunert, Brazil; Bishop James Crumley, U.S.A.; and Ephorus Soritua A.E. Nababan, Indonesia.

CHAPTER

# 7

# To Serve Christian Unity:
# Ecumenical Commitment in the LWF

## Ecumenical Commitment as Loyalty
## to the Lutheran Confession

*On the 1947 Constitution*

THE 1947 CONSTITUTION of the LWF saw the tasks and "purposes" of the Federation as not only to strengthen the harmony and communion of the Lutheran churches but also to "foster Lutheran participation in ecumenical movements."

This dual aim has been clearly sustained in the following five decades. Thus from the start it has been evident that the efforts toward gathering the Lutheran churches as a communion does not exclude or force into the background the striving for the communion of all churches and Christians. Confessional awareness and ecumenical commitment do not get in each other's way but go together. This was one of the fundamental convictions governing the formation of the Lutheran World Federation, and it continues to shape its ecumenical thinking and efforts.

Thus while the LWF was doubtless a "confessional" federation, it was never a "confessionalistic" one. The present text of the constitution, decided on at the Assembly in Curitiba (1990), reveals this even more clearly than before. "Efforts towards Christian unity worldwide" are not only among the "functions" of the LWF; they are also part of its "nature": "The Lutheran World Federation confesses the one, holy, catholic and apostolic Church and is resolved to serve Christian unity throughout the world" (Article III).

---

*Harding Meyer, Kehl-Marlen, Germany, is the author of chapter 7.*

This was also true of the Lutheran World Convention, the forerunner of the LWF. Even though the idea of ecumenical commitment was not yet directly expressed in its constitution (1929) it was nevertheless clearly present. The first meeting of the Lutheran World Convention (1923) even began with it: "The Ecumenical Character of the Lutheran Church" was the first of its three main themes. Later, in 1936, there was a statement of the executive committee of the World Convention regarding "Lutherans and the Ecumenical Movements." It linked the two: on the one hand, "fostering of Lutheran unity" or "Lutheran solidarity"; on the other, the ecumenical commitment of the Lutheran churches which—it was said—corresponded to the "ecumenical character" or "ecumenical nature of Lutheranism."

This talk of the "ecumenical nature of Lutheranism" was not an expression of Lutheran presumption but emphasized that ecumenical commitment and ecumenical effort were not placed at the discretion of Lutheran Christians and churches. Active ecumenical commitment is a matter of faithfulness to Lutheran origins and the Lutheran confession. Luther and his fellow Reformers actually never came forward with the claim to found a new church community. Wherever such a suspicion cropped up, they passionately opposed it.

Above all, it is the central concern of the Reformation itself that demonstrates that its struggles did not aim at taking people out of the church of that time and into a separate ecclesiastical existence. The issue was nothing less than the heart of the whole Christian community's life: the gospel of the unmerited grace of God in Christ, which cannot be earned. Already in his "95 Theses" Luther had said, "The true treasure of the Church is the Most Holy Gospel of the glory and the grace of God." Thus from the start, and by its very nature, the Reformation struggle had its focus on the church as a whole. Had the wish been only to create a separate church, that would have amounted to a denial of the Reformation concern. The truth of the faith and the unity of the church require each other and are in this sense inseparable.

This is clearly expressed in the Augsburg Confession (CA), especially in Article 7. If we take into account the fact that this confession of 1530 became the fundamental and binding confession of the Lutheran churches in every country and has remained so to the present, we recognize how much the ecumenical idea has been carved in the memory and consciousness of the Lutheran churches and has constituted an integral part of their Reformation inheritance. No reflection on its ecumenical commitment has in fact happened in the LWF without a clear reference—mostly explicit, sometimes also controversial—to Article 7 of the Augsburg Confession.

## The Lutheran Style of Ecumenical Effort

*From Hanover to Minneapolis*

From the start the LWF's ecumenical efforts have had marked characteristics. The Reformation convictions, particularly as they are expressed in CA 7, are also determinative in this respect. In regard to this, fundamental clarifications that have remained criteria for subsequent times were arrived at in the initial period of the LWF.

At its constitutive meeting in Copenhagen (1953) the Commission on Theology, created at the Assembly in Hanover, agreed to devote its first "Study Program" to the question of "The Unity of the Church," and was concerned with this until the 1957 Assembly in Minneapolis. The fact that this is precisely where the work of the Commission on Theology began is fresh testimony to the importance attached to the ecumenical idea and effort. Here there was a deliberate link-up with the 1954 Assembly of the World Council of Churches (WCC) in Evanston and the talk was of "taking Evanston further." At the same time the LWF's Minneapolis Assembly already came into view with its theme, "Christ Frees and Unites," which clearly included the ecumenical question. The fruits of the work were reflected in the volume *The Unity of the Church: Papers Presented to the Commissions on Theology and Liturgy of the Lutheran World Federation* (Rock Island, Ill.: Augustana Press, 1957).

What is the unity of the church we seek, and what path is indicated? This was the question. Here the point of reference was repeatedly CA 7 with its statement that "for the true unity of the church it is enough to agree concerning the teaching of the Gospel and the administration of the sacraments," or in the German version, "that the Gospel be preached in conformity with a pure understanding of it and that the sacraments be administered in accordance with the divine Word" (Tappert, *The Book of Concord*, 32).

*The Need for "Agreement in the Apostolic Gospel":*
*Freedom in the Field of Church Orders*

In interpreting and applying CA 7 one can observe among members of the Commission differences of opinion that in part have to do with the difference between its Latin and German texts. There was something like a "Scandinavian" line, which stressed agreement in the actual preaching of the gospel and administration of the sacraments; and there was something more like a "German" line, which highlighted the doctrinal character of this agreement, and thus the theological consensus. But there was agreement in the fundamental conviction: the striving for the unity of the church had to be in the form of a struggle for "agreement in the apostolic gospel" (Peter Brunner, *Unity*, p. 21).

This is where the real, promising path to the unity of the church lies, because it is the "way to the center" of Christian existence and church life (Anders Nygren, ibid., pp. 73, 78). "The way to unity by way of doctrinal agreement is the effort to reach a common understanding of the faith we live by" (Taito A. Kantonen, ibid., p. 42). If a common position is reached here in confession of the faith, that is "enough for the true unity of the church" (CA 7). "When this agreement is given, so is church fellowship, and it should be joyfully and confidently acknowledged and practiced without any anxiety or qualms" (Ernst Kinder, ibid., p. 71).

This look to the "center" frees ecumenical efforts from the compulsion and burden of having to seek agreement in those areas that may be assigned to the structure of church life but not to the saving gospel and its proclamation, that is, the church's constitution, the shaping of worship, church order, modes of piety. In these things the true unity of the church is not at stake. Here it is "not necessary" to agree or "be alike" (CA 7), but there is freedom.

It was repeatedly emphasized that this freedom does not make the sphere of church order and structure a matter of indifference. Rather it is a freedom that is willing "for the sake of love and peace and more effective service" (Kinder, ibid., p. 72) to seek fellowship here too. Peter Brunner explained this in referring to the most sensitive points and asked, "For example, why cannot a freely consummated inclusion into the fellowship of the historical episcopate also be a fitting form of expression in such church fellowship?" (ibid., p. 19).

Strictly to focus on the center of the church and on freedom in regard to everything that is not central marks, or at least should mark, the character of Lutheran ecumenical efforts. This permeated all the reflections of the LWF's first Commission on Theology. With this it really was saying nothing new, nor did it claim to do so. It only repeated and developed the conviction of the Lutheran Reformation. But it was important that this took place at such an early point of time in the LWF.

### *The Redefinition of "Confessional Fellowship" (Bekenntnisgemeinschaft)*

The Commission on Theology's reflections had to touch on a question that had occupied the attention of the ecumenical movement from its beginnings: Does the existence of different confessional churches intrinsically contradict the unity of the church, and so radically that the unity of the church is to be achieved only by abandoning confessional identity, ties, and independence?

The view predominating in the ecumenical movement at that time was moving clearly in this direction. In particular, the movement for Faith and Order had supported this view from its beginnings, and even the structure of the WCC was clearly shaped on this basis. Contrariwise, on the Lutheran side such a fundamental contradiction between "confession and ecumenism" was disputed. "We must view our confessional and ecumenical responsibility not in competition with one another, but the one through the other" (Kinder, ibid., p. 114).

The conviction that confession and ecumenism were compatible was, however, bound to lead to corrections of previous Lutheran attitudes, insofar as it was really taken seriously. This became evident particularly in the idea of the "confessional fellowship" (Bekenntnisgemeinschaft) necessary for the unity of the church. This term does not in itself have any "confessional" ring about it. It points to fellowship in confessing the apostolic faith which, indeed, is fundamental for the unity of the church. But in Lutheranism, especially in the history of efforts toward unity within Lutheranism, it had become limited to fellowship in a specific, formal church confession, namely, fellowship in the "Lutheran" confession. However, especially in the light of the conviction that confessional identity and ecumenical commitment were compatible, such a narrow understanding of "confessional fellowship" could not be sustained ecumenically without becoming "confessionalistic" and disavowing the conviction that "confession and ecumenism" were compatible.

The first Commission on Theology of the LWF was not the only place where this was clearly recognized, but it was a particularly important place. The commission opened up the concept of "confessional fellowship" (Bekenntnisgemeinschaft) again to its more comprehensive and therefore ecumenical sense, namely, that the "confessional fellowship necessary for unity is a fellowship in confessing together the one apostolic faith." This fellowship in the confession of the apostolic faith—such was the view of the Commission on Theology—may also be present where churches are and remain committed to different "confessions" (Bekenntnisse), provided that the agreement in the apostolic faith is expressed by an explicit "consensus in doctrine," by a "doctrinal agreement" (Lehrkonkordie), as it was said.

Ecumenical conversations between confessional churches separated by differences in doctrine aim precisely at that. "Conversations between churches which are doctrinally divided with the goal of reaching doctrinal agreement is the one absolutely decisive means of fulfilling our ecumenical obligations" (Brunner, ibid., p. 21). This "doctrinal agreement" (*Lehrkonkordie*) does not replace the existing church confessions but maintains their validity; it is agreement "on what we today hear, proclaim, and openly confess to be the binding content of the apostolic Word" (ibid., p. 22). The compatibility of "confession and ecumenism" is demonstrated and achieved in such doctrinal conversations. Here the way to unity opens up; confessional integrity is safeguarded, but "confessionalism" is overcome.

## The Ecumenical Goal: Church Fellowship

A specific idea or "concept" of the church's unity corresponds to the path to unity that has been described. Such a concept of unity also stands out clearly in the work of the Commission on Theology. It consciously differed from the concept of "organic union" that was mostly favored in the ecumenical movement of that time. Establishing united churches was by no means rejected; at all events we look in vain for a polemic against this concept of unity in the statements of the Commission on Theology. But another equally legitimate structuring of full church unity was indicated, which did not involve organic union or the merger of confessional churches into a new church with a new identity, a new name, and a single church leadership. The conviction was that there could be full communion among the churches without their necessarily giving up their special characters, identities, and independence. "The peculiar problem and emergency in the ecumenical movement today is not that there are various 'churches.' This situation can and must prevail. . . . The church's unity does not unconditionally need a centralized unity of organization as an expression of legal or administrative uniformity. . . . It is our conviction that *church fellowship among historical churches* is the most fitting way in which to bring the integral unity of the church of Jesus Christ to expression and reality" (Ernst Kinder, ibid., pp. 64–65). The conviction that "confession and ecumenism" are not in conflict with each other but can make common cause was thus kept up till the achievement of church unity and thus till the ecumenical goal is reached.

This form of church unity was described as "church fellowship" (*Kirchengemeinschaft*). This term as such was not new, but only then was it beginning to take on a clearer profile and become the description of a specific mode of realizing church unity. The term had a clearly programmatic resonance in the work of the Commission on Theology, and it is important in regard to later developments that the Commission on

Theology expressly and repeatedly saw the idea of "church fellowship" as taking up the idea of *koinonia* in the ancient church.

The emphasis was that "church fellowship" did not represent solely a step on the path to unity or a preliminary form of church unity. It did not only mean reciprocal admission to the Eucharist, however important that might be. "Church fellowship is confessional fellowship" understood in the sense described above as communion or fellowship in confessing the apostolic faith. Moreover, to "church fellowship also belongs necessarily a full pulpit and altar fellowship. Implicit in this is a mutual recognition of ordinations among churches" (ibid., p. 19).

Although these are certainly the basic elements of "church fellowship," they do not encompass all the modes of its expression. The wish was to leave the definition of "church fellowship" open to some degree for the inclusion of other aspects, and "not to establish boundaries in advance." Peter Brunner said, "[W]e must realize that church union manifests itself through an abundance of actually lived, concrete, historical, and of course, legally formulated relationships and forms of expression. I suggest the word 'church fellowship' (*Kirchengemeinschaft*) as incorporating all of these elements" (ibid., p. 18).

This openness of the concept of "church fellowship" would prove important. It made possible the inclusion also of structural elements in the concept of "church fellowship": "opportunities of common *assembly* as churches" in order to be able to speak and act together, as was said in preparing the Helsinki Assembly ("The Nature of the Lutheran World Federation . . . ," p. 18). Ten years later (1973) "church fellowship" for the "Leuenberg Agreement" expressly included "cooperation in witness and service to the world" (*Lutheran World*, 1973, p. 352).

Thus quite early the LWF Commission on Theology not only described the ecumenical path but also evolved a view of the ecumenical goal. A few years later one could rightly say that, given this view of the path and aim of ecumenical effort, "the Lutheran churches participate in the ecumenical movement with a positive concept" (ibid., p. 20).

The work of the Commission on Theology was indeed seen as a preparation for the 1957 Assembly in Minneapolis. Nevertheless the theses approved there on "The Unity of the Church in Christ" (*Proceedings*, Minneapolis, p. 86) ultimately remained only an impressive ecumenical appeal, however much they were welcomed at that time. Certainly they were fresh testimony to the ecumenical intention and ecumenical will of the Federation, but from the standpoint of content they still lagged behind the work of the Commission on Theology.

## Ecumenical Research and Ecumenical Dialogue

*Helsinki 1963 and the Strasbourg Institute*

The Helsinki Assembly marks—even if still hesitantly—the transition from ecumenical reflection to active, direct ecumenical engagement on the part of the LWF.

The proposal of the German National Committee that, in view of the increasingly numerous points of contact developing among the confessions, an institute for confessional research might be established, had already come before the Minneapolis Assembly. The result was the setting up of a Special Commission for Interconfessional Research which then proposed to the LWF in Helsinki the founding of a "Lutheran Foundation for Interconfessional Research," which, while closely linked to the Federation, would nevertheless be legally and financially independent. Undoubtedly the special contribution of this assembly to the LWF's ecumenical task was the fact that this proposal was accepted and the Institute was founded.

Urged on by the events in the Roman Catholic Church (the preparation for and convening of Vatican II), concrete developments had already taken place. As early as the beginning of 1960 the Danish scholar Kristen E. Skydsgaard had been busy with theological research at the behest of the Special Commission, and had devoted himself to the question of relations with the Roman Catholic Church. Assigned to the staff of the LWF, he set up a Foundation for Interconfessional Research in Copenhagen. George A. Lindbeck (b. 1923) of Yale University in the United States replaced him two years later. Both were LWF observers at Vatican II, and already in 1962 the first, well-received publication of the Institute, *The Papal Council and the Gospel/Konzil und Evangelium*, was available (*Proceedings*, Helsinki, p. 155).

All this fitted in perfectly with the ecumenical situation of the time. Thus there was unanimous acceptance of the proposal to establish a Lutheran Foundation for Interconfessional Research together with a draft constitution for it, which was submitted to the assembly in Helsinki by Bishop Hermann Dietzfelbinger of Bavaria (1908–1984), chairman of the Special Commission. With the establishment of the Foundation, the Copenhagen Institute became an institute of the Foundation; since 1965 it has been located in Strasbourg. Very soon it was employing four research professors from different geographical areas of Lutheranism—Scandinavia, North America, Germany, and Asia or Africa.

This is not the place to give a more detailed report on the Institute and the work it has done, especially in the three fields of ecumenical research, ecumenical publications and communication (seminars and lectures), and participation in the bilateral interconfessional dialogues of the LWF. Suffice it to say that its achievements have been considerable and have been widely recognized and appreciated throughout Lutheran areas and far beyond. Although in the earliest years the Institute's interests were directed particularly at Roman Catholic theology, attention to the Reformed church and Reformed theology, Anglicanism, Orthodoxy, the evangelical and Pentecostal or charismatic movements, and fundamental ecumenical questions soon followed.

The establishment of the Foundation with its Institute was significant in various respects for the general question of "Ecumenical Commitment in the LWF."

1. The Helsinki Assembly's decision to establish the Foundation and its maintenance up to the present are two powerful and effectual signs of ecumenical concern on the part of the LWF and the Lutheran churches generally. According to its constitution, "the purpose of this Foundation shall be to contribute to the fulfillment by the Lutheran churches of their ecumenical responsibility in the area of theology." With its member churches the LWF can point without presumption to the fact that it is the only one of all the Christian World Communions which has provided itself with an institution of this kind and has now been supporting it for more than three decades.

2. The main focus of the work of the Foundation and Institute clearly lies on theological ecumenical research. The constitution says, "The Foundation shall carry out its work by appropriate and critical theological research, both historical and systematic, in areas where Christian churches are divided in matters of doctrine and church order, and where theological questions are a matter of controversy."

Here again we see the special character that ecumenical efforts have to maintain according to Lutheran conviction. First and foremost, there is the struggle for the clearly recognized, affirmable fellowship in the understanding of the apostolic gospel that is the source of the church's life. The Commission on Theology held that this is the necessary and promising path to the unity of the churches that have been separated up to the present, and on this path the Foundation and Institute should serve the Lutheran churches through its theological ecumenical research.

3. The Foundation's constitution, submitted to the assembly and accepted by it, speaks of ecumenical theological research closely linked to "contacts and conversations with theologians from other churches."

A key concept had thus been voiced at Helsinki that was important for the more distant future. E. Clifford Nelson, too, had very forcefully adopted it at the end of his great address on "The One Church and the Lutheran Churches." In connection with the work of the Special Commission for Interconfessional Research he said, "research and conversation belong together," and he proposed that "this Assembly take steps to move beyond the important task of *research* to *conversation*." "Has not the time arrived," he asks, "for the Lutheran Church—previously not known for its aggressive ecumenism—to *initiate* discussions rather than to maintain a defensively withdrawn attitude while other churches seize the ecumenical initiative?" Here he had "bilateral dialogues" explicitly in mind—"bilateral confrontation of confessional groups, for example, the Lutheran and the Roman Catholic, the Lutheran and the Reformed, the Lutheran and the Anglican" (ibid., p. 293).

The proposal for establishing the Foundation for Interconfessional Research and Clifford Nelson's proposal were discussed together in the assembly's small groups. However much approval there was for the first proposal, there was just as much indecision in regard to the second. Voices were heard for the LWF's taking up bilateral interconfessional conversations, but there were also clear voices that rejected it, with the formal reason that the Federation would thus be exceeding the authority assigned to it and that it must leave such bilateral conversations to the individual churches.

Thus, as regards the decisions of the assembly, matters rested at the unanimous decision to set up the "Lutheran Foundation for Interconfessional Research." On the other hand, crossing the threshold to taking up bilateral interconfessional dialogues was still not seen as possible. Quite a number of people clearly held the view, as one of the group reports said, that while indeed "ecumenical research presupposes conversations with other confessions" it was best "if conversations were pursued within the context of such study" (ibid., p. 490).

## The Emergence of the Ecumenical Agenda

### *The First Bilateral Dialogues (1964–1974)*

In the years immediately following the Helsinki Assembly the decision was taken to do what had been considered there but was not decided on: the breakthrough to a proper "ecumenical agenda," that is, active, direct participation by the LWF in the ecumenical movement by way of bilateral dialogues. Here, too, it was to some extent true that ecumenical developments overtook the previous decisions of the LWF, and it says something for the genuineness of the Federation's ecumenical intention that it not only authorized this—and far less registered misgivings about it—but recommended and indeed welcomed it.

*The Dialogue with the Reformed Churches.*    The first steps toward the LWF's participating in dialogues already underway were made in 1963/1964. And indeed this development took place in such a way that the Federation was, as it were, drawn into dialogue by way of its member churches.

The situation was that the WCC's Commission on Faith and Order had begun Lutheran–Reformed conversations in Europe, which had entered a new stage with the "Bad Schauenburg Conversations" (1963/ 1964). Initially the Commission on Faith and Order had overall control; the Commission on Theology and the Department of Theology of the LWF played an advisory role and also seem to have supported the organizing of the conversations. At its meeting in September 1964, the LWF Executive Committee approved this development. It soon showed a clear interest in the conversations, above all in coordination among the Lutheran participants and in a better representation of the Scandinavian and Lutheran minority churches.

After the conclusion of the Bad Schauenburg Conversations, the LWF was involved to an even greater degree. Evaluation of the churches' reactions to the results of the conversations took place through a working group (April 1968), of which representatives of both the LWF and the World Alliance of Reformed Churches (WARC) were members. The proposal was that, together with the Commission on Faith and Order, both Federations should have organizational responsibility in regard to the continuation of the conversations. In view of the churches' reactions here, it was clear that matters would not be confined to theological discussion only but would now involve the question of achieving church fellowship.

"Church Division and Church Fellowship" was then the theme of the next conversations (1969–1970). Very soon they led to the "Leuenberg Agreement" (1973), the great milestone in the relation of the two Reformation churches, and thus toward church fellowship among Lutheran, Reformed, and United churches on the continent of Europe.

In the meantime, first steps had taken place toward conversations between the LWF and the WARC. Of course, this meant beginning with only an ad hoc "joint study committee," which met in January 1968 in order to evaluate the Lutheran–Reformed conversations, especially in Europe and North America. But this soon became a "Lutheran–Reformed Joint Committee," which met on several occasions from January 1970 till 1975 and had the task both of promoting Lutheran–Reformed discussions in the various countries and of looking into the possibilities for practical ecclesial implementation of theological consensus and indeed even of developing a closer working relationship between the two Federations. However, no proper bilateral dialogue between the Federations emerged.

*The Dialogue with the Roman Catholic Church.* At the same time as the LWF was drawn increasingly into the Lutheran–Reformed dialogues of its member churches, it had already seized the initiative on its own account with regard to the Roman Catholic Church. The beginnings of this dialogue lay in the fact that the LWF had appointed three theologians—Kristen E. Skydsgaard, George A. Lindbeck and Vilmos Vajta—as observers at Vatican II, who reported regularly to the executive committee. A confidential memo from Lindbeck was available at the committee's meeting in September 1964. From the memo it emerged that there was a desire on the Roman Catholic side (Secretariat for Promoting Christian Unity) for the contacts to continue beyond the Council. Entering into conversations— bilateral church conversations of an official nature—with individual world confessional families was considered to be one form of such continuing contacts. Lindbeck himself supported this idea and declared that Lutherans should be "willing to enter more and more unitedly and, when the occasion offers, 'bilaterally' into the ecumenical dialogue."

The executive committee did not at once take up this idea but first made the LWF General Secretary responsible for operating, in consultation with a small committee, as liaison officer with the Secretariat for Promoting Christian Unity, should it seek a continuation of the contacts. In 1964, in the autumn, a meeting in the Secretariat for Promoting Christian Unity took place. A joint consultation was proposed that was to examine "the possibility of future contacts and discussions, and possible themes for these." The LWF officers agreed to this proposal in January 1965, and in June the executive committee appointed the Lutheran participants of a "Joint Working Group" that went on to meet in August—and then once more in April 1966—in Strasbourg. It proposed the creation of two joint study commissions, one on "The Gospel and the Church," the other on "The Theology of Marriage and the Problems of Mixed Marriages."

The step to "bilateral international dialogue" was thus taken, something new in the history of the ecumenical movement. Thus the international Roman Catholic–Lutheran dialogue became, as it were, the "parent" of all later dialogues of this kind.

The joint study commission on "The Gospel and the Church" began its work in November 1967 and concluded it in February 1971 with the "Malta Report." In its theological clarity, breadth of theme, and ecumenical boldness this first dialogue document is important—indeed trailblazing—for all further stages of the Roman Catholic–Lutheran dialogue.

Disappointing were the "special statements" from some Roman Catholic participants who were unable to go along with the far-reaching proposals for eucharistic hospitality.

The Evian Assembly (1970) occurred during this initial stage of dialogue. Particularly at two points it belongs directly in the first stages of the dialogue. First, in his address at Evian Cardinal Willebrands, President of the Vatican Secretariat for Promoting Christian Unity, drew attention to present-day Roman Catholic research on Luther and the transformation in the Roman Catholic picture of Luther. "It is undoubtedly a good thing," he said, "to recall to mind a man for whom the doctrine of justification was the 'articulus stantis et cadentis Ecclesiae.' In this we could all learn from him that God must always remain the Lord, and that our most important human answer must always remain absolute confidence in God and our adoration of him" (*Proceedings*, Evian, p. 64).

Second, Cardinal Willebrands' visit and address was the opportunity for the LWF to request forgiveness from Roman Catholic Christians: "We are truly sorry for the offense and misunderstanding which these polemic elements [concerning their church and theology] have caused our Roman Catholic brethren. We remember with gratitude the statement of Pope Paul VI to the Second Vatican Council in which he communicates his plea for forgiveness for any offense caused by the Roman Catholic Church. As we together with all Christians pray for forgiveness in the prayer our Lord has taught us, let us strive for clear, honest, and charitable language in all our conversations" (ibid., pp. 156–57).

*The Dialogue with the Anglican Communion.* Even more clearly than the Lutheran–Roman Catholic dialogue conversations with the Anglican communion originated with LWF initiatives. The difficult course of church union negotiations, especially in India and East Africa, formed the background for these initiatives. The idea of a dialogue with the Anglican Communion was therefore first envisaged by the Commission on World Mission in 1963. There was already talk at that time of worldwide Anglican–Lutheran conversations, though directed specifically at the question of the ministry and the episcopate which had proved particularly difficult in the union negotiations. The Commission on Theology took this up in the same year. A plan was presented to the Helsinki Assembly, approved, and passed over to the two commissions for implementation. In 1962 they appointed a committee for Anglican–Lutheran conversations which met in Loccum, West Germany, in October of that year in connection with a consultation on "Agreements and Differences between the Anglican and Lutheran Churches."

In June 1967 the LWF Executive Committee approved this committee's recommendation to create a joint Anglican–Lutheran working group with the task of preparing proposals for future "worldwide Anglican–Lutheran conversations." This working group's memorandum of November 1967 was submitted to the Lambeth Conference and the Federation's Executive Committee in the summer of 1968 and was accepted by both. It outlined the present situation between the two churches and listed the reasons and possible themes for an international dialogue, the task of which should be "to define the unity that exists already, and to clarify and resolve problems that at present divide Anglicans and Lutherans, and so reaffirm and proclaim the unity of the Christian Church in a secular world."

To begin with, on the Anglican side, especially among representatives of the Church of England, a reserve clearly existed with regard to a worldwide bilateral dialogue. Multilateral dialogues as in the Commission on Faith and Order appeared to be more appropriate—and, besides, there were already conversations under way with the Evangelical Church in Germany (EKD). The votes from North and South America finally decided the issue. The dialogue itself began in 1970 and after four sessions was already able to submit its final report, the "Pullach Report" of 1972. Although the problem of the episcopate remained largely open, the report nevertheless revealed the profound fellowship of the two churches in faith and doctrine and in this respect remained fundamental for all later conversations.

Thus for the LWF the ten years following the Helsinki Assembly marked a breakthrough to direct and extremely active participation in the ecumenical movement, especially in the form of bilateral theological dialogues. It is noteworthy that in this initial period dialogue results were forthcoming which provided foundations for all further conversations with the three partner churches. This is true not only of the Leuenberg Agreement but likewise for the Lutheran–Roman Catholic Malta Report and the Anglican–Lutheran Pullach Report.

## Taking Stock of the Ecumenical Agenda

IN THE MIDDLE of these ten years came the Evian Assembly. The importance of the developments that had come about since Helsinki is reflected in the fact that the second of the assembly's three sections, "Ecumenical Commitment," was devoted exclusively to ecumenical questions. Special attention was focused on relations with the Reformed churches and the Roman Catholic Church, which, as has been noted, was represented by Cardinal Willebrands. But, at the same time, an extension of the LWF's ecumenical agenda to dialogues with Methodists and Baptists was recommended, and studies on the Pentecostal movement and the "Independent Christian Movements" in Southern Africa and West Africa were urged.

## Renewed Reflection on the Ecumenical Task

Both the LWF's involvement in bilateral dialogues and the extremely lively and active ecumenical interest that suffused individual churches down to the congregational level seemed to make two things necessary: a renewed, fundamental reflection on the ecumenical task and also practical ecumenical guidelines. This had become clear in the lead-up to Evian.

The Commission on Theology placed both on its agenda as early as 1967, also looking toward the coming assembly. After thorough preparatory work it devoted its entire 1969 session to this twofold task. The result was two documents: a study document for the coming assembly entitled, *More than Church Unity* and, closely linked with this, *Guidelines for Ecumenical Encounter* (cf. *Lutheran World* 17/1 [1970]). However, neither at the assembly nor later did these two documents take on the significance anticipated.

The *Guidelines for Ecumenical Encounter,* which clearly was focused on ecumenical practice, offering distinctions and explanations that were certainly helpful with regard to the different partners, levels, and forms of ecumenical encounters, were actually not "practical" enough. Moreover, they were part of a series of comparable guidelines produced at the time in individual Lutheran churches.

The study document *More than Church Unity* had an entirely different character based on ecumenical principles. It deliberately linked up with the work of the Commission on Theology in the fifties but also clearly took matters further in a number of respects and was compiled with concentrated effort. The characteristic stamp of Lutheran ecumenical efforts also clearly manifested itself here. Its description was more concise and precise than in the fifties. In this regard, the study document in its chapter on "Principles of Ecumenical Endeavor," scarcely three pages long, is perhaps the clearest and most concentrated description of the particular nature of Lutheran ecumenical efforts there has ever been in the LWF.

*Confessio Augustana* 7 was the point of reference. Again, two things were involved: on the one hand, "what is necessary for unity," that is, agreement in the proclamation of the gospel which is described with the help of the doctrine of justification, although without using confessional terminology (a warning against a "confessionalistic envelopment of the gospel"); and, on the other hand, "the freedom we receive," which was not seen as restrictive but as inclusive—for example, as freedom to adopt the episcopate or to recognize other historical confessions. At the same time, the study document clearly laid down new emphases. Already in its first chapter it linked the unity of the church with the "unity of mankind" (*sic*). This is the basis for understanding the title of the entire study document, *More than Church Unity*. Moreover, it went into detail in including "secular" or "non-theological factors" in the quest for the unity of the church (chapter 2). All in all, this study document surely deserves more attention than was paid to it at the time.

### The Question of Churches Forming Unions

At Evian an answer was also found to the question of how the LWF should behave in the face of negotiations for union and possible instances where by merger its member churches might form unions with other churches. This question had been repeatedly asked of the LWF by its Indian and East African member churches, but with particular directness by the WCC and organizations associated with it (Commission on Faith and Order, East Asian Christian Conference).

The question was whether the LWF was obstructing the participation of its member churches in the forming of unions or was opening up the way for them, perhaps even encouraging them. Ultimately, however, this amounted to the twofold question whether the LWF might regard a union of churches in the sense of "organic union"—which would involve the abandonment of previous confessional identities—as in principle a legitimate way of achieving church unity and whether it would continue to regard a member church entering into such a union as a member church, making its support available to that church. At the Helsinki Assembly it had not proven possible to arrive at an answer to these questions despite considerable pressure. Things were deferred to the next assembly.

The proposal for a statement answering that twofold question positively was placed before the assembly in Evian. The statement had been prepared by a small committee which included members of the Federation's Executive Committee. The assembly accepted the proposal. The crucial statement in the declaration was: "A union of churches must be seen as a proper expression of the unity of the church when uniting churches have agreed upon a confessional statement of faith that witnesses a right understanding of the gospel to serve as a guide for preaching and the administration of the sacraments. Becoming a part of a united church by a member church should not lead to a break in relationships with the LWF if the united church's confessional statement is in substantial agreement with the doctrinal basis of the LWF" (*Proceedings*, Evian, p. 142). Thus the principles of Lutheran ecumenical efforts came to be fully applied here. The assurance that "the [Lutheran] donor churches" and also the LWF itself "should continue such financial support as will benefit the receiving church" (ibid., p. 143) was only a consequence.

## Further Clarifications of the Idea of Unity and Renewed Reflections on Ecumenical Methodology

*From Evian to Dar es Salaam*

In respect to the theological and ecumenical activities of the LWF, the time between the assemblies at Evian and Dar es Salaam was the time of the Commission on Studies. This is discussed elsewhere in this volume. However, here it must be said that the Commission on Studies' aims and methods (other than in the period of the Commission on Theology) were—to put it mildly—not particularly favorable for the continuation of the LWF's previous ecumenical activity. Already at that time it was hard to avoid feeling that while there was real understanding and interest in the Commission on Studies for the Federation as an excellent "instrument," a deep concern for questions regarding "the nature" of the Lutheran World Federation and its existence was not present.

To a great extent the Federation's ecumenical activity actually shifted away from the Commission on Studies. The Desk for Interconfessional Dialogue and Ecclesiological Research remained, indeed, structurally within the Commission on and Department of Studies, but the LWF Executive Committee created for itself a Standing Committee on Ecumenical Relations that advised it. The fact that the essential decisions in ecumenical matters came to the executive committee proved important in this situation. It was also important that a close and fruitful working link developed more than previously between the Geneva Desk for Interconfessional Dialogue and Ecclesiological Research and the Strasbourg Institute for Ecumenical Research.

*"Unity in Reconciled Diversity."*    Representatives of both the Geneva Interconfessional Desk and the Strasbourg Institute were thus able to participate together in the new debate on the vision of the ecumenical goal, a debate that was resumed at the beginning of the seventies. The reason was above all the increasing number and importance of the bilateral dialogues advocated and conducted not by the WCC and its Commission on Faith and Order but by the world confessional families and their member churches.

Therefore, in a formal inquiry the Commission on Faith and Order asked the Christian World Communions, which at that time were still called families, "to clarify their understanding of the quest for unity by cooperating with the World Council of Churches" (LWF Report 15, p. 8). Immediately prior to this the Commission on Faith and Order itself in 1973 had developed a vision of the ecumenical goal: the "one church as a conciliar fellowship of local churches which are themselves truly united" (ibid., p. 4).

In 1974 two consultations of the Christian World Communions took place at which representatives of the WCC participated. The idea of a "conciliar fellowship of churches" was in every respect welcomed. However, the idea that the churches joining together in "conciliar fellowship" had to be "united local churches" in the sense of "organic," that is, trans-confessional unions, met with decided resistance. But this was precisely what the Commission for Faith and Order was aiming at: "conciliar fellowship requires organic union"; it "presupposes organic union"—such was its comment.

Over against this, the worldwide confessional bodies developed a view of unity that certainly did not deny in any way the legitimacy of such transconfessional church unions (see above, pp. 263–64, "The Question of Churches Forming Unions") but did indeed reject their claim to be the only legitimate form of locally implemented unity. On the contrary these bodies supported the view that in the implementation of church unity the variety of confessional heritages and confessional identities could be preserved, provided they lost their "exclusive" and "divisive" character. Thus the talk was of a "vision of unity that has the character of a 'reconciled diversity'" (ibid., p. 9). "Unity in reconciled diversity" has since become a crucial concept in ecumenical thinking.

LWF's representatives played an essential part in this. What was ultimately involved was the concept of "church fellowship" (*Kirchengemeinschaft*), which the LWF had supported and to which attention was drawn in the debates leading to the Leuenberg Agreement. It was logical therefore that the Dar es Salaam Assembly took up and endorsed (but did not "officially accept") the idea of unity in "reconciled diversity" as this had been worked out by the Christian World Communions.

*Ecumenical Methodology: Ecumenical Reception and Lived* Koinonia. The *Study on Ecumenical Methodology* was a second point of importance for the LWF in the period between Evian and Dar es Salaam, even though its significance has not even yet been fully recognized. The executive committee had assigned this study to the Commission on Studies in 1972 with a goal that was initially very complex but was then more clearly specified in a "Basic Document" prepared jointly by the Department of Studies and the Strasbourg Institute.

The central question was how the doctrinal consensuses worked out in interconfessional dialogues might lead to practical "fellowship between churches," to "*koinonia*, fellowship which is experienced," as was repeatedly said. Thus the issue was that of "ecumenical reception" as people have since described it. The very fact that these two concepts, reception and *koinonia*, still unusual for that time, were given a central place makes this study significant. Of particular importance was the practice-oriented use of these concepts. The question was less of what "reception" and "*koinonia*" meant as ecumenical and theological terms than of how reception was effected in practice and how *koinonia* was implemented and expressed in the life of the churches and of Christians—in worship, in church structures, in the ministry, in witness and service in the world. Over and against the increasing ecumenical disillusionment at that time it was asserted that "ecumenical efforts . . . can and must not stop at purely theological results" (*Ecumenical Methodology*, p. 5).

This, it was maintained, was not meant as a devaluation of theological dialogues and of the quest for ecumenical consensus. One could even grant it "priority." But alongside there had to be a complementary method, so it was said, which would proceed "inductively," "empirically," "contextually," "concretely related to local situations" (ibid., p. 7) and which would be suitable to take in the "nondoctrinal factors" which help to determine the actual relations between churches whether for good or ill. Such a method, it was said, required that use be made of the social sciences. In this respect, the study fitted in with the overall methodology of the Commission on Studies; it managed, however, to eschew its biases and tendency to brush aside the method of doctrinal dialogues and the pursuit of theological consensus and to restrict the quest for unity to joint activities only. That too, of course, called for fundamental reflections. They were given a place at a consultation in 1976 and summarized in a report on the consultation. But ultimately everything focused on the actual conduct of "case studies."

Locally, and with the local churches themselves participating, these case studies were designed to "identify the relationship between theological, dogmatic and nontheological (that is, historical, cultural, sociopolitical, racial, ethnic, and personal) factors and the importance of the question of church structures in efforts to bring about the unity of the Church" (ibid., p. 7). They were not, however, merely to analyze but were also to give effective help in the reception process and in the implementation of "lived community" and develop "ecumenical models" for that purpose. These case studies were in fact carried out but somehow or other became bogged down, as was self-critically admitted. The "refined techniques of the method were not always applied" (ibid., p. 28) and besides, it was said, there had been a lack of funds (ibid., p. 29).

All in all, it seems as if this general effort toward reception was premature. The theological dialogues between the churches had still not made enough progress. By contrast, things look entirely different in the present situation. Everything points to the fact that today at least the basic concern of the study of methodology—the efforts for "ecumenical reception" and for the realization of "lived community"—has taken on an incalculable urgency.

## The Jubilee of the Confessio Augustana

THE YEAR 1980 was the 450th anniversary of the Augsburg Confession. In many countries this anniversary took the shape of a jubilee of unexpected ecumenical character. An international consultation in 1978 on "The Augsburg Confession in Ecumenical Perspective," organized by the Strasbourg Institute, set the tone for this. Well-known representatives of all the churches with which the LWF was in dialogue took part in it. The consultation, as its report said, showed "a clearly positive judgment of the Lutheran Confession" (LWF Report 6/7). "It was agreed," according to the text, "that the Confessio Augustana of 1530, although it failed in its ecumenical intent at that time, now represents a very valuable starting point for ecumenical conversations—an 'ecumenical potential', a significant ecumenical document in content, spirit and method" (ibid.).

Roman Catholic participation in this jubilee was particularly strong. The reason for this lay above all in the fact that in the years prior to the jubilee the idea of a "Catholic recognition of the Confessio Augustana" had been expressed and put forward for discussion by well-known Roman Catholic theologians. At the LWF Assembly in Dar es Salaam the representative of the Vatican Secretariat for Promoting Christian Unity had talked about this idea. The assembly welcomed this initiative in a statement and expressed "the willingness of the Lutheran World Federation to engage in dialogue with the Roman Catholic Church on this subject" and "promote and carefully follow the progress of all studies of this matter" (*Proceedings*, Dar es Salaam, p. 175).

An intensive discussion and numerous publications on this question followed. A comprehensive and important investigation by Lutheran and Roman Catholic theologians, "Confessio Augustana: The Confession of the One Faith" appeared in 1980 and was followed by the response of the Roman Catholic–Lutheran Joint Commission, "All Under One Christ" (*Ways to Community*, LWF, 1981, pp. 29ff.; LWF Report 10, pp. 34ff.).

These formed the background to the pastoral letter of the German Roman Catholic Bishops, "Thy Kingdom Come" (*Dein Reich komme*) of January 1980, in which we read of the *Confessio Augustana*: "The time has come for us, in gratitude to God, to acknowledge positively everything which belongs to the substance of the Christian faith which is to be found both in this confession and in the contemporary witness of our Protestant brothers and sisters. We are happy to discover not simply a partial consensus on some truths but rather a full accord on fundamental and central truths. This makes us hope for a unity also in the sphere of our faith and of our life where, at this moment, we are yet separated" (LWF Report 10, p. 55). This statement was taken up by Pope John Paul II in his address in Mainz in November 1980, and has been repeated by him subsequently on other occasions.

This was an exceedingly significant statement. It marked a climax in the dialogue between Lutheranism and Roman Catholicism that should not be lost from sight. In a detailed reaction of the LWF Executive Committee dated August 1981, looking back on the jubilee year, this was emphatically recognized: "We therefore agree that in their mutual examination of the Augsburg Confession Catholics and Lutherans 'have discovered that they have a common mind on basic doctrinal truths which points to Jesus Christ, the living center of our faith' . . . and that therefore with regard to the Augsburg Confession one may and should speak of 'a full accord on fundamental and central truths' . . . or respectively of a 'basic consensus' of faith" (ibid., p. 76).

## Continuation of the Previous Dialogues and Starting New Ones

THE DIALOGUES BEGUN by the LWF before Evian in 1970 were continued, but further dialogues, as suggested by the Evian Assembly to the Department of Studies, were begun only when the Commission on Studies had been reconstituted after Dar es Salaam.

### Continuation of the Dialogues with Reformed, Roman Catholic, and Anglican Churches

Proper bilateral dialogues with the World Alliance of Reformed Churches began only with the "Lutheran–Reformed Joint Commission," which worked from 1985 until 1988. It closed its work with a full report, *Toward Church Fellowship* (1989), the significance of which lay and still lies in the fact that it describes the common faith and emphatically recommends to the Lutheran and Reformed churches not yet in communion to implement it.

The dialogue of the LWF with the *Roman Catholic Church* was continued in commissions that were partly of new composition. The second phase of conversations (1973–1984) produced first and foremost consensus documents on *The Eucharist* (1978), on *The Ministry in the Church* (1981), and a discussion document on forms and stages of Catholic–Lutheran church fellowship entitled *Facing Unity* (1985) [*Einheit vor uns*, 1984]. The next phase in the discussions (1986–1993) was devoted to the theme of *Church and Justification* (Geneva, 1994). Since the beginning of the fourth phase in September 1995 the Joint Commission has been officially named the "Lutheran–Roman Catholic Commission on Unity." In the framework of the theme "The Apostolicity of the Church" the prospects are that it will again concern itself with the Eucharist and continue with the question of the ministry, the episcopate, and the papacy.

The conversations on "The Theology of Marriage and the Problems of Mixed Marriages" already proposed by the Lutheran–Roman Catholic "Joint Working Group" (1965/1966; see above, p. 259) were delayed. On the one hand a pronouncement from the Vatican on mixed marriages was awaited which then took place (Paul VI's *Motu Proprio, Matrimonia Mixta*, 1970). On the other hand, conducting such a discussion together with the World Alliance of Reformed Churches seemed both possible and appropriate. After two preparatory consultations between representatives of the two world bodies (1969 and 1970) this "trilateral" dialogue began in 1971, and it ended its work in 1976 with the document entitled "The Theology of Marriage and the Problems of Mixed Marriages."

The LWF's dialogue with the *Anglican Communion* also continued, first of all in the form of a "Joint Working Group" that met twice and in 1983 published its report, and that was known thereafter as the "Anglican–Lutheran International Continuation Committee." This continued dialogue has turned out to be particularly fruitful and promising. The 1983 report—known as "the Cold Ash Report," after the venue of the consultation in England—with its definition of "full communion" clearly describes the goal set in Anglican–Lutheran dialogues and has proven decisive for those conversations in the United States that have resulted in the proposed *Concordat of Agreement* between the Evangelical Lutheran Church in America and the Episcopal Church. Of considerable importance also is *The Niagara Report* of 1988, which has opened up new possibilities for understanding in regard to the question of the episcopacy. Finally, these conversations have provided crucial impulses leading both to *The Meissen Agreement* of 1988 between the Evangelical Church in Germany and the Church of England and *The Porvoo Common Statement* of 1992 between the Nordic and Baltic Lutheran churches and the Anglican churches in Great Britain.

## Taking Up New Dialogues

*The Dialogue with the World Methodist Council.* After a December 1977 preparatory meeting in the United States, conducted by the Strasbourg Institute in agreement with the LWF Executive Committee, had outlined the theme and main emphases of the coming dialogue, the Lutheran–Methodist Joint Commission began its work in 1979. It extended over five sessions and in 1984 ended with the joint document, *The Church: Community of Grace.*

This dialogue brought fundamental clarifications of enduring importance in the relation between Methodism and Lutheranism and created a clear awareness of the breadth of common features present in faith and doctrine. But the existing differences were also clearly addressed, particularly in the understanding of justification, sanctification, and the idea that Christians continue to be sinners. Here the commission tended to see predominantly diverse "emphases." But it did not go so far as to affirm an agreement that would justify and call for full communion between the two churches. "There are some issues which we believe merit further exploration and discussion" (*The Church: Community of Grace*, p. 30), it was said. The churches were, however, invited to take steps toward full communion and were urged to provide "officially for pulpit exchanges and mutual hospitality at the table of the Lord" (ibid., p. 31). Meanwhile in Germany, Norway, and Sweden full eucharistic fellowship has been declared between Lutherans and Methodists.

*The Dialogue with the Orthodox Church.* The Lutheran–Orthodox Joint Commission was constituted in 1981. Of course, the idea of a Pan-Orthodox–Lutheran dialogue goes back very much farther. In 1967 there had been alternating visits between representatives of the LWF and the Ecumenical Patriarchate, in which initial plans for the start of a dialogue were discussed, and in 1968 the Fourth Pan-Orthodox Conference in Chambésy, Switzerland, declared itself in favor of the convening of a joint commission.

Since then the LWF has never lost sight of the idea of a Lutheran–Orthodox dialogue. In March 1974 a Lutheran–Orthodox consultation took place in Strasbourg. Continuation of reciprocal visits was recommended, and consideration was given to the appointment of contact persons. The LWF supported the setting up of a documentation center for Orthodoxy at the University of Erlangen in Germany. Later it repeatedly considered the *filioque* question, which subsequently led the Curitiba Assembly to approve a statement that concerned primarily the liturgical use of the Nicene Creed.

Finally, the formal invitation in 1977 of the Ecumenical Patriarch to an international dialogue, which the LWF Executive Committee accepted in the same year, was decisive for the formation of the Lutheran–Orthodox Joint Commission. In 1978 the appointment of fourteen Lutheran members to this commission followed—a very high number of participants in comparison with other dialogue commissions. This was due to the equally high number of Orthodox members, which was necessary because of Pan-Orthodox representation.

After several preparatory meetings among themselves in 1978, 1979, and 1980, Lutherans and Orthodox convened the first meeting of their Joint Commission in 1981. This was followed, through 1995, by seven further meetings. Three short texts have been approved: "Divine Revelation" in 1985, "Scripture and Tradition" in 1987, and "The Canon and the Inspiration of the Holy Scripture" in 1989 (see *Lutheran–Orthodox Dialogue: Agreed Statements, 1985–1989*). Obviously this dialogue is still in its early stages.

*The Dialogue with the Baptist World Alliance.*    The dialogue with the Baptist World Alliance, which had already been recommended at the Evian Assembly came about only in the years 1986–1989. Correspondence between the LWF and the Baptist World Alliance had taken up the idea of such a dialogue, but there were repeated delays in starting the discussions. Although the executive committee had invited the Baptist World Alliance to conversations in 1981 and in 1982 had already nominated Lutheran participants for the dialogue, the first meeting of the Joint Commission took place only in 1986. It closed its work in 1989.

This dialogue did not aim at achieving church fellowship. Rather the issue was to "suggest ways of overcoming present difficulties and recommend ways to improve mutual knowledge, respect and cooperation between our churches" (*Baptists and Lutherans in Conversation: A Message to Our Churches*, Geneva, p. 5). In this the question of the Lutheran doctrinal condemnations against the Anabaptists in the sixteenth century also played an important part.

The final document of the conversations, which was the fruit of intensive theological struggle, does in fact reveal important common features, especially in the understanding of faith and grace, but also in the understanding of the church, of authority in the church, and of the church's ministry. But it also shows that the "problem of baptism, . . . which has come to symbolize theological differences between us" (ibid., p. 6), and in particular the "most controversial question . . . (i.e. the evaluation of infant baptism by Baptists), . . . could not be solved in our dialogue" (ibid., p. 22). This tension was made more acute by the fact that on the Baptist side reference was made to "the problem of indiscriminate baptism" (ibid., p. 23) in the Lutheran sphere. It is rightly said that the question of baptism must not be an encumbrance on common witness to the world. But, at the same time, it has proven true that differences still exist that cannot remain without further clarifications—for instance, as to the Lord's Supper, the church's confession, and even in the understanding of church and ministry.

*Conversations with the Adventists.*   This dialogue is the most recent of all the interconfessional conversations of the LWF. In its goal it can be compared most closely with the Baptist–Lutheran dialogue: the issue is better mutual understanding, the overcoming of stereotyped views of each other, the highlighting of the bases of faith, and the precise identification of real and supposed points of friction. The first consultation in 1994 served the purpose of probing and planning for three further consultations in the period 1996–98.

*Studies on Pentecostal Churches, the Charismatic Movement, and the Evangelical Movement.*   The Evian Assembly's recommendation to conduct a "study" of the Pentecostal churches was taken up by the Strasbourg Institute. Initially it was bound up with the Institute's more comprehensive study on "New Transconfessional Movements" of 1976, which dealt with charismatic, evangelical, and action-orientated movements. In addition, there were two separate publications of the Institute on the Charismatic Movement (Carter Lindberg, *The Third Reformation? Charismatic Movements and the Lutheran Tradition* [Macon, Ga.: Mercer University Press, 1983] and Carter Lindberg, *Charismatic Renewal and the Lutheran Tradition*, LWF Report 21 [Geneva: LWF, 1985] and a very thorough presentation, sustained by a clear sympathy for the evangelical movement (Mark Ellingsen, *The Evangelical Movement: Growth, Impact, Controversy*, Dialog [Minneapolis: Augsburg, 1988]).

*The National Dialogues and the Multilateral Conversations of the Commission on Faith and Order.*   All the churches with which the LWF conducts dialogues internationally also have national dialogues with various LWF member churches, apart from the Adventists. The LWF has conscientiously tried hard and with considerable success to interlock these two forms of dialogue and foster a relationship between them. This positive interchange between national and international dialogues can easily be verified from the dialogue documents. There have been no differences and few discrepancies worth mentioning. For the dialogues of the LWF the numerous national conversations with the Reformed, the conversations with Anglicans (in North America, the Nordic countries, Germany, and Eastern and Southern Africa) and with Orthodox churches (in Finland, Germany, and North America), but, above all, the Roman Catholic-Lutheran dialogues in the United States and Germany have been particularly important.

There have been similarly close links with the multilateral conversations undertaken by the Commission on Faith and Order of the WCC, especially the "Lima Statement," *Baptism, Eucharist and Ministry* (Geneva: WCC Publications,1982; cf. Michael Seils, *Lutheran Convergence? An Analysis of the Lutheran Responses to the Convergence Document "Baptism, Eucharist and Ministry" of the World Council of Churches Faith and Order Commission*, LWF Report 25 [Geneva: LWF, September 1988]). References to this statement run through almost all the reports of the LWF dialogues.

## "The Goal of Unity" and the Return to the Idea of koinonia/communio

### From Budapest to Curitiba

Twenty years of active participation in the ecumenical movement plus the Budapest Assembly were the occasion for the LWF to summarize its repeated reflections on the goal of ecumenical efforts. The statement was also to take stock of ecumenical efforts in the past and the direction in which things might go in the future. This statement of the Budapest Assembly on "The Unity We Seek" came in a period when the ecumenical rebirth of the idea of *koinonia/communio* in the New Testament and the early church began to become apparent (*Proceedings*, Budapest, p. 175).

Chapter 6 in this volume deals with the idea of *koinonia/communio* and its importance for the development of the self-understanding of the LWF as such. However, in the LWF the term *koinonia* crops up at a very early date, particularly in the ecumenical context; the taking up of the idea of *koinonia/communio* in the eighties signified the readoption of a concept that was already familiar.

As already shown, the ecumenical concept of "church fellowship"—as developed above all by the Commission on Theology in the 1950s and taken further at a later date—was explicitly understood as an adoption of the idea of *koinonia/communio* from the New Testament and the early church. At that time, the works of Werner Elert had both a direct and an indirect effect on the reflections of the Commission on Theology. Years later, at the Helsinki Assembly, E. Clifford Nelson's address, to which reference has already been made, on "The One Church and the Lutheran Churches" again took up explicitly the *koinonia* concept. Later this term again appeared—programmatically—in the study of *Ecumenical Methodology*, mentioned above, with a focus particularly on "lived communion," including reference to social contexts.

These were, so to speak, the three stages in the history of the LWF in which the term *koinonia/communio* appeared as such and was the subject of reflection before it became, as it has since the mid-1980s, one of the most frequently appearing and central terms in the ecumenical vocabulary. These stages, moreover, marked the path to the Budapest Assembly's statement "The Unity We Seek," which was substantively directly in line with the same assembly's "Statement on the Self-understanding and Task of the Lutheran World Federation" (ibid., p. 176). In both statements, *koinonia/communio* is clearly at the center. When this was not terminologically self-evident through the use of the word *koinonia* the reason was that this Greek word, like its Latin equivalent *communio,* had not yet passed into the normal ecumenical vocabulary—which was to happen in only a few more years. At all events it is significant that the word "communion" in its English usage corresponds to the German word *Gemeinschaft*—not "fellowship" as was previously most usual.

This term, *Gemeinschaft*/communion is unmistakably the central one in the statement on "The Unity We Seek," being found repeatedly in the short text—eight times in all. It embraces almost all the dimensions and aspects that are specific to the term as it was developed in the succeeding years, up to the assemblies of the LWF in Curitiba and the WCC in Canberra (1991) and the World Conference on Faith and Order in Santiago de Compostela (1993): the trinitarian and the eschatological dimensions of *koinonia; koinonia* in the faith, the sacraments, and the ministry; common confessing and witnessing; common worship and intercession for all human beings; the diversity and differentness inherent in *koinonia;* solidarity with the poor and oppressed; common responsibility for the world and for society; and also the necessary structural aspect of *koinonia.*

For the first time in its history the LWF gave a pregnant description of the goal of its ecumenical efforts in this Budapest statement. Undoubtedly it stands on the shoulders of the formula for unity of the 1961 New Delhi Assembly of the WCC, but it is also something like a further development of that formula, especially—though not only—where the issue is that of the relation between unity and diversity. Just as the New Delhi formula for unity has undergone further development, the Budapest Statement is open to development and new emphases. But for the time being it may be regarded as what it is intended to be: an account of the ecumenical efforts of the LWF to date and guidance for these as they continue.

## The Fruits of the Dialogues So Far

IF WE LOOK at the LWF's dialogues at the same time as we take into consideration those conducted by its member churches, a complex picture emerges which is constantly shifting and can be described here only in its main features. What follows are six general observations and facts:

1. The intensive participation of the LWF in the ecumenical movement since the 1960s, especially in the form of bilateral dialogues, has been supported by the member churches and not called into question. It is true that again and again voices are heard that criticize the fact that the ecumenical commitment is more or less limited to theological dialogue; such a critique cannot merely be dismissed. Moreover, some of the dialogue results themselves have been critically assessed. But in both cases the critique is not directed against the dialogues as such.

2. We may say that the mode of "bilateral" dialogues has proved itself. The initial fears of some have not been realized—that this form of conversation, which deliberately and directly takes stock of the specific controversial questions between two churches without involving the participation of (so to speak) "neutral" and "neutralizing" partners, would lead only to a renewal and hardening of previous conflicts. None of the dialogues has had to be broken off. Even if in individual instances expectations were not fully met and there were disillusionments, none of the dialogues has so far foundered.

3. Partner churches have learned from each of the dialogues how great the common elements are in faith, doctrine, and life, even between churches which are still divided. Consequently the range of what divides the churches becomes recognizable in its real and clearly limited extent. The divisions between the different churches do not have their roots in radical "fundamental differences," which class everything as divisive and poison everything.

4. A similar observation is true of individual controversial problems as such. Looking back on the dialogues one will scarcely be able to mention any controversial question in which dissent had proven to be "total." It has always turned out that, in each of these controversial questions, before actual dissent begins an important range of common fundamental convictions takes priority. It is true that this does not in any way remove dissent,

but it has shown the limited extent of disagreement, and at the same time it has revealed possible starting points for overcoming it.

5. In the discussion of individual controversial questions, the dialogues have not aimed at the complete removal of each and every difference. The goal has been achieved when there has been common recognition and when one could say that existing differences have lost the acuteness which have hitherto divided the churches. At such moments the necessary and also sufficient "consensus" for unity has been achieved.

6. The final and comprehensive goal of the dialogues corresponds to this view of an "ecumenical" consensus, that is, a consensus necessary for church unity. Dialogues that aim at the realization of church fellowship and not only seek to achieve a better mutual understanding are carried out with the understanding of this goal as "a communion of different churches," no matter what term they use to describe this—whether "church fellowship," "full communion," or "unity in reconciled diversity."

This confronts us with the question, how much progress have the individual LWF dialogues made? What have they so far achieved?

The answer must be a differentiated one, and this differentiation between the individual dialogues is not always clear. If we look at the overall spectrum of the dialogues that have been conducted, two points at opposite ends of the spectrum first stand out clearly:

On the one hand there is the dialogue with the *Reformed churches*. This dialogue has so far been the only one of which one can say that it has overcome the controversial questions separating the churches. This can be seen not merely in the fact that church fellowship between Reformed and Lutheran churches has been achieved in many countries. The international dialogue between the LWF and WARC has also confirmed this and has accordingly been able to invite and encourage all Lutheran and Reformed churches which so far have not been living in communion with each other to take this step.

At the other end of the spectrum is the new dialogue with the *Adventists*. It does not—yet—aim at church fellowship. Rather, its goal is better mutual understanding, highlighting common bases of faith, overcoming tensions between the churches, identifying more precisely areas of controversy and friction, and exploring possibilities for cooperation. The dialogue with the *Baptist churches* also does not explicitly aim at church fellowship.

Within these two ends of the spectrum lie the other dialogues. We may say that the dialogue with the *Anglicans* has proved particularly fruitful and promising both internationally and nationally, particularly in the last fifteen years. The first phase of conversations in the international dialogue

(1970–1972) confirmed that ultimately only the question of the episcopate stood in the way of full church fellowship. This proved to be so in the national conversations too. In the United States and Germany these led initially to the declaration of eucharistic fellowship or "interim eucharistic sharing" (U.S.). But the national dialogues pushed on further. Between the Anglican churches in Great Britain and Ireland and most Nordic and Baltic Lutheran churches the Porvoo Common Statement of 1992 has led to full communion between the churches, and in the United States the proposed *Concordat of Agreement* is at present with the Evangelical Lutheran Church in America and the Episcopal Church for decision. Its acceptance would likewise mean a declaration of full communion. These developments might and probably would lead to similar decisions in other geographical areas, particularly if the path followed in the United States proves successful, so that something similar to the achievement of Lutheran–Reformed Dialogue would then hold good for the Anglican–Lutheran Dialogue.

All things considered, the dialogue with the *Methodists* has lately faded into the background. Nevertheless, in view of the fact that in Germany as well as in Norway and Sweden church fellowship or communion in the Lord's Supper has been declared between Lutherans and Methodists, the LWF should resume the dialogue with the World Methodist Council and examine how far it can invite and encourage its other member churches to implement church fellowship with Methodist churches.

The important dialogue with the *Orthodox churches of the East* has so far proved to be most protracted at the international level. It is still only in its initial stages, and the discussion of church-dividing issues has hardly begun. The longer national conversations in Germany, North America, and especially in Finland have made more progress. But it appears to be difficult to use the results of national conversations—for example, between the Finnish Lutheran Church and the Russian and Finnish Orthodox Churches—for the dialogue with the whole of Orthodoxy.

The dialogue of all dialogues to which through almost three decades the LWF and also its member churches have directed most attention theologically and organizationally has undoubtedly been that with the *Roman Catholic Church*. Since 1967 this dialogue has been continued virtually without pause. Here too controversial questions dividing the churches have been central but at the same time joint statements on the *Confessio Augustana* and on Luther have been achieved. One of the dialogue documents even dealt with the questions of implementing Roman Catholic–Lutheran church fellowship. As has been stated repeatedly and in the new designation of the Joint Commission, the aim of this dialogue is the "unity" of the two churches. Central controversial questions such as the doctrine of justification and the understanding of the Eucharist have been dealt with repeatedly both internationally and nationally, with substantially the same positive results. The same thing is true of the question of the ministry, if the issue of the historical forms of the ministry in the episcopate and the papacy are left aside. This situation calls for ecclesial reception and enactment of the dialogue results achieved, in order to proceed further with the questions that remain open.

## Tasks and Prospects

If we follow the development through which the LWF has passed in taking its ecumenical commitment seriously, two tasks automatically stand out.

### Continuation of the Dialogue

The first task is the *unwavering continuation of the individual bilateral dialogues* to the point where the LWF on its own responsibility understands itself able theologically to commend to its member churches fellowship with the respective partner churches. This is true at least in regard to all those dialogues which have as their goal the realization of church fellowship. It can, moreover, often be assumed that some individual member churches will already have taken these steps on their own initiative. This reciprocal relation between the Federation as such and its member churches is fully in line with the self-understanding of the LWF.

Such an "end to the dialogue" as has already been reached in the Lutheran–Reformed dialogue is no longer a far-off goal in regard to the Anglican churches. This is likewise true of the dialogue with the Methodists, a partner which should not be dropped or lost to view even if there is presently something of a pause in the conversation. The dialogue movement must be continued and there should not be undue concern if, in continuing this or other dialogues, questions which have been dealt with previously are again taken up. As has often been the case, this is no empty duplication but rather signifies a deepening and confirmation of what has already been achieved. Moreover, in this way the churches' critical reactions to previous dialogue results can be taken into account and answered.

Things are different in regard to the dialogues with the Roman Catholic Church and the Orthodox Churches of the East. Although there is a considerable lack of synchronism between the two dialogues, in the sense that the one with the Orthodox is still in its initial stages, and the one with the

Roman Catholics has already led to agreements in important and contro-versial questions, in neither instance is the "end of the dialogue" an immediate goal.

The Lutheran–Roman Catholic dialogue does, however, present a spe-cial picture. On the one hand, it undoubtedly calls for patient continua-tion on a national and a global level, but, on the other, it already reveals results which from the standpoint of theological dialogue may be regarded as definitive. These "definite dialogue results" should be "ratified," and thus protected from the repeated questioning to which such results are constantly exposed. This would happen most appropriately through offi-cial joint Roman Catholic–Lutheran statements, the content of which would both summarize the agreement or consensus reached and declare that on these points earlier doctrinal condemnations no longer apply to the partner church. Such joint statements would be important milestones on the way. The dialogue should no longer fall behind, even if here and there conversation and discussion may go further in line with free theo-logical opinion and debate. Ecumenical dialogue and the question of church unity are much too important to be made dependent on individual theological trends and opinions. Here there is a need—as repeatedly has been so in church history, and not least the history of the Lutheran churches—for doctrinal statements *by the churches* that they regard as binding even if they neither wish nor are able to break off continuing theological discussion.

## Ecclesial Reception of the Dialogue Results

Such actions as the "lifting of condemnations,"whether as comprehensive or only partial ecclesial confirmation of the results of dialogue, are within the logic of official interchurch dialogues as the LWF has resolved to con-duct them. To think that such actions could not in principle be carried out would amount to degrading the dialogues into merely free theological dis-cussions. Thus the LWF faces a new ecumenical task which it has so far hardly begun to tackle: *ecclesial reception of the theological agreements reached in the interchurch dialogues.*

Just as the LWF crossed the threshold from ecumenical theological research to ecumenical dialogue between churches, so too it will have to progress from dialogue to ecclesial reception of the results of dialogue: ecumenical responsibility, which the LWF has acknowledged from the start, cannot be regarded as being already fulfilled by the fact that a series of interesting consensus documents has been produced that, however, do not bind the church and thus remain ineffective. The Federation's ecumenical responsibility will not permit it to excuse itself from ecclesial reception of the consensuses that have been reached—all the less so with the widening consciousness in the LWF of its own ecclesial nature and of its capacity for joint action, a consciousness which found constitutional expression at the Curitiba Assembly.

Nevertheless, the question may presumably be asked—as it was at Helsinki—whether the Federation is not exceeding its powers by doing so. But undoubtedly it will not exceed its powers if it proceeds as indicated above and as it seems to have proceeded already with regard to the Lutheran–Reformed relationship: on its own responsibility it can state—and can justify the point theologically—that, for instance, between Reformed and Lutherans or between Anglicans and Lutherans, the hitherto divisive questions of doctrine and ministry have been overcome, and that it therefore recommends to and encourages its member churches to enter into church fellowship with Reformed and Anglican churches insofar as they have not already done so on their own initiative. Or, on its own initiative, it can state and justify theologically that, for instance, specific divisive controversial questions between Lutheranism and Roman Catholicism have been overcome and that it recommends and encourages its member churches to endorse such a statement or make it independently. Indeed, the proposed *Joint Declaration on the Doctrine of Justification* between the Roman Catholic church and the Lutheran World Federation, anticipated for common action in 1998, represents precisely such an action.

The concern that with such a process differences capable of endangering the LWF as a communion might arise between individual member churches seems unfounded and unrealistic. For this communion has for quite some time been living with the fact that there are many churches within it that have already made binding ecumenical decisions on their own initiative, without these decisions having been shared to date by all the member churches of the LWF. The statement of the Evian Assembly that member churches which have formed a union with non-Lutheran churches may also remain within the LWF (cf. pp. 263–64 above) is directly relevant here.

Something entirely similar holds regarding the concern that the development of individual bilateral dialogues might disturb the development of other dialogues and thus bring the entire network of dialogues out of kilter. This concern about the "compatibility" of dialogues is artificial and to a great extent premature. It easily forgets that all the dialogues are moving toward the ecumenical goal and are not static entities whose differences or affinities can be clearly measured or defined.

But the great task of "ecumenical reception" goes far beyond formal ecclesial reception of the results of dialogue. If we adopt the central term of the study on "Ecumenical Methodology" (see pp. 265–67 above), the issue is primarily that of actual implementation of "lived *koinonia*" among churches which have so far been separated. But inasmuch as "lived *koinonia*" is something directly related to actual situations, a "*World* Federation"—which, after all, is farther removed than its individual member churches from actual local situations—here comes up against the limits of its possibilities. Nevertheless, one of the LWF's important future tasks will be to examine and look for a way in which it may serve its churches in this reception process and thus exercise its ecumenical responsibility.

There might be a need for renewed reflection on "church fellowship" and thus on the ecumenical goal. In taking into account all previous reflections, the Budapest Assembly clearly defined this goal with its statement "The Unity We Seek." In fresh reflections the question will not be to leave this statement behind but to take it further and so to bestow on it new directional power for the future.

## Bibliographical Notes

### I. Printed Documents

> Højen, Peder, ed. *Ecumenical Methodology: Documentation and Report.* Geneva: Lutheran World Federation, 1978.
>
> LWF Commission on Theology, *More than Church Unity: Study Document for the Fifth Assembly. Lutheran World*, Volume 17, No. 1. Geneva, 1970, pp. 43-50.
>
> *Lutheran World/Lutherische Rundschau,* passim.
>
> "The Nature of the Lutheran World Federation: Commentary on Articles II, III and IV of its Constitution," *Document 4, Fourth Assembly of the Lutheran World Federation, July 30–August 11, 1963, Helsinki, Finland.* Geneva: Lutheran World Federation, 1963; also Opinion on "the Status of Document 4 [above]," *Lutheran World,* Volume 11, Geneva, 1964, pp. 172–203.
>
> *Proceedings* (all LWF Assemblies).

### II. Dialogue Reports

> Meyer, Harding, and Vischer, Lukas, eds., *Growth in Agreement: Reports and Agreed Statements of Ecumenical Conversations on a World Level.* New York/Ramsey: Paulist Press; Geneva: World Council of Churches, 1984. Cf. also Harding Meyer, Damaskinos Papandreou, Hans Jörg Urban, and Lukas Vischer, eds. *Dokumente wachsender Übereinstimmung: Sämtliche Berichte und Konsenstexte interkonfessioneller Gespräche auf Weltebene,* vol. 2. Paderborn: Bonifatius Druckerei/ Frankfurt: Otto Lembeck Verlag, 1992.

This volume includes the following reports from LWF dialogues:
1. Anglican–Lutheran Conversation—pp. 13ff.
   Pullach Report, 1972
2. Lutheran-Roman Catholic Conversations—pp. 167ff.
   Malta Report, 1972
   The Eucharist, 1978
   Ways to Community, 1980
   All Under One Christ, 1980
   The Ministry in the Church, 1981
3. Lutheran–Reformed-Roman Catholic Conversations—pp. 267ff.
   The Theology of Marriage and the Problem of Mixed Marriages,
   1976

Additional dialogue reports available as separate documents include:

Anglican–Lutheran International Continuation Committee, *The Niagara Report: Report of the Anglican-Lutheran Consultation on Episcope 1987.* London: Anglican Consultative Council Publishing House and Geneva: Lutheran World Federation, 1988.

Roman Catholic–Lutheran Joint Commission, *Facing Unity: Models, Forms and Phases of Catholic–Lutheran Church Fellowship.* Geneva: Lutheran World Federation, 1985.

Lutheran–Roman Catholic Joint Commission, *Church and Justification: Understanding the Church in the Light of the Doctrine of Justification.* Geneva: Lutheran World Federation, 1994.

Rusch, William G., and Martensen, Daniel F., *The Leuenberg Agreement and Lutheran–Reformed Relationships: Evaluations by North American and European Theologians.* Minneapolis: Augsburg, 1989. Includes the text of the Leuenberg Agreement of 1973.

Lutheran–Reformed Joint Commission, *Towards Church Fellowship.* Geneva: Lutheran World Federation, World Alliance of Reformed Churches, 1989.

Lutheran–Methodist Joint Commission, *The Church: Community of Grace.* Geneva: Lutheran World Federation and Lake Junalaska, NC: World Methodist Council, 1984.

Lutheran–Orthodox Joint Commission, *Lutheran-Orthodox Dialogue: Agreed Statements, 1985–1989.* Geneva: Lutheran World Federation, 1992.

Baptist–Lutheran Joint Commission, *Baptists and Lutherans in Conversation: A Message to Our Churches.* Geneva: Baptist World Alliance, Lutheran World Federation, 1990.

*Baptism, Eucharist and Ministry:* Faith and Order Paper No. 111. Geneva: World Council of Churches, 1982.

III. Monographs and Selected Writings

Burgess, Joseph A., ed. *Lutherans in Ecumenical Dialogue: A Reappraisal.* Minneapolis: Augsburg, 1990.

Department of Theology, LWF, ed. *The Unity of the Church: A Sympo-*

*sium. Papers Presented to the Commissions on Theology and Liturgy of the Lutheran World Federation.* Rock Island, Ill.: Augustana Press, 1957.

Gassmann, Günther, and Meyer, Harding, eds. *The Unity of the Church: Requirements and Structure.* Geneva: LWF Report 15, June 1983.

Institute for Ecumenical Research, *Communio/Koinonia: A New Testament-Early Christian Concept and Its Contemporary Appropriation and Significance.* Strasbourg: Institute for Ecumenical Research, 1990.

*The Meissen Agreement: Texts.* Occasional Paper No. 2. London: Council for Christian Unity of the General Synod of the Church of England, 1988.

Meyer, Harding. *Ökumenische Zielvorstellungen.* Göttingen: Vandenhoeck & Ruprecht, 1996. Eng. transl. forthcoming, Grand Rapids: Wm. B. Eerdmans Publishing Co.

———, ed. *The Augsburg Confession in Ecumenical Perspective: With Anglican, Baptist, Methodist, Orthodox, Reformed, and Roman Catholic Contributions.* Geneva: LWF Report 6/7, December 1979.

———, ed. *Lutheran/Roman Catholic Discussion on the Augsburg Confession: Documents — 1977–1981.* Geneva: LWF Report 10, August 1982.

———, ed. *Luthertum in der Ökumene.* Pp. 275–300 in Vajta, Vilmos, ed. *Die evangelisch-lutherische Kirche,* 2 Aufl. Frankfurt: Otto Lembeck Verlag, 1983.

Meyer, Harding, and Heinz Schütte, eds. *Confessio Augustana: Bekenntnis des einen Glaubens. Gemeinsame Untersuchung lutherischer und katholischer Theologen.* Paderborn: Bonifatius Druckerei/Frankfurt: Otto Lembeck Verlag, 1980.

Norgren, William, and Rusch, William, eds. *"Toward Full Communion" and "Concordat of Agreement": Lutheran–Episcopal Dialogue, Series III.* Minneapolis: Augsburg; Cincinnati: Forward Movement, 1991.

Schieffer, Elisabeth, *Von Schauenburg nach Leuenberg: Entstehung und Bedeutung der Konkordie reformatorischer Kirchen in Europa.* Paderborn: Bonifatius Druckerei, 1983.

*Together in Mission and Ministry: The Porvoo Common Statement with Essays on Church and Ministry in Northern Europe.* London: Church House Publishing, 1993.

25. Professor E. Clifford Nelson,
U.S.A., speaking at the
Helsinki Assembly, 1963.

26. The Institute for Ecumenical Research, 8, rue Gustave-Klotz,
Strasbourg, France.

27. Joint Working Group planning for the LWF–Roman Catholic dialogue, Strasbourg, 1965. At the head are the cochairs, Bishop Hermann Dietzfelbinger of Munich, Lutheran, and Cardinal Hermann Volk of Mainz, Roman Catholic. Cardinal Johannes Willebrands is seated next to Cardinal Volk.

28. Fourth Meeting of the Lutheran–Orthodox Joint Commission, Crete, 1987.

# Dimensions of Communion: Inclusive Participation in the LWF

IN AN OBVIOUS but perhaps ambiguous way, the growth of the Lutheran World Federation in the five decades of its history has reflected—or at least been parallel to—the twentieth-century movement toward inclusiveness.

In spite of its claim to being a global movement, traceable at least to 1923 and the formation of the Lutheran World Convention, the LWF was established in Lund in 1947 with official delegates from only two countries—China and India—outside the European and North American orbit. Since the Curitiba Assembly in 1990, it has been a requirement of the LWF that half of the elected members of the Federation council be from member churches of the Southern Hemisphere.

Similarly, at Lund in 1947, according to various and conflicting accounts, the number of women delegates to the assembly was 2.8% of the total delegation, although some documents indicate an even smaller percentage. At the Budapest Assembly of 1984 it was mandated that women should make up at least 40% of the next assembly's body of official delegates, and that that figure should be increased to 50% for the Ninth Assembly. A similar growth in the number of official youth delegates and participants can easily be traced.

What accounts for these changes toward a more inclusive Federation? Clearly, society itself has, in the past decades, become more global, more gender inclusive, and vastly more aware of the contributions of laity, youth, the disabled, and other groups that have traditionally been on the margins of church life. Has the Federation's participation in these devel-

*Anza Lema, Arusha, Tanzania, Dorothy Marple, Philadelphia, Pennsylvania, Julius Filo, Bratislava, Slovak Republic, Prasanna Kumari, Madras, India, and Norman A. Hjelm, Wynnewood, Pennsylvania, are the authors of chapter 8.*

opments been determined by forces originating in secular movements? Or has the Federation, in its growth toward *communio*, been marked by a new realization of and commitment to authentic catholicity in its life? The answer to these questions is not a simple one, and the growth to be described in the present chapter has not been without struggle and sharp controversy. White, male church leaders from the North have not always moved with alacrity to share leadership in decision making. The force of entrenched power characteristic of all institutions has not been absent from the Lutheran World Federation. Yet, however slowly and grudgingly given, there have been changes in the LWF consistent with concerns for justice and human rights and with the deeper meanings of *communio*. In what follows, the story of these changes will be described in respect to the inclusion of the Lutheran churches of the South, of women, of youth, and of persons with disabling conditions. It will be seen, moreover, that, as in so many facets of Federation life, the development of an inclusiveness consistent with full *communio* is not yet complete.

## Lutheran Churches of the South

FROM THE VERY BEGINNING there was a clear intention to make of the Lutheran World Federation a global organization. Prior to 1923, efforts to create unified expressions of Lutheranism had been regionally based. In the United States, as an example, Lutheran churches in 1918 had formed the National Lutheran Council. In Europe the situation was radically different: in the Nordic countries Lutheran state or folk churches had existed alongside few, if any, other strong Christian ecclesial bodies; in Germany there were regional churches, *Landeskirchen*, whose efforts to achieve a united Lutheran expression had resulted in the creation of a national conference of Lutheran churches even prior to 1923. Thus, in the early years of the twentieth century, Lutheran relationships and cooperation had taken place within the prevailing national boundaries of the Northern countries.

After World War I the task that occupied the North was the reconstruction of cities and nations devastated by war, and that task proved so enormous that it demanded cooperation across national boundaries. Specifically, the resources of Lutheran churches in North America and the Nordic countries, unravaged by the war, needed to be shared with the churches of Germany faced with the results of deprivation and destruction. In this situation, the National Lutheran Council in the United States and the Church of Sweden in particular sent resources of personnel and material assistance to aid those continental churches that had suffered greatly from the war. These contacts and experiences of assistance led to the formation in 1923 of the Lutheran World Convention as an agency for greater contact and cooperation between Lutheran churches from both sides of the Atlantic.

By the third meeting of the Lutheran World Convention, held in Paris in 1935, there was some evidence of an emergence of a perspective wider than just Europe and North America. This was reflected in a later statement that the Convention's purpose was "to bring the Lutheran Churches and organizations of the world into an enduring and intimate relationship with one another" (Ralph H. Long, "The Place of the Lutheran World Federation in the World Today," *Proceedings*, Lund, p. 126).

This description came, it must be admitted, from after World War II, a war that was far more devastating in its global impact than the war of 1914–1918. The experiences of this second war, coupled with a relatively vague recognition that Lutheranism had been kept alive and had even prospered in the missionary areas of Asia, Africa, and Latin America, persuaded the Lutheran churches of Europe and North America in 1947 to lead in the establishment of the Lutheran World Federation.

There was in 1947 a desire, not always boldly expressed, to include within the new Federation Lutheran churches outside the North Atlantic region. The question, however, was, Where were these Lutheran churches, and who were their leaders? There were very few established Lutheran churches in what later came to be called the Third World; the most that could be said was that there were many Lutheran missions in Africa and Asia, and congregations of immigrant European Lutherans in Latin America. Inevitably, then, the Lund Assembly was by and large an assembly of delegates from Europe and North America; the few representatives of the South were missionaries and a small number of Asian church leaders.

Yet a spirit of incipient inclusiveness was imprinted in the Federation's constitution as adopted on July 1, 1947 by unanimous vote. That document indicated the following under the rubric of "Membership":

> All Lutheran Churches previously affiliated with the Lutheran World Convention, which through their representatives participate in the adoption of this Constitution, shall continue to be members of the Lutheran World Federation. Other Lutheran churches which declare their acceptance of this Constitution shall be eligible to membership in the Lutheran World Federation. (LWF Constitution, Article IV, 1947)

The second sentence of this article made it quite clear that membership in the new body was open to any Lutheran church in the world that was prepared to accept the Federation's constitution. This stood as a significant—although not yet actual—move of world Lutheranism away from the virtual limitation to European and North American participation which had marked the Lutheran World Convention.

The planners of the Lund Assembly had anticipated this development by inviting Lutheran churches in China and India to send delegates. Missionary pastors from British Guiana, Madagascar, and South Africa also attended, but there was no indigenous representation from the Lutheran congregations of those regions.

The delegates, few in total number, from China and India participated actively in the assembly. Dr. P'eng Fu (1888–1975), President of the Lutheran Church of China, was one of three speakers at the major service of worship in the Lund Cathedral. The Rev. Prof. S. W. Savarimuthu of the Tamil Evangelical Lutheran Church in Madras, India, was also one of the assembly's keynoters (ibid., pp. 144–46).

Whether all of the delegates to the Lund Assembly understood it or not, the inclusion of P'eng Fu and Savarimuthu among the assembly speakers was a recognition that non-Northern churches had a contribution to make to the Federation. They were from societies vastly different from those of the North Atlantic countries, and they came to Lund from cultures that had very little in common with the civilization of the "Christian West." Their churches were tiny minority groups living within milieus shaped by some of the oldest and largest religious traditions of the world, and the great majority of those at Lund had little or no appreciation for their experience of religious isolation.

A further concrete example of the first small movement of the Federation toward global inclusiveness was the election at Lund of the Rev. Joel Lakra (1894–1974), President of the Gossner Evangelical Lutheran Church of India, to the first LWF Executive Committee. What are now self-evident questions about the meaning of inclusiveness were, to be sure, neither addressed nor clarified at Lund. Was it a notion restricted to participation at gatherings such as assemblies and official committee meetings? Did it mean fully equal representation of all member churches at every important Federation event? Did it mean the inclusion of, for example, women and youth in all delegations from individual church bodies? It is clear that "representation" involved church leaders, and this ipso facto sharply restricted the involvement of women and youth. Only much later and then often under the influence of the women's and youth movements of society at large, were these questions addressed. Clarity was to come only with pain and by struggle.

By the time of the Second LWF Assembly, in 1952, the Federation's executive committee had begun to take some concrete steps toward the actualization of the organization's global character. Churches in the Southern Hemisphere had been visited by LWF leaders prior to the assembly, and there was a concerted effort to make of the assembly a multiracial event. In the period between its first and second assemblies, the LWF had approved fourteen applications for membership, including churches from India, Brazil, British Guiana, Argentina, and Japan. There were also accredited delegates at Hanover from Indonesia and official visitors from Lutheran churches in Chile, Madagascar, and South Africa. In addition, mission societies sent representatives from Lutheran missions in Ethiopia, Liberia, Southern Rhodesia, South West Africa, and Tanganyika. Thus it was that the Second Assembly was considerably more representative of global Lutheranism than had been the case in the past.

This fact was underscored by the executive of the LWF Commission on World Missions, Fredrik A. Schiotz, who, in his report to the assembly, stated that "none of us could escape the absolute necessity for providing younger churches with representation through their own nationals on the new commission that will carry on after Hanover. The church of Jesus Christ is being outdistanced by secular forces in the recognition that larger responsibilities can and must be posted in the hands of younger churchmen" (*Proceedings*, Hanover, 1952, pp. 36–41).

At the assembly itself two presentations were made by Lutherans from the South: the Rev. Joel Lakra of India spoke on "The Lutheran Churches of the East," and Präses Schlünzen of Brazil spoke on behalf of congregations of Eastern European immigrants to Latin America (ibid., p. 15). The executive committee of the Federation, elected at Hanover, included the Rev. A. M. Gopal of India and Dr. Hermann Dohms of Brazil.

At Hanover it was argued from Australia that, while it was extremely important to strengthen cooperation among all Lutheran churches, it needed to be recognized that not all churches had made a decision to join the Federation even though they were often involved in cooperative work with the LWF and its member churches. The executive committee, accordingly, was asked to investigate the possibility of creating additional categories—consultants, affiliated or associate members—of relationship to the Federation. It was agreed, in giving this task to the executive committee, that under all circumstances Article II of the constitution, the confessional basis of the LWF, must be accepted "as norm for their teaching and practice" (ibid., p. 23). At the Third LWF Assembly in Minneapolis in 1957, the executive committee reported on this issue. Its conclusion was that it would be difficult if not impossible to establish affiliate or associate membership without creating "two grades of Lutheran churches" (*Proceedings*, Minneapolis, p. 157). However, the executive committee did recommend to the assembly that a number of Lutheran communities be given the status of "recognized congregations."

Four South American congregations, in Columbia, Equador, Peru, and Venezuela, were given this status. Additionally, churches from Hong Kong, Mexico, Madagascar, and Tanganyika were accepted as full members of the Federation at Minneapolis. Official visitors from nonmember churches at this assembly numbered 125, including representatives of church bodies in Asia, South America, and Africa (ibid., pp. 181, 197–201). Thus it was that the Third Assembly of the LWF became by far the most representative assembly of the first decade. Lutheran churches of the South were no longer represented exclusively or even primarily by missionaries; church leaders of all races and many nationalities met in Minneapolis as official delegates of their churches.

At the Helsinki Assembly, eleven new churches—from Eritrea, Ethiopia, Southern Rhodesia, South Africa, South West Africa, and Tanganyika—were accepted into full LWF membership, and a parish in Bolivia was added to the list of recognized congregations (*Proceedings*, Helsinki, 1963, pp. 57–62, 98–100, 512). The executive secretary of the Federation (the title then in use), Kurt Schmidt-Clausen, commenting on the number of new member churches, claimed that this underlined "still further the inter-continental character of a Lutheran World Federation binding many peoples together" (ibid., p. 65).

One of the four main lectures at Helsinki was given by Dr. Andar Lumbantobing (b. 1920), President of Nommensen University, then at Pematangsiantar, Sumatra, Indonesia, "The New Song of Praise." In this lecture an interpretation of the Lutheran heritage in the context of the experience of Batak Christians in Sumatra was given. The gospel, Dr. Lumbantobing declared, "was not for the benefit of a certain class or race, but for the whole '*oikumene*,' for all of mankind, so that the whole cosmos may be transformed into a Temple of God" (ibid., p. 127). The significance of this address was highlighted by Bishop Hanns Lilje in his response. Dr. Lumbantobing, Lilje pointed out, was a theologian from the Batak church, yet he had succeeded in setting forth Lutheran theology "in an unmistakable and winning manner":

> Thus one can see that this approach to the Gospel is really ecumenical in significance and is not bound simply to cultural backgrounds. I consider that to be an important event . . . and I should like to add that I hope each one of us has appreciated the fact that here members of a church which started a hundred years ago and were long described by us as mission churches have been amongst us now as mature Christian brethren bearing witness to Christ. That is a great event which we must make ourselves aware of. . . . (ibid., p. 134)

The executive committee elected at Helsinki consisted of nineteen persons, five from younger churches in the Southern Hemisphere: Bishop Leonard Auala, Namibia; Bishop Rajah Manikam, India, who was also among the first Vice Presidents of the Federation from the South; Bishop Stefano Moshi, Tanganyika; Dr. Ernesto Schlieper, Brazil; and Mr. Bernhard Silitonga, Indonesia. The retiring President of the LWF, Franklin

Clark Fry, summed up his Helsinki memories: "Eclipsing all other memories, the voices of a host of men [sic], yellow and black and white and brown, from east and from west, speaking in the accents of six continents and a half hundred languages, rose in testimony to the Lamb. To Him be the praise!" (ibid., Foreword, p. 10).

The Fifth Assembly of the LWF, held at Evian, France, in 1970, has come to be regarded by many as a critical turning point in the life of the Federation. It was, moreover, said of this assembly that "never before had the churches of Asia and Africa played so active a role" (André Appel, *Proceedings*, Evian, p. 9).

The assembly, centered on the theme "Sent into the World," had been planned with high hopes. When the first venue chosen, Weimar in the German Democratic Republic, proved unworkable, the offer of the Evangelical Church of the Lutheran Confession in Brazil to hold the assembly in Porto Alegre was eagerly accepted. It seemed most appropriate, in light of the chosen theme, that the Federation should for the first time hold its assembly outside the North Atlantic orbit. The last-minute decision again to change the venue, to Evian, was seen by many as a cause for disappointment and frustration. Did "Sent into the World" mean no further than Evian? According to the general secretary, André Appel, "the beginning of the Assembly was marked not by harmony but by a difficult confrontation arising from a situation of conflict." It was as if for the first time churches shaped by differing cultural contexts which had evolved under varying historical and sociopolitical circumstances were required to take seriously their different responses to the gospel. For the first time, too, the younger churches of the South voiced strong concerns that became central issues for the assembly. Yet the spirit that finally prevailed was not one of antagonism; rather, what emerged was "an Assembly of dialog, a dialog broad enough to include groups which often find too little opportunity of making their voices heard in ordinary ecclesiastical assemblies" (ibid.).

These changes in venue—Weimar to Porto Alegre to Evian—brought home anew to the entire LWF the reality of world suffering and the inadequacy of the churches' response. Professor Marc Lienhard (b. 1935) of Strasbourg, France, declared, in his sermon at the opening Eucharist of the assembly:

> There are our fellow believers in Brazil who have been deeply shaken by the change of Assembly site from Porto Alegre to Evian. They believe that they have been forsaken and their country falsely accused. But there are also others whose suffering, crying, and pain from this same country can be heard. Can we now calmly relax here at the lake and not hear all of this? (ibid., p. 15)

In a plenary debate at Evian, disappointment was expressed that the intention to hold the assembly in the Third World had been betrayed by Northern churches. Many were of the view that there was little respect for the views of the Third World churches and no desire to consult with them. The younger churches, having attained independence, discovered the reality that the Northern churches, larger and with great financial resources, were the dominant churches of the LWF: "Is the LWF not another form of domination?" a delegate from the South intoned (ibid., p. 122).

At and after Evian, it became crystal clear that church leaders from the South were no longer content merely with being onlookers. They were determined to assert themselves by bringing forward their views as shaped by their own traditions and cultures. From the South the LWF could expect little by way of material support, but that did not prevent strong and insightful voices from being raised which were to give new dimensions to the theology of the Federation. It was a letter from the officers of the Ethiopian Evangelical Church Mekane Yesus, which prompted the vigorous debate on "Proclamation and Development" during the 1970s, a debate that was determinative for much of the life of the Federation. Furthermore, it was to be an initiative by black Lutherans from South Africa that raised the central question of *status confessionis* in respect to the practice of apartheid in Lutheran churches of Southern Africa, and this was to lead in 1984 to the suspension of the LWF membership of white Lutheran churches in South Africa and Namibia.

The extent to which the Lutheran World Federation took seriously the Evian Assembly can perhaps be measured by the achievement of the Sixth Assembly held at Dar es Salaam, Tanzania, in 1977. The outgoing President of the Federation, Mikko Juva of Finland, highlighted the challenge of the younger churches to the Federation:

> If I should have to define the most substantial aspect in the development of our fellowship, I would like to speak about growing global partnership. The sheer numerical strength of European and American churches combined with their strong organization, established tradition and sophisticated theology had during the initial decades of the Federation given them an undisputed leadership. In many ways Evian was a turning point. With the theme of the Fifth Assembly, "Sent into the World," it was inevitable that the focus of deliberations would concentrate on the problems of Africa, Asia and Latin America, just those parts of the world where the injustices experienced were most severe and the need for correction most urgent.

> Evian demonstrated a remarkable step towards real partnership, but not yet its full realization. Most initiatives in the area of human rights and international justice came from Europeans and North Americans. Western as well as East European criticism was louder than Asian or African. After Evian, this is no longer the case. In the discussion going on in the LWF we have experienced

how in the areas just mentioned the churches of the developing countries have seized the initiative. In the Executive Committee, in commissions, consultations, seminars and periodicals the representatives of Africa, Asia and Latin America have spoken to our community in a clear and distinct voice. There is no need to wait for some progressive theologian from the West to analyze the abuses and defects of our world and put the grievances into words. All our member churches now speak for themselves strongly and convincingly as full partners. (*Proceedings*, Dar es Salaam, p. 12)

In his report, Carl H. Mau, Jr., the LWF General Secretary, said: "The member churches of Asia, Africa, and Latin America pressed the Assembly to face the social-political implications of the Christian faith. The statement on human rights is a significant step forward from the statement made at the Evian Assembly, which at that time had also broken new ground for Lutherans" (ibid., p. 8).

Significantly, it was at the Sixth Assembly that the Lutheran World Federation for the first time elected a church leader from the South, Bishop Josiah Kibira of the Evangelical Lutheran Church in Tanzania, as its president. His words to the assembly were very much to the point:

[I]n electing me as the first President from Africa . . . this Assembly has taken one small step in realizing the substance of the new community in Christ. . . . I regard this as an expression of the Assembly's confidence in the host church as a mature and equal partner in the task of our global ministry. . . . Evian pointed us clearly to a new understanding of the full gospel to be preached to the whole human being on all continents, an obligation laid upon every church. Dar es Salaam, it seems to me, represents a further step in consolidation of the vision of Evian. (ibid., p. 64)

There were at Dar es Salaam yet other manifestations of the increased role being played in the LWF by the younger churches. Three of the seven key addresses on the assembly theme, "In Christ A New Community," were by speakers from Asia and Africa: Yoshiro Ishida of Japan, Nicolas Maro of Tanzania, and Manas Buthelezi of South Africa. Additionally, the executive committee elected at Dar es Salaam included, out of twenty-eight members, five from Africa, four from Asia, and two from Latin America. Finally, it is important to note that the LWF Executive Committee in its report to the Sixth Assembly noted "an increase of staff coming from Asia, Africa and Latin America, as well as of women executives. Efforts are continuing to provide a greater balance of staff coming from all member churches" (ibid., p. 167).

Even as the Sixth Assembly recognized in a new and concrete way the global character of the LWF, the Seventh Assembly at Budapest is to be interpreted as a new sign of the solidarity of Lutheran churches with their brothers and sisters in the then-Communist world. The general secretary, Carl Mau, noted in his report that since the decision to hold the assembly in Hungary,

> international tension between East and West has increased and, therefore, the challenge of the Assembly being held in an Eastern European socialist country is all the greater. By being here we, as the worldwide Lutheran community, want to affirm that the church of Christ is not subservient to any political ideology and that it transcends political, cultural, and other boundaries separating peoples. . . . As part of the body of Christ, we are prepared to share one another's joys, struggles, and sufferings and also share all the ambiguities involved in being in the world but not of the world. (*Proceedings*, Budapest, pp. 172–73)

At this point in the Federation's history attention was also directed to the genuinely international character of the staff of the secretariat. In the 1960s employment of staff from the Southern Hemisphere was really a matter of tokenism: the Rev. Dr. Yoshiro Ishida (b. 1926) of Japan was the first person from the non-European/American world to be appointed, as Asia Secretary in the Department of World Mission; he later returned to Geneva as the LWF Director of Studies. Also, the Rev. Donald September of South Africa was Assistant Secretary for Africa, and Mr. Joel Ngeiyamu of Tanzania was Study Secretary for a brief term.

In the early 1970s the staff began more seriously to reflect the global reality of the LWF. Dr. Wong Yong Ji of Korea succeeded Dr. Ishida as Asia Secretary, the Rev. Amon Mwakisunga of Tanzania became the first African to serve as Executive Secretary for Africa in the Department of Church Cooperation, and the Rev. Albertus Maasdorp (b. 1936) of Namibia became, in 1973, the second person appointed to the post of associate general secretary of the Federation. From that point on, it could be said that the staff of the Federation was a fair reflection of the overall membership of the organization.

By virtue of its consideration of the meaning of communion, the Eighth Assembly of the LWF, held in Curitiba, Brazil, in 1990, became an event of great importance in the Federation's history. In his introduction to the assembly proceedings, Gunnar Staalsett, LWF General Secretary, noted that

> at this Assembly the Lutheran World Federation gave formal recognition to the development of its self-understanding in terms of the *communio* of God's people in the church. The delegates, officially designated by the one hundred five member churches of the LWF, gave formal approval to a constitutional statement which makes unambiguously clear that the churches of the Federation understand themselves to be an expression of the worldwide commu-

nion of Lutheran churches. In place of the former constitutional description of the Federation as a "free association of Lutheran churches," the Assembly adopted language which gives new testimony to the intimate and binding relationship—based on faith, mission, and service—which unites Lutheran churches throughout the world: "The Lutheran World Federation is a communion of churches which confess the triune God, agree in the proclamation of the Word of God and are united in pulpit and altar fellowship." (*Proceedings*, Curitiba, p. 1)

The assembly itself reflected this understanding of communion. Women comprised 43% of the delegates; there were equal numbers of women and men speakers; and four of the eight section addresses were given by speakers from Africa, Asia, and Latin America. A milestone was reached, further, in the decision of the assembly—in line with Federation restructuring—that the chief governing body between assemblies, the LWF Council, was to be composed of 50% of persons from churches of the Southern Hemisphere and 50% of persons from churches of the Northern Hemisphere. This parity or equality between North and South, in spite of divergences in numbers and financial strength, has been marked as potentially a concrete realization of the Federation's theological/ecclesiological commitment to the inclusiveness of *communio*.

The foregoing chronicle of the development of the full inclusion of Lutheran churches of the Southern Hemisphere into the life of the Lutheran World Federation is only partially adequate to the task of this chapter. The question remains: how truly inclusive is the LWF? Some general observations are in order.

Prior to the Evian Assembly of 1970, the involvement of persons from the South in the "inner circles" of the LWF was primarily of a symbolic nature, a token gesture of good will on the part of the churches of the North. Yet it is to be remembered that Evian took place in the midst of an era of enormous global social change. The revolts of students and youth in the 1960s questioned the traditional values of the West; age-old customs were challenged and shaken mercilessly in many parts of Europe and North America. Colonial patterns died, governments tumbled, and entrenched political leaders frequently passed from the scene. And the churches, including those of the Lutheran World Federation, were not immune to these upheavals.

The movement toward inclusiveness within the LWF thus took place in this global context and was, indeed, abetted by its challenges. As in other national and international organizations, the Federation saw its doors cracking open to allow representatives of hitherto ignored groups of people into its decision-making processes. At Evian leaders of Lutheran churches of the South began to take a rightful place in the highest levels of Federation activity. In consequence of the Fifth Assembly, women were afforded a serious role in the Federation when a women's desk was created in the Geneva secretariat's Department of Studies.

Even so, more than a movement toward equal representation has been required for the Federation genuinely to progress on the road to inclusiveness. Theological structures, language practices, and patterns and rules of procedure have also had in an ongoing process to be made more open and inclusive. And, perhaps most crucially, the inhibitions of deprivation and poverty that mark churches and institutions of the South remain to be overcome.

In each of these areas—theology, language, rules of order, and economic power—inclusiveness is yet fully to be achieved in the life of the LWF. To be sure, Lutheran churches of the South and of the North have much in common: an apostolic faith seen through the prism of the Reformation, an understanding and practice of liturgy and worship which truly unites, common convictions concerning ecumenical mission and service to the world. Yet the road toward inclusiveness, *communio*, has not reached its end.

## Women in the Life of the Federation

FOR WOMEN, three central affirmations are deeply etched in their quest for a truly inclusive LWF: the creation of women and men equally in the image of God, the baptism of both into the body of Christ, and the bestowal of gifts by the Holy Spirit on both for service in church and society. Women in the LWF have vigorously pursued a recognition of God-given gifts and opportunities to use them with grace and competence. Their journey has been a search for global consciousness, for leadership opportunities, for response to social conditions that dehumanize and spawn injustice, and for changing organizational structures to allow for representation and full participation in the Federation.

### Preparing the Way

The social upheaval created by the outbreak of World War II shattered boundaries that delineated traditional spheres for women and men. "Everywhere in the world—in Europe and America, in Asia and in Africa—woman is called upon to assume her share of responsibility in the establishment of a new order," asserted a study booklet prepared for the

Hanover Assembly in 1952. "A new code governing the life of man and woman must be found" (Carl E. Lund-Quist, ed., "The Living Word in a Responsible Church," Geneva, 1952, p. 160).

In a remarkable way, this study booklet—prepared by both men and women, theologians and laity—both illustrated the interplay of societal issues and biblical interpretation and addressed basic questions at a time of social transformation:

> To what extent has the Church begun to realize in its practice what Christ actually brought to womanhood? Must we honor the patriarchal order of society which made woman the servant of man . . . as an unconditional command of God, to be scrupulously obeyed till the end of time? . . . Is there any possible way of overcoming, in the administrative groups of our churches, the spirit of excessive objectivism, of cold bureaucracy, which fails to see the living human being? (ibid., pp. 161, 196)

In retrospect, such questions were portents of those to be raised again and again during ensuing decades. Even in response to the latter question, a tentative answer, "invite women to hold membership in all official boards of the church" (ibid., p. 197) and train them for such service, foreshadowed the accelerated activity for women's representation in decision-making structures, leadership development, and ordination that marked later years.

A fundamental divergence in perspective also emerged at this time in respect to the quest of women for inclusiveness. Even though the 1952 assembly planners had requested that a presentation of a Lutheran theological understanding of the two sexes be included in the study booklet, the LWF General Secretary, Carl Lund-Quist, described the women's and youths' sections as "sociological divisions" in contrast to four other "theological sections" (ibid., p. v). The Women's Section at the assembly, seeing itself as "Lutheran women of the world," had another perspective: "We wish to say with all possible emphasis that we are not interested in securing rights for ourselves. Something much more vital is at stake: the proper place, the God-intended place, of women in the fellowship of the Christian church" (*Proceedings*, Hanover, p. 167). Women regarded themselves by virtue of their baptism to be incorporated in the body of Christ. For them inclusion in the LWF was based on a fundamental theological conviction and was not merely a matter of sociology or human rights.

### Expectations Unfulfilled

The inclusion of a Women's Section at the Hanover Assembly raised high expectations about the participation of women in the life of the LWF and its member churches. This stood in contrast to the Lund Assembly held five years earlier when laymen and laywomen met together as a "special interest group" for only one evening's discussion. Women neither received nor apparently requested any special consideration at Lund. The expectations at Hanover, however, led to the conclusion that in future LWF assemblies women should find their place in general sections according to their own interests, experience, and gifts. The Hanover delegates suggested that the Commission on Women, a forerunner of the first Advisory Committee for the Women's Desk appointed in 1975, be maintained.

Women leaders in the United States and Europe who corresponded regularly were restive about the limited participation of women in the LWF during its early decades. They viewed the absence of a women's section at the Minneapolis Assembly in 1957 as a missed opportunity. Increased selection of women delegates to assemblies was painfully slow. At Lund, women represented 2.8% of the delegates; at Hanover they represented 6.4%; and at Minneapolis 6.9%. One woman, Sr. Eva Benedictine Lyngby of Denmark, was noted as a "consultant of the Executive Committee" at Hanover. Appointments to other LWF structures showed little commitment to the inclusion of women who were actually most noticeable by their absence on committees at all of the first three assemblies.

They fared no better in appointments to commissions until three women were named, following Hanover, to the Commission on Stewardship and Congregational Life. Women leaders learned, further, that initiative for their increased participation was not forthcoming from the member churches or the LWF itself. It would need to come from women themselves. Their efforts to hold global conferences for preassembly preparations received minimal LWF response. Plans for such a conference prior to the Minneapolis Assembly never materialized, although Bishop Hanns Lilje, LWF President at the time, gave his assent, with the provision that the discussion center on practical, not theological matters. Authorization for a similar global gathering to be held in Schmalensee, Germany, prior to the Helsinki Assembly was given, although funding came solely from women's organizations, and no LWF executive staff attended.

The findings of the Schmalensee Conference echoed the frustration of women who lacked opportunity to use their gifts in the church. The report was presented to the Helsinki Assembly through the Commission on Stewardship and Congregational Life which included women's concerns within its mandate. "Are women encouraged in the best stewardship of their lives?" the findings inquired. "Their God-given gifts are waiting to be used." The findings reinforced the earlier expectations expressed at Hanover. A "standing world-wide representative committee" with the possible assistance of a woman staff member was recommended to provide theological study, worldwide communication among women's groups, and to explore a "closer working relationship between men and women in ful-filling the task of the church" (*Proceedings*, Helsinki, p. 496).

This standing committee met twice. Financial limitations precluded both the appointment of a woman staff member and support of a request for a Women's Pre-Assembly Conference in 1967. However, funding from U.S. national women's organizations and LWF national committees in the United States, Germany, and Sweden ultimately made possible the Pre-Assembly Conference which was held in Båstad, Sweden, in 1969. Recommendations from this conference to the Evian Assembly in 1970 became the initial blueprint for program development by the women's desk, later named the Office for Women in Church and Society (WICAS). These recommendations centered on two main points: (1) full partnership of women in the work of the LWF including appointment to LWF policy, planning, and decision-making commissions and (2) programs "in which people would be enabled to help themselves," including regional leader-ship training experiences upon request and the exchange of information. The Båstad Conference further recommended that the LWF employ a woman staff member and appoint a committee to advise staff and the appropriate Federation commission (*The Continuing Journey*, pp. 32ff.).

## Pioneer Work

The Evian Assembly authorized the LWF Executive Committee to take steps toward the "serious consideration" of these recommendations. Upon referral to the newly organized Commission on Studies, action was taken in 1970 and 1971 "to incorporate women more strongly in the studies of LWF" and to nominate a woman to the new staff position (LWF Commis-sion on Studies, Minutes, November 3–10, 1970). The broad staff assign-ment brought together concerns for church structures, church law, worship, and women's concerns. The appointment of the Rev. Eva Zabolai-Csekme (b. 1943), a Lutheran pastor from Hungary, thus placed women's concerns within a larger position description. The appointment came at a time of rapid social change.

Despite significant differences in cultures, political and economic sys-tems, and physical environments, common themes emerged throughout the world reflecting changes in family structures, relationships between women and men, and the overall roles of women in church and public life. The women's movements in the United States and Europe, each with its own characteristics, had gained momentum and were receiving media attention. In Africa, Asia, and Latin America, where women's lives were being shaped by national efforts toward economic development and mili-tary security, basic concerns and problems gained increasing visibility.

The evident need to reassess the place of women in global society prompted the United Nations to proclaim 1975 as International Women's Year.

These social changes had an impact on the LWF. The staff of the women's desk identified the need for reevaluating the role of women in church and society as part of the larger church structure study—the "Identity" study—authorized by the Commission on Studies (cf. pp. 194–97 above). Through extensive staff contacts, the necessity for differentiating programs was quickly recognized. African women described "burning needs" for leadership development. Long established women's organizations in Europe and the United States cited the search for new goals and directions. Traditional "women's work" in the churches required rethinking and restructuring. Worldwide, women were gaining a new consciousness of their God-given gifts and of the need for a church community in which women and men could serve together in Christian freedom.

Although few changes in the representation of women within LWF decision-making structures had taken place since the Lund Assembly, the Commission on Studies approved programs developed by the women's desk. These programs provided the framework for spurring the drive for the inclusion of women in all ministries of the churches and the LWF as such. There was, to be sure, controversy in some member churches about the need for a women's desk, but this was inevitable at a time which called for pioneer work in cracking open time-honored beliefs and customs about the "proper role" of women in the church.

Information sharing through a newsletter, WOMEN, opened up global communication. An LWF Advisory Committee for the Women's Desk set directions in the quest for inclusiveness, demonstrating a high degree of collegiality in working relationships between volunteer advisors, staff, and the Commission on Studies. Seminars, designed as the core program, educated and equipped women to exercise leadership within the churches. Employing a variety of approaches, these seminars, held initially in Africa, Asia, Eastern Europe, and Latin America, grounded women's leadership in a biblical framework and sought to empower women to be full partners in the community of women and men. Three ten-week advanced leadership seminars funded by the LWF Scholarship Office were also conducted for women who were employed by or serving as volunteers in their churches.

The women named by their churches to participate in these seminars were largely from outside LWF decision-making structures. No longer willing to be marginalized by a lack of opportunity for participation, women used the seminars as the arena most accessible to them for voicing their concerns. Wide ranging recommendations flowed freely to the LWF Executive Committee, to LWF commissions, and to member churches. Common themes of such recommendations—the exposure of discrimination and sexism, a call for equality and justice for women in both church and society—pointed to the need to integrate these concerns into the regular programs of the LWF and its member churches. Such concerns, it was held, should not be solely the responsibility of the women's desk or of the Commission on Studies.

In spite of these initiatives, there was little positive response from either the churches or the LWF. Nevertheless, voices from these seminars grew louder as the Dar es Salaam Assembly approached. Preparation for this event dominated an LWF International Consultation for Women held in Sri Lanka. New theological perspectives and biblical insights, societal changes, shifts in the roles of women and men, stronger voices from the Two-Thirds World, and an overall drive for shared power and resources converged to have an impact on this consultation and the forthcoming assembly itself.

### A Turning Point

The Dar es Salaam Assembly, more than any other such event, was different in regard to women's participation. Women comprised 22% of the delegates, an increase from the 9.6% at the Evian Assembly. Six women were elected to the new LWF Executive Committee. For the first time, a woman, Elizabeth Bettenhausen, a lay theologian from the United States, was a Bible study presenter. The Rev. Gudrun Diestel (b. 1929) was named chairperson of the Commission on World Service and eleven women were appointed to commissions and committees, representing about one-fourth of the total membership of those groups.

The Dar es Salaam debate and adoption of a "Statement on Women in Church and Society" signaled for the first time in an LWF assembly the intention of the Federation to articulate a theological foundation for the partnership of women and men. The statement centered on the biblical understanding of the image of God (Gen. 1:27) and oneness in Jesus Christ (Gal. 3:28). It underscored

> the salvation given in Christ [and] the promise of a new community between women and men. . . . The new community in Christ is not only an eschatological gift but something which should get visible realization in the life of God's people. . . . The realization of a new community in which men and women have equal rights and dignity should be an issue of high importance for the member churches of the LWF. (*Proceedings*, Dar es Salaam, p. 175)

The Dar es Salaam theme, "In Christ—A New Community," set broad directions for the LWF. "Women's concerns" were identified as an interdepartmental priority. Under the leadership of its director, Yoshiro Ishida, the Department of Studies took the lead within the LWF in addressing this emphasis and established for the first time a full-time desk for women. Emphasizing the biblical mandate, "to equip the whole people of God," the commission continued to articulate a theological foundation for the community of women and men. Zabolai-Csekme, in a major presentation requested by the commission, elucidated the theological themes of the assembly statement on "Women in Church and Society." She described the church as the community called by the gospel

> to set a sign to the kingdom of God . . . which is present wherever the liberating, saving and transforming power of Christ is incarnate. Therefore, the question of women in the church is not a marginal issue, but one which touches the core of the church's identity and mission. . . . The struggle for the acceptance of women is at the same time a struggle for the trustworthiness of the church's proclamation. For the communication of the Gospel does not only happen through words but also through actions, structures and relationships. (*The Community of Women and Men—Rooted in the New Creation*, LWF Women's Desk, 1972–1980, p. 136)

Further exploration of both theological and sociological factors that influenced the partnership of women and men and the life of the church as an inclusive community was undertaken in *Women in the Ministries of the Church*, a document that appeared as an LWF Study in May 1983. It is also to be noted that the LWF Study of October 1983, *The Lutheran Understanding of Ministry*, also included a section on "Women in the Ministries of the Church."

The Commission on Studies through the women's desk, headed in 1980 by Eva von Hertzberg (b. 1932) of the Federal Republic of Germany, continued to give major attention to leadership development for women in seminars and regional consultations. Requests for assistance from member churches increased considerably. Five women were appointed and trained as regional consultants in India, Malaysia, Hong Kong, Liberia, and Tanzania in order to enable and equip women to participate more fully in the lives of their local churches.

Openness to integrating concern for equality and justice for women in other projects within the Department of Studies and other LWF departments began to emerge during the 1980s. With facilitation from the women's desk, research and studies were expanded to include issues such as women's rights and human rights, women in ordained ministry, and women and men as partners in development. The Commission on Studies endorsed staff cooperation and authorized financial assistance for the World Council of Churches initiative, "The Community of Women and Men in the Church."

On the global scene, women participants in LWF seminars and consultations continued to advocate strongly for a more inclusive community within the LWF itself. An International Consultation for Women, held in Geneva in 1984, became a springboard for such advocacy at the Budapest Assembly. Recommendations addressed issues coming before the assembly and called special attention to the matter of violence against women. Dissatisfaction with the number of women chosen to serve on LWF governing bodies and as Federation executive staff was intense. The consultation called on the LWF to set an initial goal of at least one-third women in all such bodies and on the Geneva staff.

## Actions for Change

In his report to the Budapest Assembly, Carl Mau, LWF General Secretary, buttressed the need for the LWF to continue pressing for greater participation of women at both the policy and staff levels: "Experience has amply demonstrated that this more just and equitable partnership of women and men in the church is a source of great new blessing and renewal for the churches" (*From Dar es Salaam to Budapest 1977–1984*, LWF Report 17/18, April 1984, p. 35).

A number of churches responded affirmatively to repeated admonitions to increase the number of women in their delegations to the Budapest Assembly. Of the total delegation, 34% were women. Assembly committees showed greater representation of women than in any previous assembly. Margaret Wold (b. 1919), a North American laywoman, was one of four major plenary speakers. In a dramatic move, a number of women delegates requested a place for women at the assembly podium, a move that was accepted by acclamation. Later, Bodil Sølling (b. 1922) of Denmark and Dorothy Marple (b. 1926) of the United States chaired plenary sessions. The assembly elected seven women to the new LWF Executive Committee. This committee subsequently named one of the women, Susannah Telewoda (b. 1941), a Liberian laywoman, an LWF Vice-President, and three laywomen as chairpersons of Federation commissions: Ruth Abraham of Ethiopia, Communication; Christina Berglund of Sweden, Studies; and Dorothy Marple of the United States, Church Cooperation.

Actions of the Budapest Assembly deepened the drive for inclusiveness within the LWF. "The Unity We Seek" and "Self-Understanding and Task of the Lutheran World Federation," official statements, laid the foundation for redoubled efforts to elucidate the theology of *communio* and prove its implications for inclusiveness. Amidst considerable debate, the assembly also authorized development of a plan for the use of a formula to assure specific increases in the percentage of women delegates at all subsequent assemblies, in the composition of the Federation Executive Committee

and its officers, and on all governing commissions and committees. To further address the sin of sexism, the assembly asked that the number of
women employed as program and supervisory staff in Geneva be increased
until at least 50% of the persons in such positions were women. Other resolutions pressed for continued leadership training and more research in
biblical anthropology as related to the identity of women and men. All
member churches were called upon to ordain women and to deal with the
many forms of social and family behavior that result in violence to
women.

These actions both stimulated debate and accelerated activity after the
assembly. The formula for representation was attacked on theological and
ecclesiological grounds, yet the actions establishing the formula and
describing the LWF in terms of *communio* were clearly seen as mandates.
Department directors' and commission reports to the executive committee—from World Service, the Community Development Service, and
Communication—began to show the small steps being taken for equality
of women and their partnership with men. The Commission on Studies
continued its major role as advocate by underlining the necessity for all
LWF studies and programs to aspire to the wholeness of the person and
move toward inclusiveness of community. Through the revamping of the
scholarship program, the commission set aside at least 40% of scholarship
funds for women on each continent.

## Expanding Opportunities

The women's desk, now known simply as WICAS (Women in Church and
Society) and after 1988 headed by Musimbi Kanyoro (b. 1953) of Kenya,
introduced new approaches to the development of shared leadership that
demonstrated the readiness of women fully to participate in decision-making responsibilities. Gender analysis and gender sensitive approaches to
planning and decision making became important tools in seminars and
workshops. Awareness-raising programs both accentuated women's contributions to national and family economics and spoke to the need for
intensive study of the many forms of violence against women found
throughout the world. After the fall of the Berlin Wall, contacts with
women in Eastern European churches increased considerably. South/North
and West/East exchanges of seminar leaders and participants reduced
dependence on the Geneva secretariat and Western-based professional
leadership. Through the joint efforts of WICAS and the theological education desk in the Department of Studies, more women were encouraged to
study theology and to make their unique contribution to that discipline.

Extensive reflections on the theological foundations and practical real-

izations of *communio* were given by Gunnar Staalsett, LWF General Secretary, in major addresses over the period of 1985–89. At the Joint Meeting
of Commissions, held in Geneva in 1987, Staalsett spoke at length about
sexism and the partnership of women and men:

> The issue of full and inclusive partnership of women and men in all aspects of
> the life of the church is a dimension of Christian unity, a full and complete
> communion of all believers regardless of gender, race and color. . . . If there is
> one issue where the Gospel challenges culture and inherited social structures
> and mores, that is the issue of the role of women in the church. . . . (Report to
> the Joint Commission Meeting, Geneva, April 1987, p. 11)

Staalsett subsequently asked LWF member churches to evaluate their
own activities in regard to the participation of women. Only eight of the
then 104 member churches responded. This gave an indication, as the
report stated, of the importance—or lack thereof—that the member
churches attributed to the subject of women in the church. The LWF Executive Committee, however, saw the need for increased participation of
women and adopted recommendations that the general secretary
described as a milestone for women. These recommendations related to
representation, planning, and the use of inclusive language at the 1990
assembly; the recruitment of women to executive staff positions in the
Geneva secretariat; the establishment of an LWF interdepartmental staff
committee on women; and support for the World Council of Churches'
"Ecumenical Decade of the Churches in Solidarity with Women."

An International Consultation for Women, held in Mexico City in 1989,
brought women together to prepare for the 1990 assembly and to plan for
future WICAS work. The human side of poverty, debt crises, militarism,
violence, integrity of creation, and church structures—all issues for
Curitiba—were emphasized as expressions of women's common suffering
and longing for justice. Recommendations to LWF commissions, member
churches, women's organizations, and WICAS itself called for intensified
efforts in education, training, advocacy, and action in the quest for inclusiveness and justice for women.

Signs of movement toward an inclusive community were distinctive at
the Curitiba Assembly. The total delegation numbered 40% women; both
women and men made plenary and major section addresses; women
shared assembly committee responsibilities in equal numbers with men;
elections to the new LWF Council reflected the formula for participation
adopted at the Budapest Assembly. Christina Rogestam (b. 1943) of the
Church of Sweden was elected as the first woman to hold the position of
LWF Treasurer.

The Message of the Curitiba Assembly to the Churches reinforced the concept of communion as foundational to the churches' life, work, and witness, but noted:

> We do not everywhere have that visible unity between our churches to which we are summoned: full communion—between women, men, youth, lay, ordained, regions, cultures—remains a goal. If our communion is to prove faithful . . . , we must grow ever more closely together. (*Proceedings*, Curitiba, p. 20)

Commitments to intensify inclusive communion in the world required in every member church a "Clear Plan of Action" to express the equality of men and women and thus enable the churches to benefit from women's potential (ibid., p. 82). The LWF Council responded to this assembly message by adopting such a plan which set goals and strategies reflecting priorities identified by women in all regions. Member churches were reminded to demonstrate commitments made in the message and to adopt their own plans of action.

The Curitiba Assembly's decision to authorize a major restructuring of the Federation summoned the churches to greater integrity in their relationships. It also emphasized closer LWF working relations with member churches and new integration and coordination in a reorganized Geneva secretariat. WICAS, now located within the Department for Mission and Development, established the compelling objective "to affirm women's faith, women's hope, and women's actions rooted in the good news of the bible" and to advocate justice for all persons, regardless of gender, physical condition, or other circumstances (*A Clear Plan of Action*, LWF Department for Mission and Development, Office of Women in Church and Society, Geneva, 1992, p. 2). Ishmael Noko, then the first Director of the Department for Mission and Development, aimed to facilitate the penetration of this objective throughout the entire work of the department. Staff of departmental area desks were counseled to collaborate with WICAS and with member churches in recognizing the gifts of women and in dealing with issues of equality and justice. Advocacy and training for women has been bolstered by this cooperation, leadership training for young women becoming a special focus.

## The Continuing Agenda

The vision of a new community in Christ has undergirded the relentless persistence of women in policy and decision making roles within the Lutheran World Federation—with ever increasing support from men—for the affirmation in the Federation of women, their equality and partnership with men, and for justice for them in church and society. The formula for representation of women, first adopted in 1984 at Budapest, has been adopted throughout the LWF. Noteworthy strides have been made in the involvement of women in LWF policy- and decision-making structures. Yet the minimum goal of at least 40% representation of women in LWF-related consultations and workshops has not been reached in at least two-thirds of such events.

The Federation reported in 1995 that 38% of program staff in Geneva were women who had been chosen on the basis of competence. However, the number of women serving on the secretariat's cabinet has never been more than three. It was not until 1980 that the first woman, Christa Held of the Federal Republic of Germany, Director of the Community Development Service, was named to that group. The number increased to two with the appointment in 1987 of Erika Reichle (1939–1993), also of the Federal Republic of Germany, as Director of the Department of Studies. Christine Grumm (b. 1950) of the United States was appointed Deputy General Secretary for Planning in 1991 and served in that role through 1995, being succeeded by Agneta Ucko (b. 1949) of Sweden. Two other women have served on the nine-member LWF Cabinet: Anneli Janhonen (b. 1936) of Finland, Director of the Office for Communication Services, and Gertrude Livernois (b. 1945) of the United States, Director of the Office for Personnel.

Formulas for just representation have opened certain LWF doors for women. Nevertheless, full justice, equality, and partnership between women and men has not been achieved. Structures of language, thought, and action reveal that there has been less than adequate progress beyond the patriarchal models that have been under question for several decades. The ideals of shared power and authority advanced by women in point of fact carry little weight with many male church leaders. Social realities in the struggle for power and control undermine the full possibilities that being "a communion of churches" hold for the Federation. Repeated admonitions by LWF assemblies regarding, for example, the ordination of women have not been heeded by at least 30% of the member churches; indeed, one member church, the Evangelical Lutheran Church of Latvia, has recently suspended a prior decision to allow the ordination of women. The record questions the seriousness of member churches regarding *communio* both within and between churches.

These and comparable issues facing women were again faced by the LWF at an International Lutheran Consultation on Women held in Geneva, October 22–28, 1995. The consultation offered proposals and recommendations on six issues: Living in Communion, Sitting at the Table as Equals, Ordination of Women, Education and Leadership Training, Economic Justice, and Safe Places for Women and Children in Church and Society (cf. *We Are Witnesses*, LWF Report No. 39, March 1996).

The Curitiba declaration regarding the LWF as *communio* does point, after decades of evolving ecclesial self-consciousness, to authentic identity, community, and mission. For women, communion must be embodied in visible ecclesial fellowship where both women and men are held responsible before God for human dignity, the quality of human relationships, and the care of creation. Just as there is to be no separation between Christ and the baptized, so there is to be no separation between the baptized people themselves. Communion thrusts women and men, young and old, persons in all conditions of life toward inclusive community. Yet again, the road toward that communion has not reached its end.

## Youth in the Life of the Federation

THE LUTHERAN WORLD FEDERATION from its inception has been prepared to accept the challenge of youth. It has recognized that the church by its very nature must be open to the reception of new generations of baptized members, for by that act of reception it is enriched and strengthened for its mission and understanding of the world in which it lives. At times this reception has involved risks as well as joys and challenges, since youth bring to the church new and sometimes radical visions, hopes, emphases, and understandings. The inclusion of youth in the LWF has involved processes of growth, change, and confrontation.

Several pictures or vignettes may show the quality of the contribution brought over the past decades by young people to the global Lutheran communion.

*Visits between Families.*   Josiah Kibira, Bishop of the Evangelical Lutheran Church in Tanzania and President of the LWF from 1977 to 1984, in a 1985 interview was asked about his future dreams for the Federation. His answer made much of the value of youth visitation programs, interchurch contacts between young persons who are not normally numbered among "official" church representatives. Youth bring to such contacts not only a note of authenticity, but also a sign of the completeness of the communion.

*Windows to the World.*   At the Fifth LWF Assembly in Evian, 1970, youth were sharply critical of the Federation's decision to move the venue of that assembly from Porto Alegre, Brazil, to Evian, France. The decision not to meet in Brazil "illustrates LWF's fear to deal with the social and political issues of the world in which it operates. The LWF refuses to discuss politics, including and especially the political situation in Brazil, pre-

ferring rather an abstract safe theological discussion. . . . The lack of information dissemination by LWF member churches about all the issues
involved in the decision demonstrates LWF's desire to hold an assembly in
silence" (*Proceedings*, Evian, p. 117). It has been part of the vocation of
youth in the LWF to call for openness to the world, to raise the consciousness of the LWF to the realities and needs of the world.

*A Handful of Rice.*   Again at the Evian Assembly, youth distributed to
the delegates and visitors a handful of rice to make visible the actual daily
diet of millions of people in all parts of the world. Throughout the history
of the LWF it has been a permanent quest of young people to make the
global context in which the churches live concrete and immediate. At
Budapest in 1984 young persons issued a call to the assembly to observe a
"day of fasting" to demonstrate solidarity with poverty and starvation.
From the Buenos Aires Pre-Assembly Youth Conference in 1990, youth
sent a message to the Curitiba Assembly both that at all future assemblies
housing for the delegates be provided in low-cost accommodations and
that the Federation should give serious consideration to moving its secretariat from Geneva in affluent and costly Switzerland to a country where
the world's poverty is seen and where costs are less.

*Breaking the Wall.*   At the Eighth Assembly in Curitiba, young persons
presented a skit—within the context of the *Kirchentag* event that brought
thousands of Brazilian Lutherans into contact with the assembly—on
"how to break the wall between youth and the church." After nearly fifty
years of LWF history how large and how thick is that wall? It can be
described both culturally and spiritually; it has to do with the mutual sharing of responsibilities within the church.

*Flowers—In Conflict and Disagreement.*   At the conclusion of the
Curitiba Assembly youth also gave a flower and a letter to each participant. The letter expressed sharply critical views of the assembly; the
flower was a sign of the love of youth for the whole Federation.

These vignettes describe with some eloquence the way in which youth
have contributed to the deliberations and decisions of the Federation.
Their desire has been to serve the communion. With what themes have
young people been concerned over the past fifty years of LWF history?

## The Contribution of Youth to the LWF

Young people have throughout the history of the Lutheran World Federation insisted on giving priority to reflection on the mission of the church.

It is remarkable, however, that such reflection has varied greatly in different periods of the Federation's history.

Central to this reflection has been Bible study, virtually an obligatory framework for youth involvement in all periods. One of the first LWF sponsored activities, a youth gathering in Berlin in 1952, identified Bible study as the inner center of the meeting. In the earliest days of the LWF, then, there was a clear attempt to uncover the biblical and theological roots of "youth work" and thereby to show the imperative for the church's engagement in such work. From the outset there was a contrast between, on the one hand, the church's mission to youth, and, on the other hand, the involvement of youth directly in the church's total mission. Are youth to be understood as an object for discussion or as integral participants in that discussion? Was the "evangelization of youth" a goal in itself, or did it have as its aim the involvement of youth in the mission of the church? The report of Section V, "On Students and Youth," at the 1952 Hanover Assembly perhaps illustrates this contrast:

> [T]he youth of our church everywhere definitely place the Bible in the very center of their life. Our young people are coming to the church of the living Word in their quest for the right orientation of their lives. They are not looking for the easiest road to "security," but for a fountain of strength for a life of consecrated service; they want to follow the Master in all sincerity. . . . The Word of God calls forth its own response when it is preached and taught to youth, and when the response is one of faith, youth will assume its share of responsibility in the church and in the world. (*Proceedings*, Hanover, p. 163)

Subsequently in LWF history, contrasts were sharpened. New gaps were evident at an International Youth Consultation held in Urach, Federal Republic of Germany, in July 1981. A German observer, Susanne Kasch, noted:

> [I]n contrast to the youth of the '60s and the early '70s the youth represented in Urach no longer have guiding and motivating goals. They rather seem to feel encircled by problems. Thus topics discussed in detail in Urach were the alienation of youth from church and society, unemployment and educational problems, questions of human relationships like "marriage—yes or no," divorce and the difficulties of family life. . . . The participants did not find equivalent solutions for all these problems. This could be clearly seen in the regional reports. In the course of the consultation the participants of different regions (Europe, North America, Latin America, Asia, and Africa) met to describe the situations in their respective areas. And here the reports of the Europeans and Americans read like long problem catalogs. The group reports of Asia and Africa are a little different. They focus on the subject of evangelism with the attempt to develop mission strategies and educating people for this. (*Youth Newsletter*, No. 5, October 1981, p. 7)

In line with these insights, LWF youth study programs have, over the years, been developed in response to the vexing question as to why young people—especially in the Northern churches—have increasingly been alienated from the church. The contributions of youth from the South have, in the context of these studies, been of particular importance in light of their pervasive, lively, and deep spirituality and sense of mission.

Well-developed programs of youth exchange have since at least 1952 played an extremely important role in the LWF youth program. These exchanges have been of two kinds: long-term internships organized either through the Geneva secretariat or bilaterally between member churches; and short, youth visitation programs organized chiefly around LWF assemblies.

Worship and spirituality have, perhaps, been the chief hallmarks—as motivating experience and source of renewal—of the contribution of young persons to the life of the Lutheran World Federation. At the World Encounter of Lutheran Youth held in Thonon-les-Bains, France, prior to the 1970 Evian Assembly, youth expressed sharp criticism both of the LWF as such and of "traditional ways of expressing faith." Yet for many participants, it was the worship which provided the most meaningful climax— "in the closing worship a real unity grew up." The closing Eucharist of this event was a celebration offering, though prayers in many languages, a new kind of communication for many participants. "It was a new Pentecost," an African participant stated. Dr. Kunchala Rajaratnam of India, subsequently elected for the first time to the LWF Executive Committee, described this Eucharist as the most exciting experience of his life (cf. Jeziorowski, Jürgen, ed., *Kirche vor den Herausforderungen der Zukunft. Evian '70* [Stuttgart: Kreuz Verlag, 1971] pp. 78–79).

Worship and spirituality also became central themes for LWF youth during two subsequent periods: from 1985 to 1990 three events were sponsored by the Federation's Youth Desk, at Rättvik, Sweden, in August 1987; at Madras, India, in March 1989; and at Bossey, Switzerland, in June and July 1989. The results of these events were used for an evaluative study, *Renewing Worship*, published by the Youth Desk of the Department of Church Cooperation (subsequently the Department for Mission and Development) in 1990. During the second of these periods a youth study team was also organized to understand the attraction for youth from all parts of the world of Neo-Buddhist spiritual experience in Nepal (cf. *Youth Newsletter*, no. 35, October 1993).

Youth have also played a significant role in the development of the social consciousness of the Lutheran World Federation. Conferences, workshops, and other gatherings have consistently been marked by the sharp, sometimes abrasive, concerns of youth for such issues. The final report of the 1990 Pre-Assembly Youth Consultation, held in Buenos Aires, registered concerns over the following topics: apartheid in South Africa, the international debt crisis, militarism, human rights, the environment, "domination in evangelization," and AIDS, together with statements regarding particular areas of conflict—Central America, Namibia, Central and Eastern Europe, and Palestine. At the Buenos Aires meeting there were, in addition to such statements, acts of social solidarity such as participation in the regular Thursday demonstration of the "Madres de Plaza de Mayo," the Argentinean human rights movement. This act was, of course, in line with the lively tradition started by young persons at the 1984 Budapest Assembly in organizing all-night prayer vigils as a sign of solidarity with the impoverished and oppressed of the world.

In spite, however, of the strength of such concerns—study, worship, spirituality, and social action—the question of the depth of the actual participation of young people in the *communio* of the LWF remains. Obstacles to authentic inclusiveness have been evident: member church structures with no provision for the participation of youth, a pervasive lack of familiarity with the processes and procedures of an international organization such as the LWF, the limitations of language, and general discrimination against youth.

## The Federation's Work with Youth

A concern for "youth work" was visible even before the 1947 LWF Assembly at Lund. Prior to that assembly, Sylvester Michelfelder, first LWF Executive Secretary, consulted with representative young persons concerning the "rightful place of youth in the Federation" (cf. the account given in the Report of the Commission on Stewardship and Congregational Life, 1952–1957, p. 23). In consequence of this, the Lund Assembly created a Commission of Youth Activities. Specific work with students also marked the early years of Federation activity. A special international conference orienting youth and students to the coming Hanover Assembly was held in early July 1952 at Sachsenhain in the Federal Republic of Germany; at the Hanover Assembly itself a youth gathering was held with 1200 young people in attendance; and just after that assembly a Lutheran Student and Youth Leaders' Conference was held in Berlin. In 1958 a Committee on Student Work was formed, consisting of four members.

Subsequently, in 1967, what was then called the Sub-Committee on Youth Work and the Committee on Student Work were merged into the LWF Commission on Stewardship and Evangelism. This subcommittee, functioning within that commission, dealt with particular youth concerns and developed both the Lutheran Youth Exchange and a series of Lutheran Youth Leaders Conferences, such as that held at Lislelund, Slagelse, Denmark, in 1958 with fifty participants. In this fashion, LWF youth work was carried on until 1970 and the Evian Assembly.

Prior to Evian a World Encounter of Lutheran Youth was held at Thonon-les-Bains, France. Forty-nine young persons in the 18–28 age group participated in this event, seven of whom were subsequently named to the business committee of the assembly itself. As has been indicated above, this event was marked by vocal disappointment at the last minute decision of the Federation to hold its Fifth Assembly in France rather than Brazil.

The shape of youth participation in Federation assemblies changed considerably by action of the Seventh Assembly in Budapest, 1984. A resolution at Budapest called for a goal of 20% youth in the roster of official assembly delegates. At Curitiba in 1990 this figure was not reached, but 15.6% of the official delegates were youth, a significant increase over previous assemblies.

In the 1950s the Department of World Mission designated two young people to come to Geneva to serve as assistants in that department, thus anticipating a later program of youth internship. Those who came to the Department of World Mission were the Rev. Christopher Polson of India and the Rev. David Rasolofosaona of Madagascar. In 1981 these initiatives were renewed when the Youth Consultation held at Urach, Federal Republic of Germany, proposed the formation of the LWF "youth internship" program. The Rev. Julius Paul of Malaysia was the first incumbent; his work in Geneva with the LWF secretariat actually prepared the ground for the establishment of the LWF youth desk. Other talented youth have served as interns in various offices of the secretariat. Two interns prepared the Pre-Assembly Youth Conferences: Joan Lofgren of the United States was key to the success of the 1984 Budapest event, which numbered two hundred fifty participants, half of them from Eastern Europe; Matti Peiponen of Finland was a leader in preparing for the 1990 event in Argentina, which involved two hundred youth.

Following the Budapest Assembly the LWF as a matter of policy named at least one youth to each of its program commissions, and four youth were named to three-year terms on the Federation Executive Committee. The first youth members of the executive committee were Annie Marava of Tanzania, Kim Schuster of the United States, Nirmala J. Abishegam of Malaysia, and Nikolaus Voss of the German Democratic Republic. At the Curitiba Assembly in 1990, six youth were elected as full members of the LWF Council, formed there for the first time.

Initial discussion concerning the possible establishment of a youth desk within the LWF Geneva secretariat began at the Evian Assembly. The matter was referred to the LWF Executive Committee and to the Commission on Studies. A variety of factors, not least the rather stormy reaction of the Pre-Assembly Youth Conference to LWF policies and decisions, led to this decision. The *Proceedings* contain the following note:

> Reference was made to the suggestion that a youth and student desk be established at the LWF headquarters. It was pointed out that the World Encounter of Lutheran Youth had refrained from requesting a special youth desk, but instead requested places for youth in the whole decision-making process of the LWF. (*Proceedings*, Evian, p. 134)

At Dar es Salaam in 1977 action was taken. It is perhaps worth quoting a lengthy extract from the *Proceedings*, an extract that describes well the whole matter of the inclusion of youth in the total life of the Federation.

> The Rev. Jacques Fischer (Ev. Lutheran Church of France) in discussion . . . argued that establishment of a youth desk would isolate rather than integrate youth in the life of the church. He was opposed by the argument that sometimes a specific structure is required to put partnership into practice. . . . It was noted that a proposal for a youth desk made at the Evian Assembly had not been met; therefore youth delegates had initiated this proposal. After full discussion action was taken. The Assembly resolved to request the Executive Committee of the Lutheran World Federation
> - to consider establishing a Youth Desk with a Youth Advisory Committee by 1978;
> - to identify the following as being among the tasks of the Youth Desk:
> - to integrate youth in the work of the Lutheran World Federation;
> - to facilitate within two years international and/or regional consultations which would be part of the process of identifying and meeting the needs of youth and sharing experiences;
> - to assist in developing youth leadership training programs as requested by the churches;
> - to build a communication network among youth and initiate exchange programs. (*Proceedings*, Dar es Salaam, pp. 207–8)

Establishment of the youth desk ultimately took place within the Department of Church Cooperation; in 1990, with LWF restructuring, it was placed within the Department for Mission and Development. The first person to hold the position was the Rev. Alf Idland (1943–1995) of Norway, 1981–84; he was succeeded by the Rev. Julius Filo (b. 1950) of Czechoslovakia, 1985–90, the Rev. Siv Limstrand (b. 1961) of Norway, 1991–94, and the Rev. Ondrej Prostrednik (b. 1963) of Slovakia, 1995–.

The work of the youth desk has been seen quite explicitly in terms of strengthening the youth work of LWF member churches. Several main programs have marked its activities: global youth conferences and Pre-Assembly Youth Gatherings, regional and sub-regional youth consultations, participation by youth in the work and consultations of other LWF program entities, youth exchange and visitation programs, and the publication of a regular newsletter for youth leaders. Through this desk the voices of Lutheran youth have been heard in the life of the LWF itself, with special contributions to Federation involvements in regional social and political issues. Moreover, youth work in the LWF has always had a strong ecumenical component as is indicated in one personal reaction to the Urach Youth Consultation, 1981: "To me the most important result of this consultation was the clear commitment of the participants to the ecumenical movement. Intensifying LWF youth work is not happening for the self-interest of the Lutheran churches, but as a contribution to ecumenism" (*Youth Newsletter*, no. 5, October 1981, p. 7).

## The LWF and People with Disabilities

THE UNITED NATIONS declared the years 1983–1992 as the Decade of Disabled Persons. The LWF, when preparing for its Seventh Assembly at Budapest in 1984, recognized the significance of ministry to persons with disabling conditions by providing a special plenary presentation and a working group on the issue of disabilities.

This working group based its recommendations on Galatians 3:27–28 as well as on St. Paul's words concerning the inclusive nature of the Christian community in 1 Corinthians 12:12–22 and concluded:

> Therefore, there is a need to reconsider the concept of ministry as it relates to the persons serving and being served (able and/or disabled), regardless of condition. As the church carries out this ministry, it has been given the commission to reach out to all who have need of the gospel of Jesus Christ. (*Proceedings*, Budapest, p. 205)

The Seventh Assembly resolved that among the priorities for the future, the establishment of a special desk should be considered to facilitate the inclusion and participation of disabled persons in the life of the LWF and its member churches. It also resolved that in preparation for the next assembly, LWF member churches be requested to be intentional in the selection of persons with disabilities as delegates.

A year later, in 1985, a new program, Ministry with Persons with Disabling Conditions, was added to the LWF Christian Education Desk. An international and interdepartmental working group convened by Riitta Virkkunen (b. 1931) of Finland, then the LWF Secretary for Christian Education, laid down its policy guidelines. It was stated that facilitating the sharing of information in the member churches regarding the program would be the special service provided by the LWF. For this purpose a network and data bank would be necessary, and this would be done in cooperation with the World Council of Churches. High priority was placed on awareness building regarding the variety of problems faced by disabled persons as they participate in church and society.

In April 1986 the LWF Cabinet agreed that the LWF should have a joint program with the World Council of Churches for ministry with persons with "disabling conditions" and that the Federation would contribute to the budget of that program. A WCC office with executive staff had already been established for this work, and the Federation Executive Committee authorized the LWF to approve the work of a part-time administrative assistant in that office.

In 1989, the LWF held a workshop in Geneva on ministry with persons with disabling conditions. Its report contained, in addition to valuable information on work actually being done in member churches, concrete recommendations for the Eighth Assembly. Sandra Holloway (b. 1942) of the United States, LWF Secretary for Christian Education, 1988–1994, coordinated this workshop and served as coopted staff to the WCC Program on Disabilities at its Canberra Assembly in 1991; she also moderated a WCC consultation on disabilities in 1994.

The WCC desk on ministry to persons with disabilities was discontinued in 1991, but in 1993 was reopened as a Consultancy for the Differently Abled and the LWF staff resumed its formal cooperation in this program. Since June 1996 the Consultancy has again been discontinued.

United Nations sources reveal that the total number of disabled persons in the world is now between five and six hundred million. In most countries, at least one person in ten is disabled by mental, physical, or sensory impairment. The greatest single cause of disabilities is poverty. Many LWF member churches have addressed the issue of disabilities with much concern and have set up effective programs both for advocacy and ministry.

How the person with disabilities is treated by the world is a matter of fundamental human dignity and right. How they are treated by the church is a matter of faith. Being inclusive will not merit God's grace, of course, but it will be a sign of whether the faith that is professed is a living faith or a dead faith. (LWF brochure, *LWF Disabilities*, 1989)

## Bibliographical Notes

I. Unpublished Documents

LWF Archives, Geneva.

Particularly the records for the Desk for Women in Church and Society and the Youth Desk, including predecessor entities and minutes of related discussions and decisions.

II. Printed Documents

*Proceedings* (all LWF Assemblies).

Kanyoro, Musimbi, ed. *The Witness of Women.* Geneva: LWF Studies 1, 1995.

Leffler, Lois, and Marple, Dorothy, eds. *The Continuing Journey: Women's Participation in the Lutheran World Federation.* Geneva: Lutheran World Federation, Department for Mission and Development, Women in Church and Society, 1992.

*LWF Disabilities.* Geneva: Lutheran World Federation, brochure, 1989.

Marple, Dorothy, and Kanyoro, Musimbi, eds. *We Are Witnesses: Platform for Action from the LWF Consultation on Women, 22–28 October 1995.* Geneva: LWF Documentation 39, March 1996.

*Women: A Clear Plan of Action.* Geneva: Lutheran World Federation, Department for Mission and Development, Women in Church and Society, 1992.

*Women Magazine.* Geneva: Lutheran World Federation, Department for Mission and Development, Women in Church and Society, passim.

*Youth Newsletter.* Geneva: Lutheran World Federation, Department for Mission and Development, Youth in Church and Society, passim.

29. Participants from the Huria Kristen Batak Protestan at the Minneapolis Assembly, 1957.

30. Dr. Kunchala Rajaratnam of India here giving a lively account of his four decade involvement with the LWF. He is flanked by Professor Jens Holger Schjørring, left, and Dr. Viggo Mortensen, right.

31. Women at the Hanover Assembly, 1952. Sister Eva Lyngby, Denmark, first woman elected to the LWF Executive Committee, is on the right.

32. André Appel, LWF General Secretary, with some of the more than forty participants at the International Lutheran Women's Consultation held in Båstad, Sweden, 1969.

LWF Photo—Peter Williams

33. A demonstration during the Budapest Assembly, 1984, concerning the role of women in the LWF.

34. Participants in the first International Consultation of Lutheran Women Theologians, Karjaa, Finland, August 1991.

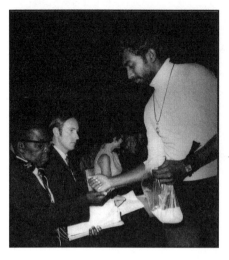

35. Herman Rao, a student from India, distributes rice to the Rev. Roland Payne of Liberia, during a youth demonstration on world hunger at the Evian Assembly, 1970.

36. Youth Workshop on HIV/AIDS, sponsored by the LWF and the WCC, Windhoek, Namibia, May 1993.

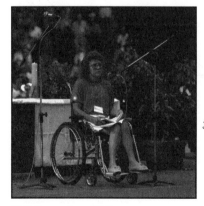

37. Ms Clarice Cid Heisler de Oliveira of the Evangelical Church of the Lutheran Confession in Brazil, lector at a Eucharist at the Curitiba Assembly, 1990.

LWF-Photo—Peter Williams

# Responsibility for the World: The Public Role of the LWF

## Lutherans and Political Responsibility

ACCORDING TO WIDELY HELD BELIEFS, social ethics is the step-child of the Lutheran confessional family. "Lutheran quietism" has become almost proverbial. Above all, Karl Barth's polemics against the problematic behavior of some leading German Lutherans (for example, Paul Althaus and Werner Elert) during National Socialist times and the reserve of many Lutherans vis-à-vis the Confessing Church discredited the Lutheran doctrine of the two kingdoms. "Fear plus the two kingdoms doctrine"—this is how a Synod of the Evangelical Church in Germany (EKD) characterized the Lutheran position in the church struggle (Espelkamp, 1955). This prejudice has prevailed for quite a long time. It is a common charge that Lutherans claim that the gospel has to do with God's private rule in human hearts and the that orders of creation are left to the law.

Nevertheless, it must not be overlooked that leading Lutherans such as the Norwegian Bishop Eivind Berggrav resolutely demanded that National Socialism be opposed and tyranny resisted even by violent means. Bishop Hanns Lilje, too, a leading figure in German Lutheranism and in the Lutheran World Federation, was an opponent of National Socialism.

It is true, however, that the foundation of the Lutheran World Convention, the predecessor of the Lutheran World Federation (see chapter 1 above) was due at first to a purely confessional concern. Thus for the Lutheran World Convention issues concerning confession and doctrine, proclamation and sacraments, ministry and church order were in the fore-

---

*Günter Krusche, Berlin, Germany, and Dennis Frado, New York, New York, are the authors of chapter 9.*

ground. Yet, while the constitution of the Lutheran World Convention was limited to spiritual tasks, an awareness of the problems of the time was not excluded. At its third meeting in Paris in 1935, the World Convention adopted resolutions that clearly address problems of the church under totalitarian regimes (cf. Eugene L. Brand, *Toward a Lutheran Communion*, LWF Report 26, Geneva, June 1988, p. 36).

## New Beginnings after World War II

IN THE LIGHT of the worldwide changes that took place in Europe and in the so-called Third World and especially during the Cold War era, this tendency changed after the Second World War. Of course, the statements of the first assemblies after the Second World War include indications and references to political events in the world, for the delegates came with their specific agendas. Especially the extension of Lutheran World Service (see chapter 3 above) meant that the Lutheran churches were confronted with the challenges of the times. Totalitarianism in the eastern part of Germany and the Soviet Union provoked the protests of Lutherans. The obstacles put into the path of the Lutheran delegates from Eastern Europe who wanted to participate in the Helsinki Assembly led to an official protest; the names of the participants unable to come were listed in the assembly *Proceedings*.

At the Fourth Assembly in 1963 in Helsinki, which dealt mainly with the doctrine of justification, the Finnish professor for social ethics, Heikki Waris (1901–1988), gave the third keynote address under the theme "Divided Humanity—United in Christ." He described the dynamic changes in the world and identified the three major oppositions that tear humanity apart and jeopardize peace: North–South opposition, East–West opposition, and the tension between believers and nonbelievers. He contrasted this to the unity already given in Christ and concluded: "This unity in Christ is the independent constant in our human equation" (*Proceedings*, Helsinki, p. 118). Thus the political tensions were identified while at the same time being sublimated to an affirmation of faith; no operational criteria were provided yet.

In his report on the—yet small and barely operational—Commission on International Affairs, Bishop Lilje once again affirmed the decision taken at Hanover (1952) and Minneapolis (1957) that the LWF refrain from independent intensive work on these questions and envisage instead a cooperation with the Commission of the Churches on International Affairs (CCIA) of the World Council of Churches. This was not a sign of a lack of interest but rather of an ecumenical spirit, since it was believed that only common witness by all churches would be effective. In this connection, Lilje criticized the fact that for many Lutheran churches issues of political responsibility had a low priority: "It would be an extremely questionable indication of the theological integrity and strength of the LWF if it were to fail to recognize the theological relevance of these questions of international politics. This would mean that the Lutheran church in the world would be cutting itself off, in one of the most important areas, from the translation of its faith into action" (*Proceedings*, Minneapolis, p. 193). In this connection, he underlined especially the need to work for the realization of human rights.

## On the Road to Evian

THESE CONSIDERATIONS gave rise to the proposal made to the LWF Executive Committee to consider a new structure which would better accommodate the Federation's political responsibility. This was the impulse for the basic restructuring of the LWF agreed on in 1969 by the executive committee and confirmed in Evian in 1970. The Commission on Theology commissioned a study, "The Quest for True Humanity and the Lordship of Christ." The study document was published even before the Fifth Assembly in Evian under the title "Christ and Humanity." In the preface, the chairperson of the Commission on Theology and later LWF president, Mikko Juva, stated that the study "has not departed from the usual Lutheran tradition, but to a certain extent has gone beyond it" ("Christ and Humanity," p. ix). He identified three basic problem areas: first, the relation of Christian ethics to humanity; second, the critical revision of the doctrine of the two kingdoms; and, third, the relation of Lutheran ethics to changes in society, including revolution. Thus the LWF caught up with the social-ethical debate in the ecumenical movement. In preparation for the ecumenical world conference for church and society in Geneva in 1966, William H. Lazareth, professor of systematic theology in the United States, wrote: "Lutherans must now be challenged to make their contribution to this mighty ecumenical effort" (*Christian Social Ethics in a Changing World*, ed. John C. Bennett [New York: Association Press; London: SCM Press, 1966], p. 131).

    With some self-criticism the editor of "Christ and Humanity" noted two weaknesses of this study: its predominantly deductive methodology and the continued predominance of the Northern hemisphere. Consequently, a new methodology and increased participation of churches from the South were required. This gap was to be overcome after the Fifth Assembly.

326

## Breakthrough: Lutherans Discover
## Their Responsibility for the World

THE FIFTH ASSEMBLY in Evian in 1970 took place against a turbulent background that cannot be described in detail here (see chapter 2 above and pp. 382ff. below). Originally it was planned to hold the assembly in Porto Alegre, Brazil, but under pressure from critical public opinion it was shifted at short notice to Evian, France. The reason was that a military regime had assumed power in Brazil and human rights were being severely violated. The LWF would have had to face a situation where it would run the risk either of jeopardizing the orderly proceeding of the assembly or of giving obeisance to the military regime.

Due to this political and social involvement, topical issues prevailed at the Evian Assembly, especially human rights issues, questions of development and revolution, the many situations of injustice in the world, and East–West tensions. Student revolts of 1968 were still in people's minds, the repression of the Prague spring had not yet been forgotten. In fact, reflections on the missionary task of the Lutheran churches were designed to determine the agenda: "Sent into the World." But the relevance of the situation turned out to be more powerful than the conference organizers' planning. The Fifth Assembly became the "Assembly of Responsibility for the World."

The paper presented by the Heidelberg social ethicist Heinz Eduard Tödt (1918–1992) with the title "Creative Discipleship in the Contemporary World Crisis" (*Proceedings*, Evian, p. 31) did pioneer work as far as the opening of world Lutheranism to the church's sociopolitical responsibility was concerned. With reference to Gerhard Gloege's (1901–1970) paper on justification presented in Helsinki in 1963, Tödt interpreted the message of justification "as human event, as a cosmological event" (p. 32). Gloege had already stated: "The narrowing down of God's action in justification to the spiritual sphere of piety denies the goal which the coming Kingdom has for the world" (*Proceedings*, Helsinki, p. 72). For Tödt this explicitly meant that there is a "pivotal co-responsibility to help orientate science toward freedom and humanity" (*Proceedings*, Evian, p. 37). In the assembly's "Statement on Servanthood and Peace" an attempt was made to draw the necessary consequences from this perspective. Especially significant was the Resolution on Human Rights under the keyword Brazil:

> The section of the Assembly dealing with "Responsible Participation in Today's Society," and particularly that portion which relates to "Human Rights and Economic Justice," could not overlook the fact that there are dramatic and evident violations of human rights in the nation we once anticipated as the site of this Assembly.

Yet Brazil is not the only issue. Our concern is far more broad, reaching into an almost universal crisis symbolized by increasing violation of human rights. Brazil is simply a demonstration of a circumstance which exists in many other countries. The concern of this Assembly is directed to the deprivation of God-given human rights wherever, whenever, and for whatever reason it may occur. (*Proceedings*, Evian, p. 148)

This concern gave birth to the human rights program of the new Commission on Studies. In 1977, it was introduced in Dar es Salaam under the title "Theological Perspectives on Human Rights" (see below, pp. 327–31).

## The New Commission on Studies

THE NEW COMMISSION on and Department of Studies, created after the new structure agreed on in the 1960s took effect, became particularly significant for issues of sociopolitical responsibility within the LWF. Along with the Commission on World Service and the new Commission on Church Cooperation, there was now also a Commission on Studies. The name had been chosen intentionally: this commission was not supposed to deal only with theology but, rather, theology was to be a response to the topical challenges facing the church in interdisciplinary dialogue, especially with the empirical sciences. The commission was to conduct decentralized interdisciplinary studies with the broad participation of many individuals, groups, institutes and organizations. Grassroots were to be involved (see chapter 5 above).

The contemporary issues were divided into four project areas:

I.   Life and work of the churches
II.  Interconfessional dialogues
III. Peace—justice—human rights
IV.  Marxism—China study—interfaith dialogue.

In this connection it must be said that the LWF's new structure in general and the new concept of studies in particular did not meet only with approval. In particular, former General Secretary Kurt Schmidt-Clausen raised the concerned question: "Whither LWF?" A concern for the confessional profile of the LWF was expressed especially within the Lutheran churches of the Northern hemisphere. Thanks to the support of General Secretary André Appel and under the leadership of the chairmen of the Commission on Studies, Kent Knutson (1970–72), Fred Meuser (1972–75), and Karl Hertz (1975–77), the controversial study work led to a change of awareness in the member churches which was not to be undone.

# A New Interpretation of Luther's Doctrine
## of the Two Kingdoms

SOCIAL ETHICAL ISSUES were taken up in the study work of the Federation in continuation of the work of the Commission on Theology and in fulfillment of assembly mandates. The role of *Luther's doctrine of the two kingdoms*—quite controversial, especially in Germany—was to be clarified. According to studies conducted under the leadership of the new director of the Department of Studies, Ulrich Duchrow, Luther's doctrine of the two kingdoms (a) was not an articulated doctrine as dogma but, rather, was based on occasional statements on the topic, and (b) had in the nineteenth and twentieth centuries been frequently and ambivalently reinterpreted, even instrumentalized.

With the help of authentic statements made by Luther and the Reformers, the dichotomy between church and world was overcome. The findings of the study can be summed up as follows:

1. The church is not identical with God's kingdom, since the eschatological struggle between God and Satan takes place in both realms (the secular and the spiritual).
2. Neither is the world identical with the "Kingdom of Evil," for there, too, God's law is binding (*usus politicus legis*).
3. The distinction between law and gospel is not identical with the distinction between church and world.

With regard to the Christians' and the church's responsibility for the world this means the following:

1. In the area of the secular realm Christians and non-Christians cooperate together on the basis of reason; it is thus not outside God's kingdom.
2. Reason and love are not mutually exclusive. Reason provides the responsibility for the world with the dimension of reality. Love sets limits to reason. The "well-being of the neighbors" can become the goal of Christian responsibility in the world. Thus the decade-old argument on the distinction between the doctrine of the two kingdoms and the doctrine of Christ's lordship was settled, nay, unmasked as a false alternative. For although God is the Lord in the two ways of governance (spiritual and temporal), the struggle between the two realms (God's and Satan's) is still raging. The empirical church is where the dispute over sanctification takes place. (Duchrow, ed. *Lutheran Churches — Salt or Mirror of Society?* passim)

## Human Rights from a Holistic Perspective

ANOTHER MAJOR TASK for the Commission on Studies was that of theological reflection on human rights. On the basis of the Resolution on Human Rights adopted at Evian (see above), it started reflection on "The Theolog ical Perspective on Human Rights." Due to the historical and universal nature of human rights, it was not considered necessary to begin with a theological argumentation on the basis of, say, natural law. Rather, what was at stake was to advocate for the implementation of human rights as part of responsibility for the world. The cooperation of experts from all contexts (East–West, North–South) meant that human rights were defined holistically; individual and social rights must not be played off against each other, freedom and justice belong together. Both aspects are held together by a "basic configuration of human rights" (Tödt). This study was conducted in close cooperation with the World Council of Churches which, inspired by the Helsinki process (Conference on Security and Cooperation in Europe) in the seventies, had also put human rights on its agenda and in 1974 held a consultation on human rights in St. Pölten, Austria. These reflections led to the Statement of the WCC Assembly in 1975 in Nairobi concerning the Helsinki process and the identification of "basic rights" which must not be defined as individual rights but come prior to personal freedom and justice as prerequisites for everything else, for example, the right to life, to cultural identity, and so on.

In preparation for the assembly in Dar es Salaam, the LWF Department of Studies organized a consultation on human rights held from June 29 to July 3, 1976 in Geneva at which three working groups deliberated on human rights. First and foremost there was the question of the appropriate theological access to this issue which had actually been taken up only quite recently by Protestant churches.

Working Group I concentrated on this aspect and submitted a definition of human rights. Since this definition is still valid let us quote it here:

> Three types of rights have crystallized out [sic] in the agreements to date on codes of human rights:
>
> First, the rights to freedom and protection. They demand that, notwithstanding the integration of the individual into the community, the inviolability of the person should be respected and every arbitrary intervention in the realm of his personal life omitted.
>
> Secondly, the rights of equality. They demand the cessation of all discrimination, and seek to draw together human beings as persons with equal rights into just relationships with each other.
>
> Thirdly, the rights concerning participation. They seek to guarantee that no decisions are taken in government or in society in which those concerned can-

not participate and express their own wishes, and that the social and cultural achievements of the state and the benefits of society are for the good of all citizens. (*Theological Perspectives on Human Rights*, Lutheran World Federation, Geneva, 1977, pp. 11-12)

Referring to concrete reality, the text goes on:

These three groups of rights compete with each other as far as their concrete realization is concerned. For this reason one group of rights is frequently played off against another and sometimes directly absolutized in different societies. This is offensive to the meaning of human rights. They refer to an indivisible whole, to something which is for the benefit of all human beings, as human beings, independently of all empirical circumstances and conditions. Whoever is concerned for man (sic) must struggle for the realization of all aspects of human rights. (ibid., p. 12)

Reason enlightened by faith should deal critically and creatively with the human rights belonging to God's temporal kingdom, "critical, because it knows how to distinguish between ideological shamming and the realization of human rights; creative, because, inspired by faith, it perceives and promotes in an unconstrained way the good thing which appears at any given moment. That takes place in the hope that the kingdom of God also draws near to us in this world" (ibid., p. 16).

Working group II dealt with "Interpretations of Human Rights in Different Cultures and Social Systems." In spite of existing tensions it pleaded for the protection of all aspects of human rights without fear of cooperating with all partners of good will. Aware of the fact that the process of humanization was still ongoing it was emphasized that peace is a precondition for any human right. The ecological dimension was also addressed which again underlines the holistic nature of human rights: "full realization of human rights can only happen in a world which deserves to be called humane and in which an equilibrium of life is maintained" (ibid., p. 24). Working Group III developed concrete recommendations on the church's responsibility for the implementation of human rights and thus sharpened the awareness of member churches. On the basis of these findings, a small group met in January 1977 in East Berlin to evaluate the results and draw consequences for the forthcoming assembly (Dar es Salaam).

The resolution on human rights adopted at the Sixth Assembly of the LWF in Dar es Salaam in 1977 can be considered to be the result of the work done in the Department of Studies. Against the background of human rights violations in Zimbabwe, South Africa and Namibia but also in view of the Helsinki Process, it was stated: "Being together here as LWF member churches under the theme 'In Christ—A New Community' we know that we are in solidarity with all those who stand for humaneness. . . . We affirm that it is our task as Christians to promote, together with those who have different beliefs, the realization of full freedom of thought, conscience and religion. . . . Above all voices must be raised against the misuse of power by the powerful where they ignore or circumvent the rights of the weak . . ." (*Proceedings*, Dar es Salam, pp. 178f., cf. also p. 400 below).

## The Ecclesiology Study: Confession and Responsibility for the World

THE ECCLESIOLOGY STUDY "The Identity of the Church and Its Service to the Whole Human Being" played a key role in this overall development. Its aim was to explore the marks of the church (*notae ecclesiae*)—"that which makes the church the church." The method was called participatory: contributions were to come from various contexts; the methodology was "grassroots-oriented, multidimensional and interdisciplinary." The concrete local context was to be related to the claims of the gospel. Thus, at a first consultation held in 1974 in Addis Ababa, Ethiopia, the societal context which gives rise to the church's witness was discussed. A second consultation, held in Bossey, Switzerland, in 1975 related to the question of the identity of the church (*notae ecclesiae*). Finally, in 1976 in Arusha, Tanzania, the two issues were summarized in a final report prepared for the 1977 assembly. Important insights on the church as a participatory, inclusive and holistic community led to the realization that ethical questions were also relevant for the identity of the church since faith and action belong together. So, the identity of the church does not stand or fall depending on the preservation of a traditional confessional position but is determined by obedience to God and service to the whole gospel and all people (see chapters 5 and 6 above).

A direct consequence of the ecclesiology study was the sensational resolution at Dar es Salaam on "Confessional Integrity" in which apartheid as practiced in Southern Africa was defined as a *status confessionis:*

> Under normal circumstances Christians may have different opinions in political questions. However, political and social systems may become so perverted and oppressive that it is consistent with the confession to reject them and to work for changes. We especially appeal to our white member churches in southern Africa to recognize that the situation in southern Africa constitutes a *status confessionis* (*Proceedings*, Dar es Salaam, p. 180).

On the basis of this highly controversial resolution, the membership in the LWF of two white member churches which were not in a position to comply with the resolution was suspended at the assembly in Budapest.

## Dar es Salaam: In Christ—A New Community

IT WAS NO COINCIDENCE that the theme for the Sixth Assembly was "In Christ—A New Community," given the fact that the ecclesiology study aimed at showing the connection between lived confession and the form of the church. Thus a "docetic understanding" of the church was rejected. The criteria for the churchliness of the church must always be communicated within the concrete society which challenges the church's witness. Without critically reflecting on the shape of the church there is no confession of the faith. In so doing, the New Testament form of the church, the *koinonia*, the community of different but reconciled individuals, was rediscovered. Thus Carl Mau, the general secretary of the LWF, wrote in preparation for the assembly in 1977:

> The motto of the VIth Assembly of the Lutheran World Federation, "In Christ—A New Community," reminds us of the liberating power of the gospel in a world of broken and distorted human relationships. This theme will be discussed in three seminars, each of which is divided into a series of issues. The seminar topics ask how our mission, our life as a church, and our responsibility in the world are shaped by the fact that we are indeed a new community in Christ. ("In Christ—A New Community": A Study Guide in Preparation for the Sixth Assembly of the Lutheran World Federation in June 1977 in Tanzania [LWF, Geneva, n.d., p. 1])

The South Africa resolution with its declaration of a *status confessionis* was a turning-point for the LWF member churches. Those who, from a classical Lutheran perspective, consider the identity and hence the unity of the church to be grounded only in the "proper understanding of the gospel" will—even when opposed to apartheid—not be inclined to declare a *status confessionis* because it is "merely" a matter of responsibility for the world. Those, however, who regard the "identity of the church" to be grounded in "the service to the whole human being" will not be able to eschew raising the issue of *status confessionis* when the unity of the body of Christ is threatened by political, social, racist, or other societal barriers. Doubtless, the declaration, "Southern Africa: Confessional Integrity" (*Proceedings*, Dar es Salaam, pp. 179–80) is a milestone in the history of the LWF. Without the preceding ecclesiology study, this keener awareness would not have been possible.

## From Dar es Salaam to Budapest: Increasing Responsibility for the World

THE EARLIER PORTIONS of the Sixth Assembly's statement "Socio-political Functions and Responsibilities of Lutheran Churches" are worth noting:

The churches cannot withdraw from their responsibility as a part of the society in which they live. They must find a way between the extremes of a complete adap[ta]tion to their surroundings and a complete withdrawal from them. Both extremes tempt the church to identify consciously or unconsciously with the structures which support social and economic injustice and to see these structures as legitimate. The churches are called to be in the world but not of the world. Therefore, they must find in each society a way of critical engagement that expresses their dependence on God and their solidarity with the world, but that does not at the same time serve worldly powers in an idolatrous way.

Our Lutheran tradition offers guidance for such critical engagement in the doctrine of the Two Kingdoms. While this doctrine has at times been both misinterpreted and seriously misused, the doctrine clearly intends not only to affirm God's sovereignty over the whole creation but also to direct the church to witness and Christians to participate in the structures by which their daily life is organized, as a form of responsible care for the creation, mutual service to the neighbor and to all humankind, and involvement in the struggles for greater freedom and justice for all.

Advocacy for justice is an essential, integral part of the mission of the church. It belongs inherently to the proclamation of the word. Justice under the law of God is a witness to the universal sovereignty of God's law over all his creation. (*Proceedings*, Dar es Salaam, p. 176)

The statement then went on to identify two areas that needed special attention: (1) studies of the root causes of social and economic injustice (and affirmed "the need for radical changes in the world's economic systems as one essential step toward attaining peace"); and (2) advocacy by the member churches with their governments in signatory states to the Helsinki Final Act (1975) to assure further implementation of the provisions of the Act. (On 1 August 1975 in Helsinki, heads of the 35 participating States signed the Helsinki Final Act of the Conference on Security and Co-operation in Europa also known as the Helsinki Accords. The Act established basic principles for behavior among the participating States and of governments toward their citizens. The Helsinki Final Act is not a treaty, but a politically binding agreement. It is divided into three main categories, or "baskets" concerning: [1] Questions relating to Security in Europe; [2] Cooperation in the Field of Economics, Science and Technology, and the Environment; and [3] Cooperation in Humanitarian and other Fields.)

Two other areas discussed at the Sixth Assembly were the need for criteria for public pronouncements or official silence in situations where human rights are violated, and attention to global stewardship, limited resources, environment, energy, and nuclear power, including the theological and ethical dimensions, within the context of the concern for the root causes of social and economic injustice (cf. *From Dar es Salaam to Budapest: Report on the Work of the Lutheran World Federation, 1977–1984*, p. 38).

A programmatic effect of the actions in the area of socio-economic issues was that the Federation undertook a number of projects, primarily, but not exclusively, with staff from the Departments of Studies and World Service. An interdepartmental staff committee on the root causes of social and economic injustice functioned from 1977 until about 1989 to promote coordination of efforts throughout the Federation. The Studies Department engaged Béla Harmati (b. 1936) from Hungary for work on social systems and Eckehart Lorenz (b. 1945) from the Federal Republic of Germany for work in the area of social issues. The Department of World Service appointed Sibusisu M. E. Bengu from South Africa to work in the area of research and social action. While other staff, notably those in the general secretariat and the Department of Church Cooperation, were involved in sociopolitical issues, full-time efforts were most concentrated with these three staff for the earlier part of the 1980s and, in the case of Dr. Bengu, for almost the entire decade.

The approaches of the two departments were rather a study in contrast. The Department of Studies tended toward a more deductive style, in pursuit of conceptual clarity, while the Department of World Service tended toward an inductive method linked to action for justice on the basis of experience. The styles reflected, to a degree, the academic and social orientations and background of the staff and led to lively interdepartmental debates on the issues being addressed in the respective units.

## Social and Economic Justice

PROGRAMMATIC ACTIVITIES between 1977 and 1984 in follow-up to these areas of concern included, for the Department of Studies, clarification of *status confessionis;* coordination of Lutheran efforts for peace; theological foundations of and interconfessional studies on human rights; women's rights or human rights for women; violence and nonviolence; the two kingdoms concept at the parish level; unemployment; ethical and theological problems of Third World development; Christian ethics and property; the church in "nation building"; the church and civil religion; and the church and the ideology of national security. For the Department of World Service, areas of special concern included research and study resources for churches on economic, social, and political dimensions of injustice as they relate to development; dissemination of information and educational materials including the periodical, *Development Education Forum*; assistance in development education and awareness building; assistance to local churches in the conduct of local and regional programs related to social and economic injustice; assistance with workshops, seminars, conferences, and consultations on these issues; initiation, support, and promotion of social action, including advocacy, for a more just economic order; liaison with the United Nations and other intergovernmental and voluntary organizations; identification of new topics and trends related to social and economic injustice; and development of strategies that address social and economic injustice in programs and projects within the Department of World Service.

The decade of the 1980s involved much international debate about appropriate development assistance. The Federation participated in this very substantially with the studies mentioned above, but also through its World Service programmatic work in Operational Service Programs, the Community Development Service (CDS), and Research and Social Action office. The field programs of the Department of World Service—also known as Operational Service Programs or locally as Lutheran World Service (LWS)—reflected the need: (1) for assistance in emergencies, primarily due to natural disasters, (2) to assist refugees and displaced persons, and (3) to attend to endemic needs which local churches and government lacked a capacity to address on a large scale. Often the World Service response to a short-term emergency led to governments and/or churches requesting it to transform the aid into a longer-term rehabilitation and/or development program. While these transformations were, for the large part, successful, the process was not always smooth and, inevitably, local churches and/or financial donors raised questions about whether a program should continue and, more often, who should operate it—LWS or the local churches (see chapter 3 above).

Even though very generous amounts of resources—some years exceeding $100 million—continued to flow and met the needs of literally millions, the operational approach was disputed. It must be observed that the discussions took place in the context of not only the global debate over the proper mix of aid and justice but also while local churches were gaining more experience in administering their own projects and wanting to exercise more control over the service programs in their country. At the same time, government aid agencies, with whom the churches and the LWF worked, offered major funding, and churches and donors debated whether there was a role for operational programs or whether only locally directed programs were appropriate. This latter discussion had intra-departmental and ecumenical ramifications inasmuch as the LWF Community Development Service and the World Council of Churches both maintained a largely nonoperational approach. In addition, the partnership debate touched the sensitive issues of power—money, management, and accountability—between the churches of the North and those in the South. Concretely, the relationship between the churches and World Service evolved through a series of memoranda of understanding and/or the formation of local advisory committees to World Service programs. These initiatives, in which World Service Director Eugene Ries played a significant role, gave the churches greater say in the way activities were undertaken, all the while maintaining World Service's mandate to assist all people in need "irrespective of race, sex, creed, nationality or political conviction." As the discussion evolved, in 1989 World Service prepared a paper on partnership for the Eighth Assembly at Curitiba. The exchange of views has continued as World Service held a similar consultation on the same topic in April 1995.

The role of CDS, which later continued its work as part of the Department for Mission and Development as a consequence of the reorganization of the Federation after the Curitiba Assembly, was to work with churches to find resources—human, financial, and technical—to enable member churches in Asia, Africa, and Latin America to undertake their own development programs. Some of the more frequent project activities included water and sanitation; agricultural development; health and medical care; primary and vocational education; forestry; income-generating small-scale industry and, last but not least, awareness building to identify local problems and work for social change. It was in this latter area that the work of CDS and the Office for Research and Social Action converged. The two units held joint workshops with member churches, such as with the Evangelical Lutheran Church in Tanzania (1982) and the Evangelical Church of the Lutheran Confession in Brazil (1983).

In addition to the workshops, the Research and Social Action office began publication of *Development Education Forum*, a magazine that appeared approximately semi-annually. The periodical discussed concepts of development, transnational corporations, the debate over the New International Economic Order, energy issues, food, population, and development and trade, to name a few. The office took active part in UN meetings related to development, such as the UN Conferences on Trade and Development (UNCTAD). It also undertook case studies (for example, in Papua New Guinea and Peru) of how World Service projects and programs addressed the root causes of social and economic injustice.

A particular area of focus was the international debt crisis. This topic was covered in *Development Education Forum* and was the subject of study undertaken by the Research and Social Action office in cooperation with the interdepartmental staff committee on the root causes of social and economic injustice. That paper was conveyed to the Eighth Assembly in Curitiba in 1990. Its assessment of the scope of the problem led the assembly to devote a section of its message to the debt crisis and economic injustice, urging the member churches to *inter alia* "call for the organization of popular movements to campaign for a solution to the debt crisis and the cancellation of unjust debts" (*Proceedings*, Curitiba, p. 86).

It was also in the middle of the 1980s that World Service initiated two new operational programs in Latin America. In response to civil strife in El Salvador a program of aid to displaced persons was begun which led to a longer-term development effort. A program to assist Haitians on a regional basis was also launched in response to their dispersion throughout the Caribbean and into the United States as well. In addition to its unique (for World Service) regional nature, the activities focussed on community development and agricultural assistance within Haiti and the Dominican Republic, and, in the face of the Duvalier regime, legal and social assistance to Haitians residing outside their home country. Efforts were made to strengthen local community organizations within Haiti to assist them in the struggle to better their lives and lay the basis for assuming greater civil responsibilities once the regime was removed. Assistance accelerated with the arrival of democratically elected leadership in Haiti in 1991. Following the military coup d'état against President Jean-Bertrand Aristide in September of that year and continuing through 1994 advocacy for a return to democracy was pursued while assistance continued to community groups.

In June 1991 Dr. Bengu returned to South Africa, and the office was vacant for a few years. In 1993, Rebecca Larson (b. 1950), a development education specialist from the Evangelical Lutheran Church in Canada, arrived to take up the tasks assigned to a reorganized office for Research and Development Education. She revived the dormant *Development Education Forum* and placed emphasis on plans for the 1995 World Summit for Social Development, the problem of child soldiers, and an international campaign to ban landmines, among other topics. The office sought more closely to relate issues such as these to the activities under way in World Service operational programs.

## Human Rights

THE DAR ES SALAAM ASSEMBLY'S statement on human rights recalled the 1970 assembly's resolution on the same topic. Meeting in Africa, the Sixth Assembly was even more keenly aware of the many violations of human rights then underway in the southern Africa region due to apartheid.

However, it also noted atrocities in Uganda and "numerous violations of human rights in many nations on our earth . . ." (*Proceedings*, Dar es Salaam, p. 179). Of particular note was "a wide gap between declared norms and concrete implementation" in the area administered under the terms of the Final Act of Helsinki (ibid., pp. 178–79). The statement then called on the churches "to take the steps necessary and possible in each situation" to implement human rights in a comprehensive fashion, promote the rights of underprivileged groups (such as women, youth, the aged, and minorities), represent dispossessed and tortured citizens with governments and authorities, provide legal aid to the persecuted, displaced, and stateless, and consult with and make full use of the legal systems to have a practical impact in each country as a result of international human rights agreements.

The signing of the Final Act at Helsinki in 1975, though viewed with some skepticism at first, proved to be helpful in the work of the Federation in widening the doors for and affirming religious and other freedoms in Eastern and Central Europe as well as many forms of exchange and dialogue with the churches there. Indeed, the "Human Dimension" provisions of the Final Act were a rationale for the LWF's efforts to increase contact and communication, formal and informal, among churches in the European–North American region covered by the Final Act. For example, through dialogue with government officials, the Europe Desk of the then-Department of Church Cooperation and General Secretary Carl Mau were able to receive permission to visit the German-speaking Lutheran churches in Siberia and Kazakhstan with whom communication had been virtually nonexistent (ibid., pp. 51–52, 116; see also pp. 170–71 above).

## The Seventh Assembly in Budapest 1984 and Its Consequences

THE OPENINGS MANDATED by the Helsinki Final Act and the resulting better church-state climate in some countries of Central Europe also contributed to the choice of Budapest for the Seventh Assembly in 1984. While a variety of factors were present, including the quest for a reduction of political and military tensions—and thus peace—in Europe, advances in the field of human rights were significant ones. This surge of energy was reflected in a number of resolutions and statements on human rights and related topics at the Seventh Assembly: Human Rights; Peace and Justice; Southern Africa; Confessional Integrity; Partnership of Women and Men; Toward Social and Economic Justice; Racism in Church and Society; Promoting Human Rights (Civil, Political, and Religious); Christian Life in

Different Social Systems; and Our Responsibility for Peace and Justice (*Proceedings*, Budapest, passim).

In 1986 the LWF Executive Committee issued a "Declaration and Recommendations for the Continuation of the Helsinki Process," which called attention to the Vienna Review Conference and affirmed the mandate from Budapest to continue to monitor subsequent follow-up meetings related to the Final Act (*From Budapest 1985 to Curitiba 1989*, p. 48).

Meanwhile, the new LWF General Secretary, Gunnar Staalsett, had requested authorization to create two new assistant general secretary positions, one of which was for International Affairs and Human Rights. This was in fulfillment of the Seventh Assembly's request that human rights be given higher priority in the life of the Federation and that a desk for that subject be created (cf. *Proceedings*, Budapest, p. 247). Paul Wee (b. 1937), general secretary of the U.S. National Committee for the LWF, was named to the post in 1986. Staalsett and Wee undertook subsequently a number of initiatives that encompassed elements involving both human rights and the quest for peace.

Parallel to this initiative, the humanitarian work being undertaken through the Department of World Service carried with it activities which reflected a concern for human rights, particularly in the economic and social areas, such as the right to food, right to adequate shelter, and the rights of refugees. In the area of civil and political rights this concern was sometimes less obvious, but nonetheless present. In a number of humanitarian responses, such as those in areas governed by repressive regimes, World Service took a posture of quiet diplomacy, choosing to "speak into" a situation, through dialogue with government officials, rather than speaking out publicly.

This approach sometimes led the Federation as such to a similar practice—most clearly in the case of Ethiopia in the 1980s, but also with respect to eastern Europe—whereby it chose carefully the timing and mode of overtly raising human rights concerns. The degree of hesitancy was partially determined by the countervailing needs both to respect the situation of the local member church and to be able to continue to provide humanitarian assistance in government-controlled areas. Major interdepartmental debates ensued over when and how to speak and the effects of such speaking on the ability of the Federation to continue its witness in the face of state pressures. The Studies Department held a workshop in February 1984 that compiled a list of criteria for public pronouncements or official silence in cases of human rights violations (see *To Speak or Not to Speak: Criteria for Pronouncements in Situations of Human Rights Violations*, LWF Studies, 1984).

Another aspect of the problem was revealed when, in the instance of

Ethiopia, the Lutheran response to the drought of the mid-1980s was, *de facto,* to have World Service work in government-controlled areas while Lutheran related agencies from Europe and North America worked through areas controlled by political insurgents. Though necessarily kept out of the limelight at the time, this tacit arrangement was understood by almost all of the parties and, no doubt, saved many lives. This harmonization of efforts did not violate the principle of nondiscrimination with respect to aid recipients but rather reflected the ability of different members of the Lutheran family to work where they could and thus meet many needs.

On other occasions, World Service chose to be more explicit in its defense of human rights in humanitarian situations. Some examples include the work in El Salvador from the mid-1980s onward and support for the deployment of human rights monitors in Rwanda during the mid-1990s. These developments reflected a recognition that working for justice is intrinsic to the humanitarian aid and development mandate.

## Peace

IN THE EARLY 1980s most LWF efforts in the area of peace focused on the instability created by the Cold War. This was typified by the executive committee's 1981 Statement on Peace and a November 1981 consultation of European and North American church leaders (*From Dar es Salaam to Budapest,* pp. 116–17). Peace was also a focus of the work of Eckehart Lorenz and Béla Harmati in the Department of Studies, particularly the coordination of Lutheran efforts for peace, mentioned earlier, studies on Christian peace ethics, the use of the two-kingdoms doctrine in congregations, and the ideology of national security. This work involved both common consultations and the development of study materials.

As noted above, the concern for human rights was often interwoven with that for peace. In Europe, the Final Act of Helsinki provided a vehicle for taking up human rights concerns and, at the same time, promoting mutual understanding and trust despite the fact that Lutherans lived within different social systems.

The Federation's search for peace was also reflected in ongoing activities with respect to the Middle East. Following up a first consultation in 1975, a second one was held in 1982 on Cyprus, which examined all aspects of Lutheran activities in the Holy Land and sought better coordination of these efforts, including those for peace (ibid., pp. 50–51). While that consultation recommended that the Federation establish and maintain a liaison officer in the region, the proposal never came to fruition.

Even so, the arrival of Paul Wee in the office for International Affairs and Human Rights in 1986 made it possible for the Federation to have additional resources to pursue Middle East peace concerns. Subsequently, when the LWF Executive Committee, meeting in 1986 at Munich, Germany, decided to study the issue, it was able the next year to issue a public statement on the Palestinian–Israeli issue. It affirmed the rights of the Jewish and Palestinian peoples, including the right of both "to live on the land of Palestine with safe and secure borders and with binding guarantees for full and equal political, economic and social life. It is upon this assumption, namely that both Jews and Palestinians have a legitimate claim to this land on which they can raise their children and bring forth the fruits of their labors without fear, that negotiations on the future of Palestine must rest . . ." (Minutes, LWF Executive Committee, Viborg, Denmark, 1987, Paras. 4, 5, pp. 191–92).

As a result, the general secretary visited the region in the wake of the beginning of the *intifada* in late 1987; a consultation on the Palestinian-Israeli question was held in February 1988; and members of the LWF Executive Committee visited the region a year later to press the Federation's pursuit of peace (*From Budapest to Curitiba*, pp. 28–29). These activities implemented many of the principles established at Viborg, which included calling for an international peace conference under UN auspices, appealing on behalf of persons detained by the Israeli government, and urging the member churches to provide spiritual, moral and financial support to the region, including the Evangelical Lutheran Church in Jordan and the Middle East Council of Churches.

Meanwhile humanitarian assistance from the member churches to the Palestinian people in the Occupied Territories was affirmed as well as provided through the LWF World service field program in Jerusalem. Other efforts included dialogue with the Jewish and Muslim communities to deepen understanding of the issue and dynamics involved in building a just peace in the area.

## Recent Features since the Eighth Assembly in Curitiba

IN A RESOLUTION the Eighth LWF Assembly in Curitiba reiterated its support for the Viborg principles as well as a 1989 appeal by heads of churches in Jerusalem for greater international attention to a resolution of the Israeli-Palestinian conflict. It also encouraged the member churches to join a regional ecumenical program, "Christians for Peace in the Holy Land," from Holy Week to Pentecost 1990 (*Proceedings*, Curitiba, p. 103).

The LWF Council in 1991 continued to press for an international peace conference, peace-building efforts, respect for human rights and the provision of spiritual, humanitarian, and economic assistance, particularly to the Palestinian people. In June 1994 the council expressed appreciation to the Israelis and Palestinians, other governments and nongovernmental organizations, including the churches, for the efforts that led to the signing of the Declaration of Principles between Israel and the Palestine Liberation Organization. They also called for governments to support infrastructure in Jericho and the Gaza Strip (*An Agenda for Communion*, p. 92).

The 1995 resolution by the council further commended the peace process as well as the efforts of local churches to promote understanding with other religious communities, pluralistic perceptions of Jerusalem, and work for reconciliation and healing. It also affirmed the spiritual significance of Jerusalem for the Jewish, Christian, and Muslim faiths as well as for Palestine and Israel. The equal rights of all residents in the region were reconfirmed, and Israel and the co-sponsors of the peace process were urged to recognize, respect, and support these rights (*A Communion of Hope*, LWF Documentation 36, pp. 60–62).

A special fund for peacemaking, with a focus on the peaceful resolution of conflicts in the Middle East and Central America, was established in 1988.

Perhaps the most concrete results in the search for peace in recent years by the Federation can be seen in the Guatemala peace process. The Seventh Assembly in Budapest had placed the Central America human rights and peace agenda before the Federation (*Proceedings*, Eighth Assembly, p. 261) and considerable support, both financial and advocacy, was provided by member churches and through the Federation to the Lutheran church and ecumenical community in El Salvador during the late 1980s and into the 1990s.

The Federation also played a unique role in the Guatemala peace process as it gained the confidence of the parties (the government and the opposition Guatemalan National Revolutionary Unity [URNG]) to be an impartial mediator in the quest for peace. Between 1989 and 1991, with encouragement from the Norwegian government, their financial assistance as well as that of church offices in Norway, Sweden, and Finland, the LWF held a series of meetings that enabled the parties to make internal contacts and then meet. This led to agreements on a number of confidence-building measures in the areas of human rights and on the role of the civil sector of society. In Oslo (March 1990), a Basic Agreement on the Search for Peace by Political Means was reached. It was followed by a number of meetings in different cities, some of which also involved the civil sectors. In April 1991, the Agreement of Mexico was signed, elaborating on the peace process.

As the encounters took on a more recognized character, the United Nations and interested countries (the so-called "Group of Friends" of the UN Secretary General) became more directly involved. In 1994, the UN's role as mediator was institutionalized and the Federation's role as initiator and sustainer receded. Since then the Federation has stood behind the process and encouraged the parties despite ebbs and flows in the speed of the process toward a comprehensive peace accord. The persistence of both the general secretary, Gunnar Staalsett, and the assistant general secretary, Paul Wee, in maintaining contact with the parties and constantly pressing them to move forward were essential elements in the progress of the process from its early stages through to 1994. It should be noted that, in addition to the perseverance and commitment of these two officials, the Federation's ability to be an impartial agent for peace was related to the valid perception of both parties that the Federation had nothing to gain materially from the effort. There were few Lutheran churches in the country and, as a mainline Protestant denomination (rather than being directly related to local evangelical churches), the Federation was not seen as having a self-interest. Beginning with the early stages of the process the Federation kept in contact with the Roman Catholic Church, both in the region and at the Vatican, about its efforts and, thereby, maintained its confidence. This led to cooperative efforts with Bishop Quezada Toruño, who was Conciliator and chair of the National Reconciliation Commission and, later, chair of the Assembly of Civil Sectors, a group which represented a wide range of community-based organizations, including indigenous peoples.

## Bibliographical Notes

I. Printed Documents

*An Agenda for Communion.* LWF Documentation 35. September, 1994.

*A Communion of Hope.* LWF Documentation 36. October, 1995.

*Consultation on the Quality of Partnership.* Report on a Consultation, Loccum, Germany, April 3–5, 1995. Geneva: Lutheran World Federation, Department for World Service, 1995.

*Development Education Forum.* Geneva: Lutheran World Federation, Department for World Service, passim.

*From Budapest 1985 to Curitiba 1989.* Geneva: LWF Report 27, November 1989.

*From Dar es Salaam to Budapest 1977–1984.* Reports on the Work of the Lutheran World Federation. Geneva: LWF Report 17/18, April 1984.

*The Identity of the Church and Its Service to the Whole Human Being,* 3 vols. Geneva: Lutheran World Federation, Department of Studies, 1977.

Krusche, Günter, "Human Rights in a Theological Perspective: A Contribution from the GDR," in Lissner, Jørgen, and Sovik, Arne, eds. *A Lutheran Reader on Human Rights.* Geneva: LWF Report 1/2, September 1978.

Lissner, Jørgen, ed. *Theological Perspectives on Human Rights.* Report on an LWF Consultation on Human Rights, Geneva, June 29–July 3, 1976. Geneva: Lutheran World Federation, 1977.

Lorenz, Eckehart, ed. *The Debate on STATUS CONFESSIONIS. Studies in Christian Political Theology.* Geneva: LWF Studies, 1983.

———, ed. *How Christian are Human Rights? An Interconfessional Study on the Theological Basis of Human Rights.* Report on an Interconfessional Consultation. Geneva, April 30–May 3, 1980.

———, ed. *Justice through Violence? Ethical Criteria for the Legitimate Use of Force.* Geneva: LWF Studies, 1984.

———, ed. *To Speak or Not to Speak? Proposed Criteria for Public Statements on Violations of Human Rights.* Geneva: LWF Studies, 1984.

Planer-Friedrich, Götz, ed. *Frieden und Bekenntnis: Die Lehre vom gerechten Krieg im lutherischen Bekenntnis.* Geneva: LWB–Studien, Dezember 1991.

———, ed. *Peace and Justice: Toward an Ecumenical Peace Ethic.* Geneva: LWF Studies, March 1990.

*Proceedings* (all LWF Assemblies).

*Public Statements and Letters in the Area of International Affairs and Human Rights Issued by the Lutheran World Federation.* Geneva: The Lutheran World Federation. Three volumes: *1984–1990, April 1990–May 1991, and May–December 1991.*

*Reports 1963–1969,* prepared for the Fifth Assembly, Porto Alegre Brazil, 14–24 July 1970. Geneva: Lutheran World Federation, 1970.

*Reports 1970–1977,* prepared for the Sixth Assembly, Dar es Salaam, Tanzania, 13–26 June 1977. Geneva: Lutheran World Federation, 1977.

II. Monographs and Selected Writings

Asheim, Ivar, ed. *Christ and Humanity: Basic Questions in Ethical Orientation Today.* Philadelphia: Fortress Press, 1969.

Duchrow, Ulrich, ed., in collaboration with Dorothea Milwood. *Lutheran Churches—Salt or Mirror of Society? Case Studies on the Theory and Practice of the Two Kingdoms Doctrine.* Geneva: Lutheran World Federation, Department of Studies, 1977.

Huber, Wolfgang, and Tödt, Heinz Eduard. *Menschenrechte. Perspektiven einer menschlichen Welt.* Stuttgart/Berlin, 1977.

Krusche, Günter. *Bekenntnis und Weltverantwortung. Die Ekklesiologiestudie des Lutherischen Weltbundes, ein Beitrag zur ökumenischen Sozialethik.* Berlin, 1986.

Mortensen, Viggo, ed. *War, Confession and Conciliarity: What does 'just war' in the Augsburg Confession mean today?* (with German text, *Krieg, Konfession, Konziliarität*). Hanover: Lutherisches Verlagshaus, 1993.

38. The LWF coordinated international and ecumenical funding for legal aid during a trial in Swakopmund, Namibia, when six Namibians were charged under the Terrorism Act of the apartheid regime.

39. Delegates to the Pre-Assembly Youth Conference, held prior to the Curitiba Assembly, participating in a demonstration of the "Mothers and Grandmothers of May Square" for 30,000 children who disappeared during the post–1976 military dictatorship of Argentina.

40. and 41.
LWF General Secretary Ishmael Noko met in March 1996 in
Gaza City with Yassir Arafat of the Palestinian Liberation Orga-
nization (plate 40) and in Jerusalem with Israeli Prime Minister
Shimon Peres (plate 41).

# Conclusion:
# Identity, Development, and Tradition

PRECISELY AT THE TIME of the preparation of the present volume, the Lutheran World Federation has been focusing its attention on its Ninth Assembly, to be held in July of 1997 in Hong Kong. As has earlier been mentioned, this assembly marks the fiftieth anniversary of the founding of the Federation and is, consequently, to be an event permeated by historical awareness. It is anticipated, moreover, that the Ninth Assembly will be notable for a variety of even more immediate reasons.

The venue for this gathering is notable since this is to be the first LWF assembly to be held on the Asian continent. Thus, the global and inclusive character of the communion of Lutheran churches will again be dramatized. That drama, moreover, is being marked by a serious LWF concern expressed by a second "China Study" (cf. pp. 171–72, 198 above), undertaken largely in preparation for this assembly, which has focused on new dimensions both of the relation between faith and culture and on the nature of the Christian mission at the end of the second millennium.

Additionally, and this has lent controversy to the selection of the Ninth Assembly's venue, this assembly is to take place just at the time when Hong Kong becomes an integral part of the Peoples' Republic of China. That event, which is vastly more than a matter of political arrangement, will be the object of international attention insofar as it represents the coming together of what have for long been regarded as antithetical and hostile ideologies. Moreover, delicate questions of human rights and religious freedom, which have since 1970 been central among LWF concerns, are likely to be seen in new and perhaps problematic and debatable ways.

The Hong Kong Assembly, furthermore, is of signal importance in the history of the Federation insofar as it is to be the first assembly after the Curitiba declaration that the LWF understands itself as "a communion of Lutheran churches." This gradually articulated self-understanding, to which the present volume has pointed as an important outcome of fifty years' history, is regarded by some as a mere slogan or simply a convenient principle for organizational or institutional arrangements. The assembly will, in contrast, be a proving ground for the ecclesiological significance of *koinonia/communio* as the reality of the relationships between the Lutheran churches of the world. Perhaps at no point in the assembly's deliberations will this *communio* be tested more fundamentally than in the discussion of momentous ecumenical proposals aimed at declaring the sixteenth-century condemnations between Lutherans and Roman Catholics concerning the "Article of Justification" as not applicable in the present situation and thus no longer being of a church-dividing character.

In bringing the foregoing chapters of *From Federation to Communion* to a close, these few comments concerning the Ninth Assembly of the Lutheran World Federation are not intended to be an exercise in agenda-setting for the programs of coming years. They are intended rather, and only briefly, to point to the fact that the themes of the foregoing chapters— diaconic service, mission, ecclesiology, ecumenism, inclusiveness, political affairs and human rights, all construed theologically—remain restlessly active concerns for the LWF. Ecclesial history is the account of how Christian identity is maintained even as it develops and is altered in response to the challenges of unanticipated events and new contexts. The trajectories that have here been traced rest firmly, on the one hand, on the ecumenical identity of the churches of the Lutheran confession; they also rest lightly, on the other hand, on the shifting grounds of the challenges and contexts of changing times.

To shift the terms slightly, one may say that the history of the Lutheran World Federation must be understood—as must the history of both Christian doctrine and ecclesial life—in terms of development, identity, and tradition. Jaroslav Pelikan has written trenchantly in just those terms that

> development is real but . . . it goes on within the limits of identity, which the tradition defines and continues to redefine. Like any growth, development may be healthy or it may be malignant; discerning the difference between these two kinds of growth requires constant research into the pathology of traditions. But it is healthy development that keeps a tradition both out of the cancer ward and out of the fossil museum. (Jaroslav Pelikan, *The Vindication of Tradition* [New Haven and London: Yale University Press, 1984], p. 60)

The Lutheran World Federation, whose five decades of history have been outlined in this volume, stakes its life on the identity of ecumenical Lutheranism, the shifting grounds of its development in time and space, and on the vitality of the enduring Christian tradition. Whether its continuing development is to be healthy or malignant is not given to the present generation to know. If, however, the life of the Lutheran *communio* is to be healthy, in theology and mission, its history must be accurately and critically read before future challenges can be creatively accepted.

This volume—marked as it inevitably is by lacunae, misreadings, and at times failure of critical nerve—is but a first step in the raising of an authentic and critically aware historical consciousness within the global communion of Lutheran churches which is the LWF. It will be the responsibility of others, in regional and local settings as well as in the global context, to undertake further research, and more sharply to identify the way in which the identity of ecumenical Lutheranism is to develop for the sake of its contribution to a more comprehensive ecclesial tradition which itself sustains and nourishes Christian witness in the world. The words of Johann Wolfgang von Goethe in *Faust* are to the point:

> Was du ererbt von deinen Vätern hast,
> Erwirb es, um es zu besitzen.

> What you have as heritage,
>   Take now as task;
> For thus you will make it your own!

*For the Editorial Group*
*Norman A. Hjelm*

# A Handbook of the
# Lutheran World Federation

1. ASSEMBLIES OF THE LWF
Lund 1947
Hanover 1952
Minneapolis 1957
Helsinki 1963
Evian 1970
Dar es Salaam 1977
Budapest 1984
Curitiba 1990


2. PRESIDENTS OF THE LWF
Anders Nygren
Hanns Lilje
Franklin Clark Fry
Fredrik A. Schiotz
Mikko Juva
Josiah Kibira
Zoltán Káldy
Johannes Hanselmann
Gottfried Brakemeier


3. GENERAL SECRETARIES OF THE LWF
Sylvester C. Michelfelder
Carl Elof Lund-Quist
Kurt Schmidt-Clausen
André Appel
Carl Henning Mau, Jr.
Gunnar Johan Staalsett
Ishmael Noko

# 1

## ASSEMBLIES OF THE LWF

## LUND 1947

### The First Assembly
### of the Lutheran World Federation

| | |
|---|---|
| Dates: | June 30–July 6, 1947 |
| Location: | Lund, Sweden |
| Theme: | "The Lutheran Church in the World Today" |
| Number of Participants: | 200 voting delegates, 400 visitors |
| Presiders: | Archbishop Erling Eidem of Uppsala, Sweden, presided in his capacity as retiring president of the Lutheran World Convention. |
| | Professor Anders Nygren of Lund was elected the first president of the Lutheran World Federation. |
| Executive Secretary: | Dr. Sylvester C. Michelfelder of the United States, who had served as acting executive secretary, was confirmed as the first executive secretary of the LWF. |
| Main Decision: | Adoption of a constitution for the LWF. |
| Principal Addresses: | "The Place of the Lutheran World Federation Today" |
| | *Dr. Ralph H. Long, United States* |
| | "The Testimony of the Lutheran Church" |
| | *Professor Anders Nygren, Sweden* |
| | "We Must Work While It Is Day" |
| | *Bishop Lajos Ordass, Hungary* |

Author: *Jens Holger Schjørring, Aarhus Denmark*

"The Lutheran Church and Its Tasks in the World"
*Bishop Hanns Lilje, Germany (FRG)*
"Christ, the Hope of the World"
*The Rev. S.W. Savarimuthu, India*


*The Moment in History*

Opposites were joined when two hundred voting delegates came together in
Lund, Sweden from June 30 to July 6, 1947, for the assembly that marked the
foundation of the Lutheran World Federation. The meeting itself took place in
untouched classical circumstances: the twelfth-century cathedral of roman-
esque design and the illustrious university symbolized historical continuity
and unbroken tradition. The location was one of undisturbed tranquillity provided by a provincial town seemingly far removed from the hectic atmosphere
characteristic of the modern metropolis.

Yet many of the delegates came from bombed cities, from countries that had
been drawn into the seemingly unceasing maelstrom of World War II. Many
came from church administrations or theological faculties that had engaged
totalitarian ideologies in a struggle for life or death. These delegates were
greeted by a host, the Church of Sweden, which wanted to be described as a
"folk church," a majority confession that worked closely with the state. This
host church was a privileged church which lived unmarked by the ravages of
the war in a stable democracy led by a thoroughly organized public administration.

The visitors to Lund, in contrast—or at least a considerable number of
them—came from religiously pluralistic countries in which the Lutheran
church occupied a minority position. Frequently, Lutherans lived in tension
with an atheistic state or in tenuous coexistence, as a minority, with Roman
Catholic or Orthodox churches. In some situations, as the United States, the
religious situation was marked by rigorous separation of church from state and
kaleidoscopic pluralism.

The physical situation of many of the delegates was also strikingly different
from what they found in Lund. Sweden had a relatively stable food supply, and
this was noticed at once by many who in the immediate aftermath of the war
were accustomed to hunger, deprivation, cold, endless crowds of refugees, and
widespread homelessness. They could not help but be reminded at every turn
that their host country had, through World War II, remained neutral. And what
is more, many of the delegates were from nations that had so recently been at
war with each other.

This encounter of opposites was the historical moment for the Lund Assembly of the Lutheran World Federation. How could such diversity be bridged?
Would it be possible for the assembly to forge for the Lutheran churches of the
world an instrument of viable cooperation? The answer to such questions lies
probably in the simple fact that the majority of participants arrived with a
determination to forgive, to put aside the enmities of war, to dismiss the
visions of "the enemy" created during nearly a decade of hostility. There was
now an intense desire to create an atmosphere of mutual understanding. There

was a commitment to seize the moment for new ways of living together in Christian communion.

For these persons in Lund in 1947 to worship together was a liberating experience, precisely when seen against this vivid joining of opposites. The message of undeserved forgiveness, the call to allow a common confession of guilt to be followed by a common dedication to serve the needs of the world—this message was at the heart of the experience of the First Assembly of the LWF.

Finally, the moment presented a large number of pressing issues which formed the agenda of the assembly, issues that could be faced only in a spirit of cooperation. The program committee, meeting in 1946 in Uppsala in preparation for this assembly, had already outlined a thematic plan for Lund:

### The Lutheran Church in the World Today

I. The Faith by which she lives
   a. The Word
   b. The Sacraments
   c. The Church
II. The Mission she should fulfill
   a. Evangelism
   b. Foreign Mission
   c. Helping one another
III. The Problems she must face
   a. Relations to other churches
   b. Relations to the state
   c. Secularism

This scheme was further developed by the committee. An assembly agenda was devised that included among its first items the following:

1. to cooperate in the aim of relief for the needy;
2. to establish a coordinated strategy with regard to the missionary tasks that had been set back as a consequence of the war;
3. to develop a common attitude and a coordinated initiative toward the ecumenical challenge which was now recognized as a commitment that could no longer be neglected;
4. to proceed in a common effort with regard to theological reflection concerning the shared heritage that had to be translated into appropriate expression in terms of modern thought.

### The Host Church

The Church of Sweden, Lutheran since the time of the Reformation, was particularly qualified to serve as host for the assembly. Its Lutheran tradition was pronounced and vigorous, and it had already, largely because of the tireless work of Archbishop Nathan Söderblom, accepted a major ecumenical role. He had developed in the first three decades of the twentieth century a broad international network of contacts, especially among the churches of Germany, France, and the English-speaking world. His work as chairperson for the pioneering "Life and Work" conference in Stockholm, 1925, was marked both by his brilliant churchmanship and by his leadership in the world of theological scholarship.

Additionally, and not least in the short period of time following the end of World War II, the Church of Sweden had consistently pursued close relationships with Lutheran churches and theological faculties in Germany and with the Church of England in Great Britain. At a time when world Lutheranism needed support for a critical reexamination of its tradition, which had suffered so much and had had so many questions put to it in consequence of the war, the Church of Sweden presented its many resources. Its contribution to this fundamental rethinking—for example, a critical reinterpretation of Luther's social ethics as they formed dominant attitudes toward the state—was considerable.

It should, moreover, be remembered that Archbishop Erling Eidem of Uppsala had in 1945 been appointed acting president of the Lutheran World Convention and in that capacity assumed leadership in planning the First Assembly of the Lutheran World Federation.

## Participants

Approximately two hundred delegates registered for the 1947 assembly in Lund, with the largest groups—about the same number in each case—coming from Germany, the United States, and the Nordic countries. The next largest group came from European countries in which Lutheranism was a minority confession.

Altogether, forty-seven churches from twenty-six countries were represented by official delegates to the Lund Assembly. There was a very small representation from churches outside Europe and North America—for example, from India (including delegates from indigenous groups) and China. The Chinese theologian P'eng Fu made noteworthy contributions to the assembly and the Indian theologian Joel Lakra was elected a member of the first executive committee of the LWF.

## Assembly Worship

The assembly opened and closed with Divine Service in the historic Lund cathedral. The Message of the Assembly bore witness to the deep significance of these communal acts of worship: "We began our assembly with sermon and sacrament in a historic sanctuary," leading to a "fellowship before the altar and pulpit." Archbishop Eidem chose Colossians 3:12–17 as the text for his opening sermon. The tenor of the archbishop's words, "We are truly brothers," became a *leitmotif* persisting throughout the assembly: Lutheran brothers and sisters of faith are in fact closely related. This proclamation of "the spirit of love" was supplemented by an emphasis on "the peace of God, and the thankfulness to God for his grace which pointed to community and solidarity, even where need seemed abundant, and humanly conditioned controversies divisive."

Eidem's plenary address, as acting president of the Lutheran World Convention, struck similar notes. "We are bleeding . . ." was his candid assessment of the overall situation in which the assembly was meeting. Yet he did not engage solely in lamentation—either over distress or guilt. "Christ is stronger than the powers of darkness," he proclaimed. To be conscious of this and of this alone was what was needed to meet the enormous challenges facing the churches. But, as he soberly added, genuine frankness of faith would easily be bewildered if it indulged in expectations of "extraordinary results." Thus he concluded with an appeal to realize that the efforts of this first LWF Assembly were no more than a modest beginning.

## The Constitution of the LWF

It was the approval of a new constitution—the first for the Lutheran World Federation, replacing that of the former Lutheran World Convention—that was the Lund Assembly's signal structural accomplishment. In order to evaluate properly both the continuity and discontinuity between these two documents, it is appropriate to cite in toto the first three articles of the new document. The entire constitution comprised thirteen articles (cf. Appendix, pp. 527ff. below). It was proposed to the assembly by a committee headed by Abdel Ross Wentz of the United States, who had been at work on these constitutional issues since the 1930s.

I. Name. The name and title of the body organized under this Constitution shall be The Lutheran World Federation.
II. Doctrinal Basis. The Lutheran World Federation acknowledges the Holy Scriptures of the Old and New Testaments as the only source and the infallible norm of all church doctrine and practice, and sees in the Confessions of the Lutheran Church, especially in the Unaltered Augsburg Confession and Luther's Catechism, a pure exposition of the Word of God.
III. Nature and Purposes.
1. The Lutheran World Federation shall be a free association of Lutheran churches. It shall have no power to legislate for the churches belonging to it or to interfere with their complete autonomy, but shall act as their agent in such matters as they assign to it.
2. The purposes of the Lutheran World Federation are:
    (a) to bear united witness before the world to the Gospel of Jesus Christ as the power of God for salvation;
    (b) to cultivate unity of faith and confession among the Lutheran churches of the world;
    (c) to promote fellowship and cooperation in study among Lutherans;
    (d) to foster Lutheran participation in ecumenical movements;
    (e) to develop a united Lutheran approach to responsibilities in missions and education; and
    (f) to support Lutheran groups in need of spiritual or material aid.
3. The Lutheran World Federation may take action on behalf of member churches in such matters as one or more of them may commit to it.

LWF Photo

42. Dr. J. P. van Heest, President of the Evangelical Lutheran Church in the
    Kingdom of the Netherlands, signing the first Constitution of the LWF at
    the 1947 Lund Assembly. Other persons at the signing included, seated from
    the left: Dr. Abdel Ross Wentz, U.S.A. and Bishop Hanns Lilje, Germany;
    archbishop Erling Eidem of Sweden, last President of the Lutheran World
    Convention and presiding officer at the Lund Assembly, is standing at the
    right.

Article IV dealt with membership in the Federation, and Article V specified
that the LWF would exercise its functions through (1) the assembly, (2) an executive committee, (3) national committees, and (4) special commissions. In
light of subsequent LWF history it is worth pointing out that this constitution
could be amended "by a two-thirds vote of those present at any regularly called
Assembly, provided notice of intentions to amend shall have been made the
preceding day."

Some comments regarding the first three articles of this 1947 constitution
are in order.

First, concerning the name. It was imperative that "Convention" be
replaced, since that name implied that cooperation between the Lutheran
churches was to be seen as occasional and noncommittal. "Federation"
described an association of a much more binding and lasting character, to
which churches and not individuals were making a commitment. Incidentally,
John A. Morehead of the United States had proposed this name for the
Lutheran churches of the world as early as 1920.

Second, concerning the "Doctrinal Basis." This paragraph retained without
change the text from the constitution of the Lutheran World Convention.
After World War I a strong statement regarding doctrine was seen as necessary

to counteract the inroads of liberal Protestantism. Similarly, the experience of World War II in, for example, the Confessing Church in Germany and in the church struggles of Norway, called for a strong and "orthodox" reliance on Bible and Confessions. The emphasis in this text on a number of exclusive adjectives—Holy Scriptures as the only source and infallible norm; the Confessions as a pure exposition—indicates a clear intention to preserve the tone of the Augsburg Confession. Such an intention, frequently in connection with the so-called formal principle of Lutheran theology, was, however, not intended as a self-contained matter of principle. Rather, it was intended as the necessary precondition that enables subsequent exposition of the real content of the Christian message. This is characteristic of the Lutheran theological movement: *sola scriptura* is the incontestable condition for the correct interpretation of the Article of Justification, the center of the church's message. *Sola scriptura, solus Christus, sola fide.* The challenge to the churches embedded in this doctrinal basis was to maintain confessional integrity, on the one hand, and the ability to translate this message to meet the needs of immediate contexts, on the other. Specifically: Would Lutheran churches be able "to cultivate unity of faith and confession" without neglecting "to foster Lutheran participation in ecumenical movements"?

Finally, concerning "Nature and Purpose." The 1947 constitution has a striking emphasis on the free character of cooperation between Lutheran churches. The Federation "shall have no power to legislate for the churches belonging to it or to interfere with their complete autonomy, but shall act as their agent in such matters as they assign to it." This is followed by an enumeration of a number of tasks that need to be taken up and may only be carried out if the Lutheran churches act jointly. These tasks (cf. the "four pillars" of chapter 1 in the present volume) gave the LWF its profile and also tested its solidarity in cooperation. Yet here was another question to be faced in the Federation's future: Would it be possible for the LWF to combine the cooperation of a "free association" with the discipline needed because of the urgency and complexity of the tasks it faced and within the limitations implied in the doctrinal basis?

## Elections

The two main elections at the Lund Assembly were those of president and executive secretary. There was a move to elect someone from the host church to serve as LWF president and since Archbishop Eidem was unwilling to stand for office, the assembly elected, by a near unanimous vote, Professor Anders Nygren, the internationally known systematic theologian from the theological faculty at Lund. Sylvester C. Michelfelder, who as executive secretary of the Lutheran World Convention had been instrumental in setting up a secretariat in Geneva, Switzerland, was confirmed as the first executive secretary of the LWF.

The Lund Assembly elected an executive committee of sixteen persons, four each from Germany, the Nordic Countries, the United States, and other countries. Subsequently, on July 6, 1947, this new executive committee elected its officers—President: Anders Nygren of Sweden (ex officio); First Vice-President: Abdel Ross Wentz of the United States; Second Vice-President: Bishop Lajos Ordass of Hungary; and Treasurer: Ralph H. Long of the United States.

## Bibliographical Notes

*Unpublished Documents*

LWF Archives, Geneva.
A. Nygren's papers, University Library, Lund.
Danish Committee of the Lutheran World Federation, State Archives, Copenhagen.

*Publications*

Nelson, E. Clifford. *The Rise of World Lutheranism: An American Perspective.* Philadelphia: Fortress Press, 1982.
*Proceedings*, Lund.
Schmidt-Clausen, Kurt. *Vom Lutherischen Weltkonvent zum Lutherischen Weltbund.* Gütersloh: Gütersloher Verlagshaus Gerd Mohn, 1976.
Solberg, Richard. *As Between Brothers: The Story of Lutheran Response to World Need.* Minneapolis: Augsburg, 1957.

# HANOVER 1952

## The Second Assembly
## of the Lutheran World Federation

| | |
|---|---|
| Dates: | July 25 to August 3, 1952 |
| Location: | Hanover, Federal Republic of Germany |
| Theme: | "The Living Word in a Responsible Church" |
| Number of Participants: | 227 delegates, 207 alternates, 801 visitors |
| Presidents: | Bishop Anders Nygren of Lund, Sweden, was president of the LWF at the time of this assembly. Landesbischof Hanns Lilje of the Evangelical Lutheran Church of Hanover, Federal Republic of Germany, was elected the second LWF president on August 1, 1952. |
| Executive Secretary: | Dr. Carl E. Lund-Quist, United States |
| Main Decisions: | Constitutional amendment (at least four members of the executive committee have to be laypersons); establishment of a Department of Theology, a Department of World Service (merger of Interchurch Aid and Service to Refugees), and a Department on World Missions; publication of a Lutheran world encyclopedia; inclusion of youth in future assemblies; creation of the LWF Archives. |
| Principal Addresses: | "The Living Word in a Responsible Church" |
| | *Bishop Dr. Anders Nygren, Sweden* |
| | "Our Church Service" |
| | *Professor Peter Brunner, Germany (FRG)* |
| | "Lutheran Ethics and Missionary Practice" |
| | *Professor Gustav Stählin, Germany (FRG)* |
| | "Lutheran Theology and World Missions" |
| | *Professor Gustav Wingren, Sweden* |
| | "State and Church Today" |
| | *Bishop Eivind Berggrav, Norway* |
| | "Lutheran World Service" |
| | *Dr. Paul C. Empie, United States* |
| | "Service to Refugees" |
| | *Dr. Stewart W. Herman, United States* |

Author: *Hans Otte, Hanover, Germany*

## The Context—The City and the Host Church

The assembly met in a city that was marked by the Second World War; practically all of the old city had been destroyed and only some of the ruins had been cleared away. It was manifest, however, that there had long been a will to reconstruct. In order to create a modern, car-friendly city, large areas were cleared in the old city and new avenues built. Thanks to the American Marshall Plan (European Recovery Program), the first successes of the *Wirtschaftswunder* appeared: the city was able to present itself and the economic power of the Federal Republic in the new "Hanover Industrial Fair." The recovery was particularly visible when compared to conditions in the German Democratic Republic, which was only 100 km away. The iron curtain was not yet tightly closed, and refugees from the GDR arrived at the station every day.

Since 1945 Germany had been split, and since 1949 it had been organized in two states: the Federal Republic of Germany (FRG) and the German Democratic Republic (GDR). Neither state had yet gained full sovereignty; each was integrated into the political bloc to which it belonged. In the Federal Republic, a heated discussion took place on how close the ties to the Western powers should be. Under the leadership of Federal Chancellor Konrad Adenauer, the government advanced the integration of the Federal Republic into the Western alliance and stepped up rearmament to enable the Federal Republic's entry into NATO. It was a controversial issue not only on the political scene but also within the church of how to deal with the East–West conflict and the growing gap between the two Germanies. One part of the Protestant church, under the leadership of the church president, Martin Niemöller from Darmstadt, and the former minister of the interior, Gustav Heinemann, used national Protestant arguments to violently oppose the course the Federal government was taking. The majority of the United Evangelical Lutheran Church of Germany, however, under the leadership of Landesbischof Hans Meiser supported the chancellor's policies. Political and church political options increasingly overlapped and thus the discussions became very involved.

The Protestant church was divided into several organizations, the most important of which was the Evangelical Church in Germany (EKD). This was a loose association of churches whose membership consisted of all Protestant territorial churches (Landeskirchen) and which represented the members' interests vis-à-vis the political institutions of the FRG and the GDR. Along with the EKD, there were other church associations based on confessional affiliation—Lutheran, Reformed, United. Most of the Lutheran territorial churches belonged to the United Evangelical Lutheran Church of Germany (VELKD), which, on behalf of its member churches, dealt with questions of confession, order of worship, and legislation concerning pastors. The EKD and the VELKD had been founded after the Second World War. In the founding period of the two organizations, violent clashes had taken place between the advocates of a separate confessional association such as the VELKD, and the opponents of a confessionally structured Protestant church, the aftermath of which was still to be felt.

With the arrival of refugees from the former German regions in the East, the

43. A memorial service for victims of war throughout the world was held during
the 1952 LWF Assembly amidst the ruins of the Aegidienkirche in Hanover.

host church, the Evangelical Lutheran Church of Hanover, had become the
numerically largest church in Germany. In its region, that is, the major part of
Lower Saxony, about 70 percent of the population belonged to it. It had the
structure of a folk church, which was mostly accepted as a matter of course.
The Landeskirche was a member of the EKD and the VELKD. To begin with,
it was quite isolated in the VELKD since its longtime Landesbischof, August
Marahrens, was accused of having kept too little distance from the National
Socialist regime. The election of Hanns Lilje to the office of Landesbischof
ended this isolation; the church now tried to mediate in the inner-church disputes between the EKD and the VELKD. In 1948, one of its leading theologians, Heinz Brunotte, had been elected president of the church office of the
EKD and, at the same time, president of the church office of the VELKD, and
Hanns Lilje, in addition to his function in the VELKD, was also a deputy chairman of the EKD Council.

## The Participants

Since in the minds of the GDR government the VELKD was particularly sup-
portive of the integration of Germany into the western alliance, it had no
interest in providing assembly participants with the necessary permits to

leave the GDR. Thus, only a few delegates from that part of Germany were able to take part in the meeting and hardly any GDR citizens could participate in the major events for laypersons which took place on the fringes of the assembly. At that time, the GDR pushed a radically anti-church course, and it not only refused to issue "interzone" passes, but even harassed transit passengers. The assembly was overshadowed by the East-West conflict. Unlike the daily press, the West German organizers had no interest in playing up the difficulties with the GDR; for this reason the inner-German problems were not emphasized in assembly sessions.

Only a few participants had come from the Eastern bloc states: the Lutheran churches of Poland and Czechoslovakia had not nominated any delegates; the Baltic churches were present only by representatives of the exile churches. The Hungarian church, however, sent a delegation. Its representative in the LWF and member of the executive committee was Bishop Lajos Ordass. As he was under house arrest, he did not obtain an exit visa. The Hungarian church was thus represented by bishops Laszlo Dezséry and Lajos Vetö, who were more compliant vis-à-vis the Communist state. When Landesbischof Hanns Lilje in his opening sermon remembered those who "cannot be present in our midst, whom we would love to welcome here," the Hungarian delegates considered this to be an allusion to Bishop Ordass and threatened to leave. When their right to speak at the assembly was once again confirmed, Bishop Lilje could calm down the Hungarians and avoid a major incident.

Compared with the assembly in Lund, there were more delegates from Latin America and Asia, above all because of the presence of several Lutheran churches from the now independent India. There were, however, no African church delegates present at all; individual Africans participated as official visitors of mission boards.

### Discussions and Decisions at the Assembly

Since its founding meeting in Lund, the work of the LWF had shown that there were more commonalities than one had thought at the foundation. These commonalities had resulted from practical work such as the joint administration of the missions in Africa and Asia orphaned because of the war, the strengthening of refugee aid, and the material aid provided for the reconstruction of churches. The Geneva staff urged that the work be tightened. At the same time, the wish was that the common work should become more binding so that Lutheran churches that had not yet joined the LWF because of the non-committal nature of the statements concerning the applicability of the Lutheran confession could also become members. Moreover, the issue was raised in the Nordic churches whether it was necessary to reshape the church work since the economic boom provided church members not only with money but also with new ways of spending their free time. In his opening lecture, the outgoing president pleaded strongly against any form of restoration; "Forward to Luther!" was his slogan for a church that was consciously to accept responsibility in the world.

## Theological Work

The assembly did not try to give new answers to the complex question of the legal position of the confessional basis. This problem was to be taken up by the newly established Department of Theology in its future study work. The members of this department were to engage permanently in theological work, enable regular exchange between theologians and church people, and improve communication between the Lutheran churches through additional publications. One topic that promised more commonality in the interpretation of the theological heritage was the question of the understanding of worship. For this reason one main lecture was on the theology of worship, which was also to be the subject of future studies.

## Organizational Changes

After the First World War, the Lutheran World Convention had lost its practical function for the member churches, when material interchurch aid was no longer necessary. The convention had then quickly become a noncommittal forum for discussion. The Geneva secretariat was aware of this danger and wanted to tighten the work in respect to aid in order better to be able to help and to publicize the needs. For this reason, it proposed the establishment of a Department of World Service, which would embrace the refugee work done by the individual national committees of the LWF and the interchurch aid work thus far done separately. In other words, it was to coordinate aid for refugees, for pastors and church workers, as well as aid for the extension of churches and church institutions.

The aim of establishing the Department of World Missions was to avoid organizational and theological tensions. At the beginning of the Second World War, the U.S.A. National Committee as well as the mission boards of other neutral states had taken over the "orphaned" mission stations whose contacts with their original mission boards had become impossible because of the war. The negotiations with government offices and with the mission boards, which were gradually able to take up contact with their field offices again, had shown that it was helpful when a transnational organization led the negotiations and served as a mediator. For this reason, the LWF had increasingly become involved in mission work. The Department of World Missions was to ensure that the work was not dependent on the personal preferences of those concerned; at the same time, there was a wish to reach agreement on missionary practice. Two assembly lectures dealt with these questions, especially the problem of adopting indigenous rites and social orders. This was also to show that the discussion within the LWF was not confined to the questions of the "old" churches. As chairman of the LWF Commission on World Missions, Fredrik Schiotz urged that consequences be drawn from the need that "larger responsibilities can and must be posited in the hands of younger churchmen." One problem, however—namely, relations with other Protestant mission boards and the International Missionary Council (IMC)—was referred to the LWF Executive Committee and the Department of World Missions. No solution to that problem was in view.

Two further assembly resolutions were aimed at dismantling structural shortcomings. A quota for laypeople in the executive committee was decided on: four additional laypeople should sit on it, and in the future these seats should continue to be reserved for laypeople. Moreover, in the future youth delegates were to have voice and vote in the assembly and all its sections.

## Public Resonance

These discussions and resolutions had mainly to do with inner-church matters. The echo in the media concentrated on two other topics, namely, the relationships between church and state, and church social order. Because of the existence of Lutheran churches in the Eastern bloc this was particularly explosive. This issue was introduced in the keynote lecture by Bishop Eivind Berggrav from Norway, who, at the same time, presented theses developed by the Norwegian National Committee on the same topic. As primate of the Church of Norway, Berggrav had, during the Second World War, participated in the resistance against the government put in place by the National Socialists, and for this reason his words met with a resounding public echo. When he warned against the traditional misunderstandings of Luther's doctrine of the two kingdoms, he also referred to his experience during that period. A government that bends the law does not need to be obeyed. "To obey such a satanic government would be nothing short of sinful." It was not up to the church to organize a rebellion, he said, but it had to watch over the freedom of the proclamation of the word and diakonia. In the second part of the paper, he explained why he rejected a mistaken doctrine of the two kingdoms. He warned against the dangers of a "welfare state" whenever it had totalitarian traits, when its effect was "to sterilize the social welfare work of the church," and when it wanted to regulate individual lives. Berggrav outlined a model of the church as advocate of freedom which must claim the necessary space for parents and children as well as for social welfare work. What Berggrav had in mind, above all, was the communist states, but he carefully avoided direct political polemics.

Another point that was extensively discussed in the media had to do with the future role of laypeople in the church. The American model of stewardship was not only introduced and discussed in several sections but also promoted in the meetings of laypeople taking place parallel to the Hanover Assembly and in the Berlin meeting arranged after the assembly for the GDR. The proposed commitments to regular financial contributions, the offer to make oneself available to the church on certain days in the week or in a special period of one's life, or the possibility of lay visitation services in the congregations were an attempt to transpose elements of the American volunteer church to the German folk churches. Given the rapid adoption of an American lifestyle in these years, this model of church work seemed promising. Thus the proposals with regard to stewardship in the church had a positive response; this seemed to open a new way of participation for laypeople who wanted to take on responsibility.

## Conclusion

The Hanover Assembly was intended to strengthen the LWF as an organization. The times of improvisation had come to an end. The direction the LWF was to take was still open. Positive decisions were taken concerning several matters: a Department of Theology was created for those interested in theology; for those urging direct action, Lutheran World Service was established; for those who demanded the promotion of church work in the congregations, the concept of stewardship was propagated. Thanks to these organizational changes, the Federation gained enough efficiency to retain its importance in the coming years. It was probably due to the great echo the assembly met with in the host country that it was not reduced to adopting organizational changes but indeed gave new impulses for the further work of the LWF. For Germany, the meeting was significant because it was the first time that a large international organization met in Germany and elected a German to be its president. This strengthened German self-assurance and enabled the German Lutherans to bid farewell to loyalty to the traditional authoritarian state and to commit themselves more strongly to a Lutheranism open to the world.

**Bibliographical Notes** _____

*Unpublished Material*

LWF Archives, Geneva.
Lutheran Church Archives, Hanover, on the Second LWF Assembly.
Papers of Landesbischof D. Hanns Lilje, Lutheran Church Archives, Hanover.

*Published Material*

Andersen, Wilhelm. *Das wirkende Wort: Theologische Berichte über die Vollversammlung des Lutherischen Weltbundes. Hannover 1958. Sektion I: Theologie.* Munich: Evang. Presseverband für Bayern, 1953.
Bachmann, E. Theodore. *Epic of Faith: The Background of the Second Assembly of the Lutheran World Federation.* New York: National Lutheran Council, 1952.
*Bankrott der dienenden Liebe!* Rufe in die Gemeinde, 3. Hanover: Feesche Verlag, 1952.
*Frauen in aller Welt danken, bitten und arbeiten: Begegnung der Frauen auf der Lutherischen Weltbundtagung.* Rufe in die Gemeinde, 2. Stein b. Nürnberg: Laetare Verlag; Munich: Claudius-Verlag, 1952.
Hahn, Elisabeth. *Partnerschaft: Ein Beitrag zum Problem der Gleichberechtigung von Mann und Frau auf Grund der Arbeit von Sektion VI, Frauen in der Kirche.* Nürnberg: Laetare Verlag 1953.
*Jugend für Christus: Berichte und Erzählungen von der Jugend- und Studententagung des Lutherischen Weltbundes, Hannover 1952.* Rufe in die Gemeinde, 4. Oldenburg: Jugenddienst-Verlag; Munich: Claudius-Verlag, 1952.

*Die Liebesarbeit der lutherischen Kirche: Theologische Berichte über die Voll-versammlung des Lutherischen Weltbundes, Hannover 1952, Sektion III, Innere Mission.* Edited by Johannes Wolff et al. Munich: Evang. Presseverband für Bayern, 1953.

*The Living Word in a Responsible Church.* Study documents, Lutheran World Federation Assembly, July 25–August 3, 1952. Edited by Carl E. Lund-Quist. Hanover, 1952.

*Proceedings,* Hanover.

Reich, Herbert. *Boten aus aller Welt: Ein Bildband von der Tagung des Lutherischen Weltbunds in Hannover.* Hanover: Lutherhaus Verlag, 1952.

Rendtorf, Heinrich. *Es soll durch seinen Geist geschehen: Die drei Bibel-arbeiten von Heinrich Rendtorff, gehalten auf der Lutherischen Woche in Hannover sowie Predigten und geistliche Ansprachen während der Voll-versammlung des Lutherischen Weltbundes.* Rufe in die Gemeinde, 6. Munich: Claudius-Verlag 1952.

Schäfer, Walter. *Stewardship: Der Dank-Dienst des Christen. Bericht und Gespräch. Theologische Berichte über die Vollversammlung des Lutheri-schen Weltbundes in Hannover, Sektion IV.* Munich: Evang. Presseverband für Bayern, 1953.

*Der wahre Schatz der Kirche: Ansprachen über die lutherische Kirche während der Vollversammlung des Lutherischen Weltbundes in Hannover.* Rufe in die Gemeinde, 9. Munich: Claudius-Verlag, 1952.

Wölber, Hans-Otto. *Jugend und Heilsgewißheit: Theologische Berichte über die Vollversammlung des Luth. Weltbundes in Hannover, Sektion V, Jugend und Studenten.* Munich: Evang. Presseverband für Bayern, 1953.

# MINNEAPOLIS 1957

# The Third Assembly
# of the Lutheran World Federation

| | |
|---|---|
| Dates: | August 15–25, 1957 |
| Location: | Minneapolis, Minnesota, United States |
| Theme: | "Christ Frees and Unites" |
| Number of Participants: | 241 delegates, 146 official visitors from member churches, 125 visitors from nonmember churches. |
| Presidents: | Dr. Hanns Lilje, Landesbischof of the United Evangelical Lutheran Church in Germany (VELKD). On August 24, 1967, Dr. Franklin Clark Fry was elected the new president. He was president of the United Lutheran Church, United States. |
| Executive Secretary: | Dr. Carl E. Lund-Quist, United States (1951–1960) |
| Main Decisions: | Constitutional change regarding new member churches (acceptance by LWF in assembly, or in the interim by the executive committee "if not more than one third of member churches raise objections within one year"); acceptance of four new member churches and seven congregations; approval of a study of the Commission on Theology on the significance of the Lutheran Confessions in the life of the church today, focusing on "justification." |
| Principal Addresses: | "Christ Frees and Unites" |
| | *Bishop Dr. Hanns Lilje, Germany (FRG)* |
| | "The Freedom We Have in Christ" |
| | *Dr. Chitose Kishi, Japan* |
| | "The Unity of the Church in Christ" |
| | *Professor Hans Werner Gensichen, Germany (FRG)* |
| | "The Freedom to Reform the Church" |
| | *Bishop Bo Giertz, Sweden* |
| | "Free for Service in the World" |
| | *Dr. Edgar M. Carlson, United States* |
| | "Free and Untied in Hope" |
| | *Bishop Friedrich-Wilhelm Krummacher, Germany (GDR)* |

Author: *Eric W. Gritsch, Baltimore, Maryland*

44. Delegates and official visitors at the assembly in procession behind the banners of their churches on their way to the opening worship of the Assembly in the Minneapolis Auditorium.

## Historical Context

The assembly met on the occasion of the tenth anniversary of the Lutheran World Federation. Although many difficulties of the postwar situation had been overcome, Lutherans and other Christians still faced various problems around the world. Newly emerging nations in Africa struggled with political and socioeconomic issues in their attempt to overcome the burden of colonialism. Christianity in China as well as in other Asian regions faced political opposition from Communist and nationalist ideologies. The "cold war" between East and West kept Lutherans divided in Europe. Delegates from Eastern Europe had difficulties traveling to the United States, although some managed to attend. Bishop Lajos Ordass from Hungary had been imprisoned, but was permitted to attend this assembly for reasons only his totalitarian government understood. His opening sermon was a moving testimony to spiritual freedom in Christ in the face of human tyranny. Other voices also testified how difficult it was in many parts of the world to be free. They referred to "The Voice of the Critical World" that often made a mockery of the church's claim to be free in Christ. "The Voice of the Critical World" was summarized in a brief statement, dealing with one of the five subtitles of the theme. A "witness" then offered a brief response.

The largest Lutheran church in the United States at the time was the United Lutheran Church in America, led by President Franklin Clark Fry. The second-largest Lutheran church, not a member of the LWF, was the Lutheran Church-Missouri Synod, led by President John W. Behnken. Lutherans were mostly concentrated in the east, especially in Pennsylvania, and in the Midwest, particularly in Minnesota. The second decade after the end of World War II in 1945 was marked by prosperity and a sense of optimism about the future of institutional religion. Many churches and Sunday school buildings were being erected in anticipation of increased church membership. Moreover, Lutherans and other Christians in America used the high value of the dollar to finance missionary and diaconal work abroad. Citizens saw themselves as representatives of a country dedicated to democracy and to peace keeping in the world. Americans had continued to fight for peace in Korea under the auspices of the United Nations, even though the war ended only with an uncertain truce, protected by South Korean and American arms. There also was progress at home regarding racial segregation. In 1954 the United States Supreme Court had ordered the racial integration of public schools. Lutheran and other Christian denominations began to support the voting rights of black citizens, the first sign of a "civil rights" movement advocating equal rights for the black population. The National Lutheran Council, headquartered in New York, provided opportunities for dialogue and cooperation. Negotiations had begun for future mergers of Lutheran church bodies as a way to overcome ethnic division and to be liberated for greater ecumenical work and mission.

The themes of freedom and unity seemed quite appropriate in a world still plagued by tyranny and a church burdened by divisions. This assembly asked, in a phrase of Franklin Clark Fry, all Lutherans "to think together" in mutual trust.

## The Host Church

The Third Assembly of the LWF was the first assembly held on the North American continent. The invitation to come to the United States had been issued by the various Lutheran churches represented in the National Lutheran Council. Minneapolis was a city where Lutherans outnumbered other Christian denominations. Minneapolis, and its twin city, Saint Paul, the capital of Minnesota, had a population of about 850,000, with some of the largest Lutheran churches in the United States and a concentration of Lutheran institutions, focusing on education, publication, mission, and other enterprises. The assembly met in the gigantic Minneapolis Municipal Auditorium, equipped with the latest communication systems, including television. The president of the United States, Dwight D. Eisenhower, the governor of the state of Minnesota, and the mayors of the Twin Cities sent cordial greetings to the delegates. Local, regional, and national mass media covered the assembly meetings through the well-known American way of "press conferences."

Opening, closing, and daily worship services were conducted in the large assembly auditorium. Daily Holy Communion services were held in English at Central Lutheran Church. Ordained delegates presided or preached at churches in the Twin Cities on the two Sundays, August 18 and 25. Delegates could also attend Communion services of various national churches. The official languages of the assembly were German, one of the Scandinavian languages (Swedish, Norwegian, or Danish), and English. Formal receptions were held at the rotunda of the State Capitol in Saint Paul. The LWF Executive Committee arranged a reception and dinner at the well-known Minneapolis Athletic Club. Delegates attended various cultural events, such as concerts, public lectures, and film presentations on Martin Luther and on various Lutheran enterprises around the world. The entire lower level of the auditorium contained the most comprehensive physical display ever built to interpret Lutheranism. The exhibit showed what members of LWF churches "believe and do" in fourteen types of work, focusing on education, arts, communication, and historical development. Local business corporations provided free office space, translation equipment, and the use of fifty passenger cars. In addition, patrons, sponsors, and donors made financial contributions to help facilitate the work of the assembly. Its work was divided into plenary sessions, assembly committees, and discussion groups.

## Participants

The 241 delegates represented global Lutheranism reflecting the various geographic concentrations of Lutherans: 145 came from Europe, especially from Germany (67) and Scandinavia (48); 60 represented the United States and Canada; 16 came from Asia; 7 from Latin America; and 5 from Africa. Delegates from Eastern Europe still had difficulties traveling to the United States, but East Germany, Czechoslovakia, Hungary, and the Baltic states were able to send delegates. Bishop Lajos Ordass from Hungary was permitted to attend only the assembly, even though he served as second vice-president. Visitors came from LWF member churches, from LWF-recognized congregations, from nonmember churches and groups, from ecumenical groups, and from confessional alliances (Reformed, Baptist, Methodist, and others). There also were special guests from Germany, Switzerland, and the United States, as well as women's representatives and youth visitors. Dr. Willem A. Visser 't Hooft, general secretary of the World Council of Churches, offered a special word of greeting.

## Discussions

The theme of the assembly, "Christ Frees and Unites," was the main item on the agenda. It was treated in twenty discussion groups (of no more than thirty-five persons) whose findings were evaluated by group leaders, recorders, and theological advisors under the leadership of Dr. Franklin Clark Fry. The discussions were based on a study document prepared by the Commission on Theology, with the theme as its title. Main presentations were scheduled in the first five days on the five subtitles of the study document, whose theme was introduced in the opening message to the assembly by the LWF President, Bishop Hanns Lilje. The special group, led by Dr. Fry, formulated "Theses" for discussion and acceptance by the assembly. The theses were transmitted to all Lutherans around the world with a covering letter by President Lilje.

Five Departments (on theology, world missions, world service, information, and Latin America) and six Commissions (on stewardship, education, inner missions, liturgy, international affairs, and the projected Lutheran World Encyclopedia) reported and offered recommendations to the assembly in the plenary sessions. The LWF Department of Information had been created in 1953 by the executive committee.

## Theological Work

The assembly invested most of its time in the discussion of the theme. The final theses on the theme, called the "Minneapolis Confession" by some interpreters, explicate the five subtitles: (1) "The Freedom We Have in Christ" means deliverance from a fractured God-relationship through Christ, who brings hope for the future despite the many aspects of the demonic, present in idolatry and tyranny. (2) "The Unity of the Church in Christ" is defined in Article VII of the Augsburg Confession as unity in word and sacraments and thus as a call to inter-communion over which churches should not be deadlocked. (3) "The Freedom to Reform the Church" is based on the fact that the church is the pilgrim people of God, which needs to recapture its apostolicity and catholicity in every age, especially in Asia and Africa, where the church must face anti-Christian ideologies, political turmoil, and ethical relativism, often imported from other parts of the world. (4) "Free for Service in the World" means to serve, above all, justice. That is the painstaking task of the Christian call to witness to God in Christ. (5) "Free and United in Hope" is a word that exorcises from the illusions of a christianized world and a kingdom of God on earth. Baptism commissions to service of the neighbor in need in the certain hope that all salvation comes through Christ alone.

The Commission on Theology recommended the formation of a subcommittee to prepare a study on the topic "The Lutheran Confessions in their Significance for the Life of the Church Today." Its purpose was to use the Lutheran Confessions as a resource for the spiritual and practical decisions which confront the church today. At the center of the study should be the topic of "justification." Such a study should also look at the constitution of the LWF from a theological and ecclesiological angle because "in this sphere many things are still unclear and there are even misunderstandings" regarding membership and cooperation.

## Organizational Decisions

The Credentials Committee recommended, and the assembly approved, the seating of delegates representing three new member churches (from Germany,

Hong Kong, and Mexico) and seven LWF-recognized congregations (from Colombia, Ecuador, Peru, and four from Venezuela). The assembly changed Article IV of the constitution regarding new membership by stipulating that new member churches may be accepted by assembly vote, or in the interim by the LWF Executive Committee "if not more than one-third of the member churches raise objections within one year."

The assembly appointed a subcommittee to deal with the recommendation of the Commission on Theology to study the relationship between the Lutheran Confessions and contemporary issues in global Lutheranism, specifically the nature and purposes of the LWF in terms of theological and ecclesiological dimensions.

Dr. Franklin Clark Fry, president of the United Lutheran Church of America, was elected president of LWF on August 24, 1957. The executive committee was composed of 27 members, some of them newly elected.

**Bibliographical Notes** _____

*Assembly Manual: The Third Assembly of the Lutheran World Federation, Minneapolis, Minnesota. August 15–25, 1957.* In English, German, and Swedish.
*Christ Frees and Unites: Messages of the Third Assembly: The Lutheran World Federation.* Minneapolis: Augsburg Publishing House, n.d. The opening worship sermon, keynote address, subtheme lectures and the resulting theses of the Third Assembly.
*Christ Frees and Unites: Study Document for the Third Assembly of the Lutheran World Federation.* Geneva: Department of Theology of the LWF, 1956.
Marty, Martin E. "Postscript to Minneapolis." *Lutheran World* 4 (1957–58): 42–64.
"A 'Minneapolis Confession'?" *Lutheran World* 4 (1957–58): 335–36.
*Proceedings*, Minneapolis.
Terray, László G. *He Could Not Do Otherwise: Bishop Lajos Ordass 1901–1978*, trans. Eric W. Gritsch. Grand Rapids: Eerdmans, 1997.

# HELSINKI 1963

## The Fourth Assembly of the Lutheran World Federation

Dates:                    July 30–August 11, 1963
Location:              Helsinki, Finland
Theme:                  "Christ Today"
Number of Participants: 267 delegates, 413 other participants
Presidents:           Dr. Franklin Clark Fry, president of the Lutheran Church of America, was LWF president up to the Fourth Assembly. On 10 August 1963 Dr. Fredrick A. Schiotz, president of the American Lutheran Church, was elected to be the new president of the LWF.
General Secretary:    The Rev. Dr. Kurt Schmidt-Clausen, Evangelical Lutheran Church of Hanover, was general secretary from 1959 to 1965.
Main Decisions:      Document on justification was *not* accepted. Establishment of the Foundation for Inter-Confessional Research; constitutional and structural issues.
Principal Addresses:   "Christ Today"
     *Dr. Franklin Clark Fry, United States*
"Grace for the World"
     *Professor Gerhard Gloege, Germany (FRG)*
"Faith Without Works?"
     *Dr. Helge Brattgård, Sweden*
"Divided Humanity—United in Christ"
     *Professor Heikki Waris, Finland*
"The New Song of Praise"
     *Dr. Andar Lumbantobing, Indonesia*
"The One Church and the Lutheran Churches"
     *Professor E. Clifford Nelson, United States*

*The Historical Context*

The historical context of the Fourth Assembly of the LWF was characterized by increasingly close and quick communication between countries and conti-

Author: *Reinhard Brandt, Hanover, Germany*

nents. One lecture referred to the jet planes that had brought most visitors to Helsinki. Technical progress was praised. The postwar period had been "overcome," and new challenges had to be tackled. This influenced the deliberations. Thus, the fact that the LWF had installed a broadcasting service, Radio Voice of the Gospel, in Addis Ababa was welcomed. Structures for more efficient work and more timely aid were being sought. The growth of the LWF—since 1957 and up to Helsinki twenty-one new churches had joined—was also part of this context.

The spiritual challenge created by the new global situation was clearly recognized. At times of progress and secularization, Luther's rediscovery of God's grace should be proclaimed in theology and practice in such a way that it becomes palpable for the modern person. This led to the assembly's consideration of the doctrine of justification. Moreover, the spiritual challenges facing the assembly included the fact that some LWF member churches still allowed no pulpit and altar fellowship. This was repeatedly deplored at Helsinki even though the necessary consequences were not drawn.

Finally, a few important ecumenical events were also part of the historical context: In 1961 in New Delhi, the Russian Orthodox Church and other Orthodox churches joined the World Council of Churches (WCC); furthermore, the International Missionary Council (IMC) merged with the WCC; in October 1962 the Second Vatican Council began in Rome, and the Fourth World Conference for Faith and Order met immediately before the LWF in July 1963 in Montreal. At a time of ecumenical breakthroughs, the LWF did not want to be left out but wished to add its own position to the ecumenical dialogue. This, too, played an important part in the debate on justification and subsequently in the creation of the Foundation for Interconfessional Research.

## The Host Church

After Lund, Hanover, and Minneapolis, the Fourth Assembly of the LWF took place in Finland. In addition to a small Orthodox church (70,000 believers), there was in Finland a large Lutheran folk church whose members made up about 94 percent of the population (4.4 million people) including a Swedish-speaking diocese. Since in Finland the state of affairs in the church had not been deplorable, the Reformation was introduced without radical changes. A deep sense of attachment to the folk church as well as close relations between church and state developed over the years. Moreover, in the eighteenth and nineteenth centuries the Finnish church was characterized by four revivalist movements, which continue to be marked by an intense biblical piety and a strong missionary commitment. Just like the political entity, the Finnish church also consciously functioned as a builder of bridges between East and West.

With the exception of the worship services in the cathedral and the congregations, the assembly itself took place in the halls and rooms of Helsinki University, especially in the Main Hall.

## Participants

There were 267 official delegates to the Helsinki Assembly. Of these, 61 came from North America, 59 from Germany, 58 from Northern Europe, 37 from the small diaspora churches in Europe, and 52 from Latin America, Asia, Africa, and Australia. This last figure shows that an increasing number of churches from the southern hemisphere were joining the LWF and were subsequently represented at the assembly. Especially Bishop David from India, Bishop Fosseus from South Africa, Dr. Lumbantobing from Indonesia (not only as speaker), and Bishop Moshi from Tanzania played important roles at the assembly.

## The Discussion on Justification

The main attention of the assembly was given to a discussion of the doctrine of justification and the ultimate failure of the final vote on Document 75, "Justification Today." Advance notices had led the delegates—as well as theologians and leaders in wider church circles—to expect that the assembly would issue a solemn statement on the subject. There was obviously considerable disappointment after the final vote, although from the perspective of the history of dogma it may well have turned out to be productive since it meant, on the one hand, that the unfinished task was still to be pursued and, on the other hand, that there remained an openness vis-à-vis other issues such as those in the area of social ethics.

The way in which the theme was developed pointed to the tensions that emerged later. The Third Assembly in Minneapolis had mandated an examination of confessions used by LWF member churches. This was done from Geneva, and the results were published in a volume edited by Vilmos Vajta and Hans Weissgerber, *The Church and the Confessions: The Role of the Confessions in the Life and Doctrine of the Lutheran Churches* (Philadelphia: Fortress Press, 1963). Moreover, the Commission on Theology questioned the relevance of the message of justification, the core of the Lutheran tradition, in the teaching and practice of the churches of the time. Thus, a working program was developed according to which exegetical, historical, and eventually systematic aspects of the doctrine of justification were to be examined. This research was integrated in a preparatory document (Document 3: "On Justification," which was sent in advance to all member churches for comment). The document included a brief analysis and an updated commentary for pastors, a sort of *apologia variata* to articles I–VI of the Augsburg Confession. Throughout, however, it was the main interest of the LWF executive committee to foster the proclamation of the message of justification to people *today* and thus to make it useful to the way the church expresses its faith and life. Clearly, the fact that these various interests did not all carry the same weight contributed to the ultimate deadlock at the assembly.

Substantially, what the preparations and the assembly were about was to establish the relationship between justification and experience. During the Reformation, the message of justification was directly connected to what people had experienced; this is different today, and thus experience had to be envisaged anew. Attempts to do so were made—or not made—in different contexts:

- In order for the assembly to proclaim the presence of the risen one, the executive committee, in 1961, decided on "Christ Today" as its theme. At the same time, the theme indicates that the doctrine of justification is only one way to formulate the message of Christ.
- At the same meeting, key words from Ephesians were chosen to guide the main lectures and the Bible studies at the assembly. The ecclesiology found in this letter was to shed light on the churches' experiences with justification.
- The Commission on Theology concentrated especially on the experience of the last judgment, the eschatological horizon. Because of manifold experiences of failure people today have to be faced with God's judgment before they can hear the good news of the gospel; for this reason law and judgment need to be preached first and foremost. At the assembly's discussions of the final document, reservations of this type were heard time and again. Much less emphasis was placed on the fact that according to Luther a Christian can only properly realize his or her guilt on the basis of forgiveness.
- Today, human beings justify themselves before ever-changing forums, no longer before God's forum. Since this, along with the reflections on the issue of judgment, was understood merely as a history of decline, the chance to apply the idea of justification from grace alone to other constraints and forums human beings are confronted with was ruined. This path was taken after the Evian Assembly.
- The belief that God alone acts in matters of salvation and the doctrine of the bondage of the will, which for Luther were at the center of the doctrine of justification, played only a marginal role at the assembly. Instead, issues were treated in a somewhat pietistic tradition and included the following: the decision to believe, the acceptance of justification and baptism, and the distinction between the objective (God acts in Christ) and the subjective aspects (we must accept this) of justification. It quite obviously seemed easier in this way to express justification's relationship to experience. Other voices were raised too, but it never became entirely clear that a basic theological controversy should have been settled here. Rather, the final statement tends to omit these questions.
- "The experience of justification" was the ulterior theme of the main lectures: Professor Gloege of Germany ("Grace for the World") addressed experience in the relation of faith to the world; in the discussion he was immediately told that the individual is the recipient of justification. Dr. Brattgård of Sweden ("Faith Without Works?") lodged experience in the fruits of faith. Dr. Waris, professor for Social Politics in Helsinki ("Divided Humanity—United in Christ"), described the contemporary societal situation (South–North and East–West oppositions, different church constitutions) and thus identified the conditions in which faith today must grow and prove its worth. Finally, Professor Lumbantobing of Indonesia ("The New Song of Praise") spoke about the many forms faith can take, especially in the

context of his Batak church. All these lectures addressed the relation of justification to experience; however, the debate remained either too abstract or too specialized for the transition to "people of today" to be achieved.

A final contribution had been prepared prior to the assembly and was largely rewritten following the deliberations in the groups, the plenary, and a hearing. Again, objections were made during the final debate so that, after voting on several proposed amendments, the document was finally referred back to the Commission on Theology for further work. The Commission on Theology then published it with only minor revisions in August 1964 (Supplement to *Lutheran World* No. 1, 1965). The reasons for the failure have partly already been mentioned: (1) The genre and objective of the document were not clear enough. It should have accurately described the Lutheran doctrine of justification while at the same time informing ordinary people about the Protestant faith. Both tasks are legitimate but cannot be performed on the same linguistic level. (2) The tension that had been clearly visible during preparations was expressed in the many questions that were raised as to whom the document was addressed to—questions that were never agreed on. (3) Theological reasons for the failure included the fact that the relation between justification and experience was not pursued in several areas but rather the document concentrated only on the aspect of judgment. In addition, Luther's belief that God alone acts in matters of salvation was not really considered. (4) In spite of the fact that the document was only to be "received" as a report on the work in the discussion groups, it would have been perceived publicly as a solemn declaration of the Lutheran churches on justification. This was rightly mentioned in the discussions. Thus, the conference logistics somewhat got out of kilter, which meant that the document was referred back to the Commission on Theology and publication was given up temporarily.

After the assembly vote it was emphasized that all Lutheran churches agreed in their adherence to the Lutheran confession even though the formulation of a common theological statement had not been possible.

Finally, a short greeting was adopted in the last plenary meeting. Rather than asking, How can I find a gracious God? people today are asking the more radical, fundamental question, Where is God? This formulation was often criticized, even at the assembly itself. What is more important is that here a new formulation of the message of justification was attempted in the context of the question of meaning. The preparations never pursued this approach.

## Other Decisions

The discussion on justification was an important part of the assembly, but it remained merely a part. The reports of the different commissions and committees were received and discussed in the sections and in the plenary; new mandates were formulated. The reports on the establishment of Radio Voice of the Gospel in Addis Ababa planned by the LWF since 1958 aroused public interest. The station was inaugurated with a solemn celebration in February 1963, an initiative emphatically welcomed by the assembly.

Moreover, a minor constitutional amendment was decided on. The fifth main lecture, by Professor Nelson, church historian at St. Paul, Minnesota ("The One Church and the Lutheran Churches"), dealt with this. Reflections on the nature of the LWF in connection with more "ecclesial density" were not pursued; the wording remained: "The Lutheran World Federation is a free association of Lutheran churches." More importantly, proposals had been presented on a reform of the structure and working style of the LWF. It had been suggested that the Committee on Latin America, the Committee on Student Work, the Commission on International Affairs, the Commission on Inner Missions and the Committee on Women's Work within the Commission on Stewardship be dissolved and the work done in different structures (e.g., in pre-assemblies and in the Commission on World Service). Eventually, the new executive committee was mandated by the assembly to proceed to these changes in the institutional framework of the LWF.

Finally, an important decision was made when the Lutheran Foundation for Inter-Confessional Research was established. Within the framework of a scholarly institute, research professors were to bring Lutheran positions into conversation with other voices from the ecumenical movement. A special committee had been established to prepare for this foundation; some preliminary research jobs had already been commissioned. The assembly decided on the establishment of this foundation that later was to become the Institute for Ecumenical Research in Strasbourg.

**Bibliographical Notes** _____

*Preparatory Lectures*

*Lutheran World* 8/1–2 (June 1961).
*Lutheran World* 9/3 (July 1962).

Baur, Jörg. "Zur Vermittelbarkeit der reformatorischen Rechtfertigungslehre: Noch einmal: Helsinki 1963 und die Folgen." *Tragende Traditionen: Festschrift für Martin Seils zum 65 Geburtstag,* edited by Annegret Freund, Udo Kern, and Aleksander Radler. Frankfurt/Main, 1992.
Brandt, Reinhard. *Die ermöglichte Freiheit: Sprachkritische Rekonstruktion der Lehre vom unfreien Willen.* Hanover, 1992.
Brunner, Peter. *"Rechtfertigung" heute: Versuch einer dogmatischen Paraklese. Lutherische Monatshefte* 1 (1962): 106–16.
*Justification Today—Studies and Reports.* Edited by the Commission and Department of Theology, LWF = Supplement to *Lutheran World* No. 1, 1965. Includes Jörg Rothermundt, *Discussion on Justification 1958–1963.*
*Proceedings,* Helsinki.
Wilkens, Erwin, ed. *Helsinki 1963: Beiträge zum theologischen Gespräch des Lutherischen Weltbundes.* Berlin/Hamburg, 1964.

45. A solemn celebration of the Eucharist was held daily during the Helsinki Assembly of 1963 in that city's cathedral of the Evangelical Lutheran Church of Finland.

# EVIAN 1970

## The Fifth Assembly
## of the Lutheran World Federation

The Fifth Assembly of the Lutheran World Federation, held in July 1970 in Evian, France (near Geneva), had a greater impact on the development of the Federation than any previous or subsequent assembly (see chapter 2 above, pp. 59ff.). The key issues raised were the following: a theological reconsideration of the relationship between the nature of the church and social ethics, notably human rights; the relationship between North and South and between Eastern and Western Europe; the nature and influence of an assembly.

Each one of these issues became a focal point during the period leading up to the assembly. This turned into a highly dramatic journey, an odyssey that captured the attention not only of the LWF but also of the media, and it is therefore necessary to describe in some detail the background before turning to the assembly itself.

### Background

The first four assemblies had been hosted by member churches in the so-called First World. After the Helsinki Assembly it was felt that the time had come to hold the next assembly in a different context. At its meeting in 1964 the LWF Executive Committee discussed Vienna or Addis Ababa as possible venues for the next assembly. The following year the committee resolved that the invitations from the Austrian and the (East) German National Committees be gratefully received and that a final decision be taken following further investigations. Furthermore, it was decided that the theme of the assembly would be "Sent into the World."

At a preparatory meeting in East Berlin in March 1966, LWF president Schiotz and general secretary André Appel met with German Democratic Republic state secretary for church affairs, Hans Seigewasser, who orally confirmed that the assembly could be held at Weimar (LWF Archives, Geneva, AS Vth, Evian, I Arrangements A. Site). In turn, a delegation representing the GDR authorities for church affairs was invited to visit Geneva in May of the same year. The LWF's main aim was to prepare the way for a stronger, global

Author: *Jens Holger Schjørring, Aarhus, Denmark*

46. A youth delegate to the Evian Assembly of 1970, Carl-Henric Grenholm of
Sweden, addresses the plenary. Seated are the Rev. Stanley Tung and Miss
Sophia Huang, both of Taiwan.

participation of the GDR Lutheran churches. During the negotiations several
other sensitive issues were raised and the GDR delegation indicated that it
rejected the West German government's claim to be the only proper legal German authority. It would, moreover, not tolerate any form of opposition and
would not hesitate to take firm action.

The LWF's delegation addressed a number of issues, essentially precondi-
tions, that would have to be met if the Federation were to make further
arrangements for holding the assembly on East German soil. GDR's import
restrictions on ecumenical literature were mentioned, for example the fact
that the GDR authorities allowed no more than twenty-two copies of
*Lutheran World* (= *Lutherische Rundschau*) to be imported for general distribution. Moreover, ways were sought to enable GDR churches to participate in
interchurch aid projects, including projects in the Third World.

Despite several points of disagreement both sides considered it be realistic
to pursue plans for holding the assembly at Weimar. Hence, Hans Seigewasser's letter dated July 14, 1966, informing Appel that plans would have to
be canceled came as a considerable surprise. Seigewasser put the blame
entirely upon the West German government.

> You know full well, Mr. General Secretary, that the *Bundestag* in Bonn has
> passed legislation which violates all norms in international law, for it extends

the jurisdiction of the Bonn state to citizens of the German Democratic Republic and even to persons who lived within the borders of the *Reich* as they existed in 1937. In view of such an obstinate and dangerous attitude of the Bonn government, which is supported by the West German church leadership, complications and difficulties will be inevitable at the Fifth Assembly of the LWF and this is something which nobody wishes to happen.

This obviously delayed the work of the planning committee. In view of the fact that the WCC's assembly had been postponed to 1968, it was decided to defer the assembly to either 1969 or even 1970. Cancellation of the plans to go to Weimar constituted a serious setback in the LWF's comprehensive strategy to ensure a more substantial participation from the churches behind the iron curtain, and to give these churches as much support and sympathy as possible. Paradoxically, the outcome turned out to be contrary to what one might have expected. It was thought important to define for the LWF a strategy that reached beyond a rigid cold-war attitude. Reaching ad hoc agreements with the authorities through silent diplomacy became a priority that was enacted first and foremost by the LWF Europe secretary, Paul Hansen of Denmark, in a pragmatic course of small steps.

At its meeting in 1967 the executive committee voted to accept the invitation extended by the Evangelical Church of the Lutheran Confession in Brazil to hold the assembly in Porto Alegre in the second half of July 1970. The Lutheran Church in Brazil was founded in 1949 following the merger of four synods. Its president, Ernesto Schlieper, who was influenced by Karl Barth, hoped that hosting the assembly might strengthen his church's identity. At the same time he was determined to encourage a process of assimilation to the Latin American context since his church had until World War II been dominated mainly by German immigrants.

It was also high time that an assembly be convened outside the First World in order for delegates to experience the conditions of life in the South. Members of the Geneva secretariat, including André Appel and Carl Mau, visited Brazil in order to negotiate with the political authorities and the planning committee of the host church. It became obvious that once again obstacles of a purely political nature might cause serious embarrassment.

At the LWF officers' meeting in January 1967 the LWF Press Service presented a report on Latin America, including documentation on political incidents affecting the lives of the local churches. Whereas these could become a stumbling block for church groups from overseas, the decision to go to Brazil remained unquestioned throughout 1969 and was reaffirmed at the officers' meeting that summer. This decision (LWF archives, Geneva, AS Vth. Evian. I. Arrangements. A. Site) was based on reports by both the general secretary and the associate general secretary. Nonetheless, a number of staff and some people in the member churches were stirred up by persistent reports in the media. Uncertainty urged the officers to seek assurance concerning a number of questions, each one of them considered vital for the holding of an assembly: Could they obtain guarantees that visas would be granted to all duly appointed delegates, freedom of speech be respected, and no censorship of press releases sent outside Brazil? Furthermore, plans to move forward should be contingent on further negotiations with the host church and the political authorities in Brazil.

This did not satisfy the growing number of critics from the outside who continued to oppose the plans to go to Porto Alegre. As early as January 1969 the director of the Swedish National Committee reported that two Christian youth organizations there were pressing for a change of venue. Information from Brazil included reports on the murder of Indian tribes, tensions between the Brazilian government and the Roman Catholic Church, the torture of Catholic priests, and lists of political prisoners. Criticism of the determination to stick to Porto Alegre grew stronger during the fall of 1969. Critics included prominent church leaders and theologians, such as Archbishop Martti Simojoki of Finland, Bishop Heinrich Meyer of Lübeck, Germany, and Prof. Mikko Juva of Helsinki, Finland.

Heated discussions continued into 1970. Protests became even stronger when Pastor Guido Tornquist, representing the planning committee of the host church, sent a letter to Carl Mau on March 16 which included a list of guests of honor and a draft invitation (in Portuguese) to State President Medici. This step was seen as unnecessary capitulation to the Brazilian government's repressive policies. The insistence on the inviolability of human rights and a statement of solidarity with those Roman Catholic brothers who had courageously resisted the authorities were regarded as being the only responsible countermove. This view gained ground first and foremost in Western Europe and North America, but to some extent also elsewhere. The fact that the critics were seen and heard in the media proved to be decisive. Those who remained loyal to earlier decisions were forced into a position of having to apologize or remaining silent.

Yet the officers reaffirmed the decision to go to Porto Alegre when they met on May 21, 1970. Adding to a statement on the nature of the church and its obligation to address specific challenges in the various contexts they declared,

> When accepting the invitation of the host church to hold its Assembly in Brazil, the LWF was mindful that it would have to include in the discussion of the Assembly the Latin American and Brazilian as well as the world context with its human, social, religious and political components. We, the Officers express the hope, that the Assembly participants will come with the openness which is derived from the freedom given in faith to respond to the challenges of the situation. We have been assured that entry will be granted to all participants, and that the Assembly may freely express itself. Since they are coming from various backgrounds with differing and sometimes limited information, it is of utmost importance that the Assembly give its witness in dialogue with the host church and other churches in Brazil. We are determined that the shape of the program be strictly that of a working assembly." (LWF Archives, Geneva, AS Vth. Evian. I Arrangements. A. Site)

With the expression "a working assembly" one wanted to avoid the impression of submitting to the totalitarian attitude of the Brazilian government. Quite clearly, this had become an emergency situation. One of the main rea-

sons for choosing Latin America as a venue for the assembly was for visitors
to experience the local context and thus to take seriously the missionary character of the global cooperation of Lutheran churches, as attested to in the
assembly theme "Sent into the World."

In yet another attempt to settle the differences of opinion, the general secretary went to Brazil seeking to interpret the officers' resolution. The host
church's representatives asked for understanding regarding the invitation
extended to the state president, whom they did not expect to make a political
speech. In fact, they assumed that President Medici would not come at all, but
believed that inviting the president was a matter of courtesy and a sign of
national solidarity.

In an atmosphere of tension and hectic activity a number of mistakes were
made. For instance, Geneva staff erroneously attributed a document supporting President Medici's fight against Communism to the church's newly
elected president, Karl Gottschald. Gottschald had submitted a number of controversial documents to Geneva in order to illustrate the complex situation
prevailing in his country. No less ironic was the fact that Geneva only learned
about the "Curitiba Declaration" drafted by the Lutheran theological faculty
at Sao Leopoldo (May 1970) and subsequently adopted by the church synod in
October 1970, which was directed against Brazil's military government
(quoted in LWF Report 1–2, Sept. 1978, pp. 40) when it was already too late. It
needs to be recorded that once it became clear that Medici's presence at the
assembly might not be appreciated, even cause difficulties, Gottschald personally asked him not to attend, to which Medici agreed.

In light of the fact that, on the one hand, the flood of protests from member
churches, mainly in the so-called First World, was matched, on the other hand,
by the seemingly unyielding determination of the LWF leadership to hold the
assembly in Brazil, it needs to be asked, What suddenly provoked the LWF
leadership to change its mind? It would be far too superficial to understand this
exclusively as a result of media pressure, although it must be admitted that the
press increasingly became a determining factor with arguments that were at
times reasonable and at other times purely sensationalistic.

The following factors were decisive when the general secretary resolved to
change the venue, after having consulted a group of advisors in Geneva and
after lengthy discussions with President Schiotz in Minneapolis:

  a. anxiety, because a considerable number of delegates (individuals and
     groups) had withdrawn from participation.
  b. concern to express solidarity with those church groups in Latin America,
     mainly Roman Catholic, that struggled against military dictatorship,
     economic injustice, and violations of human rights. At least some of the
     leaders in the host church were suspected of silently bowing down to the
     political authorities.
  c. fear that political issues might predominate and attention be drawn away
     from the real points on the agenda, if not cause estrangement or even a
     split among the delegates.
  d. considerations regarding the role of the church facing continuous viola-
     tions of church freedom and basic human rights.

Point (d) indicates the importance attributed to such deliberations. So does the resolution on human rights which was to become one of the most important products of the Fifth Assembly.

A group of experts, namely, Professor Mikko Juva of Finland, Professors Heinz Eduard Tödt and Trutz Rendtorff of West Germany, Dr. William Lazareth of the United States, Dr. Kunchala Rajaratnam of India, and Dr. Ivar Asheim representing the Geneva secretariat was convened to incorporate the consequences to be drawn from the discussion about venue into the addresses by the president and the general secretary. With its statement of June 18 the group presented to President Schiotz background material for his keynote address. According to the statement,

> a wound has broken up which is in fact the symptom of a deep-going crisis from which no nation or part of the world is exempted. The issue is an increasing number of violations of human rights. But the human rights question should not be viewed in an abstract idealistic way. It has to be seen in the wider context of the growing discrepancy between privileged and underprivileged classes and nations and as something which has its roots in the lack of human solidarity on the part of the privileged and in the lack of possibilities for creative participation on the part of the poor and oppressed. (LWF Archives, Geneva, TH I 1, Assembly/Helsinki. Correspondence 1969–1970).

It continues,

> we discovered that we already were living the assembly theme, we *were* involved in the problems of today's world. It is an illusion to think that the church can isolate itself from the world on the basis of a rigid separation of e.g. religion and politics. We welcome this discovery, because it leads us to discover aspects of the church's task in the world that we perhaps have tended to neglect. It belongs to the very nature of the church as sent to be involved in the world's problems. The basic question to be answered in the light of a biblical understanding of the church's mission then is not *whether*, but *how* to participate in the life of society. (ibid.; cf. *Christ and Humanity: A Workshop in Christian Social Ethics*, ed. Ivar Asheim [Philadelphia: Fortress Press, 1970])

Yet the group strictly avoided a politicizing of the gospel. It was the church's task "not to give directives, but to give direction." Notwithstanding such concessions to the traditional Lutheran distinction between the two kingdoms, the determination to point the Lutheran churches toward a process of reconsideration was clearly expressed: "There are situations when the church as a corporate body, perhaps through organizations like the LWF, if it will be true to its responsibility, *has* to speak out. Such a situation we have in today's increasing violation of elementary human rights" (ibid.).

There is an obvious continuity between this statement and the discussion in the seventies on *status confessionis*. It needs to be added that the group took great pains to go beyond the question of relocation as a dividing point in order to face the real challenge, namely, the task of coming to a united witness along the lines mentioned. Therefore the group concluded, "if we only agree on the necessity of this witness it does not matter that on other points the participants have a different judgment as to whether the disputed action in the complex situation of Porto Alegre was adequate. The point is that in discussing our disagreements (which may be unavoidable) we should not forget that witness which unites us!" (ibid.).

The host church felt very differently about the question of relocation. Many felt deceived; others were outraged by the decision taken by fellow Lutherans, including the leading members of staff and executive bodies. The council of the Evangelical Church of the Lutheran Confession in Brazil issued a statement, to be presented to the assembly delegates, claiming to have given consistent and correct information to the general secretariat on all issues related to assembly preparations. One-sided press reports were regarded as having been the main reason for the sudden cancellation. Moreover, the council felt it to be incomprehensible and unacceptable that responsible church leaders and theologians had yielded to such reports, without having carefully consulted the host church and local experts. Furthermore, the council raised basic questions concerning the nature of an assembly and the relationship between an international, confessional body of churches on the one hand and a complicated political context on the other:

> Is it imperative that certain political conditions must be met before a church can give its witness in a particular place? Does not the Assembly of the LWF, through the change of site, get just the political character, which it should not have? The Assembly of the LWF became an instrument of political tendencies at the moment in which the question regarding the location was isolated from the watchword 'Sent into the World', and decided in accordance with the laws of political expediency. In our opinion, Christian witness cannot be given in avoiding political and human conflicts, even when this is meant to be a sign or when it happens out of tactical reasons. (Statement, dated July 1970, printed in *Proceedings*, Evian, pp. 124f.)

The Lutheran Church in Brazil expressed its profound regret. While the lack of trust on the part of other churches prevented it from being represented in Evian as if nothing had happened, it did not merely want to dwell on the injustice to which it had been subjected.

> It follows from what has been said that our church, toward which insufficient trust has been extended, will not be represented at Evian in the way foreseen. Too much trust has been gambled away for us to be able to justify before our congregations, before the other churches in Brazil, and before the public, the appearance as though nothing had happened. Since we are of the opinion that the church must also bear tensions and human mistakes, from which we do not seek to absolve ourselves herewith, we are not withdrawing from the work. Christian cooperation must be possible also in times of inner-church crises. We believe that the LWF must now become clear about what is its actual task and which working methods correspond to this task. (ibid.)

The final decision of the LWF leadership to hold the Fifth Assembly in Evian, France, a spa on the shores of Lake Geneva, was made at extremely short notice. The Geneva staff endured extraordinary pressure in order to ensure that the assembly could take place only five weeks after the decision to relocate had been taken. The fact that there was no local host church added a special touch to the assembly. Services were held in the local Roman Catholic parish church which in itself became a sign of ecumenical progress, an important legacy of the assembly.

### Evian 1970

| | |
|---|---|
| Dates: | July 14–24, 1970 |
| Location: | Evian, France |
| Theme: | "Sent into the World" |
| Number of participants: | 216 voting delegates, 164 visitors, advisors, and consultants |
| Presidents: | Dr. Fredrik A. Schiotz, United States |
| | Professor Mikko Juva of Finland was elected LWF president on July 22, 1970 |
| General Secretary: | Dr. André Appel, France |
| Main Decisions: | Adoption of a new LWF structure; resolution on human rights; recommendation of pulpit and altar fellowship between LWF member churches |
| Principal Addresses: | Sermon at the Opening Service of Holy Communion |
| | *Professor Marc Lienhard, France* |
| | Opening Address |
| | *Dr. Fredrik A. Schiotz, United States* |
| | "Creative Discipleship in the Contemporary World Crisis" |
| | *Prof. Heinz-Eduard Tödt, Germany (FRG)* |
| | "Sent into the World" |
| | *Johannes Cardinal Willebrands, the Vatican* |
| | "The Response of the Lutheran Churches to the Roman Catholic Church and Theology today" |
| | *Professor Kent S. Knutson, United States* |

### Participants and Program

The Fifth Assembly, conceived as a "compact" assembly, became even more compact than originally intended. There were 216 delegates in total; because of disappointment at the change in venues among Latin American delegates, only eleven turned up. More than half of the delegates, 113, came from Europe—yet another paradox, since this assembly had been intended as the breakthrough for the churches from the South. 164 official visitors, advisors, and observer-consultants were registered in addition to staff and press.

It was a young assembly. Thirty of the delegates were between eighteen and twenty-five years old. The executive committee had decided to invite the member churches to send youth representatives to a preassembly youth conference, held in a neighboring resort, Thonon-les-Bains, France. The conference appointed thirty delegates to the assembly, who were granted full voting rights. This growing involvement of youth must be seen in its proper historical context. At the WCC's assembly in 1968 in Uppsala, youth representatives had been a decisive factor in the emphasis on human rights and the active support of the oppressed and underprivileged. Against this background it was not surprising that the youth delegates came up with a dynamic strategy at their preassembly meeting. They critically examined the preparatory studies, formulated radical alternatives, and agreed upon their strategy when meeting with the "establishment." These youth delegates made their presence felt right from the very first session demanding changes in the rules of procedure to avoid what they did not hesitate to call "manipulation." They were particularly critical of the procedure of having only one list from which to nominate candidates for the LWF Executive Committee. Undoubtedly their offensive in part explains why the average age of members of the executive committee went down from fifty-eight to fifty-one.

When in his opening address the president, Fredrik Schiotz, referring to the situation in Brazil, mentioned that there were also some positive sides to the regime, all youth delegates rose in protest, wearing black mourning bands around their arms. What is more, they stuck to their views and defended their positions as they went into committees and discussion groups.

It is true that the assembly program had been conceived along traditional lines, the formula tested at all previous major ecumenical occasions: worship, main addresses, division of the delegates into three main sections supplemented by a multitude of subgroups that generated reports, resolutions, and recommendations. In addition, a number of open hearings were scheduled during which specific aspects of the LWF's activities were presented and discussed. During the sessions it became absolutely clear that the traditional format was considered unsatisfactory. Other critics joined the outspoken youth, and frustration was openly vented in the discussion groups. It was felt that there was too little time for serious, in-depth debate as a result of which some of the highly controversial issues could not be resolved to the satisfaction of the participants.

An atmosphere of renewal, if not subversion, could be sensed in the way in which the preparatory material was being treated. Regardless of its qualities, it was used only to a limited extent. One of the sections agreed at the opening session to disregard the material, including a questionnaire, that had been produced by staff. When the secretaries presented their draft report, many participants protested, claiming that the report did not cover the discussion adequately. On such grounds one of the reports was totally rejected, and a new text had to be produced in a great hurry.

It should be noted though, that when it came to scrutinizing the LWF's practice and policies the open hearings were more fruitful. The youth delegates' concerns were registered most notably when they managed to obtain approval for an extra open hearing on the nomination procedure.

## Main Addresses

The first keynote address, "Creative Discipleship in the Contemporary World Crisis," was by Professor Heinz-Eduard Tödt of Heidelberg, West Germany. His starting point was the spreading of "a new wave of crisis consciousness" in the world. He referred to the support of the United Nations decade of partnership in world development, adding that results had been far from encouraging. The gross national product in the developing countries had stagnated. While the world was witnessing a number of staggering technological triumphs such as the expedition to the moon, for which hundreds and thousands of brains and hands had been made available, sufficient means were lacking when it came to making the face of the earth more human, to cleaning up slums, to providing a fair share of food for the undernourished masses, or modern education and social progress.

Against this background Professor Tödt questioned the old theological conclusion that this contradiction is an expression of human sin, thereby assuming that its evil consequences cannot be eliminated. He continued to review the Lutheran teaching on true humanity, mentioning in some detail Luther's interpretation of the two kingdoms. Without a doubt Tödt's perspective was shaped by his reliance on Dietrich Bonhoeffer, the catalyst for a Lutheran reinterpretation of social ethics. Tödt's thesis became quite clear as he advocated that the churches must accept a shared responsibility for the sciences, by seeking to bring them into line with human objectives. Moreover, he underlined another important sentiment, which

> has often received too little attention in the Lutheranism of the twentieth century. It concerns the dignity of man. . . . What is needed is a new sensitivity to that which we as Christians owe to those who suffer from discrimination. We know that the bread necessary for the overcoming of hunger must be provided. But do we know with the same urgency and concreteness that some members of the family of man hunger for something other than bread and nourishment, for actual equality, for actual participation in the basic decisions concerning life and humanity, for respect which protects them from being ruled over and controlled by others, ourselves included? They hunger simply for a real recognition of their human dignity. Only where this hunger is satisfied does the brotherhood before God, to which we have all been called, truly begin. (*Proceedings*, Evian, pp. 41f.)

There was a close connection between the themes of the next two lectures, which addressed the consequences of the Second Vatican Council for the relationship between the Lutheran and the Roman Catholic Church. The sixties had witnessed numerous initiatives pointing in one and the same direction: ecumenical dialogue and fellowship (see chapter 7 above). The bilateral dialogues were certainly a significant part of this development. The establishment of the Strasbourg Institute for Ecumenical Research had been a timely initiative, giving the Lutheran churches the scholarly expertise required to provide a solid theological basis for the dialogues. In addition, many of the delegates had experienced specific signs of ecumenical openness and fellowship at the regional and local levels. These impressions were reaffirmed at the opening of the assembly, when the opening worship was held in the local Roman Catholic church in Evian, and later, upon the invitation of the local church leadership, some of the discussion groups met in Catholic schools. It was against this backdrop that delegates listened to the lectures by Johannes Cardinal Willebrands, newly appointed leader of the Vatican Secretariat for Promoting Christian Unity and Professor Kent Knutson of the United States.

Willebrands's point of departure was the assembly theme, "Sent into the World." Comparing the preparatory material and the documents produced in the context of the recent Second Vatican Council he noticed clear similarities on important issues. In each case the basic thrust was the understanding that "Sent into the World" implied being sent into the world of *today*, addressing the world as it is, the women and men of today, with their dignity, quest, and demand for freedom. Referring to the phrase Vatican II had added to the opening theme "so that the world may be converted to the gospel," Willebrands concluded that the churches had not been sent into the world empty-handed.

Willebrands posed the crucial question whether the recognition of this common point of departure implied that the Roman Catholic Church and the Lutheran World Federation understood their mission in the same manner and as being similarly based. Referring to the challenge of achieving progress in ecumenical relations he stated that "450 years ago, our forefathers thought they had to separate in the name of the true gospel. Today we believe and hope to be able to overcome this separation" (ibid., pp. 55f.).

Willebrands gave a positive evaluation of Martin Luther, referring to him "as a deeply religious man who with honesty and dedication sought for the message of the gospel." He admitted that the Second Vatican Council had recognized concerns first articulated by Martin Luther. As a result of this reconsideration, overdue for centuries, many aspects of Christian faith and life could now find better expression. He pointed to Luther's insisting on the primacy of "faith" as being a key example of Luther's importance as a teacher for the church universal. Furthermore, he referred to the opinion of prominent Catholic and Protestant theologians that according to Luther "faith" should by no means be perceived as excluding either works, love, or hope. "One may well say, and with much good reason, that Luther's concept of faith, when taken in its full meaning, might not really mean anything other than what we designate by the word love in the Catholic Church" (ibid., pp. 63f.). When comparing the achievements of the Vatican Council and the growing ecumenical awareness of Martin Luther's legacy, Willebrands rejoiced in the points of agreement already reached. Nevertheless, he had to acknowledge that there were still areas of disagreement: "regarding the ministry, the authority, the infallibility, the position of the Pope, and the general questions of the ecclesial structures. I am also thinking of the position occupied by the Virgin Mary, Mother of God, in the mystery of Christ and the church" (ibid., p. 62). Willebrands did not want to conclude with the dividing points of doctrine. On the contrary, he made no secret of his ardent desire to present an impulse for promoting dialogue and unity: "If together we can give form to the Christian mission in the world, then we will also find in this mission a forceful impetus towards our full unity in Christ" (ibid., p. 65).

In his presentation of a Lutheran position, Professor Kent Knutson declared that the Vatican Council "constituted a challenge to the Lutheran church unprecedented in our history" (ibid., p. 45). He interpreted the outcome of the council as being the end of the Counter-reformation and the beginning of a new era involving the Roman Catholic Church's participation in the quest for the reconciliation of all churches. Knutson presented a very positive evaluation of some of the key statements by the Vatican Council, especially those dealing with the classic question regarding the relationship between scripture and tradition. He could not refrain, however, from remarking that "the meaning of tradition is not as clear to us." Even more far-reaching was his plea that the Roman Catholic Church undertake the next step, namely, the "full recognition that we are a true church" (ibid., p.46). Concluding his presentation, Knutson expressed the hope that a future ecumenical world assembly would include the Roman Catholic Church, "whose awakening to renewal and mission challenges us all with its breadth and intensity" (ibid., p. 53). Therefore a new great council could not be "Catholic" or "Lutheran," which was exactly the type of Ecumenical Council Martin Luther had hoped for. (At a press conference afterwards Knutson denied that his concluding remarks were meant as a serious proposal.)

## Reports and Recommendations

Considerable difficulties and disagreements had cropped up during the preparation and adoption of the assembly reports, notably regarding the issues presented for discussion, as well as procedures, and the basic structure of the Federation.

Major difficulties had arisen in the first section dealing with the theme "Sent with the Gospel." The report emphasized that, because of serious time constraints, the "wide diversity of issues," and differences of opinion among the participants, it had been a most arduous process to reach some kind of conclusion. The report sought to make virtue of necessity: "Many of us have entered into the discussions in the hope that a rather broad consensus would be reached. It has been necessary for us first to face our differences and to recognize that to strive for a false consensus would be wrong. We must recognize that the differences among us may be a gift of the Holy Spirit. A frank recognition of these differences may eventually become an enrichment of our life together" (ibid., p. 66).

In addition to this obvious disappointment there was a certain anxiety that by addressing social ethics the theological accent of the Federation might become obscured. On the initiative of Bishop Hans-Otto Wölber of Germany a special theological statement was therefore prepared and passed by the assembly with the intention of avoiding the impression that political measures were to be regarded as the sole means of addressing social misery and the needs of modern society. A more traditional theological note on human nature was added, underlining sin, conversion, and a new direction through Christ's forgiveness.

> [W]e wish to address ourselves not only to the individual's dependence on external structures, but also to the chaos within the structure of his own self. Back of all the perplexities lie not only, e.g., rapid and unmastered changes in the world or our inability to achieve better relations. Back of them lies also human greed, hunger for power and self-justification. . . . [W]e must not only understand our world better—we must undergo a change. We not only need a new consciousness, we need a transformation of our nature and our will. . . . We are convinced that back of our misery

there is that catastrophe in our relation to God, robbing us of all criteria for human existence and of any opportunity for a new spirit. (ibid., pp. 155f.)

Concern about the restructuring of the Federation, the impact of the relocations within the secretariat, the challenges arising from the redefinition of the balance between the "four pillars," as well as the relationship between South and North (see chapters 1 and 2 above), subtly influenced the discussions in section 1.

The heated discussion about the newly defined Department of Church Cooperation focused on the question whether the word "mission" should or should not be retained in the name (see pp. 154ff. above). This issue was merely the tip of the iceberg. Delegates were frustrated above all because they felt that not enough time had been allowed for an exhaustive treatment of the general perspectives. The plenary finally adopted the new wording of Department of and Commission on "Church Cooperation" (with 115 votes for and 58 against).

Similarly, the time allocated for plenary discussion on the two keynote addresses dealing with relationships to the Roman Catholic Church was insufficient. This also applied to section 2, which dealt specifically with ecumenical commitment. A special committee headed by Professor Knutson was appointed to prepare a statement. The first version of the text was criticized because it paid too little attention to the difficulties encountered when establishing a new ecumenical partnership at the local level. In its final form the statement recognized Cardinal Willebrands's lecture as "a unique and important step toward a deeper and more far-reaching understanding between our churches." At the same time it pointed out that the member churches must be prepared to "acknowledge that the judgment of the Reformers upon the Roman Catholic Church and its theology was not entirely free of polemical distortions, which in part have been perpetuated to the present day" (ibid., p. 156).

Section 2, "Ecumenical Commitment," included a paragraph entitled "What is Necessary for Christian Unity?" In the search for unity "we must not insist upon uniformity in theological formulations and in practice but use the variations rooted in the Scriptures to help bring together divided groups of people in the world into 'one body with many members'" (ibid., pp. 73f.). It was crucial for the subsequent development of the Federation that the member churches were reminded that "the goal of altar and pulpit fellowship should always be kept in mind" (ibid., p. 74).

The discussions in section 3, "Responsible Participation in Today's Society," were no exception. Once again, the lack of time was deplored, and—no less significantly—the deep divisions among the delegates due to different backgrounds and political convictions became very obvious. It was commonplace to urge the delegates and the member churches to participate in the development of a more just and humane society. The report succeeded in giving at least a few specific examples of general concern such as "the horrendous system of apartheid and colonialism as it exists in Southern Africa, or the continuing racial tension in the United States, or the discrimination against migrant laborers in Switzerland" (ibid., p. 93). These words of protest and warning were part of the extensive treatment of economic justice and human rights. Furthermore, there were discussions both of education as the only tenable way of creating new structures in society and of "Servanthood and Peace." The discussions ran into insurmountable difficulties when some of the delegates wanted to add further specific examples of human rights violations, such as the persecution of the Jewish people in the Soviet Union, or the situation of the churches in the German Democratic Republic. Finally, the most significant decision was the adoption of a strong resolution on human rights. At the same time this issue caused deeper wounds than any other theme of the assembly primarily because Brazil was the only specific example used to illustrate the violation of human rights. After several exhausting sessions, the resolution was adopted, to the disappointment of those delegates from Latin America who had decided to attend.

## Elections

The fact that the procedures of nomination and election were passionately contested, not only by the youth delegates, is a part of the historical setting of the Fifth Assembly. The nominations committee had to give way and propose more candidates for election than had been customary at previous assemblies. After a lengthy discussion, two candidates were nominated for election to the presidency, Bishop Fridtjov Birkeli of Norway and Professor Mikko Juva of Finland. Professor Juva was elected with 148 votes (Bishop Birkeli, 59 votes). A second ballot was necessary to fill all the posts on the LWF Executive Committee.

## Interpretation and Evaluation

The Fifth Assembly is a milestone in the history of the Lutheran World Federation. In some respects it was the culmination of what had been implicit in the first decades; in others it provided a new direction by introducing a number of concerns that were to become key issues, such as the inclusive participation of churches from the southern hemisphere, of women and of youth (see chapter 8 above), and a new focus on social ethics and human rights. The relationship between Lutheran identity in the more traditional sense and new concerns became evident also in other respects, such as the strong emphasis on ecumenical relations and the search for church unity. This was true also with regard to internal unity among Lutheran churches, the striving toward full altar and pulpit fellowship, as well as fellowship with other Christian churches at the local, national, and global levels. One of the paradoxical overtones of the Fifth Assembly was the growing number of resolutions. Not only were they numerous and sometimes highly controversial, but they also led to a conflict of interests. They reflected the endeavors and hopes of the delegates and presupposed an approval of increased staff and programs. In fact, the resolutions revealed the failure to formulate priorities, albeit they were meant as formulations of consensus. Hence, the executive committee was left with the unenviable task of being faithful to the assembly's decisions while defining priorities clearly. Seen from this perspective Evian appears in contrasting colors, pointing toward new tasks ahead and revealing a lack of inner clarity.


**Bibliographical Notes** _____

LWF Archives, Geneva.

Hanns Lilje papers, Lutheran Church Archives, Hanover.

Oral and written information submitted by André Appel, Martin Dreher, and Per Voksø.

*Lutheran World/Lutherische Rundschau.*

LWF Reports 1963–1969; Reports 1970–1977.

*Proceedings,* Evian.

# DAR ES SALAAM 1977

# The Sixth Assembly
# of the Lutheran World Federation

| | |
|---|---|
| Dates: | June 13–25, 1977 |
| Location: | Dar es Salaam, Tanzania |
| Theme: | "In Christ—A New Community" |
| Number of participants: | 250 delegates, 437 advisers, observers, staff, and visitors |
| Presidents: | Dr. Mikko Juva of Finland was the president of the LWF through the assembly. Bishop Josiah Kibira of Tanzania was elected the new president. |
| General Secretary: | Dr. Carl H. Mau, Jr., United States |
| Main decision: | Statement on "Southern Africa: Confessional Integrity," which declared that the racial separation of the church in compliance with apartheid in Southern Africa constitutes a *status confessionis*. |
| Other major issues: | Recognition of women as equals to men at all levels of the life of the church; endorsement of "reconciled diversity" as the lead theme of the ecumenical engagement of Lutherans; the study of "root causes" of social and economic injustice. |
| Principal addresses: | "In Christ—A New Community" |
| | *Dr. Mikko Juva, Finland* |
| | "The Mission of the Church and its Obligation to Evangelism" |
| | *Bishop Helmut Class, Germany (FRG)* |
| | "The Lutheran Church and the Unity of the Church" |
| | *Bishop Andreas Aarflot, Norway* |
| | "Development and Self-reliance" |
| | *Mr. Nicolaus J. Maro, Tanzania* |

*The First Third-World Assembly*

After the failure to meet in Brazil in 1970 there was much enthusiasm in LWF member churches for having the next assembly in Dar es Salaam and thus for

Author: *Risto Lehtonen, Helsinki, Finland*

the first time in Africa and the Third World. Tanzania was a natural location: the Evangelical Lutheran Church in Tanzania was a large and rapidly expanding member church, well equipped to act as host. Furthermore, in the minds of many, Tanzania had a special position among developing countries because of the moral values that had been accepted as a cornerstone of the country's social and economic development as envisioned by its charismatic president, Julius Nyerere.

The impact of this African context was conspicuous and made the Dar es Salaam Assembly different from earlier LWF world gatherings. It affected both the style and the proceedings. At the very beginning a fresh note was struck by the opening service of Holy Communion held in a large downtown church, with thousands of local Christians participating, and numerous choirs and brass bands assisting. The service lasted more than three hours. Following the service, the whole assembly proceeded—an hour and a half late—to a reception given by President Nyerere which took place undisturbed in a uniquely informal atmosphere in a garden enveloped by the warmth of the tropical evening. The presence of the host church was experienced throughout the assembly as church choirs from different congregations enriched the daily worship and the breaks with spirited Tanzanian musical offerings. The sense of welcome by the Tanzanian church and the local community overwhelmed the international participants and influenced profoundly the mood of the whole assembly.

The context had also many other consequences. Questions about African socialism, one-party systems, and African nationalism were deliberately put aside during the assembly, although a painful political debate erupted when it became known that the delegates from Taiwanese and South Korean churches had not been granted entry visas, contrary to earlier assurances by the authorities. The Tanzanian government acted under the pressure of the mainland Chinese who at that time were building the railway between Tanzania and Zambia. The high-pitched publicity given to the problem by the media effectively torpedoed the efforts made for discreet solutions. All this counterbalanced the euphoria about Africa and the Third World to which the pleasantness of the gathering, including the extensive visitation program to local congregations, tempted enthusiastic first-time visitors.

The site of the assembly was most significant to the African member churches of the LWF. Meeting on their continent was to them a sign of recognition of their churches as full members of the worldwide Lutheran communion. The topics taken up were no longer determined exclusively by the theologians of the North; the issues faced by African churches on their own continent came to the fore.

For most of the participants from outside Africa, meeting in an African context was a new experience. For many of them the Dar es Salaam Assembly proved an eye-opening event that brought them face to face with the dynamism of the host church and made them aware of the rapid expansion of Christianity in large parts of Africa. The context undoubtedly influenced delegates when they elected a Tanzanian the new president of the LWF.

Coming to Africa made a lasting contribution to the LWF as a whole. It was no longer wrapped only in the culture of Northern Europe and North America. It was at home as much in Africa as on any other continent.

## The Host Church

The Evangelical Lutheran Church in Tanzania (ELCT) was, at the time of the assembly, among the largest Lutheran churches on the continent and was also one of the influential members of the Christian Council of Tanzania. By 1977 it had over seven hundred thousand members, close to five hundred ordained pastors and some two thousand congregations. Its work extended beyond the borders of Tanzania to areas in East and Central Africa where Swahili was the lingua franca.

The history of the ELCT goes back to the beginnings of Lutheran mission work in East Africa in the late nineteenth century. The world wars interfered seriously with this mission work and even interrupted the work of the German mission for a while. Consequently, Tanganyika, as the area was called before independence, became one of the territories to which the LWF directed its efforts for "orphaned missions." The number of overseas partners increased and came to include mission agencies from Germany, the United States, and four Nordic countries. Cooperation between the synods and dioceses as well as between their mission partners greatly increased. In 1963 a common structure for the ELCT was formed, uniting the dioceses and synods into one church. From its early days until today the ELCT, including its predecessor units, has manifested a strong indigenous commitment to mission. This is also seen in the steady rise of its membership from 130,000 in 1946 to over two million today. Arranging to receive a large worldwide gathering was a new challenge for the ELCT, which it decided to meet with utmost dedication. Consequently, the experience gained in holding an assembly proved a breakthrough for the ELCT in its assumption of wider responsibilities for international mission and service.

## Participants

Although the number of voting delegates (250) was close to that of the previous assembly at Evian (216), a marked difference could be seen in the overall composition of the gathering. The share of delegates coming from the Third World was now 40 percent, while at Evian it had been 30 percent and at Lund only 8 percent. In addition, the proportion of women delegates increased to close to the targeted 25 percent. The number of youth delegates, however, was less than at Evian and reflected to some extent a backlash against the vocal radicalism of youth who participated in that event.

The absence, as noted, of delegates from Taiwan and South Korea was a major setback in respect to assembly participation. The debate concerning this matter, which was marked even by demands for calling off the assembly, meant that the matter of criteria for assembly sites would continue to be part of future LWF agendas.

## Major Debates and Decisions

The debate on the meaning of confessional integrity in relation to apartheid in Southern Africa and the subsequent *status confessionis* resolution represented the issues for which the Dar es Salaam Assembly is most remembered. The point at issue was quite simple. The Lutheran churches in Southern Africa were divided on the basis of race. While the "black" churches were committed to unity without regard to race, the "white" churches did not welcome black Christians to common worship or to participation in the Sacrament of the Altar. Further, the white churches were at best ambiguous in their attitude toward governmental policies of separate racial development (apartheid). The question was thus raised: Is it possible to accept such racial division without denying the confessional foundation of the church?

What made the debate so heated was, first, the presence of the delegates of the white Lutheran churches of South Africa and Southwest Africa (Namibia) and their attempt to interpret their view and their pleas for time and patience. They were almost alone against the others, who remembered that already the Evian Assembly had debated the same issue and voted on a clear resolution rejecting racial division at the Communion table. There was a mounting impatience about the implementation of the Evian statement, but after seven years none was in sight. A second element concerned the term *status confessionis*, which some feared could afterwards be too easily introduced into debates on other social and political issues on which Christians legitimately have different opinions and on which clear-cut criteria of confession cannot be applied. A third concern centered on the ecclesial self-understanding of the LWF and whether the LWF as a federation of churches had a constitutional mandate to declare a *status confessionis* even if its members were in complete agreement about the ethical and political issues concerned. The assembly did finally adopt a carefully worded statement entitled "Southern Africa: Confessional Integrity," in which the assembly appealed "to our white member churches" in Southern Africa to recognize that the situation "constitutes a *status confessionis*" and that this means that, "on the basis of faith and in order to manifest the unity of the church," churches are publicly and unequivocally to reject the existing apartheid system.

This debate further catalyzed other discussions of social and political concerns, including a comprehensive consideration of the overall sociopolitical functions and responsibilities of Lutheran churches. The report on this discussion recommended that studies of root causes of social and economic injustice be launched, that advocacy of human rights be expanded, and that the question of "women in church and society" be faced. It is evident that the Dar es Salaam Assembly brought to the foreground the necessity of the LWF and its member churches to intensify their involvements in contemporary social-ethical issues and in the advocacy of human rights on the basis of the Lutheran confessional heritage.

Another set of issues received almost equal attention: the ecumenical task and vision of the LWF. A keynote address with two responses and one of three assembly seminars provided considerable theological material for these discussions. The statement "Models of Unity" summed up the consensus of the assembly by endorsing as its key concept the notion of "reconciled diversity." This was presented as a complement to the concept of "conciliar fellowship," which, according to the statement, "seems to take insufficiently into account the legitimacy of confessional differences." The report articulated a vision of

47. Plenary sessions of the 1977 LWF Assembly were held in Nkruman Hall at the
    University of Dar es Salaam.

church unity in which faithfulness to "the abiding value of confessional forms
of Christian faith in all their variety" can lose its divisive character, strengthen
a "binding ecumenical fellowship," and express visibly a "universal unity in
Jesus Christ." "Christian unity means unity in diversity, not uniformity."
This theme, reconciled diversity, has played a significant role in virtually all
subsequent ecumenical conversation.

## Other Issues

Assembly actions and resolutions touch inevitably a wide variety of issues,
although only a few make a long-term impact on member churches, on the
LWF, or on the ecumenical movement. The Dar es Salaam Assembly made an
effort to give a boost to the concerns for global mission after the low point
experienced at the Evian Assembly. The statement "A Challenge to the
Churches" summed up in a succinct form a Lutheran view on motivation for
and objectives of involvement in mission and emphasized the need for equipping Christians and congregations for witness and for developing global partnership in mission on all six continents. In addition to this concise mission
statement the assembly acted on related recommendations touching various
dimensions of the church's mission and the nature of global partnership and
self-reliance. These recommendations as such hardly made much impact on
member churches, but they were taken up in LWF work on mission in subsequent years.

The youth delegates together with the stewards of the assembly reopened the question of LWF role among young people. The report approved by the assembly endorsed the establishment of a Youth Desk and a Youth Advisory Committee.

The assembly marked a new emphasis on the role of women in churches and within the LWF. Women delegates and other women participants formed an influential lobby that drove the main point home. In the recommendations that the assembly addressed to different audiences, the most weighty were those addressed to the member churches calling them to study the obstacles "which prevent realizing full, equal, joyful and creative partnership between men and women in the life of the church," to create models of a new community, and to study the issue of the ordination of women. The LWF Executive Committee was asked to establish a full-time Women's Desk.

Constitutional matters played a relatively small role at Dar es Salaam. No changes were made that altered the basic concept and nature of the LWF. The most significant change approved was the expansion of the size of the executive committee in order to increase the geographical distribution of the membership from twenty-three to thirty members.

The election of the president provided at Dar es Salaam more excitement than at most previous assemblies. The reason for this was that the Nominations Committee presented three candidates, all from the Third World, two of them from Africa. After the first ballot, which gave none of the candidates the required absolute majority, a second ballot was cast, giving Bishop Josiah Kibira 130 votes and Bishop A. W. Habelgaarn of South Africa 117. There was great jubilation in the assembly hall after the result was declared and it continued with dance, shouting, and song led by Tanzanians. Obviously the election of an African president was a particularly significant event for the Tanzanians and the African churches.

**Bibliographical Notes** _____

*Proceedings,* Dar-es-Salaam.
*In Christ—A New Community: A Study Guide in Preparation for the Sixth Assembly of the Lutheran World Federation.* Geneva: LWF, 1976.

# BUDAPEST 1984

# The Seventh Assembly
# of the Lutheran World Federation

| | |
|---|---|
| Dates: | July 22–August 5, 1984 |
| | [Youth Assembly: July 12–20, 1984] |
| Location: | Budapest, Hungary |
| | [Youth Assembly: Budapest] |
| Theme: | "In Christ—Hope for the World" |
| | (Sub-themes) |
| | "In Christ—Hope for Creation" |
| | "In Christ—Hope for Humankind" |
| | "In Christ—Hope for the Church" |
| Number of Participants: | 315 voting delegates from 97 member churches |
| | 300 youth participants |
| | 50 members of LWF staff, Geneva |
| | 270 press and media representatives |
| | 1,500 advisers, observers, and official guests from more than 100 countries, five continents |
| Presiders: | The Rt. Rev. Dr. Josiah Kibira, Tanzania, President |
| | Landesbischof Dr. Johannes Hanselmann, Bavaria, Germany (FRG), Vice-President |
| | The Rev. Dr. Andrew Hsiao, Hong Kong, Vice-President |
| | Bishop David W. Preus, United States, Vice-President |
| General Secretary: | The Rev. Dr. Carl H. Mau, Jr., United States |
| Main Decisions: | Suspension of membership in the LWF of two white churches from Southern Africa—the Evangelical Lutheran Church in Southern Africa (Cape Church) and the German Evangelical Lutheran Church in South West Africa (Namibia), on the basis of their continued support of the system of apartheid and their failure to end the division of their churches on racial grounds; a constitutional statement declaring |

Author: *Jens Holger Schjørring, Aarhus, Denmark, with draft notes from Gyula Nagy, Budapest, and László Terray, Råde, Norway.*

that all member churches understand themselves to be in pulpit and altar fellowship; the agreement that at least 40 percent of the delegates to the Eighth Assembly be women, and that at least 50 percent of the delegates to subsequent assemblies be women.

Principal Addresses:     Opening Address
                         *Bishop Josiah Kibira, Tanzania*
                         "In Christ—Hope for the World"
                         *Prof. Dr. Klaus-Peter Hertzsch, Germany (GDR)*
                         "In Christ—Hope for Creation"
                         *Dr. Emmanuel Abraham, Ethiopia*
                         "In Christ—Hope for Humankind"
                         *Prof. Carl Friedrich von Weizsäcker, Germany, (FRG)*
                         "In Christ—Hope for the Church" (Presentation on Mission)
                         *Dr. Margaret Wold, United States*
                         "In Christ—Hope for the Church" (Presentation on Ecumenics)
                         *The Rev. Dr. William Lazareth, United States*

## The Host Church

The Seventh Assembly of the Lutheran World Federation was the first assembly to be held in what has sometimes been called the "Second World," the countries of Central and Eastern Europe that were then living under socialist rule. It is therefore appropriate to provide a brief historical sketch of twentieth-century Hungary in order to understand the context in which the host church for this assembly was living.

Up to 1984 it could be said that no country in Europe had had its national borders more radically changed in the twentieth century than Hungary. As a result of the Treaty of Trianon (1920) and the dissolution of the Austro-Hungarian Empire, Hungary's territory was reduced to one-third of what it previously had been. A period of relative political stability between the two world wars had been followed at the end of World War II by a short, bloody interlude of the dictatorship of a "Quisling regime" of Szálasí, followed by devastation of the country and mainly its capital Budapest. During these last years of the war some government and opposition circles sought contact with Western allies, and the radical socialists turned toward Moscow for support.

At the end of World War II the Soviet army "liberated" Hungary. After a brief period of political instability, a Communist one-party government gained total power. There was a brief but internationally noted heroic and hopeless revolution, a fight against the Stalinist dictatorship in October 1956, which was brutally suppressed by the Red Army. The long-term effect of this was, paradoxically, a comparatively mild type of Marxist rule under the leadership of János Kádár. Gradually, Hungary achieved the status within the Eastern bloc of European nations of a relatively "economically flourishing" state.

The Lutheran Church in Hungary (Magyarországi Evangélikus Egyház) dates from the earliest years of the Reformation, 1520–21. By the mid-sixteenth century it accounted, together with its Calvinist sister church, for more than half the population of Hungary. Religious dominance shifted, however, to the Roman Catholic Church during the long period of the Habsburg reign over the Austro-Hungarian Empire. The two Reformation traditions were for a time a persecuted minority but later were treated with greater tolerance. At the midpoint of the twentieth century the Lutheran Church in Hungary was a small but lively body of approximately 430,000 members, roughly 6 percent of the total population. In spite of its limited size, it exerted considerable influence on the cultural and scientific development of the country largely as a result of its well-developed and highly respected school system.

In 1947 this church was among the founding members of the Lutheran World Federation. Its ties with both German and Nordic Lutheranism were traditionally strong, a situation that changed after the Communist Party took control of Hungary. During the first decade of this totalitarian rule, the church was led by the courageous Bishop Lajos Ordass, whose career has been traced at several points in the present volume. During the 1960s, as we have also seen (see especially chapter 2 above), the relationship of the Hungarian church both to the state and to the LWF secretariat in Geneva changed.

This change in relationship was never, to be sure, formulated in official strategy. It was a quiet result either of cautious diplomacy or of pragmatic cooperation. The prevailing reality was one of compromise in a variety of forms: at times a genuine balance of interests, at times a clear subservience to the totalitarian state, at still other times an unsettled situation dominated by palpable tensions.

The Seventh Assembly of the Lutheran World Federation, convened in Budapest in 1984, was thus held in most sensitive circumstances. For the host church it was an occasion for exchange with sisters and brothers from parts of the world with which there had been no substantive contact for decades. For the LWF itself it was an opportunity to manifest its presence in the framework of a Marxist state. Precisely these circumstances brought a number of sensitive topics to the surface at the assembly: broad issues concerning the church and socialism, questions concerning human rights, and strategies regarding the rights of the church in society.

Many measured this assembly by the remarkable historical fact that it was the first time a major international Christian organization had gathered in a country under Marxist rule. There was full awareness by most participants that it was necessary in this situation to operate in terms of the mostly unspoken rules of the one-party socialist state. Others were inclined far more to emphasize the necessity of remaining faithful to the identity of the Lutheran tradition with regard especially to its doctrinal basis and theological development during the Federation's earliest decades. This latter emphasis resulted in the advocacy of firm opposition to any form of totalitarian suppression of expression, even at the price of open confrontation with the host church or the government. A sharp question at the Seventh Assembly was which of these attitudes—or strategies—would prevail.

It was clear from the outset of the assembly that leading members of the LWF Geneva staff favored the first strategy; they had followed that track during careful preparatory negotiations with state and local authorities in Budapest. Similarly, it was evident that critics of this strategy were present from the time when the first decisions about the assembly were made. Some among these critics, using the witness of Bishop Ordass as a base point, went so far as to allege that the Federation in planning for the assembly had allowed itself to be manipulated by forces alien to the church.

## The Participants

Budapest, a city of history and beauty, was in 1984 an attractive venue for an LWF assembly precisely because it was then located in a socialist state. This context was, as already noted, unprecedented in the history of major international ecumenical conferences, a fact that itself brought to the assembly much public attention, even on a global scale. Members of the Assembly Planning Committee, assisted by staff from Geneva, had done their utmost to make certain that no one from outside Hungary would be denied entrance to Hungary and that freedom of expression would be respected throughout the assembly. The Hungarian State Secretary for Church Affairs, Mr. Imre Miklós, had provided outstanding cooperation to the Federation in reaching these agreements. In all such respects this assembly was largely a remarkable achievement even if certain incidents marred its perfection.

The host church, notably, exhibited an extraordinary interest in the Seventh Assembly. A considerable number of subcommittees from all regions of the country had provided careful preparatory assistance. The opening and closing Services of Worship were attended by ten to twelve thousand participants each. Moreover, the assembly participants from outside Hungary were shown remarkable hospitality when they visited Sunday services in more than one hundred congregations throughout the country. In terms of retrospective evaluation, this encounter between the international visitors and local congregations stands out as a memorable moment during the assembly.

## Main Events

The Seventh Assembly was opened with a solemn Eucharist, at which Bishop Zoltán Káldy preached, using Hebrews 12:1-2 as his text. From the worshipers more than nine thousand persons communed at sixty provisional altars placed throughout the huge Budapest Sports Hall.

The chief presiding officer for an LWF assembly is the President of the Federation; at Budapest this was Bishop Josiah Kibira of the Evangelical Lutheran Church in Tanzania. Since, however, Bishop Kibira was not physically able to undertake the arduous task of parliamentary leadership of so large a gathering, responsibilities for presiding were shared among the three LWF vice-presidents, Bishop Johannes Hanselmann of Bavaria, the Rev. Dr. Andrew Hsiao of Hong Kong, and Bishop David Preus of the United States. Bishop Kibira's presidential address to the assembly was read by Dr. Anza Lema of the Evangelical Lutheran Church in Tanzania, associate general secretary of the LWF; he read the address as Bishop Kibira sat nearby.

The assembly theme—"In Christ—Hope for the World"—proved to have been well selected in light both of the serious tensions that dominated world politics in that time of the cold war and of the pressures, both external and internal, that marked the daily living conditions of many of the LWF member churches. The assembly was obviously under challenge: Would it prove possible to respond to this theme in concrete terms, or would these tensions require the delegates to act without taking explicit positions?

A more procedural challenge also faced the delegates, and it was a classical dilemma for nearly all such international meetings: How would it be possible to combine a large number of substantial presentations (seventeen platform addresses including designated responses) with sufficient time for plenary discussion? And would there be adequate time for the assembly's necessary consideration of reports from more than fifteen working groups and committees? These latter groups produced resolutions which themselves occupied sixty-one printed pages. Further: Would there be an opportunity for serious attention to the decisions and resolutions adopted by the Youth Assembly, which had taken place just prior to the main assembly itself?

There was thus an imbalance between the ambitions of the assembly and what could realistically be accomplished within the allotted time. The themes assigned to working groups ranged broadly: Mission and Evangelism Today; Worship and Christian Life; Enabling Ministry; Ecumenical Commitment and Lutheran Identity; Relating to the Information Age; Partnership of Women and Men; Youth in Church and Society; Toward Economic and Social Justice; Caring for God's Endangered Creation; Racism in Church and Society; Promoting Human Rights; Christian Life in Different Social Systems; and Our Responsibility for Peace and Justice. The solution to the dilemma caused by this multiplicity of discussion themes was to transmit the many resolutions—some estimate more than 350—to all LWF member churches with recommendations for further study and action. A post-assembly Committee on Program Priorities continued to wrestle with the problem caused by the large number of actions taken by the Seventh Assembly.

Any account of the Seventh Assembly would be incomplete without due attention to ecumenical participation at the assembly, participation which gave a particular depth of meaning to frequent assembly affirmations of ecumenical commitment on the part of the LWF. A large number of outstanding church leaders represented churches, other confessions, and ecumenical organizations, including the Roman Catholic, Orthodox, Anglican, and Reformed traditions. Some of these persons gave important platform presentations to the assembly: Archbishop Johannes Cardinal Willebrands, president of the Vatican Secretariat for Promoting Christian Unity, on "Ecumenical Cooperation: A Roman Catholic Perspective," and Dr. Lukas Vischer, ecumenical officer for the Federation of Protestant Churches of Switzerland, on "Ecumenical Cooperation: A Reformed Perspective."

These ecumenical contributions are to be seen in direct relation to certain specific actions taken by the Seventh Assembly on matters involving the unity of the church. A major statement entitled "The Unity We Seek" was adopted, as was a crucial report from the working group entitled "Ecumenical Commitment and Lutheran Identity" (see chapter 7 above). Further, this latter working group report together with an assembly statement entitled "The Self-

Understanding and Task of the LWF" went far to illuminate the Federation's growing awareness of itself as *communio*, a global communion of Lutheran churches and not simply a voluntary association of churches. In the latter connection, the Seventh Assembly's action to amend the LWF Constitution's article on "Nature, Functions, and Scope" by adding the sentence: "The member churches of the Lutheran World Federation understand themselves to be in pulpit and altar fellowship with each other," has proven to be a decision of considerable ecclesiological importance.

No less significant, perhaps, was the participation in the LWF's Seventh Assembly of a delegation from the World Jewish Congress led by its retired general secretary, Gerhart M. Riegner. Dr. Riegner addressed the Federation on the matter of "The Church and the Jewish People," an address that marked the first official participation of a leader of the world Jewish community in an LWF assembly. The discussion of the relation of Lutheran churches to the Jewish people had started some two decades earlier in the life of the Federation. In spite of those initiatives, however, a widespread perception has persisted that Lutherans have not come to terms with the Holocaust and its meaning for churches of the German Reformation. In Budapest, if not earlier, the LWF went far to remove that perception, as the important presentation of Dr. Riegner was supplemented by a substantial assembly report prepared by a special committee headed by the Rt. Rev. Mikko Juva of the Evangelical Lutheran Church of Finland, a past president of the Federation (cf. pp. 450–56). That report, "The Church and the Jewish People," noted that the 1983 LWF consultation in Stockholm entitled "Luther, Lutheranism, and the Jews" "marked a historic breakthrough in Jewish/ Lutheran relationships, for it spoke to the most critical problems in our common history, and it did so in a spirit of reconciliation and hope."

Another action of the Seventh Assembly that reflects an extremely deep concern within Lutheran churches for total inclusiveness was the decision, following the report on "Partnership of Women and Men," "to develop a plan that would, with the cooperation of the member churches and the national committees, become effective at the Eighth Assembly and provide that 40 percent of the delegates at the Eighth LWF Assembly be women, and that 50 percent of the delegates at the Ninth and all subsequent LWF Assemblies be women." To this was added specific requests to the LWF Executive Committee substantially to increase the presence of women on all Federation governing bodies as well as in the staff of its secretariat. This action has provided impetus for the attainment of comprehensive inclusiveness—women, youth, and persons with disabling conditions—in all aspects of LWF life (see chapter 8 above).

## Confessional Integrity

By far the most striking action of the Seventh Assembly was the suspension of membership in the Federation of two churches of Southern Africa whose lives had been organized on a principle of "whites only"—the Evangelical Lutheran Church in Southern Africa (Cape Church) and the German Evangelical Lutheran Church in South West Africa (Namibia). This decision marked the culmination of the discussion concerning *status confessionis* begun at the Sixth Assembly in Dar es Salaam in 1977 (see pp. 399–400 above). Indeed, the fact that the proposal was dealt with as a matter of "Confessional Integrity" reemphasized the fundamentally ecclesiological character of the decision.

In preparations for the Budapest Assembly it had been made unmistakably clear, in statements of President Josiah Kibira as well as in actions of the staff, that a decision to suspend the membership of these churches was the only appropriate one. The two churches had, in point of fact, utterly failed even to begin to come to terms with the demands of Dar es Salaam. The decisive proof of this failure was the continuation in these churches of apartheid as a criterion for participation in the Eucharist.

It is important to note that whatever reluctance there was at the Seventh Assembly to take this step—and there was an articulate minority—was to be found among theologians of the First World, most notably from Lutheran churches in the Federal Republic of Germany. This reluctance served to strengthen ties between representatives of churches in Central and Eastern Europe and those from churches in the Third World.

Attendant to these discussions were also serious questions about traditional Lutheran hesitance to make decisions with direct sociopolitical implications, as well as questions about the ecclesiological propriety of disciplinary action by the Federation in respect to member churches. This action of the Lutheran World Federation to suspend the two churches from Southern Africa was widely hailed in ecumenical circles, at the time and in subsequent years, as a decisive ecclesial action in the struggle against apartheid. (It is to be noted that in the course of historical development, the LWF after careful and pastoral analysis of changes in the two Southern African churches lifted the suspension in 1991; cf. "Churches in Communion," *LWF Documentation*, No. 30, December 1991, pp. 29ff.)

## The Election

As indicated elsewhere in this book, Zoltán Káldy, presiding bishop of the host church, had made no secret of his wish to be elected president of the Federation (see pp. 468–69 below). As one of his chief arguments in this regard, Káldy referred to the "tradition" that the president be elected from among the leaders of the church which served as host to the assembly. It is clear, further, that Káldy had in effect been preparing for this over a period of time when general relations between the churches of Eastern Europe and the rest of the LWF were changing.

Nonetheless, the election turned into high drama, which some have even described as sensational. Káldy had himself contributed to tension that came to a conclusion only when on the final ballot he defeated Bodil Sølling of Denmark, the first woman to stand as a candidate for the LWF presidency. In the initial ballot Bishop David Preuss of the American Lutheran Church and Professor Roger Nostbakken of the Evangelical Lutheran Church of Canada had also received votes. The result of that first ballot was Káldy, 136 votes; Sølling, 78 votes; Preus, 52 votes; Nostbakken, 31 votes. On the second and final ballot, Káldy received 173 votes and Bodil Sølling 124. It is to be noted that an

48. The opening service of the 1984 LWF Assembly was held in the giant
    Sports Hall of Budapest.

important argument against Ms Sølling's candidacy centered on the widespread perception that the next general secretary of the Federation would be
the Norwegian Gunnar Staalsett (see pp. 510–14 below) and that it would be
difficult to have Scandinavians as both president and general secretary.

The opposition to Káldy centered not so much on his advocacy of the controversial "theology of diakonia" as on the self-willed style that he had consistently shown as leader of his church. There were, to be sure, many who
regarded Bishop Káldy's treatment of his predecessor, Lajos Ordass, as a matter of shame not alleviated by attempts to "rehabilitate" Ordass. Many delegates, further, were offended by a perception that LWF staff had been less than
evenhanded—even manipulative—in advocacy for Káldy during assembly
preparations. The issue, of course, had been that of Federation relations to
churches and governments in socialist societies. Leading staff had been
anxious to maintain cordial relations with the leadership of both the Hungarian church and the Hungarian government and at all costs to avoid giving
offense to those authorities. Critics of this position—and of Káldy's candidacy—held that it was suppressive of legitimate objection and ran counter to
the freedom of the assembly..

As if this tension were not enough, the atmosphere was further compromised by the unpleasant intermezzo of the "Dóka affair." Zoltán Dóka, a pastor in the Lutheran Church of Hungary, had written a statement, circulated
among assembly delegates, strongly critical both of Bishop Káldy's theological
views and of his leadership style. Some charged that the Federation staff had

worked to keep Dóka's charges secret, fearing that its circulation would severely damage the whole assembly. At any rate, as this matter became public it was widely noted in the media and received a great deal of attention, which focused in part on the controversial election. In retrospect it seems clear that this whole matter was handled in an inexpedient way largely because of an inordinate desire not to upset the general course of assembly events. Similarly, it is obvious that press and media coverage of the Dóka incident was determined by its sensational aspects rather than by journalistic balance.

In the end, Bishop Zoltán Káldy was elected president of the Lutheran World Federation. In light of the circumstances of the election, the new LWF Executive Committee, also elected at the Seventh Assembly, perhaps provided a needed balance between large "majority" churches and small "minority" churches as well as between representatives from the North and from the South.

The summary in the Message from the Budapest Assembly reads: "Our gathering here and the hospitality we received here showed us that in the church of Christ we can have confidence in each other and can build bridges between people across political and ideological boundaries" (*Proceedings*, Budapest, p. 11).

## Bibliographical Notes _____

*Unpublished Documents*

LWF Archives, Geneva.
Archives of the Lutheran Church of Hungary, Budapest.
Ordass Archives, Oslo.
Oral information from a group of leading theologians and Hungarian church officials, Budapest, February 1995.

*Printed Documents*

"From Budapest to Curitiba, 1985–1989." LWF Report 27. Geneva: LWF, 1989.
"From Dar es Salaam to Budapest." LWF Report 17/18. Geneva: LWF, 1983.
*Proceedings*, Budapest.
"Signs of Hope: Considerations and Questions." LWF Documentation 15/16. Geneva: LWF, 1983.
Terray, László. "Was the 'Reality' Cut Out?" *Occasional Papers on Religion in Eastern Europe*. Vol. V, No. 6 (1985): pp. 1–17.

# CURITIBA 1990

# The Eighth Assembly
# of the Lutheran World Federation

| | |
|---|---|
| Dates: | January 29–February 8, 1990 |
| Location: | Curitiba, Brazil |
| Theme: | "I Have Heard the Cry of My People" |
| Number of Participants: | 376 voting delegates (43 percent of voting delegates were women; 15.6 percent of voting delegates were youth) |
| | 192 official guests, ex officio participants, and accompanying persons |
| | 60 stewards |
| | 211 staff (local, Geneva) |
| Presidents: | Landesbischof Dr. Johannes Hanselmann, presiding bishop of the Evangelical Lutheran Church in Bavaria, Germany, presided as LWF president. The Rev. Dr. Gottfried Brakemeier, president of the Evangelical Church of the Lutheran Confession in Brazil, was elected LWF president on February 7, 1990. |
| General Secretary: | The Rev. Dr. Gunnar Staalsett, Norway |
| Main Decisions: | Adoption of a new LWF constitution and authorization of comprehensive LWF restructuring; resolutions supporting churches in situations of political and social tension in Brazil, the Baltic states, Central America, and Palestine; ecumenical actions regarding the *Filioque* clause of the Nicene Creed and the goal of full communion between the Lutheran and Anglican traditions |
| Principal Addresses: | "Justification—Freedom—Liberation Theology" *Landesbischof Dr. Johannes Hanselmann, Germany* |

Author: *Norman A. Hjelm, Wynnewood, Pennsylvania*

"From Budapest to Curitiba"
  *The Rev. Dr. Gunnar Staalsett, Norway*
"Discerning the Call of God in the Cries of God's
People" (Keynote Address)
  *Dean Ronald F. Thiemann, United States*
"Our Common Responsibility"
  *The Hon. Gro Harlem Brundtland, Prime Minister, Norway*

Section Addresses:    "I Have Heard the Cry of My People . . ."
"For Life in Communion"
  *Bishop Manas Buthelezi, Republic of South Africa*
  *The Rev. Prasanna K. Samuel, India*
"For Salvation"
  *Professor Theodor Ahrens, Germany*
  *The Rev. Jaan Kiivit, Estonia*
"For Peace with Justice"
  *Dr. Mary B. Henry, United States*
  *President Francis Stephanos, Ethiopia*
"For a Liberated Creation"
  *Professor Anna Marie Aagaard, Denmark*
  *Ms. Loe Rose Mbise, Tanzania*

### From Porto Alegre to Curitiba

Twenty years after the tumultuous events that resulted in the shift of the venue of the Fifth Assembly of the LWF from Porto Alegre, Brazil, to Evian, France (see pp. 382ff. above), the LWF came to Brazil for its Eighth Assembly. While the situation had changed for each of the three protagonists—Brazil itself, the host church, and surely the Federation—the decision to return was not without its difficulties. There were new forms of democracy in the nation, but human, economic, and environmental problems remained unsolved. The church had progressed mightily in becoming truly a Brazilian church rather than a closed immigrant body, but resentments against the 1970 decision of the LWF remained strong in several quarters. The Federation itself was so heavily involved in internal debates both over its self-understanding as a *communio* and over a proposed restructuring that many feared the assembly would not adequately respond to the real cries of its Brazilian context, much less those being sounded throughout the world. This was, after all, just the second LWF assembly to take place in the southern hemisphere and the first assembly to take place after the fall of the Berlin Wall, and both North–South and East–West tensions had played major roles in the Federation since its founding in 1947. It was not clear that the results of this assembly would be other than ambiguous.

Perhaps two kinds of juxtapositions went far to symbolize the ambiguity. First, the location of the assembly was the Pontifical University of Curitiba, a Roman Catholic University much like a Northern liberal arts college in the modernity and comfort of its facilities and campus (except for oppressive heat in the assembly hall), and assembly participants stayed in four- and five-star hotels in the prosperous downtown area of the city. This venue was juxtaposed to a large *favela* not far from the university where thousands of poverty-stricken Brazilians—marginalized, indigenous, landless—struggled for survival. Second, in the life of the assembly itself the daily worship presented sharp juxtapositions: big-band Hispanic rhythms, German brass music born in the sixteenth and seventeenth centuries, plainsong chant with incense. To the attentive and historically aware participant, there were many such signs of ambiguity. One American pointed to these signs in saying that delegates "heard some cries of the people, but the assembly did not do a very good job of folding what Brazil is into the program. We had a Western Europe–North America pace in Latin America. We haven't gotten the essence of Brazil" (quoted by Edgar Trexler, "Hot Time," p. 9).

## Brazil and the World: Cries of the People

It is noteworthy that the theme for the Eighth Assembly, "I Have Heard the Cries of My People," based on Exodus 2:23-3:7, moved, for almost the first time in LWF assembly themes, away from the boundaries of the second article of the creed. The context of the assembly—cries of suffering people and nations, the Third World, as well as the cries of a violated creation—was seen by those who prepared for the assembly to be of greater importance than perhaps had been the case at previous gatherings.

From Brazil, as stated in an assembly resolution, the cries came from the Indian population, from the landless people, from the marginalized in the *favelas*, from the children of the streets, and from the ecologically threatened creation. The problems were not the same as in 1970, but in 1990 the Federation gathered in a country decimated by international debt, by continued human rights abuses against its own people, by extraordinary contrasts between rich and poor, by rain forests being destroyed by pollution and greed.

In one of the assembly's most memorable events, more than fifty young people from the host church told their nation's "passion history." In song, drama, and dance—doubtlessly the first time that the Latin *lambada* was performed at an LWF Assembly!—the story of *conquistadors*, slavery until 1888, transnational exploitation, the nation's thirty-one million illiterates, twelve million slum dwellers, sixteen million abandoned children, and its 3 percent per day rate of inflation was told. One commentator described the conclusion of the presentation: "And when the youth were done, having told the passion story of their people, giving voice to generations of suffering, almost all of them began to cry and embrace each other. 'This is the first time these middle-class young people have had opportunity to hear the cry of their people and give it voice,' said the author of the play. And for what seemed like a long time, the rest of us in the assembly stood and clapped rhythmically, deep in the emotion of the moment" (Karl Mattson, "Trying to Cross Over," p. 37).

Internationally, this was a time of extraordinary change. The Berlin Wall had come down; Germany—FGR and GDR—was soon to be officially reunited. Countries that had lived under Marxism–Leninism were suddenly hearing about the "market economy." The Soviet Union was breaking up; only one superpower remained. And the Third World was, in the view of many, being forgotten.

The Eighth Assembly of the LWF, then, was conceived as an opportunity for the Lutheran churches of the world to take their place in direct response to global travail. As the Assembly Message put it:

> This theme of the Eighth Assembly, "I Have Heard the Cry of My People," calls us to discern the authentic cries of humanity. It has not always been easy for the church to listen, but if we are to take up the whole mission of God to the world we must in receptive humility hear how people are crying. And we can hear only when we are with the people—in solidarity with those who are outside the community, with those who are poor, with those who are home- less, with those who suffer injustice, with those for whom life has no mean- ing. Our churches are called to listen to the people.
>
> Our theme also calls us to discern how God responds to the cries of the people. It is surely God's response of servanthood and suffering—the very mind of Christ—which the church is called to share. Communion is not for the sake of place or power, communion is for the sake of mission and service in the world. God frequently answers the cries of people in ways which startle and surprise. Grace follows roads which twist and turn, even as history itself twists and turns. It is this road, laid down in God's own surprising way, which we are called to travel. . . . (*Proceedings,* Curitiba, p. 80)

### Host Church

The Evangelical Church of the Lutheran Confession in Brazil, host church to the Eighth Assembly, has been virtually throughout its history an immigrant church, from as early as the 1820s to the resettlement era after World War II. (To be sure, the earliest professed Lutheran in Brazil was one Hans Staden, who in 1557 provided the first exact description of Brazil's Indian population.) Overwhelmingly from Germany, these immigrants, together with smaller numbers of other ethnic newcomers, formed four Lutheran synods beginning in 1886. These synods came into a federated relationship in 1949, in 1954 adopted the present church name, and in 1968 formed themselves in a new regional pattern. The church, the largest Lutheran body in Latin America, now numbers about a million members and participates with deep commitment in the ecumenical structures of South America. One of its most important ecu- menical contributions has been to bring the theology of the Lutheran Refor- mation into vital dialogue with the liberation theology that for many has in recent generations been characteristic of Latin America (e.g., Walter Altmann, *Luther and Liberation: A Latin American Perspective*). The present challenge facing the church, being seriously accepted, is authentically to become a Portuguese-speaking church of the people of Brazil rather than a church still dependent on its European forebears.

To this country and as guests of this church, came nearly 850 assembly par- ticipants, 376 of them voting delegates from virtually all of the approximately 110 member churches of the Federation. There were no longer questions about adequate representation from the churches of Asia, Africa, and Latin America—or from the churches of Eastern Europe. For the first time delegates were present from among the Lutherans of the Soviet Union, a nation soon to lose its identity. It was noteworthy, further, that 43 percent of the voting delegates to Curitiba were women, thus fulfilling the 40 percent mandated by the Seventh Assembly.

## Communio, *a New Constitution and a New Structure*

In this context and with these deep and abiding concerns, the Eighth Assembly of the Lutheran World Federation found itself also dealing with pivotal issues concerning its own nature and structure. For some participants this was a dangerous diversion, from the assembly theme to institutional matters of administration and management; for others it was both a testimony to a new awareness and calling for global Lutheranism and a practical necessity. Curitiba was preoccupied with "restructuring."

In 1987 the Federation's executive committee, meeting in Viborg, Denmark, had established a five-person committee on LWF Restructuring under the chairmanship of James R. Crumley, Jr., Bishop of the then Lutheran Church in America. Other members of the committee were President Thomas Batong of the Philippines, Ms Sieghilde Hoerschelmann of the Federal Republic of Germany, Bishop Sebastian Kolowa of Tanzania, and Ms Christina Rogestam of Sweden; the group was staffed by the Rev. Norman Hjelm and Ms Beate Fistarol of the Geneva secretariat. The rationale for restructuring was seen as threefold: to devise a structure that would more adequately express and facilitate the LWF's newly articulated (since the Budapest Assembly) self-understanding as *communio*; to increase cooperation and coordination within the units of the secretariat; and to deal with serious financial restraints as they were being faced by the Federation. There can be no doubt that the entire process was energetically driven by the LWF General Secretary, Gunnar Staalsett; indeed, his aggressive leadership became, by the time of the Curitiba Assembly, itself a matter of contention.

The work of the Committee on LWF Restructuring had been intense and had included consultation with the entire LWF constituency by means of interim reports and the solicitation of critical reactions. In 1989 the executive committee adopted a final report which was presented to the assembly. The action called for from the assembly was to be the adoption of a new LWF Constitution and the authorization of the structural implementation of that constitution by the LWF Executive Committee/Council. The assembly plenary devoted a full day to the debate with one of the LWF Vice-Presidents, Ephorus Soritua Nababan of Indonesia, presiding. Bishop Crumley addressed the issues at length and was followed by Federation President Bishop Hanselmann, who gave an unprecedented personal statement favoring the entire proposal. Nearly forty interventions—pro and con—were made from the floor, and positions were taken in respect to a large number of issues. The relation of the proposed constitution and structure to the theology and ecclesiology of *communio* was keenly debated, the key constitutional proposal being "The Lutheran World Federation is a communion of churches . . ." (Article III), which was a major

change from the former "The Lutheran World Federation shall be a free association of Lutheran churches." Some participants in the debate questioned the
new language as compromising the "autonomy" of member churches; others
saw the new language as faithfully reflecting the growing *koinonia* of the LWF
as demonstrated in pulpit and altar fellowship, official statements on the
nature of the Federation adopted at the Budapest Assembly, and the 1984
action—one of ecclesial discipline?—whereby the LWF membership of two
churches was suspended on the basis of "confessional integrity."

Additionally, some held that the new constitution called for a Federation
too centralized in its secretariat and, more explicitly, in the office of the general secretary. Others saw the proposed council, which was to supplant the
executive committee with a body of fifty persons equally divided between representatives of churches from the South and the North, as diminishing the
responsibility and influence of the larger and financially more powerful
churches and their agencies. The North–South dichotomy came to a head with
the public charge, never proven, that leaders of certain Northern agencies who
opposed the restructuring had during the assembly urged African delegates in
particular to vote in the negative in return for increased assistance and aid.
Parallel to this charge was the expression of a countersuspicion, also never
proven, that the Geneva secretariat had unduly influenced Third World and
particularly African churches and national committees to ensure the appointment of assembly delegates who were positive toward the structure proposals.

These and other issues—for example, a deep concern on the part of some
delegates about locating policy-making authority for LWF departments within
the council and its program committees rather than in the more independent
commissions as had previously been the case—made for vigorous and hotly
contested debate. In general it can be said that assembly delegates from the
Third World churches were keenly in favor of the new structural proposals;
opposition was centered in strong voices from Denmark and Finland, with
some German and American delegates expressing similar reservations.

It is important to note that these debates, both prior to and at the Eighth
Assembly, did not always clearly distinguish between two issues: the self-
understanding of the LWF as *communio* and the structure proposals. The
Committee on Restructuring had quite clearly taken the position that
*communio* does not necessarily lead to one particular structure; Lutheran
understandings of church polity do not allow for such absolutes. What the
committee asserted was that its proposals regarding structure were a workable
and efficient means to express and facilitate the life of the global Lutheran
communion. Consistent with this position, some representatives of member
churches were able theologically and ecclesiologically to support the view of
communion being advanced, even as they opposed all or part of the structure
proposals. Many others, however, did not seem able to make this distinction.
The debates were at times confused, and the assembly was clearly marked by
tension and even acrimony.

The proposal was to substitute the draft constitution for the constitution
that had been partially amended in 1984 (see Appendix, pp. 530–34). Bishop
Crumley, toward the end of his address, indicated to the plenary the character
of the precise proposal:

Just one further word about the constitution. What is proposed to you is what the Executive Committee believes to be necessary to implement the proposal on structure. If this proposal is adopted, several specific items will need to be included in the by-laws and this should be done by the Executive Committee within the next year.

In some ways it could be said that this proposal for a restructured Lutheran World Federation reflects the hopes of many who have worked for a united Lutheranism on a global scale. Here we set forth in constitutional language what has developed in the relationships of our member churches one with another. (*Proceedings*, Curitiba, p. 140)

A constitutional change required a two-thirds vote of those participating in the ballot; in this case 238 affirmative votes were required. Remarkably, the Eighth Assembly approved the new constitution by a vote of precisely 238 for, and 103 against. The voting and counting of ballots, nevertheless, were not smooth and there were challenges. Dean Karsten Nissen of the Church of Denmark, one of the leading opponents of the new structure, however, called for an end to the challenges, an immediate acceptance of the vote, and a common dedication to implementing the decision for the good of the Federation.

It is difficult, as close as this writing is to the decisions of Curitiba, to assess the effect of what the LWF accomplished by these actions. Gunnar Staalsett, however, was clear about the long-range significance of the decisions: "[T]his will prove to be a pivotal assembly, with the Federation having a 'before' and 'after' Curitiba history. It will take years to transfer the decisions here to the member churches and to our attitudes. When you advance the idea of a communion of equals between North and South, there is a lot of paternalism to reverse. We are speaking about the work of the LWF for the next twenty years" (quoted by Trexler, "Hot Time," p. 9).

## Additional Decisions

While the Eighth Assembly will be remembered largely as an assembly devoted to internal considerations of structure, other decisions were made. Resolutions were passed in which the LWF expressed its solidarity with member churches and regions where life was seriously affected by sociopolitical change and conflict:

- In *Brazil*: where especially the suffering of the Indian population, the landless people, those marginalized in the *favelas*, the children of the streets, and the threatened creation pose challenges to the commitment and resources of both nation and church.
- In *the Baltic states*: where, in 1990, policies of *glasnost* and *perestroika* had given rise to new but as yet unfulfilled aspirations for freedom and self-determination.
- In *Central America*: where the integrity of nations and people was threatened by "all forms of foreign intervention policies and actions . . . be they ideological, political, economic, or military. . . ."

LWF Photo—Peter Williams

49. Youth from the Evangelical Church of the Lutheran Confession in Brazil
presented a vibrant program of drama, music, and dance at the Curitiba
Assembly in 1990. The theme both of the program, which concentrated on
the difficult history of Brazil and especially the oppression of its indigenous
peoples, and of the assembly itself, was the declaration, "I Have Heard the
Cry of My People."

- In *Palestine*: where, in 1990, the people were entering the third year of
"the uprising against the Israeli occupation of the West Bank and Gaza
Strip [and] suffering and injustice continue unabated. . . ."

In respect to ecumenical matters, the LWF recommended that Lutheran
churches make greater use of the Nicene Creed at least on major festivals and
that in countries with a sizable Orthodox population that creed be used in a
version that omits the "Western" *filioque* clause. Additionally, the assembly
reviewed positively the substantial progress made in Anglican–Lutheran relationships and resolved "that the LWF renew its commitment to the goal of full
communion with the churches of the Anglican Communion, and that it urge
LWF member churches to take appropriate steps toward its realization."

Another action taken by the assembly was to call for the inclusion of 20 percent youth among the voting delegates to the Ninth Assembly, youth being
defined as persons the age of thirty or under. This action was obviously part of
the Federation's continuing response to issues of inclusiveness (see chapter 8
above). At Curitiba, as noted above, 43 percent of the voting delegates were
women and 15.6 percent were youth. The figure for women was in line with
the Budapest mandate of 40 percent women; the figure of 50 percent was at the
same time mandated for women delegates to the Ninth Assembly.

The Rev. Dr. Gottfried Brakemeier, president of the Evangelical Church of the Lutheran Confession in Brazil, was elected the ninth president of the LWF on February 7, 1990 (see pp. 477–80 below). The election was contested and Brakemeier won over Bishop Donald Sjoberg of the Evangelical Lutheran Church in Canada, 183 votes to 165. At the opening Eucharist of the Eighth Assembly, January 30, 1990, President Brakemeier had preached on Revelation 6:9–11. A paragraph from that sermon worthily summarizes the force of the theme of the assembly, "I Have Heard the Cry of My People":

> The Assembly theme asserts that God hears the cry of his people. In what way does God hear this cry? Surely, the world would look a lot different if he did so! Here is the crux of the Assembly theme, its real challenge. It rules out any stopping short at the cry of the people. Of course it is important, this cry. Of course, we must see and feel the suffering, we must not gloss over its appalling reality, we must identify ourselves with the outcry of the suffering victims of our world. Woe betide us if all we do is to talk of the sufferings of others from a safe distance and fail to join their outcry. For that would mean excommunicating ourselves from the people of God. Our Assembly theme only rings true in anguished concern, when it is an integral dimension of our worship and service. (*Proceedings*, Curitiba, p. 124)

## Bibliographical Notes

Altmann, Walter. *Luther and Liberation: A Latin American Perspective.* Trans. Mary M. Solberg. Minneapolis: Fortress Press, 1992.

Bachmann, E. Theodore, and Mercia Brenne Bachmann, *Lutheran Churches in the World: A Handbook.* Minneapolis: Augsburg, 1989. Pp. 457–77.

Brakemeier, Gottfried., ed. *Lutherans in Brazil 1990: History, Theology, Perspectives.* São Leopoldo: Post-Graduate Studies Institute and *Estudos Teológicos*, 1989.

Mattson, Karl J. "Trying to Cross Over." *Lutheran Partners* (September/October 1990): 34–39.

*Proceedings*, Curitiba.

Root, Michael. "The LWF at Curitiba." *Dialog* (Spring 1990): 135–38.

Trexler, Edgar R. "Hot Time in Curitiba." *The Lutheran* (February 28, 1990): 6–9, 23, 50.

# 2

# PRESIDENTS OF THE LWF

# Anders Nygren

ANDERS THEODOR SAMUEL NYGREN was born on November 15, 1890, in Gothenburg, Sweden. He pursued theological studies at the University of Lund, receiving his *Teol. Cand.* in 1912. The same year he was ordained into the ministry of the Church of Sweden, in which he served as a parish pastor until 1920. His graduate theological studies were at Lund and in Germany, where he worked with Carl Stange, Ernst Troeltsch, and Rudolf Otto. In 1921 he became docent in the philosophy of religion at Lund; in 1924 he was made full professor. In 1948, Nygren was named bishop of Lund, retiring in 1958. He was elected President of the Lutheran World Federation at its First Assembly, held in Lund in 1947, and served through the Second Assembly at Hanover, Germany, 1952. As bishop of Lund, he served as host for the pivotal Third World Conference on Faith and Order, 1952. Nygren was married in 1921 to Irmgard Helene Luise Brandin, a native of Pomerania in Germany; to them were born two sons and two daughters. Anders Nygren died October 20, 1978.

## Nygren the Theologian

The academic accomplishments of Anders Nygren covered a wide range of issues: seminal works in the philosophy of religion and on the principles and methods of systematic theology resulting in the development of "motif research" as an option for theological methodology. He made significant contributions also to major debates concerning contemporary challenges to the Christian gospel with particular concern for the life of the church in Nazi Germany after 1933. Among his many published works, his major work entitled "The Christian Idea of Love through the Ages" (1930, 1936) became internationally known as *Agape and Eros* (English 1932, 1938, 1953; German, 1930, 1937; also translated into Japanese and other languages). His *Pauli brev till Romarna* (1944) was translated into English as *Commentary on Romans* (1949) and subsequently into German (1951) and other languages. In his retirement he produced for an English edition, *Meaning and Method: Prolegomena*

Author: *Jens Holger Schjørring, Aarhus, Denmark*

*to a Scientific Philosophy of Religion and a Scientific Theology,* published in 1972.

Any review of Nygren's wide range of academic accomplishment requires a search for continuity and consistency within great diversity. One must also ask about the relation between Nygren's research and his service as bishop in the Lutheran Church of Sweden. How, further, was it possible for Anders Nygren, champion of a clear and individually marked theological position, to serve as President of the Lutheran World Federation in which position he consistently and with wide vision encouraged free and open dialogue? How did he contribute to the critical examination of the Lutheran tradition that was so desperately needed when he took his chair as President of the LWF, an examination designed to maintain the original vision of Lutheran identity, even as it was being reformulated for the immediate situation? A full consideration of such questions is beyond the scope of the present work. They point, however, to a whole range of issues which marked the general situation at the founding of the Federation. We can at present only briefly review the theological work of Anders Nygren in such a way that it illuminates the context in which the LWF was formed and his role at its inception.

Nygren's childhood home was marked both by deep Christian piety and by a remarkable openness toward society and culture. There is no doubt that his entire life bore these two marks, a convinced personal faith rooted in the historical continuity of church tradition and an alertness to new insights emerging from his national and cultural environment. This produced both the tension and the balance that ran through his wide range of interests and accomplishments.

Another factor that may help explain the consistency of Nygren's life and work was the unifying milieu of Lund—university and cathedral—where he lived for more than seventy years. In these surroundings, to which he was intimately attached, Nygren balanced academic concerns not only from the theological faculty but also from his constant interaction with scholars in other disciplines with the deepest concerns of the church. In this connection his especially close relations with two colleagues should be noted. Gustaf Aulén, Nygren's teacher and subsequent colleague until his own installation as bishop of Strängnäs in 1933, and Ragnar Bring, Nygren's successor as professor of theology, together with Nygren himself developed the "Lundensian" approach to theology that dominated discussions in Sweden and achieved considerable attention internationally.

Nygren's earliest writings were in the area of the philosophy of religion, principally those areas of methodology that defined the relationship between philosophy and theology. He never hesitated to emphasize the relevance of philosophy: "Its task is to give us the wide perspective, to free us from too narrow views and to clarify the perspective we must have in order to understand at all what is under discussion" (Nygren, Anders, "Intellectual Autobiography" in *The Philosophy and Theology of Anders Nygren,* ed. Charles W. Kegley). Theology, therefore, is compelled to make use of philosophy while recognizing that the latter will not lead to a recognition of the identity of Christianity. Philosophy or the *religious a priori* cannot, to Nygren, be a basis for theological insight. Of course, questions remain concerning Nygren's view:

50. Anders Nygren, Bishop of Lund, Sweden, and President of the Lutheran World Federation, 1947–1952

Did he succeed in constructing a connection between the philosophical task
and, say, the interpretation of the creeds? Is his philosophical conception too
formal or abstract without real juxtaposition to the theological task?

   On another front, Nygren's involvement with issues arising from the German church struggle during the Nazi era took on a totally different character
from the academic concerns just mentioned. Through his marriage, Nygren
had direct access to information about the dramatic developments that followed Hitler's seizure of power. He saw it as part of his inescapable obligation,
even as a theologian, closely to observe those developments, taking account of
such information as could be gathered both from within and from outside Germany. During his frequent stays in Germany, he had close contact with Birger
Forell, the pastor of the Swedish church in Berlin, and also with leaders of the

church opposition. It became apparent to Nygren as early as 1934, when his first observations on the situation in Germany were published, that the real core of the church struggle went far beyond political or journalistic observations. The "Führer" principle, which he saw as the organizing principle of the Nazi state at all levels, and its racial ideology were absolutely dominant in the new Germany. Nygren quickly judged them to be totally irreconcilable with common law and obviously with the governing principles of Christian faith. "The struggle is about the very essence of Christianity, its existence or its destruction" (Nygren, Anders, *Den tyska Kyrkostriden*, p. 116). In this connection Nygren the theologian was required to apply traditional theological research to contemporary challenges, to focus on a theological critique of culture and society. This task became increasingly important to him in ensuing years.

The work that established Nygren's international reputation was published during this same period, in the mid 1930s. It was the work originally published in two volumes, *Agape and Eros: I. A Study of the Christian Idea of Love, II. The History of the Christian Idea of Love.* Ever since his years as a student, Nygren had directed his attention toward Pauline theology as exposed in Romans. He was concerned that the main concepts of faith were often approached as though they had unambiguous meaning. It appeared to him that the concept of Christian love had in fact changed radically through the centuries of Christian tradition, notably on account of the difference of the Pauline understanding of *agape* and Augustine's notion of *amor*. As a systematic theologian he felt deeply challenged to demonstrate this "confusion of ideas":

> Yet to talk simply of Christian love is in fact to accept this confusion. The word is used without any particular meaning being given to it. For one person it will mean demanding love, for another sentimental love, for a third some sort of sublimated eros, for a fourth the agape of the cross, and so on. The only way forward is through a careful analysis of concepts and motifs. ("Intellectual Autobiography," p. 18)

The task of "motif research" was, to Nygren, clearly to identify such basic motifs as *agape* and *eros* and to describe their empirical appearance. This would subsequently lead to the possibility of a clear evaluation of the basic types. Clearly to distinguish between such description and evaluation was, to Nygren, essential if the scientific character of theological research was to be maintained. On the basis of this method, he never demonstrated doubt in justifying a fundamental juxtaposition between, on the one side, *agape* understood as divine love expressed by God the heavenly Father and directed toward humanity in a downward movement, and *eros* understood in Hellenistic terms as human aspiration directed upward toward divine perfection.

Nygren's presentation in *Agape and Eros* drew considerable international interest, although it was often misunderstood and frequently rejected. However its content and method might be judged, when viewed sixty years after publication it must be admitted that the project revealed a remarkable comprehension of the history of theology and, additionally, provided a stimulus to wide research.

Nygren was also personally convinced that Lutheran theology should take seriously the fact that it is primarily a theology of scripture. It is true that he dedicated the first decade of his university career to dogmatic questions that touched on both philosophy and history. Yet, without removing himself from those challenges, he increasingly felt compelled to participate in the modern interpretation of biblical texts. In his subsequent biblical studies he saw it as an obligation without disregarding problems in such areas as philology, text criticism, and the history of religions to present results in such a way that details would be understood within the horizon of their entirety. Nygren's biblical work was basically theological and written for a readership beyond the circle of experts.

He thus joined with colleagues from the fields of exegesis and historical theology to produce a series of commentaries on the New Testament. He himself chose to work on Paul's Epistle to the Romans, a lifelong interest deepened by his growing awareness of Luther's dependence on the letter. Moreover, he saw Romans as allowing him to take a firm stand against the kind of liberal theology which dominated the scene during the period of his own studies and which had one-sidedly reduced biblical study to the status of testimony to a remote past. Further, Nygren saw the liberal reading of the New Testament as overly accentuating differences between the Gospels and Paul and simultaneously underestimating the role of *justification* as the core of Pauline theology.

In his *Commentary on Romans*, Nygren came to the conclusion that Christology, justification by faith, the church, and the sacraments when seen together and in that order compose the fundamentals of Christian faith. Drawing further conclusions for the present time, Nygren took a firm stand against contemporary secularization, a battle which for him never ceased. By secularism he understood the temptation, based on empirical experience, to make the world autonomous with no space for divine revelation or the power of a God who speaks and acts directly in the created order. In contrast, Nygren affirmed the Pauline gospel of a new creation initiated by Christ, a new era which conquers the old and allows for a new righteousness to shine in the world of sin and death. Thus a dramatic view of history emerged and he saw the core of Paul's writings from the vantage of the struggles between opposed ages ("aeons").

Similarly, Nygren's participation in yet another collaborative project became significant not only for his personal theological development but also for the Lutheran Church of Sweden and its contribution to world Lutheranism. This was his involvement in the 1942 publication of a collection of essays, *En bok om kyrkan* (English, *This Is the Church*, 1952). These essays are notable for their international and ecumenical perspectives and for their direct concern with the contemporary challenge of secularization. The authors, led by Nygren, were convinced that the struggle for the survival of Christianity in the secular world depends on a renewed emphasis on the identity of the church.

It is appropriate to relate the publication of *This Is the Church* to the *Barmen Declaration* of 1934, the charter of the Confessing Church in Germany issued in its struggle for survival in the face of the alien Nazi ideology. In both cases there is to be seen a reformulation of the teaching of the Reformers, a reconsideration of the identity of the church based on scripture and in direct opposition to modern heresy. At the same time there is a significant difference between the two. The *Barmen Declaration* based itself on the first article of the creed with an uncompromising protest against any kind of "double revelation" or "natural theology." It thus pointed back to the so-called dialectical theology associated since the early 1920s with persons such as Karl Barth and Rudolf Bultmann. The Swedish exposition was centered, in contrast, in the third article of the creed and proceeded with different formulations. While it is not clear that this difference in accentuation should be seen as a genuine conflict of substance or as a natural expression of differing contexts and traditions, it does perhaps illuminate difficulties experienced within the Lutheran family at the time of the foundation of the Lutheran World Federation in 1947. The contribution of Anders Nygren to *This Is the Church* thus points back to the results of his *Commentary on Romans* and forward to his involvement in the formulation of a truly ecclesiological and ecumenical theology, decisive elements in his overall impact on the twentieth-century church.

## Nygren the President of the LWF

There was clearly a deliberate strategy behind the election of Anders Nygren as the first President of the Lutheran World Federation, the promotion of a candidate whose scholarship was recognized internationally not only in areas of systematic and biblical thought but also in respect to the interpretation of the theology of the Reformers, and preeminently that of Martin Luther, for the modern era.

Nygren was vigorously opposed to any mere repristination of Reformation teaching. At the Hanover Assembly of the LWF in 1952, he demonstrated contempt for the kind of Lutheran cooperation based on a sense of satisfaction "that there are so many people in every part of the world who have the same faith as we; and we would all be very well satisfied with ourselves, because we are such good Lutherans and our doctrine is so sound!" (*Proceedings*, Hanover, p. 42). Nygren maintained that something quite the reverse of such confessional self-complacency was needed. He saw it as his task as President of the LWF to insist on asking the most difficult and urgent questions, to meet substantial contemporary demands however complicated. "Our purpose is not to reiterate what the Reformers said, but to re-think our Gospel, the one and only Gospel, the whole Gospel; to study it anew, possibly from a new point of approach and to express it in the terms of today" (ibid., p. 43).

It was the fulfillment of this purpose that Nygren intended with his celebrated call, "Forward to Luther." What at first glance might be seen as stubborn self-righteousness, perhaps even a kind of Lutheran triumphalism, was in reality meant as a call to reformulate the core of biblical truth and thus to endure all the hardships that might result from such an undaunted but informed response to the basic crises of the then present era.

A reformulation of motifs behind the theology of the Reformers was for Nygren inescapably connected to a rediscovery of the eschatological kernel of their thought. At this point Nygren was strongly polemical in his judgments, perhaps to the point of oversimplification. He came close to seeing one and the same decadence in all instances of decline in church and theology through the centuries. He suspected that there had been a perennial neglect of the original power and strength of the Christian message and a consequent intrusion into the church of both "worldliness" and a mistaken reliance on the strength of purely intellectual judgments.

The Lutheran church, in Nygren's view, had also lost its eschatological dynamic. Its theology and preaching had been drawn into general secularization processes. Thus it was that great opportunities were seen to be opening up. The task is clear: the testimony of the gospel, Luther's testimony, must be given to the present world. "This, therefore, must be our watchword: Always forward toward Luther" (*Proceedings*, Lund, p. 140).

With this basic conviction, Nygren offered his energy and passion when he took the chair as the first President of the Lutheran World Federation. His clear aspiration was to make the new organization not only functional but loyal to its vision as expressed in its foundation. A few of his practical initiatives should be considered as illustrations of his determination to translate his convictions into practical action.

He was determined to take seriously the fact that the Lutheran World Federation was a global entity. The community that marked the Scandinavian Lutheran churches was his point of departure and he made no secret of it. With vigor he insisted on resuming close links, strained by World War II, with the Lutheran churches in Germany and the minority churches elsewhere in Europe. Shortly after the close of the war he had lectured in Berlin and later reported how sympathetic his audiences were, how they needed community with fellow Lutherans as an important means of support in their effort to escape the dark shadow of the immediate past. As early as the summer of 1945, moreover, Nygren went to England in order to assist in the theological education of German students who were then at Norton Camp as prisoners of war. When he became President of the LWF he did not lose sight of convictions born in these experiences. Indeed, the 1945 lectures given to German students in England served as a basis for the draft he was asked to prepare for a report of the 1947 Lund Assembly, "The World, the Sacraments and the Church" (*Proceedings*, Lund, pp. 48ff.).

Additionally, during his presidency, Nygren visited the United States several times. When speaking there he demonstrated yet further proof of his ability based on his theological/philosophical position to clarify sensitive and crucial issues even as he listened to opposing views and subsequently achieved mediation. Such a strategy was needed in respect to features in American Lutheranism that he regarded as obvious weaknesses. In particular, he pointed to the necessity of overcoming the many organizational splits which marked the American Lutheran churches at that time. Furthermore, he was critical of "American activism, sometimes expressed at the cost of a deepened insight into the meaning of the gospel" (*The National Lutheran* [Sept. 1948]). Nygren did not offer this criticism, however, without also mentioning the considerable merits for which the Lutheran churches of America deserved thanks, especially their efficient service to fellow Lutherans in churches ravaged by World War II. It was precisely this combination of criticism and praise which made clear to Nygren what could be the central contribution of the Lutheran World Federation: to bring theological reflection and practical service into a proper and productive relation.

Nygren was also concerned with the task of mediation as he visited churches in the Third World, now more accurately described as the "Two-Thirds World." In 1950 he visited India and Tanganyika (Tanzania) for lengthy periods of time. In India, he came to the conclusion that three specific issues needed particular attention and support from abroad: (1) the challenges to younger churches that wanted to participate in newly born national feelings of independence while retaining strong ties to the "sending churches" of Europe and North America; (2) the tension between Lutheran confessional identity and ecumenical involvement, notably within the framework of the new Church of South India; and (3) the challenge of syncretism, born largely in the Hindu environment, to the Christian gospel.

Nygren's stay in Africa was no less significant, and here too he was able clearly to see serious challenges facing the Lutheran churches: the problems that inevitably faced young churches seeking to take an independent course, and the particular challenges of extreme pietism and legalism raised by the Tanzanian tradition of revivalism.

## Nygren the Ecumenical Leader

It was one of the main contributions of Scandinavian Lutheran theologians that the LWF from its founding was a body characterized both by confessional identity and by ecumenical openness. Nygren was from the beginning a prominent spokesperson for this course. He insisted that the Lutheran churches must proceed "Forward to Luther" even as he assumed leadership within the Faith and Order movement associated since 1948 with the World Council of Churches. He was the host to the Third World Conference on Faith and Order held in Lund in 1952, and prior to that he had attended such world conferences at Lausanne in 1927 and at Edinburgh in 1937.

It was Nygren's contention that Lutheran theology when properly interpreted had an essentially ecumenical dimension of great significance. Nygren saw in Luther's concern to recover the fundamental "essentials" of Christian faith a contribution of far greater significance than that of the Reformer's more polemical positions. In the modern ecumenical situation Nygren insisted—like Luther—that the necessity was to locate common convictions regarding Christ as the head of his body, the church. This method brought him to the expression of a *leitmotif* that contributed greatly to the creation of an ecumenical methodology for the time: "The way to the center is the way to unity" ("Intellectual Autobiography," p. 26).

If other paths were taken, Nygren believed, the ecumenical endeavor would have negative results. Such negative options were typified, for example, in the view that participants in the ecumenical movement were to be encouraged to relinquish elements of their confessional identities in order to discover a "common denominator." Nygren objected to that methodology, affirming that the already existing unity of faith in Christ was to provide the starting point. Ecumenism was not to be the result of human endeavors but rather of the divine gift of common faith in Christ, the center. Neither earlier ecumenical attitudes of extreme enthusiasm nor confessional stubbornness was, to Nygren, sufficient to guide the quest for the unity of the church. Rather, the ecumenical movement was to move with Christ toward what Luther in his explanation of the third article of the creed called "the whole Christian church on earth."

**Bibliographical Notes** _____

*Main Writings of Anders Nygren*

1921    *Religiöst a priori—dess filosofiska förutsättninger och teologiska konsekvenser.* Lund. German ed. 1922.
1921    *Det religionsfilosofiska grundproblemet.* Lund.
1934    *Den tyska kyrkostriden: Den evangeliska kyrkans ställning i det "Tredje riket."* Lund. 2nd ed. 1935. English trans. London, 1934.
1936    *Den kristna kärlekstanken genom tiderna: Eros och Agape.* Stockholm. German trans. 1938–39. English trans.: *Agape and Eros.* Part I, *A Study of the Christian Idea of Love,* Part II, *The History of the Christian Idea of Love,* trans. Philip S. Watson. Philadelphia: Westminster Press, one vol. ed., 1951. Part I was first published, slightly abridged, by SPCK, London, in 1932; Part II was first published in two volumes in 1938–39.
1944    *Pauli Brev till Romarna.* Stockholm. English trans. 1949. German trans. 1951. English trans.: *Commentary on Romans,* trans. Carl C. Rasmussen. Philadelphia: Muhlenberg Press, 1949.
1942    Co-author and editor of *En bok om kyrkan.* Stockholm. English, *This is the Church,* 1952. German trans. 1952. English trans.: *This Is the Church,* trans. Carl C. Rasmussen. Philadelphia: Muhlenberg Press, 1952.
1972    *Meaning and Method: Prolegomena to a Scientific Philosophy of Religion and a Scientific Theology,* trans. Philip S. Watson. Philadelphia: Fortress Press, 1972.

*Printed Material*

Brohed, Ingmar, ed. *Anders Nygren som teolog och filosof: Rapport från symposiet vid 100-årsdagen av hans födelse.* Lund, 1991.
Jarlert, Anders. "Anders Nygren." In *Svensk biografiskt Lexikon.*
Kegley, Charles W., ed. *The Philosophy and Theology of Anders Nygren.* Carbondale and Edwardsville: Southern Illinois University Press, 1970.

*Unprinted Material*

Anders Nygren papers. Lund University Library, Lund, Sweden (access only by special permission. An unprinted, complete bibliography is kept there).
*Festschrift Teologiska uppsatser, Tillägnade Anders Nygren 15.11.1950.* Lund 1950.
*Welt-Luthertum heute: Anders Nygren gewidmet am 15. November 1950.* LWF Archives, Geneva, Switzerland. German and English contributions.

# Hanns Lilje

HANNS LILJE was born in Hanover, Germany, on August 20, 1899, the son of a deacon. In 1917 he acquired his baccalaureate at the local Leibniz School and was recruited for service in the First World War. From 1919 to 1922 he studied theology and history of art in Göttingen and Leipzig. After attending the theological seminary in Loccum he became student chaplain at the Technical University in Hanover in 1924. From 1927 to 1935 he was general secretary of the German Student Christian Movement, and vice-president of the World Student Christian Federation at the end of that period. From 1935, he was executive secretary of the Lutheran World Convention (the predecessor of the Lutheran World Federation) in Berlin. In August 1944 he was arrested by the Gestapo and kept prisoner in Berlin and Nuremberg until the liberation in May 1945 by the Americans.

In 1945, Lilje became Oberlandeskirchenrat in the church office of his hometown and in 1947 Landesbischof. At the same time he was a member of the newly established Council of the Evangelical Church in Germany (EKD), from 1949 to 1967 as deputy chairperson. From 1945 to 1957 he was president of the Central Committee for Inner Mission. After the death of August Marahrens in 1950, he became abbot of the monastery of Loccum. From 1955 to 1969 he was presiding bishop of the United Evangelical Lutheran Church of Germany (VELKD). He was a member of the LWF Executive Committee from 1947 to 1970 and from 1952 to 1957, its president. In 1948 he became a member of the Central Committee of the World Council of Churches (WCC) and in 1968 a member of its Presidium. In 1971 he retired as bishop of his church, while retaining important honorary offices at the ecumenical level. Lilje died on January 6, 1977, in Hanover and is buried in the monastery cemetery in Loccum.

## Theological Position

Although Hanns Lilje came from a pietistic background, he understood himself to be a Lutheran with a broad horizon, free from any confessional constrictions. His biblical understanding was untainted by fundamentalist or historical-critical questions. For him, the Bible was no sacred mystery but a book to provide guidance in everyday life. He understood God's Word to be the proof of Christ's graceful love for human beings. Moreover, Lilje always respected people who experienced and expressed hesitation and doubt.

In his thesis of 1932 concerning Luther's view of history he wrote:

> Luther's thoughts on history are of utmost significance for the understanding of his total *oeuvre*. Whenever he comes to address history, he touches upon all

Author: *Hans-Volker Herntrich, Hanover, Germany*

basic issues of his theology. He speaks of his belief in God—of God's sole effi-
cacy, his hiddenness in history's courts just like in the major historical events
and figures of the world; he speaks of Christ, the face of God turned towards
us; of the church and the hiddenness of the true congregation of Christ in the
world. He speaks of worldly orders but also of the spreading of the gospel in
the world and finally of the end of all earthly history.

For Lilje, the principle of the justification of the sinner as rediscovered and
developed in the Lutheran Reformation led to a radical revisiting of anthropology. For Lilje, Luther's anthropology turned out to be an important ferment
of modern times. In his view, neither the ontological understanding of modern
human beings nor their understanding of freedom is possible without the foundations built in the Lutheran Reformation. Luther himself described the
impact of this approach: it includes not only theology, the church's proclamation and instruction, but also poetry and philosophy, and eventually the political realm. For Lilje, there is no doubt that Luther's anthropological approach
anticipates important insights of more recent philosophy. Since justification is
a process and not something one can possess, the subjectivity of the act of cog-
nition was always characteristic for Lilje's thinking. According to Lilje, the
often crass subjectivism of Luther's understanding of faith has decisively contributed to preparing the way for understanding modern epistemology.

Related to this is the emergence of the modern concept of freedom whose
foundations—according to Lilje—were laid by Lutheran thinking. This concept, on the one hand, goes beyond the idea of an empirically realistic freedom
of the will and, on the other, eschews the danger of believing that reason is
completely autonomous. The Lutheran concept of freedom Lilje espoused is
based on a responsive relationship to God's reality and authority; this ultimate
and absolute attachment frees human beings in a fundamental way from that
which in historical relationships is penultimate. This leads to certain
approaches toward a renewal of biblical exegesis. Luther's reading of the Bible,
of the Holy Scriptures as a whole, the Old and the New Testaments, was christocentric, and Lilje deduced that this contradicted any static canonical understanding: "The authority of the Scriptures is determined by its content, not its
form." That Hanns Lilje's spiritual mindset was shaped by Luther is shown
most clearly in his anthropology. By emphasizing the justification of the sinner, his understanding of the human being was radically removed from any
optimistic assessment and evaluation of human beings. Since the uniqueness
of human existence, its immediacy with regard to God, and its dependence on
God's act of grace are decisive for the evaluation of human beings, Lilje kept
an understanding of human existence which, following Luther, was equally
removed from both idealization and nihilistic resignation.

Lilje considered this theological approach to be particularly helpful for his
concept of the state. Approvingly he quotes Luther, who claimed to have
taught more gloriously on the state than any teacher of Christianity since the
apostles' days and admitted to having a positive relationship to "God's order
of *auctoritas*." A forceful combination of the basic categories of authority, of
responsibility, and of freedom as opposed to unlimited arbitrariness, always
the result of complete human autonomy, results from such thinking. In this

51. Hanns Lilje, Bishop of Hanover, Germany, and President of the Lutheran World Federation, 1952–1957

sense, Lilje repeatedly said that the Lutheran understanding of human existence as justified sinner and the concept of authority as a God-given order can still be used for a renewal of Western thinking. According to Lilje, the modern state can no longer be a Christian state in terms of the medieval concept of *corpus Christianum*. Thus the author developed a Lutheran doctrine of the state that does away with any form of clericalism—that is, subordination of the state to the church—and gives the state, including its worldliness, plenty of room. As long as it has "good governance," God's order is fulfilled.

Already in his first publication *Das technische Zeitalter* of 1928 (The technological age), it becomes clear that Lilje recognized that Christian theologians must take technology, the natural sciences, and the whole modern consciousness seriously, if a shift from emancipation to self-isolation, a drifting into autonomy is to be avoided. Accomplishments such as technical progress and the automation of life are subject to God's law of creation. Lilje saw that traditional solutions—that is, distinctions according to the motto Technology versus Faith—were not sufficient. He described technology as "a creative activity of human beings in the original sense of the word. And for Christian faith it is thus nothing less than the continuation of God's creation." Lilje admitted himself that such thoughts were the result of his activities as student chaplain at the Technical University of Hanover.

Hanns Lilje was a theologian of above average erudition, an intellectual, and a sound skeptic. This did not affect his statements on faith, but enabled him to get involved in spiritual disputes and political decision-making processes— more so than the average church leader. On occasion, where others cautiously remained in the background, he was one of those who were most determined in their support of the EKD memorandum on displaced persons and later the social-liberal policy toward the East of the government of what was then the Federal Republic of Germany. He did not see any alternative.

### Lilje the President of the Lutheran World Federation

In August 1957, the Lutheran World Federation held its Third Assembly in Minneapolis under the theme "Christ Frees and Unites." The meeting was a milestone on the path of the Lutheran churches, since for the first time new structures of joint theological thinking were tried out. That this became possible was not least due to its president, Landesbischof Hanns Lilje, who had been at the head of the Federation since 1952.

When asked about the results of Minneapolis, Lilje asserted that community in confession, in the understanding of the biblical message, in listening to the Word of God and in the use of the sacraments has been strengthened considerably—no mean feat at the time of fifty-seven member churches from twenty-nine countries whose delegates represented fifty million Christians on five continents, of all colors and speaking all kinds of languages. The common basis of their faith was the Bible as understood on the basis of Martin Luther's Reformation. Their practical cooperation was expressed in figures, in DMarks and Swiss Francs, in pounds and dollars, collected in congregations around the globe and sent to Lutheran World Service in Geneva to enable it to support Chinese refugees in Hong Kong or Arab displaced persons in Palestine or impecunious congregations in Eastern Europe. Under Lilje's presidency the West German Lutheran churches, which during the immediate postwar period had to hold out empty hands to their benefactors and had been on the receiving end, were now able to give something themselves.

Lilje also gave other impulses to the community. Thanks to his global commitment, the young churches of Asia and Africa, which had found support and a home in the Lutheran umbrella organization, now also received increased attention. This applied especially to the Ethiopian Evangelical Church Mekane Yesus, which had close links to the Hanover Landeskirche and whose representatives moved with considerable assurance among their Northern sisters and brothers.

As President of the LWF Lilje aimed at equipping the young churches of Asia and Africa with more self-confidence, strength, and self-reliance. Without his extensive traveling and visits, without his speeches and sermons, books and letters, this would not have been possible. Quite apart from his theological and homiletical gifts Lilje had qualities rare in German Protestantism: linguistic and negotiating skills, urbanity, charisma, personality—in short, the ability to reflect on the proper understanding of the Christian message as well as to motivate people of good will to do good deeds in the world. In Lilje, world Lutheranism had a German church leader of international rank whose voice was being listened to. His influence could also be perceived in the theme of the assembly, "Christ Frees and Unites," as well as in the "Minneapolis theses" which were the result of reflection in twenty working groups (cf. pp. 372–73 above).

Lilje emphasized that all questions of practical cooperation lose their meaning unless the Lutheran church constantly rethinks its unity in creed and confession, confronts it with the problems of the times, and takes the risk of giving common answers. It was in part due to the bishop that the document from Minneapolis breathes a spirit of latent political freedom, that it does not lose sight of the needs of underdeveloped regions, and neither ignores the needs of the poor nor the contradictions between faith and ideology, Christianity and secular *Weltanschauung,* Protestants and Catholics.

With regard to the latter, the Hanover president also promoted and supported a concrete project that turned out to be of considerable significance, the Institute for Ecumenical Research at Strasbourg, which among other things explores possibilities of coming to an understanding with modern Catholicism. Even then, it was not easy for Lutherans to walk the tightrope between emphasizing their own profile and isolated sectarianism. Lilje's contribution to the LWF is an indication that confessions can and must learn from one another.

A touch of parliament, a touch of Kirchentag, a touch of theological conference—this was what assemblies of the LWF in the fifties were like. Under Lilje the meetings took on a conciliar character. Under him, it never sufficed merely to conduct noncommittal theological discussions. The aim of all theological work was always to move on to rejoice over one's own confession. "We are at the point of expressing a confession of our faith," he said in his keynote speech. "It, like any real confession, must be made in the presence of God and before the eyes of the world." Referring to the fact that the ecumenical councils of the early church continue to influence present times, and ascribing this influence to fervent spiritual and intellectual struggle with the contemporary world, he continued:

> We must not aim at anything less. As so many representatives gather here from those congregations all over the world which constitute the Lutheran Church of today, they must, to be sure, keep clearly in mind the message entrusted to them by their forefathers. But the Lutheran Church of today dare not make her confession by simply repeating the thoughts and formulations of the past. On the contrary, whatever she has to confess she must say to the

world in which we live *today.* For the moment in which we set forth our confession of the living God is the present moment, the immediate world in
whose fascinating spectrum of longing and dread, technical triumphs and
world-wide catastrophes we have been placed.

Minneapolis was an impressive end to the five-year period under Hanns
Lilje's presidency. In those five years the LWF had acquired a status and a character that had hardly been expected. This was not least due to the fact that
Lilje visited so many Lutheran churches all over the world, in Africa and Asia,
in South and North America; and wherever he went, his personality and the
style of his proclamation were able to build bridges of understanding. The
strong participation of Lutherans from the United Churches of Germany as
well as the emphasis on theological work, which alone can lead to any influence on the public realm, must be considered a specific contribution of the
Federation under the leadership of its German president.

## The Ecumenical Leader

In 1945 National Socialism ended with the death of its "Führer," Adolf Hitler.
Since then, the term "Führer" has been tainted. It is one of the abstruse developments in the church in the first twenty-five years of the postwar period that
the term again gained currency in an area where Hitler's claim to leadership
had not prevailed at all, namely, in the church and especially in the ecumenical movement. On the other hand, it was quite natural to hand over responsibility to the generation of leading churchmen who had participated in the
church struggle. Some of them, after their release after 1945, even brought a
touch of martyrdom from Hitler's prisons and concentration camps. As Martin
Niemöller said, they had also become "Führer," or, rather, "Anti-Führer."
Among them Hanns Lilje played a prominent part.

As a young theologian he was a member of the German Student Christian
Movement and soon took on leadership roles. Via the World Student Christian
Federation he came into contact and made friends with the active champions
of the modern ecumenical movement, which was beginning to take shape in
the twenties, such as the American Francis Miller, the Frenchman Pierre
Maury, the Scotsman Robert Mackie, and the Dutchman Willem A. Visser 't
Hooft. What Lilje meant at that time, both in the common ecumenical training and later as a leader in his Lutheran Landeskirche, will remain of interest
for church history.

During the time following the Third Reich, the course was set for several
important ecumenical developments in which the Christians in Germany
played a considerable role. First is the "Stuttgart Declaration of Guilt" of
October 1945 among whose signatories Lilje is included. This declaration
clearly affirmed the church's involvement and share of responsibility in the
political injustices of the past and listed a number of its failures—something
that determined the positive attitude of the World Council of Churches to the
Germans.

In 1948 Hanns Lilje was a part of the delegation of the Evangelical Church
in Germany (EKD) to the World Council Assembly in Amsterdam. He also rep-

resented the EKD at the assemblies in Evanston (1954), New Delhi (1961), and Uppsala (1968). It was not by accident that the EKD kept nominating him as a delegate, since to his activity in the World Student Christian Federation, he combined broad experience with superb expertise. It was striking that Lilje was called to be a member of the Central Committee of the WCC already in Amsterdam, a position he held until shortly before his death. To the surprise of many a foreigner and ecumenical leader, he embodied a "different" German: easy to get on with, ready and able to fit in with international opinion, and yet with wise and balanced views. Thanks to his political integrity and the trust that he enjoyed during his extensive ecumenical contacts beyond national borders, the doors to the world were once again opened to Germany after the war. Generally speaking, he tried, unbiased as he was, to heal wounds and to reunite that which had been severed. Through him the church not only became more credible but also was freed from its provincial limitations.

It was hardly surprising that the Central Committee in New Delhi elected Hanns Lilje to be a member of its smaller executive committee nor that he was elected to be one of the six presidents of the World Council of Churches at Uppsala—although it was quite unusual that for three successive terms of office one of the presidents always came from the German church. Even if one had wanted to, one could not have sidestepped Lilje, and that was a good thing. For without him and his service to the ecumenical movement, many initiatives would not have been taken and many developments would have taken another course.

## Bibliographical Notes

*Main Writings of Hans Lilje*

1928    *Das technische Zeitalter.* Berlin.
1932    *Luthers Geschichtsanschauung.* Zurich.
1933    *Christus im deutschen Schicksal.* Berlin.
1940    *Das letzte Buch der Bibel.* Berlin, 1940. English trans.: *The Last Book of the Bible: The Meaning of the Revelation of St. John,* trans. Olive Wyon. Philadelphia: Fortress Press, 1957.
1946    *Luther: Anbruch und Krise der Neuzeit.* Nürnberg.
1947    *Im finstern Tal.* Nürnberg. Reprint, Hanover, 1985. English trans.: *The Valley of the Shadow,* trans. Olive Wyon. Philadelphia: Fortress Press, 1950.
1956    *Kirche und Welt.* Munich.
1956    *Welt unter Gott.* Nürnberg.
1962    *Atheismus, Humanismus, Christentum.* Hamburg.
1967    In collaboration with Karl F. Reinking. *Martin Luther: Eine Bildmonographie.* Hamburg, 1964. English trans: *Luther and the Reformation,* trans. Martin O. Dietrich. Philadelphia: Fortress Press, 1967.
1967    *Wanderer auf dem Wege.* Stuttgart.
1968    *Gloria Deo in desertis. Predigten.* Göttingen.
1973    *Memorabilia: Schwerpunkte eines Lebens.* Stein/Nürnberg.

1983    *Martin Luther: 1483/1983.* Bonn: Inter Nationes. [Published post-
        humously in English. Note on copyright page reads: "With the kind
        permission of © Luther Verlag, Bielefeld"]

In 1948 he founded the *Deutsches Allgemeines Sonntagsblatt,* Hamburg
(today: *Das Sonntagsblatt),* whose editor he was until 1976.

*Select Bibliography*

Brunotte, H., F. Hübner, and E. Ruppel, eds. *Gott ist am Werk.* Hamburg, 1959.
Herntrich, H.-V. "Hanns Lilje—Lutheraner mit weitem Horizont." In *Luther: Zeitschrift der Luthergesellschaft* Nr. 2 (1977): 49ff.
Hube, H. W. "Hanns Lilje." In *Geschichten um Hannovers Kirchen,* 68ff. Hanover, 1983.
Kortzfleisch, S. v. "In der Epoche nach Lilje." In *Lutherische Monatshefte* Nr. 2 (1977): 67f.
Lohse, E. "Dienet dem Herrn mit Freuden." In *Der Mensch lebt nicht vom Brot allein,* 12ff. Göttingen, 1979.
Trillhaas, W., ed. *Verständigung.* Göttingen, 1969.
Zahrnt, H. "Hanns Lilje — Eine Lobrede." *Deutsches Allgemeines Sonntagsblatt* Nr. 30 (1971): 1f.

# Franklin Clark Fry

FRANKLIN CLARK FRY was born in Bethlehem, Pennsylvania, on August 30, 1900. He was the son and grandson of pastors. After early education in Rochester, New York, he studied at Hamilton College in Clinton, New York (Bachelor of Arts in 1921), and at the American School for Classical Studies in Athens, Greece. Fry graduated from the Lutheran Theological Seminary at Philadelphia (Bachelor of Divinity in 1925) and was ordained on June 10, 1925, by the New York–New England Synod of the United Lutheran Church in America (ULCA). In the same year he was called to be pastor of Redeemer Lutheran Church in Yonkers, New York. In 1929 he became pastor of Trinity Lutheran Church, Akron, Ohio. Between 1929 and 1944 Fry served on a number of boards and commissions of the ULCA, including the Board of American Missions, the Committee on Evangelism, the Committee on Moral and Social Welfare, and the Executive Board of the Church. In 1944 he was elected president of the ULCA, and he was consistently reelected through its 1960 convention. Fry was elected president of the Lutheran Church in America (LCA) in 1962, a position he held from 1963 until he resigned shortly before his death. During his presidency of both the ULCA and the LCA, Fry served in a number of Lutheran and ecumenical positions, including as president of Lutheran World Relief (LWR), elected in 1946; as a founder of the Lutheran World Federation (LWF) in 1947 and of the World Council of Churches (WCC) in 1948, and as vice-chairman of its Central Committee and later its chairman until 1968; as councillor of the National Lutheran Council (NLC) from 1945 until 1966, and a member of its executive committee from 1946 until 1966, presiding officer at the initial convention of the National Council of the Churches of Christ in the USA (NCCC) in 1950; as treasurer of the LWF in 1948 and its president from 1957 until 1963. Fry received numerous government decorations for his relief work and thirty-four honorary doctorates from institutions throughout the world. In 1927 Fry married Hilda Adrianna Drews. They had three children. On June 6, 1968, Fry died in New Rochelle, New York.

### Fry as Pastor

Franklin Clark Fry has few if any peers among the leaders of American and global Lutheranism in this century (*Time*, April 7, 1958). He was a giant who cast his shadow over virtually every area of worldwide Lutheranism and of the ecumenical movement of his day. Obviously an extremely gifted and complex person, Fry could be studied from a number of perspectives. Yet the most

Author: *William G. Rusch, New York, New York*

52. Franklin Clark Fry, President of the United Lutheran
    Church in America and subsequently of the Lutheran
    Church in America, President of the Lutheran World
    Federation, 1957–1963

satisfactory key to understanding Fry is not primarily as the church president
or the presider at ecumenical meetings, but rather Franklin Clark Fry as the
pastor.

He represented the third generation of clergy in his family. His grandfather
was a member of the faculty of the Lutheran Theological Seminary at Philadelphia; his father a pastor in Bethlehem, Pennsylvania, and Rochester, New
York, and then executive secretary of the Board of American Missions of the
ULCA. The family context must be regarded as a consequential and decisive
influence on his life. Apparently there was always the assumption that
Franklin Clark too would be a pastor. His education, beginning Greek in high
school, his years at Hamilton College with four years of training in public
speaking, and the year in Athens at the American School of Classical Studies
all furnished excellent preparation for seminary. Stories circulate about his

dissatisfaction with the seminary preparation he received (*Mr. Protestant*, 9–10; "A Palette for a Portrait," 10).

Fry served a total of nineteen years in the parish ministry, four years at Redeemer Lutheran Church in Yonkers, New York, and fifteen years at Trinity Lutheran Church in Akron, Ohio. It was in the course of these years in the parish that Fry either acquired or honed skills that would mark him the rest of his life: discipline, hard work, organization, careful use of language in writing and preaching, and the insistence that ecumenical statements come from properly organized ecumenical organizations. Yet even with this last concern Franklin Clark Fry prior to 1944 could not be described as an ecumenist. The focal point of his ministry was the parish. This would change only later.

Although Fry left the parish ministry in 1944 with his election to the presidency of the ULCA, never to return, his deep abiding love of being Pastor Fry was evident. He taught a Sunday school class on television; he preached as regularly as his presidential office allowed; over the years he communicated with his fellow pastors in the church by a series of "Dear Partners" letters. Throughout his years as president of the ULCA and LCA he would confide on occasion to friends how he longed for a return to parish ministry (see Bachmann, *History of the United Lutheran Church in America* [forthcoming] chapter 9). Thus Fry should be understood first as a pastor of the church, and only then in other capacities.

In view of the path of his career, it is not surprising that almost all of Fry's writings are occasional pieces as distinct from formal treatises. He is recalled as a writer of constitutions, and not books. Nevertheless, the corpus of his writings is fairly extensive, although scattered in many places. There are articles and addresses in a variety of journals, bulletins, and minutes. A number of his sermons have been published. Both the *ULCA Pastor's Desk Book* and the *LCA Minister's Information Service* offered a means for Fry to share what was on his mind with the church. They are primary sources to gain an understanding of his thinking and priorities.

### Fry as President of the ULCA and LCA

In October 1944 Fry's life changed decisively. At the age of forty-four he was elected president of the ULCA at its fourteenth biennial convention. Earlier Fry had served on a number of boards and committees of the ULCA, including the executive board, to which he was elected in 1942. On January 1, 1945, he became the chief pastor and executive head of his church. From that time until his death in 1968 he maintained constant dedication to his own church and was a preeminent influence in its life. Fry throughout his two presidencies gave American Lutherans a new sense of confidence and self-respect. He contributed to a sense of good order internally while turning both the ULCA and the LCA outward to acknowledge their world opportunities and responsibilities in Christian unity and service. Fry as president of the ULCA and LCA drew on his earlier strengths exhibited in the parish and outgrew his reluctant ecumenism.

The events of the unfolding years reveal his role as Lutheran church leader and ecumenist. Fry became quickly identified with the National Lutheran Council as a member of the executive committee and chairman of its work with the LWF. He worked with the NLC's program of aid to orphaned missions. Already in 1946, the second year of his presidency, Fry was elected president of LutheranWorld Relief and over the next twenty years made many trips to further church relief and reconstruction.

Between 1945 and 1948 Fry struggled hard for the formation of the World Council of Churches, insisting on confessional representation in the council (see Flesner, *American Lutherans Help Shape World Council*). These efforts took him to Europe in 1945 when he met church leaders with whom he would work for the rest of his life. At the same time Fry was a major factor in the process of the transformation of the Lutheran World Convention (LWC) into the LWF, which culminated in Lund in 1947.

Fry presided at the first session of the constituting convention of the National Council of the Churches of Christ in the USA (NCCC) in Cleveland in 1950. He played a key role in the process of defining the principles of organization for the National Council. In January 1951 he made a round-the-world flight on behalf of the "One Great Hour of Sharing" appeal of the NCCC's Church World Service.

In the swirl of all these activities Lutheran unity was never far from Fry's attention. The ULCA had long been committed to a vision of one Lutheran Church in the United States. In 1956 Fry used his president's report to the Harrisburg convention of the ULCA to address the theme of Christian unity (*Minutes of the Twentieth Biennial Convention of The United Lutheran Church* [Harrisburg, Penn., 1956] pp. 29–38). While the immediate catalyst is to be seen as Lutheran unity, the address is also evidence of the deep impact that Fry's ecumenical activities had on him. Lutheran unity is viewed in the context of the unity of the church catholic. This report is perhaps one of Fry's most impressive writings and a testimony to his leadership.

Although an all-inclusive union of the eight bodies comprising the NCL did not occur, under Fry's leadership and largely through his efforts the LCA was established in 1962. In 1956 the Joint Commission on Lutheran Unity began its work on behalf of the ULCA, Augustana Lutheran Church, American Evangelical Lutheran Church and Finnish Evangelical Lutheran Church (Suomi Synod). In six years the task was completed. Fry was elected the first president of the LCA at its constituting convention in Detroit and held that office until his resignation in 1968.

As a result of this merger and the union of churches forming the American Lutheran Church (ALC) in 1960, Fry with Dr. Paul C. Empie, the executive director of the NLC, proposed the replacement of that organization in 1966 with the Lutheran Council in the USA (LCUSA). Now for the first time the LCA and ALC were joined with the Lutheran Church–Missouri Synod (LCMS) and the Synod of Evangelical Lutheran Churches in a cooperative program of theological study and Christian service.

Under Fry's leadership, the LCA quickly grew into a unified church, enriched with the gifts of its merging churches. It took its place as a member of the NCCC, WCC, LCUSA, and the LWF. It also early in its history clarified its principles of ecumenical participation in local areas. As president of the LCA, Fry continued in pivotal ecumenical positions to which he had been elected earlier.

## Fry as President of the LWF

Fry's leadership in the LWF was felt long before he became president. Already in 1945 he was appointed to the Lutheran World Convention Liaison Committee, whose responsibilities were to oversee relief work and reorganization of the LWC. In 1945 and 1946 Fry was in Europe with colleagues from the Federal Council of Churches and the American section of the LWC. On the latter trip his goals were to reactivate the executive committee of the LWC, promote relief work and welfare agencies, and secure the support of European Lutherans for confessional rather than geographic representation in the WCC, which was about to be formed. Fry was an active participant in the meeting of the executive committee of the LWC in Uppsala in 1946, which planned the constituting assembly of the LWF in Lund in 1947. Fry considered the Uppsala meeting an "epochal victory of world Lutheran unity" (see Nelson, *The Rise of World Lutheranism*, 1987, pp. 384–86).

At the 1947 Lund Assembly, Fry was elected to the executive committee of the Federation. In the following year he was chosen to be treasurer, a position he kept until 1952. In that year at the Hanover Assembly Fry was elected first vice-president. At the Minneapolis Assembly in 1957 Fry was the logical choice to become president. He held this office through the 1963 assembly in Helsinki. His leadership at both these events was notable: at Minneapolis he was largely credited with being the author of the widely circulated "Minneapolis Theses," which provided theological explication of the theme "Christ Frees and Unites"; at Helsinki he presided over the difficult discussions concerning the proposed statement on justification, discussions that sorely tested his parliamentary expertise and elicited some criticism of his "Western" skills (see pp. 58–59 and 377–79). From 1963 until his death in 1968 Fry continued to serve on the LWF Executive Committee.

Fry's leadership within the LWF, and especially his presidency, was characterized by confessional integrity with his constant emphasis on the confessional and evangelical principles and by ecumenical commitment in reaching out to Orthodox, Anglican, Reformed, and Roman Catholic leaders—although in the last instance after some considerable hesitation (see *ULCA Pastor's Desk Book* [Dec., 1950]: 211–19; [June, 1951]: 249–55; [Nov., 1951]: 287–98). Throughout these years the three issues that engaged his attention were the relation of the LWF to the WCC, the relation of the LWF to LCMS, and a study of the nature of the LWF from the standpoint of theology and church history.

On many occasions Fry spoke of the great issues confronting the LWF or interpreted the Federation to its member churches. At his first executive committee meeting as president at Strasbourg in October 1958, Fry emphasized the balance between unity and truth as twin imperatives. The justification for the LWF was its effort to maintain the proper relationship between these imperatives. This was the theme he lifted up at the 1958 convention of United

Lutheran Church Women under the title "LWF Serves the Church in the World Today." Already in 1955 as first vice-president, Fry was sharing developments in the executive committee, which that year met in Vienna, in his *Dear Partners Letter* as part of a report on the state of the church.

### Fry as Moderator of the Central Committee of the WCC

As in the case of the LWF, Fry was a significant player in the creation of the WCC. Almost immediately after his election as president of the ULCA he became an active supporter of the proposal that the WCC must recognize the confessional principle for member church representation. Meetings took him to Europe in 1945 and 1946 to make his point to other Lutherans and to W. A. Visser't Hooft, the general secretary of the WCC in formation. One of Fry's considerable achievements was the early action of the first assembly of WCC in Amsterdam in 1948 to adopt unanimously a proposed amendment to the constitution that provided for confessional representation.

The first central committee of the WCC, meeting after the assembly, elected Fry its vice-chairman. Under the tutelage of George K. A. Bell, the Anglican bishop of Chichester, Fry had the opportunity to become acquainted with the people and the work of WCC. He served in that position from 1948 until 1954 and from 1954 until 1968 was the chairman of the WCC central committee and of its executive committee. He was first elected at the Evanston Assembly and reelected in New Delhi in 1961. He served in that capacity until his death, a few months before the Uppsala Assembly in 1968.

In 1949 and 1950 Fry was part of a small group consulted by Visser't Hooft regarding the creation of the Toronto Statement, "The Church, the Churches, and the World Council of Churches," the document approved by the central committee in 1950 to clarify the meaning of membership in the WCC. As a leader within the WCC, Fry was concerned with relations with the Orthodox including membership for the Russian Orthodox Church, the question whether to send WCC observers to the Second Vatican Council, and the challenges to the WCC as it lived through the cold war and the tensions of East and West. He was known for his skill in chairing meetings, his diplomacy, and his ability for negotiation. On occasion he represented the WCC in Communist lands with firmness and skill. For example, at the time of a WCC meeting in Hungary when delicate negotiations were being conducted for the freedom of Bishop Lajos Ordass, whom Fry supported in all possible ways, the American church leader spoke with force and articulation.

Fry effectively interpreted the WCC not only internationally but within his own church, as his *Dear Partners Letter* and the *LCA Ministers' Information Service* disclose. Over the years Fry shared—attractively and with attention to its local significance—news of WCC assemblies, central committee meetings, and the joint working group between the WCC and the Roman Catholic Church.

For approximately two decades Franklin Clark Fry kept before global Christianity confessionalism as an integral part of the ecumenical vision. He surrendered neither unity nor truth, while maintaining that all ecumenical activity must be rooted in the constituent church bodies. He never regarded it a paradox to strive for the upbuilding of his own church and at the same time for that of the church catholic.

## Bibliographical Notes

Bachmann, E. Theodore. *A History of the United Lutheran Church in America.* Forthcoming. Especially chapter 9.

Fischer, Robert W., ed. "Franklin Clark Fry: A Palette for a Portrait." Vol. 24 of *The Lutheran Quarterly* (1972).

Flesner, Dorris A. *American Lutherans Help Shape the World Council.* Dubuque, Iowa: William C. Brown, 1981.

Gilbert, W. Kent. *Commitment to Unity: A History of the Lutheran Church in America.* Philadelphia: Fortress Press, 1988.

Lazareth, William H. "Franklin Clark Fry." Pp. 96–98 in *Ecumenical Pilgrims: Profiles of Pioneers in Christian Reconciliation,* edited by Ion Bria and Dagmar Heller. Geneva: World Council of Churches, 1995.

*Mr. Protestant.* Philadelphia: The Board of Publication of the ULCA, 1960.

Nelson, E. Clifford. *The Rise of World Lutheranism: An American Perspective.* Philadelphia: Fortress Press, 1982.

# Fredrik A. Schiotz

FREDRIK AXEL SCHIOTZ was born on June 15, 1901, in Chicago, Illinois. His parents were Danish immigrants. After high school, he studied at St. Olaf College in Northfield, Minnesota (Bachelor of Arts in 1924), and at Luther Seminary in St. Paul, Minnesota (Bachelor of Theology in 1930 and Master of Theology in 1932). He was a leader in the Lutheran student movement and was ordained in 1930 as a pastor in the Norwegian Lutheran Church (from 1946 named the Evangelical Lutheran Church [ELC]), which in 1960 merged with German and Danish Lutheran churches in America to form the American Lutheran Church (ALC). Schiotz served three parishes: Zion in Duluth, Minnesota (1930–1932); Trinity in Moorhead, Minnesota (1932–1938); and Trinity in Brooklyn, New York (1945–1948). He held a variety of leadership positions related to global mission and ecumenical work: executive secretary of the Student Service Commission of the American Lutheran Conference (1938–1945); member of the board of directors of the Student Volunteer Movement for Foreign Missions (1948– 1954); executive secretary of the Commission on Younger Churches and Orphaned Missions (CYCOM) of the National Lutheran Council (1948–1954); first chairperson of the Commission of World Missions of the Lutheran World Federation 1952–1957; member of the executive committee of the National Lutheran Council (1955–1966), of the Lutheran Council U.S.A. (1967–1971); president of the ELC (1954–1960) and of the ALC (1961–1971). He was a delegate of his church to the first three assemblies of the Lutheran World Federation and was elected to the executive committee of the Lutheran World Federation (1955–1971). The Federation elected him president at the Fourth Assembly in Helsinki in 1963. Ten American academic institutions and the German University of Erlangen granted him honorary doctoral degrees. He was married to Dagny Aasen in 1928. Fredrik Schiotz died on February 25, 1989.

## Advocate for Global Mission

Fredrik A. Schiotz always understood himself as a member of a worldwide Christian movement. Experiencing radical changes in a world plagued by the two world wars, he was eager to relieve the plight of Christians and non-Christians on the basis of faith, love, and justice. He did his work as a Lutheran who was deeply grounded in the Lutheran confessions and in a piety shaped by the Haugean Awakening. (Haugeanism originated with Hans Nielsen Hauge [1771–1824], a Norwegian lay preacher and leader of the first great Norwegian Awakening. Influenced by German pietism, he advocated individual piety based on Bible study and thrifty living.) The Lutheran confessions taught

Author: *Eric W. Gritsch, Baltimore, Maryland*

53. Fredrik A. Schiotz of Minneapolis, Minnesota, President of the American Lutheran Church and President
of the Lutheran World Federation, 1963–1970

Schiotz that Christian unity is not an appendix to but the heartbeat of Christian life; and Haugean pietism taught him that personal commitment to Christ
is the presupposition for ecumenism and mission.

Schiotz summarized his life's work in a brief autobiography entitled *One
Man's Story*. In it he speaks of insights that shaped his early life as a student,
especially his inner release from a lifestyle that was bound by custom and
man-made rules (ibid., p. 41). When he discovered that customs and rules
inhibited Christians from joyful interaction or common work for justice, he
called for release from what he called "moral legalism," which he himself had
experienced in his own church. In a book entitled *Release*, he spelled out a way
in which Christians can be liberated from a narrow-minded lifestyle and thus

better suited for global mission. Schiotz used his parish experience to communicate his Lutheran stance of Christian freedom. Such freedom from the bondage of fear, sin, and self comes through "three sign posts," which read "seeing, wanting, surrendering." Healthy, critical sight, he contended, leads to proper diagnosis of human weakness, to penance as the honest desire to change. Such sight, then, leads to a desire to be forgiven and to be no longer ruled by despair and apathy. Finally, the desire to be forgiven leads to a surrender, a yielding to God by faith. According to Schiotz, release is not a pious feeling but the experience of change from the bondage of self to the bond of faith with God, who, in Christ, enables Christians to become and to remain steadfast disciples (*Release*, chaps. 1–3). Schiotz was aware that American Lutheran pietism, inherited from Germany and Scandinavia, tended to stress individualistic introspection and narrow-minded moralism. Although Bible study, Sunday schools, and summer camps can create a specific piety that contributes to spiritual renewal, it is always superseded by the Lord's Supper as the true source of a "yielded life" that unites Christians with Christ and with each other (*Release*, pp. 119–27). Such fellowship becomes the true source of Christian unity and mission, focusing on the victims of the plight of the twentieth century with its violence, tyranny, and neglect of the neighbor in need.

Schiotz was particularly concerned about the lack of a consciously Lutheran approach to mission. He developed the theological basis for such an approach in an essay entitled "A Lutheran Approach to Missions," published together with two other essays—"Missions at Home," by H. Conrad Hoyer of the National Lutheran Council's Division of American Missions, "Missions Abroad," by Andrew S. Burgess of Luther Seminary in St. Paul, Minnesota (*Go Into All the World*). Acknowledging the difference between the time of Luther and the twentieth century, Schiotz focused on the "word of God, the recovered gospel" as the foundation for the church as a community charged with the dissemination of the gospel everywhere, be it an unsystematic or a "systematic sending" ("Lutheran Approach," p. 1; this term is from the German missiologist Gustav Warneck). But the proclamation of the word of God does not become propaganda or a license to export a particular form of church organization. Rather, Christian mission is the communication of the gospel in word and sacraments as the only necessary means by which people are united with Christ. All other components of mission are functional arrangements for the sake of improving the essential communication of the word of God. Schiotz also saw the need for a proper distinction of such communication and works of love and justice. Just as the feeding of the five thousand accompanied the teaching of Jesus, so should agricultural experimentation or the establishment of a hospital find their place as a commentary on the gospel (ibid., 12).

Schiotz practiced what he preached in his contacts with churches and peoples around the globe. He was particularly concerned about the issue of ethnic differences, which had divided Christians, especially in South Africa and in the United States. Whenever he encountered racism, he opposed it, gently but firmly. Racism was pervasive, he admitted, but it had no place among Christians, and it was on its way out all over the world (*One Man's Story*, p. 127).

## An Unassuming Churchman

Schiotz never aspired to a greater office than that of being an ordained servant in his Lutheran church. Although he dreamed of going to China or other foreign territories as a missionary, he never actively pursued this dream. But doors opened for him again and again, from his time as a college student to his election as President of the Lutheran World Federation. He learned to be a leader by accepting the church's call, be it as itinerant administrator of various mission projects abroad or as the head of his church at home. He took on many assignments related to foreign missions; he negotiated critical issues; and he supplied his superiors with accurate accounts of his endeavors (see, e.g., Schiotz, "Lutheran World Missions," pp. 311–22, a meticulous account of various Lutheran missions, with critical insights into the deliberations between Lutherans and other Christians in the Batak churches of Indonesia).

When Schiotz was nominated to be president of the ELC in 1954, he made it known that he would be absent from the church assembly because he was to be at a meeting of the National Lutheran Council to report on its mission abroad. But he was elected president on the second ballot (*One Man's Story*, p. 130). He worked tirelessly to steer the ELC on a pan-Lutheran, ecumenical course. He worked hard for the reorganization of the National Lutheran Council until it was reorganized as the Lutheran Council in the United States (LCUSA) in 1966. When social and political turmoil plagued many American cities, he helped to create a Lutheran Committee on Inner-City Ministries in 1967 (CICM). Aware of the enduring Lutheran problem of biblical authority he summarized his view of the matter in a succinct way, stressing the freedom and joy in the Lutheran position with regard to the Bible and avoiding a biblical fundamentalism (ibid., p. 148).

When Schiotz was nominated for the presidency of the Lutheran World Federation at its Fourth Assembly in Helsinki in 1963 he announced that he was not seeking the office. But he was elected and continued his work as a tireless, unassuming churchman, who, however, always got things done. He was especially helpful in negotiations with churches in Communist Eastern Europe. His cool, polite manner as well as his clear communication of Christian concerns in a hostile environment kept lines of communication open with Lutheran churches burdened by Communist governments. At the same time, he refused to compromise with Fascist governments when they tried to use the Lutheran World Federation for their own purposes.

When the Fifth Assembly was to be held in Porto Alegre, Brazil, the executive committee decided under his leadership to question the invitation by the host church in Brazil to invite the highest authority in the country to greet the assembly, which had been the tradition for similar events. Normally this would have been welcomed, but given the situation, the welcome by the Brazilian government would have been the equivalent of an LWF endorsement of its actions. Brazil was under military dictatorship, and the military government was violating human rights by suppressing political opposition. Schiotz made sure that LWF member churches were informed about this difficulty, and, after thorough consultations, he advocated an assembly meeting in Europe. Evian, France, was the best available location (cf. pp. 382ff. above).

Once again, Schiotz steered the assembly through difficult situations. He succeeded in having voting privileges granted to youth delegates, who frequently criticized LWF resolutions as being too distant from the problems of the developing countries, especially in Africa and Asia. He also heartily welcomed Cardinal Willebrands, who was the first emissary of the Vatican to address an LWF Assembly, with favorable words about Luther and Lutheran relations with Rome. One year later, in 1971, Schiotz visited Rome on behalf of the LWF to express gratitude for the cardinal's participation at the assembly in Evian. But it was not just a courtesy call. Schiotz had attended sessions of Vatican II (1962–1965) and discussed various issues with the pope, including the neuralgic topic of population control. Schiotz defended it, but departed as a friend of the Vatican.

**Bibliographical Notes** _____

*Main Writings by Fredrik Schiotz*

1935    *Release.* Minneapolis: Augsburg.
1951    Together with Conrad H. Hoyer, and Andrew S. Burgess. *Go Into All the World: An Introduction to Lutheran Missions.* Chicago: Division of Student Service, National Lutheran Council.
1954    "Lutheran World Missions." *International Review of Missions* 43 (1954): 311–22.
1980    *One Man's Story.* Minneapolis: Augsburg.

# Mikko Juva

MIKKO JUVA was born on November 22, 1918, in Kaarlela, Finland. He studied history at the University of Turku (1936–1939) and theology at the University of Helsinki (1939–1944). Ordained in 1944, he served as general secretary of the Student Christian Movement (SCM) of Finland from 1944 to 1946. In 1946 he married Riitta Brofeldt. Following studies at Gettysburg Lutheran Seminary in the U.S. (1946–1947) he was a student pastor from 1948 to 1950. He earned a doctorate in history at Turku (1950) and in church history at Helsinki (1955); he was professor of Finnish history in Turku from 1957 to 1962, and professor of Finnish and Scandinavian church history at the University of Helsinki from 1962 to 1978. He also served as rector of the university from 1971 to 1973 and chancellor from 1973 to 1978. He was elected archbishop of Turku in 1978 and retired in 1982. Mikko Juva was chairperson of the LWF Commission on Theology from 1963 to 1970 and President of the LWF from 1970 to 1977.

## Scholar

Juva was born into the home of a professor of history. From his early youth he was at home in the academic community. The classical syllabus of his secondary education made him well versed in the humanistic tradition of Europe and the history of the Greco-Roman world. Majoring in history, he wrote his master's thesis on the concept of the state in St. Augustine. After graduating from the University of Turku in 1939, he moved to the University of Helsinki to study theology.

Juva's pursuit of theology was abruptly interrupted by the hundred-day Winter War, when the Soviet Union attacked Finland on November 30, 1939. He was sent to the front as an infantry soldier. When war broke out again between Finland and the U.S.S.R. in June 1941, he was, as a newly trained officer, made commander of a mortar platoon. During the lulls between the fighting he resumed his theological studies and, after a four-month study leave, he was ordained in January 1944. He came out of the war as a seasoned soldier, promoted to the rank of captain and as a young pastor whose ministry had been tested by the horrors of combat. The experience on the front left a lifelong imprint on Juva's personality and his theological outlook.

Juva received a scholarship to study at the Gettysburg Lutheran Seminary in the United States in 1946–1947. This gave him an opportunity to expand his theological training into those areas to which he had not been able to give adequate attention during the war. The main significance of the American year for him, however, was that it opened to him the reality and diversity of the worldwide church, broadened his understanding of the Lutheran communion, and helped him to step out of the confines of Finnish pietism.

Author: *Risto Lehtonen, Helsinki, Finland*

54. Mikko Juva, Professor at the University of Helsinki
    and subsequently Archbishop of the Evangelical
    Lutheran Church of Finland, President of the
    Lutheran World Federation, 1970–1977

After his return to Finland, Juva concentrated on his doctoral work in history and earned the Ph.D. at the University of Turku in 1950. His thesis dealt with the entry of religious liberalism into Finland in 1848–1869. In the following years he continued research in the intellectual and spiritual history of Finland in the second half of the nineteenth century and wrote two more books in which he dealt with the confrontation between conservatism and liberalism in church and society, the introduction of religious freedom, and the transformation of the Finnish Lutheran church from a state church into a folk church. The trilogy including his doctoral thesis became a standard work on the history of intellectual movements of that era in Finland.

Juva's second doctoral thesis, for the Department of Theology at the University of Helsinki, was on folk religiosity in Southwestern Finland in the seventeenth and eighteenth centuries. After five years of teaching history at the University of Turku, he joined the theological faculty of the University of Helsinki as a professor of church history. Subsequently, as rector, and finally as the chancellor of the University of Helsinki, he became influential in the Finnish university scene and in government policies on higher education. During the years of radical student unrest Juva played a central role in leading a successful battle for the freedom of the university from political and ideological control. He earned the respect of his adversaries among students and politicians, including spokespersons of the extreme left, as a defender of the freedom and integrity of scholarly work.

## The Making of a Church Leader

For Mikko Juva the ministry became an obvious choice when in 1936 he attended a summer conference of the Finnish Student Christian Movement (SCM). He was overwhelmed, as he himself has described it, by an experience of "spiritual illumination," which gave him a new, deeply personal grasp of the meaning of Jesus Christ. Subsequent involvement in the SCM during two decades influenced him profoundly. From the thirties until the late forties the Finnish SCM was marked by a blend of rural Finnish pietism and the Nordic evangelicalism associated with Ole Hallesby of Norway. This heritage became a significant point of departure for his later convictions and commitments.

Participation in the World Student Christian Federation (WSCF) under the leadership of Philippe Maury added vital elements to Juva's vision about the ministry of the church. His attendance in 1953 at the World Christian Youth Assembly at Kottyam, India, the meeting of the Central Committee of the WCC at Lucknow, and the General Committee of the WSCF at Nasrapur exposed him to the worldwide ecumenical movement and to the mission of the church in the midst of Asian nations' struggle for independence. The persons who had a special impact on him were W. A. Visser't Hooft of the WCC, Martin Niemöller of Germany, M. M. Thomas of India, and D. T. Niles of Sri Lanka (Ceylon).

The period after the war meant for the Finnish church a profound search for theological directions. The conservative evangelical movement in the church had grown, following a wartime spiritual revival; it presented a simple message of repentance, conversion, and acceptance of Christ, and emphasized the contrast between God's kingdom and the world. Another trend appeared among pastors who had spent years in trenches. They found it pointless to try to separate believers and nonbelievers and thereby destroy the precious sense of solidarity and communication which they had met among men on the front; their spiritual search was much wider and more multifaceted than was recognized by the pietists. Witness to God's unconditional love for creation and to his unqualified openness to people facing hardship, fear, and suffering, was for them the heart of the matter in ministry. A movement around these emphases spread into the church, drawing heavily on the theology associated with Lund, Sweden.

Juva was influenced by these developments as he formed his own theological position. He broke away from the neo-pietism of the conservative evangelical movement, but he could not identify fully with the Finnish disciples of the Swedish Lundensian school. He felt that Christian involvement in the world presupposed a background in classical Christology, which, in his view, this latter movement failed adequately to express.

His leading theme became "the church for the world." Being for the life of the world, driven by the gospel, was the heart of the missionary task of the church. It implied engagement and even confrontation in dialogue with the social and ideological movements of the day. Juva's concept meant a deliberate rejection of an introverted and defensive understanding of Christian faith. While there were many in the Finnish church who at that time were not prepared to follow this approach, which they feared promoted secularism, Juva's vision nevertheless began to gain ground in the church.

In 1954 Juva, who was being attacked by conservative theologians and pastors, was elected chairman of the Finnish Missionary Society (FMS, subsequently the Finnish Evangelical Lutheran Mission). This task was very close to his heart, and he held the position until 1980. The visits he made in this capacity to the "mission fields," especially to Namibia and Tanzania, influenced his own grasp of the struggle of African countries for independence. Moreover, they equipped him for turning the FMS from political quietism with regard to South African apartheid to opposing racism and supporting the Namibian struggle for independence.

## Participant in Public Life

In the mid-sixties Juva made a detour from his academic and church responsibilities into national politics. He joined the Liberal Party and was its chairman from 1965 to 1968, and a member of the Finnish parliament from 1964 to 1966. He soon concluded, however, that his new responsibilities in the Lutheran World Federation were more important to him than running for reelection or other positions of political leadership.

His knowledge of national politics made Juva a much-used resource person in governmental committees on church–state relationships, university policies, and the rights of refugees. This experience contributed to his alertness and realism concerning issues of Christian political and social responsibility and to his preparation for leading the LWF and the Evangelical Lutheran Church of Finland.

## President of the LWF

Juva's election as the President of the LWF at the Evian Assembly in 1970 did not follow the usual pattern. He was not from the host church of the assembly, nor was he a bishop. He had become known in the LWF as the local coordinator of the Helsinki Assembly (1963) and as an active and influential chairman of the LWF Commission on Theology (1963–1970). At that time the Commission on Theology gave much attention to the emerging "theologies of revolution," to the Lutheran contribution to the ecumenical discussion, and to action on social justice, peace, and human rights.

Juva's own understanding of the function of the presidency influenced the life of the LWF in numerous ways. He underlined strongly the character of the LWF as an organization of Lutheran churches. The president, elected by the assembly, was a trustee of the member churches and the *primus inter pares* among the members of the executive committee. But in addition to presiding over the executive committee and officers, the president was the chief representative of the LWF and, between the meetings, its highest authority. This constitutional role meant for Juva that he was to be involved in the major issues and decisions faced by the secretariat. The Geneva office under the leadership of the general secretary was in the first place the implementing arm of the executive committee. It was responsible for planning and proposing policies and programs for the approval of the executive committee and for carrying out its decisions. In Juva's concept the division of responsibilities between the executive committee, over which he presided, and the headquarters staff, which was led by the general secretary, had to be kept clear and precise. The staff should not on its own set the course of the LWF but should rely on the executive committee. Juva was not prepared to function as a rubber stamp. This division of responsibility and the implied regular communication between him and the general secretary was, in his view, essential for the health of the LWF.

Juva also was acutely aware that on current issues such as the war in Vietnam, racism in general and apartheid in particular, and human rights, the executive committee would not necessarily have enough time and, at the outset, a common viewpoint for defining well-grounded positions on these issues. Besides national and regional diversities, the tension between those emphasizing the common Lutheran doctrinal tradition and those emphasizing cultural-political contextuality made it difficult to reach a common mind. Therefore Juva put much effort into his addresses at the executive committee meetings, endeavoring to offer theological and political perspectives for the deliberations and decisions and to place on the record the major concerns of Lutheran churches in the world. After the 1970 Evian Assembly the challenge of the radicalism of youth and students continued to influence the life of the LWF. Juva resented activities that were introduced to the LWF behind the back of the executive committee, bypassing the legitimate decision makers of member churches. He was determined to contain such influence and maintain an open debate and transparency of decisions.

Juva also felt that an expansion of the membership of the executive committee would make the organization more vulnerable to staff control and would undo the necessary balance between the governing bodies and the general secretary and headquarters staff. For him such a concentration of power in the staff, which he saw happening in the WCC, was contrary to the nature of the LWF as a federation of churches and an expression of communion.

Seeing signs of what he perceived to be subversive activities among staff members made him prone to conflict. This happened in his relationship to the LWF Department of Studies and its director, Ulrich Duchrow. However, changes within the staff after 1974 helped to put an end to the escalation of conflict. This orientation began to lose its influence in the LWF, and the preparations for the 1977 assembly were carried out without excessive internal conflicts. By the time of Dar es Salaam the LWF had proceeded toward a new theological and political balance and had become free from suspicions of manipulation. Juva's passion to deal openly and fairly with clashes and the parties involved, including those with whom he disagreed, combined with his ability to place LWF debates in the context of wider social and political movements, contributed decisively to the improvement of the atmosphere within the LWF

Juva's era as the President of the LWF was a major step forward in making the Federation into a world community. Representatives of churches from Africa, Asia, and Latin America felt themselves to be no longer an appendix to an organization of European and North American churches but full members of the worldwide community of Lutheran churches.

## Church Leader

In 1978 Juva was elected archbishop of Turku and primate of the Evangelical Lutheran Church of Finland. Although he decided to go into early retirement in 1982, his leadership widened markedly the radius of the Christian message and contributed to a growing openness of the church toward the whole society, including those traditionally hostile to it. Mutual understanding between the church and the working class increased to the extent that at the time of his leaving the office the leading Communist paper published an editorial in which the writer regretted his decision.

During his term as archbishop, Juva wanted to reshape the function of his office in relation to the central administration of the church and also in relation to international concerns. His initiatives were met with considerable opposition. This, together with his desire to be freed from administrative burdens for a life of writing and opinion formation, led him to opt for early retirement. Benefits from his decision have included the publication of several significant books.

The notes on Mikko Juva would be incomplete unless mention were made of his passion as a botanist. No one in LWF circles knows the world's flora as thoroughly as he does. His escapes, at suitable moments during LWF meetings, to fields, mountains, and forests to add rare species to his collection was an encounter with that part of God's creation where he had no confrontations.

**Bibliographical Notes** _____

_Main Writings of Mikko Juva_

(In Finnish, some with English summaries)
1945    _The Concept of the State in St. Augustine_. Turku.
1950    _The Educated Classes of Finland in the Crisis of Religious Liberalism (1848–1869)_. Helsinki.
1955    _Congregational Life in South-West of Finland under Lutheran Orthodoxy 1600–1808_. Turku.
1956    _In the Wake of a Storm: The Origins of the Ideas Shaping Finland in the Eighties_. Porvoo.

1960     *From a State Church to a Folk Church: The Response of the Finnish Church to the Eighties.* Porvoo.

1964-    *History of the Finnish People I-V.* Together with Einar W. Juva.
1967     Helsinki/Keuruu.

1966     *The Gospel is the Issue.* Porvoo.

1976     *The Parliament of the Church: History of the Synods of the Evangelical Lutheran Church of Finland 1876–1976.* Helsinki.

1985     *Time to Think, Time to Believe: A Collection of Major Addresses and Lectures.* Helsinki.

1993     *I Followed the Vision of My Youth: Memoirs.* Helsinki.

# Josiah Kibira

JOSIAH MUTABUZI KIBIRA was born August 25, 1925, in Kashenye, a village in the northwestern part of Tanzania (at the time the British colony of Tanganyika). Kibira was educated at a teachers' training college near Bukoba, the largest town in northwestern Tanzania. He taught from 1951 to 1957. In 1951 Kibira married Martha, who was from the same region. From 1957 to 1959 he studied theology at Bethel, Germany, finishing with a masters degree, and he was ordained upon his return to Bukoba in 1961. He pursued further studies in Boston from 1962 to 1964, and in 1964 was ordained bishop of the North Western Diocese in Tanzania, consecrated by his predecessor, Swedish missiologist Bengt Sundkler. Elected President of the Lutheran World Federation at the Sixth Assembly in Dar es Salaam (1977), he served until the Seventh Assembly in 1984. Due to illness (Parkinson's disease) he retired from the office of bishop in October of the same year. Kibira died July 18, 1988.

## An African Church Leader with an International Outlook

Kibira's parents were first-generation Lutherans and lived on the shores of Lake Victoria. His father, a pioneering figure in the early period of evangelization, died when Josiah was only four years old. His mother outlived her husband by fifty-six years and throughout her life was a respected and beloved figure of authority in the family. Josiah had five older sisters and brothers.

Kibira was brought up in an atmosphere of solidarity marked by Christian piety. Young Kibira's personal faith was further strengthened when he came into contact with the East African revival in 1947. In later years he never sought to deny that his identity as a Christian had been marked by this encounter with revivalism. However, he always added a note of basic theological reserve in relation to this movement, which, in this part of Africa, was of crucial importance. This was noticed by the LWF's first president, Anders Nygren, during a visit to this region.

Kibira was very conscious of his background, and during the later years of his international activity, he emphasized as a matter of principle the richness of African culture and church life. This was one way of dealing with the perceived self-sufficient arrogance of many of the Westerners he encountered. Furthermore, he combined an awareness of his native background with an international outlook.

Thanks to his intellectual gifts, he was awarded a scholarship for Bethel, Germany. In the history of German Protestantism Bethel is of particular importance, having developed into a center combining diaconic institutions, missionary initiatives, and theological studies. This combination became fundamental to Kibira's position.

Author: *Jens Holger Schjørring, Aarhus, Denmark*

55. Josiah Kibira, Bishop of the North Western Diocese of
the Evangelical Lutheran Church in Tanzania and President of the Lutheran World Federation, 1977–1984

His stay in Boston a few years later was no less significant. The early sixties
were the years of the U.S. civil rights movement and the awakening of a deeper
understanding of the connection between the proclamation of the gospel and
social justice. Kibira's international and ecumenical outlook was broadened
during these years in North America. After he had been elected bishop in his
home country, he attempted to combine being a local church leader with participating in ecumenical fellowship at the local and international levels.

In 1964 Kibira was elected Bishop of Bukoba, in the North Western Diocese
of the Evangelical Lutheran Church in Tanzania. He was consecrated by his
predecessor, the Swedish bishop Bengt Sundkler, who had been his teacher,
counselor, and pastoral father. Kibira was thus not only a church leader within
the episcopal order; he was also in the apostolic succession. He was very conscious of these perspectives, aware that it was yet another qualification of his
own revivalist background with its strong lay, antihierarchical tendency. Yet
he was far from making episcopal order, or even the historical succession, a

precondition for genuine church identity. At the local level there had been some reservations regarding his election since he was extremely young, rather inexperienced, and his predecessor's favorite. His sharp tongue, hot temper, and strong opinions were feared. Yet at the same time he was very humane and had a sense of humor, a way of spontaneously showing joy and grief, and—no less important in the years to come—a sensitivity as a pastoral counselor. Hence, he soon became a respected leader among his own people and, a few years later, entered the ecumenical scene just as convincingly.

His debut on the international scene was spectacular. The All African Lutheran Conference met for the third time in October 1965, this time in Addis Ababa. Kibira was invited to present the keynote address on the theme "A Living Church in a Changing Society." As we have seen (see pp. 52–54 above), the first conference of this kind to take place on the African continent had shown the first painful attempts of the indigenous African church leaders to speak out on their own behalf in the presence of the agencies and mission societies from the "sending churches." Although things had changed to a certain extent, Kibira believed that this tension between indigenous churches and mission movements remained the main challenge, a subject he addressed openly. Having enjoyed the privilege of visiting centers of classical theological learning, he questioned why it was so immensely difficult to promote theological studies from an independent African perspective and why there was little freedom of theological inquiry.

> Today with the exception of a few cases, we can hardly think independently. We depend mostly on advisers from Europe and America. Our theological boards are very inadequate as long as they reflect American, Swedish and German Lutheran theologies rather than African theologies. But, who stops Africans from using their minds? (Quoted in Larsson, *Bishop Josiah Kibira of Bukoba*, p. 30)

He challenged African theologians to gain the self-confidence necessary to bring about changes that would have to "affect church buildings, liturgy, forms of worship and symbolism. We must realize how our African art and culture can be given Christian meaning" (ibid., p. 31). With almost prophetic vision Kibira predicted a process of vigorous debate, hard struggle, and difficult decisions, foreshadowing the focal issues he faced a decade later as an international leader with considerable responsibility. Over against the danger of withdrawing "Into the stronghold of faith, pretending to be unaware of the world outside," he told his audience that a "Christian cannot be forgiven for any cowardice in speaking out on politics, on wholesale injustices, racism, segregation or any other inhuman treatment exercised by the South African government, or any type of neocolonialism toward the children of this continent" (ibid., p. 30). The lecture was widely discussed; the speaker became known far beyond the orbit of African Lutherans. Josiah Kibira became a respected and influential church leader within the Lutheran World Federation, following his Tanzanian colleague Stephano Moshi, who already in the fifties and sixties had been given prominent positions on the executive bodies of the LWF.

Kibira participated in the third and fourth assemblies of the World Council of Churches, in New Delhi in 1961 and Uppsala in 1968. He perceived Uppsala to be an important step forward in the endeavor to combine a renewed emphasis on the mission of the church universal with an intensified struggle for just structures in the southern hemisphere.

As a result of the restructuring process within the LWF, the Fifth Assembly in 1970 reappointed members to the three commissions. Kibira was elected chair of the Commission on Church Cooperation. In his capacity as chair of this important commission, Kibira was able to elaborate on and expand the ideas he had already expressed in his address of 1965. He continued to challenge the arrogance and superstitions that marked many of the rich and powerful churches in the northern hemisphere. He saw himself as spokesperson for the southern churches, which not only claimed equal rights for themselves in the governing bodies of the LWF but primarily fought for a life in true human dignity for their congregations and their nations.

At the annual meeting of the Commission on Church Cooperation at Villach, Austria, in 1972, Kibira voiced clearly some of his anger and concern for the future. He dispelled any doubt that by dropping the word "mission" the redefinition of the commission's mandate could be interpreted as meaning a withdrawal from missionary proclamation (see pp. 154–59 above). Indeed, he saw the commission's mandate as being "to support all Lutheran churches and groups to carry out the mission imperative of our Lord." Kibira was unwilling to evade the difficult process of rethinking. He turned with indignation and sarcasm against the attitude of superiority among the sending agencies in the North and attacked the old unrealistic missionary thinking that "heathenism" is found only in Africa, Asia, and Latin America, and that Europe and North America are to regard those countries as the target of their missionary activities. Instead he turned toward the real situation in the churches of the North, asking, "How are we going to reinitiate a missionary zeal for Europe and North America? Heathens in those countries are just as heathen as those anywhere else where they are found. Our problems are common" (quoted in Larsson, *Bishop Josiah Kibira of Bukoba*, pp. 36ff.).

## President of the Lutheran World Federation

Josiah Kibira took the fact that he was a *Lutheran* church leader seriously. Among the historical commemorations during the years of his presidency were the 450th anniversary of the Augsburg Confession and the 500th anniversary of Martin Luther's birth. In his speeches on these occasions he elaborated on the Lutheran heritage and its present importance for the global family of Lutheran churches. Needless to say, he knew the classical criteria of Lutheran theology. Far be it from him, however, to repeat those in the way they had been formulated time and again. He was determined to redefine the meaning of the call "Forward to Luther" made by the first President of the LWF, Anders Nygren. So Kibira said in 1984, "Indeed Luther is 500 years young! The celebrations have made us aware that it is our task to carry to this generation the message of the free mercy of Jesus. As Martin Luther has clarified it, it is greater and more valuable than we ever realized (ibid., p. 59). Rather than giving a scholarly exegesis of Luther's testimony, Kibira spoke as a preacher who knew from his own experience what Luther's heritage involved in the lives of congregations, including those in his own diocese. Hence, he took pride in mentioning hymns in the Buhaya hymnal, which were precise renderings of Luther's central hymns, for instance *"Mir ist Erbarmung widerfahren"* (ibid.), a hymn that his people in Bukoba knew by heart. This was for him the sort of evidence that counted.

Aware of the importance of solid theological work, Kibira on several occasions fought to establish a stronger and more globally comprehensive study department in the Geneva secretariat. Nevertheless, he perceived what to him was an appalling identification of true faithfulness to the heritage of the Reformers with the European and North American way of interpreting it. This experience convinced him of the importance of an open global exchange of views. He criticized the shortsightedness of certain theologians from the North, stating not without bitter irony:

> During the celebration of the Augsburg Confession I was confronted with the following questions by a reporter at Augsburg: "You are an African, a Tanzanian. I mean you are not a German" (After all this was a platitude) "Anyhow," he went on, "What have you to do with the celebrations of Luther and his fellow reformers? Wouldn't it have been better to stay home, develop your own African religions which in my opinion would make your countrymen more stable in life as they used to live before colonialism took over Africa?" (*Has Luther "reached" Africa?* The testimony of a confused Lutheran; copy in P. Larsson's possession)

During Kibira's term as President of the LWF the heated debate on the question of *status confessionis*, a subject particularly crucial to him took place. He took a strong position in this debate on behalf of the African continent; he was not daunted by the spirit of confrontation which at times marked the atmosphere. Kibira stated in his opening address to the Budapest Assembly, an address that he could not himself deliver because of his advanced illness, but which was read as he listened attentively by his compatriot, Anza Lema, then deputy general secretary of the Federation:

> Apartheid is not just one among many problems related to violations of human rights, however important the others may be: it concerns our whole faith and the history of salvation.—For I repeat: The whole history of salvation is included in our dealings with this question of racial inequality. And we cannot condone any kind of support or legitimization of the racial policies of the South African government, as do some countries that call themselves democracies. (*Proceedings*, Budapest; see p. 406 above)

Kibira's involvement in important questions during his presidency is referred to in other parts of this book; among them, the relationship between the member churches and the executive bodies on the one hand and the Geneva headquarters on the other, and the different aspects of inclusiveness (see chapter 8 above). Another example of an imbalance that Kibira believed to have a devastating impact on the well-being of the whole Federation was the lack of exchange and community between the privileged Western European and North American churches and the underprivileged churches from Eastern Europe and the southern hemisphere. For Kibira, the choice of Budapest as venue for the Seventh Assembly became the point of departure for a renewed discussion about this tension. He turned critically against the prevailing system of dominance of the majority churches of the so-called First World. Without leaving any doubt as to the real addressee, he mentioned the impressions he had gained during a visit to the churches in the then German Democratic Republic.

> In the GDR I was impressed by an unusually deep devotion and commitment among the Lutheran Christians. It is not self-evident that a person is a Christian in a communist situation. So in many places, people had to tell us who was a Christian and who was not. This is quite different from the situation in the West where none seems to bother much whether you are a believer or not and where there is no suppression of religious freedom. I therefore felt that the Lutheran churches of the GDR were alive and theologically alert and have much to teach the majority churches of the West, which in fact may not be in the majority any longer. (Address to the 1981 meeting of the LWF Executive Committee, Turku, Finland, Minutes, Exhibit 6, pp. 3–4)

Kibira was not only interested in the character of the majority churches in liberal Western societies compared to minority churches in countries under socialist rule. He wanted to discuss the relationship between Christian churches and different political ideologies, knowing full well that his personal preference for dialogue between Christianity and socialism would meet with considerable opposition. In his presidential address in Budapest Kibira said:

> Many of us might think that churches in countries with communist governments are churches that have come to know the cross of Christ in a more discerning way than others. It is no secret that some see the root causes for the suffering of the churches in these countries as a lack of participation by earlier generations of Christians in the social transformation of their societies. Others believe that socialist ideologies and Christianity are totally incompatible. May I remind you that Tanzania, where I come from, is a socialist country with a socialism that has grown out of our own soul. In our country, many of the leaders of the government are professing Christians, and Christ is present both in witness and development work. Maybe this could be a challenge to both East and West to realize how Christ and socialism *can* live together? (*Proceedings*, Budapest, p. 16)

Such bold statements should not be taken out of context, as if Kibira had limited himself to propaganda for his own political priorities. Kibira was committed to taking seriously that the global community of Lutheran churches contained different types of church law, cultural patterns and prevailing political ideologies. With all due respect for this variety of traditions, they were all united in a common heritage and mission. Whatever society a member church was placed in, it was confronted with the danger of "conformism." Therefore Kibira considered it to be the member churches' responsibility to show critical solidarity with one another, in faithfulness to the biblical witness. He pointed out:

Still I plead: let us not accuse one another! Let us instead give each other courage by a common stand to challenge the societies in which we have to live! But each member church must decide for itself how heavy a cross it is ready to carry. Membership in our Federation should help us to have our eyes opened for our prophetic responsibilities at this difficult stage of human history. (ibid.)

## Bibliographical Notes

*Unpublished Material*

Collection of unprinted Kibira documents in possession of Pastor Per Larsson, Sigtuna, Sweden.
Information from the late Bengt Sundkler and Per Larsson.

*Published Material*

Larsson, Per. *Bishop Josiah Kibira of Bukoba in an International Perspective.* Nairobi: Uzima Press/Dodoma: Central Tanganyika Press, 1993.

# Zoltán Káldy

ZOLTÁN KÁLDY was born on March 29, 1919, in Iharosberény, Hungary. He studied from 1937 to 1941 at the Faculty of Theology of the Elisabeth University at Sopron-Pécs (Ödenburg), and was ordained in 1941 to the ministry of the Lutheran Church in Hungary (Magyarországi Evangélikus Egyház). After serving as assistant pastor in Pécs, he became senior vicar (superintendent) in the Tolna-Baranya church district of southern Hungary in 1954. In 1958 he was ordained bishop of the Southern Diocese of the Lutheran Church in Hungary and in 1967 was made presiding bishop of that church with headquarters in Budapest. Together with leading bishops of other churches, he had a seat in the Hungarian parliament. At the Federation's Seventh Assembly at Budapest in 1984 Káldy was elected seventh President of the Federation. Káldy died on May 17, 1987, following a stroke, the first President of the LWF to die while still in office. Zoltán Káldy was married in 1960 to Magdolna Esze, who later taught economics at Budapest.

## Zoltán Káldy in Context

It would not be possible to present an objective description of Zoltán Káldy's work as bishop of Hungary or as President of the Lutheran World Federation without reviewing the context—of both Hungary and its Lutheran Church—in which he lived and worked. These circumstances, marked by highly dramatic vicissitudes have already been outlined in the account of the Seventh LWF Assembly held in Budapest in 1984 (see pp. 403ff. above). Important also is the role of the Hungarian bishop Lajos Ordass in the early years of the Federation and the life of the church in post–World War II Hungary. Káldy's career both as bishop and as President of the LWF covered a span of thirty years, from the time when Ordass endeavored heroically to secure an appropriate status for the Lutheran Church of Hungary in a Stalinist society, to the mid-1980s. At that point there was a general easing of tensions, and yet it was not until the late 1980s that there were signs that Ordass would be rehabilitated. Throughout his service as bishop, Káldy directed his energy toward the preservation of his church within a socialist state. Káldy certainly had opponents from within, critics who denounced his stance vis-à-vis the Marxist government. He was frequently accused of helping Marxists in their endeavor to gain total control of power.

Káldy can be understood only against this background of tension and controversy, and even then neither complete accuracy nor objectivity can be guaranteed. It is clear that ambiguities and contradictions, both in Káldy's own life and in his role in the international church community, must be acknowledged.

Author: *Jens Holger Schjørring, Aarhus, Denmark, with draft notes from Gyula Nagy, Budapest, Hungary, and László Terray, Råde, Norway.*

56. Zoltán Káldy, Presiding Bishop of the Lutheran Church
in Hungary and President of the Lutheran World Federation, 1984–1987

## Life and Contribution

Zoltán Káldy's father was a Lutheran pastor, and his early environment both
at home and at school made the study of theology natural. The Theological
Faculty at Sopron-Pécs (Ödenburg) was part of the internationally known
Elisabeth University. There Káldy became familiar with German Luther
studies, with liturgical renewal in Sweden, and with the impact of revivalism
on Finnish theology and church life. Indeed, movements of revival had an
important impact on Káldy the young pastor, and he was often invited to
preach at revivals and evangelistic rallies. Thus he gained the confidence of
many within the church, and his election in 1958 to the position of bishop of
the Southern Diocese was met with great hope. Yet that very election took
place against a disadvantageous, if not alarming, background.

In November 1957, following the Hungarian revolution, the State Office for
Church Affairs initiated talks with the leaders of the Lutheran Church in Hun-

gary in order to discuss, among other things, matters related to personnel. The negotiations ground to a halt with the appointment of a state official responsible temporarily for the control and administration of church affairs. Dean Káldy, then senior vicar of Tolna-Baranya, showed himself willing to work for a compromise which would involve the resignation of Bishop Ordass from his episcopal office. In June 1958 Ordass was removed from that office, and in November of the same year Káldy was installed as bishop of the Southern Diocese. As part of his first responsibilities he was to carry out the removal of the pastors whom the state had judged to be unacceptable.

Even though the main features of this compromise, which were finally accepted by Káldy, were well known to the general public, Káldy's election as bishop was welcomed by many within the church. He was highly regarded as a preacher, and it was felt by many that, at a time when harsh state control was being exercised in many areas of public life, the compromise warded off even more severe restrictions on the church from the state.

In the international and ecumenical arenas, it must have been clear to Káldy that Bishop Ordass enjoyed the utmost confidence of the LWF leadership. Following the annual meeting of the Federation's executive committee in Vienna in February 1959, Káldy met with several leading members of that committee: Franklin Clark Fry, the American President of the LWF, Bishop Bo Giertz of Sweden, and the LWF executive secretary, Carl Lund-Quist. They made it quite clear to Káldy that in spite of his status in Hungary—he was under what amounted to house arrest—Bishop Ordass remained a vice-president of the Federation and a member of its executive committee even though he was unable to carry out the duties of his office.

During the early years of Káldy's service as bishop, he seemed to undergo decisive changes in his theological views. He gradually reconsidered his own "pietistic tendencies," characterizing evangelistic preaching as sterile, out of date, inaccurate, and reactionary. Accordingly, he began to revise his theological position and to develop a "theology of diakonia," which was to become his hallmark. This theology was meant to serve as a unifying point in the life of the church, enabling the church to render dynamic service in the context of a socialist state.

Káldy developed this theology on a number of public occasions during the 1960s. In connection with receiving an honorary doctorate from the Faculty of Theology at Bratislava in what was then Czechoslovakia, he described five options facing the church in its relation to modern society: the church as a ruler in society, a "hierarchy"; the church adapting to society and thereby avoiding controversy; the church as a ghetto, shielded from sinful society; the church as a force of political resistance risking persecution at the hands of dictators; and the church adopting the way of diakonia, the way of serving without exercising power, promoting the gospel through a strategy of love in action. Káldy unhesitatingly chose the last of these options. In time, moreover, this "theology of diakonia" gained status far beyond its origins, becoming the watchword of a carefully administered church policy, adherence to which was officially expected of students of theology, professors, and pastors.

Clearly, Káldy's policy—as theologian and episcopal leader—contributed greatly to the creation of an inner stability for the church, a fact strikingly apparent in any comparison of the life of the Hungarian church to that of churches in other countries behind the iron curtain. In Hungary, for example, the publication of books for church use was possible—a new translation of the Bible, a new hymnal, a new and uniform agenda for clergy use, a series of biblical commentaries. Additionally, it was possible for Káldy to negotiate higher salaries and pensions for pastors and to effect the renovation of churches and church properties.

During those years the doors of his home church were opened to the wider activities of the church. A three-year course of theological education for the laity was introduced at the Theological Academy in Budapest. With support from the Federation and partner churches in the West, a number of churches, church centers, and pastor's houses were renovated and newly constructed. In 1979 a Protestant museum was opened in the heart of Budapest. The 500th anniversary of Martin Luther's birth was celebrated. Yet, for the Hungarian church, the most important development during this period was that it was the first church in the "Marxist world" to be host to an LWF Assembly, to Lutheran churches from all five continents. As a result of personal encounters in 114 urban and rural congregations "Budapest 1984" became an unforgettable event for all foreign participants, and for the host church, and contributed to an inner strengthening of that church.

There were two main goals to Káldy's church policy. First, to strengthen the congregations from inside, through the proclamation of the gospel in many ways, as mentioned above. Second, he recognized the vital importance of close contacts between his home church and the family of Lutheran churches in the Lutheran World Federation and with the worldwide ecumenical movement. These two endeavors were decisive for his whole life and contribution in his church.

Within the span of one decade, from the late 1950s to the late 1960s, the relationship between the Geneva secretariat in the Lutheran World Federation and Bishop Káldy changed dramatically. This was a time of a general shift in LWF policy toward its member churches in Eastern Europe, a shift toward greater openness. As a result, considerable confidence was shown in Káldy and he was elected to a number of important positions in the Federation's governing bodies. As early as 1963 he served, at the suggestion of Federation staff, as a member of the LWF Committee on Nominations and as a member of the Commission on Stewardship and Evangelism. At the Evian Assembly he became vice-chairperson of the Commission on Church Cooperation, serving with Bishop Josiah Kibira, chair, and Gunnar Staalsett, second vice-chair. At the assembly at Dar es Salaam he was elected to the LWF Executive Committee, and in 1984 at the assembly at Budapest hosted by the Hungarian Lutheran Church, he was elected to the LWF presidency.

The growth of Káldy's influence in the LWF reflected more than either personal ambition or the decision of the Federation to give increased attention to one of its largest member churches in Central and Eastern Europe. Káldy became increasingly prominent within the LWF in a way that mirrored tendencies inherent in a far-reaching reorientation of general policy. One example is characteristic.

In a paper that Káldy presented to the LWF Executive Committee at its August 1975 meeting in Amsterdam, he elaborated on his theology of diakonia by an exposition of its connection between Christology and ecclesiology. Seeing Christ as both *Kyrios* and *Diakonos*, he sought to develop a similar linkage between the proclamation of the Christian gospel and Christian faith in action:

> It is the innermost secret of the life of Jesus that he is at once, in one person, equally Kyrios and Diakonos. . . . (§ 37)
> It is clear the cosmic Christology does not provide us with a Christocratic view of the world, but it furnishes a basis for our effort—also in view of Luther's teaching about the "Two Realms"—to intensify our participation in the action for bringing about a world under the sovereignty of the Kyrios by proclaiming the Gospel and doing acts of love. (§ 49) (*Minutes,* LWF Executive Committee Meeting, August 1975, Exhibit 20.1.3, pp. 9ff.)

Káldy was determined to connect a theology of diakonia with due respect for a *via crucis*. With this statement Káldy took a position also taken at that time by the Ethiopian Evangelical Church Mekane Yesus and by Bishop Josiah Kibira of Tanzania, soon to be elected LWF President. An alliance was being forged between Lutheran churches in Central and Eastern Europe, on the one hand, and sister churches in the "two-thirds world," on the other. This alliance was to become increasingly important in the life of the Federation.

> There can be no doubt that a critical function is a task also for the churches serving in different contexts of social structures; it is even more significant, however, that they contribute through service and love to the creation of a more just social order. Or, to say the same in the language of our time: mission without "humanization" is a mutilated mission. This is a lesson which the Lutheran churches in Africa and Asia have to learn. (ibid.)

## Káldy as President of the LWF

There was thus both a theological connection and a bond of cooperation between Zoltán Káldy and African church leaders such as Bishop Josiah Kibira of the Evangelical Lutheran Church in Tanzania and President Emmanuel Abraham of the Ethiopian Evangelical Church Mekane Yesus. This relation—which we call an "alliance"—helps explain why Káldy proved able to attract the majority of votes when he stood for election as president at the Seventh Assembly of the LWF in Budapest in 1984. Nonetheless, the election of Bishop Káldy was controversial.

The Hungarian bishop was admittedly interested in being elected president and in support of his own candidacy publicly cited the Federation's custom of usually electing as its president a leader of the assembly's host church. Questions were, indeed, raised by many delegates to the Seventh Assembly regarding the propriety or necessity of maintaining this custom. Moreover, there were accusations, widely noted in the press, of pressure, even of manipulation on Káldy's behalf by LWF staff. Additionally, much media attention was given to charges against the Hungarian bishop by Zoltán Dóka, a Hungarian pastor who had seriously criticized Káldy and whose publications had been withheld by Káldy. This attention perhaps forced into the background a more serious consideration of basic issues. Nevertheless, the assembly did decide for Bishop Káldy, and he took office as the seventh President of the Lutheran World Federation (cf. pp. 409–11 above).

As president, Káldy took up his duties with vigor and determination. Important travels brought him to the United States and to the Vatican. Yet his stay in office, tragically, was too brief to give him the possibility of achieving a breakthrough at the point closest to his heart—improved relations between church and state in the countries of Central and Eastern Europe. Zoltán Káldy suffered a stroke at the Zurich airport in December of 1985 en route home from a meeting with LWF staff in Geneva. He died in May 1987 and was succeeded by one of the Federation's vice-presidents, Bishop Johannes Hanselmann of the Evangelical Lutheran Church in Bavaria, who was elected to this post at the 1987 meeting of the executive committee in Viborg, Denmark. This was the first time an LWF President had been elected at a time other than an assembly.

## Other Contributions

Káldy held several ecumenical positions and was involved in many public activities. Beginning in 1960, for example, he became an active participant in the (Prague) Christian Peace Conference and in 1963 he was elected to the presidium of the World Federation of Hungarians, initially established prior to World War II and given new life in the 1950s. It was clearly a political organization under Communist leadership, which strove to engage leading non-Communists in its life and aimed at creating good relations with Hungarians in Western countries.

In 1971 Káldy was elected a member of the Hungarian parliament, an election common for leading bishops of several Hungarian churches. To be sure, the parliament met only two or three times a year and then mainly to comment on reports and approve laws proposed by the Communist bureaucracy. Yet it was a significant part of Communist strategy to recommend cooperative church leaders for election to the national parliament.

In recognition of his role in society, Káldy was honored on several occasions by the Hungarian state: in 1969 he received both the order of the Golden Degree of Work Merit and the First Grade of the Order of the Banner of the Hungarian People's Republic. He received honorary doctorates of divinity from the Lutheran Theological Academy in Bratislava, Czechoslovakia, from the Protestant Theological Institute in Cluj, Romania, and from the Reformed Theological Academy in Debrecen, Hungary. He was a leading member of the Christian Peace Conference (Prague) and the Conference of European Churches. In 1963 he became a member of the Central Committee of the World Council of Churches and retained this office for two terms.

## The Man of His Times

As already indicated, it is extremely difficult to arrive at an objective evaluation of the work and contribution of Zoltán Káldy, seventh President of the Lutheran World Federation. While the very positive aspects of his accomplishments must be acknowledged, points of critique must also be raised. At the time of this writing, 1996, there is a tendency to condemn all "compromise" made between state and church in the countries of Central and Eastern Europe while they were under socialist rule. It is therefore extremely important to do justice to Bishop Káldy and to see him first of all within his own historical, ecclesial, social, and political contexts. While it may seem premature and without claiming any finality of judgment, it is relevant to point to various elements in those contexts which will help understand his work and contribution.

In the first place, it is important to bear in mind that as a matter of principle the relationship between the Lutheran World Federation—its official policy makers, its staff, and its member churches—is based on cooperation between churches. Thus, the LWF strives to take its lead from local church leaders. This fact is to be held in tension with the fundamental duty of the secretariat to show solidarity with all who are victimized or oppressed in totalitarian states.

In the second place, it is evident that a maximum of subtle differentiation is required when interpreting the public role of churches in one-party states. Moreover, it is evident that certain shifts can be observed as having taken place during the five decades of LWF history in respect to the churches of Central and Eastern Europe and their relationships to the Marxist governments of their nations. In the case of Káldy it is particularly important to draw attention to the general shift away from a "cold war" situation toward the climate of "small steps" of rapprochement first championed in the 1960s by Willy Brandt, chancellor of the Federal Republic of Germany.

In the third place, it must be borne in mind that in the late 1960s and the early 1970s, when Bishop Káldy was leading his church and assuming a greater role in the LWF, there was a global tendency to promote understanding and cooperation between "socialism with a human face" and the churches. This was a significant dimension of LWF life during this period—the "China Study" of the Department of Studies is but one example—and gives a rationale to the approval and expectation with which Káldy was received by many church leaders, not least those from the southern hemisphere.

Finally, it is necessary to be aware of certain features of the specific national history of Hungary, the details of which go beyond the scope of this analysis. In the context of that history it is significant that it was not only Zoltán Káldy who adopted a stance favoring close cooperation between church and state in Hungary. Similar positions were taken by other Hungarian religious leaders, among them leading representatives of the Roman Catholic and Hungarian Reformed churches.

These few remarks are not offered as a conclusive statement about Zoltán Káldy, "the man and his times." His legacy—to his church, his nation, and to the Lutheran World Federation—is yet to be fully assessed. The crucial matter for the present work is that his role be seen within the framework of his ambiguous and complicated times.

## Bibliographical Notes _____

*Unprinted Source Material*

LWF Archives, Geneva.
ELCH, Budapest.
Draft manuscripts on Zoltán Káldy provided by László Terray, Norway, and Gyula Nagy, Budapest.

*Main Writings by Zoltán Káldy*

1957   *Bevezetés az Újszövetségbe* (Introduction to the New Testament).
1970   *Új úton* (Lectures, sermons, articles).
1979   *A diakónia útján* (Lectures on the theology of diakonia).

*Select Bibliography*

Ordass, Lajos. *Válogatott irások* (Selected writings). Edited by István Szépfalusi. Bern, 1982.
————. *Önéletrajzi irások* (Autobiographical writings) I, II. Bern, 1985, 1987.
Philippi, Hans, and Theodor Strohm, eds. *Theologie der Diakonie.* Heidelberg, 1989.
Terray, László. *He Could Not Do Otherwise: Bishop Lajos Ordass, 1901–1978,* trans. Eric W. Gritsch. Grand Rapids: Eerdmans, 1997.
Vajta, Vilmos. *Die diakonische Theologie im Gesellschaftssystem Ungarns.* Frankfurt/M, 1987.

# Johannes Hanselmann

JOHANNES HANSELMANN was born on March 9, 1927, in Ehingen/Ries, Germany. He studied Protestant theology and philosophy at the University of Erlangen (1946–1949), at Hamma School of Theology at Wittenberg University, in Springfield, Ohio, U.S.A. (1949–1950), and at the Hartford Seminary Foundation (1950–1951), from which he received a doctorate in philosophy, in Hartford, Connecticut. He was ordained in Germany in 1950 and first served as an assistant pastor in Grub am Forst and was subsequently director of the "Church House" in West Berlin (1957); he became Oberkirchenrat and regional dean for the Church District of Bayreuth in 1974, and in 1975 was elected Landesbischof of the Evangelical Lutheran Church in Bavaria. In 1977 he was elected one of the vice-presidents of the LWF and was returned to that office in 1984. After the mid-term death of Bishop Zoltán Káldy, President of the LWF, in 1987 he was elected Federation President by the LWF Executive Committee, meeting at Viborg, Denmark. He served as president through the Curitiba Assembly in 1990. Johannes Hanselmann retired in 1994.

## Education, Publications

Johannes Hanselmann is a theologian who never sees his discipline in isolation. Thus, when he was studying in the United States in the early fifties he availed himself of the opportunity to get an M.A. in philosophy with a paper entitled "Theology without God? A Contribution to the Problem of the Influence of Philosophy of Existence to the New Testament Theology of Rudolf Bultmann, seen from the standpoint of a Lutheran Theology of the New Testament" and a doctorate in philosophy on "Martin Heidegger's Fundamental Ontology and Its Theological Implications." Even though this showed clearly that he was interested in and suited for a scholarly career, he decided to work for the church. It is characteristic of his further career that Hanselmann, whenever asked, time and again agreed to accept new responsibilities. Not least because of a serious scarcity of pastors, he began in a rural congregation. From early on, he demonstrated convincing pastoral qualities, sensitivity in dealing with people of different opinions, the ability for integration, a balanced temper, and a fair sense of humor. In 1966, he was called to West Berlin to head the "Church House" of the Evangelical Church of Berlin-Brandenburg. At the time of the student revolts in Germany, he utilized his skills as a mediator in situations of conflict, and when, in 1975, he was elected bishop he explained why he took his capacity for mediation so seriously: "Not because I'm afraid to take positions but because I believe that there must be people who can stand to be in the middle and assume a bridge-building function" (quoted by Walter

Author: *Udo Hahn, Bonn, Germany*

LWF Photo—Peter Williams

57. Johannes Hanselmann, Bishop of the Evangelical
Lutheran Church in Bavaria, Germany, and President
of the Lutheran World Federation, 1987–1990

Allgaier, "Der gute Mann aus Bayreuth," *Deutsche Zeitung/Christ und Welt*
[2 May 1975]).

In his publications, usually addressed to ordinary parish members, Hanselmann again and again tackled the central question of what it means today to
be a Lutheran Christian. His answer is quite elementary and yet aims at the
very core: to be a Lutheran Christian means to be a member of a church that
"understands itself to be dependent on and supported by the gospel of Jesus
Christ as it was rediscovered, translated and interpreted by Martin Luther: a
church that gathers around Word and Sacrament, which is consolidated by the
confession and plans its life and its reality in the world on this basis" (*Bischofsworte für den Alltag*, p. 84). According to Lutheran understanding, Hanselmann claimed, the church cannot and must not keep aloof from the world.

Responsibility before God frees it for responsibility for the world, even though it must neither implement a political program nor attempt to rule the world from the pulpit.

An interest in church communication ran like a red thread through Hanselmann's activities. It was a stroke of luck that he presided over the Evangelical Church in Germany's Advisory Commission for Communication Work between 1977 and 1980. What he wrote in the foreword to the first comprehensive communication plan of the EKD in 1979 has lost none of its topicality:

> Whoever thinks about communication in the church encounters a certain dilemma. Whilst the number of church newsletters, information services, periodicals, and staff publications of all kinds keeps growing, no one could necessarily claim that this has led to a better-developed sense of responsibility and fellowship within the whole church. The same applies to communication between church and society: the fact that the church's public relations have in the last years increased and become more professional does not mean that it has become easier to communicate the church's witness and service today in the ongoing dialogue with society. On the one hand, there is too much information, but too little communication on the other. (*Publizistischer Gesamtplan der Evangelischen Kirche in Deutschland* [Gütersloh, 1979], p. 11)

Hanselmann was particularly concerned about the Evangelische Buchhilfe e.V. (Protestant Churches' Book Agency) founded in 1960. This institution, whose president he was from 1974 to 1990 when Germany was reunited, aimed at providing the territorial churches in the German Democratic Republic with Christian religious literature. For reasons that can well be understood, the activities of the agency were not made public, since without discretion they could not have taken place. To realize the significance of this work, it has to be kept in mind that between 1960 and 1990 about 200 meetings took place in the GDR, usually in East Berlin, and that 1.4 million books, valued at thirty million East German Marks, were made available to the GDR regional churches.

Most popular among Hanselmann's publications was his book *In jeder Sekunde geborgen: Ein Begleiter in Tagen der Krankheit* (Safe every single second: A companion for days of illness) (Munich, 1990). So far, its print run has exceeded a million copies.

### President of the Lutheran World Federation

In 1978, Johannes Hanselmann became one of the vice-presidents of the Lutheran World Federation. In 1984, at the Seventh Assembly in Budapest, he chaired plenary discussions and provided a stabilizing influence in an often tense atmosphere. It was not foreseen that he would move to the top rank of the LWF leadership; however, after the unexpected death of the Hungarian bishop Zoltán Káldy, the LWF Executive Committee meeting in Viborg, Denmark, in 1987 elected him President of the LWF. In 1990, upon completion of his term, Hanselmann became an honorary President of the Federation.

From the very beginning, the commitment of the Bavarian bishop focused on the question of how the LWF, which, according to Article III of its constitution dating from its founding year of 1947, understood itself to be a "free association of Lutheran churches" and not a church itself, could become a communion of churches. This concern is manifest in his address as newly elected president at the meeting of the executive committee that took place in 1988 in Addis Ababa (Ethiopia) under the theme "Church Community in the Lutheran World Federation."

In this address, he first recalled that at the Budapest Assembly (1984) Article III of the LWF Constitution had been amended to read: "The member churches of the Lutheran World Federation understand themselves to be in pulpit and altar fellowship with each other." He then turned against the idea of perceiving pulpit and altar fellowship in a "minimalistic sense" and explained: "Rather, pulpit and altar fellowship entails much that 'ecclesial communion' means only when further explicated: mutual recognition of the ministries, joint action and structures of joint decision-making indispensable for the latter. What is ultimately decisive is that ecclesial communion in essence is 'mutually committed communion.'" Hanselmann thus mentally anticipated what the Eighth Assembly indeed resolved: "If one day the Constitution of the Lutheran World Federation is to really reflect the development towards the concept of fellowship/communion, then the slogan 'pulpit and altar fellowship' does not suffice—no matter how fundamental it may be" ("Church Community in the Lutheran World Federation," Minutes LWF Executive Committee, Addis Ababa, June/July 1988, §§ 28–29).

### An Ecumenical Church Leader

Hanselmann is considered to be an authority on the Roman Catholic Church. For the bishop of the geographically largest Lutheran church in Germany—which, compared to ten million Roman Catholics, can be said to be in a diaspora situation in spite of its some two million members—good contacts beyond confessional borders have always been particularly important. As deputy presiding bishop of the United Evangelical Lutheran Church in Germany (VELKD), Hanselmann was responsible, on the Protestant side, for preparing the visit of Pope John Paul II to Germany in 1980. In 1984, he became the president of the Lutheran Foundation for Ecumenical Research in Strasbourg. Moreover, between 1991 and 1994 he was also the VELKD's Catholic commissioner.

Hanselmann has participated in the interconfessional dialogues with much sensitivity and theological competence. When he met with the pope in 1988, he explicitly underlined that the church neither aimed at a "return oikumene" nor any type of united church but only at a "unity in reconciled diversity" (Udo Hahn, "Partner für die Ökumene," Rheinischer Merkur [12 July 1991]). At the same time, he refused to accept the allegation of a standstill or even regression in ecumenical relations. He could rightly point to many successes in the ecumenical dialogues that had come about over the last thirty years.

Nevertheless, a few problems remain unsolved—also for Hanselmann. In his view, no quick solutions are in sight with regard to the admission to the

Roman Catholic Eucharist. His wish—to allow mixed married couples jointly to partake of the Eucharist in the Roman Catholic Church—is likely to be realized in the near future. "I personally just don't understand," he said in 1990 at a meeting of the Bavarian synod, "that, on the one hand, we complain about the lack of interest in the church, especially of the younger and middle-aged generation, and, on the other, practice such exclusion in the case of open-minded couples who seek community at the Lord's table" (ibid.). It is nevertheless true that if the ecumenical movement has made considerable progress not only in Germany but also on the international level of conversations, this can be credited not least to the work of Johannes Hanselmann.

**Bibliographical Notes**

*Main Writings of Johannes Hanselmann*

1982    *Der Herr gibt meiner Seele Kraft.* Munich.
1985    *Signale der Hoffnung.* Neukirchen-Vluyn.
1986    *Brücken zum Frieden.* Wuppertal.
1987    *Diener am Wort: Bischof der Kirche.* Munich.
        *Damit wir leben können: Die Zehn Gebote.* Wuppertal.
1988    *Kirche und Politik—kontrovers: Eine Diskussion mit Günter von Lojewski.* Munich
1992    *"Wie laut mich auch der Tag umgibt. . .": Ein evangelisches Monatsbrevier.* Munich
1994    *Bischofsworte für den Alltag: Bedenkenswertes aus 19 Amtsjahren.* Munich.

# Gottfried Brakemeier

GOTTFRIED BRAKEMEIER was born on January 4, 1937, in Cachoeira do Sul, Brazil. He studied theology in São Leopoldo from 1955 to 1956 and from 1957 to 1962 in Göttingen and Tübingen, Germany. He pursued doctoral studies at the University of Göttingen (1966–1968). Between 1962 and 1966 he was vicar and pastor in a congregation in São Leopoldo. From 1968 to 1985 he was professor of New Testament at the Faculdade de Teologia in São Leopoldo. During 1975–1978 he also served as secretary for education (Secrétario de Formação) and first deputy church president of the Igreja Evangélica de Confissão Luterana no Brasil (IECLB—the Evangelical Church of the Lutheran Confession in Brazil) from 1978 to 1985, becoming president in 1985 and serving in that capacity until 1994. From 1986 to 1990 Brakemeier was president of the National Council of Christian Churches in Brazil (CONIC). Since January 1995 he has been professor of Systematic and Ecumenical Theology at the Escola Superior de Teologia in São Leopoldo. He was elected President of the Lutheran World Federation in 1990. Brakemeier is married to Lydia Klatt from Bartin/Pomerania in Germany.

## Education, Theology, Main Writings

As the son of a German missionary and a German-Brazilian mother, Gottfried Brakemeier studied theology at a time when Brazilian Lutheranism was on its way truly to becoming a church of Brazil. The specific situation of his home church thus influenced his writings and papers which cover the whole range of theology. Again and again, solidly grounded exegesis leads to contextual theology, the question of what the church is in the context of Latin America.

For this reason, he believes that theology must reflect and define faith, love, and hope in community with the whole people of God on earth. This must go hand in hand with an examination of the tradition of the church, the historical reality and God's promise given in Jesus Christ. The aim of doing so is the promotion of a truly evangelical practice as well as preparing for and contributing to the liberation from all evil.

Therefore, theology has several indivisible functions which Brakemeier lists as critical, normative, ecumenical, confessional, ecclesial, prophetic, pastoral, and spiritual. The *critical* function of theology is the "distinction between spirits" with regard to church and society, speaking and acting, religion and theology itself. The *normative* criterion is the gospel. The *ecumenical* function of theology is grounded in God's history with his people, and seeks the unity of this people and the fulfillment of the common, God-given task. For the universality of God's grace calls the exclusiveness of faith into question

Authors: *Martin Dreher, São Leopoldo, Brazil, and Vitor Westhelle, Chicago, Illinois*

58. Gottfried Brakemeier, President of the Evangelical
Church of the Lutheran Confession in Brazil, and
President of the Lutheran World Federation, 1990–1997

and advocates fellowship and peace on earth. The *confessional* function of
theology is committed to the historical forms of confessing and life but does
not render them absolute. Oikumene must respect the confessional tradition,
but at the same time put it into question. If the tradition and its critique are
rooted in the gospel, then they mutually correct each other and intensify discipleship. The focus of the *ecclesial* function of theology is always the congregation. The congregation is committed to the gospel, and theology is called to
work with it. The *prophetic* function of theology is to proclaim God's will in
this world and to claim the creator's rights. It must remind human beings that
they have no right to arbitrariness and violence with regard to law, peace, and
creation, but that they are subject to God's judgment. The *pastoral* function of
theology is to shape, preserve, and renew life through counsel and solidarity,
proclamation and diakonia, forgiveness of sins and the call to repentance. Theology derives its *spiritual* function from the fact that when it deals with God's
mysteries and miracles it is overcome by awe and humility.

In his theological pronouncements Brakemeier is deeply committed to the
heritage of the Lutheran Reformation. He does not consider the Lutheran contribution to ecumenism to be dogmatic *topoi,* although justification alone by
grace, the *theologia crucis,* and the concept of God's twofold governance are
highly relevant for Latin America. What he considers to be more important is

the recovery of the "Lutheran distinctions" and their correlates, for instance the distinction between law and gospel. According to him, the "distinctions" are one of Lutheranism's major gifts, which need to be shared with other denominations.

Such reflections can be found throughout Brakemeier's theological writings. His exegesis, moreover, is far from "undogmatic." It has dogmatic prerequisites and implications. Hence the above-mentioned functions of theology are included in his exegetic and homiletic papers in the journal *Estudos Teológicos* and in the homiletic yearbook *Proclamar Libertação*, in his reflections on pastoral formation, in his major publications such as *Reino de Deus e Esperança Apocalíptica* (God's kingdom and apocalyptic hope); *Der "Sozialismus" der Urchristenheit: Experiment und neue Herausforderung* ("Socialism" in early christendom: Experiment and new challenge); *Testemunho de fé em Tempos Difíceis* (Confession of the faith in difficult times), in his addresses as church president to the IECLB congregations, and in his statements as President of the Lutheran World Federation.

## Brakemeier as President of the LWF

Elected at the Curitiba Assembly in 1990 by a slim majority, Brakemeier became the second President of the LWF to come from a Third-World member church. Born and raised in Brazil, of German descent and with a graduate education in Germany, he combines two theological emphases that he has insisted need to be kept in dialectical relationship: a contextual commitment as the incarnate expression of one's faith and an uncompromising faithfulness to the gospel as the *verbum externum* (President's Address, *LWF Documentation* 30, December 1991, p. 7). In his address to the LWF Council at Geneva 1994, he presented this tension as the one of discerning between solidarity and complicity in realizing the task of *koinonia*. This vision is summarized in his statement that calls for a "new 'orthodoxy'": "A praxis without faith loses direction; a faith without praxis becomes sterile" (ibid., p. 11).

Brakemeier's leadership within the LWF has been marked by this very methodological posture. He has seen, accordingly, the mission of the LWF as unfolding a double task of relating "the gospel to culture" ("President's Address, *LWF Documentation 33*, September 1993, p. 9). On the one hand, the LWF is an *expression* of the Lutheran *communio* within the universal body of Christ and, on the other, it is the *instrument* to strengthen, intensify, and bring to fruition this community. As an expression it needs to make manifest the "parables of the kingdom" that the churches in multiple contexts "set up." As an instrument it ought to enable the churches to "give assistance to people in learning faith, love, and hope" (President's Address, *LWF Documentation* 30, p. 13). This double task unfolds itself in the relationship between the church and the world. The church has the double mandate of mission and diakonia which is ruled by and expressed in terms of a balanced view of the relationship between "inculturation" and distance: "Inculturation without distance jeopardizes the gospel. Distance without inculturation renders communication of the gospel impossible" (President's Address, *LWF Documentation* 33, p. 19).

Brakemeier's approach to the ecumenical challenges that the church faces today is similar. While "confessions of faith have their locus in the people (*Sitz im Volk*)," which warrants a variety of faith expressions, it is to be maintained that "there are limits to the plurality of the expressions of faith. Faith must correspond to the 'sola gratia'" (ibid., p. 14). The LWF in its self-understanding as a *communio* sees its own vocation as being fundamentally oriented toward ecumenism, occupying a critical and mediating stance toward both the Roman Catholic tradition without succumbing to exclusivism, and the Protestant heritage without surrendering to pluralism.

As concerns the "'modern aphasia with regard to justification,'" Brakemeier finds in the central teaching of Luther a motif that should "go hand in hand with practical topicality" (President's Address, *LWF Documentation 31*, p. 7). It is in its understanding of how justification is linked to justice that the Lutheran tradition carries a particular and permanent responsibility toward society, "[i]n view of the hatred and the indifference, in view of immeasurable guilt in the past and at present, in view of the brutality of an ever more desperate struggle for survival." Justification, he claims, "requires life" and, in face of "the dangers that confronts humanity," offers "another vision of humanity, another 'eco-image'" (ibid., p. 14).

## Ecumenical Leadership

Even before Brakemeier was elected president of his Lutheran church in Brazil he participated in several ecumenical consultations. From 1983 to 1989 he was a member of the Board of the Ecumenical Institute in Strasbourg. However, the most important preparation for the office of President of the LWF and the subsequent wider ecumenical conversations was his presidency of the National Council of Christian Churches in Brazil (1986–1990) and participation in the Roman-Catholic/Lutheran International Commission (1987–1994). He also attended the assemblies of the Latin American Council of Churches and many conversations in Brazil.

## Bibliographical Notes

*Main Writings of Gottfried Brakemeier*

1984   *Reino de Deus e Esperança Apocalíptica* (God's kingdom and apocalyptic hope). São Leopoldo.

1988   *Der "Sozialismus" der Urchristenheit: Experiment und neue Herausforderung.* Göttingen. Portuguese, 1985.

1989   *Testemunho de fé em Tempos Difíceis* (Confession of the faith in difficult times). Presença Luterana, ed. São Leopoldo. German, *Glaube im Teilen bewahrt.* Erlangen, 1989.

# 3

# GENERAL SECRETARIES OF THE LWF

## Sylvester Clarence Michelfelder

SYLVESTER CLARENCE MICHELFELDER was born on October 27, 1889, in New Washington, Ohio. He graduated from Capital University and Theological Seminary, Columbus, Ohio, and was ordained a minister of the American Lutheran Church in 1914. That same year he married Florence E. Kibler. He served as pastor in Willard and Toledo, both in Ohio, from 1914 to 1945, interrupted by ten years in Pittsburgh, Pennsylvania, where he served five years as a pastor, then another five years as superintendent of the Lutheran Inner Mission. From the summer of 1945 he served in Geneva; in December 1945 he was elected executive secretary of the Lutheran World Convention; and in July 1947 of the Lutheran World Federation. He was awarded the degree of Doctor of Divinity by his alma mater, Capital University, Columbus, Ohio, and in 1949 by the University of Münster, Westphalia, Germany. Sylvester Michelfelder died on December 30, 1951, in Chicago.

*Education, Personal Background, Pastoral Experience*

As his family name indicates, Sylvester Clarence Michelfelder's ancestors had emigrated to the United States from Germany, from a region near Stuttgart, Württemberg. It so happened that important events in his development as a student and young pastor further strengthened his rootedness in a Lutheran, confessional heritage and his commitment to personal piety. His seminary in Ohio was at that time still bilingual, German and English; and in 1911 he went to Canada for missionary activity in Alberta among the settlers who were working on the Pacific railway.

In his service as a minister, he combined a gift for pastoral care and missionary preaching with remarkable abilities in establishing networks of cooperation, involving dedicated lay people as well as pastoral colleagues. These qualifications were supplemented by a full-grown sense of humor and by a no less developed skill in setting up administrative patterns of work and raising funds for church activities.

Authors: *E. Theodore Bachmann (†), Princeton, New Jersey, and Jens Holger Schjørring, Aarhus, Denmark*

Photo: R. Seemann

59. Sylvester Clarence Michelfelder of the American
    Lutheran Church, Executive Secretary of the Lutheran
    World Federation, 1947–1951

Michelfelder was not an academic theologian. It was his skill as pastor,
organizer, and team leader that caused Ralph Long, director of the National
Lutheran Council in New York, to apply to his congregation in Toledo, Ohio,
to grant him a leave in order that he could serve as commissioner of the American Section of the Lutheran World Convention to the rising World Council of
Churches.

### Executive Secretary in Geneva

Michelfelder arrived with his wife in Geneva on July 18, 1945, having crossed
the Atlantic ocean on the *Miraposa*, and traveled by rail from Cherbourg,
France, to Geneva, a trip that gave him ample evidence of emergency needs in
Europe.

In Geneva he joined the staff of the World Council of Churches, which was
then being established under the leadership of Willem A. Visser 't Hooft. During his first week in Geneva Michelfelder was encouraged and stimulated to

establish contact with church leaders in Germany, not least at the moment
when Visser 't Hooft was leading a morning service and touched on the role of
the modern martyrs in countries that had been occupied by Nazi Germany and
in Germany itself. Visser 't Hooft made specific reference to the last days of
Dietrich Bonhoeffer, quoting from Bonhoeffer's poem "Nächtliche Stimmen"
("Night Voices in Tegel," 1944). It was such a confession of guilt and repentance, followed by the forgiveness of sins, reconciliation, and a common will
to a new beginning, which lay behind Visser 't Hooft's contact with leaders
from the Confessing Church in Germany, a dialogue that subsequently
resulted in the Stuttgart Declaration of Guilt of October 18, 1945. This Declaration has received much attention in scholarly research. Less well known,
and yet no less significant is a parallel initiative, taken by Sylvester Michelfelder only ten days after his arrival in Geneva.

In a "Message to the Churches of Germany" Michelfelder went straight to
the point in mentioning "the devastation and horrors of war." But the message
was in no way dictated by gloating revenge . On the contrary, it was a letter of
sympathy for brethren in Germany with assurance of friendship and willingness to help. "Your Lutheran brethren in America seek to find the best means
to help you. Now we are limited by the authority of the armies of occupation.
For the present there are many things we would like to do but can't. The
Lutheran World Convention, American Section, which I represent, has elaborate plans for coming to your aid. Millions of dollars will be forthcoming if we
can reawaken that kinship in the faith which once was so strong."

Michelfelder went on to assure the Germans that he was conscious of the
persecution of the church, expressing his admiration for those who had perse-
vered in resisting. "We know that many of you have suffered imprisonment
and persecution for your faith and your resistance to those satanic powers
which tried to destroy the Church of Jesus Christ. We have been shocked by
the reports of how many of your brethren have suffered martyrdom for the
Cause of Christ. The blood of the martyrs is still the seed of the Church. We
believe that these hallowed dead have not died in vain. We believe that a
stronger church will arise from these ashes in the land of the Reformation."

At the same time, however, the message had an appeal to self-criticism,
repentance, and confession of guilt: "God still hates sin, but he loves the sinner. Where you have erred in judgment, recognize it and retrace your steps to
the Cross of Christ our Savior. If you have trusted cruel, godless leaders which
have misled and deceived you, pray God for the Grace and Courage to say: 'I
was wrong.' 'We were wrong.' "

In conclusion Michelfelder reassured his brethren in Germany of sympathy,
solidarity, and readiness to actions of aid, provided that their brothers and sisters in the United States should receive a message with a corresponding
application from Germany and that he personally could be admitted by the
military authorities to enter Germany. He closed with a pastoral invocation of
God's help "to the weary and tempted."

Due to the severe rules governing the occupation it was for a while impossible for Michelfelder to be granted access to Germany. His American colleague in Geneva, Stewart Herman, however, had held a job for the U.S.
government during the war, after his service as chaplain in Berlin until 1941,

and could act on behalf of Michelfelder and the Geneva offices when he attended the important synod in Treysa, Germany, in the late days of August 1945, the synod that marked the constitution of a reunited Evangelical Church in Germany (EKD). In his reports Herman gave a detailed account of his impression of the position being taken by the leading members of the Confessing Church. He made no secret of their difficulties in defining a common course of action.

In his diary from September 21, Michelfelder gave particular emphasis to the promising signs from Treysa, and to the positive effect his message had exerted.

> Treysa showed itself as a great achievement. There was a real spirit of devotion, and Christian work received its proper place of importance. Herman reported that the meeting was held in the chapel of a hospital where many crippled war veterans were housed. This in itself made the conference quite conscious of the effects of the war. The opening devotions were colored by the war situation and the German suffering particularly. Then to the amazement of Herman, Bishop Wurm read my letter to the German churches. 'It was like opening the window and letting in a ray of light and a breath of fresh air. This was a new note which had not been heard in Germany before. It changed the complexion of the meeting completely. The knowledge that American Lutherans cared made the difference.' I felt very much pleased and was very grateful. It partly compensated for my deep regret at having been kept out of Germany and away from Treysa. (Michelfelder's Diary, LWF Archives, Exec. Sec. office, Class Nr. ES / II 2)

We can hardly overestimate the ramifications of this opening gesture, which led to mutual confidence and a willingness to make a new beginning, thereby overcoming the disastrous errors, shortcomings, and cruelties of the past. It is against such a background that we have to understand the meeting in Stuttgart on October 18, 1945, when leaders from the Confessing Church in Germany met with ecumenical leaders. The Germans presented to their friends from the outside world the "Confession of Guilt." Sylvester Michelfelder was a member of the ecumenical delegation in Stuttgart, and the experience became a determining factor in his subsequent correspondence with Lutheran leaders in Germany, among them Hans Meiser and Hanns Lilje.

## Preparations for the First Assembly of the LWF

In the account of early rescue operations to Germany in the early postwar period we have quoted from the reports Michelfelder sent to the United States' agencies for relief operations (cf. p. 355 above). Suffice it here to point to the inner coherence of the development, which started with the message in July, went via the Stuttgart Declaration of Guilt, and finally led to the building of close ties of confidence and networks of cooperation, all of which was finally affirmed and lifted up to international interaction between sisters and brothers of the same faith, at the first LWF Assembly in Lund 1947.

The preparations for this gathering and its successful implementation were

Michelfelder's major accomplishment. His careful preparation included exchange of ideas with the acting president, Archbishop Eidem of Uppsala, and with his new friends in Germany, Meiser and Lilje as well. Michelfelder had clear ideas for an assembly with a three-part program: "confessing the truth in a confused world," which was to concentrate on the Word, the church, and the sacraments; a section on evangelism, stewardship, "foreign mission," and aid operations; and a final section on "facing the problems in a troubled world" (cf. pp. 354–55 above). His comments to Meiser and Lilje, as he explained his ideas in advance, drew a clear connection between pastoral concerns and their consequences in the actual political situation:

> [W]e would include under Materialism, secularism, the decline of morals, and any other isms which are giving problems to the church, Bolshevism. Under b), Race Relations, we would of course want to consider all those problems which have arisen due to intense Nationalism, racial prejudices, and deportation; then under c) refugees and Displaced Persons, we certainly would want to have findings and reports concerning the great movement of the millions, who are refugees to day throughout the world. ( Letter of Oct. 8, 1946, to Hans Meiser, with copies to H. Lilje, E. Eidem, A. Nygren, and A. Th. Jørgensen, LWF Archives, Lund Assembly, Box I, Correspondence. Drafts and manuscripts)

The varying degrees of specification in Michelfelder's assembly outline—from rather brief notes concerning the theological section to more detailed directions concerning the moral challenges in society—together with his perceptible passion, reflect both his strengths and limitations as executive secretary. Even if it is true that he was not an academic theologian but rather a gifted preacher and administrator, it should not be concluded that he did not care about the role of theology in the new LWF. He was in no doubt that solid theology, conducted within the framework of international exchange on all levels, should be given high priority in the Federation.

Without doctrinal clarity, Michelfelder constantly maintained, it would be a risky business to combine confessional identity with ecumenical openness, an interaction that Michelfelder advocated throughout his term as executive secretary. Looking back on his first four years in Geneva, his involvement in the foundation of the WCC in Amsterdam 1948, and commenting on the paragraph in the constitution, "To foster Lutheran participation in ecumenical movements," Michelfelder said to the executive committee at its annual meeting in 1949: "No church body has taken a more active part in the affairs of the World Council of Churches than the Lutheran Church. And unaccustomed as they were at that time to hear the opinion and suggestions from a Lutheran source, one can safely say today that the Lutheran representatives on the campus of the World Council of Churches are recognized as a very important factor in every discussion and meeting." ( Report of the Exec.Comm 1948–1949, Lilje papers, Hanover, L3/ III 420)

### Patterns for an Organizational Structure

His abilities as an administrator became apparent particularly in two connections: when he prepared and led the First Assembly, and when he led in the formation of a functional structure for the whole LWF, the Geneva secretariat and the national committees as well. This was his main task during his last years, when the provisional decisions of the earliest years had to be transferred into sustainable working principles. Michelfelder combined firm leadership with flexibility and sensitivity to the varying conditions in the member churches, a balance that was not at all simple at the outset and which has involved increasing challenges ever since. He introduced his suggestions for an organizational structure in a 1951 handbook as follows: "This is no rule book; it is a guide book. No two National Committees of the Lutheran World Federation are organized alike. Consequently each must adapt these suggestions as they fit the need. Some National Committees have elaborate organizational machinery, others have no paid staff. Some may want to appoint all 15 Study Committees or Study Groups, others may have to combine kindred committees." Throughout his proposed pattern it was his concern to create a dynamic interaction between the national committees with their study groups on the one hand, and the international special commissions and the Geneva headquarters on the other (Handbook for Guidance of Special Commissions, National Committees and Study Groups, in preparation for the Assembly of the LWF, Hanover 1952; rev. ed. Geneva, 1952).

Sylvester Michelfelder was in the process of bringing these ideas to fruition in connection with numerous other aspects of preparation for the Second LWF Assembly when he died on December 30, 1951 during a visit to his home church.

## Evaluation

Even in his lifetime Sylvester Michelfelder received wide recognition for his successful efforts to bring cooperation into being, efforts that may be understood against the background of the unprecedented difficulties of the historical situation. It was Michelfelder's achievement that he was able to be a catalyst and coordinator in this process.

Having granted this, however, it should not be forgotten that there were in the young LWF dispersed voices of hesitation or even suspicion. Some of the old-timers from the Lutheran World Convention were unable to adjust to the new circumstances; some were reluctant to accept the apparent dominance of an American working style that accompanied the flow of economic and material support from the U.S. relief agencies. Some were anxious that the magnanimous aid was distributed too rapidly; they feared both abuse in the distribution and the negative side effect of materialistic estrangement from the spiritual identity of the recipients. Here and there voices were heard that Michelfelder personally exhibited a style of extravagance.

Such undertones, however, should not hide Michelfelder's remarkable achievement. The president of the LWF, Anders Nygren, gave a moving expression to this, when he led a memorial service during the Second Assembly in Hanover. Nygren pointed out that it would be untimely to praise the man in whose memory they were assembled. "We Lutherans are radically opposed to the glorification of man." Instead Nygren wanted to lead this unusual, international congregation in a service of remembrance. With this purpose he took as his text Hebrews 13:7, "Remember them who have the rule over you, who have spoken unto you the word of God." Nygren found it inappropriate to speak of "rulers." He thought higher of the translation which Luther had proposed: teachers. Or, as he suggested, it might be better to say leaders, or guides.

> Dr. Michelfelder was a leader in the deepest sense of the word. He was not only the leader of one congregation, or of one church body, but of all the Lutheran churches of the world; in fact, his leadership extended even beyond the limits of our own confession.— It is perfectly clear to all of us now, that he was the right man to perform this service at this particular time; it is a proof of God's love of our Church that He gave us this chosen vessel at the right moment for the unification of Lutherans throughout the world. (A. Nygren, Sermon, in *Proceedings*, Hanover, p. 173).

## Bibliographical Notes

*Unpublished Sources*

LWF Archives, Geneva.
H. Lilje papers, Lutheran Church Archives, Hanover.
E. Eidem's papers, Landsarkivet, Uppsala.
A. Nygren's papers, University Library, Lund.
E. Theodore Bachmann. "A Michelfelder Profile: Early Times in Geneva." Unpublished manuscript.

*Literature*

Bachmann, E. Theodore. *Epic of Faith: The Background of the Second Assembly of the Lutheran World Federation.* New York: National Lutheran Council, 1952.
Besier, Gerhard, and Gerhard Sauter. *Wenn Christen ihre Schuld bekennen: Die Stuttgarter Erklärung 1945.* Göttingen: Vandenhoeck & Ruprecht, 1985.
Besier, Gerhard, Hartmut Ludwig, Jörg Thierfelder, and Ralf Tyra, eds. *Kirche nach der Kapitulation*, Bd. 2, *Auf dem Weg nach Treysa.* Stuttgart: Kohlhammer Verlag, 1989.
Greschat, Martin. Die *Schuld der Kirche: Dokumente und Reflexionen zur Stuttgarter Schulderklärung vom 18./19. Oktober 1945.* Munich: Chr. Kaiser Verlag, 1982.
Nelson, Clifford A. *The Rise of World Lutheranism: An American Perspective.* Philadelphia: Fortress Press, 1982.
Schmidt-Clausen, Kurt. *Vom Lutherischen Weltkonvent zum Lutherischen Weltbund*, 2 vols. Gütersloh: Gütersloher Verlagshaus Gerd Mohn, 1976.
Visser 't Hooft, Willem A. *Memoirs.* London: SCM Press, 1973; 2d edition, Geneva: World Council of Churches, 1987.
Vollnhals, Clemens. *Die Evangelische Kirche nach dem Zusammenbruch: Berichte ausländischer Beobachter aus dem Jahre 1945.* Göttingen: Vandenhoeck & Ruprecht, 1988.

# Carl Elof Lund-Quist

CARL ELOF LUND-QUIST was born on September 19, 1908, on a farm near Lindsborg, Kansas, U.S.A. His parents were Swedish-American. His father was born and raised on a frontier farm; his mother, a Swedish immigrant, died when Carl was eight years old. After high school, he attended Bethany College, Lindsborg, Kansas (Bachelor of Arts in 1932) and the Lutheran Bible Institute in Minneapolis, Minnesota (1929–1930), a school known for a legalistic piety that disappointed him. He found a spiritual home in the Lutheran Student Association of America (LSAA), in the World Student Christian Federation (WSCF), and in the World Sunday School Association (WSSA). After his theological education at Augustana Theological Seminary in Rock Island, Illinois (Bachelor of Divinity in 1936), and a one-year internship at Ebenezer Lutheran Church in Chicago, Illinois, he was ordained on June 14, 1936, by the Augustana Lutheran Church and called to be pastor of Concordia Lutheran Church in Chicago, Illinois (1936–1941). He also served as campus pastor at the University of Minnesota in Minneapolis (1941–1946). He held various leadership positions related to mission and Christian unity: president of the LSAA (1931–1933); member of the executive committee of the Young Men's Christian Association (YMCA) and of the executive committee of the WSCF in America (1939–1944); delegate to the World Conference of Christian Youth in Amsterdam (1939) and Oslo (1947); executive director of the Division of Public Relations of the National Lutheran Council of America (NLC) (1946–1948); assistant executive director of NLC (1948–1951); assistant to the first LWF executive secretary, Sylvester C. Michelfelder, and acting executive secretary after Michelfelder's sudden death (1951); second executive secretary of the LWF (1951–1960). He was involved in planning the First Assembly of the LWF in Lund in 1947, and he was responsible for the preparation of the assemblies in Hanover in 1952, in Minneapolis in 1957, and, to a lesser degree, in Helsinki in 1963. In failing health since 1960, Lund-Quist died on August 26, 1965. Four American academic institutions and the German University of Erlangen granted him honorary doctoral degrees. The German Federal Republic awarded him the Order of Merit in 1957. Lund-Quist never married.

## Educational and Spiritual Formation

Carl Elof Lund-Quist was nurtured in a family settled at the frontier of Midwest America and grounded in a Swedish Lutheran piety with its emphasis on Bible study, family values, and personal commitment to Christian service in the world. Rural elementary and high schools, together with the Lutheran parish Sunday school in Freemont, Kansas, laid the foundation for

Author: *Eric W. Gritsch, Baltimore Maryland*

LWF Photo—1956

60. Carl Elof Lund-Quist of the Augustana Lutheran
    Church (U.S.A.), Executive Secretary of the Lutheran
    World Federation, 1951–1960

Lund-Quist's early decision to become a pastor. He viewed this decision as a
"distinct" and "inner call," differing from an "outer call" to another, more
worldly vocation. Such terminology was common in his church, the Augustana Lutheran Church. He preached his first sermon when he was seventeen
years old and assisted pastors in small congregations before he entered college
at age eighteen. But when he encountered a legalistic piety during a brief
period of studies at the Lutheran Bible Institute in Minneapolis, Minnesota, he
rejected it as an impediment to effective ministry. His college studies showed
him a less conservative Lutheranism that did not shy away from a critical evaluation of new and challenging scientific insights and theories, such as the Dar-
winist view of biological evolution, a matter of debate at Bethany College and
at other institutions of higher learning. He soon discovered a more tolerant
ecumenical component of Lutheranism in the Lutheran student movement,
which opened the world to him. But he always retained his strong commitment to personal spiritual formation through communal Bible study, prayer
groups, and close fellowship, especially in the popular "Ashrams" (gatherings
that took their name from an Asian Indian term meaning "respite from

work"). These Ashrams began in 1936 and became very popular in the Lutheran student movement. (See Emmet E. Eklund and Marion Lorimer Eklund, *He Touched the Whole World: The Story of Carl E. Lund-Quist*, pp. 18–19.) Lund-Quist led parishioners and students to such spiritual formation during his work as a parish and campus pastor.

Lund-Quist encountered the sense and taste of international Christianity when he attended a seminar at the University of Geneva in 1936 during his travels to student conferences in Europe. There he met Hanns Lilje, the German secretary of the World Student Christian Federation, and Toyohiko Kagawa, the Japanese theologian who was one of the first significant theological voices of the world's "younger churches." In 1946 he was selected to travel for four months in Europe as the American representative of the World Student Christian Federation, with visits to universities in Germany, Scandinavia, Switzerland, and England. Such traveling offered Lund-Quist unforgettable experiences of the devastation of World War II and enriched him with insights that strengthened his desire to become involved in the ecumenical movement.

## Service in the National Church

As the first executive director of the Division of Public Relations of the National Lutheran Council of America (NLC) Lund-Quist was called "to present the faith, ideals, and programs of the Lutheran church through various means of influencing human thought and action" (Eklund and Eklund, *He Touched*, p. 33). The NLC had been launched in 1918 and had become a well-known pan-Lutheran agency at home and abroad by the end of World War II. Lund-Quist was particularly fond of the agency's radio program *March of Faith*, which was produced with the cooperation of the well-known and influential National Broadcasting Company (NBC). Lund-Quist also supervised the production of visual aids depicting the work of Lutheran World Action (LWA), which was involved in the global distribution of food and other aid programs. Such programs were complemented by Lutheran World Relief (LWR), founded in 1945 by the NLC for the purpose of collecting supplies for shipment to areas designated for international aid by the United Nations Relief and Rehabilitation Agency (UNRRA). In addition, Lund-Quist was responsible for the publication of a widely read journal, *The National Lutheran*, one of sixty-three Lutheran publications in the United States (Frederick K. Wentz, *Lutherans in Concert: The Story of the National Lutheran Council*, pp. 154–55). He was not a man of vision but a capable enabler who could realize, within a reasonable praxis, the vision of others. He was known as an administrator who did not dominate in discussions; he was a good listener who instilled confidence among his coworkers; and he could well summarize what was said in different contexts and isolate significant issues for further deliberation. It was said of him that he had "a sense of people" (from interviews conducted by Eklund and Eklund, *He Touched*, p. 37).

Lund-Quist's service at home also involved him with world Lutheranism, especially with the LWF and its First Assembly in Lund, Sweden, in 1947. He was placed in charge of press relations and met many Lutheran leaders from around the world. Moreover, he also made the travel arrangements for the

Lund delegates from the United States. After the assembly he edited its *Proceedings* and arranged the publication of Bishop Eivind Berggrav's essay on church and state (published in *Man and the State*, trans. George Aus [Philadelphia: Muhlenberg Press, 1951]). When the constituting assembly of the World Council of Churches (WCC) met in Amsterdam, Holland, in 1948 Lund-Quist assisted in making the housing arrangements for the Lutheran delegates. At the same time, he urged the executive secretary of the LWF, Sylvester C. Michelfelder, to start a program for European students to study in the United States through LWF scholarships. He also solicited essays from Lutherans in Europe for publication in Lutheran journals in the United States.

When Paul Empie headed the NLC in 1948 he made Lund-Quist the assistant executive director, authorizing him to make all decisions in his absence. Since Empie was often absent, Lund-Quist used his authority to extend the influence of the NLC. He lobbied hard to get permission for Lutheran officials to travel to war-torn Europe. Such lobbying involved visits to the United States War Department, which required many bureaucratic details for permission to gain entry into Europe. In one case Lund-Quist wrote nineteen letters in order to receive permission for one Lutheran church official to visit Finland in 1948. (The letters were written on behalf of Sigfrid E. Engstrom, executive secretary of the Augustana Board of American Missions [Archives of the Evangelical Lutheran Church in America (ELCA), cited in Eklund and Eklund, *He Touched*, p. 40]). He also was often asked to facilitate visits from European church officials to the United States. LWF General Secretary Michelfelder once sent a whole catalogue of requests to Lund-Quist, asking, for example, to find a teaching position for an acquaintance in Geneva, or to secure office supplies (excerpts from the LWF Archives in Geneva, cited in Eklund and Eklund, p. 41). Empie had full confidence in Lund-Quist's leadership, and they became and remained good friends during and after Lund-Quist's tenure at the NLC.

## LWF Executive Secretary

Following their work at the assembly in Lund in 1947 Lund-Quist and Michelfelder remained close friends. It was, therefore, not surprising that Michelfelder would call Lund-Quist as his assistant to Geneva. When he arrived in Geneva in 1951 he was given several tasks: directing the European program of NLC; managing the LWF publication *Lutherische Rundschau* (as of 1954 paralleled by the English-language edition, *Lutheran World*), which informed the world of the work of LWF; and to assist the LWF Executive Secretary in whatever ways he deemed appropriate. Both men were soon known as the team of "Carl and Micky," even though they had different personalities. Michelfelder was more volatile and lacked patience; Lund-Quist was more diplomatic. But their time together in Geneva was short. Michelfelder died in December 1951 of a heart attack shortly after a meeting with NLC committees in Chicago.

Lund-Quist assumed the work of Michelfelder, having become well acquainted with the work in Geneva. The focus of the work was the preparation of the LWF Assembly in Hanover, Germany, in 1952. Working with President Anders Nygren, he summarized his expectations in an essay entitled

"Our Tasks." It was his main contention that Lutherans had not yet been adequately faithful to their heritage, which focused on Holy Scripture and the historic confessions. If they became faithful to this heritage they would become a more effective group of Christians in witness, service, and aid to all. (The article was printed in *Information Service of the LWF* No. 13:3 [July 5, 1952]; summarized in Eklund and Eklund, *He Touched*, p. 60).

He also referred to the global political situation, which prevented Lutherans from coming to the assembly from Communist countries. As interim executive secretary, Lund-Quist was responsible for organizing the Hanover Assembly. He did this task with attention to focus and detail. He viewed worship and theology as primary, and he worked tirelessly on organizational matters. "My hours were from 6 in the morning until 2 or 3 at night. I was glad I was raised on the farm where we got used getting up early." So he wrote in a letter to his family from Geneva, November 9, 1952 (cited in Eklund and Eklund, *He Touched*, p. 73). He was especially pleased with the decision to establish a Department of Theology, and he was a key supporter of the establishment of an LWF Foundation for Inter-Confessional Research (created in 1965 as the Institute for Ecumenical Research in Strasbourg, France). Another important concern was the place of the laity and of youth. In his report to the executive committee of the LWF in 1953 he stated his satisfaction with the decision in Hanover to have a larger number of lay people on the committee (ibid., 74).

As the second LWF Executive Secretary, Lund-Quist traveled extensively in the years between the assembly in Hanover in 1952 and the Third Assembly in Minneapolis in 1957; he covered about 150,000 miles to all parts of the globe. (Wilmar Torkelson, "From a Farm Boy to Church Diplomat: The World is His Parish," *Lutheran Standard* [September 14, 1957] 18; cited in Eklund and Eklund, p. 79). He was the first LWF representative to go to Indonesia and negotiate the membership of the Batak Church on the basis of its own "confession." He helped create the first regional conferences in Africa (1955) and in Asia (1956). His organization of a Second All-Latin America Conference in 1954 helped unite the dispersed Lutherans on that continent. Lund-Quist also lifted up the plight of Lutheran minority churches, especially in Eastern Europe. Bishop Lajos Ordass of Hungary, who had been elected a vice-president of the LWF in Lund in 1947, symbolized this plight in his personal suffering under a Communist regime and in his steadfast witness. Lund-Quist managed to maintain some contact with Ordass, regarded him as a friend, and presented detailed reports to the executive committee on developments in Hungary. (The Hungarian situation is depicted in "Überblick über die neuesten Entwicklungen in der ungarischen lutherischen Kirche," LWF Department of Information, News Release, 45/56, November 30, 1956.) Lund-Quist is frequently mentioned in the Ordass biography of László G. Terray, *He Could Not Do Otherwise* (see also Eklund and Eklund, "Hungary and the Ordass Case," pp. 97–104). In 1957 he was able to make an official visit to Hungary and to present Bishop Ordass with a set of winter clothes he had smuggled in by wearing them himself (Eklund and Eklund, pp. 103–4).

The cold war between Russia and the United States overshadowed the preparations for the Third LWF Assembly in Minneapolis in 1957. Lund-Quist tried without much success to get exit visas for Lutheran delegates from behind the iron curtain. Even personal interventions in East Germany and in Hungary did not bring much fruit, though Bishop Ordass was permitted to travel to Minneapolis in the wake of a political thaw after the short-lived Hungarian revolt against Communism in 1956. Despite criticism, Lund-Quist viewed the assembly in Minneapolis as a success since it advanced the cause of Lutheran and Christian unity. He was proud that the assembly was an American event. "Certainly the work of the Federation for the next few years is going to be much easier now they have seen and know what we are trying to do." So he described his view in a letter to his family from Geneva, December 12, 1957 (Eklund and Eklund, p. 125).

In what was to be his last full report to the executive committee (October 27–30, 1958), Lund-Quist summarized the work of the LWF in its first decade. He noted his conviction that the local congregation is the best representation of the church, and that he still had a fear of bureaucracy. Regular contact with member churches is crucial, he contended, especially with minority churches (Eklund and Eklund, pp. 128–29). He was proud to have been part of the efforts to establish a radio station, Radio Voice of the Gospel, in Addis Ababa, Ethiopia, and he spent his final period of service in negotiations with Australian Lutherans who were burdened with doctrinal issues related to the tradition of the Lutheran Church–Missouri Synod. After a visit to Australia in 1959, he stated his optimism about the future since there had been much cooperation with respect to problems of immigration, home mission, and relationships with the LWF.

Already quite ill since Christmas 1958, Lund-Quist continued to work at his desk in Geneva after his return from Australia. He consulted with member churches regarding the Fourth LWF Assembly and its theme. But hypertension, depression, and strokes finally forced him to resign from his office in 1960. He never recovered and died less than a month before his 57th birthday in 1965 in Minneapolis. Friends and co-workers from around the world remember him as a man who listened well before he made a decision and as one who never lost the "common touch."

## Bibliographical Notes

*Proceedings,* Hanover.
*Proceedings,* Minneapolis.

Eklund, Emmet E., and Marion Lorimer Eklund. *He Touched the Whole World: The Story of Carl E. Lund-Quist.* Lindsborg, Kansas: Bethany College Press, 1990 and 1992.
Terray, László. *He Could Not Do Otherwise: Bishop Lajos Ordass, 1901–1978,* trans. Eric W. Gritsch. Grand Rapids: Eerdmans, 1997.
Torkelson, Wilmar. "From a Farm Boy to Church Diplomat: The World Is His Parish." *Lutheran Standard,* September 14, 1957.
Wentz, Frederick K. *Lutherans in Concert: The Story of the National Lutheran Council.* Minneapolis: Augsburg, 1968.

# Kurt Schmidt-Clausen

KURT SCHMIDT-CLAUSEN was born on October 1, 1920, in Hanover, Germany. In the forties, though interrupted by war service and imprisonment, he studied theology in Göttingen, Vienna, and Oxford. After his ordination in 1951, he became pastor at the Neustädter Church in Hanover, and in 1955 in Wunstorf (Lower Saxony). From 1960 to 1965, he was general secretary of the Lutheran World Federation in Geneva, having been a delegate of his church at the LWF Assemblies in Hanover in 1952 and in Minneapolis in 1957 and at the World Council of Churches Assembly in Evanston in 1954.

In 1965, Schmidt-Clausen became Oberlandeskirchenrat in the Hanover church office. He was in charge of the desks for mission, ecumenics, and church press. The foundation of the Protestant Press Association of Lower Saxony was due to his initiative. He coedited the *Lutherische Monatshefte*, the publication of the United Evangelical Lutheran Church in Germany (VELKD). He also chaired the VELKD's ecumenical commission. In 1970, the Hanover church senate nominated him to become Landessuperintendent for the diocese of Osnabrück, an office he held until his retirement in 1982. Moreover, he was a member of the Convent of Amelungsborn and in 1971, as successor to Christhard Mahrenholz, became abbot of the monastery. He died on January 25, 1993, and is buried in the Stöckener cemetery in Hanover.

## Theological Position

Kurt Schmidt-Clausen always underlined that the primary raison d'être of the Lutheran church lies within the framework of the ecumenical movement and consists in exercising theological responsibility: the Lutheran church must interpret the truths that came out of the Lutheran Reformation, that is, the total understanding of the Christian message purely on the basis of the gospel, and on this basis it must update this message and make it bear fruit. "Since the Holy Scriptures contain this central Good News and because this gospel of the free and boundless love of God for the sinner transcends all boundaries of language, race, ethnicity, sex, class and culture, the Reformation must be ecumenical." What is at stake is that "sinners are justified for the sake of Christ through faith alone." In other words, the biblical message as rediscovered by the Reformation needs to be set in the center again. This message of the justification of the godless through faith is said to be the center of the ecumenical renewal and evangelism movements. Schmidt-Clausen describes this not as a confessional peculiarity but as the very meaning both of the gospel and the church's existence. "What can be more universal than the question of the proper way of proclaiming salvation for lost and godless human beings?" Against this background, the Reformation and the ecumenical movement are

Author: *Hans-Volker Herntrich, Hanover, Germany*

61. Kurt Schmidt-Clausen of the Evangelical Lutheran
Church of Hanover, Germany, General Secretary of the
Lutheran World Federation, 1960–1965

not contradictory terms. For Schmidt-Clausen, the most important characteristic of the Reformation is the "attempt to put truth above everything else";
and, he continues, "one cannot speak about the truth without thinking of the
document that bears witness to truth. All action and the life of the church of
Jesus Christ needs to be tested by what in the Holy Scriptures is clearly the
will of God."

At this point, Kurt Schmidt-Clausen's attitude was clear-cut—almost intol-
erant. *Christus solus*—this was the only and exclusive content of his faith and
his theology. For him, this position quite frequently became polemical and
was at the forefront of his thinking. Nobody save Christ can pave the way to

God for human beings: "He is the only mediator between God and human beings." "It is not some belief that redeems us but solely the belief in Jesus Christ who died for us and was resurrected, the Lord of the world, the goal of our hope."

From this position, Schmidt-Clausen skeptically followed the developments of the ecumenical movement during and after the World Council of Churches assembly in Uppsala in 1968. While sympathetic to the social and political engagement of Christians and their churches, he resisted all attempts by those who wanted to transform Christianity into an element of immanent politicosocial progress. For him, the ecumenical movement was an instrument in God's hands aimed at equipping Christianity to proclaim the gospel more clearly and unanimously. The Lutheran church and its confession, in his opinion, had an indispensable service to contribute to the ecumenical movement, namely, to "keep them to this center, to the gospel, and never to tire in calling them to this center. Everything that claims to be heard in the ecumenical movement can only be of secondary significance compared to the gospel. Will the Lutheran church do justice to this task assigned to it or will it change back into an instrument of performance religion?" Self-justification by performance or justification by faith alone for the sake of Christ? This was Schmidt-Clausen's question. He answered it clearly by choosing the second alternative.

## LWF General Secretary

After the Americans Sylvester Michelfelder and the unforgettable Carl Lund-Quist, Schmidt-Clausen was the first German in this office. It cannot be underestimated what it meant that German was spoken in the general secretariat of such a worldwide organization. But, of course, it was not just a matter of language. Kurt Schmidt-Clausen's Oxford English with its Hanover intonation was admired by everyone who had learned English in other areas of the world. But it meant much more: a German found the proper tone in an international community and managed to speak in a way that even with regard to political issues did not deny anything that was part of his own history, while at the same time reflecting the ecumenical self-assurance that the German churches showed in a new way after all that had been.

To be sure, Schmidt-Clausen had not taken a direct path from his parish work in the Hanover area to Geneva and the international scene. A growing diplomatic dexterity, which can do no harm in the church either, as well as the proper mix of clear theological profile; brotherly respect for the opinions, working styles, and traditions of other churches; and profound commitment to the cause, helped Schmidt-Clausen to make his way successfully.

The then forty-two-year-old doctor of theology was ecumenically well prepared for his office. He became assistant executive secretary, then acting executive secretary during Lund-Quist's sick leave. Finally, at its meeting in Warsaw in 1961, the executive committee appointed him executive secretary (after the Helsinki Assembly, general secretary.) It is usually said that general secretaries of large organizations perform better when they are less preoccupied with details and instead concentrate on the whole. For Schmidt- Clausen, it was difficult to separate the two demands: attention to detail—important to him as a conscientious German theologian—and the overall view to which he was increasingly committed the longer he was involved in the decision making in Geneva. What every other general secretary tried to do pragmatically with the authority of being in charge, Kurt Schmidt-Clausen attempted to do according to strict theological principles. Many things became much more difficult for him, but also more colorful, more profound, livelier, and more fruitful. He was always aware of the fact that his actual strength lay in theology.

As executive secretary, Schmidt-Clausen had to prepare the assembly in Helsinki in 1963, which aimed at adopting an up-to-date formulation of the Lutheran doctrine of justification. Whether the assembly came to terms with the topic or not is still controversial today. The assembly elicited much response which, however, was rather muted in Germany. It was difficult to accept that an assembly of the world's Lutheran churches had failed to speak with one voice on an up-to-date formulation of such an important matter as the doctrine of justification, for the assembly did not adopt the final report. It does credit to the Lutheran church and its strict adherence to the truth that it did not yield to temptation and switch to quick harmonizing formulae. Schmidt-Clausen himself was always positive about the 1963 Helsinki results. The wholesale criticism that the Lutherans had not been up to the task and were thwarted by their own standards hurt him, because he considered it to be a sign of the church's freedom resulting from the Reformation understanding of faith that this church does not "live on the basis of a monolithic dogmatization." In no way did he wish to detract from the fact that the debates in the discussion groups had made manifest the existence of lively and in part considerable differences and tensions. It seemed that there were two essential trends in the Lutheran church: For some the legacy of the Reformation forefathers was so central that they had no desire to move away from it. For others, an honest confession of their faith could only be one that is proclaimed here and now and stands the test of the present.

Schmidt-Clausen's most important speeches and papers on topics of the ecumenical movement are collected in his book *Reformation als ökumenisches Ereignis* (1970). In this book he defines the ecumenical situation in a way that deserves attention. For it shows the thoughts of a man who learned his job while serving in the ranks. The most essential aspect of the book is that theological reflection is given the place due to it, namely, at the center, even with regard to supposedly marginal questions such as planning and organization. Theology is more than abstract reflection; it is, rather, reflection on the center of the biblical message as rediscovered by the Reformation. This message is about the justification of human beings by faith in Jesus Christ and, according to Schmidt-Clausen, this insight alone can credibly serve as the center of all attempts at ecumenical rapprochement.

Kurt Schmidt-Clausen was a theologian who was open to the world because he was loyal to the one who conquered the world (John 16:33). He was a decidedly Lutheran theologian and, for this very reason, perhaps particularly suitable for ecumenical conversation. He stubbornly argued that only Christians with a clear profile of their own and an unmistakable confessional identity could make a suitable contribution to ecumenical proximity and the growing together of the various churches.

**Bibliographical Notes** _____

*Proceedings*, Helsinki.

*Main Writings of Kurt Schmidt-Clausen*

1956    "Die kirchliche Entwicklung Wunstorfs seit der Reformation." Off-
        print.
1960    *Das Amt der nichtgeistlichen kirchlichen Mitarbeiter.* Hanover.
1965    *Vorweggenommene Einheit: Die Gründung des Bistums Jerusalem
        im Jahr 1841.* Berlin and Hamburg.
1970    *Reformation als ökumenisches Ereignis: Reden und Aufsätze zu
        Themen der ökumenischen Bewegung.* Berlin and Hamburg.
1976    *Vom Lutherischen Weltkonvent zum Lutherischen Weltbund.*
        Gütersloh: Gütersloher Verlagshaus Gerd Mohn.
1985    *Kloster Amelungsborn 1135–1985.* Edited with G. Ruhbach. Hanover.
1989    *August Marahrens, Landesbischof in Hannover, Wirklichkeit und
        Legende.* Hanover.


*On Schmidt-Clausen*

Henze, E. "Konfessionelle Klarheit, Zum Tode von Kurt Schmidt-Clausen."
    *Lutherische Monatshefte* 3 (1993): 11.

# André Appel

ANDRÉ APPEL was born on December 20, 1921, in Saverne, Alsace, France. He read theology first at the universities of Leipzig and Tübingen, Germany. Although he was drafted, against his will, into the German army in 1942, he was later able to escape to the free French forces. He resumed studies in Paris and completed his training at the theological faculty at Strasbourg in 1946. Having been awarded a American grant, he spent two years studying and teaching in the United States. Appel was ordained in 1949 in Wissembourg, Alsace, then appointed university chaplain in Paris in 1955. A year and a half later he became general secretary of the Protestant Federation in France. He returned to his native Alsace in 1964, where he served as pastor at one of the Lutheran churches in Strasbourg. The following year, he was appointed general secretary of the Lutheran World Federation. After serving for two terms he was elected president of his home church, the Church of the Augsburg Confession in Alsace and Lorraine, in 1974 and retired in 1987. Appel married Marjorie Rosell Pedersen of Brooklyn, New York, United States, in 1950. They have four children.

## Background and Education

André Appel's father, Georges Appel, was a Lutheran pastor who deeply identified with the relatively small minority church in Alsace but nevertheless maintained a broad international outlook. He had spent a year studying in Berlin and had served as a pastor in Milan, Italy, where he had met his future wife, Erna Meyer of Switzerland. Even after Georges Appel had become pastor in Saverne, a provincial town in Alsace, the family retained its international background, speaking German and English besides French and Alsatian. As a student André Appel broadened his cultural and linguistic horizons by spending the first years of his theological studies at German universities and, after passing his finals in Paris, going on to postgraduate studies in North America.

Appel was greatly influenced by the unstable political and cultural situation in his home country. Alsace became German in 1871* and remained a buffer zone, an area of encounter and bridge building. There can be no doubt that living in Alsace during the Nazi era and the Second World War had a decisive influence on Appel's international and ecumenical work.

Appel's stance was shaped by his background. In an interview with the News Bureau of the National Lutheran Council shortly after his nomination as general secretary of the LWF, he made specific reference to his being a mem-

---

* Editor's note: Alsace was returned to France in 1919 (Treaty of Versailles) and was occupied by German troops and under German civilian authority from 1940 to 1945. Alsace has been French since 1945.

Author: *Jens Hoger Schjørring, Aarhus, Denmark*

LWF Photo

62. André Appel of the Church of the Augsburg Confession
in Alsace and Lorraine, France, General Secretary of
the Lutheran World Federation, 1965–1974

ber of a minority church. Appel stressed that better understanding among and
closer cooperation between the Christian churches was necessary. He regarded
his taking office as a confessional leader in the World Council of Churches'
office building as an important testimony to an ecumenical commitment
which he had already experienced as general secretary of the French Protestant
Federation of Churches.

The historical context of the time was conducive to ecumenical openness.
Appel took office during the aftermath of the Second Vatican Council. In his
first interview as general secretary of the Federation, he declared, "The
Catholic Church now confronts us with the question whether we are prepared
with courage and disciplined humility to scrutinize our churches anew accord-

ing to the principles of reform. What does reformation mean, after the Second Vatican Council?"

## Appel as General Secretary of the LWF

The first general secretaries of the LWF had been North American (Michelfelder and Lund-Quist) and West German (Schmidt-Clausen). Hence, Appel's appointment signaled the dawning of a new era. He endeavored both to define a more global strategy in view of the historical process of decolonization and to accommodate the demand for a more just influence and inclusiveness on the part of women, youth, and the southern hemisphere churches. Moreover, he was faced with the necessity of having to redefine the role of the minority churches in Central and Eastern Europe. This became clear at the very beginning of his term when he started negotiating with the East German authorities with regard to holding the Fifth Assembly at Weimar, GDR. His predecessor, as a West German citizen, had been somewhat more restricted. Moreover, Appel's understanding of the political divisions in Europe was rather impartial. Negotiations regarding the Fifth Assembly drew to an end only upon the East German government's insistence (see above, pp. 383ff., for the entire account of the Fifth Assembly at Evian. Appel was, of course, a pivotal figure in all that involved that crucial LWF event; the account will not be given again in the present context).

Appel's first years in Geneva were marked by his endeavors to give a new orientation to the ecumenical dialogues and increasing the involvement of youth, women, and younger churches. All this was overshadowed by the dramatic preparations for the Fifth Assembly and the numerous important decisions resulting from it.

Appel was aware that listening to demands for renewal and reorientation while keeping a sense of proportion and preserving the true values of the Lutheran heritage would not be easy. He therefore faced an immense task when he addressed the executive committee the year after the Evian Assembly. In his report, "What Time Is It for the LWF?" Appel did not hide the fact that the LWF had witnessed a drama that had put the Federation's survival into question. Yet he urged that the challenges be faced more optimistically: "Seldom have discussions about the LWF been so passionate and stimulating." Responding to those who feared that "the not yet twenty-five-year-old organization would not survive the upheaval caused by the decision not to meet in Brazil," Appel insisted that "It has survived, but whether it can be of real value to our churches and the ecumenical movement will depend on our ability to read the signs of our time, to hear the voice of the Lord to his church and to live up to such a call." Quoting from the book of Ecclesiastes, "To everything there is a season, and a time for every matter under the heaven . . . ," he suggested that the LWF embark on a period of careful reconsideration.

The first phase would have to be "a time for listening." The assembly had marked a breakthrough, precisely because the diversity within the global community had been expressed: "We have to listen as intensely to minorities as we do to majorities; we have to put side by side the voices of delegates and the observers, of the theologians and the people, of the church leaders and the youth, of the vocal westerners and the more reserved representatives of Asia and Africa, of the journalists from the church and the secular press" (*Lutheran World* [1971] 358). Rather than considering this pluralism a troublesome or paralyzing burden, Appel encouraged the member churches to regard the diversity of the Federation as a privilege. "Combining all of this [the multitude of voices], of course gives quite a new symphony with conflicting tones. It would be an oversimplification to say that the LWF has betrayed its aims and lost its justification just because the *soli* of theologians or the *cantus firmus* of the Reformation doctrine could not be heard as loudly as in the past. The question is rather whether the basic theme, the central message of the gospel was there and expressed through the various documents and witnesses" (ibid.).

Appel's vision was marked by optimism and the plea to look forward. Nevertheless, he affirmed that it would be unrealistic if one were merely to listen without redefining the strategy and setting priorities. Here Appel particularly emphasized the role of the churches from the South, because the need to change, or at least to adjust was so evident.

> The predominance of the churches on both sides of the Atlantic is so overwhelming that some take it for granted and others are resigned to it. But today we hear the churches in Africa, Asia and Latin America telling us that, as Lutheran churches, they have their own identity and way of looking at their role which may be different from that which has come out of the sixteenth century tradition. Taking this into account, we may realize that in the past decades we have not taken full advantage of the opportunities the LWF offers for mutual enrichment. (ibid., p. 360)

A time of listening would have to precede the phases of reviewing and setting priorities. Again Appel's strategy maintained a balance between idealistic stocktaking of all concerns and interests, on the one hand, and the determination courageously to meet the challenges, on the other. Although some of the main issues raised at Evian, such as the concerns related to Brazil, South Africa, or the resolution on human rights, caused controversy and division, it would have been disastrous if the LWF were to have shirked the complex task ahead and failed to address the core of the issues.

Setting priorities demanded not only foresight and courage but also trust in the LWF's ability to survive. Appel was determined to take very seriously the essence of the Evian theme, "Sent into the World." He was prepared to set new priorities with regard to the basic meaning of "mission," the definition and implementation of a new social ethic based on inclusiveness and human rights, and the consequences of the resolution on pulpit and altar fellowship.

Appel certainly did not regard the LWF as an aging institution showing signs of growing pains, if not resignation, nor as an organization collapsing under the burden of restructuring the secretariat, implementing important resolutions, and setting new priorities while being mindful of the heritage and maintaining a real understanding for the identity of the LWF as a whole. This presupposed that the LWF would remain mobile and flexible. "The Lutheran World Federation has the advantage of being a young organization and not too much of a settled institution. It wants to be and must be a living, moving organism;

Evian also has proven this." This diagnosis would be incomplete without recognizing the cooperation among Lutheran churches as being first and foremost an attempt" to be better instruments through which God can fulfill his redemptive plan" (ibid., pp. 363ff.).

## Evaluation

The LWF experienced its most thorough revision to that time during Appel's term in office, and his activities and vision can only be assessed in the light of this transition (see chapter 2, above). It must be mentioned here that Appel was faced with a nearly impossible task. Could anyone maneuver a ship loaded with so many items, each one of them demanding specific attention and care? Could a complex vessel such as the LWF be navigated safely between Scylla and Charybdis without running aground, let alone risking a battle at sea? In 1974, when Carl Mau, who had served as Appel's associate general secretary, succeeded Appel, certain controversial issues had not been settled, which should in no way diminish Appel's accomplishments during a period of turmoil and transition.

**Bibliographical Notes** _____

Written and oral information from Michel Hoeffel (Strasbourg) to the author.
*Lutheran World.*
*LWF Reports.*
*Proceedings*, Evian.

# Carl Henning Mau, Jr.

CARL HENNING MAU, JR., was born on June 22, 1922, in Seattle, Washington, U.S.A. He was in the sixth generation of Lutheran pastors in his family, dating back to 1762 in Germany. This tradition continues with Mau's brother and daughter, both pastors in the Evangelical Lutheran Church in America (ELCA). Carl Mau received the Bachelor of Arts degree in 1944 from Washington State University in Pullman, Washington. This was followed by studies in German, with minors in mathematics and history, at Willamette University in Oregon and the University of Pennsylvania. In 1946 he completed theological studies at the Lutheran Theological Seminary in Philadelphia and was ordained into the ministerium of the then American Lutheran Church. From 1946 to 1950 he was pastor of Luther Memorial Church in Portland, Oregon, and in 1950 began his international career when he was appointed director of the LWF office in Hanover, Germany, where he specialized in aiding German Lutherans in respect to evangelism, stewardship, and relief. For this work he received, in 1957, the Wichern Medal of the German Evangelical Inner Mission and the Cross of the Order of Merit of the Federal Republic of Germany. In 1957 he returned to the United States, becoming pastor of Luther Memorial Church, Tacoma, Washington, and from 1960 to 1964 Lutheran campus pastor at the University of Wisconsin, Madison, Wisconsin. In 1963 he was elected to the post of LWF assistant general secretary, the title of which post was changed in 1965 to associate general secretary, and in the following year he assumed that post within the Geneva secretariat of the LWF. In 1972 he returned to New York City as general secretary of the U.S. National Committee of the LWF. In 1974 the LWF Executive Committee, meeting in Northfield, Minnesota, elected Mau LWF General Secretary, succeeding André Appel. He was reelected to this post in 1977 at the Sixth Assembly of the LWF in Dar es Salaam and served until 1985, when he was succeeded by Gunnar Staalsett. He returned to the United States as Associate Pastor of the Reformation Lutheran Church in Washington, D.C., where he served until his retirement in 1989. In his retirement Carl Mau served as co-chair of the ELCA Task Force on Peace, as a member of the Eminent Church Persons Groups of the World Council of Churches reviewing the apartheid situation in southern Africa, and he also spent several months working with the Lutheran churches in Namibia. He received numerous prizes from church and governmental agencies and four honorary doctorates from colleges and universities in the United States. Carl Mau died at the age of 72 on March 31, 1995, in Des Moines, Washington. He is survived by his wife, Thilda, a daughter, the Rev. Joan A. Mau, and sons, Eric and Christian; he was preceded in death by his son, Mark, who died in an automobile accident in 1973.

Author: *Norman A. Hjelm, Wynnewood, Pennsylvania*

LWF Photo

63. Carl Henning Mau, Jr., of the American Lutheran
    Church, General Secretary of the Lutheran World
    Federation, 1974–1985

## International Beginnings

Carl Mau was one of a number of younger American Lutheran pastors and students who, after World War II, volunteered their services to assist in the rehabilitation of the Lutheran churches in war-torn Europe. In 1950 Mau went to Hanover, Germany, as head of the LWF's office there, serving in fact as a pastor in the Landeskirche of Hanover. He brought to the German church uniquely American expertise in the areas of parish life, stewardship, and evangelism; this work was enhanced by his remarkable fluency in the use of the German language. It was, moreover, in Hanover that Mau first became associated with Hanns Lilje, bishop of the Hanover church and President of the Federation from the time of the Second Assembly of the LWF, held in Hanover in 1952. Lilje's influence on Mau—as mentor, colleague, pastor, and friend—was considerable. The young Mau was first exposed to the world Lutheran communion by his work at the Second Assembly.

Mau's subsequent ministry in the United States, as parish pastor in the state of Washington and as campus pastor at the University of Wisconsin was clearly marked by his initial international experience with the LWF in Germany. As early as the mid-1950s he was identified as a spokesperson in the United States for the Federation. In 1962 Mau gave part-time service to the LWF by accepting responsibility for the recruitment and testing of translators and interpreters for the Helsinki Assembly from America, Germany, England, and the Nordic countries, building up a team of forty-one volunteers. He served also as general coordinator for the Fourth Assembly in 1963.

In 1964 Mau accepted the position of assistant general secretary of the LWF (in 1965 the post was retitled associate general secretary), serving with two general secretaries, Kurt Schmidt-Clausen and André Appel. When he returned to the United States in 1972 it was to further the work of global Lutheranism as general secretary of the United States LWF National Committee, which was later known as Lutheran World Ministries. In this position Mau continued his passion for deepening the worldwide involvement of Lutherans through the extension of broad American commitment to and support of LWF projects and activities. His already keen sense of Lutheran responsibility for political and social matters was considerably sharpened during this period of service.

### LWF General Secretary

When the LWF Executive Committee met in Northfield, Minnesota, in 1974 one of its key agenda items was the election of a new general secretary for the Federation, to succeed André Appel, who had been elected president of his home church, the Church of the Augsburg Confession of Alsace and Lorraine. Mau was elected to the post, receiving one more vote than the Norwegian churchman Gunnar Staalsett, who was himself to follow Mau as general secretary in 1985.

Carl Mau's tenure as LWF General Secretary was filled with defining moments for the Federation. In addition to steering the Geneva secretariat through a time when the decisions concerning LWF structure made at Evian and before were tested, modified, and solidified, he brought the LWF to a new consciousness of its global opportunities—particularly in respect to issues within the life of African churches caused by the horrors of apartheid, and also the many tensions between East and West as they were played out in Europe. Further, his support of increased participation and responsibility for women and youth in the life of the Federation contributed greatly to the LWF's dawning self-awareness as *communio*. During his time of service the Sixth and Seventh LWF Assemblies were held in Dar es Salaam in 1957 and Budapest in 1984, the former being the first such gathering in a Third World country and the latter being the first such Christian assemblage in socialist East Europe.

At Dar es Salaam Mau played a key role in the assembly's statement on southern Africa, which he described as "the bold declaration that opposition to the system of apartheid was not for Christians primarily a political decision, but a matter of the integrity of the Christian faith (*status confessionis*)" (*Proceedings*, Dar es Salaam, p. 8). When at the next assembly in Budapest the white churches of the Republic of South Africa and Namibia had not dissociated themselves from national policies of apartheid and had not moved toward communion with their black Lutheran brothers and sisters, Mau was strongly in favor of the action to suspend those churches from LWF membership (see, e.g., pp. 408–9 above).

Similarly, in respect to East–West tensions, particularly as they impinged on the life and role of the churches in socialist societies, Mau played a key role. When it had been learned, for example, in the 1960s that thousands of ethnic Germans living in the Soviet Union had kept their Lutheranism alive even after being sent by Stalin to Siberia and the Central Asian Republics from their longtime homes in the Volga Valley, the Federation played a key role in demonstrating support and solidarity with these people. During his time as general secretary, Mau fostered contacts with these dispersed Lutheran groups by Federation gifts of Bibles and hymnals, also aiding in the supplying of pastoral services by ordained Lutheran ministers.

But the political tensions surrounding the churches in communist and socialist East Europe were far more delicate, and Mau led the Federation in playing crucial and at times controversial roles of reconciliation. The very decision to hold the Eighth Assembly in Budapest was roundly criticized, but has subsequently been acknowledged as a milestone in late-twentieth-century church history. The words of the assembly's message were by implication directly consistent with the leadership of the LWF General Secretary, Carl Mau:

> We saw a sign of that hope ["In Christ—Hope for the World"] in our coming together from all parts of the world as Lutherans who share in a common confession of faith in Christ. Meeting in Budapest, Hungary, the Federation was assembling for the first time in a socialist country in Eastern Europe. Our gathering here and the hospitality we received here showed us that in the church of Christ we can have confidence in each other and can build bridges across political and ideological boundaries. (*Proceedings*, Budapest, p. 11; see pp. 403ff. above)

The highly controversial election of Bishop Zoltán Káldy of the Lutheran Church in Hungary as president of the LWF required, at Budapest and beyond, patient and diplomatic interpretation and understanding on the part of the LWF General Secretary. This election was a further sign of reconciliation between East and West even within the Lutheran World Federation.

### Toward Communion

At the Budapest Assembly, finally, the LWF—in examining the character of its own life—adopted a milestone "Statement on the Self-Understanding and Task of the Lutheran World Federation." This statement, now recognized as a key stage on the way "from Federation to Communion," authenticated the understanding to which Carl Mau had come in his nearly thirty-five years of association with the LWF. In his valedictory report as LWF General Secretary to the Federation's Executive Committee, given in Geneva in August of 1985, Mau expressed his judgment that the "free association" language to be found in what was then the LWF Constitution urgently needed reconsideration. To say "the LWF shall be a free association of Lutheran churches" is "ecclesiologically as weak as you can say it." He proposed "fellowship" or "communion" instead (see Brand, *Toward a Lutheran Communion*, pp. 68–69). Carl Mau, who made his mark within Lutheranism not as an academic theologian but as a dedicated and at times prophetic leader, thus spanned in his career with the Federation a growing understanding of the Lutheran reality of communion which, in point of fact, he himself embodied in a perhaps unique way.

## Bibliographical Notes

LWF Archives, *passim.*

Brand, Eugene L. *Toward a Lutheran Communion: Pulpit and Altar Fellowship.* LWF Report 26, June 1988. Geneva: Lutheran World Federation, 1988.

Gilbert, W. Kent. *Commitment to Unity: A History of the Lutheran Church in America.* Philadelphia: Fortress Press, 1988.

*Proceedings,* Budapest.

*Proceedings,* Dar es Salaam.

# Gunnar Johan Staalsett

GUNNAR JOHAN STAALSETT was born on February 10, 1935, in Nordkapp, Norway. He studied theology at the University of Oslo (1954–1957) at Bethany Lutheran Seminary, Mankato, Minnesota (1957–1959), at the Free Theological Faculty, Oslo (1959–1962) and in Heidelberg, Germany, during the spring of 1964. He received his theological degree in 1961 in Oslo and was ordained in 1962 as a pastor in the Church of Norway. From 1962 to 1964 he served as youth pastor in the Diocese of Hamar, employed by the Norwegian Federation of Evangelical Students and from 1964 to 1970 he was lecturer in systematic theology at the School of Mission and Theology of the Norwegian Missionary Society, Stavanger. From 1970 to 1979 he was general secretary of the Church of Norway Council on Foreign Relations which also is the National Committee of the LWF. For two periods he served in Norwegian governmental and political posts: from 1972 to 1973 as state secretary in the Ministry of Church, Education, and Culture and from 1977 to 1979 as chairman of the Norwegian Center Party. He returned to active church service and from 1979 to 1982 was Dean of Sør Østerdal and Vicar of Elverum in the Diocese of Hamar. From 1982 to 1985 Staalsett was general secretary of the Norwegian Bible Society and the Verbum Publishing House in Oslo. During the sixties and seventies, he served on several committees and boards on the national church level, that is, as chairman of the Board on Education of the Church of Norway and as member of the Board of the Nordic Ecumenical Institute. In January 1985 he was elected general secretary of the Lutheran World Federation, assuming his duties in that position in August of that year. He resigned from the LWF in 1994 and in November of that year became rector of the Practical Theological Seminary at the University of Oslo. In the LWF, Staalsett served from 1970 to 1977 as vice-chairperson of the Commission on Church Cooperation; from 1970 to 1974 on the board of Radio Voice of the Gospel; and from 1975 to 1977 on the Commission on Communication. He was on the central and executive committees of the World Council of Churches from 1983 to 1985 and on the general committee of the United Bible Societies from 1984 to 1985. He has received doctorates in divinity and law *honoris causa* in the United States, Hungary, and Czechoslovakia. He is a recipient of several awards recognizing his international work, such as the Albert Schweitzer Humanitarian Award and the Wittenberg Award. He has also served on the Norwegian Nobel Peace Prize Committee, the Board of the Norwegian National Commission for UNESCO, as a deputy member of the Norwegian Parliament, and as a member of the Oslo City Council. In 1959 he was married to Unn Eriksen, a professor of education; they have two children.

Authors: *Per Voksø, Oslo, Norway, and Norman A. Hjelm, Wynnewood, Pennsylvania*

64. Gunnar Johan Staalsett of the Church of Norway,
    General Secretary of the Lutheran World Federation,
    1985–1994

*Education and Early Career: Church and Politics*

Gunnar Staalsett was born at Nordkapp (North Cape), Norway, the northern-
most community on the European continent in 1935. His family were Finnish
immigrants who came to Norway around the middle of the nineteenth century, a minority marked spiritually by the piety of the Swedish revivalist Lars
Levi Læstadius (1800–1861). Staalsett's father was a teacher, and Gunnar was
third in a row of seven brothers and one sister. Thus, it was necessary for him
to finance his own education as a teacher, seaman, and hotel worker.

In his theological studies, Gunnar Staalsett was especially influenced by
two of his teachers; from the years at the University of Oslo, the distinguished
church historian and patristic scholar professor Einar Molland, who was one of
the leading ecumenists of the Church of Norway; and from his years at the

Free Theological Faculty, his teacher of systematic theology, Leiv Aalen, whose strong emphasis on Lutheran confessions was combined with an ecumenical spirituality.

After his three years at the University of Oslo, in 1957 he received an invitation to study at Bethany Seminary in Minnesota, an institution of a small, conservative church body of Norwegian background, where he received his Bachelor of Divinity degree two years later. Upon his return to Norway, he entered the Free Theological Faculty, from which he graduated in 1961. He completed one year of practical theological training before ordination in 1962.

At the beginning of his ministry, he advocated a conservative Lutheranism which was critical of the ecumenism of the World Council of Churches, and together with Swedish and Danish ecumenical scholars he was instrumental in drafting an alternative mission statement to the WCC Assembly in Uppsala in 1968. At some points he also distanced himself from the form of global Lutheranism as it was then represented by the LWF. During a tenure as lecturer at the School of Mission and Theology of the Norwegian Mission Society, however, Staalsett developed his own theological position, demonstrating a strong commitment to the mission of the church in its global and ecumenical forms.

During his tenure as general secretary of the Church of Norway Council on Foreign Relations (until 1977), Staalsett brought global and ecumenical church life closer to local parish activities by a special emphasis on such human rights concerns as the struggle over apartheid in South Africa.

The global and socioethical dimensions of church life led Staalsett twice to leave his church positions to take up responsibilities in governmental and political life. In 1972 he joined the national government for one year as state secretary in the Ministry of Church, Education, and Culture, and from 1977 to 1979 he served full-time as chairperson of the Norwegian Center Party, formerly known as the Agrarian Party. He declined to stand for a second term, due to continued internal strife in the party over whether to choose coalition partners to the right or to the left, a political struggle that weakened the party in two consecutive general elections, a trend which Staalsett did not manage to turn around at the parliamentary election in 1977. Nevertheless, throughout his subsequent career Staalsett has accepted a number of public positions in the service of successive Norwegian governments, such as the Governments Council on Disarmament and Arms Control and Norway's delegation to assemblies of the United Nations. Most notable, perhaps, has been his service as a member of the prestigious Norwegian Nobel Peace Prize Committee, a five-person committee appointed by the Norwegian Parliament but otherwise totally independent.

## In the Lutheran Communion

Gunnar Staalsett's active participation in the Lutheran World Federation began most notably at the Evian Assembly, 1970. He participated vigorously in the far-reaching discussions of that assembly concerning the decision to change the name of the Commission on World Mission to the Commission on Church Cooperation and on the position of the LWF on human rights. In point of fact, he drafted a resolution by which at the end of a controversial debate, the assembly unanimously expressed the Federation's enduring commitment to mission and evangelism. Together with the Swedish professor Gustav Wingren, he was responsible for the final drafting of the assembly's foundational and far-reaching Resolution on Human Rights. Staalsett's name was nominated from the floor as an alternative to the then bishop of Oslo, as President of the Federation, but he withdrew his candidacy. He was, however, elected to the new LWF Commission on Church Cooperation.

In 1974 the name of Gunnar Staalsett again appeared for consideration by the LWF Executive Committee; this time as a candidate to succeed André Appel as general secretary. His candidacy did not, however, prevail, as he lost by one vote to Carl Mau, who thus succeeded Appel.

In 1985 Staalsett's name was again proposed, this time as successor to Mau. He was, however, not willing to comply with the procedure established for interviewing prospective candidates, and therefore did not initially wish to have his name placed in nomination. Ultimately, however, he was unanimously elected to the post and assumed his Geneva responsibilities in August 1985.

In his opening greeting to the executive committee—he declined a formal "installation" as general secretary—Staalsett indicated that during his term the "two faces" of the LWF would be in the areas of ecumenical action and human rights. He requested the executive committee to authorize the appointment of two assistant LWF General Secretaries for Ecumenical Affairs and for International Affairs and Human Rights.

Faced with the LWF's growing financial difficulties and long-felt organizational problems, the new general secretary formulated his goal as bringing about "unity of purpose, cooperation and coordination" and reducing the Geneva staff and costs by 25 percent while maintaining global services and programs. As to the unity of purpose within the LWF, it was from the outset clear that Staalsett would move aggressively to realize a vision of the LWF as a communion of churches rather than a federation or association of autonomous church bodies. In this he felt he was following the clear declaration of the Budapest Assembly, where the Federation expressed its self-understanding in terms of *communio*. In all of his reports and public statements, Gunnar Staalsett did not miss an opportunity to focus on this goal, attempting to make concrete what *communio* might mean in terms of structure and program priorities.

This focus was most clearly—and controversially—expressed in Staalsett's move toward a new structure for the Federation. In April of 1987 at a joint meeting in Geneva of all LWF commissions he declared that Federation work had often been carried on "without a clear vision and without sufficiently integrated strategy and action." Subsequently he asked the officers of the LWF to authorize the formation of a Committee on Structure, which would make concrete proposals by the time of the Eighth LWF Assembly. This committee was formed by the executive committee at its 1987 meeting in Viborg, Denmark. Bishop James Crumley of the then Lutheran Church in America was named chairperson of the committee and major staff responsibilities for the work of the committee were given to the Rev. Norman Hjelm, LWF director of communication. Through the entire process of restructuring—proposals and vigorous and sometimes bitter debate—it was doubtlessly the vision of the general secretary that guided developments. The process culminated at the Curitiba Assembly (see pp. 416ff. above).

Staalsett saw restructuring not only as a vehicle for closer coordination but as a move that caused power to shift—from the Northern churches to those of the Two-Thirds World, from the wealthy to those who were deprived. By emphasizing communion, he moved the Federation from a male and clergy dominated leadership to one in which lay people and women had a greater say. Before the Curitiba Assembly he warned against

> excelling in communion language if we are not willing to translate into structure programs and institutions which reflect a readiness to regard all member churches of the Federation as equal. Communion must be seen in relationship to established realities of dependence and domination by churches of history, wealth, size, theology, culture, and power.

Staalsett strove also to place his heavy commitment to matters of peace and human rights under the *communio* rubric. He actively supported the struggle of SWAPO, the Namibian liberation movement, and human rights efforts in Ethiopia and Eritrea; and he used the "good offices" of the Federation and of his own person to promote peace initiatives in El Salvador and Guatamala. The Southern Africa engagement, and in particular the involvement with SWAPO, drew heavy criticism from among the LWF's German constituency. During his time in office much energy was also devoted to human rights efforts in the Soviet Union and Eastern Europe, which did not soften the accusations from "mission behind the iron curtain" groups, not least in Norway as well as from other right-wing groups in the United States, that the LWF was "soft on communism."

Finally, it must be pointed out that Gunnar Staalsett saw communion also as confessional. Ecumenism for him was not incompatible with an appreciation of Lutheran identity. He developed strong links with other Christian World Communions, and initiated regular meetings between the LWF secretariat and the Vatican Secretariat for Promoting Christian Unity. Developments within the World Council of Churches received his criticism; he warned that the ecumenical movement cannot take a shortcut to "visible unity" by ignoring the significance of confessional heritage and identity. The ecumenical movement must be a *movement of churches* and is not to be turned over to "para-ecclesial movements," a development that Staalsett saw as "fraught with disaster."

The tenure of Gunnar Staalsett as general secretary of the Lutheran World Federation, nine years in length, is clearly too recent to be fairly evaluated. His initiatives and commitments were many: the ecclesiology of *communio*, human rights and peace making, the cause of women's advancement in the church, bridges to Eastern Europe, the restructuring of the Federation. Perhaps no general secretary in the five decades of LWF history has both elicited such support and given rise to such opposition. Under all circumstances, however, the judgment must be made that considerable ground on the journey "from Federation to Communion" was covered during Staalsett's tenure.

**Bibliographical Notes** _____

*Writings of Gunnar Staalsett*

1969    *Church Manual.* Stavangar: Nomi Forlag.
1969    *Mission Today and Tomorrow.* Stavangar: Nomi Forlaġ.
1970    *The Church Under Way.* Stavangar: Nomi Forlag.
1974    *God Wants Justice: Homage to Don Helder Camara.* Oslo: Det Norske Samlaget.
1993    *One Church Made New: Reports and Speeches.* Geneva: Lutheran World Federation.
1994    *Following Christ Together.* Geneva: World Council of Churches.

# Ishmael Noko

ISHMAEL NOKO was born on October 29, 1943, in Mnyabezi, Rhodesia, now Zimbabwe, to Andries and Abigail Noko. His father is a pastor, now retired, in the Evangelical Lutheran Church in Zimbabwe. Noko is the second oldest of five sons and one daughter. Noko's early education (1952–1961) was in the Mnyabezi Primary and Manama Central Schools; from 1962 to 1965 he studied at Bernard Mizeki College. He obtained a diploma in theology from the Lutheran Theological College Umpumulo in Mapumulo, Natal, South Africa. He also studied at the University of South Africa in Pretoria and received the A.B. degree in 1971 in theology from the University of Zululand. Noko was ordained a pastor in the Evangelical Lutheran Church in Zimbabwe in 1972, and in that year he taught at the Manama Secondary School, serving also as school chaplain. In November of 1972 he left Zimbabwe for Canada, in 1974 receiving a Master of Theology degree from the Lutheran Theological Seminary in Saskatoon with a thesis entitled "The Communion of Saints from the African Perspective." During his time in Saskatoon he also served as associate pastor of Redeemer Lutheran Church in that city. In September 1974 Noko became a candidate for the Ph.D. in the Faculty of Religious Studies at McGill University in Montreal, Quebec. That degree was awarded Noko in 1977; his dissertation was "The Concept of God in Black Theology: An Appreciation of God as Liberator and Reconciler." In October 1977 he returned to Africa as lecturer at the University of Botswana, serving as head of the Department of Theology and Religious Studies from 1978 to 1982; he was also dean of the Faculty of Humanities at that university from 1980 to 1982. From 1978 to 1982 Noko also held the position of secretary-treasurer of the Botswana Lutheran Liaison Committee for Refugee Aid and during that period was responsible for the scholarship program for refugees at the University College of Botswana, the Cathedral Commercial School, and the Botswana College of Administration. In May 1982 he was engaged by the Department of World Service of the Lutheran World Federation as secretary for liaison and interpretation and moved to Geneva. In October 1987 Noko became Director of the LWF Department of Church Cooperation and in 1990 he was appointed the first director of the Department for Mission and Development in the restructured Federation. The council of the LWF elected Noko general secretary of the LWF and on November 1, 1994, he took up his responsibilities as the successor to Gunnar Staalsett, the first non-American or European to hold the post. Ishmael Noko and his wife, Gladys, a registered nurse from the Republic of South Africa, have three children.

Author: *Norman A. Hjelm, Wynnewood, Pennsylvania*

65. Ishmael Noko of the Evangelical Lutheran Church in
Zimbabwe, General Secretary of the Lutheran World
Federation, elected 1994

## A Son of Africa

Ishmael Noko was born into a milieu largely shaped by the missionary efforts
of the Church of Sweden in southeastern and southwestern Zimbabwe, a
country—formerly known as Rhodesia—that did not receive its independence
from the United Kingdom until 1980. The Lutheran Church in Zimbabwe
became autonomous in 1962, but as early as 1941 had fully shared responsibility for its own life with the Swedish missionaries. It was a Swedish missionary, Miss Elsa Kälström of Skara—his "Swedish parent"—who shared with
Noko's biological parents in the responsibility of his upbringing, and the ecclesiological and liturgical character of the Swedish church marked his church
life from the beginning.

But the milieu into which Noko was born was also shaped by the independence struggles of his country from British rule. The civil war that marked the

transformation of Rhodesia into Zimbabwe pervaded the consciousness of the people with whom he lived from his earliest years. As a student in Rhodesia and in apartheid South Africa, he was nurtured like most other younger students of that time in the spirit of African nationalism. He read theology at the Lutheran Theological College at Umpumulo and at the University of Zululand. Upon returning to his native country, Rhodesia, he was ordained on February 6, 1972. He served as a pastor and a high school teacher at Manama Lutheran Mission. He was forced, together with his wife and one-year-old son, Israel, to leave his native land as an exile from the independence struggle in November of 1972. In this move he had the assistance of the then Evangelical Lutheran Church of Canada, particularly professors Martin Liesberg and William Hordern of the Lutheran Theological Seminary at Saskatoon.

Noko's academic work in Canada—first at the Lutheran Theological Seminary, now affiliated with the University of Saskatchewan, in Saskatoon and subsequently at McGill University in Montreal—bore the marks of both the ecclesial and political milieus into which he was born. His first thesis, at Saskatoon, dealt with *communio sanctorum* "from an African perspective," a topic that bore the marks of his churchly origins as shaped by the Church of Sweden's work in Africa. His doctoral dissertation at McGill was on questions raised by "black theology," which he approached from the perspectives of liberation and reconciliation, perspectives to be found at the heart of the many independence struggles that have taken place on the African continent during the second half of the twentieth century and which Noko knew at firsthand.

In Canada, moreover, Noko and his family were exiles from Rhodesia/Zimbabwe. This experience was formative of the commitment to refugee and relief work which has exercised Noko so greatly, first in Botswana, to which he returned in 1977 and where he became active in the Botswana Lutheran Liaison Committee for Refugee Aid, and subsequently in the Lutheran World Federation, to which in 1982 he was called for service as secretary for liaison and interpretation in the Department of World Service in Geneva.

## Early Work in the LWF

In three key LWF positions—in the Department of World Service and subsequently as Director of the Department of Church Cooperation and of the Department for Mission and Development—Ishmael Noko brought the perspectives born in his earliest ecclesial and political experience.

In his World Service post, Noko was responsible for establishing and maintaining liaison with LWF member churches, National Christian Councils, and other ecumenical agencies in areas where aid was being provided by the Federation. He also represented World Service to regional organizations such as the All Africa Conference of Churches, the Organization of African Unity (O.A.U.), and the Economic Commission for Africa. From 1984 to 1988 he served as chairperson for the O.A.U. Coordinating Committee on Assistance to Refugees.

As director of the Department of Church Cooperation, a post he assumed in 1987, succeeding the Finnish churchman, Risto Lehtonen, Noko was responsible for giving overall direction to global LWF work in such areas as mission and related issues, theological education, youth, and the work of regional desks for Asia, Africa, Latin America and the Caribbean, Europe, and North America. During Noko's tenure he was charged with the responsibility of working pastorally with those white churches in southern Africa which had been suspended from membership in the LWF in light of their denial of "confessional integrity" in respect to apartheid. He was able ultimately to recommend the restoration of full membership to those churches as a consequence of their commitment to full communion with their black Lutheran sisters and brothers.

When, in 1990, he assumed the directorship of the newly created Department for Mission and Development, the largest LWF department in the new structure authorized by the Curitiba Assembly, Noko faced the delicate task of bringing the Federation's Community Development Service out of World Service and into what had previously been Church Cooperation. Under his direction, Mission and Development administered approximately five hundred projects and twenty-five global programs, representing expenditures of between fifty-five and sixty million U.S. dollars.

## General Secretary

Ishmael Noko was installed as general secretary of the Lutheran World Federation on February 3, 1995, although he had assumed his responsibilities the previous November. His Service of Installation was marked by the sound of drums and hymns from southern Africa as staff, church officials, and diplomats who packed the chapel of the Geneva Ecumenical Center welcomed Noko with the Zimbabwean acclamation, "Rakanaka vangeri" ("The Gospel is good") and the South African hymn, "Thuma mina" ("Send Me, Lord").

The challenges being faced by the first LWF General Secretary from the southern hemisphere are many. Arrangements for the Ninth Assembly, scheduled for Hong Kong in July of 1997, the year of the Federation's fiftieth anniversary, are now his responsibility, and they are fraught with political, diplomatic, and logistic problems, since that assembly will be the first international gathering in Hong Kong after its unification with the People's Republic of China. It is an event of global importance, both ecclesially and politically, and requires much of the Federation and its leadership. Discussion of the proposal, a "Joint Declaration on the Doctrine of Justification" between the global communion of Lutheran churches and the Roman Catholic Church, could well lead to an act of momentous historical and ecumenical importance during his ministry.

The assembly—under the executive leadership of Ishmael Noko of Zimbabwe—brings together the LWF family as a self-understood communion. Noko has himself said that *communio* is "my own entry point" to the Federation, and he sees his responsibility as carrying through the "consequences of communion." In an interview given by Noko in June of 1996 he responded in the following way to the question, "Can you mention some important goals which have not been reached?"

The Lutheran World Federation as an expression of the global Lutheran Communion does not at this point in time represent all Lutherans in the whole world. There are three million Lutherans "not yet" in this fellowship. This means that while the LWF speaks on behalf of the majority of Lutherans worldwide, it cannot claim at all times to speak on behalf of those who do not yet find it possible to be in this global fellowship. It is nonetheless my prayerful hope for the sake of the integrity of our witness and for the one ecumenical movement that we shall achieve the goal of inter-Lutheran unity.

For many years the Lutheran World Federation has been engaged and has concluded several dialogues with other Christian World Communions on specific doctrinal and theological issues. These have been commended to both the Lutheran and partner churches for discussion and "living out." The reception process has been extremely weak on all sides. I believe the next decade will be marked by initiatives intended to harvest and expedite "reception."

In the 1960s and 1970s, the LWF work and that of other international organizations in the area of refugee work was marked by a sense of optimism. Everybody thought durable solutions were at the steps of the next decade. But we have seen the population of refugees and displaced persons increase from 4 million in the 1970s to 125 million in 1996. The disrespect for human dignity has increased in many countries and nations. (*LWF Today* [June 1996]: 6)

This answer eloquently summarizes the challenges faced by Ishmael Noko as general secretary of the Lutheran World Federation and the milieu—ecclesial and political—from which he approaches them.

# Afterword

LOOKING BACK ON HISTORY, provided such a retrospective is not limited simply to listing statistics, is a complex enterprise. It combines information on the past and self-reflection; it gives account and aims at a critical assessment of today's position. Things are not so different when reviewing the fifty-year history of the Lutheran World Federation. This volume is evidence of that.

Yet this retrospective would not be complete without acknowledgment of thanks due and thanks given. The churches that founded the Lutheran World Federation or joined it in the course of the years have without exception been enriched by their union. Much mutual aid, common witness, prophetic and charitable services, as well as many learning processes, would not have happened had the Lutheran World Federation not been in existence. Therefore thanks are due to all those who have sustained it, struggled to achieve its goals, and made its work possible. Above all, thanks are due to God—the beginning, the middle, and the end of all our doing—and who, through his Word, has provided the Lutheran World Federation with encouragement, perseverance, and direction. Without the Lord's grace our actions and exertion would be for nothing, a truth we must not lose sight of, also in this context.

The same is true in the face of historical guilt. An honest encounter with one's own history requires courage. It uncovers failures and omissions, entanglements in private and societal interests. Hence, facing up to history is often evasive or one-sided, leads to the suppression or distortion of facts, or else serves as a triumphalist self-justification. The contributions in this volume have avoided this danger. The Lutheran World Federation is free self-critically to deal with its past and guilt must not be concealed; gratitude for the good work, for exemplary solidarity, for God's miracles must not be hidden either. Together humility and gratitude guarantee that the path behind us is described as realistically as possible. The extent to which the aim of "objective" historiography has been reached is left to the readers' judgment.

In the course of years, the Lutheran World Federation has changed. It is no longer what it was fifty years ago. Maybe the difference in self-understanding, structure, and the nature of its tasks is more evident than the continuity that links it to its origins. Yet such continuity exists. Were it not so, the Lutheran World Federation would have given itself up. The four pillars—*rescue for the needy, common initiatives in mission, joint efforts in theology, and a common response to the ecumenical challenge*—still determine its work. Today, these tasks are set in another framework and have taken on new dimensions, but they have essentially remained the same. At the beginning of the Lutheran World Federation there was the churches' wish to achieve closer community even though ideas concerning the expression such community was to take diverged widely. The existential question the Lutheran World Federation faces is how in different situations it can reach a common language and common action on the basis of the common confession. This is the red thread that runs through its history. Incontestably, more communion is necessary between Lutheran churches, and the only question that remains to be discussed is how.

It is part of history's particularity that continuity is possible only through change, adaptation, and transformation. A certain limited discontinuity is the very prerequisite for continuity. The much-discussed development of the Lutheran World Federation from a free association to a communion of churches sheds light on this. To be sure, this development is rooted in a common doctrinal basis, for the church is wherever there is agreement on the understanding of the gospel and the administration of the sacraments. Thus, the development of the Lutheran World Federation into a communion with increasing "ecclesial density" was a necessary consequence of its own theological premises.

Yet there is another point of view to be considered. Would the Lutheran World Federation have been true to its original goals if, even at a time of comprehensive globalization of all areas of life, it continued to understand itself as a loose association of churches? It would have got stuck in time without facing up to the present-day challenges. These challenges require global thinking, but at the same time regional contexts must not be overlooked. The fact that many theological and structural questions concerning the Lutheran World Federation continue to be open should not worry us, since this development has been recognized to be vital in order to preserve the very identity of the Lutheran World Federation.

These problems are not specifically Lutheran. The churches and the ecumenical movement at large are facing the question regarding the meaning and shape of worldwide communion today. In this respect, the discussion about the Lutheran World Federation's nature is representative of the whole ecumenical situation and part of the larger question concerning the nature of the *communio sanctorum* as such. How to live and realize the community of faith has always been one of the major challenges for the church of Jesus Christ on earth. Yet in today's world, which has grown so much smaller, it has become incomparably more urgent. Thanks to its self-definition as a communion of churches and the intensive theological debate preceding and accompanying it, the Lutheran World Federation has to a certain extent acted as an ecumenical pioneer, although admittedly the existence of its *magnus consensus* has greatly helped it along. To implement the communion concept in the whole ecumenical movement still requires a lot of hard work.

Nevertheless, the Lutheran World Federation itself, too, will have to clarify a large number of questions, especially with regard to the structures that correspond to its claim to be a communion of churches. The relationship between the "autonomy" of the member churches and worldwide joint responsibility must be right—an old and yet a new question. Where and how does consensus come about in the Lutheran world family? Where should the "teaching authority" be located? How comprehensively does one understand communion? It has been widely accepted by now that it cannot be limited to altar and pulpit fellowship but must extend to other expressions of the congregation of Jesus Christ. Yet concrete models and notions for such a concept are lacking.

The Lutheran World Federation is not alone with these questions. Whether in church or society, "communion" has become an almost soteriological concept. Whether it will be possible to lift communion from the local, national, and regional levels to the global level and to provide it with the necessary international structures has become a question of human survival. The same is true for the church of Jesus Christ. Isolation and particularism jeopardize its credibility and thus its existence. The church needs ways to speak with one voice in today's world. The Lutheran World Federation should not be afraid of continuing to set an example.

No doubt this will be difficult. The task will have to be done with dwindling resources, which clearly sets limits to what the Lutheran World Federation can do. Nevertheless this should not be a cause for resignation. It is important to set signs no matter how small. It gives us reason to rejoice that the fifty-year history of the Federation has been so rich in such signs. There is not merely World Service's impressive work but also the remarkable integration of the churches from North and South, from East and West, the ecumenical initiatives and the fruits of theological work, not forgetting the common learning that was the result of sometimes bitter experiences. That confessional integrity also includes responsibility for society, that practice can lead to a *status confessionis*, that loyalty to the confession must not be confused with confessionalistic narrowness—all these are insights that mark the path of the Lutheran World Federation. Thus we hope that this path will continue to be marked by growing insight and that communion can be expressed also with modest means.

It would be wrong to interpret this wish in terms of a special confessional program. Ecumenism without a confessional basis is not imaginable. Loyalty to the confession and ecumenical openness are not contradictory in terms. The Lutheran World Federation has always been committed to the ecumenical movement, and it may have to pursue this commitment more energetically, including the drawing of structural consequences. A duplication of initiatives must be avoided and costs have to be saved. Nevertheless, the striving for a specifically Lutheran unity is not illegitimate. On the contrary, it is an ecumenical necessity that keeps arising when the question is asked who authentically represents the Lutheran confession and what it can contribute to ecumenical discussions. Obviously we do not advocate a confessionalistic fundamentalism. But is it really wrong when the Lutheran churches understand their Reformation heritage as a talent entrusted to them with which they are to serve the ecumenical movement? This talent has to do with theology, mission, witness—in other words, Lutheran identity. Just as confessional particularism is opposed to the Lutheran confession, so is confessional relativism. An ecumenism of "empty hands," of unclear positions, has no future. Resisting such relativism will be the task of the Lutheran World Federation also in the future.

This perspective presupposes a certain understanding of ecumenical communion. It will not eliminate diversity but reconcile it. Peace is the aim of ecumenism but peace is not possible without recognizing diversity. Diversity as such is not a problem, but the destructive elements it contains or releases. Once we have learned how diversity can be of service, communion comes about. This aim will have to remain on the Lutheran churches' agenda. The communion of churches the Lutheran World Federation has agreed to and wants to be must continue to be implemented in practice and take shape in the way people relate to one another.

The third millennium challenges us in a special way. New and dangerous conflicts need to be overcome, especially the social conflict between rich and poor, employed and unemployed, overemployed and superfluous. Increasingly, the border between First and Third Worlds will be drawn across countries. Moreover, there are cultural and religious conflicts, including atheist secularism. New religious wars threaten to break out unless the existing dynamite is defused in time. Communion will have to be lived in an increasingly polarized world.

The ecumenical commitment to more unity is in every respect of great urgency for the Lutheran World Federation—toward the "outside" and the "inside." This retrospective on the past fifty years is instructive for both and, with God's help, should provide motivation for continuing along this path also under changed circumstances

Faculdade de Teología                          *Gottfried Brakemeier*
São Leopoldo, Brazil                                     President
Reformation Day, 1996                    The Lutheran World Federation

# Appendices

1. CONSTITUTIONS OF THE LWF

2. MEMBER CHURCHES OF THE LWF

3. FINANCES OF THE LWF

# 1

# CONSTITUTIONS OF THE LWF

## Constitution of the Lutheran World Federation
## (as adopted by the LWF First Assembly, Lund, Sweden, 1947)

I.  NAME
The name and title of the body organized under this Constitution shall be
The Lutheran World Federation.

II.  DOCTRINAL BASIS
The Lutheran World Federation acknowledges the Holy Scriptures of the Old
and New Testaments as the only source and the infallible norm of all church
doctrine and practice, and sees in the Confessions of the Lutheran Church,
especially in the Unaltered Augsburg Confession and Luther's Catechism, a
pure exposition of the Word of God.

III.  NATURE AND PURPOSE
1.  The Lutheran World Federation shall be a free association of Lutheran
churches. It shall have no power to legislate for the churches belonging to
it or to interfere with their complete autonomy, but shall act as their agent
in such matters as they assign to it.

2.  The purposes of The Lutheran World Federation are:
(a)   To bear united witness before the world to the Gospel of Jesus Christ
as the power of God for salvation.
(b)   To cultivate unity of faith and confession among the Lutheran
churches of the world.
(c)   To promote fellowship and co-operation in study among Lutherans.
(d)   To foster Lutheran participation in ecumenical movements.
(e)   To develop a united Lutheran approach to responsibilities in missions and education; and
(f)   To support Lutheran groups in need of spiritual or material aid.

3.  The Lutheran World Federation may take action on behalf of member
churches in such matters as one or more of them may commit to it.

IV.  MEMBERSHIP
All Lutheran churches previously affiliated with the Lutheran World Convention, which through their representatives participate in the adoption of
this Constitution, shall continue to be members of The Lutheran World Federation. Other Lutheran churches which declare their acceptance of this Constitution shall be eligible to membership in The Lutheran World Federation.
Their acceptance into membership shall be decided by The Lutheran World
Federation in assembly, or in the interim, if no fundamental objection is
raised, by the Executive Committee.

V.  ORGANIZATION
The Lutheran World Federation shall exercise its functions through the following: (1) The Assembly; (2) The Executive Committee; (3) National Com-

mittees; (4) Special Commissions. In all the functions of the Federation, both clerical and lay persons shall be eligible to participate.

VI.   THE ASSEMBLY

1. An Assembly of the Federation shall be held every five years at the call of the President. The time and place and program of each Assembly shall be determined by the Executive Committee. Special Meetings of the Assembly may be called by the Executive Committee.

2. The Assembly shall consist of chosen representatives of the member churches of the Federation. The number of the representatives shall be determined by the Executive Committee.

   The allocation of the representatives in the Assembly shall be made to the member churches by the Executive Committee with the advice of the National Committees, and due regard shall be given to such factors as numerical size of churches, geographical distribution by continents and countries, adequate representation of the younger churches and the minority churches, and the right of each completely independent member church to have at least one representative in the Assembly. Suggestions for readjustments in the allocation of representatives in the Assembly may be made to the Executive Committee by member churches or groups of member churches, national or regional, and these readjustments shall become effective if approved by the Executive Committee and by the member churches concerned.

   The representatives in the Assembly shall be chosen by the member churches themselves. Whenever Lutheran congregations in union church bodies combine to ask for representation in the Assembly, the Executive Committee may invite them to send representatives to the Assembly in a consultative capacity. Lutheran associations and organizations designated by the Executive Committee may be invited to send representatives to the assembly in a consultative capacity in such numbers as the Executive Committee may determine.

3. The Assembly shall be the principal authority in the Federation. It shall elect the President of the Federation and the other members of the Executive Committee, shall receive reports from national Committees, shall appoint Special Commissions, and shall determine the fundamental lines of the Federation's work.

VII.  OFFICERS

The President of the Federation shall be chosen by ballot of the Assembly and a majority of the votes cast shall be necessary for an election. He shall assume office immediately after the close of the Assembly which has elected him and before the organization of the new Executive Committee. He shall be the chief official representative of the Federation. he shall hold office until the close of the following Assembly, and he shall be ineligible to succeed himself. Other officers of the Federation shall be chosen by the Executive Committee.

VIII. EXECUTIVE COMMITTEE

1. Each Assembly shall elect fifteen persons who with the President shall

constitute the Executive Committee of the Federation. Membership in the Executive Committee shall be allocated with due regard to such factors as numerical size of churches, geographical distribution by continents and countries, and adequate representation of the younger churches and the minority churches. In the choice of members from the younger churches and the minority churches, an effort shall be made to effect changes at each Assembly in order to make possible a rotation among all of them.

2. The Executive Committee shall meet at least once annually. It shall choose from its own membership two vice-presidents and a treasurer as officers of the Federation. The duties of these officers shall be those usually assigned to those officers.

3. The Executive Committee shall conduct the business of The Lutheran World Federation in the interim between Assemblies, shall supervise the appointment of National committees and receive annual reports from them, shall elect an Executive Secretary and assign him his duties, shall make a full annual report (including complete financial statements) to all member churches, shall appoint all committees and Special Commissions not otherwise provided for, and shall represent the Federation in all external relations.

4. Vacancies in the Executive Committee ad interim shall be filled by that Committee.

5. The expenses of a member of the Executive Committee in attending meetings of that Committee shall be borne by the church to which the member belongs or arranged by the National Committee in which his church is represented.

IX.   EXECUTIVE SECRETARY
Immediately following the close of each Assembly the Executive Committee shall elect an Executive Secretary who shall devote his full time to this office and who shall serve until the close of the next Assembly. The Executive Secretary shall be responsible to the Executive Committee for his work. It shall be his duty to carry out the decisions of the Assembly and of the Executive Committee under the general supervision of the President. He shall report through the Executive Committee to the Assembly of the Federation.

X.    NATIONAL COMMITTEES
The member churches in each country shall select a group of persons who together with the member or members of the Executive Committee in that country shall constitute a National Committee for The Lutheran World Federation. Each National Committee shall be asked to present to the Executive Committee an annual statement concerning the interests of The Lutheran World Federation in its country.

XI.   SPECIAL COMMISSIONS
Special Commissions shall be established under the authority of the Federation and shall be appointed either by the Assembly or by the Executive Com-

mittee. It shall be the purpose of these Commissions to discharge designated functions of the Federation. They shall report annually to the Executive Committee, which shall exercise general supervision over them.

XII. FINANCE

The Executive Committee shall prepare annually a detailed budget for the Federation, designate the allocation of funds to particular needs, and assign to each National Committee its responsibility for specific portions of the budget. The Treasurer shall be authorized to establish depositories in various countries.

XIII. AMENDMENTS

Amendments to this Constitution may be made by a two-thirds vote of those present at any regularly called Assembly, provided notice of intention to amend shall have been given the preceding day. Amendments so made shall become effective one year after their adoption by the Assembly unless objection has been filed with the Executive Committee by churches embracing in aggregate one-third of the constituency of the Federation.

# Constitution of the Lutheran World Federation
## (as adopted by the LWF Eighth Assembly, Curitiba, Brazil, 1990)

I. NAME

The name of the body organized under this constitution shall be The Lutheran World Federation.

II. DOCTRINAL BASIS

The Lutheran World Federation confesses the Holy Scriptures of the Old and New Testaments to be the only source and norm of its doctrine, life and service. It sees in the three Ecumenical Creeds and in the Confessions of the Lutheran Church, especially in the unaltered Augsburg Confession and the Small Catechism of Martin Luther, a pure exposition of the Word of God.

III. NATURE AND FUNCTIONS

The Lutheran World Federation is a communion of churches which confess the triune God, agree in the proclamation of the Word of God and are united in pulpit and altar fellowship.

The Lutheran World Federation confesses the one, holy, catholic, and apostolic Church and is resolved to serve Christian unity throughout the world.

The Lutheran World Federation:
• furthers the united witness to the Gospel of Jesus Christ and strengthens the member churches in carrying out the missionary command and in their efforts towards Christian unity worldwide;
• furthers worldwide among the member churches diaconic action, alleviation of human need, promotion of peace and human rights, social and economic justice, care for God's creation and sharing of resources;

- furthers through cooperative study the self-understanding and the communion of member churches and helps them to act jointly in common tasks.

IV.  SCOPE OF AUTHORITY
As instrument of its autonomous member churches the Lutheran World Federation may take action in matters committed to it by the member churches. It may act on behalf of one or more churches in such specific tasks as they commit to it. It may request individual member churches to assume tasks on behalf of the entire Communion.

V.  MEMBERSHIP AND OTHER FORMS OF AFFILIATION
1. Member Churches
The Lutheran World Federation consists of churches which accept the doctrinal basis set forth in Article II of this Constitution.

Each church which applies for membership in the Federation shall declare its acceptance of this Constitution.

Reception into membership shall be decided by the Federation in the Assembly, or in the interim, by the Council.

Membership in the Federation may be terminated by withdrawal. Upon recommendation of the Council, the Assembly may suspend or terminate the membership by a two-thirds vote of the delegates.

Procedures relating to membership shall be governed by the Bylaws.

2. Recognized Churches, Councils and Congregations
The Lutheran World Federation may recognize as eligible to participate in the work of the Federation non-member churches, councils or congregations which accept the doctrinal basis set forth in Article II of this Constitution (Associate Membership).

The granting, conditions and continuation of such recognition shall be governed by the Bylaws.

VI.  ORGANIZATION
The Lutheran World Federation shall exercise its functions through the Assembly, the Council, the Secretariat and appropriate instrumentalities of the member churches. In all these functions of the Federation, ordained and lay persons, men, women and youth shall be eligible to participate.

VII.  ASSEMBLY
1. The Assembly shall consist of representatives of the member churches of the Federation. As the principal authority of the Lutheran World Federation, the Assembly shall:
   - be responsible for the Constitution;
   - give general direction to the work of the Federation;
   - elect the President and the members of the Council;
   - act on the reports of the President, the General Secretary and the Treasurer.

2. The Assembly shall normally be held every six years with the time, place and program to be determined by the Council.

Special meetings of the Assembly may be called by the Council and shall be called at the request of one-quarter of the member churches.

3. The number of representatives to the Assembly and their distribution among the member churches shall be determined by the Council.

Each member church shall have the right to have at least one representative in the Assembly.

Due regard shall be given to the numerical size of member churches and their distributions by continents and countries.

4. The Council may invite representatives of the Lutheran congregations in union church bodies or of Lutheran associations and organizations to the Assembly in a consultative capacity if these are not represented by member churches.

The number of these representatives shall be determined by the Council.

VIII. COUNCIL

1. The Council shall be composed of the President, the Treasurer, and 48 persons to be elected by the Assembly.

Upon nomination by the churches, 48 members of the Council shall be elected by the Assembly by a majority of the votes cast.

The Assembly shall have the right to elect persons other than those nominated by member churches and other than those who are delegates to the Assembly provided the consent of the relevant member churches is given.

Election procedure and distribution of seats to the continents and countries shall be governed in the Bylaws. A due representation of ordained and lay persons, women, men and youth shall be observed.

The term of office of the Council shall end at the close of the next ordinary Assembly. Members of the Council shall be eligible for one reelection.

2. The Council is responsible for the business of the Federation in the interim between ordinary Assemblies; it should meet at least once a year.

3. The Council shall elect the General Secretary (Article XII.) and the Treasurer (Article X.) and prescribe their duties.

The term of office of persons elected by the Council may be terminated before expiration by a two-thirds vote of the members of the Council.

The Council shall decide on the structure of the Secretariat and present an annual report to the member churches.

4. Upon death or incapacity of the President, the Council shall elect a president within three months.

If a member of the Council can no longer be present for his/her term of office, the Council elects in consultation with the member church a deputy for the remaining term of service.

5.  The Council shall decide on the budgets of the Federation. It shall receive the audited accounts and approve them.

6.  The Council shall elect the Vice-Presidents from among its members taking into consideration the seven geographical areas.

    The Council shall elect from among its members an Executive Committee and Program Committees as required and appoint their chairpersons.

    The Executive Committee shall be composed of the following persons: The President, the Vice-Presidents, the Treasurer and the chairpersons of the Program Committees.

    For the Program Committees the Council elects for its term of office up to 30 advisers with voting rights in the committees.

    The Council may appoint Standing Committees or *ad hoc* sub-committees as required.

    The Executive Committee shall pursue the duties assigned to it by the Council to ensure the proper functioning of the Federation.

    Among other things, it determines who is entitled to sign on behalf of the Lutheran World Federation within the Council or the administration.

    The Executive Committee shall serve as the Personnel Committee. It shall also serve as the LWF Board of Trustees.

IX.   NATIONAL COMMITTEES
      The member churches in each country may constitute a National Committee to coordinate the relationships to the Federation. The right of direct communication between the member churches and the LWF shall be retained. Each National Committee shall present to the Council an annual report on its activities.

X.    OFFICERS
      1.  President
          The election of the President by the Assembly shall be by a majority of the votes cast in a written ballot.

          The President shall assume office immediately after the close of the Assembly at which the election was held. He/she shall hold office until the close of the following ordinary Assembly and shall not be eligible for a second term.

          The President shall be the chief official representative and spokesperson of the Federation. He/she shall be the presiding officer of the Assembly, the Council and the Executive Committee.

          The President shall oversee the life and work of the Federation, in consultation with the Treasurer and General Secretary.

      2.  Treasurer
          The Treasurer shall be elected by the Council at its constituting meeting and shall hold office until the close of the following ordinary Assembly.

The Treasurer shall oversee the financial activities and shall counsel the President and the General Secretary in this respect.

XI.  SECRETARIAT
The Federation shall have a Secretariat adequate to carry out its tasks.

The Council shall authorize the structure and the Terms of Reference of the Secretariat.

XII.  GENERAL SECRETARY
Without delay following the close of each ordinary Assembly the Council shall elect the General Secretary who shall devote full time to this office and who shall serve until his/her successor has taken office. The General Secretary shall be eligible for reelection.

The General Secretary shall be responsible to the Council for his/her work. He/she shall conduct the business of the Federation and carry out the decisions of the Assembly and the Council.

The General Secretary shall report to the Assembly and the Council.

XIII.  FINANCES
The Council shall authorize the Statement of Needs for transmission to the member churches, National Committees and other agencies, commending it for support through designated and undesignated contributions.

The Council shall allocate membership fees to be paid by member churches. The Council shall receive the auditor's report and adopt the annual financial report. The member churches shall receive an annual financial report.

XIV.  AMENDMENTS AND BYLAWS
1.  Amendments
Amendments to this Constitution may be made by a two-thirds majority of the votes cast at any ordinary Assembly, provided notice of intention to amend shall have been submitted through the General Secretary to the member churches, three months before the Assembly.

Amendments shall become effective one year after their adoption by the Assembly unless objection has been filed with the Council by at least one-third of the member churches.

2.  Bylaws
The Council shall adopt Bylaws to this Constitution. Such Bylaws adopted or amended by the Council shall become effective one year after their adoption unless objection has been filed with the Council by at least one-third of the member churches.

The Assembly may adopt, amend or rescind Bylaws by a majority of the votes cast. Such decisions shall become effective after one year unless objection has been filed with the Council by at least one-third of the member churches.

# 2

# MEMBER CHURCHES OF THE LWF

*Africa*

Evangelical Lutheran Church in Botswana
(Kereke ya Luthere ya Efangele mo Botswana)
Joined LWF: 1986

Church of the Lutheran Brethren of Cameroon
(Eglise fraternelle luthérienne du Cameroun)
Joined LWF: 1992

Evangelical Lutheran Church of Cameroon
(Eglise évangélique luthérienne du Cameroun)
Joined LWF: 1971

Evangelical Lutheran Church of the Central African Republic
(Eglise évangélique luthérienne de la République centrafricaine)
Joined LWF: 1974

Evangelical Church of Eritrea
(Wenghelawit Bete Kristian Be Ertra)
Joined LWF: 1963

The Ethiopian Evangelical Church Mekane Yesus
(Ye Ethiopia Wongelawit Bete - Kristian Mekane Yesus)
Joined LWF: 1963

Evangelical Lutheran Church in Kenya
(Kanisa la Kiinjili la Kilutheri Katika Kenya)
Joined LWF: 1970

Kenya Evangelical Lutheran Church
(Kanisa la Kiinjili la Kilutheri Kenya)
Joined LWF: 1992

Lutheran Church in Liberia
Joined LWF: 1966

Malagasy Lutheran Church [Madagascar]
(Fiangonana Loterana Malagasy)
Joined LWF: 1950

Evangelical Lutheran Church in Malawi
(Mpingo wa Uthenga Wabwino Wa Lutele M'Malawi)
Joined LWF: 1988

Evangelical Lutheran Church in Namibia (ELCIN)
(Ongeleki Onkwaevaangeli paLuther yomuNamibia)
Joined LWF: 1961

Evangelisch-Lutherische Kirche in Namibia (DELK)
(Evangelical Lutheran Church in Namibia/GELC)
Joined LWF: 1963

Evangelical Lutheran Church in the Republic of Namibia (ELCRN)
(!Gâi-=hôa Kerkib Lutheri dib Namibiab !na - Ongerki jEvangeli ja Luther mu
Namibia)
Joined LWF: 1970

Lutheran Church of Christ in Nigeria
(Ekklesiyar Kristi Ta Lutheran A Nigeria)
Joined LWF: 1961

Lutheran Church of Nigeria
Joined LWF: 1973

The Lutheran Church of Senegal
(Eglise luthérienne du Sénégal)
Joined LWF: 1992

Evangelical Lutheran Church in Sierra Leone
Joined LWF: 1990

Evangelical Lutheran Church in Southern Africa [ELCSA]
(Evangelies Lutherse Kerk in Suider Afrika)
Joined LWF: 1976

Evangelical Lutheran Church in Southern Africa (Cape Church)
(Evangelies-Lutherse Kerk in Suider Afrika (Kaapse Kerk))
Joined LWF: 1963

Evangelical Lutheran Church in Southern Africa (Natal-Transvaal)
(Evangeliese Lutherse Kerk in Suider Afrika [Natal-Transvaal])
(Evangelisch-Lutherische Kirche im Südlichen Afrika [Natal-Transvaal])
Joined LWF: 1992

The Moravian Church in Southern Africa
Joined LWF: 1975

Evangelical Lutheran Church in Tanzania [ELCT]
(Kanisa la Kiinjili la Kilutheri Tanzania)
Joined LWF: 1964

Evangelical Lutheran Church in Zaire
(Eglise évangélique luthérienne du Zaire)
Joined LWF: 1986

Evangelical Lutheran Church in Zimbabwe
Joined LWF: 1963

## Asia, Oceania, and the Near East

Bangladesh Lutheran Church
Joined LWF: 1986

Bangladesh Northern Evangelical Lutheran Church
Joined LWF: 1992

The Chinese Rhenish Church, Hong Kong Synod
Joined LWF: 1974

Evangelical Lutheran Church of Hong Kong
Joined LWF: 1957

Hong Kong and Macau Lutheran Church
Joined LWF: 1992

Tsung Tsin Mission of Hong Kong
Joined LWF: 1974

Andhra Evangelical Lutheran Church [India]
(Andhra Suvisesha Lutheran Sangham)
Joined LWF: 1950

The Arcot Lutheran Church [India]
Joined LWF: 1961

Evangelical Lutheran Church in Madhya Pradesh [India]
(Madhya Pradesh Evangelical Lutheran Kalisiya)
Joined LWF: 1950

Gossner Evangelical Lutheran Church in Chotanagpur and Assam [India]
Joined LWF: 1947

India Evangelical Lutheran Church [India]
Joined LWF: 1970

Jeypore Evangelical Lutheran Church [India]
Joined LWF: 1950

Northern Evangelical Lutheran Church [India]
Joined LWF: 1950

South Andhra Lutheran Church [India]
(Dakshana Andhra Lutheran Sangham)
Joined LWF: 1952

Tamil Evangelical Lutheran Church [India]
(Thamil Suvesesha Lutheran Thiruchabai)
Joined LWF: 1947

Batak Christian Community Church [Indonesia]
(Gereja Punguan Kristen Batak)
Joined LWF: 1972

Christian Protestant Angkola Church [Indonesia]
(Gereja Kristen Protestan Angkola)
Joined LWF: 1977

Christian Protestant Church in Indonesia
(Gereja Kristen Protestan Indonesia)
Joined LWF: 1975

The Indonesian Christian Church
(Majelis Pusat Huria Kristen Indonesia)
Joined LWF: 1970

Indonesian Christian Lutheran Church
(Gereja Kristen Luther Indonesia)
Joined LWF: 1994

Protestant Christian Batak Church [Indonesia]
(Huria Kristen Batak Protestan)
Joined LWF: 1952

Protestant Christian Church in Mentawai [Indonesia]
(Gereja Kristen Protestan di Mentawai)
Joined LWF: 1984

Simalungun Protestant Christian Church [Indonesia]
(Gereja Kristen Protestan Simalungun)
Joined LWF: 1967

The Evangelical Lutheran Church in Jordan*
(Al-Kanisa Al-Injiliyyeh Al-Loutheriyyeh Fi Al-Urdun)
Joined LWF: 1974

Japan Evangelical Lutheran Church
(Nihon Fukuin Ruuteru Kyookai)
Joined LWF: 1952

Kinki Evangelical Lutheran Church [Japan]
(Kinki Fukuin Ruteru Kyokai)
Joined LWF: 1976

Lutheran Church in Korea
(Kidokyo Hankuk Lutuhoi)
Joined LWF: 1972

Basel Christian Church of Malaysia
(Gereja Basel Malaysia)
Joined LWF: 1979

Evangelical Lutheran Church in Malaysia
(Gereja Evangelical Lutheran di Malaysia)
Joined LWF: 1968

Lutheran Church in Malaysia and Singapore
(Gereja Lutheran di Malaysia dan Singapura)
Joined LWF: 1971

The Protestant Church in Sabah [Malaysia]
(Gorija Protestan Sid Sabah)
Joined LWF: 1995

Evangelical Lutheran Church of Papua New Guinea
Joined LWF: 1976

Gutnius Lutheran Church — Papua New Guinea
Joined LWF: 1979

Lutheran Church in the Philippines
Joined LWF: 1973

Taiwan Lutheran Church
Joined LWF: 1960

The Lutheran Church of Taiwan [Republic of China]
Joined LWF: 1984

The Lutheran Church of the Republic of China [Taiwan]
(Chung Kuo Chi Tu Chiao Hsin Yi Hui)
Joined LWF: 1995

The Evangelical Lutheran Church in Thailand
Joined LWF: 1994

## Europe

Evangelische Kirche Augsburgischen Bekenntnisses in Österreich
(Evangelical Church of the Augsburg Confession in Austria)
Joined LWF: 1947

Evangelical Church in Croatia
(Evangelicka crkva u R. Hrvatskoj)
Joined LWF: 1951

Silesian Evangelical Church of the Augsburg Confession in the Czech Republic
(Slezská církev evangelická augsburského vyznání v Ceské republice)
Joined LWF: 1956

Evangelical Lutheran Church in Denmark
(Den evangelisk-lutherske Folkekirke i Danmark)
Joined LWF: 1947
The Dioceses of the Faroe Islands and Greenland are part of the Evangelical
Lutheran Church in Denmark.

Estonian Evangelical Lutheran Church
(Eesti Evangeelne Luterlik Kirik)
Joined LWF: 1963

Evangelical Lutheran Church of Finland
(Suomen Evankelis-Luterilainen Kirkko)
Joined LWF: 1947

Church of the Augsburg Confession of Alsace and Lorraine
(Eglise de la Confession d'Augsbourg d'Alsace et de Lorraine)
Joined LWF: 1947

Evangelical Lutheran Church of France
(Eglise évangélique luthérienne de France)
Joined LWF: 1947

Evangelische Landeskirche in Württemberg [Germany]
(Evangelical Church in Württemberg)
Joined LWF: 1947

Evangelisch-Lutherische Kirche in Baden [Germany]
(Evangelical Lutheran Church in Baden)
Joined LWF: 1968

Evangelisch-Lutherische Kirche in Bayern [Germany]
(Evangelical Lutheran Church in Bavaria)
Joined LWF: 1947

Evangelisch-Lutherische Landeskirche in Braunschweig [Germany]
(Evangelical Lutheran Church in Brunswick)
Joined LWF: 1947

Evangelisch-Lutherische Kirche in Oldenburg [Germany]
(Evangelical Lutheran Church in Oldenburg)
Joined LWF: 1957

Evangelisch-Lutherische Kirche in Thüringen [Germany]
(Evangelical Lutheran Church in Thuringia)
Joined LWF: 1947

Evangelisch-Lutherische Landeskirche Hannovers [Germany]
(Evangelical Lutheran Church of Hanover)
Joined LWF: 1947

Evangelisch-Lutherische Landeskirche Mecklenburgs [Germany]
(Evangelical Lutheran Church of Mecklenburg)
Joined LWF: 1947

Evangelisch-Lutherische Landeskirche Sachsens [Germany]
(Evangelical Lutheran Church of Saxony)
Joined LWF: 1947

Evangelisch-Lutherische Landeskirche Schaumburg-Lippe [Germany]
(Evangelical Lutheran Church of Schaumburg-Lippe)
Joined LWF: 1947

Latvian Evangelical Lutheran Church Abroad [Germany]
(Latvijas Evangeliski Luteriska Baznica àrpus Latvijas)
Joined LWF: 1947

Lippische Landeskirche [Germany]
(Church of Lippe)
Joined LWF: 1992

Nordelbische Evangelisch-Lutherische Kirche [Germany]
(North Elbian Evangelical Lutheran Church)
Joined LWF: 1977

Pommersche Evangelische Kirche [Germany]
(Evangelical Church of Pomerania)
Joined LWF: 1956

Lutheran Church in Hungary
(Magyarországi Evangélikus Egyház)
Joined LWF: 1947

Evangelical Lutheran Church — The National Church of Iceland
(Thjodkirkja Islands)
Joined LWF: 1947

Evangelical Lutheran Church in Italy
(Chiesa Evangelica Luterana in Italia)
Joined LWF: 1949

Evangelical Lutheran Church of Latvia
(Latvijas Evangeliski Luteriska Baznica)
Joined LWF: 1963

Evangelical Lutheran Church of Lithuania
(Lietuvos Evangeliku-Liuteronu Baznycia)
Joined LWF: 1967

Evangelical Lutheran Church in the Kingdom of the Netherlands
(Evangelisch-Lutherse Kerk in het Koninkrijk der Nederlanden)
Joined LWF: 1952

Church of Norway
(Den Norske Kirke)
Joined LWF: 1947

Evangelical Church of the Augsburg Confession in Poland
(Kosciól Ewangelicko-Augsburski w R.P.)
Joined LWF: 1947

Evangelische Kirche A.B. in Rumänien
(Evangelical Church of the Augsburg Confession in Romania)
Joined LWF: 1964

Evangelical Synodal Presbyterial Lutheran Church of the Augsburg Confession in
Romania
(Biserica Evanghelica Lutherana Sinodo-Presbiteriala de Confesiune Augustana
din Romania)
Joined LWF: 1964

Evangelical Lutheran Church in Russia and Other States
(Evangelisch-Lutherische Kirche in Russland und anderen Staaten)
Joined LWF: 1989

Evangelical Lutheran Church of Ingria in Russia
Joined LWF: 1994

Evangelical Church of the Augsburg Confession in the Slovak Republic
(Evanjelická cirkev augsburgského vyznania na Slovensku)
Joined LWF: 1947

Evangelical Church of the Augsburg Confession in Slovenia
(Evangelicanska cerkev A.V. v Republiki Sloveniji)
Joined LWF: 1952

Church of Sweden
(Svenska Kyrkan)
Joined LWF: 1947

Bund Evangelisch-Lutherischer Kirchen in der Schweiz und im Fürstentum
Liechtenstein
(Federation of Evangelical Lutheran Churches in Switzerland and the Principality
of Liechtenstein)
Joined LWF: 1979

Lutheran Church in Great Britain
Joined LWF: 1988

Slovak Evangelical Church of the Augsburg Confession in Yugoslavia
(Slovenská evanjelická augsburského vyznania cirkev v Juhoslávii)
Joined LWF: 1952

## Latin America

Evangelical Church of the River Plate [Argentina, Paraguay, Uruguay]
(Iglesia Evangélica del Río de la Plata)
Joined LWF: 1991

United Evangelical Lutheran Church [Argentina]
(Iglesia Evangélica Luterana Unida)
Joined LWF: 1951

Bolivian Evangelical Lutheran Church
(Iglesia Evangélica Luterana Boliviana)
Joined LWF: 1975

Evangelical Church of the Lutheran Confession in Brazil
(Igreja Evangélica de Confissão Luterana no Brasil)
Joined LWF: 1952

Evangelical Lutheran Church in Chile
(Iglesia Evangélica Luterana en Chile)
Joined LWF: 1955

Lutheran Church in Chile
(Iglesia Luterana en Chile)
Joined LWF: 1991

Evangelical Lutheran Church of Colombia
(Iglesia Evangélica Luterana de Colombia)
Joined LWF: 1966

Salvadoran Lutheran Synod
(Sínodo Luterano Salvadoreño)
Joined LWF: 1986

Christian Lutheran Church of Honduras
(Iglesia Cristiana Luterana de Honduras)
Joined LWF: 1994

Lutheran Church in Guyana
Joined LWF: 1950

Mexican Lutheran Church
(Iglesia Luterana Mexicana)
Joined LWF: 1957

Lutheran Church of Nicaragua Faith and Hope
(Iglesia Luterana de Nicaragua Fe y Esperanza)
Joined LWF: 1994

Evangelical Lutheran Church in Suriname
(Evangelisch Lutherse Kerk in Suriname)
Joined LWF: 1979

Evangelical Lutheran Church in Venezuela
(Iglesia Evangélica Luterana en Venezuela)
Joined LWF: 1986

## North America

Estonian Evangelical Lutheran Church Abroad
(Eesti Evangeeliumi Luteriusu Kirik)
Joined LWF: 1947

Evangelical Lutheran Church in Canada
Joined LWF: 1986

Evangelical Lutheran Church in America
Joined LWF: 1988

Lithuanian Evangelical Lutheran Church in Diaspora
(Lietuviu Evangeliku Liuteronu Baznycia Iseivijoje)
Joined LWF: 1947

## Australia

Lutheran Church of Australia
Joined the LWF as associate member in 1994

# 3

# FINANCES OF THE LWF

| GENERAL RESERVES | US DOLLARS |
|---|---|
| 1947 | 118,435 |
| 1950 | 10,143 |
| 1955 | 134,334 |
| 1960 | 236,204 |
| 1965 | 610,213 |
| 1970 | 702,800 |
| 1975 | 1,560,142 |
| 1980 | 2,991,748 |
| 1985 | 3,535,928 |
| 1990 | 2,393,295 |
| 1995 | 3,811,546 |

DEVELOPMENT OF LWF GENERAL RESERVES
(see Table 1)

| | TOTAL EXPENDITURE IN DOLLARS |
|---|---|
| 1947 | 138,312 |
| 1950 | 719,059 |
| 1955 | 3,297,992 |
| 1960 | 3,744,992 |
| 1965 | 9,294,676 |
| 1970 | 16,087,614 |
| 1975 | 29,797,992 |
| 1980 | 63,959,844 |
| 1985 | 63,500,944 |
| 1990 | 90,059,607 |
| 1995 | 119,817,095 |

DEVELOPMENT OF LWF
TOTAL EXPENDITURE
(see Table 2)

## Development of LWF General Reserves

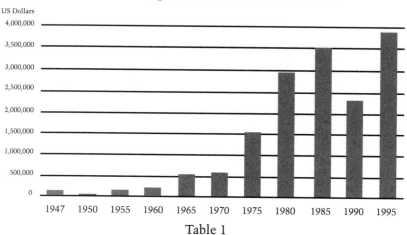

Table 1

## Development of LWF Total Expenditure

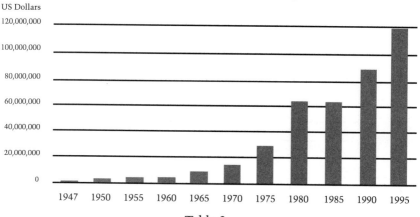

Table 2

# Index